W9-ADY-308

Praise for Aging and Mental Health

"*Aging and Mental Health* is that rare book which is both pleasurable to read and deeply informative. The science of psychiatric diagnosis and treatment is set forth through rich conceptual frameworks of gerontology and psychology, and – new in this edition – critical health service contexts. As a comprehensive and skillfully crafted resource all in one volume, the book is an indispensable gem for students and practitioners alike."

Jennifer Moye, PhD, VA Boston Healthcare System and Harvard Medical School

"The Third Edition of *Aging and Mental Health* offers far more than an update. It is a thoughtfully and creatively designed textbook poised to serve as a strong introduction to major clinical disorders, dominant models of therapy, service delivery systems, and ethical issues, together rounding out the universe of mental health and mental illness in older adults. Generous and well-selected references for each topic are provided."

Erlene Rosowsky, PsyD, Director of the Center for Mental Health and Aging and Associate Professor of Psychology, William James College

"Kudos to the authors of this updated new edition on *Aging and Mental Health.* Life span developmental theory, normative biopsychosocial processes, and models of successful aging inform clinical recommendations for mental health professionals who provide services to older adults. This is an excellent volume to read and reference if one desires to employ an evidence-based state-of-the art approach to assess and treat the mental health problems of older adults and to promote integrated care in geriatric settings."

Victor Molinari, PhD, President of the American Board of Geropsychology and Professor, School of Aging Studies, University of South Florida

"I've used *Aging and Mental Health* as a textbook for my undergraduate class in "Gerontological Counseling" and my graduate class in "Aging and Mental Disorders" for a decade. This book is unique in including reviews of fundamental issues in gerontology (e.g. age-related changes), major theoretical models of mental health, the most common mental disorders of late life, and contextual issues such as policy, housing, and caregiving issues. The text is full of vivid case studies and practical information. The Third Edition includes valuable updates, such as incorporation of the DSM-5 and recent research information. The authors bring years of experience in clinical practice, research, and public policy related to mental health to bear on the topic. This is the perfect text for instructors from diverse fields who want to engage their students in understanding mental health and aging, and help them develop a passion for providing excellent care for older adults and their families."

William E. Haley, PhD, Professor, School of Aging Studies, University of South Florida

Aging and Mental Health

UNDERSTANDING AGING

The Psychology of Adult Development

General Editor
James E. Birren

Editorial Advisory Board
Stig Berg, Dennis Bromely, Denise Park, Timothy A Salthouse, K Warner Schaie, and Diana Woodruff-Pak

During this century, life expectancy at birth has increased more for the average person than it did from Roman times to 1900: There are a greater number of old people today and they live longer than ever before. Within universities there is pressure to educate younger students about the scientific facts of adult development and aging as well as to train professionals to serve and aging society. The past 20 years have seen an exponential growth in material published.

This new series of modular texts has been designed to meet the need to integrate, interpret, and make this new knowledge available in an efficient and flexible format for instructors, students, and professionals worldwide. Each book will present a concise, authoritative, integrated and readable summary of research and theory in a clearly defined area. Bridging the gap between introductory texts and research literature, these books will provide balanced coverage and convey the excitement and challenge of new research and developments. The modular format allows the series to be used as a complete sequence in primary courses in other fields.

Published

The Social Psychology of Aging by Michael W. Pratt and Joan E. Norris

The Neuropsychology of Aging by Diana S. Woodruff-Pak

Aging and Mental Health, Second Edition by Daniel L. Segal, Sara Honn Qualls, and Michael A. Smyer

Aging and Mental Health
Third Edition

Daniel L. Segal, Sara Honn Qualls, and

Michael A. Smyer

WILEY Blackwell

Edition History
WB - Wiley-Blackwell (2e, 2011)
Blackwell Publishers (1e, 1999)

Registered Office(s)
John Wiley & Sons, Inc., 111 River Street, Hoboken, NJ 07030, USA
John Wiley & Sons Ltd, The Atrium, Southern Gate, Chichester, West Sussex, PO19 8SQ, UK

Editorial Office
The Atrium, Southern Gate, Chichester, West Sussex, PO19 8SQ, UK

For details of our global editorial offices, customer services, and more information about Wiley products visit us at www.wiley.com.

Wiley also publishes its books in a variety of electronic formats and by print-on-demand. Some content that appears in standard print versions of this book may not be available in other formats.

Library of Congress Cataloging-in-Publication Data
Names: Segal, Daniel L., author. | Qualls, Sara Honn, author. | Smyer, Michael A., author.
Title: Aging and mental health / by Daniel L. Segal, University of Colorado at Colorado Springs, Colorado Springs, CO, US 80918, Sara Honn Qualls, University of Colorado at Colorado Springs, Colorado Springs, CO, US 80918, Michael A. Smyer, Bucknell University, Lewisburg, PA, US, 17837.
Description: 3rd edition. | Hoboken, NJ: Wiley, 2018. | Includes bibliographical references and index. |
Identifiers: LCCN 2017034907 (print) | LCCN 2017035874 (ebook) | ISBN 9781119133162 (pdf) | ISBN 9781119133155 (epub) | ISBN 9781119133131 (pbk.)
Subjects: LCSH: Older people–Mental health. | Geriatric psychiatry.
Classification: LCC RC451.4.A5 (ebook) | LCC RC451.4.A5 S66 2018 (print) | DDC 618.97/689–dc23
LC record available at https://lccn.loc.gov/2017034907

Cover image: Courtesy of Michael A. Smyer
Cover design: Wiley

Set in 10/12.5pt Galliard by SPi Global, Pondicherry, India

Printed in Singapore by C.O.S. Printers Pte Ltd

10 9 8 7 6 5 4 3 2 1

Contents

Preface

What is important in knowledge is not quantity, but quality. It is important to know what knowledge is significant, what is less so, and what is trivial.
(Leo Tolstoy)

In this book, we have endeavored to take Tolstoy's maxim to heart, sorting out the significant from the trivial in the domain of aging and mental health. As we did so, we had two audiences in mind: today's clinicians and the clinicians of the future. The first group includes clinicians who are already in practice settings but who want to know more about the intricacies of working with older adults. The second group encompasses students in the professions that work with older adults (e.g., psychology, social work, counseling, nursing, psychiatry).

Both groups must face the issues of aging summarized by Michel Philibert, a French philosopher: "Of aging, what can we know? With aging, what must we do?" (Philibert, 1979, p. 384). These are also issues that older adults and their family members must face. In a way, they are variations on the questions that often arise in clinical settings. Consider the following example:

> Betty was worried about Alex. His memory seemed to be failing him more often. He would get to the store and forget half of the things she'd sent him there for. He seemed more tired than usual, with less energy for his hobbies at the end of the day or on weekends. He didn't want to go out with friends to the movies or to dinner. Alex didn't seem to notice anything different in his behavior. Betty called to ask your advice: "Should I get him tested at the local Alzheimer's Center?"

How would you answer Betty? What would you need to know? Which portion of her story is significant in forming your answer? Which less so? In answering these questions, you are implicitly answering Philibert's queries as well. You are implicitly making a differential diagnosis of Alex's situation: Is this a part of normal aging? Is this a pathological pattern? Is it a combination of the two? (Of aging, what can we know?) You may also be linking your answer to an implicit action plan. Betty certainly is: Diagnose the problem and then decide what kind of treatment is most appropriate. (With aging, what must we do?)

To fully answer Betty's question requires much more information about aging in general, about patterns of mental health and mental disorder in particular, about Alex's distinctive history and pattern of functioning, and about the contexts in which she and Alex live and receive services. We designed this book to provide you with frameworks for considering each element.

The book is divided into four parts. Part I is an overview of basic gerontology, the study of the aging process. This background information forms a context for answering the simple question often posed by clients and their relatives: Should I be worried about this pattern of behavior (e.g., Alex's apparent memory problems)? To answer this deceptively simple question requires that we sort out the influences of physical illness, basic processes of aging, and the intersection of historical and social trends as they affect older adults' functioning. In Part I, we outline the basic parameters of mental health in later life, providing the foundation upon which later chapters build.

In Part II, we consider basic models of mental disorders. Each model provides a set of assumptions about mental health and the development of mental health problems, their assessment, and their treatment. These assumptions direct the clinician's attention to specific aspects of older adults and their functioning. For example, assume for the moment that Alex's memory problems are not organically caused. The behavioral perspective might highlight the context of the older adult's behavior. Four important models of mental health and mental disorder are outlined in the chapters of Part II. In each chapter, we focus on an important question for older adults and those who work with them: How is this approach relevant to older adults and the problems they encounter in later life?

Part III focuses attention on the most commonly occurring mental health problems and disorders in later life: neurocognitive disorders, major depression, bipolar disorder, serious mental disorders (e.g., schizophrenia), anxiety disorders, post-traumatic stress disorder, sexual disorders, sleep disorders, substance use, personality disorders, and other common disorders. In each chapter, we outline the prevalence of the disorders, the most appropriate assessment approaches for older adults, and the most effective treatment strategies for older adults. We were fortunate to be able to call upon Stephen J. Bartels and his colleagues for their expertise in the diagnosis and treatment of severe mental disorders (Chapter 10).

Part IV concludes our book with several chapters focusing on the contexts and settings of contemporary geriatric mental health practice. The contexts of housing, health care settings, social service settings, and public policy affect how, where, and why older adults with mental health problems are diagnosed and treated. Families and caregiving are also addressed, as families are the primary providers of care, and caregiving is a challenge facing millions of people who are taking care of older family members and friends who need assistance. This section concludes with an analysis of ethical and legal issues facing practitioners in geropsychology and also discusses the impact of global climate change.

Colleagues and friends in several settings have helped us write this book: in the Department of Psychology, the Aging Center, and the Gerontology Center of the University of Colorado at Colorado Springs, and in the Center for Advanced Study in the Behavioral Sciences at Stanford University. We thank Brian P. Yochim and Mary Dozier for their feedback on specific chapters of the book, and we thank Lacey Edwards for her contributions to Chapter 4. We also thank Michelle Buffie for her expertise in making figures and tables. Early in the development of the first edition we benefited from the guidance and advice of Jim Birren and two anonymous reviewers. The process of revision for the second edition was supported by input and advice from our academic and community services colleagues as well as a new set of anonymous reviewers. We eagerly acknowledge our debt to each, while also admitting that any remaining flaws are ours. We also express our deepest appreciation to our friends and editors at Wiley, including Darren Reed, Monica Rogers, Roshna Mohan, Catherine Joseph, Elisha Benjamin, and Nishantini Amir, and our excellent copy-editor Katherine Carr, whose patience and diligence ensured that this third edition came to fruition. Finally, we remain grateful to our family members and friends for their ongoing love, encouragement, and support.

Our goal throughout this book is to provide information and a set of frameworks that will be useful in working with older adults and their families. In the end, we hope that you will conclude that there is much to hope for in aging, and much that we can do to foster positive mental health later in life.

Reference

Philibert, M. (1979). Philosophical approach to gerontology. In J. Hendricks & C. Davis Hendricks (Eds.), *Dimensions of aging* (pp. 379–394). Cambridge, MA: Winthrop.

Aging and Mental Health

Part I
Introduction

1

Mental Health and Aging
An Introduction

Consider the following case description:

> Grace, director of a Senior Center in your area, calls you about Mr. Tucker. Although Mr. Tucker used to come to the center three or four times a week, he hasn't come at all since the death of his good friend, Ed, four months ago. Grace had called Mr. Tucker at home to say how much he'd been missed. When she asked if he wasn't coming because he was still upset over Ed's death, he denied it. Instead, Mr. Tucker said that he wanted to return to the center, but he was in terrible pain. In fact, he was in so much pain that he really couldn't talk on the phone and he abruptly hung up. Grace was worried that Mr. Tucker might not be getting the medical attention that he really needed. She asked you to make a home visit, which you agreed to do. You call Mr. Tucker and set up an appointment.

As you prepare to visit Mr. Tucker, what are the basic questions you might ask about him and his situation? Which factors do you think are important to explore with Mr. Tucker? How would you assess Mr. Tucker's functioning?

Your answer to these simple inquiries reflects your implicit model of mental health and aging. In this book, especially in Part II, we will illustrate several different conceptual models of mental disorders and aging. In doing so, we will emphasize the links between one's starting assumptions and one's subsequent strategies for assessment and intervention. You will come to see that your philosophical assumptions about mental health, mental disorder, and aging shape the interpretive process of working with older adults and their families.

Mr. Tucker's current functioning raises a basic question: Is his behavior simply part of normal aging or does it represent a problem that requires professional attention?

Aging and Mental Health, Third Edition. Daniel L. Segal, Sara Honn Qualls, and Michael A. Smyer.
© 2018 John Wiley & Sons, Inc. Published 2018 by John Wiley & Sons, Inc.

Our answer represents implicit and explicit assumptions regarding the continuum of functioning that runs from outstanding functioning through usual aging to pathological patterns of behavior.

What Is Normal Aging?

The starting point for mental health and aging must be a general understanding of *gerontology*, the multidisciplinary study of normal aging, and *geriatrics*, the study of the medical aspects of old age and the prevention and treatment of the diseases of aging. In Mr. Tucker's case, we want to know if his reaction is a part of a normal grieving process or an indication of an underlying mental health disorder (e.g., a mood disorder, such as major depressive disorder). To answer this requires a starting definition of normal aging.

A conceptual definition

Discussions of this issue focus attention on three different patterns of aging: normal or usual aging, optimal or successful aging, and pathological aging. Baltes and Baltes (1990) provided classic definitions of normal and optimal aging:

> Normal aging refers to aging without biological or mental pathology. It thus concerns the aging process that is dominant within a society for persons who are not suffering from a manifest illness. Optimal aging refers to a kind of utopia, namely, aging under development-enhancing and age-friendly environmental conditions. Finally, sick or pathological aging characterizes an aging process determined by medical etiology and syndromes of illness. A classical example is dementia of the Alzheimer type. (pp. 7–8)

Schaie (2016) provides a somewhat different conceptual perspective of the possible trajectories of aging, distinguishing four major patterns. *Normal aging* is the most common pattern, characterized by individuals maintaining a plateau of psychological functioning through their late 50s and early 60s and then showing modest declines in cognitive functioning through their early 80s, with more dramatic deterioration in the years before death. In contrast, *successful agers* are characterized by being genetically and socioeconomically advantaged, and maintaining overall cognitive vitality until right before their death. As described by Schaie, "These are the fortunate individuals whose active life expectancy comes very close to their actual life expectancy" (p. 5). The third pattern includes *those who develop mild cognitive impairment*. Individuals in this group experience declines in cognitive functioning that are more severe than is typical. Some, but not all, in this group progress to having more substantial cognitive problems. Finally, the fourth pattern is *those who develop dementia,* in which individuals experience severe, dramatic, and diagnosable forms of cognitive impairments. (We fully discuss the dementias and neurocognitive disorders in Chapter 8).

A statistical definition

Distinguishing between normal aging and optimal aging requires us to sort out statistical fact from theoretically desirable conditions. For example, the Baltes and Baltes definition suggests that normal aging does not include "manifest illness." However, in the United States today, chronic disease is typical of the experience of aging: More than 25% of all adults and 66% of older Americans have *multiple* chronic conditions. This is an expensive issue: More than two-thirds of all health care costs in the US are for treating chronic illnesses. For older adults specifically, 95% of health care costs are for chronic diseases (Centers for Disease Control and Prevention, 2013).

Let's look at a specific condition: arthritis. Current estimates indicate that 22.7% of adults in the US reported having doctor-diagnosed arthritis, including 49.7% of people 65 years old and older (Barbour et al., 2013). Moreover, among the oldest old groups (75+ or 85+) there are substantially higher rates. Thus, from a statistical perspective, arthritis is certainly modal, and may be considered a part of normal aging. We will return to this theme in Chapter 2.

A functional definition

Another approach to defining normal aging arises from defining "manifest illness." By focusing not on presence or absence of a chronic disease, such as arthritis, but on the *impact* of that disease, we may get another depiction of "normal aging." Here, again, though, the definition of terms can affect our conclusions regarding normal aging.

Consider the prevalence of disability among older adults. Functional disability could be considered one indicator of manifest illness among older adults. So far, so good. However, how shall we define functional disability? The answer may determine our conclusion about what is or is not normal for later life. Again, Mr. Tucker's situation may help us clarify the issues:

> When you get to Mr. Tucker's house, you find an apathetic, listless, very thin man of 81. He seems to be isolated socially, having few friends and even fewer family members in the area. (He never married and he has no living siblings.) Although he seems physically able to cook, he says that he hasn't been eating (or sleeping) regularly for quite a while—and he doesn't care if he never does again.

Is Mr. Tucker functionally disabled? If so, is this normal for someone of his age? According to the US Census Bureau, most persons aged 75 years old and older have a disability: 54% of those 75–79 years old had any type of disability with 38% having a "severe disability" (Brault, 2012). In contrast, Manton, Gu, and Lamb (2006) reported that 78% of the 75–84 age group was "non-disabled." How could such differing pictures of older adults emerge?

The answer lies in the definition of disability. The Census Bureau focuses on difficulty with functional activity for its specific definition of disability. The range of functional activities is somewhat broader than traditional definitions: lifting and carrying a weight as heavy as 10 pounds, walking three city blocks, seeing the words and letters in ordinary newsprint, hearing what is said in normal conversation with another person, having one's speech understood, and climbing a flight of stairs. In contrast, Manton et al. (2006) focused on *activities of daily living* (ADLs; e.g., taking care of basic hygiene, eating, getting dressed, using a toilet) and *instrumental activities of daily living* (IADLs; e.g., managing money, doing the laundry; preparing meals; shopping for groceries).

Not surprisingly, these different definitions of disability produce different depictions of functioning and normal aging. The metric we use in assessing functional ability is important for two reasons: The specific activities may be important in and of themselves; and one's ability to complete activities (such as ADLs and IADLs) acts as a proxy for underlying physical, cognitive, emotional, and social abilities. Thus, depending upon the range of functioning we wish to assess, we may conclude that Mr. Tucker is either disabled or not and that such a pattern of functioning is either normal or unusual aging!

What Is Abnormal or Unhealthy Aging?

Thus far, we have considered merely one side of the dilemma: What is normal aging? We have also limited ourselves to *physical* and *functional* definitions, steering clear of similar issues focusing on *mental* health problems or disorders.

> You notice that Mr. Tucker doesn't mention being in any terrible pain—that is until you mention his friend Ed. When you do, Mr. Tucker grabs his side and says how much it hurts to talk. You suggest that he lie down and rest for a minute, which he does.
>
> From the couch, Mr. Tucker begins to talk about Ed. It turns out that the two men were not just "friends" as Grace had implied. They were like brothers (if not closer) and had been since they were boys. "I'm good for two things," Mr. Tucker said, "no good and good for nothing. But Ed was my buddy anyway. Don't know why he bothered with me. I never made much of my life. But I do know that it won't be hunting season without him. Just can't do it alone and nobody in their right mind would want to hunt with an old fool like me."

Again, the presentation and responses of Mr. Tucker challenge us. Does he have a mental disorder? The answer depends upon resolving other issues: How will we define mental health among older adults? Conversely, how will we define mental disorder among older adults? In Part III of this book, we will discuss assessment and treatment approaches for many specific mental disorders. Here, however, we start at the beginning: definitions of mental health and mental disorder.

Mental Health and Mental Disorder

The Centers for Disease Control and Prevention and the National Association of Chronic Disease Directors (2008) thoughtfully summarized the importance of mental health in later life:

> The World Health Organization defines health as "a state of complete physical, mental, and social well-being and not merely the absence of disease or infirmity." Because mental health is essential to overall health and well-being, it must be recognized and treated in all Americans, including older adults, with the same urgency as physical health.

Indeed, in the past two decades mental health has become more integrated into the larger public health mission. As an example, the mental health of older Americans was identified as a priority by the Healthy People 2020 objectives (US Department of Health and Human Services, 2010) and more recently by the 2015 White House Conference on Aging (US Department of Health and Human Services, 2015).

Mental health among older adults is a multifaceted concept that reflects a range of clinical and research activity, rather than a unified theoretical entity (Qualls & Layton, 2010; Qualls & Smyer, 1995). Definitions of mental health in later life combine several complex elements: statistical normality, the link between individual functioning and group norms, the extent to which specific disorders can be effectively treated or controlled, and ideals of positive functioning.

Diagnostic and Statistical Manual of Mental Disorders (DSM-5)

In contrast to definitions of mental health, there is greater agreement on definitions of *mental disorder* (for all age groups, including older adults). For both clinical and research purposes, operational definitions of mental disorder usually follow the guidelines in the *Diagnostic and Statistical Manual of Mental Disorders*, now in its fifth edition (DSM-5; American Psychiatric Association, 2013). The DSM-5 is the standard classification of mental disorders used by mental health professionals in the United States. The DSM-5 defines several hundred distinct mental disorders and lists the specific diagnostic criteria for each disorder, as well as other information such as the impact of gender, culture, and aging on the expression of the disorders. Thus, mental disorder in older adults is operationally defined by patterns of disorders in the DSM-5.

A notable feature of the DSM system is that it uses a *categorical approach* to the classification of mental disorders. In other words, mental disorders are conceptualized as either being present (the diagnostic threshold is reached for an individual) or absent (the threshold was not reached). This follows the prominent model in medicine in which one either has a disorder (e.g., cancer) or one does not. In actuality, it is clear that mental disorders are best represented using a *dimensional approach* in which the severity of any specific disorder can be rated along a continuum from absent or mild to the most severe expression. This is the approach we endorse, to think dimensionally about mental disorders rather than categorically.

Earlier editions of the DSM (the first edition was published in 1952) used Roman numerals to identify new editions (e.g., DSM-II, DSM-III, and DSM-IV). However, with publication of DSM-5, the switch was made to Arabic numerals. This change is a true reflection of the current digital age in which we now live. The premise is that minor updates to the DSM can be disseminated more regularly, using sequential annotations of DSM-5.1, DSM-5.2, and so on until a full new edition is eventually published (to be called DSM-6). Although the DSM-5 is arguably the most comprehensive and sophisticated version yet developed, it is still a human-made system that is limited by our current scientific understanding of mental disorders. In our opinion, the DSM-5 is best viewed as a *tool* to be used by clinicians and researchers, not as a definitive manifesto that is above reproach and without criticism (for a discussion of some criticisms and limitations of the DSM; see Segal, Marty, & Coolidge, 2017).

The DSM-5 is often used in conjunction with the *International Statistical Classification of Diseases and Related Health Problems* (ICD, now in its 10th edition), produced by the World Health Organization (WHO). The ICD is a more broad and comprehensive manual that includes physical health as well as mental health disorders, and it is more widely used than the DSM-5 in Europe and other parts of the world. However, regarding mental disorders, the two manuals are highly compatible due to recent and ongoing efforts in the revision process of both systems to harmonize one with the other. In fact, with the passage of the Patient Protection and Affordable Care Act of 2010 in the US, as of October 2015, ICD-10 codes for mental disorders were required for all coding and billing purposes to insurance companies. Fortunately the DSM-5 provides a table that gives ICD-10 codes for all DSM-5 disorders to assist with this transition. For organizational purposes of this book, we will use the DSM-5 categorization of mental disorders throughout because the DSM-5 is still the prominent diagnostic system in the US. It helps to know that the DSM is highly aligned with the ICD.

Now that we have defined mental health and mental disorder, let's take a look at how these play out among older adults in the US. The Centers for Disease Control's Behavioral Risk Factor Surveillance System (BRFSS) is a large interview project that assesses general mental health status in the US. Respondents are asked to report how many of the previous 30 days their mental health was not good because of stress, depression, or problems with emotions. Frequent mental distress is defined as having 14 or more mentally unhealthy days in the previous 30 days. In 2010, only 7.4% of adults aged 65–74 reported frequent mental distress and the percentage was slightly lower (6.3%) for the 75 years or older group (CDC, 2010). Older adults clearly had the lowest rates of frequent mental distress compared to the younger age groups (see Figure 1.1).

A similar pattern emerges when the focus is on diagnosed mental disorders. The National Comorbidity Survey Replication (NCS-R, 2007) includes interviews about mental disorders from a large, nationally representative sample in the US. Again, older adults had lower levels of diagnosable anxiety disorders, mood disorders, impulse control disorders, and substance use disorders compared to younger adult groups (see Figure 1.2).

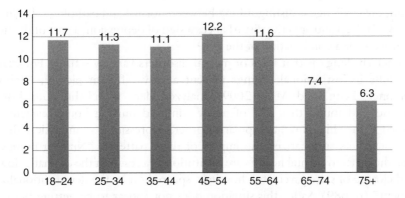

Figure 1.1   Frequent mental distress by age group in 2010 (% of respondents).
Source: Adapted from the Centers for Disease Control (2010).

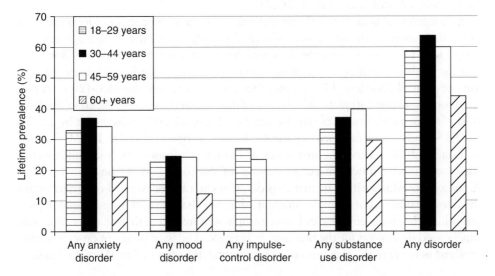

Figure 1.2   Lifetime prevalence of DSM-IV/World Mental Health Survey disorders by age group in the United States from the National Comorbidity Survey Replication sample.
Source: Adapted from the National Comorbidity Survey Replication (2007).

Depression is clearly not a part of normal aging. And, in the vast majority of cases, depression is a treatable condition, with several effective biological and psychotherapeutic approaches (Fiske, Wetherell, & Gatz, 2009). However, geriatric depression reflects the difficulty of discerning "normal aging" from pathological aging. Depression in later life appears in several guises. Depression can easily be confused with medical problems, cognitive impairment, variations in the grief process, and the normal ups and downs of later life. Only around 5.0% of adults aged 65 years or older currently have depression and 10.5% have had a lifetime diagnosis of depression (Centers for Disease Control and Prevention and the National Association of Chronic Disease Directors, 2008). However, the prevalence of depressive *symptoms* among older adults is much higher. (See Chapter 9 for a full discussion of the epidemiology of depression.)

Again, the challenge is distinguishing between normal and pathological aging: Are Mr. Tucker's sleep and appetite disturbances a sign of depression, a part of the normal aging process, or a combination of the two?

Another challenge is that rates of mental disorders vary by setting. For example, older adults in institutional settings present a very different picture. Grabowski, Aschbrenner, Feng, and Mor (2009) analyzed data from Minimum Data Set assessments and found that 27% of newly admitted nursing home residents were diagnosed with schizophrenia, bipolar disorder, depression, or an anxiety disorder. These researchers summarized the impact of these patterns: "Nursing homes have become the de facto mental health care institution as a result of the dramatic downsizing and closure of state psychiatric hospitals, spurred on by the deinstitutionalization movement" (p. 689). Sadly, this situation does not appear to be getting better, and recent data suggest that as the proportion of nursing home residents with serious mental disorders increases, the quality of care for all residents decreases (Rahman, Grabowski, Intrator, Cai, & Mor, 2013).

A final relevant issue is not simply the rates of mental disorder in older adults, but rather the pattern of the *age of onset* of mental disorders (e.g., the average age at which people tend to first experience the disorder). Informative data from the NCS-R indicate that the median age of onset was much earlier for anxiety disorders (11 years old) and impulse-control disorders (11 years old) than for substance use disorders (20 years old) and mood disorders (30 years old). For all of the mental disorders included in this large study, 50% of all lifetime cases start by age 14, 75% of all lifetime cases start by age 24, and 90% of all lifetime cases start by age 42 (Kessler, Berglund, Demler, Jin, Merikangas, & Walters, 2005). Thus, the first onset of most mental disorders is in childhood or adolescence and a much smaller percentage of disorders have an onset in later life. Among older adults with a mental disorder, it is clinically relevant to determine when the disorder began. For example, an older adult who has suffered from lifelong depression will likely have a lengthier and more complicated treatment than an older adult who experienced depression for the first time in later life. The issue of age of onset is further explored in many of the chapters on specific mental disorders in Part III of this book.

Linking the Physical and Mental in Later Life: Comorbidity

Mr. Tucker's pattern of symptoms—his lethargy, social withdrawal, and his reported physical pain—remind us of the importance of *comorbidity*: combinations of more than one mental disorder, physical illness, or combination of both. In a classic paper, gerontologist Gene Cohen (1992) provided a context for understanding comorbidity by outlining four useful paradigms for the interaction of physical and mental well-being among older adults:

- Psychogenic (or psychologically based) stress may lead to health problems.
- Health problems may lead to psychiatric disturbances.
- Coexisting mental and physical health problems may interact.
- Social and psychosocial resources may affect the course of physical or mental disorders.

Indeed, one's initial concern about a client or patient may be raised by seeing evidence of either a physical or mental health problem.

First, psychogenic stress may lead to physical health problems. In Mr. Tucker's case, abdominal pain may be a reaction to his grief over Ed's death. For Mr. Tucker, this physical symptom may be a more socially acceptable way for him to express his emotional pain. More generally, you are likely well aware of the strong connection between the mind and the body. You may have noticed in yourself or others times when stress from the environment affected you physically, for example through headaches, stomach upset, or teeth grinding.

Second, the direction of causality may be reversed, however, with a physical disorder leading to psychiatric problem. Consider the following sentence:

The five senses tend to decline with senescence.

Remove the f's, s's, c's and th's. Now try to make sense of what's left:

e ive en e tend to de line wi ene en e.

This example mimics high-frequency hearing loss among older adults and gives you a sense of how easily such a hearing loss might lead to delusions and confusion among this age group.

A third possibility is that coexisting physical and mental disorders may interact. One category of mental disorders among older adults underscores this interplay: cognitive impairment, including the neurocognitive disorders (formerly called the dementias). Cognitive impairment among older adults is a challenge for interdisciplinary diagnosis and treatment. Distinguishing among age-related cognitive change, mild cognitive impairment (MCI), and Alzheimer's disease or other major neurocognitive disorders can be difficult. (We discuss this important issue fully in Chapter 8.) In addition, differential diagnosis and prompt treatment requires ruling out a myriad of potentially reversible causes of confusional states: drug reactions, mental disorders, metabolic disorders, impaired vision and hearing, nutritional deficiencies, dehydration, brain tumors and traumas, and infections. This requires an interdisciplinary collaboration designed to assess complex patterns of comorbidity, in which distinctions between physical disorder and mental disorder become blurred.

Fourth, and finally, Cohen (1992) suggests that social and psychosocial resources can affect the course of physical and mental disorders. As we discuss in the stress and coping model (see Chapter 6), social support can buffer the negative effects of life stress and help people cope better with a myriad of problems. Even among those with a cognitive disorder, a positive social environment can enhance the person's dignity and quality of life.

Individual Differences and Assessment of Risk

Thus far, we have sketched general patterns of mental health and mental disorder among older adults, as a context for working with Mr. Tucker. One question has been implicit in this discussion: How is Mr. Tucker like other older adults of

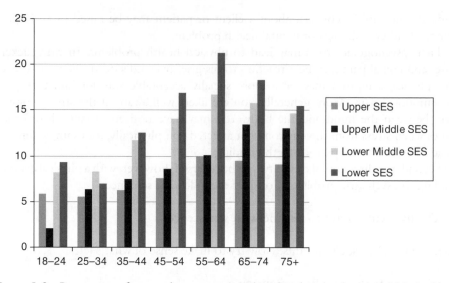

Figure 1.3   Percentage of respondents reporting that they have a chronic health problem stratified by age and socioeconomic status (SES).
Source: Adapted from Centers for Disease Control's Behavior Risk Factor Surveillance System (2007).

his age? In this section, the emphasis shifts to another question: How is Mr. Tucker different from other individuals his age?

What do we know about Mr. Tucker that would differentiate him from other 81-year-olds? What are the categories of information we would use in sorting older adults? Socioeconomic status (SES) dramatically affects the experience of aging. Consider the relationships among age, having a chronic health problem, and SES (see Figure 1.3). Data from the Behavioral Risk Factors Surveillance System (CDC, 2010) showed that individuals in the lower SES categories have the highest rates of chronic conditions throughout adulthood.

Moreover, by early mid-life (ages 35-44), those in the lower SES group already have chronic health problems at higher rates than those in the highest SES group at ages 55–64, 65–74, and 75+. Variability in risk among older adults is not limited to the physical or functional domains, however. There are similar patterns of variability in risk of mental disorders. Consider the risk for suicide. We resume our conversation with Mr. Tucker:

> … "I never made much of my life. But I do know that it won't be hunting season without Ed. Just can't do it alone, and nobody in their right mind would want to hunt with an old fool like me."

These words have a haunting finality to them. As you hear them, you begin to wonder about Mr. Tucker's will to live and his plans for the future. Should you ask him about these elements, about his potential for self-harm or suicide?

Psychiatric epidemiological data can be helpful in tracing patterns of suicide risk across the lifespan in the US (see Figure 1.4). Overall, a total of 42,773 people died

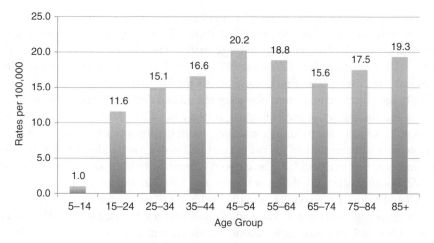

Figure 1.4 Suicide death rates per 100,000 people, ages 5 to 85+ for 2014 in the US.
Source: Adapted from Drapeau & McIntosh (for the American Association of Suicidology; 2015).

by suicide in 2014. Suicide death rates climb from early adulthood and then peak in both the 45–54 year old group and the 85+ year old group. Aggregated across later-life (65+), the threat of completed suicide is substantial, with older adults having a higher suicide death rate (16.6 per 100,000 people) than for the general population (13.4 per 100,00 people; Drapeau & McIntosh, 2015). Across the lifespan, men are much more likely to die by suicide than women, with 3.4 male deaths by suicide for each female death by suicide. White men are at especially elevated risk (24.1 per 100,000 people) with older White men at the absolute greatest risk of any group.

Armed with this knowledge of differential risk—particularly for white men over 80—you ask Mr. Tucker about his current plans and perspectives:

> "It sounds like you're feeling pretty blue. Have you ever thought about hurting yourself in any way?"
> "I may be down, but I'm not crazy!"

Mr. Tucker quickly gives you a sense of his own perspective on his problems, allowing you to follow up with specific questions regarding intent. The conversation could have gone in a different direction:

> "It sounds like you're feeling pretty blue. Have you ever thought about hurting yourself in any way?"
> "Every now and then I get that feeling."
> "I'm sorry to hear you are in so much pain. Have you thought about how you would do it?"
> "Well, I'd use that shotgun that I keep loaded next to the door—just head out to the barn, clear out the cows, and pull the trigger…"

This conversation confirms your fears—he has motivation, a way to achieve that purpose, and seemingly little concern about the consequences.

These two resolutions to the inquiry highlight the theme of variability among and between older adults. This variability is a hallmark of aging: As we grow older, we become increasingly distinct from our age-mates. This diversity among older adults (often called *inter-individual differences*) is the result of the complex patterns of both biological and biographical functioning across the life span.

The biographical elements may play a key role in two different ways: the history of the disorder and the history of the individual. In the case of Mr. Tucker's suicide potential, for example, we will want to know something about his previous experience with suicidal ideation: Has he been suicidal for many years and now grown older? Or, has he grown older and now become suicidal? These two divergent paths both arrive at suicidal risk in later life, but they offer very different suggestions for treatment attempts, the availability of social and emotional resources, and the likelihood of successful intervention.

In summary, we will want to know more about several key elements of Mr. Tucker's history: his social and economic resources, his current and past physical health, his current and past mental health, and his functional abilities. Approaches to these issues will be presented in Part II of this book.

The Context of Clinicians and Clients: Now What Do We Do?

Thus far, we have had one conversation with Mr. Tucker and we have gathered information about his current functioning, his previous history, and his future ability to continue to cope on his own. What will we do next?

Our approach to Mr. Tucker is a function of several, interrelated elements: our sense of his strengths and weaknesses (e.g., how acute is his crisis; is he a threat to himself or others; how has he handled personal challenges in the past; etc.); our assessment of his capacity to be involved in health care decision-making as an active participant in developing the treatment plan; and the service settings and contexts in which we work. These issues are discussed in detail in Chapter 17.

The context of mental health services for older adults has changed substantially since the 1970s. As part of a larger public policy of deinstitutionalization, there were increases in *both* institutional and outpatient services. In the institutional sector, inpatient services were shifted from state mental hospitals to private psychiatric hospitals, psychiatric units in general hospitals, and "swing beds" in general hospitals. As pointed out earlier, one other setting became increasingly important as a receiving site for mentally disordered older adults: nursing homes (Rahman et al., 2013).

Access to mental health services is another important issue. According to Karel, Gatz, and Smyer (2012), older adults significantly underutilize mental health services. And when older adults do receive services, they are less likely to receive care from a mental health specialist compared to younger and middle aged adults. As noted earlier, older adults represent the vast majority of the mentally disordered population in nursing homes (Rahman et al., 2013) representing an overreliance on nursing homes as a treatment setting for older adults with mental disorders. Pepin, Segal, and Coolidge (2009) examined the kinds of barriers that prevent younger and older adults from accessing mental health services, finding that stigma was at the bottom of the ranked list of barriers for younger and older adults alike. Instead, more practical issues such as concerns about paying for treatment, difficulty with transportation, and difficulty finding an appropriate mental health service provider were perceived as greater barriers. The shortage of specialists trained in geriatric mental health continues to be a problem plaguing the US mental health workforce (Institute of Medicine, 2012). This current and projected shortage can easily be deemed a crisis for the field.

These patterns of care—with a substantial bias toward inpatient, medically oriented services—are only one of two major elements that shape the availability of and access to mental health care for older adults. The second is the combined priorities of major funding sources for geriatric mental health: Medicare, Medicaid, and private insurance plans. We discuss these programs and their impacts in Chapters 14 and 15. These contextual factors—institutional patterns of service provision, insurance coverage, fee structures—affect the choices for services for Mr. Tucker. To work effectively with him, you will need to understand the coverage of mental health services that he has, the availability of services in your local community, and the range of services for which you can be reimbursed. These issues will be further discussed in Chapters 14 and 15.

The Biopsychosocial Model

We wish to round out this introduction to core issues in aging and mental health by introducing the *biopsychosocial model of mental disorders*. This popular and broad model represents current philosophical thinking about the etiology (or underlying causes) of mental disorders. In essence, the biopsychosocial model posits that the etiology of the vast majority of mental disorders is due to various intricate combinations of biological factors, psychological factors, and social factors (hence the name bio-psycho-social) (see Figure 1.5). Biopsychosocial factors are also thought to impact the manifestation and outcome of mental disorders.

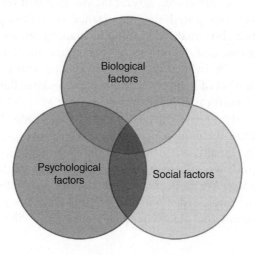

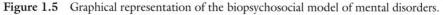

Figure 1.5 Graphical representation of the biopsychosocial model of mental disorders.

Briefly stated, *biological factors* include genetics, medical disorders, medications and other psychoactive substances, nutrition, hormones, and physical trauma (such as a head injury), whereas *psychological factors* include learned behaviors, faulty or unhelpful ways of thinking, one's coping strategies (whether effective or ineffective), defense mechanisms, self-esteem, and personality traits, all of which affect one's mental health. *Social factors* include culture, race, socioeconomic status, and religion as well as influences in one's environment that impinge on mental health and wellness, for example, adverse childhood experiences, current hassles and stressors, and larger social issues such as racism, discrimination, and political upheaval that affect people in those environments.

Viewing mental disorders through the biopsychosocial lens is especially important to ensure comprehensive assessment of all factors that could possibly play a role in the development and outcome of a mental disorder, and not just factors from one domain that at first blush seem prominent to the client or clinician. This is not to say that there are no mental disorders that do not load primarily on one domain or the other (for example, the neurocognitive disorders are known to have strong biological causes, whereas the eating disorders are known to be strongly affected by social and cultural factors). Rather the core idea is that for most people and for most mental disorders, it is best to view potential causes as having biological, psychological, and social influences, in varying degrees and combinations, as they play out in individual cases. We encourage you to keep this model in mind as we discuss the various mental disorders covered in Section III of this book. You will come to see that, with rare exceptions, biopsychosocial factors are almost always present and contribute to the etiology (and outcome) of psychopathology.

Summary and Conclusions

In this chapter, we have introduced several themes that will reemerge throughout the book. First, we highlighted the importance of philosophical assumptions regarding normal and abnormal functioning in shaping our assessment strategies, targets for intervention, and definitions of therapeutic success. Next, we emphasized the importance of individual differences in shaping our understanding of the etiology and presentation of mental health problems in later life. We also discussed briefly the fiscal and political context that shapes the availability of mental health services for older adults. These themes—ranging from individual functioning to social policy—illustrate the complexity of the task of providing mental health services to older adults. Finally, we introduced the biopsychosocial model, which is the lens through which we will strive to view the etiology of the mental disorders described in this book. We hope that these themes also reflect the excitement inherent in trying to bring order out of the chaos of needs and services, of trying to both understand the older client and match the client's needs with the services available.

Critical Thinking / Discussion Questions

1   Articulate some of the historical factors that have shaped your personal views of healthy aging and unhealthy aging, perhaps from your experiences in your family of origin. How might your personal views impact your clinical work with older adults?

2   Think of an older family member or friend who you know well. What are some of the salient biopsychosocial factors that contribute to the person's sense of well-being and/or distress?

Website Resources

American Psychological Association: Office on Aging
http://www.apa.org/pi/aging/index.aspx
American Psychological Association, Division 12, Section II: Society for Clinical Geropsychology
http://www.geropsychology.org
American Psychological Association, Division 20: Adult Development and Aging
http://www.apadivisions.org/division-20
Diagnostic and Statistical Manual of Mental Disorders (DSM-5)
www.dsm5.org
International Classification of Diseases (ICD)
http://www.who.int/classifications/icd/en
The State of Aging and Health in America (SAHA)
http://www.cdc.gov/aging/help/dph-aging/state-aging-health.html
Psychologists in Long-term Care (PLTC)
http://www.pltcweb.org
2015 White House Conference on Aging
http://www.whitehouseconferenceonaging.gov

References

American Psychiatric Association. (2013). *Diagnostic and statistical manual of mental disorders* (5th ed.). Arlington, VA: Author.

Baltes, P. B., & Baltes, M. M. (1990). Selective optimization with compensation. In P. B. Baltes & M. M. Baltes (Eds.), *Successful aging: Perspectives from the behavioral sciences* (pp. 1–34). New York, NY: Cambridge University Press.

Barbour, K. E., Helmick, C. G., Theis, K. A., Murphy, L. B., Hootman, J. M., Brady, T. J., & Cheng, Y. J. (2013). Prevalence of doctor-diagnosed arthritis and arthritis-attributable activity limitation—United States, 2010–2012. *Morbidity and Mortality Weekly Report, 62*(44), 869–873.

Brault, M. W. (2012). *Americans with disabilities: 2010, Current Population Reports, P70–131.* Washington, DC: US Census Bureau.

Centers for Disease Control and Prevention (CDC). (2010). *Behavioral risk factor surveillance system survey data.* Atlanta, Georgia: US Department of Health and Human Services.

Centers for Disease Control and Prevention (CDC). (2013). *The state of aging and health in America 2013.* Atlanta, GA: US Department of Health and Human Services. Retrieved from http://www.cdc.gov/aging/help/dph-aging/state-aging-health.html

Centers for Disease Control and Prevention, National Center for Chronic Disease Prevention and Health Promotion, Division of Population Health. (2010). Health-related quality of life (HRQOL) data. Retrieved from http://nccd.cdc.gov/hrqol

Centers for Disease Control and Prevention & Alzheimer's Association. (2007). *The healthy brain initiative: A national public health road map to maintaining cognitive health.* Chicago, IL: Alzheimer's Association.

Centers for Disease Control and Prevention & National Association of Chronic Disease Directors. (2008). *The state of mental health and aging in America. Issue Brief 1: What do the data tell us?* Atlanta, GA: National Association of Chronic Disease Directors. Retrieved from http://www.cdc.gov/aging/pdf/mental_health.pdf

Cohen, G. D. (1992). The future of mental health and aging. In J. E. Birren, R. B. Sloane, & G. D. Cohen (Eds.), *Handbook of mental health and aging* (2nd ed., pp. 893–914). San Diego, CA: Academic Press.

Drapeau, C. W., & McIntosh, J. L. (for the American Association of Suicidology). (December 22, 2015). *U.S.A. suicide 2014: Official final data.* Washington, DC: American Association of Suicidology. Retrieved fromhttp://www.suicidology.org/resources/facts-statistics

Fiske, A., Wetherell, J. L., & Gatz, M. (2009). Depression in older adults. *Annual Review of Clinical Psychology, 5,* 363–389.

Grabowski, D. C., Aschbrenner, K. A., Feng, Z., & Mor, V. (2009). Mental illness in nursing homes: Variations across states. *Health Affairs, 28,* 689–700.

Institute of Medicine. (2012). *The mental health and substance use workforce for older adults: In whose hands?* Washington, DC: National Academies Press.

Karel, M. J., Gatz, M., & Smyer, M. (2012). Aging and mental health in the decade ahead: What psychologists need to know. *American Psychologist, 67,* 184–198.

Kessler, R. C., Berglund, P., Demler, O., Jin, R., Merikangas, K. R., & Walters, E. E. (2005). Lifetime prevalence and age-of-onset distributions of DSM-IV disorders in the National Comorbidity Survey Replication (NCS-R). *Archives of General Psychiatry, 62,* 593–602.

Manton, K.G., Gu, X., & Lamb, V. L. (2006). Change in chronic disability from 1982 to 2004/2005 as measured by long-term changes in function and health in the U.S. elderly population. *Proceedings of the National Academy of Sciences, 103,* 18374–18379. Retrieved from http://www.pnas.org/cgi/doi/10.1073/pnas.0608483103

National Comorbidity Survey Replication (NCS-R). (2007). NCS-R Lifetime prevalence estimates. Retrieved from http://www.hcp.med.harvard.edu/ncs/ftpdir/NCS-R_Lifetime_Prevalence_Estimates.pdf

Pepin, R., Segal, D. L., & Coolidge, F. L. (2009). Intrinsic and extrinsic barriers to mental health care among community-dwelling younger and older adults. *Aging and Mental Health, 13,* 769–777.

Qualls, S. H., & Layton, H. (2010). Mental health and adjustment. In J. C. Cavanaugh & C. K. Cavanaugh (Eds.), *Aging in America. Vol. II: Physical and mental health* (pp. 171–187). Santa Barbara, CA: Praeger.

Qualls, S. H., & Smyer, M. A. (1995). Mental health. In G. L. Maddox (Ed.), *The encyclopedia of aging* (2nd ed., pp. 629–631). New York, NY: Springer.

Rahman, M., Grabowski, D. C., Intrator, O., Cai, S., & Mor, V. (2013). Serious mental illness and nursing home quality of care. *Health Services Research, 48,* 1279–1298.

Schaie, K. W. (2016). Theoretical perspectives for the psychology of aging in a lifespan context. In K. W. Schaie & S. L. Willis (Eds.), *Handbook of the psychology aging* (8th ed., pp. 3–13). New York, NY: Academic Press.

Segal, D. L., Marty, M., & Coolidge, F. L. (2017). Diagnostic and Statistical Manual of Mental Disorders, 5th ed. (DSM-5). In A. Wenzel (Ed.-in-Chief), *The SAGE encyclopedia of abnormal and clinical psychology* (pp. 1093–1095). Thousand Oaks, CA: Sage.

US Department of Health and Human Services. (2010). *Healthy people 2020*. Washington, DC: Author. Retrieved from https://www.healthypeople.gov

US Department of Health and Human Services. (2015). *2015 White House conference on aging*. Washington, DC: Author. Retrieved from http://www.whitehouseconferenceonaging.gov

2

Basic Gerontology for Working with Older Adults

Imagine that you have been hired as a consultant by a local nursing home. To prepare you for your first visit, the facility staff members have developed two case descriptions:

> Max won't move. He used to be a successful accountant, but he hasn't worked in several years when he began to forget things. Now he barely allows himself to be nagged out of the bed or dressed… He seems physically able to do things for himself but gently mumbles "I can't" when the nurses' aides encourage him to do anything. He looks very sad. When his photo album is brought to him he does spend some time mumbling and paging through it, but generally spends his time alone. He has been this way day in and day out, for as long as anyone can remember… (Cohn, Smyer, & Horgas, 1994, p. 152)

> Molly collects spoons, both clean and dirty, from the dining room trays and stores them very carefully in her dresser drawer. She argues violently when the nurse tries to remove them. The nurse gives long explanations of why they need to go back to the kitchen, but Molly insists that the staff are stealing her things (Cohn et al., 1994, p. 179)

Imagine that your consulting company has just landed a contract with a continuing care retirement community, commonly called a life-care community. The head of social services calls with the following referral:

> Gloria has moved to the assisted living portion of the community, following hip replacement surgery. She had lived in her own apartment for four years before the surgery. During that time, she had been an active participant in the read-aloud program at a local school, a member of the "galloping gourmet" club (featuring dinners in each other's apartment every month), and an avid bridge player.

Aging and Mental Health, Third Edition. Daniel L. Segal, Sara Honn Qualls, and Michael A. Smyer.
© 2018 John Wiley & Sons, Inc. Published 2018 by John Wiley & Sons, Inc.

Now Gloria is demanding to move back to her apartment. She complains that she wants more scheduling freedom, that she wants to cook her own meals again, and that she doesn't need any more "help." The social worker is concerned about Gloria's physical abilities and her capacity to make decisions on her own. Is Gloria's demand for "freedom" a sign of good mental health or a denial of her changed physical and mental abilities?

As any good consultant, you're immediately faced with a simple challenge: Do my knowledge and skills allow me to respond effectively? In these scenarios, the consultant also needs to ask him or herself: What do I need to know to work effectively with older adults?

This chapter is designed to provide an initial answer to that simple question. We begin with a brief depiction of the basic developmental issues necessary for a full understanding of aging and mental health. We end the chapter with a two-part question: How is clinical work with older adults similar to working with younger people? How is it different?

Developmental Issues in Mental Health and Aging

According to Schaie (1995), there are several key developmental issues that provide a useful foundation for clinical work with older adults. His suggested topics form an outline of mental health and aging: normal and pathological aging, individual differences in aging, age differences and age changes, changing person/environment interactions, and reversibility of age-related behavior changes.

Normal and pathological aging

As noted in Chapter 1, gerontology is the study of the process of aging. Geriatrics is the study and treatment of the diseases associated with aging. The boundaries between these two fields have become more and more blurred as researchers and clinicians question our basic assumptions about the course of development.

How can we differentiate normal from pathological aging? As noted in Chapter 1, if we take a statistical view, we might assume that chronic physical illness is part of normal aging. Consider arthritis, for example. Although approximately 50% of adults 65 and older have some form of arthritis, the condition is not a *universal* part of aging and, therefore, is not part of the normal process of growing older. Rather, arthritis would be considered an *age-related illness*. This means that rates for arthritis increase with age, but aging itself does not cause arthritis. An example of another age-related illness or disorder is a neurocognitive disorder, formerly called dementia (described in detail in Chapter 8). Although the rates of neurocognitive disorders increase with age, even substantially so, becoming cognitively impaired is still not a normal part of aging. Like arthritis, an underlying disease process causes the conditions.

Similarly, consider the epidemiological data on the prevalence of frequent mental distress and diagnosable mental disorders at different ages presented in Chapter 1 (see Figures 1.1 and 1.2). Several trends in these data are important. First, the percentage of adults experiencing frequent mental distress decreases as age increases. Second, older adults have the lowest rate of mental disorder of any age group. As Kessler et al. (2005) put it: "Prevalence was always lowest, sometimes substantially so, in the oldest age group (≥60 years)." One notable exception to this pattern is regarding cognitive impairment which is relatively more common among older adults (discussed fully in Chapter 8). Third, at any age, and especially in later life, only a minority of adults have a diagnosable mental disorder. Thus, having any type of mental disorder is definitely *not* a part of normal aging. Recent estimates suggest that approximately 26% of adults 60 years old and older meet the criteria for a mental disorder (Kessler et al., 2005). Even with mild cognitive impairment—which is presumed to be a marker for Alzheimer's disease and other neurocognitive disorders—it is a minority of older adults who are afflicted.

In sum, it is important to recall the distinctions among normal, optimal, and pathological aging. Equating age with disease is mistaking gerontology for geriatrics— a mistake in both research and clinical work.

Individual differences

Throughout life, three systems of influence work to assure that differences among people *increase with age*: normative age-graded influences, normative history-graded influences, and non-normative influences (Baltes, 1987; Riffin & Lockenhoff, 2015).

Normative age-graded influences are universal, time-ordered biological, psychological, and sociocultural processes that affect development. Age-norms or developmental tasks that are age-linked illustrate this type of influence. For example, in the United States most children enter first grade at age six or seven, representing a socially constructed influence. Some examples of biologically based normative age-graded influences include puberty, menarche, and menopause, all of which are events that usually mark a major change in a person's life.

Normative history-graded influences are events that most people in a specific culture experience at the same time. For example, the Great Depression (Elder, 1974), the holocaust (Hartman, 1997), school desegregation (Clotfelter, 2004), and the impact of AIDS (Elwood, 1999) were major social developments anchored in particular historical conditions that affected the development of children and adults. A more contemporary example includes the terrorist attacks on the World Trade Center on September 11, 2001, that profoundly impacted the views about personal safety and national security among many people in the United States. Yet another example is the impact of Hurricane Katrina on many older adults, their families, and their communities in the Southern part of the US (see Box 2.1).

The aging of our global society is another example of a normative history-graded influence on development (see Figure 2.1) (He, Goodkind, & Kowal, 2016).

Demographic data portray two simple facts: Over the coming decades we will witness both increasing numbers and increasing proportions of older adults in the United States and across the globe. At the global level, in 2012, one out of every nine persons was 60 years old or older. By 2050, one out of every five persons is projected to be over 60 years old (United Nations, 2012). Moreover, by 2050 the global population of people 60 years old and older is expected to surpass, for the first time in

Box 2.1   A historic event: The impacts of Hurricane Katrina

Wendell Pierce is an actor and Tony-award winning producer who is probably best known for his starring roles in *The Wire* and *Treme* on HBO, as well as his roles in films like *Selma, Ray,* and *Waiting to Exhale*. In his memoir, *The Wind in the Reeds* (Pierce, 2015), Pierce recounts his boyhood in his native New Orleans and the traumatic impacts of Hurricane Katrina on his then-elderly parents and their flood-ravaged black, middle-class neighborhood of Pontchartrain Park:

> The fate of Pontchartrain Park was sealed shortly after nine a.m., when the eastern walls of the London Avenue Canal, a drainage canal running through Gentilly two miles east of my family's home, began to bulge outward from the surge rushing in from the lake and finally gave way. The flood cascaded downhill, drowning the eastern half of Gentilly and submerging Pontchartrain Park, the bottom of the bowl, under as much as twenty feet of water—among the most severe flooding in New Orleans…
>
> Katrina left New Orleans later that day, but for three days the water kept relentlessly gushing into the city from swollen Lake Pontchartrain. By then 80 percent of New Orleans was underwater. Except for the French Quarter and the Garden District, both built on the city's highest ground, every neighborhood in the city took on water. Nearly fifteen hundred people were dead. Half the houses in the city had four feet of water in them, or more. There was no electricity or clean water in the city; looting and the breakdown of civil order would soon follow. Tens of thousands of New Orleanians were stranded in the city with no way out; many more evacuees were displaced, with no way back in. (pp. 214–215)

Pierce recounts his family's struggle to return to the city, to rebuild their lives and their neighborhood. His family's struggles and his parents' efforts were part of a larger story of devastation and resilience after Hurricane Katrina.

Kessler and his colleagues (Kessler et al., 2008) interviewed residents of the region five to eight months after the storm and one year later to assess the psychological impacts. They found three demographic variables were most predictive of psychological distress (serious mental illness, post-traumatic stress disorder, or suicidal ideation): age; income; and current living arrangements. Middle-aged adults were most at risk for continuing distress, as were those with lower incomes and those not living in the same town as before the storm. A common theme in these demographic factors was the ongoing nature of the catastrophe: Those in mid-life felt responsible for family members and friends; for those with few economic resources or not in their homes, the daily struggle of coping continued. In many ways, Pierce's family understood the need to restore their own family home and the community of Pontchartrain Park, reflecting individual and community resilience, and the support that community members provide each other.

When physical disorders were considered, however, older adults were disproportionately at risk. After Hurricane Katrina, almost half of the deaths immediately following Katrina were among adults 75 and older (Brunkard Namulanda, & Ratard, 2008). Among the oldest old—those 80 or older—patterns of death and disease were equally striking: They accounted for 41% of emergency treatment visits for illness due to chronic diseases after Katrina (Sharma et al., 2008).

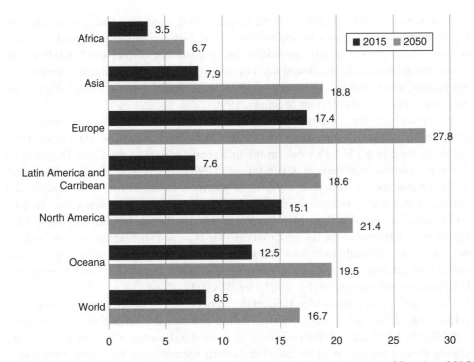

Figure 2.1 Percentage of population aged 65 years and older by major world region, 2015 and projected 2050.
Source: Adapted from He, Goodkind, & Kowal (2016).

history, the number of children under 15 years of age (United Nations, 2012). Like much of the rest of the world, the United States is in the midst of a longevity revolution, primarily due to the massive numbers of Baby Boomers marching into later life. Beginning in 2012, nearly 10,000 Americans turn 65 every day, essentially becoming an "older adult." Currently, about 14% of the US population is 65 or older. By 2030, more than 20% of the US population will have passed their 65th birthday, representing over 72 million people (US Census Bureau, 2014).

A fast growing subpopulation of older adults in the US is the oldest-old group (those 85 years old and older), who are also the frailest. This group is projected to increase from the current 5.5 million people to 8.9 million by 2030, to 14.1 million by 2040, and to 17.9 million by 2050 (US Census Bureau, 2014). The centenarian population (individuals 100 years old and older) in the US is also growing. The 2010 census (US Census Bureau, 2012) counted 53,364 centenarians, and this group was overwhelmingly comprised of women. For every 100 centenarian women, there were only about 21 centenarian men. Almost all of these centenarians (about 92%) were between the ages of 100 and 104. Being a "supercentenarian" (defined as those ages 110 and older) represented less than 1% of all centenarians.

The culmination of these trends has generated a profound impact on modern society—for the first time in human history, surviving into later life is an expected part of the life cycle in all of the developed parts of the world. These demographic patterns influence the experience of aging across the lifespan.

Finally, *non-normative influences* are random, rare, or idiosyncratic events that are highly important to a specific individual person but are not experienced by most people. These unique events are neither age-graded nor history-graded influences. Some examples include the distinctive impact of genetic predispositions, family configurations, and individual life events, such as winning the lottery, being adopted, or surviving a plane crash (Martin & Smyer, 1990).

Importantly, all three types of influences interact continually across the lifespan. In addition, the same influence may affect individuals differently depending upon their age at the time (e.g., Elder's work on the differential effects of the Great Depression) or the interaction of influences. Grundmann (1996), for example, studied the impact of father-absence on different cohorts of German men. Those who experienced father-absence either before or after World War II, when such absence was socially non-normative, delayed their own transition to fatherhood. In contrast, those who experienced father-absence linked to World War II, when such absences were socially normative, accelerated their own transition to fatherhood. A final example is the varied impacts and meaning of the terrorist attacks on the World Trade Center and US Pentagon on September 11, 2001 (see Box 2.2).

Other important aspects of individual differences are interindividual (between individuals) variability and intraindividual (within individuals) variability. For example, variability is a hallmark of older adults with a mental disorder. We must differentiate among three patterns of older individuals with mental disorder: those who had a mental disorder early in life and maintained the same disorder into later life; those who grew old and experienced mental disorder for the first time in later life; and those who came to later life with a liability (e.g., genetic influence, life stress, etc.) that was exacerbated by the conditions of later life, producing mental disorder (Fiske, Wetherell, & Gatz, 2009).

In sum, our clinical work must place older adults in a variety of contexts that produce individual differences: social, historical, and individual. We must understand

Box 2.2   Differential impact of an event: 9/11

In *The Reluctant Fundamentalist*, Mohsin Hamid (2007) depicts the impact of the 9/11 attacks on a young man from Pakistan who studied in the United States. The reaction to the novel, however, differed strongly by age/generation. One of us (MAS) participated in two discussions of the book. In one, the average age was 65+. This was a community book-reading discussion and the conversation became increasingly heated. It was clear that individuals' opinions about the book were directly related to their understanding of and interpretation of the 9/11 attacks. The other discussion occurred with a group of 16 first-year college students who had read the book as an assignment for all incoming students. As the discussion started, the students were asked how old they were when 9/11 happened. One raised his hand: "That was my first day of kindergarten." These young adults had a very different view of the events and themes embodied in 9/11 and in *The Reluctant Fundamentalist*. Same event, different impacts.

the various influences that shape development across the lifespan and produce the variability that accompanies aging.

Age differences and age changes

Understanding aging and its effects requires assessing several influences at once. Consider some of the basic questions of gerontology and geriatrics: Does intelligence decline with age? Is the risk of suicide greater in later life than in young adulthood? How would you investigate these questions?

One approach compares adults of different ages at one point in time, called a *cross-sectional* approach. This approach is appropriate for assessing age *differences*, because participants are all assessed at the same point in time, but it does not tell us much about age *changes* per se. Indeed, a cross-sectional approach confuses several elements at once: age differences, age changes, cohort effects, and time of measurement effects.

A second approach would follow the same people over a long period of time, measuring them at several different ages. This *longitudinal approach* allows for observation and measurement of actual age changes in the individuals' functioning. This approach, however, has the limitation of following only one cohort of individuals. In doing this, one might mistake the characteristics of that particular cohort's experience for general patterns of aging.

Data on intellectual functioning across the lifespan offer a compelling demonstration of the difference between cross-sectional and longitudinal views (Willis & Boron, 2015) (see Figure 2.2 and Figure 2.3). These data represent performance on several broad domains of cognitive functioning, from the famous Seattle Longitudinal Study (Schaie, 2015). The cross-sectional results in Figure 2.2 represent age differences.

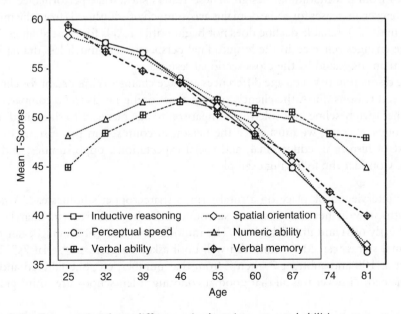

Figure 2.2 Cross-sectional age differences in the primary mental abilities.
Source: Schaie (2013).

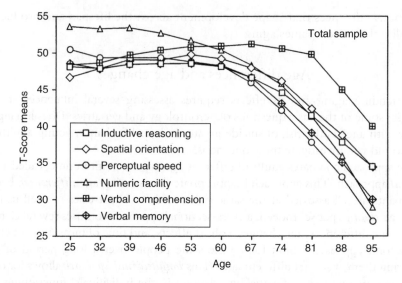

Figure 2.3   Estimated age changes in the primary mental abilities.
Source: Schaie (2013).

The pattern suggests that younger adults generally perform better than middle-aged adults, who generally perform better than older adults. If these findings were interpreted as age changes, we might think that there is a steep decline in most abilities around mid-life, but this, in fact, would be incorrect. Figure 2.3 represents actual age changes from a longitudinal design. These results show that performance remains stable or even increases for some domains across much of adulthood (from the mid-20s to the mid-50s); reliable decline does not begin until the 60s for most abilities. Thus, the age changes reflected in the longitudinal perspective are much less dramatic and severe than suggested by the cross-sectional results.

The distinction between age differences and age changes is important for clinicians for several reasons. First, the client's current functioning needs to be compared with his or her own baseline, not solely in comparison to age mates or to those in different age groups. Second, we must place the person in context—in this case in a cohort context of historical, educational, and social expectations, opportunities, and challenges. Consider the following example:

> The interview took place on a rural farm, a sharecropper's homestead. Mrs. Ella Smith, now in her late 80s, was surrounded by her children (in their late 50s and early 60s) and grandchildren. The multidimensional assessment began with a mental status test. Mrs. Smith did well until asked to perform "serial 7s": Please start at 100 and subtract 7, then 7 from that number, etc. She faltered and then explained: "I never was all that good at counting. I left school after third grade."

In Mrs. Smith's case, school was not one of the opportunities available to her rural cohort. Mrs. Smith was clearly educationally impaired. As it turns out, she was not also cognitively impaired. Her self-report reflected a comparison to her former functioning ("I never was good at counting"), a self-report confirmed by her children. In short, to equate her current inability with an age-related decline would have been off the mark.

Changing person/environment interactions

In his classic book, pioneering behavioral and social psychologist Kurt Lewin (1935) alerted us more than 80 years ago to the importance of concentrating on the inter-action between the person and the environment. Since then, a number of scholars have focused on the importance of the environment for the ongoing functioning of older adults (e.g., Aldwin & Igarashi, 2012; Lawton & Nahemow, 1973; Pynoos, Caraviello, & Cicero, 2010).

Several themes are important in conceptualizing the interplay between person and environment in later life. Some suggest that the optimal environment provides the best "fit" to the older person's changing abilities (e.g., Lawton, 1982; Kahana & Kahana, 2003). For some, the concept of fit includes notion of an optimally challeng-ing environment—a context that demands that the older person stretch a bit and use her abilities to the utmost.

Baltes and his colleagues (e.g., Marsiske, Lang, Baltes, & Baltes, 1996) suggest that the basic dynamics of later life reflect two subtle and profound shifts: First, there is a changing balance between gains and losses, with increasing social, psychological, and physical losses; second, there is an increasing investment of the individual's reserve capacity toward maintenance of functions, rather than toward growth. These gener-alizations, of course, provide a framework for assessing an older individual's unique combination of gains and losses, and her idiosyncratic combination of physical, psychological, and social growth and maintenance. An overview of the "balance sheet" of losses and gains in later life is presented in Table 2.1.

Neither an overly pessimistic or negative view of aging (e.g., associating later life with decrepitude, loneliness, and melancholy) nor an overly positive view of aging (e.g., the image of a sweet old grandmother baking cookies all day) serves the clini-cian and researcher well. Instead, to fully appreciate the challenges and opportunities experienced by a specific older person requires a realistic perspective of aging.

Table 2.1 A balance sheet of losses and gains in later life

Losses	Gains
Physical deterioration	Verbal skill
Speed of cognitive processing and capacity of working memory	Social judgment
Income	Emotional balance and self-regulation
Risk-taking	Values clarity
Declines in vision and hearing	Family and role choices
Social network	Expertise and wisdom
Social and work roles	Personality complexity

Like trying to get a photo into focus, we have to emphasize the unique experiences and qualities of the individual while understanding that variability increases with age. For example, if you take a group of 7-year-olds and a group of 77-year-olds, which group will have more variability on almost any measure of psychological functioning? The answer is the 77-year-olds.

Gatz and her colleagues (1996) described the mental health impact of the changing dynamics between the environment and older adults' vulnerabilities that contribute to this increasing variability. They emphasized three, interrelated elements: biological vulnerability (including genetic influences); stressful life events (including physical and social losses or challenges); and psychological vulnerability or diathesis (including pessimistic thinking and poor coping skills). For our purposes, the lesson is simple: Understanding the interaction between an older person and the social, physical, and psychological environment is essential for successful assessment and treatment of mental disorders in later life. Viewing the individual out of context will lead to an incomplete understanding of the person's difficulties and to subsequent ineffective treatment.

Reversibility of age-related behavior change

How inevitable are the losses associated with aging? Can you teach an old dog new tricks? Is there anything we can do about the most common mental disorders in later life? In the 1950s and 1960s, much of the research and clinical lore focused on depicting the expectable losses of old age, with an emphasis on prompt treatment of excess disability.

More recently, however, attention has shifted to preventive interventions and effective strategies for coping with the most common problems of later life. A common theme has emerged: the "plasticity" of behavior in later life (Kuhn & Lindenberger, 2016; Niederehe, 2015). In short, results from a number of areas confirm that there are a variety of strategies and approaches that can be effective in reducing some of the deficits commonly associated with later life.

Consider the area of intellectual decline with age. Several studies have documented the impact of training interventions designed to improve the functioning of older adults. In either small group or individual sessions, Schaie and his colleagues have documented the impact of five-hour training programs on older adults' cognitive functioning on laboratory tests and everyday functioning. Building on Schaie's earlier work, psychologist Sherry Willis developed a longitudinal research project, Advanced Cognitive Training for Independent and Vital Elderly (ACTIVE), to assess the modifiability of cognitive changes in later life. The project compared the effects of training on one of three cognitive interventions: memory, reasoning, or speed of processing. She and other colleagues have documented the lasting impact of such interventions on cognition, everyday functioning, and other behaviors, such as driving, with follow-ups 7 and 14 years later (Willis & Boron, 2015). (For more detailed summaries of this work, see Unverzagt et al., 2009; Willis & Bellville, 2016).

A variety of approaches can mitigate some of the losses of later life. The challenge for both the clinician and the older adult is to assess realistically the rewards of improvement likely to come from an investment of time and personal attention. These important issues will be considered in more detail throughout Part III of the book.

The Complexity of Working with Older Adults: Contexts, Cohorts, and Specific Challenges

Most mental health practitioners who work with older adults are not geriatrics or gerontology experts (Institute of Medicine, 2012; Qualls, Segal, Norman, Niederehe, & Gallagher-Thompson, 2002). For example, the American Psychological Association's Center for Workforce Studies reported that only about 1% of psychologists who were surveyed identified geropsychology as their primary specialty (American Psychological Association [APA], 2010; Stamm et al., 2016). Across all respondents, only 8.5% of psychologists' health service provider time was spent with older adults (APA, 2010). Licensed psychologists who reported at least occasionally providing care to older adults spent an average of 8.7 hours per week providing direct services and 1.6 hours providing services to family members or other caregivers.

Many professionals have come to serve older adults after working with other populations. Even those who have specialty training in geropsychology must focus on a simple question when working with older adults: Are the basic approaches to assessment and treatment different when working with older adults or are they the same as when working with other adult populations? Our answer is similar to the advice attributed to Yogi Berra: When you come to a fork in the road, take it. Working with older adults is both different from and similar to working with other age groups. In this section, we will briefly review both aspects. Our discussion is guided by the template provided by Knight (2004) and Knight and Pachana (2015), who have proposed the Contextual, Adult Life-Span Theory for Adapting Psychotherapy (CALTAP) to guide psychotherapeutic work with older adults. Table 2.2 provides an overview of this model.

Table 2.2 An overview of individual, cohort, and contextual elements affecting assessment and psychotherapy with older adults

Elements of maturity	Specific challenges	Cohort effects	Contexts
Cognitive and emotional complexity	Chronic physical illnesses and disability	Cognitive abilities and education	Age-segregated communities
Expertise	Grieving for the loss of loved ones	Word usage	Aging services agencies
Areas of competence	Caregiving	Values	Senior recreation sites
Multiple family experiences	Changes in cognitive functioning	Normative life paths	Medical settings and long-term-care settings
Accumulated interpersonal skills	Changes in economic resources	Social-historical life experiences	Age-based laws and regulations

Sources: Adapted from Knight (2004) and Knight & Pachana (2015).

Differences

The differences in psychotherapeutic approach to working with older adults stem from changes over time in the older adult herself, differences between the contexts of older people and younger people, cohort differences, specific challenges commonly experienced in later life, and potential differences in the therapeutic alliance.

Interpersonal qualities and maturation   Two aspects of older adults' functioning may differentiate them from younger adults: an increasing cognitive maturation and a changing sense of time.

Knight (2004; Knight & Qualls, 1995) has suggested that older adults develop increasing expertise in family, work, and social relationships across the lifespan. In addition, older adults may show increasing emotional complexity, with a greater understanding and control of their affective states (Carstensen & Mikels, 2005). From a psychotherapeutic perspective, this may offer an opportunity to collaborate with the older client in reflecting on the current problem within a perspective of past problem-solving successes: "How have you handled similar challenges in the past?"

Another frequently differentiating aspect of working with older adults is their sense of time (Lang & Carstensen, 2002). First, there is the obvious difference that more time has passed for older adults—giving them both more experience and the opportunity for greater perspective, an opportunity unfortunately missed by some.

A frequent benchmark used by one of our older friends reflects this greater perspective. When faced with a problem, he routinely asked: "Will it matter a year from now?" If the answer was no, he would not worry too much about that particular problem.

A second aspect of time reflects a subtle change in older adults' temporal calculus: Oftentimes there is a shift from focusing on time lived to concentrating on the time left to live (e.g., Carstensen, Isaacowitz, & Charles, 1999; Wade-Benzoni, Tost, Hernandez, & Larrick, 2012). These important differences in the perception of time left in life typically lead younger adults and older adults to differ in the types of goals they pursue. Younger people tend to pursue goals that expand their horizons and provide new social networking opportunities; older adults tend to pursue goals that are more emotionally meaningful (Carstensen, Fung, & Charles, 2003; Carstensen et al., 1999). For some, shuttling between these two represents one of the psychotherapeutic challenges—how to keep focused on the present and the future, without either denying or being consumed by the past.

Contextual complexity   Working effectively with older adults requires recognizing the complexity of their lives and the impact of their contexts. We discussed the potential impact of the physical environment earlier. Here, we focus on the complexity of two aspects of the social, interpersonal environment: family members and those who provide care and support to the older client.

Knowing a person's age can provide some information about the historical time and cohort experiences to which she has been exposed. Knowing her generational position can also tell us much about the resources and demands presented by family members, about the give and take of family members and friends. Consider two men:

> Bryce is a 67-year-old CEO of a billion-dollar-a-year company. He is a middle generation adult, with caregiving concerns for his 89-year-old mother and his two children in their 20s.
>
> Charles is a 38-year-old professional. He also is a middle generation adult who divides his time and resources among his 80-year-old mother and his children who are in elementary school.

These men differ in age and life stage, but they share a generational position that affects their psychological well-being. Focusing solely on their ages would overlook the psychological and social complexity of their generational positions.

Family members and friends provide the majority of assistance to older adults who need help because of physical or mental health problems (Coughlin, 2010). In the United States, 52 million caregivers provide assistance to someone 18 or older with a disability or illness, including approximately 40 million family caregivers providing 37 billion hours of care to adults with activity limitations (Couglin, 2010; Reinhard, Feinberg, Choula, & Houser, 2015). Oftentimes, however, the family caregivers are complemented by formal and informal services provided by physicians, social agency staff members, and friends. Again, to understand effectively the life context of the older client, the clinician must assess the availability of two types of support: emotional support in the give and take of daily interactions, and support that would be available in a time of crisis. In addition, the mental health professional must understand the affection and support that the older client provides to other family members.

The older population is also becoming more ethnically and racially diverse (Ortman, Velkoff, & Hogan, 2014), yet another factor that influences the contextual complexity of work with older people. For example, the Hispanic portion of the over-65 population will increase from its current rate of 7.3% to 18.4% by 2050; at the same time the Non-Hispanic White proportion of older adults will shrink from 79.3% to 60.9%, while the Black portion of the older population will rise from 8.8% to 12.3% during the same time frame (Ortman et al., 2014). These racial and ethnic categories may mask additional diversity. For example, 26 census-defined sub-ethnic groups make up the category of Asian Americans, coming from more than two dozen countries (APA, 2009). Other important aspects of diversity include the growing number of older adults who are lesbian, gay, or bisexual or who are transgender and gender nonconforming, who require competent and affirming services from health and mental health professionals (Cooper et al., 2016). Indeed, effective practice with older adults requires multicultural competency in aspects of assessment and treatment (APA, 2009), a theme we return to later in this chapter.

In many cases, older adults' contextual complexity requires clinicians to leverage their gerontological expertise. This means sharing problem-solving approaches with those who have the most frequent contact with the older client: family members, friends, and other service providers, especially primary care physicians. Collaboration is a keystone in effective assessment and treatment of mentally disordered older adults, a theme we will return to in Part IV of this book.

Cohort differences   Each of us carries with us the imprint of the culture and time in which we live. Think of today's oldest old: born 80 or more years ago, witnesses to almost unimaginable technological changes, witnesses to world war and cold war, survivors of economic upheavals, and among the earliest beneficiaries of Medicare and Medicaid. These experiences affect the ways that older adults encounter the challenges of later life. Consider, for example, one of our older clients who for the past 20 years wore a fresh pair of socks every day, donating the "old" socks to a charity at the end of each month. At first blush, this behavior may appear unusual until one considers the context: As a young boy growing up during the Great Depression, he and his family were extremely poor and could not afford clothing for the children, even socks to wear to school. In his later years, he "treated himself" to fresh socks each and every day as a reminder of the early struggles he had overcome.

Members of different cohorts, for example, may use different language to describe similar reactions.

Hazel reported that she was "frustrated" when the hospital social worker reported that Medicare would not pay for her medications.

The mental health professional probed Hazel's frustration. It became clear that younger clients might have used another word: angry.

Cohorts may also differ in their patterns of help-seeking and problem definition. When faced with a mental health problem, today's older adults might first seek out a primary care physician, a minister, or a neighbor—but not a mental health professional. Many older adults in the current cohort grew up with especially pejorative and stigmatized views of mentally ill individuals and mental health treatment. Indeed, "treatment" at that time was reserved only for the most severe forms of mental disorder (e.g., a psychotic disorder like schizophrenia) and usually meant long-term stays in locked units of state psychiatric hospitals. Effective psychiatric medications, such as major tranquilizers for the treatment of schizophrenia and other forms of psychosis, were not developed until the 1950s, meaning that treatments prior to that time for people with severe mental disorders were notoriously ineffective, and oftentimes cruel and inhumane, at least through the later part of the nineteenth century. There is some evidence that younger cohorts have higher rates of mental disorders (e.g., Kessler et al., 2005). Tomorrow's older adults, therefore, may be much more comfortable with mental health treatment, perhaps changing the profile of where mental health treatment is provided for older adults.

Another important aspect that interacts with cohort is diversity, including the impacts of what Bronfenbrenner (2005) called the individual's "social address" on the older person's experience as part of a specific cohort: the individual and combined effects of race, culture, ethnicity, gender, and sexual orientation (Tazeau, 2011). For example, Moen (2016) recently highlighted the impact of three elements—education, gender, and timing within a cohort—on poverty rates among older adults. Drawing on census data, she found that overall about one in 10 Baby Boomers was in poverty in 2014. But the rates varied by gender: 11.8% of Boomer women and 9.9% of Boomer men were living below the poverty line. Moen also divided the Baby Boomers into Leading Edge (born between 1946–1954) members, who were born after the end of World War II and during the Korean conflict, and Trailing Edge (born between 1955–1964) members, born during period of economic prosperity before the Vietnam war escalation. The Leading Edge and Trailing Edge categories were also proxies for age within the Boomer cohorts. As Moen (2016) points out, age and gender intersect with education to affect rates of poverty in late life: Trailing Edge Boomer men with a college degree had the lowest rate of poverty (5%), while one in three (33.5%) of Leading Edge Boomer women without a high school diploma was likely to be poor.

Aspects of culture and diversity impact, sometimes in profound ways, how individuals express, experience, and cope with feelings of distress, the stigma associated with mental health treatment, and the preferences for and barriers to treatment for mental health problems (US Department of Health and Human Services, 2001). The American Psychological Association's guidelines for psychological practice with older adults emphasize the importance of understanding the interactions among sociocultural factors (e.g., gender, ethnicity, sexual orientation, socioeconomic status) and the experience and expression of psychological and health challenges in later life (APA, 2004). The American Psychological Association's Committee on Aging (2009) summarized the importance of these issues:

> …racial and ethnic minorities are overrepresented in many subgroups at high risk for the development of mental illnesses, and they have less access to mental health services than Whites, are less likely to receive needed services, and often receive a lower quality of care. As a result, they incur a disproportionately high disability burden. This is especially the case with the minority elder who has a serious mental illness (Karlin, Duffy, & Gleaves, 2008).

(We return to the significant concerns of older adults with serious and chronic forms of mental disorders in Chapter 10.)

The specificity of challenges in later life   In sharp contrast to the increased maturity associated with normal development throughout the lifespan discussed earlier, it is equally important to be aware of the serious challenges of growing older. According to Knight (2004) there are several problems that, although not unique to later life, are commonly experienced by older adults. These areas include chronic physical illness and disability, grieving the loss of loved ones, and caregiving for an ill family member. An important premise of Knight's work is that these problems are conceptualized as "challenges" that can be overcome with rehabilitation, psychotherapy, or other types of intervention. This perspective helps us recognize that it is not normal to become clinically depressed, severely anxious, or have difficulty managing one's day to day activities at any stage of the lifespan and that when signs of mental disorder are recognized, appropriate treatments should be offered.

Disability, chronic illness, and medication use The Americans With Disabilities Act defines a disability as an individual's physical or mental impairment that substantially limits one or more of the individual's major life activities. By this definition, 38.7% of those 65 years old and older reported having one or more disabilities (He & Larsen, 2014), reflecting limitations in hearing, vision, cognition, walking or climbing stairs, self-care, or independent living. The rates of disability increased with increasing age: 74%

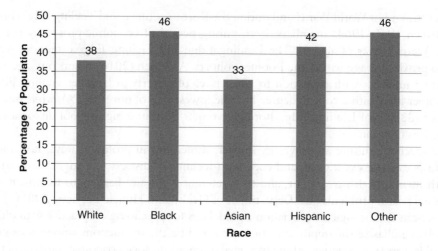

Figure 2.4   Percentage of United States population aged 65 and over with a disability by race. *Source*: Adapted from He & Larsen (2014).

Note: "Other" in race includes the categories of American Indian or Alaska Native, Native Hawaiian or Other Pacific Islander, some other race, and two or more races.

of those 65–74 had no disabilities; 55% of those 75–84 had none; and only 28% of those 85 years old and older had none.

Increasingly, though, the definition of disability focuses attention not only on the individual, but also on the social and physical contexts, which are clearly linked to differential rates of disability. For example, the rates of disability for those 65 and over varied by race and Hispanic origin (see Figure 2.4; He & Larsen, 2014), with Blacks and those of Other/Mixed race having the highest rates (about 46% in both groups).

Similarly, the rates of the combination of disability and poverty varied by racial or ethnic group. Among older adults with a disability, 11% of Whites lived in poverty, 17% of Asians lived in poverty, and 24% of Blacks lived in poverty (He & Larsen, 2014). The living arrangements for older adults with disabilities also varied by racial or ethnic origin: 15% of disabled Asian older adults lived alone, compared to 31% of Whites and 31% of Blacks (He & Larsen, 2014). Finally, disability rates varied across states, ranging from 35% of older adults in Arizona to 48% of Mississippi's older adults. These local and regional contexts shape the settings for collaboration in responding to disability.

Drawing on data from the National Health and Aging Trends Study, Freedman and his colleagues proposed a new measure of disability and functioning (Freedman et al., 2011) that combines both disability and the individual's ability to compensate and continue to function. In addition to traditional measures of activities of daily living, Freedman and his colleagues focused on the physical capacity needed to carry out tasks at home and in the neighborhood. Their survey questions assessed one's

> ability in the last month to carry out, without devices or help from another person, the following validated pairs: walk 6 blocks/3 blocks, walk up 20 stairs/10 stairs, lift and carry 20 pounds/10 pounds, kneel down/bend over (without holding on to anyone or anything), put a heavy object on a shelf overhead/reach up over head, open a sealed jar using hands only/grasp small objects.

They suggest dividing older adults into five groups (Freedman et al., 2014):

> Those who (1) are fully able; (2) have successfully accommodated declines by using assistive technology or environmental features; (3) have reduced their activity frequency but report no difficulty, (4) report difficulty doing activities by themselves, even when using any accommodations they may have in place; and (5) receive assistance from another person.

Once again, the individual's social address is related to the stage of disability. For example, 45% of those in the highest income level were "fully able," while only 23% of those in the lowest income quartile were "fully able." Similarly, the rates of those who needed assistance from others varied from 19% for Whites to 33% for older adults of Hispanic origins (Freedman et al., 2014).

Another indicator of health is the presence or absence of chronic disease, such as hypertension, coronary heart disease, stroke, cancer, diabetes, obesity, hepatitis, and arthritis (Centers for Disease Control and Prevention, 2012). As of 2012, about half of all adults had one chronic health condition, and about 1 in 4 had multiple chronic health conditions, but the prevalence rates varied by race/ethnicity and age (Ward et al., 2014). When race and ethnicity were considered across all ages, two groups stood out: those who self-reported as Hispanics and non-Hispanic Asians. Of those who identified themselves as Non-Hispanic Whites, Blacks, or Other Races, 47–50% reported having no chronic conditions. In contrast, approximately 65% of Non-Hispanic Asians and Hispanics reported having no chronic conditions (Ward et al., 2014). When age was considered, only 14% of those 65 and older had no chronic conditions, in contrast to those 18–44 (74%) and 45–64 (37%). At the other end of the spectrum, 33% of older adults had three or more chronic conditions, whereas those in younger age groups had much lower rates: 18–44 (2%); 45–64 (14%) (Ward et al., 2014).

Chronic conditions are likely to be part of the treatment landscape for those working with older adults. In addition, recent analyses suggest cohort differences in rates of disability and chronic conditions (Martin & Schoeni, 2014). When compared to the 40–64 population of a previous generation, those in that age range during 2004–2010 had higher rates of disability and chronic conditions. This suggests that they may arrive in later life with higher rates of disability than today's cohort of older adults.

Given this profile of older adults' chronic conditions and disabilities, it is not surprising that older adults report taking more prescription medicines than members of other age groups (National Center for Health Statistics, 2014). Almost half of all Americans reported taking at least one prescription medicine in the last month, but the pattern of use varied by age: Only 10% of those 65 and older reported taking no prescription medicine, while 61% of those 18–44 and 34% of those 45–64 reported no prescription use. In contrast, 40% of older adults reported using five or more prescription medicines (National Center for Health Statistics, 2014). Among older adults, a large majority (71%) took at least one cardiovascular agent and almost half took a cholesterol-lowering agent in the last month. Other frequent categories include anti-acid reflux medicines, antidiabetics, anticoagulants, analgesics, and antidepressants (National Center for Health Statistics, 2014). (Thirteen percent of older adults reported using an antidepressant in the last month.)

Besides taking more medications, older adults also metabolize medications more slowly than younger adults and it is common for them to take numerous medications prescribed by multiple providers. As a consequence, older adults are at a much greater risk for adverse reactions to a medication or to combinations of medications than younger adults. (We will return to the challenge of polypharmacy and its potential impacts in Chapter 8.)

Apart from a modest developmental change of central nervous system slowing, the major physical challenges for the mental health professional and the older client involve the interrelationship of physical and mental health. As noted in Chapter 1, there are four paradigms for examining the links between physical and mental health, reflecting the complexity of physical and mental interactions for older adults:

- Psychological or psychogenic stress may lead to physical health problems.
- A physical disorder may lead to a psychiatric disturbance.
- Coexisting physical and psychiatric disorders may interact.
- Social and psychological resources can affect the course of a physical disorder.

These complex interactions of physical and mental health for older adults require clinicians to monitor closely the older client's physical well-being. Thus, clinicians must have a solid understanding of the various kinds of chronic medical illnesses common in later life and the psychological impact of these illnesses, pain control techniques, and strategies to increase medication adherence (Knight, 2004). Close collaboration is needed among the range of people who interact with the older client: family members, friends, the primary care physician, and other health care and social service providers. (We will return to this collaborative theme in Chapter 14.)

Grieving losses A sad reality of aging is that with advanced age we will inevitably outlive some if not many of the people whom we have loved. As an example, one of our older family members (a grandmother to DLS) had a prized possession of photo of 20 couples who were present at her wedding in 1936. Many of the individuals depicted had remained lifelong friends. On her 90th birthday, she realized that she had outlived everyone in the photo, including her husband of 65 years. Thus, a common theme in psychotherapy with older adults involves grief work (Knight, 2004), in many cases, multiple losses over a period of time. Besides helping an older client come to grips with the loss and accept the loss, the focus of psychotherapy also typically turns to the future, helping the older person craft a meaningful existence despite the loss of loved ones.

Caregiving Given the high rates of physical illness in late life, many relatively healthy older adults find themselves providing care for a family member who is physically frail, cognitively impaired, or in many cases, failing both physically and cognitively (Knight, 2004). Due to the caregiving demands, many caregivers become overwhelmed and experience high levels of emotional distress (Knight, 2004). Specific forms of psychotherapy have been developed and tested to help caregivers manage extremely difficult and taxing caregiving situations, with promising results (e.g., Gonyea, O'Connor, & Boyle, 2006; Knight, Lutzky, & Macofsky-Urban, 1993;

Qualls & Williams, 2013). We will return to the theme of caregiving in Chapter 16; caregiving in the context of caregiving challenges for an individual with cognitive impairment is addressed in Chapter 8.

Countertransference issues   Encounters with older adults as clients likely elicit a range of responses from the clinician, including stereotypical assumptions, fantasies, and projections about aging and older adults (Knight, 2004; Knight & Pachana, 2015). At times, the countertransference issues raised may be either current issues in the clinician's own relationship with his or her parents or grandparents, or future issues on the horizon in the clinician's own family. Similarly, working with older adults may raise concerns about one's own aging, frailty, dying, and death. In each instance, the clinician must first be aware of the potential for countertransference processes and then depend upon supervision or collegial support to help differentiate the clinician's projections from the client's reality.

Similarities

Although Knight's work describes many important aspects of later life that should be thoughtfully considered and understood in clinical work, working with older clients is not entirely different from working with other groups. Throughout this book, we will be discussing approaches to assessment and treatment that build upon techniques developed and used with other age groups. In some cases, there have been modifications to accommodate age-related changes (e.g., large print versions of assessment instruments). In other cases, there has been a relatively straightforward application of previously developed approaches to the problems of later life (e.g., cognitive-behavioral therapy). Important findings from psychotherapy outcome studies with older adults have demonstrated unequivocally that psychotherapy with older adults is effective, roughly equivalent to the psychotherapy with younger adults and to the effects of psychiatric medications with older adults (see reviews by: Ayers, Sorrell, Thorp, & Wetherell, 2007; Gallagher-Thompson & Coon, 2007; Pinquart & Sorenson, 2001; Lichtenberg & Mast, 2015; Knight & Pachana, 2015; Powers, 2008; Satre, Knight, & David, 2006; Scogin, Welsh, Hanson, Stump, & Coates, 2005). A note of caution about these findings, however, is that there is very little research on the efficacy of various psychotherapies among the oldest-old group (i.e., 85+ years). Our working assumption is that the essential skills that contribute to an effective clinician are also necessary for working effectively with older adults—necessary but not sufficient. In addition, the wise clinician must also call upon an appreciation of the developmental influences at work in later life.

Summary and Conclusions

In this chapter, we have provided a broad overview of the major concepts and themes of gerontology, highlighting aspects of aging that are critical for the further understanding of mental health and mental disorder. Clinical work with older adults requires knowledge about normal age-related changes, disease processes, cohort effects, specific challenges associated with aging, and the distinct social environment of older adults in our society. In working with older adults, knowledge about individual differences and the diversity of the experience of the aging process is also necessary. Explicit and implicit models of aging shape clinicians' approaches to older adults and older adults' own expectations of later life. In the next chapter, we explore several dominant themes that provide a context for our psychotherapeutic work.

Critical Thinking / Discussion Questions

1   Consider the specific demographic profiles of the older adults in your county or service area. What are the implications of their social addresses for developing and implementing assessment and treatment approaches?
2   Develop a timeline of normative age-graded, history-graded, and non-normative events for members of today's older adult cohort. Develop a timeline for your own cohort. Compare and contrast them, with particular attention to how the similarities and differences might affect your work together.
3   What advice would you give to today's teenagers to best prepare them for later life?
4   What do you find most challenging about your prospects for working with older adults? Conversely, what do you find most attractive about working with older adults?

Website Resources

A resource for thinking about developmental tasks across the lifespan
https://www.apa.org/pi/aging/lifespan.pdf
American Psychological Association: Guidelines for Psychological Practice with Older Adults
http://www.apa.org/practice/guidelines/older-adults.pdf
Multicultural Competency in Geropsychology
http://www.apa.org/pi/aging/programs/pipeline/multicultural-competency.pdf
Healthy Aging
http://www.ghc.org/healthAndWellness/index.jhtml?topic=adult/seniorHealth
The Seattle Longitudinal Study
https://sharepoint.washington.edu/uwsom/sls/Pages/default.aspx
Demographic Resources
http://www.un.org/esa/population/publications/2012PopAgeingDev_Chart/2012
    PopAgeingandDev_WallChart.pdf
The US Census: An Aging World
https://www.census.gov/library/publications/2016/demo/P95-16-1.html

References

Aldwin, C., & Igarashi, H. (2012). An ecological model of resilience in late life. *Annual Review of Gerontology and Geriatrics, 32,* 115–130.

American Psychological Association. (2004). Guidelines for psychological practice with older adults. *American Psychologist, 59,* 236–260.

American Psychological Association, Committee on Aging. (2009). *Multicultural competency in geropsychology.* Washington, DC: American Psychological Association. Retrieved from http://www.apa.org/pi/aging/programs/pipeline/multicultural-competency.pdf

American Psychological Association. Center for Workforce Studies (2010). *2008 APA survey of psychology health service providers.* Retrieved from http://www.apa.org/workforce/publications/08-hsp/index.aspx

Ayers, C. R., Sorrell, J. T., Thorp, S. R., & Wetherell, J. L. (2007). Evidence-based psychological treatments for late-life anxiety. *Psychology and Aging, 22,* 8–17.

Baltes, P. B. (1987). Theoretical propositions of life-span developmental psychology: On the dynamics between growth and decline. *Developmental Psychology, 23,* 611–626.

Bronfenbrenner, U. (2005). *Making human beings human: Bioecological perspectives on human development.* Thousand Oaks, CA: Sage.

Brunkard, J., Namulanda, G., & Ratard, R. (2008). Hurricane Katrina deaths, Louisiana, 2005. *Disaster medicine and public health preparedness, 2*(4), 215–223. doi:10.1097/DMP.0b013e31818aaf55

Carstensen, L. L., Fung, H., & Charles, S. (2003). Socioemotional selectivity theory and the regulation of emotion in the second half of life. *Motivation and Emotion, 27,* 103–123.

Carstensen, L. L., Isaacowitz, D. M., & Charles, S. T. (1999). Taking time seriously: A theory of socioemotional selectivity. *American Psychologist, 54,* 165–181.

Carstensen, L. L., & Mikels, J. A. (2005). At the intersection of emotion and cognition aging and the positivity effect. *Current Directions in Psychological Science, 14*(3), 117–121.

Clotfelter, C. T. (2004). *After Brown: The rise and retreat of school desegregation.* Princeton, NJ: Princeton University Press.

Centers for Disease Control and Prevention. (2012). *Chronic disease and health prevention.* Retrieved from http://www.cdc.gov/chronicdisease/overview

Cohn, M. D., Smyer, M. A., & Horgas, A. L. (1994). *The ABCs of behavior change: Skills for working with behavior problems in nursing homes.* State College, PA: Venture.

Coughlin, J., (2010). *Estimating the impact of caregiving and employment on well-being: Outcomes & Insights in Health Management, 2*(1).

Elder, G. H., Jr. (1974). *Children of the Great Depression: Social change and life experiences.* Chicago, IL: University of Chicago Press.

Elwood, W. N. (Ed.). (1999). *Power in the blood: A handbook on AIDS, politics, and communication.* Mahwah, NJ: Erlbaum.

Fiske, A., Wetherell, J. L., & Gatz, M. (2009). Depression in older adults. *Annual Review of Clinical Psychology, 5,* 363–389. doi: 10.1146/annurev.clinpsy.032408.153621

Freedman, V. A., Kasper, J. D., Cornman, J. C., Agree, E. M., Bandeen-Roche, K., Mor, V.,…Wolf, D. A. (2011). Validation of new measures of disability and functioning in the National Health and Aging Trends Study. *Journal of Gerontology Series A: Biological Sciences and Medical Sciences, 66*(9), 1013–1021.

Freedman, V. A., Kasper, J. D., Spillman, B.C., Agree, E. M., Mor, V., Wallace, R. B., & Wolf, D. A. (2014). Behavioral adaptation and late-life disability: A new spectrum for assessing public health impacts. *American Journal of Public Health, 104*(2), e88–e94. doi: 10.2105/AJPH.2013.301687

Gallagher-Thompson, D., & Coon, D. W. (2007). Evidence-based psychological treatments for distress in family caregivers of older adults. *Psychology and Aging, 22,* 37–51.

Gatz, M., Kasl-Godley, J. E., & Karel, M. J. (1996). Aging and mental disorders. In J. E. Birren & K.W. Schaie (Eds.), *Handbook of the psychology of aging* (4th ed., pp. 365–382). San Diego, CA: Academic Press.

Gonyea, J. G., O'Connor, M. K., & Boyle, P. A. (2006). Project CARE: A randomized controlled trial of a behavioral intervention group for Alzheimer's disease caregivers. *Gerontologist, 46,* 827–832.

Grundmann, M. (1996). Historical context of father absence: Some consequences for the family formation of German men. *International Journal of Behavioral Development, 19,* 415–431.

Hamid, M. (2007). *The reluctant fundamentalist.* New York, NY: Harcourt.

Hartman, A. (1997). Aging holocaust survivors and PTSD. *Dimensions, 4*(3), 3–5.

He, W., Goodkind, D., & Kowal, P. (2016). US Census Bureau. International Population Reports, P-95/16-1, *An aging world: 2015.* Washington, DC: US Government Publishing Office.

He, W., & Larsen, L. J. (2014). US Census Bureau, American Community Survey Reports, ACS-29, *Older Americans with a disability: 2008–2012.* Washington, DC: US Government Printing Office.

Institute of Medicine. (2012). *The mental health and substance use workforce for older adults: In whose hands?* Washington, DC: National Academies Press.

Kahana, E., & Kahana, B. (2003). Contextualizing successful aging: New directions in age-old search. In R. Settersten, Jr. (Ed.), *Invitation to the life course: A new look at old age* (pp. 225–255). Amityville, NY: Baywood.

Karlin, B. E., Duffy, M., & Gleaves, D. H. (2008). Patterns and predictors of mental health service use and mental illness among older and younger adults in the United States. *Psychological Services, 5*(3), 275–294.

Kessler, R. C., Berglund, P., Demler, O., Jin, R., Merikangas, K. R., & Walters, E. E. (2005). Lifetime prevalence and age-of-onset distributions of DSM-IV disorders in the National Comorbidity Survey Replication. *Archives of General Psychiatry, 62,* 593–602. doi: 10.1001/archpsyc.62.6.593

Knight, B. G. (2004). *Psychotherapy with older adults* (3rd ed.). Thousand Oaks, CA: Sage.

Knight, B. G., Lutzky, S. M., & Macofsky-Urban, F. (1993). A meta-analytic review of interventions for caregiver distress: Recommendations for future research. *Gerontologist, 33,* 240–248.

Knight, B. G., & Pachana, N. A. (2015). *Psychological assessment and therapy with older adults.* New York, NY: Oxford University Press.

Knight, B. G., & Qualls, S. H. (1995). The older client in developmental context: Life course and family systems perspectives. *Clinical Psychologist, 48*(2), 11–17.

Kuhn, S., & Lindenberger, U. (2016). Research on human plasticity in adulthood. In K. W. Schaie & S. Willis (Eds.), *Handbook of the psychology of aging* (pp. 106–124). San Diego, CA: Academic Press.

Lang, F. R., & Carstensen, L. L. (2002). Time counts: Future time perspective, goals, and social relationships. *Psychology and Aging, 17,* 125–139.

Lawton, M. P. (1982). Competence, environmental press, and the adaptation of old people. In M. P. Lawton, P. G. Windley, & T. O. Byerts (Eds.), *Aging and the environment: Theoretical approaches* (pp. 33–59). New York, NY: Springer.

Lawton, M. P., & Nahemow, L. (1973). Ecology of the aging process. In C. Eisdorfer & M. P. Lawton (Eds.), *The psychology of adult development and aging* (pp. 619–674). Washington, DC: American Psychological Association.

Lewin, K. (1935). *A dynamic theory of personality: Selected papers of Kurt Lewin.* New York, NY: McGraw-Hill.

Lichtenberg, P. A., & Mast, B. T. (Eds.). (2015). *APA handbook of clinical geropsychology.* Washington, DC: American Psychological Association.

Marsiske, M., Lang, F., Baltes, P. B., & Baltes, M. M. (1996). Selective optimization with compensation: Life-span perspectives on successful human development. In R. A. Dixon & L. Backman (Eds.), *Compensating for psychological deficits and declines: Managing loss and promoting gains* (pp. 35–79). Mahwah, NJ: Erlbaum.

Martin, L. G., & Schoeni, R. F. (2014). Trends in disability and related chronic conditions among the forty and over population: 1997–2010. *Disability and Health Journal, 7*(10), S4–14. doi:10.1016/j.dhjo.2013.06.007

Martin, P., & Smyer, M. A. (1990). The experience of micro- and macroevents: A life span analysis. *Research on Aging, 12*, 294–310.

Moen, P. (2016). *Encore adulthood: Boomers on the edge of risk, renewal, and purpose.* New York, NY: Oxford University Press.

National Center for Health Statistics. (2014). *Health, United States, 2013: With special feature on prescription drugs.* Hyattsville, MD: US Department of Health and Human Services, Centers for Disease Control and Prevention.

Niederehe, G. (2015). Research trends in geropsychology. In P. A. Lichtenberg & B. T. Mast (Eds.). (2015). *APA handbook of clinical geropsychology* (pp. 135–176). Washington, DC: American Psychological Association.

Ortman, J. M., Velkoff, V.A., & Hogan, H. (2014). An aging nation: The older population in the United States. *Current Population Reports*, P25–1140. Washington, DC: US Census Bureau.

Pierce, W. (2015). *The wind in the reeds: A storm, a play, and the city that would not be broken.* New York, NY: Riverhead Books.

Pinquart, M., & Sorenson, S. (2001). How effective are psychotherapeutic and other psychosocial interventions with older adults? A meta-analysis. *Journal of Mental Health and Aging, 7*, 207–240.

Powers, D. V. (2008). Psychotherapy in long-term care: II. Evidence-based psychological treatments and other outcome research. *Professional Psychology: Research and Practice, 39*, 257–263.

Pynoos, J. Caraviello, R., & Cicero, C. (2010). Housing in an aging America. In J. C. Cavanaugh & C. K. Cavanaugh (Eds.). *Aging in America. Vol. 3: Societal issues* (pp. 129–159). Santa Barbara, CA: Praeger Perspectives.

Qualls, S. H., Segal, D. L., Norman, S., Niederehe, G., & Gallagher-Thompson, D. (2002). Psychologists in practice with older adults: Current patterns, sources of training, and need for continuing education. *Professional Psychology: Research and Practice, 33*, 435–442.

Qualls, S. H., & Williams, A. A. (2013). *Caregiving family therapy.* Washington, DC: American Psychological Association.

Reinhard, S. C., Feinberg, L. F., Choula, R., & Houser, A. (2015). Valuing the invaluable: 2015 update. *AARP Public Policy Institute: Insight on the issues.* Retrieved from http://www.aarp.org/content/dam/aarp/ppi/2015/valuing-the-invaluable-2015-update-new.pdf

Riffin, C. A., & Lockenhoff, C. E. (2015). Life span developmental psychology. In N. Pachana (Ed.), *Encyclopedia of geropsychology* (pp. 1–11). Singapore: Springer Science + Business Media. doi: 10.1007/978-981-287-080-3_107-1

Satre, D., Knight, B. G., & David, S. (2006). Cognitive behavioral interventions with older adults: Integrating clinical and gerontological research. *Professional Psychology: Research and Practice, 37*, 489–498.

Schaie, K. W. (1995). Training materials in geropsychology: Developmental issues. In B. G. Knight, L. Teri, P. Wohlford, & J. Santos (Eds.), *Mental health services for older adults: Implications for training and practice in geropsychology* (pp. 33–39). Washington, DC: American Psychological Association.

Schaie, K. W. (2013). *Developmental influences on adult intelligence: The Seattle Longitudinal Study* (2nd ed.). New York, NY: Oxford University Press.

Scogin, F. R., Welsh, D., Hanson, A., Stump, J., & Coates, A. (2005). Evidence-based psychotherapies for depression in older adults. *Clinical Psychology: Science and Practice, 12*, 222–237.

Sharma, A. J., Weiss, E. C., Young, S. L., Stephens, K., Ratard, R., Straif-Bourgeois, S.,... Rubin, C. H. (2008). *Disaster Medicine and Public Health Preparedness, 2*(1), 27–32.

Stamm, K., Hamp, A., Karel, M., Moye, J., Qualls, S. H., Segal, D. L.,...Lin, L. (2016, January). Datapoint: How many psychologists provide care to older adults? *Monitor on Psychology, 47*, 17. Washington, DC: American Psychological Association.

Tazeau, Y. (2011). Individual and cultural diversity considerations in geropsychology. In V. Molinari (Ed.), *Specialty competencies in geropsychology* (pp. 103–114). New York, NY: Oxford University Press.

United Nations, Department of Economic and Social Affairs, Population Division. (2012). *Population ageing and development wallchart 2012*. Retrieved from http://www.un.org/esa/population/publications/2012PopAgeingDev_Chart/2012PopAgeingandDev_WallChart.pdf

Unverzagt, F. W., Smith, D. M., Rebok, G. W., Marsiske, M., Morris, J. N., Jones, R.,... Tennstedt, S. L. (2009). The Indiana Alzheimer Disease Center's Symposium on Mild Cognitive Impairment. Cognitive training in older adults: Lessons from the ACTIVE Study. *Current Alzheimer Research, 6*, 375–383. Retrieved from http://www.ncbi.nlm.nih.gov/pubmed/19689237

US Census Bureau. (2012). *2010 Census Special Reports, Centenarians: 2010, C2010SR-03*. Washington, DC: US Government Printing Office.

US Census Bureau. (2014). *65+ in the United States: 2010, P23-212*. Washington, DC: US Government Printing Office.

US Department of Health and Human Services. (2001). *Mental health: Culture, race, and ethnicity – A supplement to mental health: A report of the Surgeon General*. Rockville, MD: US Department of Health and Human Services, Substance Abuse and Mental Health Services Administration, Center for Mental Health Services.

Wade-Benzoni, K. A., Tost, L. P., Hernandez, M., & Larrick, R. P. (2012). It's only a matter of time: Death, legacies, and intergenerational decisions. *Psychological Science, 23*(7), 704–709.

Ward, B. W., Schiller, J. S., & Goodman, R. A. (2014). Multiple chronic conditions among US adults: A 2012 update. *Preventing Chronic Disease, 11*, 130389. doi: 10.5888/pcd11.130389

Willis, S., & Belleville, S. (2016). Cognitive training in later adulthood. In K. W. Schaie & S. Willis (Eds.), *Handbook of the psychology of aging* (pp. 220–244). San Diego, CA: Academic Press.

Willis, S., & Boron, J.B. (2015). Cognitive aging and cognitive training. In P. A. Lichtenberg & B. T. Mast (Eds). (2015). *APA handbook of clinical geropsychology* (pp. 195–216). Washington, DC: American Psychological Association.

3

Psychological Bases of Positive Mental Health

Consider the following late life experiences:

Virginia lived to be 102. She was a vital force in her community, having seen it change from a horse-and-buggy town to a vibrant university center. Throughout the changes, she actively reached out to young and old friends, who gathered in her living room and at her dining room table for insightful and clever conversation. In her early 90s, though, things started to change for Virginia and her family. Friends and relatives noticed a little forgetfulness at first. Later, her daughters were worried about leaving Virginia at home alone. For the last couple of years of her life, Virginia was content to sit and watch the birds at the feeder outside of her window. She was no longer capable of quick or clever conversation. Throughout it all, however, she remained physically strong.

John, Bill, and Tom were close to their parents. They watched as their mother smoked and eventually had a fatal heart attack in her 50s. Now 30 years later, the brothers have had health challenges of their own. John, the oldest, doesn't smoke, is active and exercises every day, mindful of his mother's unexpected death in mid-life. He has had lifelong asthma. Bill, a year younger than John, struggles with his weight, being at least at 80 pounds overweight. He has already had a stent put in, and he is trying to walk three to four times a week. Tom, five years younger, was born a "blue baby," leaving him legally blind. He also has a heart murmur that his physician is monitoring. At a family reunion, they talked about what the next phase of life holds for each of them.

These life experiences reflect some of the basic challenges in understanding aging processes. We need to account for both intraindividual (within individual) variability and interindividual (between individuals) variability. The divergence of Virginia's mental and physical functioning illustrates one of the paradoxes: How do we account

---

for different rates of change across different areas of functioning in the same individual? The differences between and among John, Bill, and Tom illustrate another challenge: How do we account for differences in rates and types of changes between individuals?

In this chapter, we will outline three theories of adult development and aging that highlight several elements contributing to positive mental health in later life: Rowe and Kahn's theory of successful aging (1987, 1998); Paul Baltes's theory of selective optimization with compensation (Baltes & Baltes, 1990; Baltes, 1997; Lang, Rohr, & Williger, 2011); and Aldwin's framework of resilient or optimal aging (Aldwin & Igarashi, 2015, 2016).

We will also highlight theories of psychological functioning developed for other purposes: *stereotype threat* (e.g., Levy, 2009) and *positive psychology* (e.g., Hill & Smith, 2015). For each area, we will ask a simple question: How can this theory aid us in understanding the psychological bases of positive mental health in later life? Before turning to specific models, however, let's consider what we can expect of an effective model or theory.

What do Models have to Account for?

Psychologist Paul Baltes was a major proponent of life-span developmental psychology (Baltes, 1987, 1997; Baltes, Lindenberger, & Staudinger, 2006). He suggested that models of adult development and aging had to account for four elements: multidirectionality, plasticity, the historical context, and multiple causation.

Regarding multidirectionality, Baltes reminded us that development includes both growth and decline. For example, an individual's vocabulary typically increases across the lifespan, while reaction time typically slows down. This is also a reminder that in the clinical setting we should attune ourselves to both the strengths and the weaknesses of our clients: What has improved with age? What has been lost? And perhaps, what has remained the same.

By plasticity, Baltes reminds us that many skills can be developed and that training to compensate for losses may be effective in later life. Kuhn and Lindenberger (2016) differentiate plasticity and flexibility. They define *plasticity* as "long-lasting alterations in the brain's chemistry, gray matter, and structural connectivity in support of behavior" (p. 106). *Flexibility*, in contrast, is "the adaptive reconfiguration of the existing behavioral repertoire in the absence of macroscopic structural changes" (p. 106). In considering the dynamics of plasticity and flexibility across the lifespan, Kuhn and Lindenberger offer three conclusions: "plasticity decreases from childhood to old age"; "flexibility increases from childhood to middle adulthood and declines thereafter"; and "relative to childhood, plasticity in adulthood and old age is more associated with maintenance, and less with growth" (p. 107). This is a clear reminder that aging is a bio-, psycho-, and social-development process. Understanding an individual's current functioning requires assessing all three aspects, including current capacity for behavioral flexibility.

Baltes's emphasis on the historical context reminds us that each cohort or generation encounters the tasks of development in a particular set of historical conditions. The divergent views about the post-9/11 themed novel *The Reluctant Fundamentalist* (Hamid, 2007) cited in Box 2.2 in Chapter 2 are an example. The discussions were conducted by one group of participants who were on average in their late 60s when 9/11 occurred and by a second group who were first-year college students, including one student for whom 9/11 was her first day of kindergarten. This is a small reminder of Baltes's larger lesson: The historical context shapes an individual's understanding of and response to events near and far.

Baltes's focus on multiple causality is a reminder that a variety of forces together produce development and its aberrations. Again, an emphasis on the intersection of biological, social, psychological, and historical factors will help us guard against a simple and sometimes simplistic focus on a single cause for our client's underlying distress or impairments. For example, a couple we knew spent a sabbatical year halfway across the country, a prestigious award for the wife. After the move, it became clear that her husband had a neurocognitive disorder of some sort (eventually diagnosed as Alzheimer's disease). The move did not cause the underlying disorder, but it made apparent the extent to which his physical and social environment had been carrying much of the "cognitive load" for him for some time. Understanding the complex interaction of biology, social support, and family function helped the family fully comprehend the situation and begin to plan for treatment. Their situation reflected the old adage "Complex problems require complex solutions."

With this context, let's now turn to three models of adult development and aging.

Successful Aging

Thirty years ago, geriatrician Jack Rowe and psychologist Robert Kahn published an article on usual and successful aging (Rowe & Kahn, 1987). Although others (e.g., Butler, 1974; Havighurst, 1961) emphasized successful aging before Rowe and Kahn, their article and a subsequent book (Rowe & Kahn, 1998) had a significant impact. They differentiated usual or normal aging from "successful" aging. Their work stood in contrast to earlier investigations of "normal aging" (e.g., Palmore, Nowlin, Busse, Siegler, & Maddox, 1985) that emphasized central tendencies of community-dwelling older adults. In contrast, Rowe and Kahn sought to highlight variability across individuals and optimal functioning (Martin et al., 2015). Success in this context had three elements: freedom from disease and disability, high cognitive and physical functioning, and active engagement with life.

Rowe and Kahn's (1987) initial article focused on the individual. Their subsequent book (Rowe & Kahn, 1998), drawn from the work of the MacArthur Foundation network of research on successful aging (Berkman, Seeman, & Albert, 1993), also focused primarily on individual adaptation. Subsequent works by Rowe and others, including the MacArthur Foundation Research Network on an Aging Society, have focused on the societal contexts of successful aging (Carr, Fried, & Rowe, 2015; Rowe, 2015).

As we shall see when we consider the work of Erik Erikson (1963; Erikson, Erikson, & Kivnick, 1986) in Chapter 4, Rowe and Kahn were not the first to focus on vital involvement and active engagement in later life (see Peterson & Martin, 2015, for an historical review). However, their emphasis on success has resulted in a deep and rich set of investigations into many aspects of successful aging.

Some, however, have also been critical of the successful aging framework. (See *The Gerontologist*'s 2015 special issue on Successful Aging for a recent review). It is useful to consider the criticisms within the framework of Rowe and Kahn's three criteria for success: freedom from disease or disability, high cognitive and physical functioning, and active engagement with life.

As reviewed in Chapter 2, many older adults are faced with both chronic diseases and acute medical challenges. More than 66% of older Americans, for example, have multiple chronic conditions (Centers for Disease Control and Prevention, 2012). Thus, the argument goes, Rowe and Kahn have left many older adults out of their definition of success. For example, using data from the Health and Retirement Survey, McLaughlin and her colleagues (2010) found that no more than 12% of those 65 and older met Rowe and Kahn's criteria for success in any one year. Hank (2011) replicated the McLaughlin et al. (2010) study, using cross-national comparisons. He found that the 12% "success rate" in the US placed it in the middle of the countries reviewed, while Denmark, Sweden, and the Netherlands topped the list. Hank (2011) also reported that income inequality was related to rates of success: higher inequality, lower rates of success. In a follow-up study with relaxed, expanded criteria, McLaughlin and her colleagues (2012) found that the prevalence of success ranged from 3% to 34%. Two themes emerged from this work: the need to expand the definition of success when encountering disease and disability, and the need to consider resilience in the face of disability as one element of success in this domain.

If we return to Virginia, described at the opening of this chapter, it was clear that she faced the challenges of chronic disease in later life, particularly the effects of dementia. However, she had defined aging at home as her goal; by this definition, she was able to succeed despite the presence of increasing disability.

Virginia's perspective highlights another shortcoming of the successful aging framework: the "missing voices" of older adults themselves (Martinson & Berridge, 2015). Rowe and Kahn initially focused on objective indicators, without taking into account subjective views of older adults. Subsequent work indicated that both subjective and objective elements are important in predicting outcomes for older adults. Older adults' views of their lives are an additional component of success. For example, Pruchno and her colleagues (Pruchno et al., 2010) found that objective functioning in the areas of functional abilities, pain, and chronic diseases and subjective views of how successfully they have aged, how well they are aging, and how they rate their lives were correlated but provided unique information (see Figure 3.1).

Jeste and his colleagues (2010) reported on the interaction of objective and subjective measures of successful aging. In a sample of 1,979 women (from the San Diego site of the Women's Health Initiative), they found a contrast between the objective and subjective measures (see Table 3.1). Note that 71% of the women achieved normal cognitive functioning, based on a self-administered cognitive screening test. While it is not clear that this criterion would correspond to Rowe and Kahn's initial high cognitive functioning, it is consistent with earlier findings that about 1/3

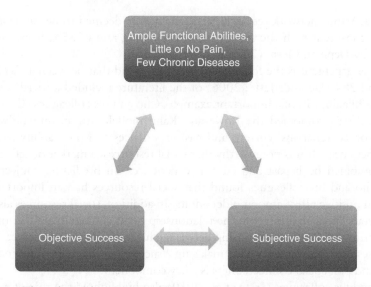

Figure 3.1 The relationship among objective success, subjective success, and indicators. *Source*: Adapted from Pruchno et al. (2010).

Table 3.1 Percentage of sample successfully aging

Domain	Operational definition	% of sample meeting criteria
Absence of disease[1]	Absence of self-reported cancer, diabetes, high blood pressure, heart attacks, other heart disease, stroke, osteoporosis, Parkinson's disease and respiratory disease	15%
Freedom from disability	SF-36 scored of "no limitation" in the ability to a) lift or carry groceries, b) climb one flight of stairs, c) bend/kneel/stoop, d) walk one block or e) bathe /dress oneself[2]	38%
Normal cognitive functioning	Score of 18 or higher on self-administered Cognitive Assessment Screening Test	71%
Active engagement with life	Visiting family and/or friends at least once a week and having three or more close friends[2]	74%
Self-rated successful aging	Scores ranging from 7 to 10 on a 1–10 scale item asking "Where do you rate yourself in terms of successful aging?"[2]	90%

Source: Adapted from Jeste et al. (2010).
[1] As outlined by Phelan & Larson (2002).
[2] Modeled after Strawbridge et al.'s (2002) definition of successful aging. Percentage reported from Montrose et al. (2006).

of the MacArthur network research participants were deemed to be successful agers. It is also consistent with the median successful aging rate of 35%, from the studies reviewed by Depp and Jeste (2006).

When engagement is the focus, meta-analyses found that between 13% (Bowling, 2007) and 28% (Depp & Jeste, 2006) of the literature included a social component of successful aging. In one important example, Cho and his colleagues (Cho, Martin, & Poon, 2015) combined the Rowe and Kahn model with an integrative model, focusing on centenarians' current and past experiences and their ability to adapt to those experiences. It was noteworthy that social resources, a marker of active engagement, combined both past and current experiences. In predicting subjective well-being, Cho and his colleagues found that social resources had an important direct impact on positive affect among older adults. In addition, social resources also played an important mediating effect in the relationship between cognitive functioning and positive affect, and in the relationship between education and positive affect. In short, when assessing the elements that make up "success" in later life, the individual's current and past social connectedness is a key component.

Jeste and his colleagues (Jeste et al., 2010) also highlighted the role of depression as a negative correlate with self-rated successful aging. For the clinician, one takeaway is that the individual's self-rated success at aging is likely to be positively correlated with optimism, resilience, cognitive ability, and perceived quality of life—but not with the presence or absence of chronic disease. Moreover, a perceived lack of success at aging is not a part of normal aging.

As with any model, it is important to analyze the overlap between the successful aging framework and other theoretical perspectives like the selective optimization with compensation model (discussed next in this chapter) (Martin et al., 2015). We turn to this element, often viewed as a process to achieve successful aging.

Selective Optimization with Compensation (SOC)

Consider the following proverbs:

> Those who follow every path never reach any destination.
> If at first you don't succeed, try, try again.
> There are many hands; what one cannot do, the other will.
> 　　　　　　　(Drawn from Freund & Baltes, 2002a)

These selections of folk wisdom represent three processes that help adults manage the gains and losses of aging: selection, optimization, and compensation (Baltes & Baltes, 1990). Within the selective optimization with compensation (SOC) framework, adults are active in setting, pursuing, and maintaining goals despite the challenges of changing biological, social, cognitive, and cultural resources (Freund, 2002).

Selection encompasses developing, elaborating, and committing to personal goals (Freund, 2002). According to Freund, there are two broad types of selection: elective selection and loss-based selection. *Elective selection* refers to the process of delineating goals to match the individual's needs and motives with appropriate resources in order to achieve a higher level of functioning. *Loss-based selection*, in contrast, aims at either maintaining function when faced by a loss of previously available resources or preventing further loss. This may require either helping an individual change her goals or set priorities among her goals since prior resources are no longer available to achieve all of them. Alternatively, another strategy is to compensate for a loss of resources or abilities through engaging others or the larger environment. The Age-Friendly community movement of the AARP (formerly the American Association of Retired Persons), for example, seeks to establish an environment that supports older adults' SOC.

Lang, Rohr, and Williger (2011) highlight the importance of person/environment fit (e.g., Lawton, 1989; Lawton & Nahemow, 1973) within the SOC framework. They remind us that both elements are important in thinking about the SOC processes at work: adults actively interacting with their environments; and environments that include interpersonal resources, familial resources, organizational resources (e.g., nursing homes; see Baltes, 1996), and technological resources (e.g., Charness & Schaie, 2003).

As Jopp and Smith (2006) point out, the SOC model complements other approaches such as models of coping (e.g., Lazarus & Folkman, 1984) or problem solving (e.g., Blanchard-Fields, Chen, & Norris, 1997). Proponents of the SOC model argue that it is useful in considering both adaptation to loss and the process of setting and achieving goals (Baltes & Carstensen, 1999). Others have applied the SOC framework in various contexts: industrial-organizational psychology (e.g., Baltes & Dickson, 2001); long-term care (e.g., Molinari, Kier, & Rosowsky, 2006); with older adults with cognitive impairment (e.g., Rapp, Krampe, & Baltes, 2006); and in "retiring" older drivers from the road (e.g., Pickard, Tan, Morrow-Howell, & Jung, 2009).

Paul Baltes and his colleagues (e.g., Ebner, Freund, & Baltes, 2006) suggest that there is a natural shift across adulthood from growth and gain (e.g., "I want to improve my physical fitness") to maintenance ("I want to stay physically fit") or prevention of loss (e.g., "I do not want my physical fitness to deteriorate"). This shift, they argue, allows people to manage the shifting balance between gains and losses and to maintain subjective well-being in the process. Within this general shift, Jopp and Smith (2006) found that SOC strategies were particularly useful buffers for the oldest old with low resources—a reminder of the person/context fit and how it may change across the lifespan.

As one application of the SOC model, for example, Carstensen (2006) and her colleagues (Carstensen, Isaacowitz, & Charles, 1999) suggest that the individual's sense of time also changes across the life course, along with a growing awareness of gains and losses. In mid-life, our attention shifts to the time left to live, a process that leads to a "pruning" of our commitments, including some extraneous social ties. Carstensen has focused on this "socioemotional selectivity" as one domain in which older adults set priorities and focus their attention and energies on a "smaller set of goals and a highly selected group of loved ones."

Three elements of the SOC model may be particularly important: the meaning that the older adult ascribes to her current goals and life situation; the resources available to her; and the older adult's capacity to engage in the process of selection, optimization, and compensation. As a start at assessment linked to the SOC framework, Freund and Baltes (2002b) provide a 48-item self-report questionnaire focused on four strategies: elective selection (e.g., "I concentrate all my energy on a few things"); loss-based selection (e.g., "When things don't go as well as before, I choose one or two important goals"); optimization (e.g., "I think carefully about how I can best realize my plans"); and compensation (e.g., "When things don't work the way they used to, I look for other ways to achieve them"). This measure may enable older adults or clinicians who work with them to use the SOC framework to reflect on their current explicit and implicit strategies in responding to the gains and losses of aging.

Resilience

In addition to successful and optimal aging, Aldwin and her colleagues have suggested that another model of aging is helpful in characterizing the experience of many older adults: resilient aging (Aldwin & Igarashi, 2015). Aldwin and Igarashi (2016) argue that there are three dimensions of resilient aging: effective coping to maintain functional health, developing a comfortable life structure, and achieving a sense of purpose in life and wisdom. In a similar vein, Garroway and Rybarczyk (2015) suggest that there are three main characteristics in various definitions of resilience: recovery, sustainability, and growth. "Resilience involves recovery from an adverse event, maintenance of values and purposeful life pursuits, and new learning or advances as a result of the adversity" (Garroway & Rybarczyk, 2015, p. 572). In addition, there are cultural and ethnic variations and emphases within each characteristic.

In later life, recovery is often experienced in the context of chronic illness. As noted in Chapters 1 and 2, the vast majority of older adults (approximately 80%) are faced with at least chronic disease or acute medical challenge. At the same time, older adults face more stressful life events than younger adults (e.g., personal losses, disease, and functional limitations) (Allen, Haley, Harris, Fowler, & Pruthi, 2011). In this context, sustainability in later life often requires moving ahead despite ongoing challenges (Zautra, Arewakisporn, & Davis, 2010).

The resilience framework incorporates two important elements: emerging challenges that are the result of an interaction of biological and structural forces, as well as the individual's own agency or response; and a dynamic interaction between the immediate social context and the individual. (This framing has echoes of Lewin's (1935) assertion that behavior is a function of the person and the environment, mentioned in Chapter 2). Figure 3.2 summarizes these interactions.

Within this framework, stress or adversity in the environment offer an opportunity for continued growth and development in later life (Aldwin, Levenson, & Kelly, 2009). Stress-related growth and resilience embody five characteristics: enhanced coping strategies; better social relationships; changes in values away from materialism; increased self-knowledge; and, for some, increased spirituality (Tedeschi & Calhoun, 1995). For the clinician, it may be useful to assess whether the client's current reaction to stress embodies any of these hallmarks of resilience.

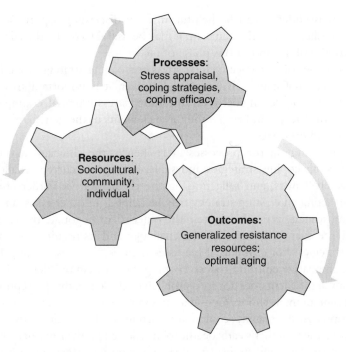

Figure 3.2 Resilience and aging.
Source: Adapted from Aldwin & Igarashi (2016).

When resources are the focus, the resilience framework draws our attention not only to the individual's capacities, but also to the larger community and cultural contexts within which she lives (Aldwin & Igarashi, 2016). For example, what are the formal and informal resources available to the older client? Are there aging services available in the community? Senior centers? Is the client active in a religious or spiritual community? Similarly, what are the cultural values about aging and resilience that the client has grown up with? Are there age-friendly policies in her current community?

The resilience framework highlights two types of outcomes: generalized resistance resources (GRRs) and optimal aging. GRRs (Antonovsky, 1987) include both social capital (e.g., social support systems, financial resources, etc.) and individual capital (e.g., values, a sense of mastery, purpose in life, etc.). As pointed out in our earlier discussion of "social address" in Chapter 2, the larger context of community and sociocultural resources also affects the development of GRRs, as do the processes of stress and coping.

Optimal or resilient aging, in this framework, has three main components: functional health, life satisfaction, and purpose in life. In the area of health, for example, note that the emphasis is not on disability; instead, the emphasis is on functioning in the face of challenge. In addition, Aldwin and her colleagues (e.g., Aldwin & Igarashi, 2015, 2016) emphasize the importance of self-transcendence. Koltko-Rivera (2006) defined self-transcendence as seeking "to further a cause beyond the self and to experience a communion beyond the boundaries of the self through peak experience" (p. 303; quoted in Aldwin & Igarashi, 2015). Aldwin and Igarashi emphasize that self-transcendence can be helpful, in both discerning a purpose in life and in achieving resilience. For the clinician, it may be useful to probe the client's own views of the purpose of life and of this phase of life.

The processes of resilience include stress and coping strategies. We focus on these in more detail in Chapter 6. For now, however, it is important to emphasize two dynamics: active processing between and among stress appraisal, coping strategies, and indications of efficacy; and across the three elements of the general model (resources, outcomes, and processes).

When focusing on the processes of resilience, the clinician may usefully assess already-existing coping strategies and skills, linking the current challenge to previously met challenges, and reflecting on the efficacy of the earlier efforts. In some cases, reenacting an existing strategy may be helpful. In other cases, a modification of the coping strategy is needed to help the older client negotiate the current problem. Similarly, the client's appraisal of the challenge and its requirements will affect her coping strategies. For example, if her assessment is "there is nothing I can do," she may well emphasize emotion-focused coping, rather than problem-solving coping.

Similarly, if the client does not see a problem or challenge, that perception could be the starting point for intervention. Consider our example of John and his brothers at the start of this chapter. At their family reunion, the starting point for their discussion of the future was the past: their mother's early death. John reflected on their mother's history of heart disease and smoking and decided to pursue a consistent program of exercise and diet choices. His brother Tom also knew the history but did not see a threat; eventually, he needed a cardiac stent intervention, with physician-ordered exercise three times a week.

Standard coping inventories may not capture some of the sophisticated coping strategies older adults use (Aldwin, 2011). For example, *decentering*, which is an understanding that someone else's needs may be greater than your own, is often not captured. Similarly, downward social comparison may also be important for older adults coping with functional limitations (Behel & Rybarczyk, 2012). This strategy adjusts the client's self-expectation relative to a self-created peer group (e.g., "I am in good shape for an 80-year-old widow"). (For more on coping appraisal, strategies, and efficacy, see Chapter 6.)

There has been relatively little investigation of cultural and ethnic differences in both the conceptualization of resilience and in its processes and outcomes (Aldwin & Igarashi, 2016). Aldwin and Igarashi (2016) suggest that the three key elements of resilience (effective coping in the service of maintaining functional health; developing a comfortable life structure; and achieving a sense of meaning or purpose in life and wisdom) are both specific enough to allow development of measures and broad enough to be applied with differing cultures emphasizing different elements.

Contributions from Psychological Science: Stereotype Threat and Positive Psychology

Gatz and her colleagues (Gatz, Smyer, & DiGilio, 2016) recently highlighted the important implications of psychological science for the well-being of older adults. Their message was simple: Developments in other areas of psychology (e.g., neuroscience or behavior change) may have direct relevance for older adults. With this context, we will consider two areas of psychology—stereotype threat and positive psychology—for their importance for working with older adults.

Stereotype threat

Consider the following exchanges one of us (MAS) has recently had with transportation security administration (TSA) agents in three different airports:

TSA AGENT: "How are you, young man?"
TSA AGENT: "Do you have a pacemaker?"
TSA AGENT: "Do you have any implants (knee, hip)?"

Each question reflected an attitude and assumption about aging. In one case, it was condescension. In the others, it was an assumption of disability. Together, these remarks reflect common stereotypes of aging, what Cuddy and Fiske (2002) summarize as "doddering but dear," high in warmth but low in competence. Together, these comments were just the most recent examples of explicit and implicit assumptions about aging that form an important context of aging (Hinrichsen, 2015).

The title of a recent *Wall Street Journal* article (Tergesen, 2015) summarized the impacts that social expectations and stereotypes can have on older adults' own expectations and performance: "To age well, change how you feel about aging; negative stereotypes about getting older can become a self-fulfilling prophecy. How to improve your mind-set—and well-being." The article outlined the important implications of psychological research on stereotype threat that first started with children.

In the 1990s, Steele and Aronson (1995) found that being the target of a stereotype can negatively affect those targeted, who may be concerned that they may confirm the stereotype. The targets do not need to believe or internalize the stereotype to have it affect their performance.

Subsequently, the concepts of stereotype threat have been applied to older adults (Meisner, 2012). For example, Levy (Levy, 2009; Levy, Zonderman, Slade, & Ferrucci, 2009; Levy, Ferrucci, Zonderman, Slade, Troncoso, & Resnick, 2016) has undertaken a series of studies to assess the impact of negative stereotypes of aging on cardiovascular health and brain structures. Using data from the Baltimore Longitudinal Study, Levy and her colleagues found that negative views of aging were associated with higher rates of cardiovascular incidents, even decades after the initial views were assessed. Similarly, negative stereotypes of aging were associated with brain changes that often accompany Alzheimer's disease (reduced hippocampal volume and neurofibrillary plaques and tangles); the association was found 25 years after the stereotypes were assessed.

Some have suggested that older adults incorporate age stereotypes into their subjective views of their future selves (Diehl et al., 2014). Levy suggests that there is a two-step mechanism: stereotypes contribute to stress, and chronic stress contributes to pathological changes in the brain and in other systems. In addition, Levy and her colleagues (2015) have shown that negative stereotypes are robust: They "resist change as well as generate it." On the other hand, Levy and her team (2014) have also demonstrated that interventions focusing on implicit positive stereotypes can be beneficial for older adults' physical well-being.

There are several takeaway messages for clinicians. First, stereotypes and expectations about aging are pervasive and pernicious. Second, they have long-lasting effects on physical and mental health. Third, older adults are likely unaware of the impact of their own expectations on their experience of aging. It may be helpful to gauge your client's views and expectations as you start to work together. Finally, each of us has our own expectations and stereotypes about older adults and aging. As Hinrichsen (2015) points out, it is essential to assess your own biases as you start to work with older adults. The Age Implicit Association Test (https://implicit.harvard.edu/implicit/takeatest.html) is a good place to start.

Positive psychology

Advocates of positive psychology suggest that we need to attend to individuals' strengths, as well as weaknesses, and to the meanings that they attribute to their circumstances (Lopez & Gallagher, 2009). Although Maslow (1954) first focused attention on psychology's relative emphasis on the "negative than on the positive side," renewed interest in positive psychology emerged when Seligman and Csikszentmihalyi (2000) called for a shift of attention from an almost exclusive focus on disease and pathology to a broader emphasis on the scientific study of strengths:

> A science of positive subjective experience, positive individual traits, and positive institutions promises to improve quality of life and prevent the pathologies that arise when life is barren and meaningless. The exclusive focus on pathology that has dominated so much of our discipline results in a model of the human being lacking the positive features that make life worth living." (p.5)

Two aspects are noteworthy about positive psychology approaches: They are focused on helping individuals and organizations reframe problems as life challenges, and they are focused on "meaning centered" resources to enable individuals to improve their well-being (Hill & Smith, 2015). Thus, the subjective meaning that individuals attribute to events matters within the positive psychology framework. Three specific meaning-centered approaches often used within positive psychology are forgiveness, altruism, and gratitude interventions, with emerging empirical evidence of intervention effectiveness and sustainability (Bolier et al., 2013; Hill & Smith, 2015).

As reflected in Chapters 1 and 2, the majority of older adults are physically and psychologically healthy. Despite chronic illnesses, most rate themselves as satisfied with life and "successful" at aging, and most continue to make contributions to their families and their communities until very late in life. These self-perceptions are important for the positive psychology framework with its emphasis on the impact that a person's framing of experience has on the individual's well-being (Hill & Smith, 2015; Williamson & Christie, 2009).

Robert Hill has been a leader in applying the positive psychology framework to the processes of aging (Hill, 2005, 2008, 2011). As with the work of Baltes on selective optimization with compensation, Hill and others acknowledge that older adults must cope with both the gains and losses that accompany aging. He suggests that there are four characteristics of someone who is aging positively: the ability to mobilize latent social or psychological capacities; flexible thought and behavior; decision-making that affirms psychological well-being, even in the face of loss; and optimism, despite processes of decline that accompany aging (Hill & Smith, 2015).

One approach for working with clients within the positive psychology framework uses the Ottawa Personal Decision Guide for people who are making tough social or health decisions (a link to the guide is provided at the end of the chapter). The guide was developed by the Research Institute at the Ottawa Hospital to help clinicians and clients assess several elements: the framing of the decision; what is needed to make the decision (e.g., support, knowledge, clarity about the values at work in the choices, and how much uncertainty the client perceives); who can assist in making the decision to meet those needs (adding the social support dimension); and mapping out specific next steps. There is also a version of the guide for use with couples in decision-making. The guide embodies several elements of the positive psychology approach: the importance of the individual's perception and framing of the decision; using individual and social resources; and an optimistic assumption that valued decisions can be made, even in the face of uncertainty and loss.

Are There Secrets to Aging Well?

Recently, one of us (MAS) was asked to write a book review essay, covering several books on aging and later adulthood that have been written for a popular audience (Smyer, 2016). The books took different approaches in integrating gerontology and geriatrics with takeaway lessons for their readers. The books may be useful for clinicians and clients as a starting point for exploring expectations of aging and how to achieve optimal or resilient aging.

We have already discussed Rowe and Kahn's (1998) *Successful Aging*. Psychologist Laura Carstensen's (2009) book, *A Long Bright Future*, draws on gerontology and geriatrics to shape life lessons for living to 100, a realistic prospect for many of today's young adults. *National Geographic* writer, Dan Buettner, also focused on the long view. In *The Blue Zones* (2008), he sought out life lessons from those who live in regions with a disproportionate number of centenarians.

Psychiatrist George Vaillant (2002, 2012) took a different approach in following a sample of Harvard men across their lives, gleaning lessons for the rest of us from his longitudinal study, *Aging Well* (Vaillant, 2002). Sociologist Karl Pillemer (2011) took a direct approach, getting advice directly from today's older adults, whom he characterizes as the "wisest Americans." He solicited information from them using both surveys and interviews for his book, *30 Lessons for Living*.

Are there secrets to aging well? Yes and no. There are some simple rules that will help you and your clients achieve optimal aging, but they are not secret. For example, Vaillant suggests that there are seven simple rules: don't smoke, don't abuse alcohol, exercise regularly, maintain your weight, have a stable marriage, get an education, and control your stress. In putting together his nine rules for long life, the only one of Vaillant's rules that Buettner didn't emphasize was education (but then he wasn't following a sample of Harvard men!). Carstensen points out that, after age 70, four of these elements reduce mortality by 60%: exercise, not smoking, moderate alcohol consumption, and a Mediterranean diet (fruits, vegetables, and healthy fats like olive oil) to maintain weight. Notice that these rules contradict one of the myths of aging, that one's DNA is Destiny. As Carstensen (2009) points out, behavioral choices can be aging accelerators or aging decelerators. Pillemer's older adults put it well: "Act now like you'll need your body for 100 years."

Finally, sociologist Phyllis Moen (2016) drew lessons from gerontology to offer advice to the Baby Boomers who are getting ready to take advantage of the "longevity bonus," which refers to the added years of health that are part of today's experience of longer life. Moen calls her book *Encore Adulthood*, emphasizing the active crafting of a life structure for this part of the lifespan. For many of us, the years between 65 and 80 are similar to our 20s. We are faced with similar issues: How can we support ourselves? Where shall we live? Where will our family members and friends be? One big difference, though, is that we face these issues with different resources (personal and fiscal) and a lifetime of experience. Consider, for example, the role of friends in later life. As mentioned earlier, Carstensen suggests that there is a natural pruning of social relationships, focusing on those most important to us in late life, in what she calls socioemotional selectivity. At the same time, she notes that having fewer than three people we feel emotionally close to is a risk factor for physical and mental health problems. In fact, feeling socially isolated is as great a risk factor for poor health and death in late life as cigarette smoking.

For clinicians and clients alike there are several lessons to be drawn from this translational literature: Lifestyle choices make a difference; and both physical and mental health are linked to our perception of our social resources, as well as our expectations of what aging will bring. A starting point for discussing these issues is a simple lifespan calculator (a link to one is provided at the end of the chapter). Our experience is that using a site like this is a good conversation starter about current behaviors and choices. Pillemer sought takeaway messages from his older adults, what he called the refrigerator magnet messages. They summed it up: "Time is of the essence." Live as though life is short, because it is, even if you live to be 100!

Summary and Conclusions

In this chapter, we have highlighted three theories of aging and their implications for assessment and further clinical work. Each theory—successful aging, selective optimization with compensation, and resilient aging—focuses our attention on the challenges of aging, the gains, and the losses that accompany later life. They also highlight potential attitudes toward aging that clients may have, as well as potential expectations for the processes of aging that lie ahead. In addition, we have used two other areas of psychology—stereotype threat and positive psychology—to illustrate the relevance of broader fields of psychology for clinical geropsychology. We will return to this theme in the next section of the book, as we consider different models of psychological functioning.

Indeed, throughout the lifespan, theoretical perspectives of the etiology, assessment, and treatment of disorders mold the clinician's approaches. In the next section, we will introduce several models, emphasizing those aspects that are most salient in each. Our working assumption is that the clinician's implicit and explicit models shape problem identification and treatment, regardless of the age of the client. The challenge, therefore, is to identify the strengths and shortcomings of each model, especially as they apply to older adults and the context of later life. We turn to this challenge in the next section.

Critical Thinking / Discussion Questions

1   How would you define "successful aging"? How does your definition accommodate the challenges of changing circumstances that often accompany later life?
2   Apply the Selective Optimization with Compensation framework to your own life. What do you currently optimize? How do you compensate?
3   What advice would you give a 70-year-old for successfully making the transitions to retirement?

Website Resources

Selective Optimization with Compensation
http://www.margret-baltes-stiftung.de/PBB-Website/SOC.html
Ottawa Personal Decision Guide
https://decisionaid.ohri.ca/decguide.html
The Age Implicit Association Test
https://implicit.harvard.edu/implicit/takeatest.html
The Legacy Project: Lessons for Living from the Wisest Americans
http://legacyproject.human.cornell.edu/
A Longevity Calculator
https://www.northwesternmutual.com/learning-center/tools/the-longevity-game

References

Aldwin, C. N. (2011). Stress and coping across the lifespan. In S. Folkman (Ed.), *The Oxford handbook of stress, health, and coping* (pp. 15–34). New York, NY: Oxford University Press.

Aldwin, C. N., & Igarashi, H. (2015). Successful, optimal, and resilient aging: A psychosocial perspective. In P. A. Lichtenberg, B.T. Mast, B. D. Carpenter, J. L. Wetherell (Eds.), *APA handbook of clinical geropsychology. Vol. 1: History and status of the field and perspectives on aging* (pp. 331–359). Washington, DC: American Psychological Association. doi: 10.1037/14458-014

Aldwin, C. M., & Igarashi, H. (2016). Coping, optimal aging, and resilience in a sociocultural context. In V. L. Bengtson & R. A. Settersten, Jr. (Eds.), *Handbook of theories of aging* (3rd ed., pp. 551–576). New York, NY: Springer.

Aldwin, C. M., Levenson, M., & Kelly, L. (2009). Life span developmental perspectives on stress-related growth. In C. L. Park, S. C. Lechner, M. H. Antoni, & A. L. Stanton (Eds.), *Medical illness and positive life change: Can crisis lead to personal transformation?* (pp. 87–104). Washington, DC: American Psychological Association. doi: 10.1037/11854-005

Allen, R. S., Haley, P. P., Harris, G. M., Fowler, S. N., & Pruthi, R. (2011). Resilience: Definitions, ambiguities, and applications. In B. Resnick, K. A. Roberto, & L. P. Gwyther (Eds.), *Resilience in aging: Concepts, research, and outcomes* (pp. 1–13). New York, NY: Springer. doi: 10.1007/978-1-4419-0232-0_1

Antonovsky, A. (1987). *Unraveling the mysteries of health: How many people manage stress and stay well.* San Francisco, CA: Josey-Bass.

Baltes, B. B., & Dickson, M. W. (2001). Using life-span models in industrial-organizational psychology: The theory of selective optimization with compensation. *Applied Developmental Science, 5,* 51–62.

Baltes, M. (1996). *The many faces of dependency in old age.* New York, NY: Cambridge University Press.

Baltes, M. M., & Carstensen, L. (1999). Social-psychological theories and their application to aging: From individual to collective. In V. L. Bengtson & K. W. Schaie (Eds.), *Handbook of theories of aging* (pp. 209–226). New York, NY: Springer.

Baltes, P. B. (1987). Theoretical propositions of life-span developmental psychology: On the dynamics between growth and decline. *Developmental Psychology, 23,* 611–626.

Baltes, P. B. (1997). On the incomplete architecture of human ontogeny: Selection, optimization as foundation of developmental theory. *American Psychologist, 52,* 366–380.

Baltes, P. B., & Baltes, M. M. (1990). Selective optimization with compensation. In P. B. Baltes & M. M. Baltes (Eds.), *Successful aging: Perspectives from the behavioral sciences* (pp. 1–34). New York, NY: Cambridge University Press.

Baltes, P. B., Lindenberger, U., & Staudinger, U. M. (2006). Life span theory in developmental psychology. In R. M. Lerner (Ed.), *Handbook of child psychology* (6th ed., pp. 569–664). Hoboken, NJ: Wiley.

Behel, J. M., & Rybarczyk, B. (2012). Physical disability and body image in adults. In T. F. Cash (Ed.), *Encyclopedia of body image and human appearance* (vol. 2, pp. 644–649). San Diego, CA: Academic Press.

Berkman, L. F., Seeman, T. E., & Albert, M. (1993). High, usual and impaired functioning in community-dwelling older men and women: Findings from the MacArthur Foundation Research Network on Successful Aging. *Journal of Clinical Epidemiology, 46,* 1129–1140.

Blanchard-Fields, F., Chen, Y., & Norris, L. (1997). Everyday problem solving across the adult life span: Influence of domain specificity and cognitive appraisal. *Psychology and Aging, 12,* 684–693.

Bolier, L., Haverman, M., Westerhof, G.J., Riper, H., Smit, F., & Bohlmeijer, E. (2013). Positive psychology interventions: A meta-analysis of randomized controlled studies. *BMC Public Health, 13,* 119. doi:10.1186/1471-2458-13-119

Bowling, A. (2007). Aspirations for older age in the 21st century: What is successful aging? *International Journal of Aging and Human Development, 64,* 263–267.

Buettner, D. (2008). *The Blue Zones: 9 lessons for living longer.* Washington, DC: National Geographic.

Butler, R. N. (1974). Successful aging and the role of the life review. *Journal of the American Geriatrics Society, 22,* 529–535.

Carr, D. C., Fried, L. P., & Rowe, J. W. (2015, April 1). Productivity and engagement in an aging America: The role of volunteerism. *Daedalus, 144*(2), 55–67. doi:10.1162/DAED_a_00330

Carstensen, L. (2009). *A long, bright future: An action plan for a lifetime of happiness, health, and financial security.* New York, NY: Broadway Books.

Carstensen, L. L. (2006). The influence of a sense of time on human development. *Science, 312*, 1913–1915. doi:10.1126/science.1127488

Carstensen, L. L., Isaacowitz, D. M., & Charles, S. T. (1999). Taking time seriously: A theory of socioemotional selectivity. *American Psychologist, 54,* 165–181. doi:10.1037/0003-066X.54.3.165

Centers for Disease Control and Prevention. (2012). *Chronic disease and health prevention.* Retrieved from http://www.cdc.gov/chronicdisease/overview

Charness, N., & Schaie. K. W. (Eds.) (2003). *Influence of technology on successful aging.* New York, NY: Springer.

Cho, J., Martin, P., & Poon, L. (2015). Successful aging and subjective well-being among oldest-old adults. *The Gerontologist, 55,* 132–143. doi.10.1093/geront/gnu074

Cuddy, A. J. C., & Fiske, S. T. (2002). Doddering but dear: Process, content, and function in stereotyping of older persons. In T. D. Nelson (Ed.), *Ageism: Stereotyping and prejudice against older persons* (pp. 3–26). Cambridge, MA: MIT Press.

Depp, C. A., & Jeste, D. V. (2006). Definitions and predictors of successful aging: A comprehensive review of larger quantitative studies. *American Journal of Geriatric Psychiatry, 14,* 6–20.

Diehl, M., Wahl, H. W., Barrett, A. E., Brothers, A. F., Miche, M., Montepare, J. M.,...& Wurm, S. (2014). Awareness of aging: Theoretical considerations on an emerging concept. *Developmental Review, 34,* 93–113. doi: 10.1016/j.dr.2014.01.001

Ebner, N. C., Freund, A. M., & Baltes, P. B. (2006). Developmental changes in personal goal orientation from young to late adulthood: From striving for gains to maintenance and prevention of losses. *Psychology and Aging, 21,* 664–678.

Erickson, E. H. (1963). *Childhood and society* (2nd ed.). New York, NY: Norton.

Erickson, E. H., Erickson, J. M., & Kivnick, H. Q. (1986). *Vital involvement in old age.* New York, NY: Norton.

Freund, A. M., (2002). Selection, optimization, and compensation. *Encyclopedia of Aging.* Retrieved from Encyclopedia.com. http://www.encyclopedia.com/doc/1G2-3402200367.html

Freund, A. M., & Baltes, P. B. (2002a). The adaptiveness of selection, optimization, and compensation as strategies of life management: Evidence from a preference study on proverbs. *Journals of Gerontology: Psychological Sciences, 57B,* 426–434.

Freund, A. M., & Baltes, P. B. (2002b). Life-management strategies of selection, optimization, and compensation: Measurement by self-report and construct validity. *Journal of Personality and Social Psychology, 82,* 642–662.

Garroway, A. M., & Rybarczyk, B. (2015). Aging, chronic disease and the biopsychosocial model. In P. A. Lichtenberg, B. T. Mast, B. D. Carpenter, J. L. Wetherell (Eds.), *APA handbook of clinical geropsychology. Vol 1: History and status of the field and perspectives on aging* (pp. 563–586). Washington, DC: American Psychological Association. doi: 10.1037/14458-024

Gatz, M., Smyer, M. A., & DiGilio, D. A. (2016). Psychology's contribution to the well-being of older Americans. *American Psychologist, 71*(4), 257–267.

The Gerontologist. (2015). *Special issue: Successful Aging, 55*(1). doi:10.1093/geront/gnu131

Hamid, M. (2007). *The reluctant fundamentalist.* Orlando, FL: Houghton Mifflin, Harcourt.

Hank, K. (2011). How "successful" do older Europeans age? Findings from SHARE. *The Journals of Gerontology: Series B, Psychological Sciences and Social Sciences, 66B,* 230–236. doi: 10.1093/geronb/gbq089

Havighurst, R. J. (1961). Successful aging. *The Gerontologist, 1,* 8–13. doi: 10.1093/geront/1.1.8

Hill, R. D. (2005). *Positive aging: A guide for mental health care professionals and consumers.* New York, NY: Norton.

Hill, R. D. (2008). *Seven strategies for positive aging.* New York, NY: Norton.

Hill, R. D. (2011). A positive aging framework for guiding geropsychology interventions. *Behavior Therapy, 42,* 66–77. doi:10.1016/jbeth.2010.04.006

Hill, R. D., & Smith, D. J. (2015). Positive aging: At the crossroads of positive psychology and geriatric medicine. In P. A. Lichtenberg, B. T. Mast, B. D. Carpenter, J. L. Wetherell (Eds.), *APA handbook of clinical geropsychology. Vol 1: History and status of the field and perspectives on aging.* (pp. 301–329). Washington, DC: American Psychological Association. doi: 10.1037/14458-013

Hinrichsen, G. A. (2015). Attitudes about aging. In P. A. Lichtenberg, B. T. Mast, B. D. Carpenter, J. L. Wetherell (Eds.), *APA handbook of clinical geropsychology. Vol 1: History and status of the field and perspectives on aging.* (pp. 363–377). Washington, DC: American Psychological Association. doi: 10.1037/14458-015

Jeste, D. V., Depp, C. A., & Vahia, I. V. (2010). Successful cognitive and emotional aging. *World Psychiatry, 9*(2), 78–84.

Jopp, D., & Smith, J. (2006). Resources and life-management strategies as determinants of successful aging: On the protective effect of selection, optimization, and compensation. *Psychology and Aging, 21*(2), 253–265. doi: 10.1037/0882-7974.21.2.253

Koltko-Rivera, M. E. (2006). Rediscovering the later version of Maslow's hierarchy of needs: Self-transcendence and opportunities for theory, research, and unification. *Review of General Psychology, 10,* 302–317. doi:10.1037/1089-2680.10.4.302

Kühn, S., & Lindenberger, U. (2016). Research on human plasticity in adulthood: A lifespan agenda. In K. W. Schaie & S. L. Willis (Eds.), *Handbook of the psychology of aging* (8th ed., pp. 105–123). Amsterdam, Netherlands: Academic Press. doi:10.1016/B978-0-12-411469-2.00006-6

Lang, F. R., Rohr, M. R., & Williger, B. (2011). Modeling success in life-span psychology: The principles of selection, optimization, and compensation. In K. L. Fingerman, C. A. Berg, J. Smith, & T. C. Antonucci (Eds.), *Handbook of life-span development* (pp. 57–85). New York, NY: Springer.

Lawton, M. P. (1989). Behavior-relevant ecological factors. In K.W. Schaie & K. Schooler (Eds.), *Social structure and aging: Psychological processes* (pp. 57–78). Hillsdale, NJ: Erlbaum.

Lawton, M. P., & Nahemow, L. (1973). Ecology and the aging process. In C. Eisdorfer & M. P. Lawton (Eds.), *Psychology of adult development and aging* (pp. 619–675). Washington, DC: American Psychological Association.

Lazarus, R. S., & Folkman, S. (1984). *Stress, appraisal, and coping.* New York, NY: Springer.

Levy, B. (2009). Stereotype embodiment: A psychosocial approach to aging. *Current Directions in Psychological Science, 18,* 332–336. doi: 10.1111/j.1467-8721.2009.01662.x

Levy, B. R., Ferrucci, L., Zonderman, A.B., Slade, M., Troncoso, J., & Resnick, S. M. (2016). A culture-brain link: Negative age stereotypes predict Alzheimer's disease biomarkers. *Psychology and Aging, 31,* 82–88.

Levy, B. R., Pilver, C., Chung, P. H., & Slade, M. D. (2014). Subliminal strengthening: Improving older individuals' physical function over time with an implicit-age-stereotype intervention. *Psychological Science, 25,* 2127–2135. doi: 10.1177/0956797614551970

Levy, B. R., Slade, M. D., Chung, P. H., & Gill, T. M. (2015). Resiliency over time of elders' age stereotypes after encountering stressful events. *The Journals of Gerontology. Series B, Psychological Sciences & Social Sciences, 70,* 886–890. doi:10.1093/geronb/gbu082

Levy, B. R., Zonderman, A. B., Slade, M. D., & Ferrucci, L. (2009). Age stereotypes held earlier in life predict cardiovascular events in later life. *Psychological Science, 20,* 296–98.

Lewin, K. (1935). *A dynamic theory of personality: Selected papers of Kurt Lewin*. New York, NY: McGraw-Hill.

Lopez, S. J., & Gallagher, M. W. (2009). A case for positive psychology. In S. J. Lopez & C. R. Snyder (Eds.). *The Oxford handbook of positive psychology* (2nd ed., pp. 3–6) New York, NY: Oxford University Press. doi: 10.1093.oxfordhb/9780195187243.013.0001

Martin, P., Kelly, N., Kahana, B., Kahana, E., Wilcox, B. D., Wilcox, D. C., & Poon, L. (2015). Defining successful aging: A tangible or elusive concept? *The Gerontologist, 55,* 14–25. doi: 10.1093/geront/gnu044

Martinson, M., & Berridge. C. (2015). Successful aging and its discontents: A systematic review of the social gerontology literature. *The Gerontologist, 55,* 58–69. doi: 10.1093/geront/gnu037

Maslow, A. H. (1954). *Motivation and personality*. New York, NY: Harper & Row.

McLaughlin, S. J., Connell, C. M., Heeringa, S. G., Li, L. W., & Roberts, J. S. (2010). Successful aging in the United States: Prevalence estimates from a national sample of older adults. *The Journals of Gerontology. Series B, Psychological Sciences & Social Sciences, 65B,* 216–226. doi:10.1093/geronb/gbp101

McLaughlin, S. J., Jette, A. M., & Connell, C. (2012). An examination of healthy aging across a conceptual continuum: Prevalence estimates, demographic patterns and validity. *The Journals of Gerontology: Series A, Biological Sciences and Medical Sciences, 67,* 783–789. doi: 10.1093/gerona/glr234

Meisner, B. A. (2012). A meta-analysis of positive and negative age stereotype priming effects on behavior among older adults. *The Journals of Gerontology. Series B, Psychological Sciences and Social Sciences, 67,* 13–17. doi:10.1093/geronb/gbr062

Moen, P. (2016). *Encore adulthood: Boomers on the edge of risk, renewal, and purpose*. New York, NY: Oxford University Press.

Molinari, V., Kier, F. J., & Rosowsky, E. (2006). SOC, personality, and long-term care. In L. Hyer & R. C. Intrieri (Eds.), *Geropsychological interventions in long-term care* (pp. 139–155). New York, NY: Springer.

Montrose, L. P., Depp, C., & Daly, J. (2006). Correlates of self-rated successful aging among community-dwelling older adults. *American Journal of Geriatric Psychiatry, 14,* 43–51.

Palmore, E., Nowlin, J., Busse, E., Siegler, I., Maddox, G. (1985). *Normal aging III*. Durham, NC: Duke University Press.

Peterson, N. M., & Martin, P. (2015). Tracing the origins of success: Implications for successful aging. *The Gerontologist, 55,* 5–13. doi:10.1093/geront/gnu054

Phelan, E. A., & Larson, E. B. (2002). "Successful aging" – where next? *Journal of the American Geriatrics Society, 50,* 1306–1308.

Pickard, J. G., Tan, J., Morrow-Howell, N., & Jung, Y. (2009). Older drivers retiring from the road: An application of the selection, optimization, and compensation model. *Journal of Human Behavior in the Social Environment, 19,* 213–229.

Pillemer, K. (2011). *30 lessons for living: Tried and true advice from the wisest Americans*. New York, NY: Penguin.

Pruchno, R. A., Wilson-Genderson, M., & Cartwright, F. (2010). A two-factor model of successful aging. *Journals of Gerontology, Series B: Psychological Sciences and Social Sciences, 65,* 671–679. doi: 10.1093/geronb/gbq051

Rapp, M. A., Krampe, R. T., & Baltes, P.B. (2006). Adaptive task prioritization in aging: Selective resource allocation to postural control is preserved in Alzheimer's disease. *American Journal of Geriatric Psychiatry, 14,* 52–61.

Rowe, J. W. (2015, April 1). Successful aging of societies. *Daedalus, 144*(2), 5–12. doi:10.1162/DAED_a_00325

Rowe, J. W., & Kahn, R. L. (1987). Human aging: Usual and successful. *Science, 237*, 143–149.

Rowe, J. W., & Kahn, R. (1998). *Successful aging.* New York, NY: Pantheon Books.

Seligman, M. E. P., & Csikszentmihalyi, M. (2000). Positive psychology: An introduction. *American Psychologist, 55*, 5–14. doi: 10.1037/0003-066X.55.1.5

Smyer, M. (2016). Is there a secret to aging well? *Solutions, 7*(1), 55–61. https://www.thesolutionsjournal.com/article/how-shall-we-age

Steele, C. M., & Aronson, J. (1995). Stereotype threat and the intellectual test performance of African Americans. *Journal of Personality and Social Psychology, 69*, 797–811. doi: 10.1037/0022-3514.69.5.797

Strawbridge, W. J., Wallhagen, M. I., & Cohen, R. D. (2002). Successful aging and well-being: Self-rated compared with Rowe and Kahn. *The Gerontologist, 42*, 727–733.

Tedeschi, R. G., & Calhoun, L. G. (1995). *Trauma and transformation.* Thousand Oaks, CA: Sage.

Tergesen, A. (2015, October 19) To age well, change how you feel about aging; Negative stereotypes about getting older can become a self-fulfilling prophecy. How to improve your mind-set –and well-being. *Wall Street Journal* (online). Retrieved from https://www.wsj.com/articles/to-age-well-change-how-you-feel-about-aging-1445220002

Vaillant, G. (2002). *Aging well: Surprising guideposts to a happier life.* New York, NY: Hachette Books.

Vaillant, G. (2012). *Triumphs of experience: The men of the Harvard Grant Study.* Cambridge, MA: Harvard University Press.

Williamson, G. M., & Christie, J. (2009). Aging well in the 21st century: Challenges and opportunities. In S. J. Lopez & C. R. Snyder (Eds.). *The Oxford handbook of positive psychology* (2nd ed., pp. 165–170) New York, NY: Oxford University Press. doi:10.1093.oxfordhb/9780195187243.013.0015

Zautra, A. J., Arewakisporn, A., & Davis, M. C. (2010). Resilience: Promoting well-being through recovery, sustainability, and growth. *Research in Human Development, 7*, 221–238. doi:10.1080/15427609.2010.504431

Part II
Models of Mental Health in Later Life

Discussions about the mental health of any population often begin with disclaimers about the ambiguity of the construct of mental health or mental disorder. A serious conversation with your peers that focused on the task of defining mental health would generate quite diverse ideas and a fair amount of controversy. Conceptions of health and disorder are varied, at least in part, because of the variety of assumptions made concerning the nature of human beings and their interactions with the environment.

Major texts on psychopathology or abnormal psychology typically summarize the major strategies for describing normal or abnormal behavior using a core set of definitions of abnormality that includes statistical definitions (i.e., what is non-normative), moral definitions (i.e., what is socially and culturally unacceptable), definitions of disability or dysfunction (i.e., what impairs social or occupational functioning), definitions of dyscontrol, and definitions based on what is personally distressing. The current edition of the *Diagnostic and Statistical Manual of Mental Disorders* (DSM-5) provides the following definition:

> A mental disorder is a syndrome characterized by clinically significant disturbance in an individual's cognition, emotion regulation, or behavior that reflects a dysfunction in the psychological, biological, or developmental processes underlying mental functioning. Mental disorders are usually associated with significant distress or disability in social, occupational, or other important activities. An expectable or culturally approved response to a common stressor or loss, such as the death of a loved one, is not a mental disorder. Socially deviant behavior (e.g., political, religious, or sexual) and conflicts that are primarily between the individual and society are not mental disorders unless the deviance or conflict results from a dysfunction in the individual, as described above. (American Psychiatric Association, 2013, p. 20)

Aging and Mental Health, Third Edition. Daniel L. Segal, Sara Honn Qualls, and Michael A. Smyer.
© 2018 John Wiley & Sons, Inc. Published 2018 by John Wiley & Sons, Inc.

These definitional components can be used to examine the presence or absence of mental health problems of older persons. Each provides some insights, but each also runs into conceptual conundrums. If a disorder process or organ deterioration is normative among 85-year-olds, does that mean it is normal? How can we talk meaningfully about what might be normal for 85-year-olds that would not be normal in 25-year-olds (i.e., is age per se a moderator of our definition of normal)? Perhaps we might acknowledge differences based on age in the area of memory or attention, but what about depression, anxiety, or substance abuse?

Mental health or well-being is no easier to define than abnormality. Definitions may focus on competence, maturity, emotional resilience, responsibility for actions, or freedom to love and work. Jahoda (1958) provided six highly cited criteria of positive mental health: positive self-attitudes, growth and self-actualization, integration of the personality, autonomy, reality perception, and environmental mastery. We appreciate the qualitative richness of the definition offered by Birren and Renner (1980) that, at any age, mentally healthy people "have the ability to respond to other individuals, to love, to be loved, and to cope with others in give-and-take relationships" (p.29). Qualls (2002) drew on Ryff and Keyes' (1996) empirically supported theoretical framework for psychological well-being in later life with the following definition.

> A mentally healthy person, therefore, accepts the current self, with its strengths and weaknesses, uses the strengths available to him or her to maintain maximum autonomy by mastering their environment, and maintains positive relations with others, all with the overarching purpose of enacting personal meaning in life and personal growth. (p. 12)

Clinical work with older persons is sometimes challenging simply because it forces us to articulate our general conceptions of positive mental health, and then adjust them (as needed) for older persons. As Birren and Renner (1980) acknowledged, the conceptual dichotomies implicit in most distinctions of mental health and mental disorder become even more complicated when applied to older adults: "The conceptual dichotomies…—health and illness, competence and incompetence, and intrapsychic and interpersonal processes—seem, in the minds of the present authors, to have rather different implications for older adults in which there can be may coexisting features" (p. 7). The person described in the following case study challenges us to clarify our definitions of normality.

> Joan Rankin is a 74-year-old woman who lives in her home in a small rural community. Her husband, Jim, died two years ago, following a five-year bout with cancer. Now that she is alone, Joan is tempted to move closer to her children, but cannot quite make up her mind. Her house is paid for, and she is not sure she could buy a comparable house in a city with the proceeds from a sale of this house. She has a modest pension that will be sufficient unless she needs major medical care. Sometimes she worries about not having enough money to carry her through. She chooses to live frugally with an occasional indulgence.
>
> Joan belongs to the local garden club, but is not a particularly active member. She does enjoy working in her own small flower garden during the nice weather seasons. She also attends church almost weekly. Joan has a few close friends, but many of those friendships were strained by the period of Jim's illness. Even two years after his death, she is not sure how to fill her days. Her nights are usually

tolerable although sometimes she lies awake for long periods in the middle of the night. At those times she feels overwhelmingly alone and scared.

Joan is generally healthy, although she has high blood pressure and some difficulties with thyroid and arthritis. She takes ibuprofen for the arthritis, propranolol for blood pressure, and synthroid to regulate her thyroid.

Joan's two children live 300 miles away in major cities. Her daughter, Jeannie, is married, has three children (ages 4, 7, and 10), and teaches school. Her son, John, a very successful Realtor, is currently engaged to be remarried. He was divorced four years ago from his wife of 18 years, who has custody of their two children, ages 8 and 13. Jeannie and John have never been very close. Nor was John close to his father, although he confided his troubles and joys to his mother privately.

Joan has two younger sisters still living, and had two older brothers who died more than five years ago. Her sister Betty lives only two blocks away from Joan, and calls her daily. Sometimes Joan resents the call because Betty is so perky and enthusiastic about life. Betty insists that Joan get out to social events regardless of how tired or sick Joan is feeling. Betty has always been the cheerful one, encouraging all those around her to enjoy life. Recently she has hinted that she might like to move in with Joan to share expenses.

Her other sister Vivian lives with her husband 30 miles away on a farm. They stay busy with farm responsibilities, and with their children and grandchildren. Joan sees them only at family gatherings on holidays. Vivian has always been the quiet, solid one in the family. Joan would like to spend more time with her, but can see that she is too busy with daily responsibilities to socialize.

Her brothers, Elwood and Milt, were in business together in a city 150 miles from Joan's home. They died of heart attacks exactly one year apart. They left their families quite well off financially, and their children and grandchildren have continued their business. Joan only visits with her sisters-in-law or their offspring at the annual family reunion each summer.

To what extent is Joan mentally healthy or disordered? Clinicians would readily recognize several symptoms in this brief description of Joan that might be clinically meaningful. For example, she has difficulty with decision-making, worries, has mild insomnia, and is socially withdrawn. Could she be diagnosed with a mental disorder? Is her current distress caused by her recent widowhood, her health, her struggle to create meaning, the family and social systems conflicts, or some inadequacy in her personality that inhibits her coping? Given her circumstances, what would mentally healthy look like? Where would you begin to look for additional information to help you understand Joan's well-being? Recall the biopsychosocial approach we introduced in Chapter 1. This important model gives clinicians and researchers entry points with which to begin to explore the nature of mental disorders and mental health.

A systematic examination of conceptualizations of the mental health of older persons leads us to examine the broader paradigms of psychology. A paradigm is a framework used to construct our understanding of the world. Such frameworks make basic assumptions about the nature of human beings, including assumptions about motivation, cognition, emotion, personality, and behavior. Built on those assumptions are postulates or theories that attempt to explain particular behavior patterns, including patterns defined as mental health and mental disorder.

In the section that follows, a series of chapters describes four basic paradigms used often by psychologists: the psychodynamic, cognitive-behavioral, stress and coping, and family systems paradigms. These models represent the psychological aspects within the larger biopsychosocial frame. Each chapter will review the basic assumptions and core theoretical contributions of one paradigm. Specifically, we offer descriptions of the assumptions about what well-being looks like and how mental disorders are defined and conceptualized. Because approaches to assessment and intervention are rooted in the assumptions about mental health and mental disorder, we also include in each chapter a description of the major approaches to assessment and intervention that have arisen from each paradigm.

Gerontology has not produced totally new paradigms for defining and examining human lives. It has instead applied existing frameworks to the unique and common problems of older persons. There is no single way to answer the questions raised at the beginning of this introduction regarding Joan Rankin. As will become evident, each paradigm produces a different (although perhaps related) explanation of Joan's mental health.

Regardless of paradigm or theory, gerontologists have developed a profound respect for the influence of culture and cohort experience on well-being. Subcultures offer specific definitions and mechanisms for demonstrating mental health and disorder. These definitions and mechanisms for experiencing well-being also vary by the historical period into which individuals are born and live (birth cohort). If Joan Rankin were Chinese, German, or Cherokee, how would that influence your understanding of her behavior and your analysis of her well-being? How would her experience be different and what different meanings would be embedded in her behavior if she lived in the seventeenth, twentieth, or twenty-first century?

As you study the chapters in Part II, engage yourself in the challenge of creating meaningful models for understanding mental health and disorder in older adults. What paradigms explain behavior most adequately and parsimoniously? What tenets from each paradigm seem most credible? As you read, you may find it useful to write an analysis of Joan Rankin's story from each paradigm. When you have completed all four chapters, consider writing an integration essay that articulates your personal model of mental health and mental disorder in older adults.

References

American Psychiatric Association. (2013). *Diagnostic and statistical manual of mental disorders* (5th ed.). Arlington, VA: Author.

Birren, J. E., & Renner, V. J. (1980). Concepts and issues of mental health and aging. In J. E. Birren & R. B. Sloane (Eds.), *Handbook of mental health and of aging* (pp. 3–33). Englewood Cliffs, NJ: Prentice-Hall.

Jahoda, M. (1958). *Current concepts of positive mental health.* New York, NY: Basic Books.

Ryff, C., & Keyes, C. L. (1996). The structure of psychological well-being revisited. *Journal of Personality and Social Psychology, 69,* 719–727.

Qualls, S. H. (2002). Defining mental health in later life. *Generations, 25,* 9–13.

4

Psychodynamic Model

Co-author: Lacey Edwards, PhD[1]

The psychodynamic model of psychological functioning is one of the earliest comprehensive models of psychological well-being and disorder, but a relatively late contributor to models of mental health in later life. The progenitor of this line of theory was Sigmund Freud's psychoanalytic model. Subsequent contributors (e.g., Carl Jung, Erik Erikson) developed varied approaches to the inner dynamics of personality, but stayed true to core assumptions about the importance of intrapsychic functioning, the balance of genetic and environmental influence on personality, and the key role of relationships in normal and abnormal development. The interpersonal school shifted focus to the social contexts in which the personality structures were formed and maintained (e.g., Karen Horney, Harry Stack Sullivan). Thus, although the theories covered in this chapter offer a wide range of constructs and explanations, they share a common focus on the motivational and personality aspects of human beings whose social contexts have powerful effects.

Maria Jiminez is increasingly isolated because she often just does not feel like getting out. Up until a few years ago her home was the constant gathering place of the extended family. After her husband's death, however, the nieces and nephews quit coming around. Her children and grandchildren visit, but seem to resent it. The entire family continues to mourn the death of Juan, the warm, generous, and fun-loving patriarch of the family. Although Maria had always cooked for the family, she was not known for a generous spirit. In family gatherings she usually kept to herself, portraying a rather quiet person who waited for others to notice what she needed or wanted. Her daughters feel obligated to care for their mother, but it is a fairly joyless relationship on both sides. The girls can never quite get it right—if they make apple pie, she wanted peach. If they clean the kitchen, she laments about the dirt in the bathroom. The doctors don't pay enough attention to her, the home health

---

1 Post-Doctoral Fellow at the University of Colorado at Colorado Springs Aging Center

---

aide "is just working for money" and "doesn't genuinely like me." Everyone recognizes Maria's depression and encourages her to seek help from a mental health professional. She resists because "any woman would feel depressed if she had a life like mine," but has made it to your office to tell you her sad story. She obviously likes having you listen to her, but tells you that she is sure you can't help her.

Introduction to the Model

How does the psychodynamic model describe and explain Maria's distress? As with any model, basic assumptions about human beings are the core constructs used to explain behavior. In the case of psychodynamic theory, the basic personality, developmental processes, and interpersonal relationships are the main foci of the theory.

The psychodynamic view of human beings emphasizes the complex interrelationships among cognition, emotion, and motivation in the formation of personality. The complexity into which these highly evolved structures are organized gives humans a tremendous advantage over other species of animals in the task of managing their basic needs (e.g., food, shelter, procreation). However, the struggle to survive, along with the knowledge that survival is tenuous, generates anxiety.

Managing anxiety is a primary task of the executive function of the personality, the ego. Freud initially postulated that anxiety was generated by conflict between the primitive life energy (libido) that resides in an animalistic structure called the id, and the societally imposed conscience structure called the superego. The ego's task, according to Freud, is to modulate the inevitable conflict between the two structures. Later, ego psychologists emphasized the interpersonal contexts in which the developing capability of the ego or Self emerges and forms a distinctive style. Other theorists postulate that the process of creating meaning is a key potential of the ego. What is shared in common by psychodynamic theorists, however, is their attempt to describe the organization and functioning of the basic structures of personality and suggest ways to assist people to gain insight into the functioning of those structures so they can make more conscious choices regarding their motives, emotions, behavior, thoughts, and values.

Basic personality structures are established very early in life as the infant and very young child experiences its basic needs and the external world's response to them. The primary relationships for infants are known as their attachment relationships (Bowlby, 1969). Attachment figures are the persons who teach infants and toddlers about the external world (e.g., its safety, trustworthiness, and availability of nurturance) through their interactions. Because all humans begin as helpless, dependent creatures, the early experience of helplessness generates very basic survival anxiety.

Strong nurturing caretakers, who teach the child that Others are trustworthy, become internalized as parts of the Self that will be experienced as sharing those characteristics. Conversely, Others whose behavior increases anxiety or rage will teach the child not only about an unreliable, unsafe external world, but are also internalized as representations of the world as an unsafe, unreliable Self. These early experiences shape the form of the child's cognitive schema, emotional response patterns, and motivations. The resulting personality structures subsequently serve the function of buffering individuals from the core anxiety about living life and facing death. Thus, early relationships are where basic linkages are forged between thoughts, feelings, and motivations that culminate in an external worldview. Similarly shaped by early relational experiences, internal self-protective structures, called *defense mechanisms*, are one's primary ways of managing basic anxiety about life and death.

The development and evolution of these structures was once solely the purview of child psychologists interested in the initial structuring of personality during the first five years of life. Certainly, the experiences of childhood continue to be recognized as particularly profound because the early experiences establish styles or strategies for managing internal conflicts and adapting to external changes that have lifelong effects. For example, childhood attachment styles link to subsequent patterns of adult relationships (Shemmings, 2006). In adulthood, secure attachment styles are expressed as mutuality in the processes of caregiving, intimacy, and sexuality. Avoidant attachment styles, in contrast, constrain the individual's subsequent ability or willingness to give or receive care, or to emotionally connect within a sexual relationship (leading to distancing or promiscuity). Most current psychodynamic theorists recognize the potential for growth and development across the lifespan as intrapsychic processes evolve in response to life experience as well as the critical importance of childhood experiences.

Adult Development: The Context for Aging

Developmental processes of adulthood provide new opportunities to mature in the course of responding to the many tasks and crises faced by all adults in the course of normal adulthood. Colarusso and Nemiroff (1979) offered seven classic hypotheses regarding the nature of development in adulthood that can be viewed as basic postulates of psychodynamic views of adult development (see Table 4.1). These statements claim that there is more continuity than discontinuity between child and adult developmental processes, with distinctions primarily in form and content. The basic structures through which development is evoked and expressed remain the same.

Table 4.1 Psychodynamic model of adult development

Hypothesis I	The nature of the developmental process is basically the same in the adult as in the child.
Hypothesis II	Development in adulthood is an ongoing, dynamic process.
Hypothesis III	Whereas childhood development is focused primarily on the *formation* of psychic structure, adult development is concerned with the continuing *evolution* of existing psychic structure.
Hypothesis IV	The fundamental developmental issues of childhood continue as central aspects of adult life but in altered form.
Hypothesis V	The developmental processes in adulthood are influenced by the *adult* past as well as the *childhood* past.
Hypothesis VI	Development in adulthood, as in childhood, is deeply influenced by the body and physical change.
Hypothesis VII	A central, phase-specific theme of adult development is the normative crisis precipitated by the recognition and acceptance of the finiteness of time and the inevitability of personal death.

Source: Adapted from Colarusso & Nemiroff (1979).

Thus, aged adults come to the last part of their lives heavily influenced not only by childhood events, but by adult events and adaptations.

> The individual enters late life with a personality structure that reflects a long history of life experiences. Idiosyncratic means of managing internal sexual and aggressive impulses and of coping with external stresses have been established, a well-engrained sense of self has been formed and shaped, providing an internalized representation that guides behavior and experiences, and child, adolescence, and adulthood disappointments and traumas have marked the individual with particular areas of psychological strength and weakness. In late life, the adult confronts age-correlated events (retirement, physical changes and illness, loss through death of friends and family) and internal psychological changes that can re-evoke long-unresolved but defended against internal conflicts, undermine the sense of self, and increase demands on ego resources and defense mechanisms, thus requiring a new level of integration and development or resulting in depression, anxiety, or psychotic disturbance. (Newton, Brauer, Gutmann, & Grunes, 1986, p. 208)

The effects of a lifetime of experiences are embedded in the internal structures of personality. Despite the importance of external events to the adjustment to aging, the personality is considered a primary mediator of adaptation in later life.

Adult developmental processes have been outlined in terms of the tasks that provoke change (e.g., marriage, entry of children), the effects of adult events on development of the Self (e.g., Kohut, 1971), or the development of internal structures such as defense mechanisms (e.g., Vaillant, 1977). A popular framework for conceptualizing development is to divide the lifespan into stages. Stage theorists attempt to divide the lifespan into discrete phases that are characterized by common life tasks, especially those related to family development and work roles (Gould, 1978; Levinson, Darrow, & Klein, 1978).

Erik Erikson's (1963) early model of development across the lifespan (Figure 4.1) is one of the most influential stage models. Adults have opportunities to mature in response to the major tasks of the life course by restructuring internally. In the last formulation of his model, Erikson, Erikson, and Kivnick (1986) describe specific life themes that, although present throughout the lifespan, are most salient at the point in the life cycle when internal and external pressures highlight one particular theme. These themes are experienced within the dynamics of the personality as children and adults struggle with the use of their personality strengths and weaknesses to address life tasks. For example, the theme of autonomy that emerges so powerfully in toddlerhood as the child first experiences the power and frustration of the will, is again significantly addressed in adolescence, and again in old age. The substantive issues that generate the struggle vary, but the thematic focus on autonomy is similar. The struggle with the opposing alternative responses to life challenges is what produces the potential for growth of character or virtues. A balance between the alternatives generates growth toward maturity.

The basic principles of Erikson's model are shared by most psychodynamic theorists: People use the styles and strategies consistent with their personality structure to address the psychosocial tasks of their life stage. The tasks or crises of adulthood challenge the familiar styles and strategies, however, creating an opportunity for development of more complex and mature personality structures. In the course of responding to life challenges, heightened anxiety may result if the task is not being

Older Adulthood	57	58	59	60	61	62	63	64 Integrity & Despair WISDOM
Middle Adulthood	49	50	51	52	53	54	55 Generativity & Self-Absorption CARE	56
Young Adulthood	41	42	43	44	45	46 Intimacy & Isolation LOVE	47	48
Adolescence	33	34	35	36	37 Identity & Confusion FIDELITY	38	39	40
School Age	25	26	27	28 Industry & Inferiority COMPETENCE	29	30	31	32
Play Age	17	18	19 Initiative & Guilt PURPOSE	20	21	22	23	24
Toddler-hood	9	10 Autonomy & Shame/Doubt WILL	11	12	13	14	15	16
Infancy	1 Basic Trust & Basic Mistrust HOPE	2	3	4	5	6	7	8

Figure 4.1 Psychosocial themes and stages of life.
Source: Adapted from Erikson et al. (1986).

managed well using familiar methods. Increased anxiety sets the stage for either growth within the personality, or a breakdown in functioning (regression), perhaps even to the ultimate level of psychosis.

Development in the Second Half of Life

What new potentials for growth exist in later life that are not possible early in the life cycle? Beginning in mid-life, humans alter their perspective on their own lifespan. Neugarten (1979) hypothesized that people begin to count time in terms of time until death rather than in terms of time since birth, a perspective that impacts relationship priorities, for example (Carstensen, Isaacowitz, & Charles, 1999). Having achieved a stable life structure, and given increased awareness of the limits of their lifespan, humans are prompted to reexamine their life for unused opportunities and unknown aspects of the self.

Jung (1933) noted the tendency for some men and women to become more androgynous by exploring characteristics of the other gender during the second half of their life. Men explore their feminine side while women are drawn to explore their underdeveloped masculine characteristics. Beginning in late mid-life, then, adults are drawn to explore new interests, skills, and interpersonal styles. For example, high-powered business executives may choose to paint, garden, and build close ties to family. Extroverts may explore their introverted side through journaling, meditation, or interests that draw upon the inner resources of creativity. Gutmann (1987, 1992) expanded on this theme by arguing that parenting is the organizing life structure of early adulthood that is sufficiently demanding that couples organize their work into constraining but efficient roles, traditionally along gender-based lines. Once the "chronic parental emergency" ends, individuals are free to resume the full range of their development, both masculine and feminine.

Erikson (1963) argued for the potential for wisdom in later life, as the individual makes peace with his or her life as it was lived. Like all of the other Eriksonian themes, the basic polarity of ego integrity versus despair is present in all stages of life. Yet a special perspective is available at the end of life.

> Throughout life, the individual has, on some level, anticipated the finality of old age, experiencing an existential dread of "not-being" alongside an ever-present process of integrating those behaviors and restraints, those choices and rejections, those essential strengths and weaknesses over time that constitute what we have called the sense of "I" in the world. In old age, this tension reaches its ascendancy. The elder is challenged to draw on a life cycle that is far more nearly completed than yet to be lived, to consolidate a sense of wisdom with which to live out the future, to place him- or herself in perspective among those generations now living, and to accept his or her place in an infinite historical progression. (Erikson et al., 1986, p. 56)

Mental Health in Later Life

A developmental approach to personality dynamics would imply that positive mental health requires a richer definition than merely the absence of pathology. Is it positive mental health when a frail older person maintains basic personality integrity despite the significant decline of physical abilities? Or when an older adult adapts to tremendous loss with only modest regression? Psychoanalysts have focused on pathology or maintenance of function in the face of loss and deterioration far more than on positive potentials, with rare exceptions. Emotional integration or deepening of personality is described by some developmentalists as a positive developmental potential in old age (Butler, Lewis, & Sunderland, 1998; Ryff, 1982). Kivnick (1993) suggests that vitality reflects the infusion of meaning into daily activities.

> Throughout the life cycle, everyday mental health may be described as an attempt to live meaningfully, in a particular set of social and environmental circumstances, relying on a particular collection of resources and supports. Simply said, we all try to do the best we can with what we have. Part of this effort involves developing internal strengths and capacities; part involves identifying and using external resources; part involves compensating for weaknesses and deficits. (p. 24)

Yet another proposed component of mental health is deriving meaning. Meaning must be worked out for the entire life cycle in the form of a coherent *narrative* that explains the continuity of an individual life in the face of interruptions and adverse events (Cohler, 1993; Schiff & Cohler, 2001).

Development of Psychopathology

Psychodynamic theorists who focus on developmental tasks unique to each life stage typically link later life to themes of loss such as: (1) grief over loved ones within one's intimate circle; (2) loss of roles; (3) loss of physical capacity and resulting dependency; and (4) loss of opportunity to alter one's life course. The belief that the loss theme dominates the aging experience often leads newcomers to the field of aging to assume that depression rates are particularly high in older adults. Surprisingly, however, older adults report lower rates of clinical depression than most adult populations (see Chapter 9). Clearly, the tasks of later life alone do not explain the emergence of psychopathology.

Psychodynamic theory points to internal rather than external causes of psychopathology because the external events or challenges associated with aging are experienced by far more older adults than those who develop psychiatric symptoms. Explanations of the etiology of psychopathology presume one or more of the following causal factors: (1) losses of later life reenact significant childhood losses; (2) an underdeveloped self or immature defense mechanisms provide insufficient strength for handling the psychological challenges of later life; (3) loss of physical, cognitive, and emotional strengths with advanced old age undermine the functioning of the ego; and/or (4) one's personal narrative cannot meaningfully integrate the events and transitions of later life. As outlined below, each of these explanations is evident in the brief description of Maria Jiminez at the beginning of the chapter.

Losses

Classic psychoanalytic theory proposes that loss is particularly threatening to older adults if it evokes strong unresolved grief over a childhood loss. The model emphasizes the critical negative impact of childhood loss on formation of intrapsychic structures. Specifically, loss of an attachment figure evokes extremely powerful grief that overwhelms the young child's adaptive capacity. More recent research examines the role of childhood trauma and post-traumatic stress disorder on subsequent physical and mental health problems (e.g., Choi, DiNitto, Marti, & Choi, 2017). The legacy of childhood experiences of death or trauma is anxiety about living in a profoundly unstable, unprotected world. Early experiences are significant wounds that may never heal, or may produce significant emotional scar tissue that is embedded in the organization of the brain. Defense mechanisms may protect an individual from severe depression, until such time as the defense mechanisms themselves are taxed by a life event or task too momentous for adaptation by the current psychological structures. The significant losses of later life leave a person particularly vulnerable to reexperiencing the feelings evoked during the childhood grief experience. When the grief over significant attachment figures reenacts the childhood loss, this model predicts a regression in functioning into some form of psychopathology. However, the loss model may only address the latest phase of the lifespan when social and physical losses are pervasive (Gutmann, 1987).

> The fact that Maria Jiminez was unable to give much nurturance to others during her adult life would lead a psychodynamic clinician to suspect that she failed to receive sufficient nurturance in her own childhood to have a fully functioning ego. It turns out that Maria was the sixth of nine children in a very poor and busy household. Her mother was very ill for several months after her birth, leaving Maria in the care of her 8-year-old sister. This type of chronic, pervasive loss of parenting at a critical period limited her potential to engage in rich attachment relationships. Always seeking a caregiver, Maria had limited care to give.

Underdeveloped self or immature defenses

Throughout the lifespan, developmental tasks are most challenging to those who lack internal structures sufficient to support adaptation. In his model of successive tasks, Erikson (1963) noted that those who have not mastered previous developmental challenges when faced with adult tasks are considerably handicapped in their efforts to adapt. One study that attempted to examine the idea of maturation across the lifespan was a study of Harvard sophomores that was launched in the early 1940s. Although containing an obviously limited sample (e.g., bright, well-to-do White men selected by the Deans at Harvard for being academically and emotionally strong, and who were not involved in World War II), the longitudinal nature of the study has offered an opportunity to study change in personality structures over time through in-depth clinical interviews. Twenty-five years later, interviews illustrated the themes of stability and change as changes in defensive styles were studied. One question guiding the research was whether these men who had society's most ideal developmental conditions in young adulthood (financial and educational resources, social status, and personality strength) would continue to mature throughout adulthood. Under what conditions would they mature, and what would stunt the maturational process? Specifically, would the men mature through a hierarchy of defense mechanisms as they experienced the challenges of adulthood (see Table 4.2 for a listing of the defenses within the hierarchy). Results of the clinical interviews when the men were 25, 30, 47, and 57 showed that there was a tendency for the men to use increasingly mature defense mechanisms with increased age, and those who failed to mature in defensive style had the worst outcomes (Vaillant, 1977; Vaillant & Vaillant, 1990).

Within the loss model described above, early childhood trauma is postulated to inflict permanent personality scars that become points of vulnerability in old age. Gutmann (1987) used an immune system analogy to describe the relationship between personality defenses and loss. The pathogen (loss) is powerful only to the extent that the immune system (personality structure) is vulnerable to that pathogen. Later life losses are particularly lethal to persons whose personality structures adapted to early losses in immature ways. Thus, an underdeveloped self exacerbates the power of loss to evoke distress and psychopathology in late life.

Table 4.2 Schematic table of adaptive mechanisms

Level 1	Psychotic mechanisms	Denial
		Distortion
		Delusional projection
Level II	Immature mechanisms (common in severe depression, personality disorders, and adolescence)	Fantasy
		Projection
		Hypochondriasis
		Passive-aggressive behavior (masochism, turning against the self)
		Acting out (compulsive delinquency, perversion)
Level III	Neurotic mechanisms	Intellectualization (isolation, obsessive behavior, undoing, rationalization)
		Repression
		Reaction formation
		Displacement (conversion, phobias)
		Dissociation
Level IV	Mature mechanisms	Sublimation
		Altruism
		Suppression
		Anticipation
		Humor

Incomplete development can result from less traumatic sources as well. Gutmann's model suggests that the demands of mid-life are sufficient to limit the full range of individual development. Once the chronic parental emergency is past, adults can continue with their development in a wider range of domains. Young-old adults may experience the urges and drives to continue that development by exploring the unknown parts of the personality. As wishes and urges surface, the young-old find their personal myths (or narrative) threatened by parts of the self that have not previously been integrated into the myth. Anxiety over the need to learn about new parts of the self and integrate them into the myth can spawn pathological reactions such as anxiety, depression, or more primitive psychotic reactions.

Maria used primitive defense mechanisms to protect her from the terror of being unnurtured in a dangerous world. She commonly projected her feelings onto other family members and neighbors, was a noted hypochondriac, and dealt with her anger consistently in passive-aggressive ways. The children knew not to ever confront her version of reality directly, or she would withdraw for days at a time, after which she always had a new illness "because of the stress of this family." Prior to her husband's death, Maria had fared considerably better because she had managed to marry a nurturer who doted on her with tremendous amounts of warmth and affection. As the children perceived it, he was the "giver" and she was the "receiver" throughout their lives. Juan never complained, but the children could see his frustration at her constant manipulation of circumstances to ensure that her desires were met. After his death, Maria obviously was bereft of her primary caretaker and often behaved like a lost child.

Compensation for lost ego strength

Self psychologists describe the devastating impact on the self of the many age-correlated experiences such as loss of physical strength, cognitive abilities, and energy. Diminished capacity and energy is postulated to undermine self-esteem, forcing the person to find restitution for the loss. If the environment is insufficient to maintain the ego functions, a frail older adult may use compensatory mechanisms that appear pathological, such as recounting past glories or blaming others for lost items.

> After her husband's death, Maria's environment clearly lacked sufficient structure and caretaking to maintain her highest possible level of functioning. Her constant blaming of the daughters for not doing enough was insufficient to make her feel better, but protected her from the reality that a perfect caretaker was simply unavailable. If she could just keep at them, the daughters could take care of her well enough, she was sure.

Inability to preserve or build a coherent narrative

Later life is the period in which individuals are particularly challenged to integrate a meaningful ending to their life narrative that is also internally consistent with the entire story (Cohler, 1993).

> From this perspective, the so-called wisdom achieved in later life consists of the ability to maintain a coherent narrative of the course of life in which the presently remembered past, experienced present, and anticipated future are understood as problems to be studied rather than outcomes to be assumed. The question is not whether older adults are able to realize wisdom but rather how these older adults are able to continue to experience a sense of coherence while confronting factors associated with the loss of personal integrity, as well as feelings of fragmentation and disruption of the life story across the course of their lives. (Cohler, 1993, p. 119–120)

Cohler postulates that the life constructs from earlier adulthood may not be adequate to integrate the experiences and expectations of later life into the personal narrative, necessitating a true developmental shift. If the shift cannot be made, the individual is vulnerable to psychopathology characteristic of personal fragmentation. Even events as traumatic as the holocaust are rewritten with multiple, and at times, paradoxical meanings for the human life (Schiff & Cohler, 2001).

> Maria's adolescence and young adulthood were a Cinderella story. Raised doing the hard labor of women in a poor family, Maria was rescued by Prince Charming who was the only person who truly recognized her for the princess that she really was. Unfortunately, he took her to a blue-collar subsistence in a small town rather than a true castle, a failing for which she never quite forgave him. The world could never know just what she could have become if the circumstances had been right, and now it never would. Not only is it hard to be an aging princess, but her prince is gone. No one else treats her like she deserves; if she doesn't demand good work, they will all do just the minimum. Maria sees herself as stuck in a bad fairytale that

won't force the wicked stepsisters to recognize the true beauty of a princess. The narratives of old age that describe contentment from a life lived well and making peace with lost opportunities and the limited accomplishments of a human life are a foreign language to Maria.

Assessment

Psychodynamic theorists and clinicians focus assessment on internal personality structures and relational patterns grounded in beliefs, narratives, emotional responses, values, meanings, and behaviors. A developmental history of the individual life cycle is a key starting point, including developmental stages, tasks, and themes (Nemiroff & Colarusso, 1990). Early childhood experiences hold obvious importance within this model that presumes that early development constrains later developmental styles. Of particular importance are the critical events or traumas, and the attachment relationships within which the earliest experiences were processed.

Important for treatment is assessment of the capacity for insight. Psychodynamic treatments rely upon the patient's insight into his or her own personality to make conscious the structures and processes that influence behaviors and self-perception. To bypass the requirement for insight, projective assessment techniques can be used to elicit information about personality structure and function. For example, Thematic Apperception Test cards allow respondents to project their basic assumptions about relationships into the stories they tell about standardized pictures. The Projective Assessment of Aging Method (Starr, Weiner, & Rabetz, 1979), a Thematic Apperception Test designed specifically for assessing dynamics of later life, depicts older adults during reflection and social interaction. Projective tests continue to be used for a variety of clinical and research purposes, although their use is declining (Norcross, Hedges, & Castle, 2002) and debate and significant controversy exist about the empirical justification for projective tests (Mihura, Meyer, Dumitrascu, & Bombel, 2016).

Kivnick (1993) developed an interview schedule for eliciting information specifically about life strengths. Drawing on her interview experience with older participants in the longitudinal study reported by Erikson et al., (1986), she designed this instrument to reflect the language and themes relevant to the psychological work typical of old age. The interview is designed to solicit primarily positive aspects of development.

Treatment

The goal of psychodynamic treatment with older adults is to (1) provide direct support to a fragile ego, (2) modify personality structure, or (3) strengthen the psychosocial functioning of the person. Psychodynamic psychotherapy engages clients in an intensive, and at times, long-term revisitation of the experiences of childhood during which the core self was constructed from experience with parental caregiving styles. The foci of psychodynamic therapies include affect and expression of emotion, attempts to avoid distressing thoughts and feelings, recurring themes and patterns, past experience, interpersonal relationships, the therapeutic relationship, and fantasy life (Shedler, 2010). For the client, the therapeutic relationship offers a new relational experience and the opportunity for reworking the interpersonal experience base for defining the self.

Brief psychodynamic psychotherapy is one of the therapeutic approaches that has a sufficient empirical research base to categorize it as an evidence based treatment for depression in older adults (Scogin, Welsh, Hanson, Stump, & Coates, 2005). Other psychodynamic therapeutic approaches are now being applied to older adults (e.g., interpersonal psychotherapy and narrative therapy) with interesting results. Supportive psychotherapy represents a low-intensity less directive approach that may also be appropriate when the capacity for insight, which is necessary to produce personality change, is absent or limited.

Time-limited dynamic psychotherapy

Time-limited dynamic therapy (TLDP) was created to meet the need for a shorter model of psychodynamic therapy that was also effective and allowed for more people to receive services. Brief, or time-limited, dynamic therapy differs from traditional psychodynamic therapy by offering a short-term model that centers around a specific theme. TLDP is an effective treatment for adults with symptoms of depression, anxiety, and somatic disorders (Driessen et al., 2015; Shedler, 2010). Many studies have shown that the benefit of brief dynamic therapy increases long after the client has ended treatment, as the client continues to focus on personal development related to the pattern identified in therapy (Levenson, 2010; Shedler, 2010).

TLDP is built on seven foundational principles that provide a conceptualization for difficulty and treatment. The principles are: People are innately motivated to search for and maintain human relatedness; maladaptive relationship patterns are learned early in life and underlie many presenting difficulties; these patterns persist because they are maintained in current relationships; clients are understood as stuck rather than sick; maladaptive relationship patterns are reenacted in the therapeutic relationship; treatment will focus on the primary problematic relationship pattern; and the change process will continue after therapy has ended (Levenson, 2010). The seven principles support the understanding that relational patterns learned early in life influence present-day experience, and new ways can be learned in the context of a safe therapeutic relationship, which builds upon past experiences and is able to become a new model for relational engagement even after therapy has ended.

The therapist begins the initial session by allowing the client to tell his or her story, including when problems arose, and exploring interpersonal changes during the times of difficulty. The therapist and client identify the length of time therapy will continue, with the general expectation of completion within approximately 16 to 22 sessions. The therapist utilizes an assessment to identify the primary relational difficulty called the Cyclical Maladaptive Pattern (CMP). The CMP identifies the client's behavior, the client's expectations of others' reactions, how others respond to the client, how the client acts toward the self, and the interactive countertransference of the therapist toward the client (Levenson, 2010). The focus of therapy centers around the identified CMP, and therapy is duly concluded by 22 sessions. TLDP affirms the strengths of the client, and highlights the ability to continue to grow and generalize learning after therapy is completed rather than encouraging engagement in long-term therapy (Levenson, 2010).

TLDP has significant research supporting its effectiveness and the long-term gains evidenced for clients (Driessen et al., 2015), yet, it does not have specific research supporting its use with older adults. However, the themes and tenets of the theory are applicable for adults of all ages. As generational norms often influence a client's receptiveness toward therapy, a brief model is often beneficial for older adults who may desire to address a pattern and then personally continue the work outside of therapy. TLDP provides an effective and time-limited model for engagement with older adults, affirming their strengths and ability to effect change both within the self and in relationships with others.

Interpersonal psychotherapy

Interpersonal psychotherapy (IPT) was developed to treat major depression (Klerman, Weissman, Rounsaville, & Chevron, 1984) by addressing the interpersonal difficulties that often lead to depression. IPT was formally structured in a treatment manual for depression (Weissman, Markowitz, & Klerman, 2000) and has been the focus of clinical trials for a wide range of client populations and mental health diagnoses (Cuijpers, Donker, Weissman, Ravitz, & Cristea, 2016). Four particular interpersonal problem areas are addressed in IPT: grief, interpersonal role disputes, role transitions, and interpersonal deficits. Clients are assessed for symptom intensity as well as for difficulties in these four areas. Assessment findings are shared with clients, and one or two problem areas are chosen by therapist and client together as a focus of therapy. The time-limited treatment approach begins with an assessment and education phase in which the therapist explains to the client how depression was created by the interpersonal difficulties. The middle phase of therapy is when the therapist applies well-elaborated strategies to address very specific problems identified in the interpersonal life of the client. The approach is essentially collaborative and hopeful as the therapist points to the array of options that can be used to address each problem. The final phase addresses the termination process, including review of progress as well as remaining challenges, feelings about ending the relationship, and possible need for additional treatment. Although rooted in the interpersonal school of psychiatry and thus broadly construed as a psychodynamic model, the focus is on the here-and-now and on cognitive and behavior change, which represents a significant departure from traditional psychodynamic psychotherapy and also shares much in common with problem-solving therapy (covered in Chapter 5).

IPT has been demonstrated to be effective in treatment of depression (Mello, Mari, Bacaltchuk, Verdeli, & Neugebauer, 2005) through empirical validation (Cuijpers et al., 2011). IPT also shows probable effectiveness with depressed populations of all ages, including adolescents and older adults for whom the limited research literature offers less powerful support than with adults generally (David-Ferdon & Kaslow, 2008; Scogin et al., 2005). Trials of IPT for other disorders, including anxiety disorders, post-traumatic stress disorder, and eating disorders, have also been conducted in recent years, with growing evidence of the value of the approach for preventing and treating a range of problems (Cuijpers et al., 2016). Older adults may be particularly well situated to benefit from IPT because of the significance of social losses in later life (Hinrichsen, 2008; Hinrichsen & Clougherty, 2006).

Narrative therapies

Narrative therapies build upon the tendency of humans to write and rewrite their autobiography throughout the lifespan. Indeed, humans construct their core self through stories that define identities and interpersonal positions, and create meaning (White & Epston, 1990). The telling of a narrative inevitably involves the selection and discarding of information that is relevant to the immediate story or stories through which meaning is created. Clinicians using this approach focus on the process of telling, inviting clients to tell and retell the stories, reframing experiences in ways that open possibilities for creating change in behavior, meaning, and identity.

Erickson claimed that life review is a natural developmental process that must be embraced in order to achieve a sense of ego integrity in old age when decline and loss become themes. His approach emphasized the importance of proactive self-management of ego functioning in later life when the salience of limited time left to live constrains the urge to revise one's life mistakes. Furthermore, the assaults on the sense of the integrity of one's life are not only internal. Ageism and negative stereo-types of aging have powerful effects on the day-to-day functioning and well-being of older adults (Levy & Macdonald, 2016). Narrative therapies provoke conscious reflection on a life lived, inviting an active reexamination of the meaning of the particular life one lived, linked with a focus of how one would like to engage in the here-and-now given the narrative meaning of one's life.

Reminiscence therapy is one of the earliest psychotherapies developed for older adults, drawing upon the power of narrative to combat depression or the loss of purpose or identity. At its simplest level, reminiscence engages an older adult in revisiting pleasant periods of life as a reminder of what has been. At a far more complex level, life review reminiscence offers the option of reassigning meaning to events and relationships through which the core self has been created and interpreted. Reminiscence and other narrative therapies offer older adults the option of exploring how a long developmental history intersects with immediate life challenges to shape the meaning of a life. Evidence of the effectiveness of reminiscence therapies provides support for their usefulness in treating symptoms of depression and anxiety, while also increasing a personal sense of mastery (Bahr, 2014).

Supportive therapy

Non-directive supportive psychotherapy shows somewhat less effectiveness than other psychotherapies (Cuijpers, van Straten, Andersson, & van Oppen, 2008), yet meta-analyses of supportive psychotherapy provide evidence of sustained positive growth even when compared with more conventional talk therapies (Cuijpers et al., 2012). In addition, there may be clients for whom it remains the only available treatment approach due to the level of ego strength needed to participate and benefit from depth-oriented psychotherapy. For example, research provides evidence that supportive therapy is associated with positive treatment results for late-life depression, likely due to therapeutic factors shared in many therapies such as therapist warmth, unconditional positive regard, and provision of empathy (Huang, Delucchi, Dunn, & Nelson, 2015).

Later life may challenge the personality structures of older adults through cognitive impairment or by stripping away psychosocial supports, leaving few psychological resources to engage in psychotherapy. If environmental enrichment is not possible, or is insufficient to rebuild the ego functions, supportive psychotherapy may be all that is appropriate. In such cases, support is provided until the ego or core self is shored up or the environment is enriched to provide more external support for basic ego functioning. Traditional psychodynamic therapies work to facilitate insight that may increase the client's level of anxiety; in traditional psychodynamic theory, an increase of anxiety is viewed as a positive catalyst for promoting change within the client. Supportive psychotherapy differs from traditional psychodynamic therapy by working toward the goal of building self-esteem and thereby lowering the client's level of anxiety, to facilitate increased ego strength and adaptive responding to internal stimuli and the external environment (Winston, 2014).

For example, supportive therapy might be used with older adults with personality disorders or those with more primitive defense mechanisms that are too well defended for insight. Given the intensity with which the ego functioning can be undermined by the losses of later life, there are occasions when it is most appropriate to begin with supportive therapy and progress to insight-oriented therapy only when it is evident that the ego has regained sufficient strength to tolerate depth work (Gutmann, 1992). On the other hand, therapists should not assume that aging or frailty keep a person from engaging in anything other than supportive psychotherapy (Roseborough, Luptak, McLeod, & Bradshaw, 2013). Many therapies have been demonstrated to be effective with older adults, and therapists should use supportive therapy only when other therapies clearly did not work yet the person shows capacity to benefit from supportive therapy.

> Maria Jiminez would likely be considered an appropriate candidate for supportive psychotherapy. Her capacity for insight is probably quite limited. She has used immature defense mechanisms her entire life, and is only now in exceptional distress because the environment no longer supports her sufficiently. As she becomes more physically dependent on others, she will likely become more depressed unless given sufficient support. Supportive therapy may focus on helping her adjust to being an unrecognized princess in a foreign land. Given enough nurturance from the therapist, Maria's ego strength may be sufficient to engage in less destructive interpersonal relationships. For example, although the therapist's nurturance may be perceived as her due, Maria may be sufficiently gratified that she reduces her verbal abuse to her daughters.

Psychotherapy process

As with younger adults, the patient–therapist relationship is a primary tool for treatment. Indeed, Newton et al. (1986) acknowledge the potency of the relationship in particular for persons who live isolated, lonely lives. Such persons experience tremendous validation of the self merely from interaction with an empathic, caring figure. For most older clients, however, the relationship is experienced through the transference and the therapy process. Transference is the process by which a client projects onto the therapist characteristics of significant persons (e.g., parents) whose interactions with the client shaped his or her basic beliefs about human beings and interactions. These projections are not based on the real interactions of client and therapist, but on projected assumptions about how the relationship functions. In contrast, countertransference is the therapist's own process of projecting onto the client or the interaction with the client perceptions that are not based on the real interaction or person, but on the therapist's own conceptual and emotional framework.

Transference processes can be particularly complex, because a lifetime of powerful relationship experiences is available for projection onto the therapist of an older client. The therapist may become a lover of 40 years ago, a parent, a child, a grandchild, or a significant mentor. The therapist is encouraged to identify the patient's "secret inner age" that holds the key to the transference projection (Berezin, 1972).

Countertransference reactions are also complex because therapists are generally younger than their older adult patients and thus have not personally experienced either the historical period or the developmental stages that impact the client (Knight, 2004). Novice younger therapists are likely to experience a reaction to aging itself. The effects of biological aging (e.g., physical limitations, reduced energy, changing physical appearance) and the functional consequences of aging (e.g., limited autonomy, social stigma, reduced activity level) must be acknowledged and experienced empathically by younger therapists for whom such experiences are "off time". A certain amount of courage is needed to tolerate handling the psychological work of another developmental period, even after the younger therapist comes to understand it (at least cognitively).

Less emotionally powerful but equally important is the vivid understanding needed by younger therapists regarding the historical contexts in which their older patients have lived their lives. As Knight (2004; 2010) describes, the terminology, customs, idioms, and preferences of birth cohorts vary systematically. Therapists must be familiar with the ways in which emotions are expressed and described by the children of the World War II, for example. Thus, real differences between therapists and clients are typical of therapy process with older adults, and must be acknowledged as real. In addition, projections can distort perceptions of the immediate interaction, sometimes complicating efforts to track the process of psychotherapy.

The psychotherapy process uses a variety of techniques to prompt insight into the developmental processes described above. Life review or reminiscence is commonly used to assist the patient's integration of life experiences into a coherent narrative, and as an assessment strategy. The life review may rewrite the story several times during the course of psychological work. Traditional strategies such as interpretation of dreams, analysis of defenses, and exploration of ambivalence are also used with older adults.

As with any developmental task unfamiliar to a patient, it is often useful to educate the older patient about the aging process. Distortions and cultural myths can lead to inappropriate expectations or service underutilization. For example, the belief that memory loss with age is normal may keep an older woman from recognizing an organic disease process in her husband. Similarly, the belief that it is inappropriate to ask one's children for assistance can leave an older adult quite vulnerable to isolation and feeling excessively overwhelmed in the face of significant care giving responsibilities.

Confirmation of the patient's strengths in the face of mounting deficits is an important role for therapists working with frail older persons (Newton et al., 1986; Greenberg, 2016). The battered ego may need to be supported by a therapist who can hold up a mirror to the patient's life so it is easier to see the full array of strengths and resources that have sustained the person throughout the lifespan. The therapist helps regain perspective on the entire life as it was lived, a process that gives courage to a fragile ego whose capacities have diminished. At times, therapists need to encourage particularly depleted clients to engage in self-enhancing behaviors, just to regain some semblance of experienced strength.

In general, the process of therapy with older adults does not vary dramatically from that used with adults of any age. Knight (2004) recommends that therapists modify the process somewhat for older adults. For example, therapists should take a more active role in therapy, be less formal in the structuring of the role, and be more flexible with the termination process. The other differences relate primarily to the transference and countertransference components of the relationship, recognition of normal aging processes, and the unique historical context in which older persons have lived.

Summary and Conclusions

In summary, the psychodynamic model provides an effective lens for treatment across the lifespan. By alerting the therapist to the continuing impact of early events, current losses, and the unique aspects of the therapeutic relationship, the framework provides a coherent focus for assessment and treatment of older adults. Psychodynamic models invite us to examine the ways inner processes shift over the lifespan. They maintain a strong focus on development and maturation of strategies for coping with inevitable tensions between one's inner life and the outer world. Interpersonal dynamics continue in later life to influence quality of life, building on a lifetime of experience of one's self in the context of other people.

Critical Thinking / Discussion Questions

1 How have your early relationships shaped your view of life?
2 What influence have relational experiences had on your choice of career or your expectations of family roles in later life?
3 Within the psychodynamic approaches, which therapeutic approach would you prefer? What aspects draw you to that modality?
4 How would a mental health provider know if an older adult did or did not have the capacity for insight that would allow him or her to benefit from a depth-oriented psychotherapy?

Website Resources

American Psychological Association, Division 39: Psychoanalysis
http://www.apa.org/about/division/div39.aspx
International Psychoanalytic Association
http://www.ipa.world
Intensive Short Term Dynamic Psychotherapy Institute
http://istdpinstitute.com

References

Bahr, S. S. (2014). Reminiscence therapy: A review. In N. A. Pachana & K. Laidlaw (Eds.), *The Oxford handbook of clinical geropsychology* (pp. 675–690). New York, NY: Oxford University Press.

Berezin, M. A. (1972). Psychodynamic considerations of aging and the aged: An overview. *American Journal of Psychiatry, 128,* 1483–1491.

Bowlby, J. (1969). *Attachment and loss. Vol. 1: Attachment.* New York, NY: Basic Books.

Butler, R. N., Lewis, M., & Sunderland, T. (1998). *Aging and mental health: Positive psychosocial and biomedical approaches.* New York, NY: Merrill.

Carstensen, L. L., Isaacowitz, D. M., & Charles, S. T. (1999). Taking time seriously: A theory of socioemotional selectivity. *American Psychologist, 54,* 165–181.

Choi, N. G., DiNitto, D. M., Marti, C. N., & Choi, B. Y. (2017). Association of adverse childhood experiences with lifetime mental and substance use disorders among men and women aged 50+ years. *International Psychogeriatrics, 29,* 359–372.

Cohler, B. J. (1993). Aging, morale, and meaning: The nexus of narrative. In T. R. Cole, W. A. Achenbaum, P. L. Jakobi, & R. Kastenbaum (Eds.), *Voices and visions of aging: Toward a critical gerontology* (pp. 107–133). New York, NY: Springer.

Colarusso, C. A., & Nemiroff, R. A. (1979). Some observations and hypotheses about the psychoanalytic theory of adult development. *International Journal of Psycho-Analysis, 60,* 59–71.

Cuijpers, P., Donker, T., Weissman, M. M., Ravitz, P., & Cristea, I. A. (2016). Interpersonal psychotherapy for mental health problems: A comprehensive meta-analysis. *American Journal of Psychiatry, 173,* 680–687. doi: 10.1176/appi.ajp.2015.15091141

Cuijpers, P., Driessen, E., Hollon, S. D., van Oppen, P., Barth, J., & Andersson, G. (2012). The efficacy of non-directive supportive therapy for adult depression: A meta-analysis. *Clinical Psychology Review, 32,* 280–291. doi: 10.1016/j.cpr.2012.01.003

Cuijpers, P., Geraedts, A. S., van Oppen, P., Andersson, G., Markowitz, J. C., van Straten, A. (2011). Interpersonal psychotherapy for depression: A meta-analysis. *American Journal of Psychiatry, 168,* 581–592. doi: 10.1176/appi.ajp.2010.10101411

Cuijpers, P., van Straten, A., Andersson, G., & van Oppen, P. (2008). Psychotherapy for depression in adults: A meta-analysis of comparative outcomes studies. *Journal of Consulting and Clinical Psychology, 76,* 909–922.

David-Ferdon, C., & Kaslow, N. (2008). Evidence-based psychosocial treatments for child and adolescent depression. *Journal of Clinical Child and Adolescent Psychology, 37,* 162–104.

Driessen, E., Hegelmaier, L. M., Abbass, A. A., Barber, J. P., Dekker, J. J. M., Van, H. L., Jansma, E. P., & Cuijpers, P. (2015). The efficacy of short-term psychodynamic psychotherapy for depression: A meta-analysis update. *Clinical Psychology Review, 42,* 1–15. doi: 10.1016/j.cpr.2009.08.010

Erikson, E. H. (1963). *Childhood and society* (2nd ed.). New York, NY: Norton.

Erikson, E. H., Erikson, J. M., & Kivnick, H. Q. (1986). *Vital involvement in old age.* New York, NY: Norton.

Gould, R. L. (1978). *Transformations: Growth and change in adult life.* New York, NY: Simon & Schuster.

Greenberg, T. M. (2016). *Psychodynamic perspectives on aging and illness* (2nd ed.). New York, NY: Springer.

Gutmann, D. L. (1987). *Reclaimed powers: Toward a new psychology of men and women in later life.* New York, NY: Basic Books.

Gutmann, D. L. (1992). Toward a dynamic geropsychology. In J. W. Barron, M. N. Eagle, & D. L. Wolitzky (Eds.), *Interface of psychoanalysis and psychology* (pp. 284–296). Washington, DC: American Psychological Association.

Hinrichsen, G. A. (2008). Interpersonal psychotherapy as a treatment for depression in later life. *Professional Psychology: Research and Practice, 39,* 306–312.

Hinrichsen, G. A., & Clougherty, K. E. (2006). *Interpersonal psychotherapy for depressed older adults.* Washington, DC: American Psychological Association.

Huang, A. X., Delucchi, K., Dunn, L. B., & Nelson, J. C. (2015). A systematic review and meta-analysis of psychotherapy for late-life depression. *American Journal of Geriatric Psychiatry, 23,* 261–273. doi: 10.1016/j.jagp.2014.04.003

Jung, C. G. (1933). *Modern man in search of a soul.* New York, NY: Harcourt Brace.

Kivnick, H. Q. (1993). Everyday mental health: A guide to assessing life strengths. In M. A. Smyer (Ed.), *Mental health and aging* (pp. 19–36). New York, NY: Springer.

Klerman, G. L., Weissman, M. M., Rounsaville, B. J., & Chevron, E. S. (1984). *Interpersonal psychotherapy of depression.* Northvale, NJ: Jason Aronson.

Knight, B. G. (2004). *Psychotherapy with older adults* (3rd ed.). Thousand Oaks, CA: Sage.

Knight, B. G. (2010). Clinical supervision for psychotherapy with older adults. In N. Pachana, K. Laidlaw, & B. G. Knight (Eds.), *Casebook of clinical geropsychology: International perspectives on practice* (pp. 107–117). New York, NY: Oxford University Press.

Kohut, H. (1971). *The analysis of the self.* New York, NY: International Universities Press.

Levenson, H. (2010). *Brief dynamic therapy.* Washington, DC: American Psychological Association.

Levinson, D. J., Darrow, C. N., & Klein, E. B. (1978). *The seasons of a man's life.* New York, NY: Alfred A. Knopf.

Levy, B. R., & Macdonald, J. L. (2016). Progress on understanding ageism. *Journal of Social Issues, 72,* 5–25.

Mello, M. F., Mari, J. J., Bacaltchuk, J., Verdeli, H., & Neugebauer, R. (2005). A systematic review of research findings on the efficacy of IPT for depressive disorders. *European Archives of Psychiatry and Clinical Neuroscience, 255,* 75–82.

Mihura, J. L., Meyer, G. J., Dumitrascu, N., & Bombel, G. (2016). On conducting construct validity meta-analyses for the Rorschach: A reply to Tibon Czopp and Zeligman. *Journal of Personality Assessment, 98,* 343–350.

Nemiroff, R., & Colarusso, C. (1990). Frontiers of adult development in theory and practice. *New dimensions in adult development* (pp. 97–124). New York, NY: Basic Books.

Neugarten, B. L. (1979). Time, age and the life cycle. *American Journal of Psychiatry, 136,* 887–895.

Newton, N., Brauer, D., Gutmann, D. L., & Grunes, J. (1986). Psychodynamic therapy with the aged: A review. *Clinical Gerontologist, 5,* 205–229.

Norcross, J. C., Hedges, M., & Castle, P. H. (2002). Psychologists conducting psychotherapy in 2001: A study of the Division 29 membership. *Psychotherapy: Theory, Research, Practice, Training, 39,* 97–102.

Roseborough, D. J., Luptak, M., McLeod, J., Bradshaw, W. (2013). Effectiveness of psychodynamic psychotherapy with older adults: A longitudinal study. *Clinical Gerontologist, 36,* 1–16.

Ryff, C. (1982). Successful aging: A developmental approach. *The Gerontologist, 22,* 209–214.

Schiff, B., & Cohler, B. J. (2001). Telling survival backwards: Holocaust survivors narrate the past. In G. M. Kenyon, P. G. Clark, & B. de Vries (Eds.), *Narrative gerontology: Theory, research, and practice* (pp. 113–136). New York, NY: Springer.

Scogin, F., Welsh, D., Hanson, A., Stump, J., & Coates, A. (2005). Evidence-based psychotherapies for depression in older adults. *Clinical Psychology: Science and Practice, 12,* 222–237.

Shedler, J. (2010). The efficacy of psychodynamic psychotherapy. *American Psychologist, 65,* 98–109.

Shemmings, D. (2006). Using adult attachment theory to differentiate adult children's internal working models of later life filial relationships. *Journal of Aging Studies, 20,* 177–191.

Starr, B. D., Weiner, M. B., & Rabetz, M. (1979). *The projective assessment of aging method (PAAM)*. New York, NY: Springer.

Vaillant, G. E. (1977). *Adaptation to life*. Boston, MA: Little, Brown, & Co.

Vaillant, G. E., & Vaillant, C. O. (1990). Natural history of male psychological health, XII: A 45-year study of predictors of successful aging at age 65. *American Journal of Psychiatry, 147,* 31–37.

Weissman, M. M., Markowitz, J. C., & Klerman, G. L. (2000). *Comprehensive guide to interpersonal psychotherapy*. New York, NY: Basic Books.

White, M., & Epston, D. (1990). *Narrative means to therapeutic ends*. New York, NY: Norton.

Winston, A. (2014). Supportive psychotherapy. In R. E. Hales, S. C. Yudofsky, & L. W. Robert (Eds.), *The American psychiatric publishing textbook of psychiatry* (1161–1186). Arlington, VA: American Psychiatric Publishing.

5

Cognitive-Behavioral Model

The nursing home staff are very annoyed at Anna Tweed because she constantly stands at the nurses' station asking them questions. Even if they answer her queries, Anna simply won't go away. When the staff try to involve her in something else, she returns to the nurses' station within a few minutes. Nurses and certified nursing assistants (CNAs) complain that they get headaches from trying to write their notes or answer phones while Anna is constantly talking. Staff understand that she has a severe memory problem, but they don't know how to get her to stop asking the repeated questions.

Joanna Jenkins came to the mental health clinic because her daughter insisted that she do so. Joanna's daughter is worried and frustrated that her mother appears lethargic and uninterested in life. Joanna doesn't believe you can do anything for her because nothing in particular is wrong with her. She is just old, and she says she is waiting to die.

Introduction to the Model

As its name suggests, the cognitive-behavioral model is actually a combination of two important but distinct approaches in psychology. The behavioral model was founded in the 1920s by American psychologist John B. Watson (1878–1958) as a reaction to the predominant psychodynamic approach and its emphasis on introspection and the unconscious, topics that were difficult to quantify and measure clearly. The cognitive model was developed in the 1960s based on the work of two American pioneers, psychiatrist Aaron Beck (1921–present) and psychologist Albert Ellis (1913–2007), who highlighted the primary role of thought processes (or cognitions) in mental health, mental distress, and psychotherapeutic treatment strategies. Despite their

Aging and Mental Health, Third Edition. Daniel L. Segal, Sara Honn Qualls, and Michael A. Smyer.
© 2018 John Wiley & Sons, Inc. Published 2018 by John Wiley & Sons, Inc.

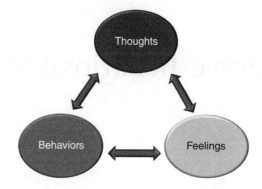

Figure 5.1   The reciprocal nature of thoughts, feelings, and behaviors in the CBT model.

distinct origins, the two approaches have been largely unified into the cognitive-behavioral model which places emphasis on one's cognitions or thought patterns and one's specific measurable observable behaviors or actions. An overarching theme of the model is the multiple and reciprocal interactions among thoughts, feelings, and behaviors (see Figure 5.1). That is, each aspect influences and is influenced by one another, and a positive change in one domain will usually result in positive changes in the other two. In the cognitive-behavioral model, the emphasis for interventions is usually on thoughts and/or behaviors as the entry point, since it is more difficult to change feelings directly. As a learning exercise, apply these principles to yourself: Choose any entry point into the model (thoughts, feelings, or behaviors) and then try to articulate an example of how actions or experiences in that area affect the other two areas. Then, alter the entry point and repeat the analysis.

The type of psychotherapy associated with this approach is called *cognitive-behavioral therapy* (CBT). Although there are behaviorists or cognitive therapists who focus heavily on the primary domain of interest, the vast majority of clinicians and researchers who identify in the cognitive and behavioral areas appreciate the impact of overt behaviors and internal thought patterns on psychological functioning. Good CBT clinicians also appreciate the importance of developing a strong therapeutic alliance with their clients. As a learning tool, we will next describe the cognitive and behavioral aspects of the model separately, fully appreciating that in modern-day practice the two models are not only compatible but synergistic in their combination.

Cognitive Aspects of the CBT Model

Cognitive theory focuses on the contributions of thoughts and beliefs to maladaptive behaviors and negative emotions. As neuroscience evolved, the complexity of the brain/behavior relationships required more explanatory variables than were provided by learning theories. Several different cognitive-behavioral approaches emerged to describe how various cognitive processes influenced the acquisition and performance of behaviors. For example, attention, expectancies, internalized rules, performance standards, self-instruction, observation, and imagery all influence behavioral performance. At the most general level, all cognitive theories share three fundamental hypotheses (Dobson & Dozois, 2010; Dozois, Frewen, & Covin, 2006):

1   that cognition affects emotion and behavior,
2   that cognition can be monitored and changed, and
3   that by altering cognitions, one can exert desired emotional and behavioral changes.

To elaborate, cognitive theory suggests that an event, in and of itself, is not the cause of one's emotional response, but rather it is how one *interprets* or *perceives* that event (i.e., it is the accompanying cognitive processes) that causes one's emotional reaction. Consider the death of a loved one as an example. It might be assumed that this death would automatically make someone feel sad and despondent, but that is not always the full picture. The death of an older person that ends the person's struggle with a long, painful, and debilitating disease might result in other feelings in the survivors such as relief, as well as some normal degrees of sadness. Indeed, in this example, the extent to which one feels intense despair or relief (or sometimes combinations of various feelings) depends on the *meaning* that one attaches to the death. Thus, according to cognitive theory, our attitudes and beliefs about external events give rise to our emotions and not the events themselves.

This central idea that thought processes are an important determinant of emotions and behaviors is, in fact, quite old. Centuries ago, Phrygian Stoic philosopher Epictetus (c. 101 AD) expressed his view in *The Enchiridion* that "Men are disturbed not by things, but by the view which they take of them" (Epictetus, c. 101/1955). In many respects, this idea is empowering: People are not always in control of what happens to them. Bad things do sometimes happen to good people. But, people are always in control of the attitude or perspective they take about those unfortunate events and how they respond to those events. This mantra and its derivatives are widely used by cognitive therapists.

Direct application of cognitive-behavioral principles to mental health problems has been made by cognitive therapy theorists, including Aaron Beck and Albert Ellis. Beck's approach focuses on the role of distorted or unhelpful thoughts in the production of disorders such as depression and anxiety (Beck, Emery, & Greenberg, 1985; Beck, Rush, Shaw, & Emery, 1979). These theorists and clinicians identified a specific set of inaccurate core worldview assumptions and related thought distortions that produce and maintain mental disorders. Beck and others developed interventions that restructure cognition patterns to produce more adaptive and realistic appraisals of self, the world, and the future than is typical of depressed and anxious persons' ways of thinking.

Beck's theory emphasizes three levels of cognition. The first level is called *schemas* or core beliefs. Schemas are often expressed as unconditional evaluations about the self and others. Some examples include beliefs that: "I am incompetent," "I am defective," "I am unlovable," "I am special," "Others are hurtful and not to be trusted," "Others need to take care of me," and "Others must love and admire me." Schemas are generally thought to be formed early in life and tend to persist into adulthood and later-life if conscious efforts are not made to identify, examine, and challenge them (Dozois et al., 2006). Schemas are believed to influence perceptions and thoughts at a more conscious level.

The second level is called *information-processing biases* that are represented as dysfunctional or unhelpful beliefs (sometimes called cognitive distortions) that many people can learn to recognize. Some of the commonly occurring cognitive distortions include:

- all-or-none thinking (seeing personal qualities or situations in absolutist "black and white" terms, and failing to see shades of gray in between),
- catastrophizing (perceiving negative events as intolerable catastrophes, commonly referred to as "making mountains out of molehills"),
- labeling (attaching a global label to oneself [e.g., I am a loser] instead of referring to a specific action or event [e.g., I did not handle that particular situation very well]),
- magnification and minimization (exaggerating the importance of negative characteristics and experiences while discounting the importance of positive characteristics and experiences),
- personalization (assuming one is the cause of an event when other factors are also responsible),
- "should" statements (using *should* and *have-to* statements to provide motivation or to control behavior, often resulting in guilt and sadness when one does not live up to one's self-created demands).

Finally, the third level of cognition in Beck's models is *automatic thoughts* which refer to the stream of cognitions that people have throughout the day (e.g., "I'm such a failure," "I can't handle this situation," or "People think I'm stupid."). Such thoughts stem directly from core beliefs (schemas), cognitive distortions, and current life events. Automatic thoughts are easily accessible by simply "thinking about one's thinking," in essence, by paying attention to the thoughts that float through one's mind in any given situation. In Beck's most current iteration of the cognitive model, Beck and Haigh (2014) emphasize the continuity between normal cognitive processing and psychopathology, whereby cognitive distortions and unhelpful beliefs are best understood as being on a continuum from none to extreme levels. It is likely that you may have noticed examples of some of the cognitive distortions (presented earlier) in yourself or others, at least a little bit. Psychopathology emerges when these distortions or biases reach a severe magnitude, which can occur at any point in the lifespan, often as a result of potent life events or stressors. Beck and Haigh also describe common cognitive processes in psychopathology as well as unique cognitive features for many specific mental disorders.

The methods developed by Albert Ellis are consistent with those developed by Beck, and are based on a simple premise: When people are faced with unfortunate life circumstances, they make themselves feel miserable, frustrated, and upset, and they behave in maladaptive ways because they construct irrational beliefs about themselves and their situations (Ellis, 1991; Ellis & Dryden, 2007). More adaptively, people can craft adaptive feelings and behaviors by adopting more reasonable and rational thoughts.

An important aspect of Ellis's approach is the ABC model which purports that emotional and behavioral consequences (C) are not directly precipitated by an activating event (A) or life stressor such as becoming physically ill or becoming a widow, but rather that one's beliefs about the event (B) mediates the relationships (Ellis & Dryden, 2007). For Ellis, similar to Beck, beliefs, feelings, and behaviors are viewed as interrelated processes, although beliefs are given primary importance in causing psychological problems. A final important aspect of the cognitive approach is its emphasis on education about the client's symptoms and about the cognitive therapy model so that the process is transparent, fully understood by the client, and collaboratively carried out with the therapist and client as active and equal participants.

Note that in the cognitive paradigm, it is typical for some thoughts or beliefs to be referred to as "dysfunctional" as part of the model. Although the difference may seem slight, we much prefer to not use the term dysfunctional to refer to a client's thoughts during clinical work, but rather refer to such thoughts as being "unhelpful" or as "getting in the way of the client's emotional well-being or happiness." Rest assured, no matter how maladaptive an individual's thoughts or beliefs may seem, those thoughts likely developed for a good reason in the person's life and at one point were either adaptive or the best effort the person could muster under adverse if not traumatic circumstances. We think this is a less pathologizing way to essentially implement the exact same cognitive formulations and interventions, but in a way that incorporates a more kind, gentle, and supportive use of language.

Behavioral Aspects of the CBT Model

The classic behavioral model focuses attention on measurable, overt *behaviors* rather than emotions, motives, or biological factors (Kazdin, 2013). An individual's behavior results from the interaction between the person and his or her environment. In general, adaptive and maladaptive behaviors function in the same way. They evolve from the interaction between one's behavior and contextual factors in the environment. Environmental events and cues influence the acquisition, performance rate, and termination of specific behaviors according to principles of learning theory. The focus is primarily on observable behaviors although some private events (e.g., thoughts and feelings) are considered to be equally under the influence of learning principles (discussed in more detail below) and thus modifiable by behavioral techniques.

The behavioral model emphasizes the benefits of empirical scientific research, and organizes its assessments and interventions accordingly. Behaviorally oriented clinicians draw heavily from the empirical literature that reports on the efficacy of interventions whose impact has been evaluated according to rigorous scientific criteria (i.e., with research designs that control for alternative explanations). Training in single subject designs (Barlow, Nock, & Hersen, 2008) as well as group designs is considered imperative for effective implementation and evaluation of behavioral interventions.

The application of behavioral interventions with older adults (oftentimes called *behavioral gerontology*) has a growing literature base in recent years. Behavioral gerontology covers a wide range of behaviors including self-care, social interaction and participation, memory and language, health maintenance, anxiety, depression, sexual problems, sleep difficulties, and disruptive behaviors (LeBlanc, Raetz, & Feliciano, 2012). The empirical results are clear: Many behaviors previously believed to be a normal product of aging have been demonstrated to be modifiable by changes in the environmental context. Perhaps most dramatic are the effects of behavior management programs in institutional settings with particularly low functioning ill older persons (e.g., Allen-Burge, Stevens, & Burgio, 1999; Teri, McKenzie, & LaFazia, 2005) and behavioral interventions for depressed care-givers of individuals with dementia (Gitlin et al., 2003; Gallagher-Thompson & Coon, 2007).

Assessment and intervention in behavioral therapies generally focus on observable variables—what people do. As we discuss more thoroughly below, cognitive-behavioral clinicians include self-reports of cognitive activity or thought processes in the category of observable variables. The focus on observable characteristics from the behavioral model can be contrasted with other models whose domain of work is motives, drives, traits, or unconscious processes that are inferred from patient behavior but cannot be observed directly. There are many specific behavioral techniques used by clinicians to help people change maladaptive behaviors to more adaptive and fulfilling behaviors. At its core, however, the behavioral aspects of CBT focus on helping clients increase access to reinforcing and positive experiences (e.g., the identification and subsequent scheduling of pleasant events) and training in specific skills (e.g., assertiveness or com-munication skills).

Behaviorists observe human behavior in context because behavior is believed to be an adaptive response to help individuals meet their needs in a particular environment. The principles used by behaviorists to describe human behavior link the behavior to the information available to the person in the environment, especially information contiguous in time with the behavior. *Antecedents* refer to the information available to the person immediately prior to the target behavior, whereas *consequences* refer to the information available immediately following the behavior.

Traditional learning theory offers three primary learning mechanisms to explain the acquisition and maintenance of human behavior: classical conditioning, operant conditioning, and modeling. Notably, the same learning mechanisms are thought to account for adaptive behavior as well as maladaptive (abnormal) behavior. We discuss each next.

Classical conditioning, as articulated by Russian physiologist Ivan Pavlov (1849–1936), occurs when a previously neutral stimulus elicits a response that is reflexive or automatic in the presence of a stimulus. Drawing from his famous experiments in which hungry dogs learned to salivate to the sound of a bell that immediately preceded the presentation of their food, Pavlov created labels for the natural and conditioned stimuli. The reflexive or automatic response to a natural (Unconditioned) stimulus was called an Unconditioned Response. Classical conditioning occurs when the Unconditioned Stimulus (UCS) is paired with a previously neutral stimulus (now the Conditioned Stimulus; CS) to produce the target response (e.g., salivating) without the UCS ever being presented. When Pavlov's dogs salivated to the sound of the bell (CS) alone, the target response was called a Conditioned Response (CR). Classical conditioning theory explains behavior that occurs in the presence of an apparently neutral stimulus by demonstrating that the behavior is under the control of the antecedent conditions. As an example, classical conditioning would be operating in the case of an older woman who becomes trapped in an elevator, and comes to subsequently associate all elevators with fear.

Operant learning theory maintains that the acquisition and performance of behavior is controlled by the consequences of behaviors, an idea popularized by American psychologist B. F. Skinner (1904–1990) in his classic book *Science and human behavior* (1953). The principle of reinforcement states that behaviors will increase in frequency if they are followed closely in time by positive events (e.g., being praised by someone after doing a kind deed; receiving a good grade on an exam after studying hard for the exam; feeling happier after a vigorous workout). The positively experienced event is called a reinforcer if it reliably increases the rate of behavior, and this process is called *positive reinforcement*. In a similar vein, *negative reinforcement* also increases behavior, but it does so by the response-contingent removal of an unpleasant stimulus (e.g., an older woman increases her avoidance of uncomfortable social situations because her anxiety is reduced each time she avoids unpleasant situations; a cat stops pawing at the face of its sleeping human companion when he or she starts to pet the cat). Negative reinforcement is also commonly implicated in the maintenance of substance-abuse disorders. As the effects of an addictive but pleasurable substance (for example, alcohol or cocaine) wear off, the person may ingest the substance again to eliminate general feelings of unhappiness or uncomfortable physical and emotional signs of withdrawal.

In contrast to reinforcement patterns that serve to increase behaviors (whether adaptive or maladaptive), *punishment* aims to reduce or curb behaviors by the provision of a negative consequence following undesired behavior. In most clinical treatment settings, punishment is rarely used because reinforcement strategies are more powerful and humane, and because punishment is generally not effective in promoting long-term behavior change. In nursing homes, for example, staff are commonly encouraged to pay attention to residents (reinforce them) when they engage in appropriate self-care behaviors, like eating, dressing, and toileting.

The third form of learning, modeling (often referred to as observational learning), is defined as learning new behaviors by imitating the behavior of another person. The new wrinkle here is that people do not have to receive consequences themselves to learn new behavior, but that they can learn by observing the consequences experienced by others. Consider, for example, a newly admitted resident to a nursing home who sees that another resident gets a great deal of attention, albeit some of it negative attention, when she complains vociferously to the staff. The new resident begins to grumble more having imitated the behavior from the other resident. As an exercise, consider the types of behaviors you have learned by watching others. Can you identify some positive behaviors that have been modeled? Can you identify some less adaptive ones? Finally, we should emphasize here that the mechanisms of learning frequently co-occur. For example, both modeling and operant principles are in play when a person tries a new behavior because of observing another person demonstrate it and then the person receives a reward following the new behavior (assuming it's an adaptive prosocial one).

Mental Health from the Cognitive-Behavioral Model

From the behavioral perspective, adaptation is defined as the capacity to meet one's own needs effectively within the environment, a preferred alternative to the term "mentally healthy." Behaviors that meet an individual's physical, social, and emotional needs within the particular relevant environment are considered adaptive. Persons who cannot meet their needs effectively are viewed as having problems in living that occur because of one of the following:

• they have learned maladaptive behavior or frameworks,
• they have failed to learn effective or appropriate behavior or frameworks because of a poor learning environment or because of their particular learning history,
• they are responding to the wrong environmental contingencies or are self-regulating poorly.

In contrast to the pure behavioral perspective, cognitive-behaviorists use adaptation and subjective distress to measure well-being. Distress is experienced when an individual is unable to meet his or her own goals, including internalized goals in the form of standards or expectations, which are cognitive constructs. For example, a common problem for depressed persons is negative self-evaluation that occurs when a perfectionistic standard cannot be met. As Ricky Bobby said in the movie *Talladega Nights,* "If you ain't first, you're last." A reasonable goal for treatment in this case might be to reduce the person's perfectionistic standards, allowing the person to be less self-critical, and thus less distressed. As another example of a cognitive goal, a depressed person may want to increase her sense of hope. Hope is her own goal, and exists solely in her mind as a cognition, but is a perfectly legitimate goal for a cognitive-behavioral clinician to support. Cognitive-behaviorists must balance the individual's subjective sense of distress with some objective judgment about adaptability to the immediate environment.

The two cases presented at the beginning of the chapter show the value of using multiple criteria for defining disorder. Anna Tweed is not particularly distressed, but her behavior is not adaptive in that environment. Or is it? Her constant questioning may gain her additional staff attention, interpersonal interaction, and cognitive stimulation that may be lacking elsewhere in the nursing home. Her behavior is disruptive for staff more than for her, although over time Anna will probably receive negative attention from frustrated staff members. Of course, the ethics of intervening with an individual's behavior for the good of the institution must be examined carefully. Joanna Jenkins is distressed but does not seek help because she does not believe there is help or that there is hope for change. Her behavior is also not adaptive because she is no longer attempting to meet her own social needs due to her lethargy and her learned helplessness.

Mental Health in Older Adults

The CBT definition of mental health for older persons would be the same as for any other population—a pattern of thoughts, beliefs, values, and behaviors that lead to healthy adaptation and adjustment to one's environment and a lack of significant personal distress or impairment in one's functioning. However, some changes commonly associated with aging may make the processes of adaptation and adjustment more challenging. For example, changes with age may occur in the array of available antecedents and consequences, the contingent relationships among antecedents-behaviors-consequences, and the needs of the individual. In the young-old years (60s and early 70s), adults are likely to live within environments and contingency patterns similar to those of middle adulthood. With advanced age, physical impairments may limit mobility, dull sensation, and may force changes in the environments within which older adults live and meet their needs.

Changes in the living environment may simply alter the array of antecedents and consequences, or may enrich or deplete the available options. For example, moving from one's suburban home to a senior high-rise apartment complex may significantly enrich the array of social stimuli, or may simply change which social relationships are available while holding steady the amount and reinforcement value of the relationships. On the other hand, the presence of dozens of other residents in the high-rise may not compensate for the loss of access to close friends in the former neighborhood.

In old age, physical illnesses may restrict very old persons' range of activities. Limited mobility, restricted vision and hearing, fatigue, or cognitive impairment may alter abilities of older adults to respond to environmental contingencies. Yet freedom from some demanding roles that are characteristic of young and mid-life adulthood (e.g., raising a family, maintaining a career) may enhance older peoples' responsiveness to environmental stimuli. For example, a recent retiree may experience the freedom to be much more socially responsive to neighbors and friends or to engage more vigorously in desired political activism.

As described in Chapter 3, Baltes and Baltes (1990) suggest that older adults show high rates of adaptability or *behavioral plasticity*. Recall that early behavioral research demonstrated that behaviors commonly thought to be typical of old age were actually under the control of environmental contingencies. Baltes and Baltes go a step further to argue that older adults naturally modify their behavior in predictable ways to adapt to changing capabilities and changing environments, a process reflecting the role of adaptability in mental health. Specifically, they suggest that older adults draw upon their areas of competence to compensate for areas in which they have lost function or in which the environment is more impoverished. As discussed in Chapter 3, this process of adaptation involves *selective optimization with compensation*.

Despite this natural process of adaptation, certain environments are clearly more challenging than others. For example, nursing home life presents a serious challenge to the mental health of many older residents (Molinari, 2000; Rosowsky, Casciani, & Arnold, 2008). Although only 5% of older adults live in a nursing home at any one point in time, the effects of the institution on mental health warrants comment. Institutions such as traditional nursing homes provide few natural reinforcers because the institution regiments so many aspects of daily life, including bathing, dressing, sleep schedules, food schedules and selection, and may even structure social interaction. Residents of nursing homes are typically physically frail and often cognitively impaired, which limits further the sources of pleasure available to them and their capacity to respond to environmental contingencies. The rates of mental disorders are particularly high in nursing homes, as might be predicted by the environmental contingencies, although environment is only one factor in the high rates of mental disorders (physical illness and cognitive disorders are two other important factors). These challenges notwith-standing, behavioral techniques have been shown to be effective for diverse mental health problems among nursing home residents (Burgio et al., 2002; Meeks, Looney, Van Haitsma, & Teri, 2008; Meeks, Shah, & Ramsey, 2009; Molinari, 2000), but implementation and sustainability are not easy or cheap. (We will return to the challenges of effective nursing home care in Chapter 14.)

Assessment

Refer back to the case scenarios presented at the beginning of the chapter. Consider yourself a consultant to these two women. What kind of assessment needs to be done to design the best intervention to help Anna Tweed and Joanna Jenkins? Take a moment to review the principles we have presented, and develop a conceptualization and hypothesis for the two cases. Your framework for the problem will, of course, determine where you begin with assessment. In both cases, you will obviously need considerably more information than was given initially. What do you need to know, and how will you gather the information (for example, e.g., from whom and in what format)?

Purposes of assessment

Assessment from the cognitive-behavioral model focuses on the two important domains identified within the model: cognitions and behaviors, which are often intertwined. Assessment focuses on clarifying behavior patterns and identifying cognitive and environmental variables that mediate behavior. The primary purpose of assessment is to assist with the design and evaluation of interventions. Assessment for the purpose of a richer understanding of the client, or even to formulate an accurate diagnosis, is most valuable to the extent that it directly benefits the intervention. Although cognitive-behaviorists do not necessarily ascribe to the medical model of diagnosis on which the DSM-5 is based, they support the use of diagnostic categories if they are used for scientific purposes of producing homogeneous client groups in which to test interventions. Indeed, an active and growing research base on cognitive and behavioral interventions for a broad array of mental disorders is an important strength of the cognitive-behavioral model.

Assessment also serves as a baseline for determining progress in treatment. Assessments are used as feedback for the therapist and the client regarding the impact of particular interventions. Clients often begin to change simply because of the clear feedback about their own behavior that is provided by cognitive and behavioral assessment (i.e., the assessment may function as an intervention itself).

Principles of cognitive-behavioral assessment

Cognitive and behaviorally oriented mental health providers follow general practice guidelines for older adults by initially examining the medical data available to ascertain if the problem could be caused by disease or medication. For example, although the therapist would recognize that Joanna Jenkins's scenario matches the general profile of a depressed person, the description is also consistent with physical illness (including medication-induced delirium) or even an organic brain disorder. If Joanna Jenkins has not received a thorough physical examination to rule out potentially reversible medical causes of the symptom profile, such an evaluation would be the first order of business. Only after physical causes of the symptoms have been ruled out would a strictly cognitive-behavioral approach to assessment and intervention be appropriate. For the sake of clarity, let us presume that an appropriate medical evaluation has been completed and that Ms. Jenkins is physically healthy and not using any medications that could produce this behavior profile.

With the strong commitment to gathering empirical data regarding behavior, a cognitive-behaviorally oriented mental health provider would focus assessment on *specific problem behaviors,* in what is commonly called a *behavioral assessment.* If staff or family members have framed the problem as "she's manipulative" or "her life has no purpose," the therapist would ask questions about specific behaviors until the exact behaviors that are problematic are defined in terms that render the behavior directly observable. Exactly what does Joanna do, and when does she do it? How is this different from one or five years ago? How much distress does she report or show? What self-care behaviors does she do for herself? In the Anna Tweed scenario, exactly when and for how long does Anna stand at the nurses' station? How many questions does she ask? What is the content of her questions? What do staff do in response to Anna's questions? How does Anna respond when her questions are answered or not? Careful questioning of the exact behavior patterns observed by staff will give a mental health consultant enough information to form hypotheses about the reinforcement contingencies. Other methods for obtaining behavior information are described below.

The assessment also focuses on the *context* of the problem behavior. Exactly when and under what conditions does Anna leave the desk? What is the exact context when she asks questions (e.g., who is present; are others also talking or does she wait for a break in conversation)? What time of day does the questioning either intensify or reduce? The behavioral assessment will show the contextual variables that serve as reinforcers and punishers (increasing or decreasing the frequency of specific behaviors).

The assessor would also want to identify times when the problem behavior is not present. When does Anna Tweed leave the nurses' station? Are there ever occasions when she maintains attention focused on something other than the nurses' station? Do alternative behaviors exist within the client's behavioral repertoire that are not being used to meet her goals? How sensitive is she to social cues? She may have appropriate behaviors, but they are not being controlled by appropriate cues and contingencies. In the case of Joanna Jenkins, one might ask when she shows the most animation and energy? Are there days or hours when she feels better than other times?

The process of obtaining a full assessment from the cognitive-behavioral model typically requires several methods of data collection. Self-reports of distress may be obtained from the clients and the involved care providers. For example, Anna Tweed may be asked about the goal of her questioning behavior because her behavior may be explicitly goal directed. In this particular case, Anna Tweed is actually experiencing a dementia that produces such severe memory impairment that she is unaware of how frequently she asks questions in her attempt to try to orient herself to time, place, and purposive activity.

	Client's response
1. Are you basically satisfied with your life?	Ⓝ
2. Have you dropped many of your activities and interests?	Ⓨ
3. Do you feel your life is empty?	Ⓨ
4. Do you get bored often?	Ⓨ
5. Are you hopeful about the future?	Ⓝ
6. Are you bothered by thoughts you can't get out of your head?	N
7. Are you in good spirits most of the time?	Ⓝ
8. Are you afraid that something bad is going to happen to you?	N
9. Do you feel happy most of the time?	Ⓝ
10. Do you often feel helpless?	N
11. Do you often get restless and fidgety?	Ⓨ
12. Do you prefer to stay at home, rather than going out and doing new things?	Ⓨ
13. Do you frequently worry about the future?	Ⓨ
14. Do you feel you have more problems with memory than most?	N
15. Do you think it is wonderful to be alive now?	Ⓝ
16. Do you often feel downhearted and blue?	N
17. Do you feel pretty worthless the way you are now?	Ⓨ
18. Do you worry a lot about the past?	N
19. Do you find life very exciting?	Ⓝ
20. Is it hard for you to get started on new projects?	Ⓨ
21. Do you feel full of energy?	Ⓝ
22. Do you feel that your situation is hopeless?	N
23. Do you think that most people are better off than you are now?	N
24. Do you frequently get upset about little things?	Ⓨ
25. Do you frequently feel like crying?	N
26. Do you have trouble concentrating?	Ⓨ
27. Do you enjoy getting up in the morning?	Ⓝ
28. Do you prefer to avoid social gatherings?	Ⓨ
29. Is it easy for you to make decisions?	Ⓝ
30. Is your mind as clear as it used to be?	Ⓝ

Note: In scoring the GDS, each item is scored 0 or 1 depending upon whether the item is worded positively or negatively. The total score on the scale is the number of depressive responses, as follows.

      For items 2–4, 6, 8, 10–14, 16–18, 20, 22–6, 28 the scoring is: Yes = 1; No = 0
      Items 1, 5, 7, 9, 15, 19, 21, 27, 29, 30 are reverse scored as follows: No = 1; Yes = 0

The depressive responses for Joanna Jenkins are circled. Her GDS Total Score = 21

The GDS is in the public domain and available for free from the following website: http://www.stanford.edu/~yesavage/GDS.html.

Figure 5.2   Geriatric Depression Scale responses for Joanna Jenkins (baseline).

Joanna Jenkins has more obvious subjective distress and thus she would likely be asked to complete a self-report depression scale as part of a diagnostic evaluation. Data on the severity of depression would also serve as a baseline against which treatment progress can be evaluated. Several self-report inventories for depression are described in Chapter 9. The responses of Ms. Jenkins to a popular one, the Geriatric Depression Scale (GDS; Yesavage et al., 1983), are shown in Figure 5.2. As you can see, she has scored 21 out of 30, indicating a severe range of depressive symptoms.

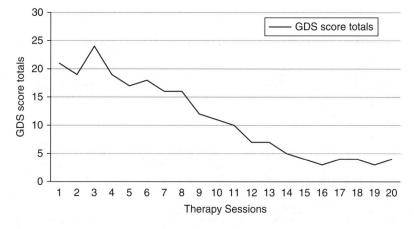

Figure 5.3   Geriatric Depression Scale total scores for Joanna Jenkins across sessions.

Take a moment to look at the specific symptom description you get from this instrument. Now look back at the initial description of her problem in the first lines of this chapter. Based on the GDS data, you know that Ms. Jenkins is experiencing boredom and a sense of emptiness. She reports having trouble with concentration and excessive worry. She also reports feeling worthless. A clinical interview would be done to follow-up on this valuable type of data to elicit further details about each symptom. For example, what kind of worry? How much difficulty with concentration? Brief self-report symptom inventories are used throughout the intervention to track progress. A graph like that shown in Figure 5.3 would provide evidence of the effectiveness of an intervention.

More objective data may be requested to clarify the actual frequency and context of specific behaviors. For example, Joanna Jenkins may report her activities and mood in a mood and behavior log. For Anna Tweed, the staff at the nursing home may be asked to keep a record of the frequency of questions asked during each hour of the day to identify variations in the frequency pattern during the course of a day. A behavioral observer may collect descriptive data regarding the frequency, content, and context of the questions over the course of a day. A typical behavior recording chart of a scenario like Anna Tweed's is shown in Figure 5.4.

You will note that there is a pattern evident in this record of behavior. Ms. Tweed's question asking is more intense when more persons are present. When the staff leave the nursing station, so does Ms. Tweed. What hypothesis might you form about the reinforcement contingencies for Ms. Tweed's question-asking behavior? Further assessment may be needed to determine how she meets her information goals when staff are not available at the nurses' station. As noted above, the recording of specific details is what made a pattern evident. Staff might have stated, "she's there all of the time," a fact that matches their experience while they are at the nurses' station, but was not the whole picture.

The role of assessment in designing an intervention is illustrated in the treatment of Joanna Jenkins. As described in more detail in Chapter 9, the cognitive-behavioral model for treating depression postulates that depression is caused and maintained

Date	Time Start	Time End	Who was Present?	Content of Questions	How Questioning Ended?
3/16	0830	0840	Nurse, CNA, Activity Director	When is lunch?	Activity Director took to room
	0915	0930	Nurse, CNA	What to do next?	Nurse took to day room
	1110	1145	Nurse, QA Staff	When is lunch?	CNA took to lunch
	1430	1450	Nurse, Social Worker, CNA	Where is her daughter?	Activity Director took to activity
	1500	1530	2 Nurses	Where is her daughter?	CNA took to activity
	1600	1620	Nurse, family member	When is dinner?	CNA took to dinner
	1730	1740	CNA	Where is daughter?	Volunteer took to day room
	1820	1845	Nurse, family member	What happened to sweater?	Nurse took to room
3/17	0840	0850	Nurse, CNA	When is lunch?	CNA took to bath
	0955	1005	Nurse, Activity Director	What to do next?	Activity Director took to activity
	1050	1100	Nurse, Activity Aide	When is lunch?	CNA took to lunch
	1320	1330	Nurse, CNA	What to do next?	CNA took to room and turned on TV
	1610	1625	Nurse	Where is daughter?	Activity Aid took to hairdresser
	1730	1745	Nurse, family member	Where is daughter?	CNA–TV in Day room
	1930	1950	Nurse	Needs pill	Nurse took to room

Figure 5.4   Record of questioning behavior by Anna Tweed.

by a deficiency in the amount of response-contingent positive reinforcement as well as negative thought patterns that contribute to the negative views of self, the world, and the future. The deficiency may be caused by several factors, the most common of which are a low rate of engagement in pleasant activities, high levels of anxiety that interfere with actually experiencing the pleasantness, high rates of unpleasant activities, or cognitive schemas that are pervasively gloomy and negative.

Therapists begin detailed assessment with daily mood monitoring (completed by the client). Depressed clients tend to believe that they always feel bad and that nothing ever happens to make them feel good. They do not believe the depression is under their control, or even under the control of environmental factors (e.g., pleasant events). Daily mood monitoring demonstrates to the client that although their mood may never be great, it does indeed fluctuate, indicating that some days are better than others, or, as the depressed client would report, some days are worse than others. Figure 5.5 shows Ms. Jenkins's first week of mood monitoring. Typical of persons who are depressed, she reports that her mood fluctuates along the lower end of the mood scale. Can you see any pattern in the days that are better versus those with the lowest mood scores?

Joanna Jenkins would also be asked to complete a Pleasant Events Schedule on which she would indicate the frequency with which she engages in a set of different activities that many older persons find pleasant. The Older Person's Pleasant Events Schedule (Teri & Lewinsohn, 1982) contains activities commonly enjoyed by older adults. On this scale Ms. Jenkins would also rate each activity as to its subjective pleasantness for her. A few items from Ms. Jenkins's scale are recorded in Figure 5.6.

Daily Mood Rating Form

1. Please rate your mood for this day; i.e., how good or bad you felt, using the nine-point scale shown below. If you felt good put a high number on the chart below. If you felt "so-so" mark five and if you felt low or depressed mark a number lower than five.

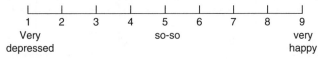

2. On the two lines next to your mood rating for each day, please briefly give two major reasons why you think you felt that way. Try to be as specific as possible.

Date	Mood Score	Why I think I felt this way
Monday, 5/10	1	1. Bored. Watched TV. 2. Home all day, alone.
Tuesday, 5/11	1	1. Worried about daughter. 2. Worried about bills.
Wednesday, 5/12	4	1. Son and children stopped by. Good to see them. Brought candy! 2. Played my piano for 15 minutes (hand started to hurt).
Thursday, 5/13	2	1. Neighbor took a walk with me. 2. She criticized my blouse.
Friday, 5/14	1	1. Worried about checkbook balance. 2. Worried about falling.
Saturday, 5/15	6	1. Grandchildren brought new puppy to visit. Puppy licked me. 2. Old friend called and we had a nice long walk.
Sunday, 5/16	5	1. Church and lunch with friends. 2. Neighbor stopped by for tea after dinner.
		1. 2.
		1. 2.
		1. 2.

Figure 5.5 Daily Mood Rating Form for Joanna Jenkins.

Specific items that she rated low in frequency but high in pleasantness would then be selected for daily monitoring. She would be asked to indicate whether she engaged in that activity each day. The therapist would begin graphing her mood and the rate at which she engaged in pleasant activities. This is both an assessment and an intervention tool, because in a short time Ms. Jenkins would be able to see quite clearly the relationship between her mood and enjoyable activities. During treatment, she likely would be helped to increase participation in several positive activities, in order to gain more control over her mood and to enhance positive feelings.

	Frequency Rating			Pleasantness Rating		
	Often	Sometimes	Never	Very Pleasant	Somewhat Pleasant	Not at all Pleasant
Listening to music	3	2	①	③	2	1
Shopping	3	②	1	3	2	①
Smiling at people	3	2	①	3	②	1
Arranging flowers	③	2	1	3	②	1
Solving a problem, puzzle, or crossword	3	2	①	3	②	1
Baking a new recipe	3	2	①	3	2	①
Going to church	3	2	①	3	②	1
Thinking about people I like	3	2	①	③	2	1
Listening to birds sing	3	2	①	3	②	1
Having a clean house	3	2	①	③	2	1
Looking at stars or moon	3	②	1	3	②	1

Figure 5.6 Older Person's Pleasant Events Schedule completed by Joanna Jenkins.

Another popular checklist specifically designed for older adults is the California Older Person's Pleasant Events Schedule (COPPES; Rider, Gallagher-Thompson, & Thompson, 2004). The COPPES contains 66 items representing a broad array of age-appropriate pleasant or enjoyable activities. Items load on one of five subscales: Socializing (item example: Complementing or praising someone); Relaxing (Listening to music); Contemplating (Thinking about people I like); Being Effective (Having a daily plan); and Doing Things (Doing volunteer work). There is some overlap of items between the COPPES and the Older Person's Pleasant Events Schedule but they each have their own unique items. Interested readers may download the COPPES and its scoring protocols from http://med.stanford.edu/oafc/coppes.html. Finally, a version of the Pleasant Events Schedule modified for use in nursing homes or long-term-care settings is available, called the Pleasant Events Schedule-NH (Meeks at al., 2009).

Cognitive aspects of Ms. Jenkins's depression would become the focus of therapy as well. Interviews are often used to identify thought patterns, assumptions, and world-views with a specific focus on those cognitive patterns that produce negative affect (e.g., depression or anxiety). One popular instrument used to identify the specific thought patterns and their relationships to mood states is the Thought Record. A sample record for Joanna Jenkins is shown in Figure 5.7.

Many other specific tools can be created to assist cognitive-behavioral therapists in measuring and recording subjective experiences, thoughts, and behaviors. Furthermore, older adults respond well to use of cognitive-behavior therapy self-help books, even without the assistance of a therapist (Floyd, Scogin, McKendree-Smith, Floyd, & Rokke, 2004). When used with a therapist or on one's own, CBT

Daily Thought Record

	SITUATION	EMOTION(S)	AUTOMATIC THOUGHT(S)	RATIONAL RESPONSE	OUTCOME
Date	Describe: 1. Actual event leading to unpleasant emotion, or 2. Stream of thoughts, daydreams or recollection, leading to unpleasant emotion	1. Specify sad/anxious, angry, etc. 2. Rate degree of emotion 1–100	1. Write automatic thought(s) that preceded emotion(s) 2. Rate belief in automatic thought(s) 0–100%	1. Write rational response to automatic thought (s) 2. Rate belief in rational response(s) 0–100%	1. Re-rate belief in automatic thought(s) 2. Specify and rate subsequent emotions 0–100
5/11	*Worry about daughter*	*anxious = 85* *sad = 70*	*She is going to be an unhappy lonely old woman now that she is divorced 95%*	*Divorce doesn't have to mean she is lonely.* *She might not be unhappy forever .* *Maybe she will find a better partner.* *She deserves it.* *My worrying about her does not help her and only makes me miserable 70%*	*40% –still anxious but I can't worry forever and worrying won't do her any good; anxious = 50 sad = 40*

Explanation: When you experience an unpleasant emotion, note the situation that seemed to stimulate the emotion. (If the emotion occurred while you were thinking, daydreaming, etc., please note this.)Then note the automatic thought associated with the emotion. Record the degree to which you believe this thought 0%–not at all, 100%–completely. In rating degree of emotion, 1 = a trace, 100 = the most intense possible.

Figure 5.7   Daily Thought Record for Joanna Jenkins.

assessment tools provide rich data about the frequency, intensity, and context of problem behaviors, thoughts, and feelings. These data serve as excellent prompts for behavior change because the problem is so clearly defined.

The cognitive-behavioral model provides a straightforward, easily understood framework within which a psychological or behavioral problem can be analyzed. Individualized assessment tools are frequently developed to facilitate tracking of specific targeted thoughts, feelings, and behaviors for a particular client.

Treatment

CBT is a time-limited, learning-based approach and is considered a short-term psychotherapy. The goal of CBT is indeed to help clients change their unhelpful thoughts and behaviors into more adaptive or helpful thoughts and behaviors. As such, self-monitoring of thoughts and behaviors (and recording of those observed thoughts and behaviors) is a true cornerstone of effective CBT practice. The CBT approach maintains a present-day focus on current thoughts or behaviors the client wishes to change, and focuses on factors believed to maintain the current problem(s) rather than on factors believed to cause the problem initially. CBT includes instructional and educational components, to familiarize the client with the basic tenets and language of the model, and clients and therapists frequently work in partnership to design homework assignments for clients to complete outside of the therapy sessions, which can also shorten the therapeutic process. The process is designed to be highly collaborative—that is, the therapist and client set concrete goals together, and they work together to monitor progress toward the goals. Flexibility inherent in CBT is ideally suited to the complex nature of problems experienced by many older adults seeking treatment (Karlin, 2011; Satre, Knight, & David, 2006).

Behavioral aspects of CBT

In a nutshell, the behavioral aspects of CBT aim to decrease the frequency of maladaptive or unhelpful behaviors and increase the frequency of adaptive or helpful behaviors, with the ultimate goal of increasing flexibility in the client's behavioral repertoire. The principles by which behavior can be changed are typically quite simple and straightforward (Kazdin, 2013). Behavior therapy has been applied in numerous settings with a wide variety of populations, including older adults (Laidlaw, 2015; Laidlaw, Thompson, Dick-Siskin, & Gallagher-Thompson, 2003).

Behavioral activation and engagement in pleasurable activities   Behavioral activation refers to helping the client become more *active* in his or her life, especially by helping the client to identify and schedule specific positive, enjoyable, or value-congruent activities in which to participate on a regular basis to increase contact with meaningful sources of enjoyment (i.e., positive reinforcement). Altering the contingencies for behavior involves changing or adding reinforcers to produce the desired behavior more often or adding disincentives to decrease the frequency of undesirable behavior. To change the reinforcement contingencies, a true reinforcer must be identified. Pleasant events or rewards for good behavior may be experienced as positive, but are not considered to be a reinforcer unless they actually change the rate of the targeted behavior. Similarly, an aversive consequence to a behavior is only a true punishment contingency if it decreases the rate of behavior.

A pleasant events reinforcement intervention might be appropriate for Anna Tweed. The first step would be to identify the desired behavior. The goal in this case is to decrease the frequency of a behavior that is noxious to staff (asking questions at the nurses' station), so a desirable behavior that is incompatible with the undesirable behavior must be identified. The goal behavior might be engaging in pleasant activity in the day room. The next step would then be to identify a reinforcer for her, that is, some event or item that is so valuable to her that she increases the frequency of the desired behavior in order to obtain or experience it. Nursing staff may have noticed that when one of them talks with Anna in her room she does not engage in the constant questioning behavior, nor does she seek to return to the nurses' station. Staff attention is likely to be a reinforcer for her that could be administered contingent on the targeted behavior. A behavioral program might be designed in which staff members talk with her in the day room contingent on her engaging in a certain period of appropriate behavior that does not include questioning. Staff attention is being used to reinforce her for engaging in activities away from the nurses' station. Punishments are unlikely to be used to decrease this particular behavior because it is generally considered unethical to use punitive strategies in an institutional setting to control behavior that is not harmful to self or others.

Joanna Jenkins might be engaged in a more collaborative process of activity monitoring and then activity scheduling as part of her outpatient psychotherapy, with emphasis on helping her to create an individualized list of realistic and doable activities in order to help her increase her participation in these activities. As we noted earlier, these targeted behaviors would be expected to give her a sense of mastery, accomplishment, or enjoyment. In order to reduce or work around some barriers and increase chances of success, it is often helpful to discuss barriers to engagement in rewarding activities while the weekly plan is being devised in session. Therapists usually help clients start with easier, readily available activities and then progress to more complex ones as momentum in treatment builds. As we will discuss in Chapter 9, behavioral activation is a well-known and effective treatment for depression in adults and older adults.

Apply differential reinforcement Often, the desired behaviors are occurring, but in an inappropriate context. Perhaps the behavior occurs where it is annoying to others, or perhaps the behavior is simply not achieving the desired effects for the older person. For example, a perfectly appropriate question asked to a person with severe hearing impairment may yield no effect. The questioning behavior was appropriate, but the context was not appropriate to yield the desired effects. Interventions can be established to differentially reinforce the behavior in one context but not another. For example, Anna Tweed might be given attention for asking questions of staff if the behavior occurs in her room, but not at the nurses' station.

Generalization of stimuli and responses While new behavior patterns are being established, reinforcement contingencies and eliciting stimuli are tightly controlled to maximize the efficiency with which the behavior is learned. Typically, however, the desired outcome is for the client to be able to perform that behavior in a variety of appropriate settings. Stimulus generalization refers to the process by which a person learns to perform the desired behavior in the presence of a wider variety of stimuli. If a reinforcement training program were established for Anna Tweed, it might be implemented by one or two staff initially. Eventually, however, the goal would be for Anna to be able to distinguish between a broader category of "busy staff" and "staff available to talk." This latter discrimination requires her to generalize her initial learning about talking with staff only in the day room and never at the nurses' station, to a much broader set of cues that indicate that staff are busy.

Response generalization refers to the fact that reinforcement of one response may increase the probability of other responses that are similar. Reinforcing Anna Tweed's conversations with staff who enter the day room may not only increase her rate of interaction with staff, but may lead her to increase her interaction with other people. Combined with stimulus generalization, the effects of response generalization would create for Ms. Tweed a more appropriate, active social life away from the nurses' station.

Shaping and chaining   Desired behaviors do not always occur spontaneously in the environment in which we want to reinforce them. The procedure of shaping involves reinforcing tiny steps toward the desired behavior. In the classic animal paradigms, pigeons were initially reinforced for turning toward the stimulus with which they were to interact. Once they were consistently turning toward the stimulus, they were reinforced only if they took steps toward the stimulus. Eventually, they had to complete the full behavior of turning, walking, and pecking the stimulus (the desired behavior) to be reinforced. The pecking behavior was shaped through reinforcement of small successive approximations of the desired behavior. As long as Joanna Jenkins is depressed, she may never spontaneously behave in a way that would elicit positive social reinforcement for her in a natural environment. A therapist or family member might establish a shaping procedure in which she is initially reinforced for behaving in a slightly less negative way than is typical for her. As Joanna becomes slightly less negative, she would have to behave in increasingly more positive ways over time in order to elicit reinforcement, until she is behaving in ways that will more naturally elicit positive social reinforcement from her natural social network.

Chaining refers to the process by which a person learns to produce a series of behaviors in a particular sequence. Reinforcement is initially given for a single behavior. Later, another behavior is required before the reinforcer is given. Finally, the full series of behaviors must be accomplished prior to reinforcement. Older adults who have experienced a stroke may need to relearn how to dress. Dressing is a long series of discrete behaviors that must be accomplished in order. A chaining procedure might be created to teach the steps of dressing oneself.

Extinction   Behaviors decrease if the positive reinforcement contingencies are removed. The gradual elimination of behavior following the removal of reinforcement contingencies is called extinction. Many behaviors are maintained by positive social consequences such as attention or praise. Removal of attention in response to the performance of the targeted behavior will result in a lower frequency of that behavior. This principle is particularly useful when working with behaviors that are either self-defeating or aversive to others. For example, Anna Tweed's behavior at the nurses' station may be inadvertently reinforced by social interaction from nurses during the time she stands at the station and asks questions. An extinction intervention would require all staff to ignore consistently Anna's presence and her verbalizations while she is standing at the nurses' station. Unfortunately, nursing home residents are often on an extinction paradigm for behavior the staff actually desires, such as independent social behaviors and self-care behaviors. Extinction techniques usually work quite well for externally reinforced behaviors but are less effective for behaviors that are principally internally reinforced or pleasurable for example, drinking alcohol to reduce anxiety or compulsively masturbating.

Exposure techniques and relaxation training   Exposure techniques are typically applied to a wide array of anxiety-based problems or disorders. The nature of exposure therapy is to repeatedly expose a person to the thoughts, events, objects, activities, and situations which are causing the person intense anxiety. Exposure may be to the actual object or situation or via imagery. The idea is that after being exposed to the anxiety-provoking stimuli on a regular basis, and seeing that they pose no real threat, the person will eventually become desensitized to them and experience less anxiety. More commonly, relaxation training is combined with exposure so that the person learns to relax in the presence of the feared object or situation and no longer has to rely on avoidance (which is sometimes inadvertently reinforced and keeps the fear and anxiety going). Exposure usually starts with less threatening aspects of the object or situation and progresses to more threatening aspects, using a fear hierarchy that is developed by client and clinician. In systematic desensitization, for example, the client learns to replace excessive or irrational fear with relaxation in a step-by-step learning process. Many resources are readily available for the client to learn and practice a diverse array of relaxation techniques, of which there are hundreds (see *The Relaxation and Stress Reduction Workbook*; Davis, Eshelman, & McKay, 2008). Exposure techniques are especially helpful for reducing anxiety symptoms since avoidance of anxiety-provoking situations is usually negatively reinforced, and exposure combats this avoidance and promotes facing one's excessive fears, which eventually reduces them.

Skills training Powerful and widely used techniques in behavior therapy involve helping clients, at all levels of functioning, to initiate, practice, and/or refine new behavioral skills. A diverse set of skills may be targeted during treatment including: assertiveness, communication, relaxation, problem-solving, emotion regulation, and coping skills. For example, some older adults with schizophrenia would benefit by enhancing their social skills, like initiating friendships and carrying on conversations, as a way to reduce isolation which is common among those with severe mental disorders. As another example, consider an older woman who describes herself as a "doormat" who lets others "walk all over her." She likely lacks appropriate assertiveness, which is the ability to express one's thoughts and feelings in a direct way without violating the right of others.

During assertiveness training, the client and therapist might role-play various scenarios from the client's life so that the client can model some assertive responses from the therapist and also practice assertive responding in a safe environment before trying them out in her life. These techniques are called *role-playing* and *behavioral rehearsal*, respectively. Participating in *behavioral experiments*, or trying out the new behaviors and observing their impacts, are critical for the client to learn and improve their skills. Among older adults, it can take time for a client to effectively implement new skills, especially in cases where the he or she has been practicing unhealthy behaviors for many years (sometimes more than 50 or 60 years). It may be important to understand why the client learned to be unassertive (in the current example the client was repeatedly and harshly punished as a young child for expressing her feelings, so she learned to completely shut down as a way to protect herself), but understanding why is not always possible nor is it always necessary for the person to learn and practice more adaptive behaviors. Even if the client experiences a failure when trying out a new behavioral skill, this is still valuable therapeutic material to process in session so his or her next attempts are more likely to be successful. This iterative process continues in treatment until the skill is solidified in diverse contexts in the client's life.

Cognitive aspects of CBT

In a nutshell, the cognitive therapy approach involves the recognition of distorted, biased, or unhelpful thoughts with the goal of replacing such thoughts with less distorted and more adaptive ones. A therapeutic outcome occurs when clients learn to identify their unhealthy thinking patterns and then alter their thoughts accordingly (Reinecke & Clark, 2004). In practice, cognitive therapy is highly pragmatic and strongly emphasizes individualized effective treatments. The identification of the client's particular pattern of misperceptions, attitudes, assumptions, core beliefs (schemas), and interpersonal strategies is crucial for cognitive therapy to proceed. Cognitive therapists, therefore, emphasize the recognition of biased and harmful thinking and the learning of self-counseling skills (Reinecke & Clark, 2004).

The distinction may seem subtle at first, but it is very important for the cognitive therapist to help the client to learn to identify and challenge her own negative thinking rather than the therapist challenging the client directly. The hope is that as the client becomes effective at implementing a wide array of cognitive techniques, the therapist becomes obsolete, although ongoing or intermittent consultation is sometimes necessary for lower-functioning clients.

Cognitive therapy has been adapted for older adults and widely applied to diverse types of problems common in later life (see excellent resources by Laidlaw, 2015; Laidlaw & Kishita, 2015; Sorocco & Lauderdale, 2011). Indeed, the individualized treatment approaches that cognitive therapists have developed adapt well to the unique challenges experienced by many older adults, contrary to some pejorative earlier reports that older adults would not be able to do much cognitive work due to the rigidity of thinking that was associated with later life. This notion is clearly a myth that has been debunked. It certainly is possible to "teach old dogs new tricks," and much research data attest to the positive impact of cognitive therapy among older clients (see Laidlaw, 2015; Satre et al., 2006). Some of the specific strategies used to help clients (of all ages) learn and apply methods of challenging negative thinking are described next.

The first step in the process is to help the client identify his or her own automatic negative thoughts. Because some people confuse thoughts and feelings (e.g., "I feel like a failure" rather than "I think I am a failure"), use of the Thought Record can help clients pinpoint the beliefs that mediate between a life event and an affective state. This often takes some practice but the vast majority of cognitively intact people of all ages can learn to identify their own thought processes. Once unhelpful thoughts are identified, the therapist then teaches the client a set of specific skills to combat, defeat, or neutralize the negative thinking. The typical strategies include:

1   Examining the evidence: What information or data support the negative belief? What evidence does not support the belief?
2   Examining the consequences of maintaining the belief: To what extent does holding the belief make the person miserable, depressed, anxious, scared, etc...? Is it worth it to continue to hold the belief?
3   Examining how somebody else would see the situation: Would a friend or family member look at the situation in the same way that the client does and draw the same conclusion that the client has drawn? Often people are able to recognize

the unhelpful or misguided nature of their beliefs by stating that a friend would not agree with their perspective or interpretation of some events.

4   Considering alternative beliefs: Are there other possible explanations of the situation? What are some other possible ways to view the situation that are backed up by some data and would have some potential benefit to the person to adopt the new way of thinking? Once a series of alternative thoughts are generated, each one can be scrutinized more fully to determine the validity or usefulness of the new way of thinking.

Problem-solving therapy

An important offshoot of traditional CBT is problem-solving therapy (PST). PST's underlying core premise is that one's mental and physical health can be enhanced by learning how to use a step-by-step process to find solutions to different types of problems that arise in life (Nezu, Nezu, & D'Zurilla, 2013). The PST approach consists of teaching clients two major strategies. The first is applying a *problem-solving orientation to life* which involves appraising problems as challenges to be solved, believing that problems can be solved, and understanding that effective problem solving requires time and systematic efforts. The second component of PST is learning how to effectively implement specific *problem-solving behaviors*. The specific problem-solving skills include:

1   selecting and defining the problem,
2   establishing realistic and achievable goals related to the problem,
3   generating a range of ideas to address or solve the problem,
4   implementing decision-making guidelines (thinking about the pros and cons of each idea),
5   choosing the most promising solution,
6   implementing the preferred solution (making a specific and doable action plan),
7   evaluating the outcome.

To help individuals manage emotion dysregulation, which is a frequent barrier to effective problem solving, clients are taught to use the SSTA method for coping with stress, where S=Stop, S=Slow down, T=Think, and A=Act. The process of PST is structured and intensive, involving written and oral presentations of the problem-solving steps by the clinician, guided practice in applying the model in session, and homework assignments to apply to model to real problems. PST has been found to be effective and helpful in a wide variety of populations and situations including major depression in younger adult patients, adult medical patients suffering from a variety of chronic diseases, developmentally disabled adults, sexual offenders, and individuals experiencing anxiety, suicidal ideation, schizophrenia, personality disorders, and post-traumatic stress disorder (Nezu et al., 2013).

The skill-building, flexible, and practical approach of PST is often very attractive to older adults who frequently experience complex environmental challenges. In fact, the model has been applied successfully to diverse groups of older adults, including depressed older adult outpatients (Areán et al., 1993), depressed medically fragile, homebound older adult patients (Gellis, McGinty, Horowitz, Bruce, & Misener, 2007), depressed older adult primary care patients (Areán, Hegel, Vannoy, Fan, & Unuzter,

2008), and depressed older adults with comorbid executive dysfunction (e.g., having difficulties with initiation, perseveration, and response inhibition) (Alexopoulos, Raue, Kanellopoulos, Mackin, & Areán, 2008; Areán et al., 2010), a group known to be especially resistant to conventional pharmacotherapy for depression. A variant of PST that also included caregivers to help depressed and cognitively impaired older adults was effective in reducing depression and disability in the participants (Kiosses et al., 2015). Further application of this model will hopefully extend the suitability and effectiveness of PST to caregivers of individuals with a cognitive disorder. These studies as a whole suggest that PST is an important and viable therapeutic option for many older adults with clinical depression.

Third wave approaches in CBT

The practice of CBT has continued to morph and evolve in recent years. Several important offshoots, commonly referred to as "third wave" or "third generation" approaches, are briefly described next. These treatments share in common their focus on *acceptance-based strategies*. The primary emphasis in these approaches is on accepting one's unwanted thoughts or emotions rather than trying to directly change or control them.

Acceptance and Commitment Therapy (ACT; Hayes, Strosahl, & Wilson, 2012) includes two primary foci. The first is to help the client learn to deeply and mindfully observe and accept her thoughts and feelings. The second emphasis is to help the client clarify her values in order to help her change or persist in behavior that aligns most closely with chosen values. The end goal is to increase the flexibility of clients in the service of their own clarified value-driven goals. Mindfulness Based Stress Reduction (MBSR) and Mindfulness Based Cognitive Therapy (MBCT) both focus on increasing mindfulness, which involves acceptance of one's experiences without resistance or judgment, in the present moment, in contrast to either ruminating about the past or worrying about the future. In this way, mindfulness is the opposite of experiential avoidance (defined as attempts to avoid or suppress unpleasant thoughts, feelings, memories, and bodily sensations, which is usually harmful in the long run). The origin of mindfulness strategies is from Buddhist meditation techniques which have been practiced for thousands of years.

Finally, Dialectical Behavior Therapy (DBT; Linehan & Koerner, 2012) combines acceptance-based strategies with skills training in the areas of mindfulness, distress tolerance, emotion regulation, and interpersonal effectiveness. These skills are usually tackled and addressed in successive modules that include extensive role-playing, rehearsal, implementation, and refinement over time. There is an increasing body of literature in support of the efficacy of these newer CBT approaches with diverse populations, including older adults (e.g., Alonso, Lopez, Losada, & Gonzalez, 2013; Lenze et al., 2014; Lynch et al., 2007), and we are excited about future prospects for adapting these techniques more specifically to aging populations and playing on the strengths, like wisdom and experience, that often come with advancing age.

Additional Comments about the Cognitive-Behavioral Model

The power of environmental contingencies (e.g., classical and operant conditioning) to develop and maintain behavior has been illustrated in several naturalistic settings with older adults. One illustrative research program has examined the effects of antecedents and consequences for controlling behavior in nursing homes in the United States and Germany. Margret Baltes and colleagues famously demonstrated that staff in nursing homes reinforce dependency behavior from residents, but extinguish (fail to reinforce) independent behavior from residents (Baltes, 1988). Staff tend to interact with residents most, and most warmly, when the residents are receiving hands-on care. In other words, if residents want warm social contact with staff they must "need" care from staff. Obviously, this line of research illustrates several principles of cognitive-behavioral theory. Staff appear to extinguish independent behavior by not providing even an intermittent reinforcement schedule. At the same time, they are reinforcing dependent behavior. In contrast, altering staff behavior so it reinforces desired independent behaviors has been shown to be effective (Burgio, Burgio, Engel, & Tice, 1986; Cohn, Smyer, & Horgas, 1994).

Interventions to alter cognitions and behavior always require careful examination of ethics. When designing interventions for frail persons who either cannot collaborate in the establishment of treatment goals (e.g., cognitively impaired persons) or whose power to refuse the intervention is compromised (e.g., in a nursing home), cognitive-behavioral clinicians must be particularly careful to examine the ethical implications of their decision to intervene. For example, when is family or staff displeasure a sufficient reason to intervene? How much understanding must be present for informed consent to be truly informed? Cognitive-behavioral clinicians must respect the burden of ethical consideration that is placed on them by the very power of their tools. (We return to a range of ethical issues in Chapter 17.)

Summary and Conclusions

In summary, the cognitive-behavioral model is rooted in a scientific approach to investigating efficiency and effectiveness of interventions. As such, the amount of evidence supporting the utility of this model to explain mental health problems and to design interventions for older adults is impressive (e.g., Gallagher-Thompson & Coon, 2007; Karlin, 2011; Laidlaw, 2015; Satre et al., 2006; Scogin & Shah, 2012; Scogin, Welsh, Hanson, Stump, & Coates, 2005; Stanley et al., 2003). Cognitive-behaviorists working with cognitively intact persons have demonstrated significant impact with challenging problems like depression, anxiety, negative health behaviors, distress in caregivers, and insomnia. Many interventions, especially more behaviorally focused ones, have been successful even with cognitively impaired individuals (e.g., incontinence programs and self-care programs), suggesting robust application of the model to older persons with diverse levels of functioning.

Critical Thinking / Discussion Questions

1   Some students have a natural preference for one aspect of the model (that is, cognitively focused work versus behaviorally focused work). Which aspects of the model are most appealing to you and which aspects are least appealing? Provide the rationale for your preferences.

2   What do you envision would be some of the unique opportunities in implementing cognitive and behavioral interventions with older adult clients? Conversely, what would be some of the challenges to such implementation?

3   What modifications to the CBT approach would you consider making if your client was a healthy 60-year-old person compared to a frail 90-year-old person?

Website Resources

Association for Contextual Behavioral Science
https://contextualscience.org
Association for Behavioral and Cognitive Therapies
http://www.abct.org/Home
Association for Behavior Analysis International
https://www.abainternational.org/welcome.aspx
Beck Institute for Cognitive Behavior Therapy
https://www.beckinstitute.org

References

Alexopoulos, G. S., Raue, P. J., Kanellopoulos, D., Mackin, S., & Areán, P. A. (2008). Problem solving therapy for the depression-executive dysfunction syndrome of late life. *International Journal of Geriatric Psychiatry, 23,* 782–788.

Allen-Burge, R., Stevens, A. B., & Burgio, L. D. (1999). Effective behavioral interventions for decreasing dementia-related challenging behavior in nursing homes. *International Journal of Geriatric Psychiatry, 14,* 213–232.

Alonso, M., Lopez, A., Losada, A., & Gonzalez, J. (2013). Acceptance and commitment therapy and selective optimization with compensation for older people with chronic pain: A pilot study. *Behavioral Psychology, 21,* 59–79.

Areán, P., Hegel, M., Vannoy, S., Fan, M. Y., & Unuzter, J. (2008). Effectiveness of problem-solving therapy for older, primary care patients with depression: Results from the IMPACT project. *The Gerontologist, 48,* 311–323.

Areán, P. A., Perri, M. G, Nezu, A. M., Schein, R. L., Christopher, F., & Joseph, T. X. (1993). Comparative effectiveness of social problem-solving therapy and reminiscence therapy as treatments for depression in older adults. *Journal of Consulting and Clinical Psychology, 61,* 1003–1010.

Areán, P. A., Raue, P., Mackin, R. S., Kanellopoulos, D., McCulloch, C., & Alexopoulos, G. S. (2010). Problem-solving therapy and supportive therapy in older adults with major depression and executive dysfunction. *American Journal of Psychiatry, 167,* 1391–1398.

Baltes, M. (1988). The etiology and maintenance of dependency in the elderly: Three phases of operant research. *Behavior Therapy, 19,* 301–320.

Baltes, P. B., & Baltes, M. M. (Eds.). (1990). *Successful aging: Perspectives from the behavioral sciences.* Cambridge, England: Cambridge University Press.

Barlow, D. H., Nock, M. K., & Hersen, M. (2008). *Single-case experimental designs: Strategies for studying behavior change* (3rd ed.). Boston, MA: Allyn & Bacon.

Beck, A. T., Emery, G., & Greenberg, R. L. (1985). *Anxiety disorders and phobias: A cognitive perspective.* New York, NY: Basic Books.

Beck, A. T., & Haigh, E. A. P. (2014). Advances in cognitive theory and therapy: The generic cognitive model. *Annual Review of Clinical Psychology, 10,* 1–24.

Beck, A. T., Rush, A. J., Shaw, B. F., & Emery, G. (1979). *Cognitive therapy of depression.* New York, NY: Guilford Press.

Burgio, L. D., Burgio, K. L., Engel, B. T., & Tice, L. M. (1986). Increasing distance and independence of ambulation in elderly nursing home residents. *Journal of Applied Behavior Analysis, 19,* 357–366.

Burgio, L., Stevens, A., Burgio, K., Roth, D., Paul, P., & Gerstle, J. (2002). Teaching and maintaining behavior management in the nursing home. *Gerontologist, 42,* 487–496.

Cohn, M. D., Smyer, M. A., & Horgas, A. L. (1994). *The ABCs of behavior change: Skills for working with behavior problems in nursing homes.* State College, PA: Venture Publishing.

Davis, M., Eshelman, E. R., & McKay, M. (2008). *The relaxation and stress reduction workbook* (6th ed.). Oakland, CA: New Harbinger.

Dobson, K. S., & Dozois, D. J. A. (2010). Historical and philosophical bases of the cognitive-behavioral therapies. In K. S. Dobson (Ed.), *Handbook of cognitive-behavioral therapies* (3rd ed., pp. 3–38). New York, NY: Guilford Press.

Dozois, D. J. A., Frewen, P. A., & Covin, R. (2006). Cognitive theories. In J. C. Thomas & D. L. Segal (Eds.), Personality and everyday functioning. In M. Hersen & J. C. Thomas (Eds.-in-Chief), *Comprehensive handbook of personality and psychopathology* (Vol. 1, pp. 173–191). New York, NY: Wiley.

Ellis, A. (1991). *Reason and emotion in psychotherapy.* New York, NY: Citadel.

Ellis, A., & Dryden, W. (2007). *The practice of rational emotive behavior therapy* (2nd ed.). New York, NY: Springer.

Epictetus. (1955). *The enchiridion.* (G. Long, Trans.). New York, NY: Promethean Press. (Original published c. 101 AD).

Floyd, M., Scogin, F., McKendree-Smith, N. L., Floyd, D. L., & Rokke, P. D. (2004). Cognitive therapy for depression: A comparison of individual psychotherapy and bibliotherapy for depressed older adults. *Behavior Modification, 28,* 297–318.

Gallagher-Thompson, D., & Coon, D. W. (2007). Evidence-based psychological treatments for distress in family caregivers of older adults. *Psychology and Aging, 22,* 37–51.

Gellis, Z. D., McGinty, J., Horowitz, A., Bruce, M. L., & Misener, E. (2007). Problem-solving therapy for late-life depression in home care: A randomized field trial. *American Journal of Geriatric Psychiatry, 15,* 968–978.

Gitlin, L. N., Belle, S. H., Burgio, L. D., Czaja, S. J., Mahoney, D., Gallagher-Thompson, D., ... Ory, M. G. (2003). Effect of multicomponent interventions on caregiver burden and depression: The REACH multisite initiative at 6-month follow-up. *Psychology and Aging, 18,* 361–374.

Hayes, S. C., Strosahl, K. D., & Wilson, K. G. (2012). *Acceptance and commitment therapy: The process and practice of mindful change* (2nd ed.). New York, NY: Guilford Press.

Karlin, B. E. (2011). Cognitive behavioral therapy with older adults. In K. H. Sorocco & S. Lauderdale (Eds.), *Cognitive behavior therapy with older adults: Innovations across care settings* (pp. 1–28). New York, NY: Springer.

Kazdin, A. E. (2013). *Behavior modification in applied settings* (7th ed.). Long Grove, IL: Waveland Press.

Kiosses, D. N., Ravdin, L. D., Gross, J. J., Raue, P., Kotbi, N., & Alexopoulos, G. S. (2015). Problem adaptation therapy for older adults with major depression and cognitive impairment: A randomized clinical trial. *JAMA Psychiatry, 72,* 22–30.

Laidlaw, K. (2015). *CBT for older people: An introduction.* Thousand Oaks, CA: Sage.

Laidlaw, K., & Kishita, N. (2015). Age-appropriate augmented cognitive behavior therapy to enhance treatment outcome for late-life depression and anxiety disorders. *GeroPsych: The Journal of Gerontopsychology and Geriatric Psychiatry, 28*(2), 57–66.

Laidlaw, K., Thompson, L. W., Dick-Siskin, L., & Gallagher-Thompson, D. (2003). *Cognitive behavior therapy with older people*. New York, NY: Wiley.

LeBlanc, L. A., Raetz, P. B., & Feliciano, L. (2012). Behavioral gerontology. In W. W. Fisher, C. C. Piazza, & H. S. Roane (Eds.), *Handbook of applied behavior analysis* (pp. 472–486). New York, NY: Guilford Press.

Lenze, E. J., Hickman, S., Hershey, T., Wendleton, L., Ly, K., Dixon, D., …Wetherell, J. L. (2014). Mindfulness-based stress reduction for older adults with worry symptoms and co-occurring cognitive dysfunction. *International Journal of Geriatric Psychiatry, 29*, 991–1000.

Linehan, M. M., & Koerner, K. (2012). *Doing dialectical behavior therapy*. New York, NY: Guilford Press.

Lynch, T. R., Cheavens, J. S., Cukrowicz, K. C., Thorp, S. R., Bronner, L., & Beyer, J. (2007). Treatment of older adults with co-morbid personality disorder and depression: a dialectical behavior therapy approach. *International Journal of Geriatric Psychiatry, 22*, 131–143.

Meeks, S., Looney, S. W., Van Haitsma, K., & Teri, L. (2008). BE-ACTIV: A staff-assisted behavioral intervention for depression in nursing homes. *Gerontologist, 48*, 105–114.

Meeks, S., Shah, S. N., & Ramsey, S. K. (2009). The Pleasant Events Schedule – nursing home version: A useful tool for behavioral interventions in long-term care. *Aging & Mental Health, 13*, 445–455.

Molinari, V. (Ed.). (2000). *Professional psychology in long term care: A comprehensive guide*. New York, NY: Hatherleigh Press.

Nezu, A. M, Nezu, C. M., & D'Zurilla, T. J. (2013). *Problem-solving therapy: A treatment manual*. New York, NY: Springer.

Reinecke, M. A., & Clark, D. A. (Eds.). (2004). *Cognitive therapy across the lifespan: Theory, research and practice*. Cambridge, England: Cambridge University Press.

Rider, K. L., Gallagher-Thompson, D., & Thompson, L. T. (2004). *California Older Person's Pleasant Events Schedule: Manual*. Retrieved from http://oafc.stanford.edu/coppes.html

Rosowsky, E., Casciani, J., & Arnold, M. (Eds.) (2008). *Geropsychology and long-term care: A practitioner's guide*. New York, NY: Springer.

Sadavoy, J. (2009). An integrated model for defining the scope of psychogeriatrics: The five C's. *International Psychogeriatrics, 21*, 805–812. doi: http://dx.doi.org.libproxy.uccs.edu/10.1017/S104161020999010X

Satre, D., Knight, B. G., & David, S. (2006). Cognitive behavioral interventions with older adults: Integrating clinical and gerontological research. *Professional Psychology: Research and Practice, 37*, 489–498.

Scogin, F., & Shah, A. (Eds.) (2012). *Making evidence-based psychological treatments work with older adults*. Washington, DC: APA Books.

Scogin, F. R., Welsh, D., Hanson, A., Stump, J., & Coates, A. (2005). Evidence-based psychotherapies for depression in older adults. *Clinical Psychology: Science and Practice, 12*, 222–237.

Skinner, B. F. (1953). *Science and human behavior*. New York, NY: Free Press.

Sorocco, K. H., & Lauderdale, S. A. (Eds.) (2011). *Cognitive behavioral therapy with older adults: Innovations across care settings*. New York, NY: Springer.

Stanley, M. A., Hopko, D. R., Diefenbach, G. J., Bourland, S. L., Rodriegues, H., & Wagner, P. (2003). Cognitive-behavior therapy for late-life generalized anxiety disorder in primary care: Preliminary findings. *American Journal of Geriatric Psychiatry, 11*, 92–96.

Teri, L., & Lewinsohn, P. M. (1982). Modification of the pleasant and unpleasant event schedules for use with the elderly. *Journal of Consulting and Clinical Psychology, 50*, 444–445.

Teri, L., McKenzie, G., & LaFazia, D. (2005). Psychosocial treatment of depression in older adults with dementia. *Clinical Psychology: Science and Practice, 12*, 303–316.

Yesavage, J. A., Brink, T. L., Rose, T. L., Lum, O., Huang, V., Adey, M. B., & Leirer, V. O. (1983). Development and validation of a geriatric depression screening scale: A preliminary report. *Journal of Psychiatric Research, 17*, 37–49.

6

Stress and Coping Model

Consider the following examples:

Donna is a 68-year-old retired teacher and principal. She and Steve married late in life, after Steve's wife died. It was a wonderful match: Both of them had been teachers and principals; both enjoyed hiking, going to plays and museums, and spending time with family members and friends. They left the northwest and moved back east to where Steve had grown up. They had just started making new friends when all of that changed: Steve was afflicted with a degenerative spinal disease. He became increasingly limited in his mobility, eventually relying on a scooter to get around. And Donna became increasingly involved in providing and organizing his care. She told friends that she wasn't sure she could continue to cope for very much longer. The stress of 24/7 caregiving responsibility was overwhelming her.

Pat, aged 70, was increasingly concerned about her younger son, Mike. He and some friends had started a company on the West Coast. Pat and her husband invested a large sum of money to keep the operation afloat. After two years, Pat became aware of the excessive amount of time it took for her to clean up the bookkeeping and provide business leadership for the fledgling, and failing, enterprise. Just about that time, Pat began gaining weight, had times of deep depression, and started experiencing periods of rapid heart rates. She also had a biopsy for a possible colon cancer. Her physician asked if she was under any stress.

Mrs. C. is an 80-year-old African American woman whose adaptation in late life is plagued by disruptive relocation and very poor health. Not surprisingly, she exhibits severe psychological distress, and her medical chart includes a diagnosis of clinical depression. She is currently surviving on the barest social, economic and health resources. She is also socially isolated. "My family—they're all dead,

Aging and Mental Health, Third Edition. Daniel L. Segal, Sara Honn Qualls, and Michael A. Smyer.
© 2018 John Wiley & Sons, Inc. Published 2018 by John Wiley & Sons, Inc.

my mama, my papa, everyone." She had been married in her late teens and widowed before 30—"so long ago I can hardly remember it." Her son and a grandson died many years previously, and she subsequently lost contact with a second grandson. Before retiring because of illness, she worked as a domestic for 40 years. Currently she subsists on Supplemental Security Income (SSI). Compounding her many losses, she was recently evicted from an apartment where she had resided for 30 years. This event was especially traumatic because it removed her from a familiar neighborhood, proximity to her church, and friends of long standing. She complains of loneliness and believes that her doctor is her only confidante. Her declining physical health is a serious factor in her current distress. According to her medical charts, she was recently diagnosed as having cervical cancer and nodular shadows were seen on her chest X-ray. She and her doctors were most troubled about the possibility of a serious systemic disease (Johnson & Johnson, 1992, p. 233).

Jason is a mason. He is proud to be a union member and proud of his ability to work on technically challenging jobs, like commercial firebrick applications. At age 61, decades of heavy work are taking their toll. He has chronic back pain, high blood pressure, and a kidney disorder, and his doctor said he might need to have cataract surgery. Jason is worried about how to pay for his medical care: If he quits work, his coverage will end. But he is too young for Medicare. Besides, he likes being on the job site each day, joking with the guys, and feeling that he is making a difference; but he worries how long he can continue to work.

These situations pose challenges for each older adult and for those who are working with them. How do we conceptualize their problems? What can we do for them and with them? Not surprisingly, all of these older adults have a series of challenges that they are coping with, including concerns about money, concerns about family members, and concerns about their own health and well-being.

Introduction to the Model

This chapter outlines a stress and coping perspective that may be useful for working with older adults like Donna, Pat, Mrs. C., or Jason. We draw upon research and clinical work from several different disciplines to help sketch an understanding of the stress and coping process and its implications for assessment and treatment.

Well-being

Have you ever been "stressed out"? How do you know?

In developing your answer, you worked from an implicit model of what stress is and how it works. For some, stress is experienced as a physical reaction: quickened heartbeats, upset stomach, neck pain, sweating. For some, stress is experienced as a combination of feelings: worry, fear, apprehension, or hopelessness. For others, stress is identified with external problems: problems in paying bills, too much work and too little time, conflict with a friend or family member.

Consider a softball player. Her team is tied in the bottom of the last inning. She is at bat with two strikes called against her. Is this situation stressful? Is it unhealthy for her? Your answer depends upon your implicit model of the stress process and its implications for well-being. A more formal definition of stress is in order. *Stress* may be defined as a physical, mental, or emotional response to events that makes you feel threatened or upsets your balance in some way. In small amounts, stress can be positive in that it may motivate you to perform well. In contrast, high levels of chronic stress are usually unhealthy for the mind and body. Aldwin (2011) put it this way: "Appraisals of stress arise when environmental demands exceed the individual's resources, especially in situations that are personally significant." This definition emphasizes the interaction among the individual, the context, and the environment.

A lifespan developmental perspective of stress and coping emphasizes several elements: stress and coping processes change across the lifespan; it often takes a multidisciplinary perspective to fully depict stress and coping, since a complex and complete understanding entails biological, social, and cultural elements; we should not underestimate the impact of the immediate context; and we must be aware of individual differences and individual coping trajectories in reacting to similar stresses (Aldwin, 2011).

Aldwin (2007) outlined an integrative perspective on stress, coping, and development. She suggested that it is useful to think of stress and coping as a process with three key elements: an internal state of the person, called *strain*; external events or *stressors*; and an experience that derives from the interaction of the person and environment, called *transactions*. These themes echo McEwen's (2015) emphasis on life course health development, integrating developmental processes at the individual and environmental levels.

Strain

The concept of strain encompasses reactions that are physiological (e.g., sympathetic activation; parasympathetic suppression; neuroendocrine changes; immune function changes) and emotional (e.g., negative feelings; positive feelings, emotional numbing). Growing interest in the connection between the mind and the body spurred the development of the field of psychoneuroimmunology (PNI), the study of the interaction between psychological processes and the nervous and immune systems of the human body (Ader, 2007; Daruna, 2012; Vedhara & Irwin, 2005). Indeed, the links between stress and immune system functioning have received a great deal of research and clinical attention (Kiecolt-Glaser, 2009). In an early review of this literature, Herbert and Cohen (1993) highlighted several important themes: First, both objective stressful events and subjective reports of stress are related to immune changes; second, objective events have a greater impact than subjective reports;

and, third, the nature of the events (e.g., interpersonal stress vs. nonsocial events) affects the type of immune response.

How does this help us understand Pat's situation? To begin with, we might attend to the objective stressful events that have occurred for her, and their likely impact on her physiological functioning. For example, consider only two aspects of her situation: depression and cancer. There is a substantial link between clinical depression and compromised immune system functioning (Gruenewald & Kemeny, 2007) and these effects are greatest among older and hospitalized patients. Similarly, there is a clearly established link among the stress of cancer diagnosis and treatment, other life stresses, and subsequent health or illness (e.g., Penedo & Dahn, 2005). Thus although depression and cancer are not directly related, they both relate to poorer health outcomes.

In short, there is good reason to suspect that the stresses of clinical depression and a cancer diagnosis and subsequent treatment regimen—apart from any of the other objective stressors or subjective perceptions—put Pat at risk for suppressed immune functioning and poor disease prognosis.

In addition to cancer, financial strain is a chronic stressor for Mrs. C. Her career as a domestic suggests that she has not been highly paid, and her current subsistence on SSI confirms this suspicion. Mrs. C.'s financial stress and challenging living situations embody a larger pattern of cumulative disadvantage first described by Crystal and Shea more than 25 years ago (Crystal & Shea, 1990) and recently updated (Crystal, 2016; Crystal, Shea, & Reyes, 2017). Crystal (2016) recently summarized the growing inequality in income and wealth in later life:

> Between 1983–84 and 2010, the share of total income received by 65-to-74 year-olds in the lower 40% of the income distribution went down from 17% to 14%, while the share of the best-off 20% increased from 46% to 48%. For people 75 and older, the share received by the lower 40% decreased from 15% to 14%, while the share of the top 20% increased from 47% to 50%, with the lower 80% receiving only 50%.
>
> Concentration of wealth among older people also increased. By 2010, the top 20% accounted for 62% of total annuitized value of wealth.

As Abramson (2016) put it: "Late life is not the end of inequality; it is inequality's end game."

Low income also put Jason and Mrs. C. at risk for poorer health. As Hardy (2016) points out, one of the enduring challenges is the persistent relationship between health and socioeconomic status. Hardy suggests that a stress paradigm may be one of the frameworks that help us understand this persistent relationship. (We will consider the impact of the larger social context more fully in Chapter 17.)

Krause (1995a) summarized the impact of chronic financial strain on older adults' social and mental well-being, noting that financial strain has a significant impact on depressive symptoms—second only to the impact of a physical illness. In Mrs. C.'s case, we might ask what the impact of this chronic stressor has been for her depressive symptoms (Krause, 1995a): Has it caused depression to occur for the first time in later life? Has it prolonged an already-existing depressive episode? Has it caused a relapse of a previously diagnosed disorder? These are leads that we may want to pursue in our history-taking with Mrs. C.

Stressor

Examples of external events or stressors include traumatic or upsetting experiences (e.g., being a victim of crime; undergoing a contentious divorce; death of a parent; being fired from a job), aversive physical environments (e.g., being too hot, too cold, in pain), role strain (e.g., simultaneously having to care for an ill older parent and younger children), and daily hassles (e.g., facing traffic each day on the way to work). These stressors cause the experience of stress. A distinction between strain and stressors is that strains are generally chronic whereas stressors are generally acute.

The concept of stressor shifts our attention to the social, historical, and physical context that surrounds older adults. As noted in Chapter 2, three types of influences shape the individual's life course: age-graded, history-graded, and non-normative events. Age-graded influences are associated with a specific chronological age, for example, entering school or graduating from high school are usually linked to a narrow age band. History-graded influences are linked to the particular historical period in which the individual has lived (e.g., the Great Depression; the Vietnam War; the Oklahoma City bombing; the 9/11 terrorist attacks; Hurricane Katrina or Tropical Storm Sandy). Non-normative events are influences that occur at any time in the lifespan but are not part of the "expected" life pattern (e.g., death of one's parents at an early age; winning the lottery). As we discussed earlier, these influences vary across the lifespan.

In the case of Mrs. C., we might use these frameworks to consider all three of the history-graded, age-graded, and non-normative influences that have shaped her development. An 80-year-old, she was born in the 1930s. She experienced the Great Depression as young child, married after WWII, and was widowed during the Korean War. She has had other non-normative events befall her: death of a grandson and eviction from her home.

The deaths of her family members remind us that Mrs. C.'s life events are interwoven with the events of her family members and friends. Pruchno, Blow, and Smyer (1984) call these "life event webs" as a way of reminding us of interdependent lives. Mrs. C. has lost potential sources of support through the deaths of her husband, son, and grandson.

In addition, Mrs. C. has recently lost the support of her familiar surroundings, a place where she had lived for 30 years. Moving means that she has to establish new social ties and links to a new physical and social community, another challenge at an already difficult time. New friends can become important sources of support for older adults but they are unlikely to replace the bonds of friendship forged over many years and even decades.

Transaction

The third element of the stress process is transaction, the interaction between the person and the environment. The basic assumption is that the person's *perception* of the stressor affects his or her coping response, highlighting a cognitive dimension to the stress process. For example, imagine that you are taking an important course and a final exam is coming up. You might view this impending stressor in at least two different ways: a threat to your mental health and educational well-being, or a challenge to your intellectual skills and an opportunity to hone your knowledge on the course topics. How you view the stressor may very well affect what you do about it. An appraisal of the intensity of the stressor (e.g., weak, moderate, strong, ambiguous) is another aspect of the stress process. Stressors appraised with stronger intensity typically yield stronger emotional, behavioral, and physiological responses.

McEwen (2015) reminds us that the "brain is the central organ of stress and adaptation" (p. 233). He suggests that we take a "top down" approach to stress, realizing that stress affects the brain's capacity for self-regulating anxiety and mood, as well as working and episodic memory, executive functioning, and decision-making. Through the neuroendocrine, autonomic, immune, and metabolic systems, the brain regulates the body. McEwen (1998; 2015) offers a useful summary of the brain's central role in stress and adaptation, along with key mediators of stress (see Figure 6.1). He emphasized that the most potent immediate stressors may be the social and physical environments.

McEwen differentiated between allostasis, which is the body's initial adaptation to stressors and allostatic load, which may reflect cumulative change (e.g., hypertension, body fat) resulting from chronic stress and a subsequent unhealthy lifestyle. Eventually, these adaptations may lead to allostatic overload evidenced in diseases like diabetes or cardiovascular disease. Pat's case example illustrates these themes.

Adler and Prather (2015) also emphasized the role that stress linked to physical and social environments can play in the processes and outcomes of aging. They suggested two mechanisms for how social conditions "get under the skin" to affect morbidity and mortality: cellular aging and epigenetics.

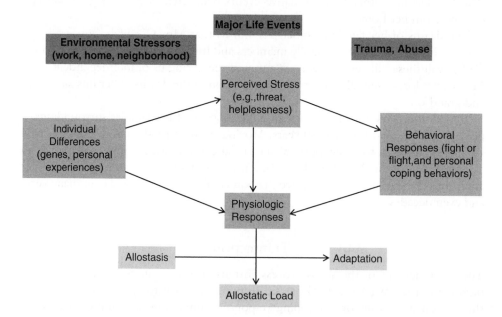

Figure 6.1 Central role of the brain in the protective and damaging effects of the mediators of stress and adaptation.
Source: Adapted from McEwen (1998).

On a cellular level, telomere length in immune cells offers an index of accelerated senescence (Adler & Prather, 2015):

> Telomeres are DNA-protein complexes that cap the ends of the chromosome, conferring chromosomal stability…. When critically short, they can send cells into replicative senescence, causing cell cycle arrest and malfunction. Short telomere length in immune cells may serve as a marker, and possibly a mechanism, of earlier onset of diseases of aging." (p. 414)

Adler and Prather (2015) point out that accelerated telomere attrition has been linked to social determinants, including aspects of socioeconomic status (e.g., income, education, employment status) and the neighborhood social environment (Adler et al., 2013; Carroll, Diez-Roux, Adler, & Seeman, 2013; Needham et al., 2014).

In addition to cellular aging, early life experiences of trauma and abuse may also have long-term consequences through the mechanisms of epigenetics. Epigenetic mechanisms "change DNA gene activity or expression by altering DNA organization without modifying the genetic code of the DNA" (Boyce, 2015, p. 220). Adler and Prather summed up the importance of epigenetics: "It provides a mechanism through which the environment can regulate the transcriptional control of a gene that can persist for prolonged periods, even across generations" (p. 414). Animal models suggest that early rearing can affect the individual's lifelong response to stress, through modifying their hypothalamic-pituitary-adrenal (HPA) axis.

Govia and her colleagues (Govia, Jackson, & Sellers, 2011) provide a link between the challenges of a lifetime of low socioeconomic status and low immune system functioning. They highlight the impacts that cumulative disadvantages have across the lifespan, including differential life expectancies and rates of disease (see Chapter 2 for more on this topic). They note that racial disparities in physical and mental health are complicated, particularly with lower rates of mental distress among African American elders, but high rates of chronic disease. As they put it: "Why do Blacks do worse than Whites in physical disorders but have positive disparities in mental health disorders?" (p. 737).

Jason's and Mrs. C.'s experiences illustrate the blurring of the lines across biological and behavioral domains, suggesting that we take a life course health development view (McEwen, 2015). Govia and her colleagues suggest that chronic environmental stressors (e.g., living in an unsafe neighborhood; racial discrimination) and personal stressors (e.g., Jason's financial hardships) activate the HPA axis and related hormonal systems. Chronic activation of the HPA axis, along with poor health behaviors (e.g., smoking, drinking, overeating), may lead to physical health disorders, while, paradoxically, easing stress and psychiatric disorders (Jackson, Knight, & Rafferty, 2010). Jackson and his colleagues (2010) summarized the interaction of chronic stress, physical health outcomes, and mental health outcomes:

> Many Black Americans live in chronically precarious and difficult environments… These environments produce stressful living conditions, and often the most easily accessible options for addressing stress are various unhealthy behaviors (e.g., smoking, drinking, drug use, and so on)…. these behaviors may alleviate the symptoms of stress through

the same mechanisms that are hypothesized to contribute to some mental disorders: the HPA axis...negative health behaviors, such as smoking, overeating (especially comfort foods), drinking alcohol, and drug use also have direct and debilitating effects on physical health. Thus, although these activities have the effect of alleviating or masking the ostensible symptoms of stress, they contribute—along with difficult living environments—to the disparities in mortality and physical health morbidity observed between Black and non-Hispanic White populations." (p. 938)

Conceptualizing Coping

How shall we think about older adults' response to stress? In a now-classic dichotomy, Lazarus and his colleagues highlighted two basic approaches to coping that are linked to the perception of stress: *problem-focused coping* and *emotion-focused coping* (Folkman, Lazarus, Pimley, & Novacek, 1987; Lazarus & Folkman, 1984). Problem-focused coping is aimed at managing or altering the problem that is causing distress, whereas emotion-focused coping is aimed at regulating distressing emotions. Both styles of coping include behavioral and cognitive strategies. The type of coping used depends upon an individual's appraisal of the situation, namely, whether or not the stressful problem is perceived as being amenable to change. In general, problem-focused coping is directed at conditions that are assessed as amenable to change whereas emotion-focused coping is directed at conditions where nothing ostensibly can be done to alter the challenging situation. Typically, use of problem-focused coping or emotion-focused coping do not preclude each other; rather, individuals use some combination of both when handling a stressful problem. Indeed, the type of coping that is used in response to a particular stress is a function of the individual's perceptions, the specific types of stress, and the context for coping.

Skinner and her colleagues (2003) have criticized the dichotomy of problem-focused and emotion-focused as too simplistic. After an extensive review of the literature, they suggested that there are five basic coping strategies: problem solving; support seeking; avoidance; distraction; and positive cognitive restructuring. Aldwin (2011) summarized these approaches:

> Problem solving includes not only behavior (instrumental action) but also cognition (e.g., planning) and motivation (perseverance). Support seeking includes reaching out to others for behavioral, cognitive, and emotional support. Avoidance also includes both behavioral and cognitive strategies such as denial. This should not be confused with distraction, which includes positive behaviors and cognitions to minimize stress. Positive cognitive reconstruction involves reinterpreting problematic situations, looking for potential positive facets and outcomes. (p. 22)

Skinner and her colleagues suggested three other negative strategies (rumination, helplessness, and social withdrawal) and one positive one (emotion regulation). Others have emphasized prayer (e.g., Pargament, 2011) or finding meaning or benefits coming from stress (e.g., Park, 2005).

Aldwin (2011) notes that, in general, older adults use fewer coping strategies, but maintain their self-rated effectiveness. She cautions, however, that we need to distinguish between coping effort and coping ability when considering older adults' strategies. Older adults may seek to conserve energy by using less effort, but that does not mean that they are less effective.

A central element of perception is the individual's sense of control over the event (Skaff, 2007). In a classic study in this area, Zautra, Reich, and Newsom (1995) focused on the links between sense of control, loss of autonomy, and mental health among older adults. They found that it is important to assess the individual's sense of control that derives from experience with the possibility of shaping the events of life—both positive and negative. They focused on mental health and adaptation in the face of a loss of autonomy because of either physical disability or conjugal bereavement. Their results were impressive: A sense of personal control over events was associated with positive mental health and adaptation in the face of increased disability or decreased autonomy. In general, the consensus of recent literature suggests that entering later life with a strong sense of control is highly adaptive (see review by Skaff, 2007).

What about our case examples at the start of the chapter? How do the individuals depicted view the stressors in their lives? How much control do they perceive themselves to have? Their comments about caregiving, moving, finances, or health care suggest that some of them may perceive having little sense of control over their life situations, which likely adds stress for them.

Stress and Coping: Normal and Abnormal Adaptation

Are the profiles of strain, stressors, and transactions (described in the case examples) normal for older adults? Although a great deal of knowledge about stress and its impact on older adults has been synthesized (Aldwin, Park, & Spiro, 2007), much remains unknown. We simply cannot chart the normal ebb and flow of stress and coping across the lifespan for all older adults. A more pragmatic approach might be asking about the individual's own development, and deviations from her own baseline of functioning. For each individual, successful coping with stress is a function of three elements: the individual's level of vulnerability, the stress that the individual encounters, and protective factors (Gatz, Kasl-Godley, & Karel, 1996). Individual vulnerability includes genetic influences, acquired biological vulnerabilities, and psychological factors that affect the individual's adaptation (e.g., a tendency to be pessimistic or think negatively; poor problem-solving skills; poor communication skills). Stress incorporates psychosocial and environmental elements, as well as the individual's perception of these elements. Protective factors include biological, psychological, or social elements that can either buffer the older adult from stress or moderate its impact, for example, being physically active, eating healthily, having effective coping skills, and relying on a solid social support network.

With all of our older adult clients, we might begin by asking how their current adaptation compares to their earlier situation. For Mrs. C., we know that many of her social supports are no longer available. We also know that her familiar physical environment has changed, after she was evicted. In some of the other case examples, we highlighted how the older person's medical status is threatened (e.g., with a cancer or cardiovascular diagnosis) and how one's current psychological adjustment may be poor (with a diagnosis of depression).

As we review their histories and consider their current adjustments, we have an implicit view of the interaction between these older adults and their interpersonal, social, and physical environments. This perspective is consistent with Lewin's (1935) classic emphasis on the interaction between person and environment and with seminal work in geropsychology focusing on the interaction between the individual's capacity and environmental characteristics that may affect the development and course of disorders (e.g., Lawton, 1980, 1982). As described in Chapter 1, the biopsychosocial model is a sound framework to depict the factors that affect the probability of developing any particular mental disorder in later life (see Figure 1.5). The important element is the dynamic interaction among the individual's biological vulnerability or predisposition, the situational stressors of life events or life circumstances, and the individual's psychological coping mechanisms. This conceptualization provides a framework for assessment and subsequent intervention, which we turn to next.

Assessment Strategies

Litt and his colleagues (Litt, Tennen, & Affleck, 2011) reviewed approaches for assessing stress and coping. They began by defining coping, the major focus of assessment, as "the cognitive and behavioral effort of the person in response to stressors that determine how those stressors will affect physical and emotional well-being" (p. 387). They remind us that from the outset of this field, the relationships among stress, coping, and health indicators were considered dynamic (see Figure 6.2). Several aspects interact to affect the individual's physical or mental stress, including: dispositional factors (e.g., personality; past history); situational factors (e.g., the appraisal of the situation; the individual's situation-specific self-efficacy); and the individual's coping skills.

Aldwin (2011) reviewed more than 90 measures of coping. Given the interactional nature of the stress and coping model, she emphasized process models of coping that highlight both the individual's perceptions and coping strategies and the specific nature of the stress or challenges. Skinner and her colleagues (2003) summarized the situation well:

> If one takes the coping system, which included not only the individual's way(s) of coping but also the specific stressor(s) and demands, individual appraisals, and currently available personal and social resources, as the focal unit, then a particular pattern of coping can be considered diagnostic of the state of the entire system."(p. 230)

To implement an interactive, ecological approach, assessment within the stress and coping framework usually focuses on the individual's vulnerabilities, the stresses to which she is exposed, and the protective factors that may mitigate the stress process.

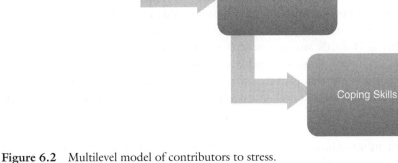

Figure 6.2 Multilevel model of contributors to stress.
Source: Adapted from Litt, Tennen, & Affleck (2011).

Assessing individual vulnerabilities

One of the key elements for assessment is the older adult's biological vulnerability. For example, two aspects are particularly important when getting Mrs. C.'s history: her experience of chronic illness (Garroway & Rybarczyk, 2015), and previous episodes of mental disorder, in this case depression.

The interaction of physical and mental health in later life is a complex, interdependent process. From the brief case description, we know that Mrs. C. is currently coping with cervical cancer and the possibility of other health problems. It will be important to assess Mrs. C.'s history of coping with chronic illness since this chronic strain is a robust predictor of poor mental health in later life (Krause, 1995a). Thus, we need to understand where in the coping process we encounter Mrs. C. as she faces the chronic illness of cancer and its treatment.

Moos and Schaefer (1984) suggested that illness brings with it seven coping tasks, three specifically linked to illness and four more-general: dealing with the physiological consequences of the illness (e.g., symptoms, pain, disability); dealing with the treatment environment (e.g., hospital, rehabilitation facility, etc.); developing and maintaining good working relations with the health care staff; maintaining emotional equilibrium; maintaining a sense of self, including a sense of one's own competence and mastery (and self-efficacy, Zautra, Hoffman, & Reich, 1996); maintaining good relations with one's social support system (family members and friends); and preparing for what the future might bring (Aldwin, 2011). Returning to Mrs. C., these seven areas offer a framework through which clinicians may explore the impact of her physical condition (cancer) and its impacts.

Another focus of assessment should be the history of the mental disorder itself: Is this Mrs. C.'s first bout of depression? Is it a recurrent pattern? Did Mrs. C. have significant depression earlier in life, only to have it vanish until recently? Each of these patterns would have different implications for treatment and the likely course of the disorder. (See Chapter 9 for a fuller discussion of major depression and its impacts.)

Assessing life stresses

Two aspects of life stresses should be assessed: the individual's subjective perception of the stress, and the "objective" indicators of stress. Each component must be understood, as distinct and in interaction with the other (Aldwin, 2007, 2011).

In Donna's case, her subjective perception of stress focuses us on a simple question: What is Donna's assessment of how stressful, upsetting, or overwhelming her situation is? Cohen, Kamarck, and Mermelstein (1983) developed a set of 10 self-report questions for this purpose, the Perceived Stress Scale (PSS), which has remained a popular tool in clinical and research contexts. Some sample items of the PSS include the following:

- In the last month, how often have you been upset because of something that happened unexpectedly?
- In the last month, how often have you felt that you could not cope with all the things that you had to do?
- In the last month, how often have you felt difficulties were piling up so high that you could not overcome them?

Cohen et al. found that perceived stress was associated with illness, illness symptoms, and a range of health behaviors. The PSS illustrates the usefulness of a standardized inquiry into the individual's perceptions.

Objective assessments of stress have typically focused on checklists of life events. A classic example of this type of measure is the Social Readjustment Rating Scale (SRRS; Holmes & Rahe, 1967), which asks respondents to rate the degree to which a large number of life events are stressful. The SRRS considers both positive and negative events as stressful, because even positive events (e.g., getting married; having a baby) require an adjustment that may be perceived as stressful. Most stress, however, comes from a series of little stressors, or daily hassles, that include irritations and demands that occur in daily life. In general, the number of daily hassles that are reported on a weekly basis tend to decrease with age, most likely due to the fact that, as social roles decrease with age, so do the hassles associated with those roles (Aldwin, Yancura, & Boeninger, 2007).

A good example of an elder-specific stress checklist is the Elders Life Stress Inventory (ELSI; Aldwin, 1990), which includes 31 items that measure whether or not the respondent has had specific stressful experiences over the past year. A helpful aspect of the ELSI is that it encompasses both stressful events (e.g., death of a spouse; death of a child; major personal illness or injury; retirement) and stressful processes (e.g., deterioration of relationship with a child or spouse) that affect older adults. However, there are some limitations to checklists. If Donna merely endorses an item, it tells us little about the impact of that event on her subsequent adjustment and it reveals little about the specific context in which the event occurred.

Instead of checklists, a structured interview or a clinical interview may be used to assess current stresses. For example, a structured approach designed to understand age-specific stressors is the Louisville Older Persons Stress Scale (LOPES; Murrell, Norris, & Hutchins, 1984) which includes 54 items that are administered in an interview format. For each stressful event that is identified as having occurred in the past six months, the interview evaluates salient characteristics of the stressful event, including information about the degree of change required by the stressor, desirability of the changes, novelty of the stressor, preoccupation with the stressor, and the exact date of the occurrence. According to Murrell et al., the most frequent stressful life events among adults were health problems whereas the most undesirable life events were the loss of a home and the death of a loved one—all challenges Mrs. C. has faced.

Emphasizing a clinical interview approach to understanding stressors, Krause (1995b) listed life stresses under the major roles that older adults play, such as spouse, parent, grandparent, etc. In addition to a standardized list, it is also helpful to ask an open-ended question at the end of each section. For example, under the section on the parental role, it is useful to ask whether anything else had happened with their children (Krause, 1995b). This question would allow Pat to discuss her current concerns about her son's company and its finances. Another follow-up inquiry may focus on whether the life stress was desirable or undesirable. In short, by using an interview format, the clinician can gauge three elements of the older adult's life stresses: their frequency, their perceived saliency, and their desirability. In Jason's case, the interview might reveal the importance of his long-standing and valued role as a union member and the negative impact that possibly losing this role has had on his well-being.

Assessing protective factors

It is important to assess two types of protective factors: the individual's own coping capacity and the environment that can either help or hinder effective coping.

Individual coping   There are two basic approaches to assessing an individual's coping: a trait approach or a state approach (see Aldwin, 2007 and 2011 for thorough reviews). The trait approach assumes that the individual's coping style is fairly stable, regardless of the particular type of stress that she encounters. In contrast, the state approach assumes that the process of coping may vary across time, depending upon the particular stressor encountered. These different assumptions have different implications for assessment strategies.

Those who focus on coping styles as traits use standardized questionnaires to assess the individual's general pattern of coping, often called *dispositional coping*. A popular dispositional measure is the Coping Orientations to Problems Experienced scale

(COPE; Carver, Scheier, & Weintraub, 1989) consisting of 60 self-report items. The COPE provides scores on three main clusters of strategies (Problem-focused coping; Emotion-focused coping; Dysfunctional coping) with each cluster containing five specific scales (see Table 6.1 for a full description of the COPE scales and a sample item for each scale). Notably, a brief version of the COPE containing only 28 items is available (Carver, 1997).

Cross-sectional research has documented that individuals of different ages use dissimilar dispositional coping strategies. For example, Folkman et al. (1987) found that older adults used more positive reappraisal and distancing as coping strategies whereas younger adults tended to seek social support more often and used more confrontive coping styles. Diehl, Coyle, and Labouvie-Vief (1996) found that older adults used a combination of coping strategies indicative of greater impulse control and they tended to evaluate conflict situations more positively than younger adults. Segal, Hook, and Coolidge (2001) used the COPE to examine dispositional coping styles in younger and older adults and they found that older adults used dysfunctional coping strategies at lower levels than younger adults. Specifically, older adults were less likely to use focusing on and venting of emotions, mental disengagement, and alcohol or drugs to cope with their problems. In the problem- and emotion-focused clusters, older adults were more likely to use restraint coping and religion, but less likely to use humor.

Important cultural differences also have been found in the factor structure of the brief COPE. In a sample of African American and White dementia caregivers, for example, Kim, Knight, and Longmire (2007) found three factors: active coping, avoidant coping, and faith-oriented coping. In contrast, in a sample of Korean American caregivers, Kim and Knight (2008) found only two factors: active-cognitive coping and social support. These findings illustrate the broader point that standard measures of coping must be viewed through the lens of cultural differences, as well as individual differences.

In contrast to dispositional measures of coping, the process-oriented measures focus on the individual's reaction to a specific stressor or type of stressor. The most widely used process measure of coping is the Ways of Coping Questionnaire (WCQ; Folkman & Lazarus, 1988). The WCQ is designed to identify the thoughts and actions an individual has used to cope with a *specific* stressful encounter, and as such, it measures coping processes, not coping dispositions. It contains 50 self-report items and provides scores on eight empirically derived factors (see Table 6.2 for descriptions of the factors and sample items).

Aldwin (2011) notes that many current assessment approaches fail to appreciate the nuances of coping in later life. To illustrate, she described a woman who used avoidant coping to handle a tricky situation: Her daughter-in-law ordered her out of the delivery room, despite the grandmother's eager expectation of the grandchild's arrival. The woman left, without making a comment. On a checklist, this might be categorized as avoidance—leaving the scene. When interviewed, the grandmother said that she knew the daughter-in-law was in a difficult time of the delivery and her "hormones were talking." In addition, the grandmother knew that having a good relationship with her daughter-in-law for the long term was more important than being in the room for the grandchild's birth. She realized that the event was not about her, but about her daughter-in-law and new grandchild. Aldwin (2011) noted

Table 6.1 COPE clusters, specific scale definitions, and sample items

Strategy type	Definition	Example
Problem-focused cluster		
Active coping	Taking active steps to try to remove or circumvent the stressor or to ameliorate its effects	I concentrate my efforts on doing something about it.
Planning	Thinking about how to act upon a stressor	I try to come up with a strategy about what to do.
Suppression of competing activities	Putting other projects aside or trying to avoid becoming distracted by other events	I keep myself from getting distracted by other thoughts or activities.
Restraint coping	Waiting until an appropriate opportunity to act presents itself	I restrain myself from doing anything too quickly.
Seeking social support for instrumental reasons	Seeking advice, assistance, or information	I try to get advice from someone about what to do.
Emotion-focused cluster		
Seeking social support for emotional reasons	Seeking moral support, sympathy, or understanding	I get sympathy and understanding from someone.
Positive reinterpretation and growth	Reappraising a stressor in positive terms	I try to see it in a different light, to make it seem more positive.
Acceptance	Recognizing the reality of a stressful situation	I learn to live with it.
Turning to religion	Utilizing religious beliefs	I pray more than usual.
Humor	Taking a light-hearted approach to a stressful situation	I laugh about the situation.
Dysfunctional cluster		
Focus on and venting of emotions	Focusing on the distress one is feeling and ventilating those feelings	I let my feelings out.
Denial	Refusing to believe that the stressor exists or trying to act as though the stressor is not real	I say to myself, "This isn't real."
Behavioral disengagement	Reducing one's effort to deal with the stressor	I just give up trying to reach my goal.
Mental disengagement	Reducing one's thoughts about the stressor	I turn to work or other substitute activities to take my mind off things.
Alcohol/drug use	Using alcohol or drugs in response to a stressor	I use alcohol or drugs to make myself feel better.

Source: Adapted from Carver et al. (1989).

Table 6.2 WCQ factors, definitions, and sample items

Scale name	Definition	Example
Confrontive coping	Aggressive efforts to alter the situation and suggests some degree of hostility and risk-taking	I stood my ground and fought for what I wanted.
Distancing	Cognitive efforts to detach oneself from the situation and to minimize its significance	I went on as if nothing had happened.
Self-controlling	Efforts to regulate one's feelings and actions	I tried to keep my feelings to myself.
Seeking social support	Efforts to seek informational support, tangible support, and emotional support	I talked to someone to find out more about the situation.
Accepting responsibility	Efforts to acknowledges one's own role in the problem with a concomitant theme of trying to put things right	I apologized or did something to make up.
Escape-avoidance	Wishful thinking and behavioral efforts to escape or avoid the problem	I hoped for a miracle.
Planful problem solving	Deliberate problem-focused efforts to alter the situation, coupled with a rational approach to solving the problem	I made a plan of action and followed it.
Positive reappraisal	Efforts to create positive meaning by focusing on personal growth	I changed or grew as a person in a good way.

Source: Adapted from Folkman & Lazarus (1988).

that this mature coping strategy—decentering, understanding that someone else's needs were more important—is typically not included in standard checklists.

In Donna's case or in Mrs. C.'s case, we might focus on how she has coped with depression in the past, perhaps using the Self-Help Inventory (Burns, Shaw, & Crocker, 1987) which consists of 45 items that include behavioral strategies (e.g., "get busy"), cognitive strategies (e.g., "remind myself that my upset will pass and I will feel good again"), and interpersonal strategies (e.g., "talk to a friend or relative that I like").

The coping environment It is also important to assess the individual's coping environment, including the physical environment: Does it present additional challenges in the face of impairment? Does it facilitate her adaptation? Consider Mrs. C.'s situation: She has recently moved from a familiar physical environment (her home of 30 years) and she reports a dwindling social environment.

We should not focus solely on her friends and family, however. It is also important to gauge the range of institutional and organizational resources that Mrs. C. can call upon (Smyer, 1995). For example, we know that Mrs. C. receives SSI. Is she also linked to the "aging network" in her community? Does she receive meals-on-wheels? Does she attend programs at her local senior center? Because many older adults do not receive formal services from agencies or organizations but rather obtain informal help from friends and family members, both informal and formal elements of support must be gauged when assessing the coping environment. Assessing these resources often leads directly to the development and implementation of a treatment plan.

In their review of assessment approaches, Litt et al. (2011) highlight three short-comings of the conceptualizations of stress and coping: Most schemes are static, not reflecting the dynamic interactions of elements; the majority of the literature treats coping as a trait, relatively stable across time and situations; and few assessment approaches take into account the variability of changing situations.

When they turn to assessment strategies, Litt et al. (2011) again raise important concerns. Most approaches are cross-sectional in nature, asking for current reports on stress and coping. They tend to be general, not tailored to the specifics of the situation as perceived by the individual. They are often retrospective—asking for recall across different time spans (a day, a week, a month, a year). Finally, they tend to be "always adaptive," with a strong bias in many measures to ask about adaptive responses to stress.

Litt and his colleagues (2011) suggest that today's technologies offer solutions to many of these problems in that they allow the collection of real-time data on stress and coping, as the stress arises and the coping unfolds, using individual self-report mechanisms (e.g., provided via cellphone reports). They urge the use of intensive, longitudinal designs to reflect the "ebb and flow" of coping processes in people's lives. Although such approaches are labor-intensive for both research and clinical enterprises, they argue that they produce "a richer, and admittedly more complicated, view of human adaptation, in which appraisals, coping, expectancies, and adaptational outcomes all may change over days or over minutes, and which in turn will set the stage for all these factors at the next moment in time" (Litt et al., 2011, p. 400). Aldwin (2007) strikes a similar theme as she emphasizes the usefulness of ecological momentary assessments, provided through personal digital assistants, to capture the daily processes of stress and coping.

General Treatment Strategies and Health Psychology

The field of *health psychology* is strongly associated with the stress and coping model. Health psychology is the branch of psychology that investigates the psychological factors related to wellness and illness, including the prevention, diagnosis, and treatment of medical problems. Clinical health psychology (and clinical health geropsychology) has come of age and flourished due to the mounting evidence for effectiveness of interventions used by psychologists to help medically ill patients and growing opportunities for reimbursement (Qualls & Benight, 2007). Health psychology has also expanded as the traditional dichotomy between mind and body has been replaced by the more integrative biopsychosocial framework that considers each area important to mental and physical health. Many clinical health psychologists focus their work on psychophysiological disorders, which are medical problems caused by an interaction of psychological, emotional, and physical difficulties (Molton & Raichle, 2010) and on the management of chronic illnesses (e.g., diabetes, cardiovascular disease, arthritis).

An important policy development for the practice of health psychology was the creation and development in 2002 of health and behavior (H&B) codes which allowed psychologists to bill Medicare for services provided to help older adults manage chronic medical problems. Qualls and Benight (2007) summarized the variety of services covered by these codes, including assisting patients with:

- adherence to medical treatment,
- symptom management (e.g., pain management),
- reduction of negative health behaviors (e.g., smoking),
- adjustment to the medical disorder.

These codes provide validation for the important role that psychologist can play in the management of health problems as part of a multidisciplinary team and they provided the impetus for the critical expansion of psychology's role in health care. (See Chapter 17 for a full discussion of the policy context of practice.)

Treatment Strategies

As in the other frameworks, treatment within the stress and coping paradigm follows directly from the assessment approaches. A comprehensive assessment should highlight those areas needing prompt intervention and those that form longer-term objectives. A comprehensive treatment plan should include social, physical, and mental well-being. Throughout, realistic goals should be established, focusing on those elements that are controllable. Finally, the initial assessments should be viewed as a baseline against which to judge the impact of treatment at follow-up.

When reviewing the impact of stress and coping on mental health outcomes, Aldwin (2007) summarized the literature and sounded a cautionary note: "Put simply, due to a large number of individual and situational constraints, there is no 'silver bullet' in coping that works for everyone. However, in the midst of conflicting and counterintuitive results, a much more complex picture of adaptation has emerged." (p. 182)

With this caveat in mind, five major treatment strategies are consistent with a stress and coping theoretical framework (Gatz, 1992):

- eliminating stressors,
- modifying the physical and social environment,
- teaching coping skills,
- providing social support,
- improving health practices.

As this list suggests, often the clinician must pursue several simultaneous intervention strategies, depending upon the client's life history and life circumstances. Each strategy is discussed next.

Eliminating stressors

If life stress is a major contributing factor to one's mental disorder, then one effective intervention may be to eliminate (or reduce) as many stressors as possible. The clinician can use the assessment information regarding the client's perceptions of stressors to target specific stresses for elimination. In Mrs. C's case, for example, a major stressor seems to be her recent relocation from her familiar neighborhood, with its links to friends and the church. One intervention strategy, therefore, might be to explore the possibility of relocating Mrs. C. back into her old neighborhood, in a setting that she can afford. As Mrs. C.'s situation reflects, interprofessional approaches to health and mental health are critical, with health providers collaborating not only with mental health professionals, but also with case managers, social service providers, and other community resources. Similarly, Donna's case and Jason's cases reflect the importance of comfort in working outside of traditional modalities, such as psychotherapy, to know how to effectively engage community resources with and on behalf of older adults. For example, in Donna's case, a referral was made to the Area Agency on Aging for an initial assessment of eligibility for services to assist Steve with his activities of daily living, giving Donna some relief from direct caregiving.

Modifying the environment

Within the interactionist perspective on stress and coping, the context directly affects the individual's well-being. Therefore, intervention strategies can target aspects of the physical or social environment that work against the client. For example, the physical environment may act as a barrier to the older client's active social involvement (see Box 6.1). Assessing the impact of the environment may

---

Box 6.1 Prevention starts at home: Eliminating potential problems in the physical environment

The physical environment may present additional stresses for an older adult. Several areas are important as potential sources of trouble:

1 Medications: Are they stored and labeled in easy-to-read letters?
2 Stairways: Are they free from clutter? Are there gates to prevent falls?
3 Water temperature: Is the water heater set to 120^0 or lower? Are hot water pipes insulated or exposed?
4 Is the kitchen safe? Is there clutter near the stove? Are the knobs on the stove or the settings clearly indicated?
5 Is the bathroom safe? Are there grab bars near the toilet and the shower or tub? Is there a bath mat that might slip? (Could it be replaced with bathroom carpeting?) Is there a skid-resistant mat in the shower or tub?

Source: Adapted from Mace & Rabins (2001).

require mental health professionals to collaborate with occupational therapists or others to optimize their client's functioning.

Consider the case of an older woman with deteriorating arthritis in her knees. She lives on the second floor of a duplex, with steep stairs. She enjoyed gardening for many years, but she can no longer bend or stoop in the garden. She refuses to change apartments to the ground floor: "It's too dangerous. You never know who's going to break in and knock you in the head." Yet she complains that there's nothing left for her to do. The solution? Consider a window garden, or involving her in a local gardening program that can bring gardening enthusiasm and aid to her apartment. The specifics will vary by location and the resources available. The universal element, however, is that the clinician broadens the therapeutic role to consider the ecology of the coping that the client brings with her, the fit between the client's capacities and the demands of the physical and social environment.

Teaching coping skills

A third strategy focuses on improving the client's skills for coping with current and future stressors. Consider the case of mild to moderate depression. A skill-based approach has been developed focusing on the client's skills in identifying the proximal causes of negative and positive mood changes, the link between daily events and mood, and the client's control over these elements (Lewinsohn, Munoz, Youngren, & Zeiss, 1992). This approach has been extended to older adults, with impressive results (Gallagher-Thompson & Thompson, 2010; Thompson, Dick-Siskin, Coon, Powers, & Gallagher-Thompson, 2010).

Similarly, interventions have been designed to increase older clients' sense of control over positive events and mastery of negative events (e.g., Reich & Zautra, 1989, 1990). In this case, the focus was not solely on depressed older adults. The target audiences were recently bereaved or disabled people. The common element, however, was a skill-building emphasis on increasing self-initiated positive events and responding effectively to negative events. Mindfulness meditation is another skill that has garnered empirical support for the treatment of health problems including pain, depression, and anxiety (see review by Davis, Zautra, Johnson, Murray, & Okvat, 2007).

Acceptance and commitment therapy (ACT) has become a highly visible treatment approach to help older adults adapt to what they cannot change while changing what they can (Wetherell et al., 2011). As an alternative, values-based approach, ACT now complements strategies for improving coping that have been emphasized in past decades (e.g., Problem-Solving Therapy) (Bower & Wetherell, 2015). Wetherell and her colleagues summarized the ACT approach:

> The goal of ACT is not to reduce the frequency or severity of aversive internal experiences (e.g., thoughts, emotions, sensations, memories, urges), but rather to reduce the struggle to control or eliminate these experiences and increase engagement in meaningful life activities. Over the course of treatment, ACT balances acceptance with commitment to value-directed behavior change. The acceptance component includes mindfulness techniques designed to foster nonjudgmental awareness of experience, such as noticing thoughts without perseveration or avoidance of the thought content. (p. 127)

The impact of interventions will vary depending on their timing within the stress and coping processes and the goodness of fit between the coping strategy and the situational demands. Problem-focused strategies are more likely to lead to a decrease in psychological symptoms in situations that are perceived as controllable. In contrast, emotion-focused efforts are associated with lower symptom levels in situations that are perceived as uncontrollable (Aldwin, 2011).

In Mrs. C.'s case, we might try to increase her skill at controlling her depressed mood by helping her identify what she can do to give herself some pleasure in her day, as well as what she can do to avoid the day's negative stresses, and by increasing her awareness of positive moods. By giving her skills to manage moods, we may improve her adaptation, even in the face of chronic, challenging stresses (Gallagher-Thompson & Thompson, 2010).

Providing social support

A common strategy for those encountering life stresses is to find others who are coping with similar problems. For many older adults, however, this is easier said than done. Consider the case of a 90-year-old widow who has outlived her older friends, her age-mates, and even many of her younger friends. Her children are in their late 60s, coping with the challenges of their own aging. Mrs. C., our 80-year-old, reflects this situation in her lament: "My family—they're all dead, my mama, my papa, everyone." Perhaps one tack for the therapist is to engage others as social supports for Mrs. C.

Two challenges quickly arise, however: What type of support and how? Two major types of support are emotional support and instrumental support. The timing of these, however, may vary depending upon when we encounter the client:

> The needs of clients may vary depending upon where clients are located temporally in the natural history of an event. Early in the history of a stressor, emotional support may be most useful, but later on tangible assistance may be more helpful as the client becomes more willing to take concrete steps to reconstruct his or her life. (Krause, 1995a, p. 213)

In Mrs. C's case, for example, she may need emotional support in coping with the recently discovered cancer diagnosis. A support group that can provide a shared sense of experience and understanding may be an important first-step of linking her to outside help. Later on, she may call upon group members for their advice on how to handle the details of chemotherapy and its accompanying unpleasant side effects.

All social support is not the same, however, and the context in which support is offered is critical to determining its perceived effectiveness (Uchino, 2009). Some peers may encourage you to "lean on me—let me share your burden." Others might encourage you to "pull yourself up by your bootstraps." This advice is fairly common from relatives and friends of clients with depression. Which type of support is best?

Evidence suggests that the effectiveness of each strategy depends upon the timing of the support in relation to the impairment:

> It comes as no surprise that healthy individuals gain in mental health with a social net-work that encourages self-reliance. For those with an established impairment, these types

of messages may also ease feelings of helplessness. It is during the time of loss that the social network messages of self-reliance are incongruent with the person's experience and his or her needs. During this period of crisis, receiving messages that you can rely on others, the "lean on me" message, appears to play a valuable part in limiting the damage caused by the crisis events, perhaps by providing ways of maintaining a sense of control. (Zautra et al., 1995, pp. 167–168)

In Mrs. C.'s case, she may be in need of emotional support that allows her to rely on others, as she copes with the recent diagnosis of cancer. Thus, the nature of the support group that she joins may be very important. In Donna's case, joining a caregiver support group may provide emotional support, affirmation that she is not alone in feeling the stress of caregiving, and practical tips for day-to-day caregiving and stress reduction.

Improving health practices

The interaction of physical and mental well-being in later life makes working with older adults a challenge. Chronic stress can adversely affect the client's immune system functioning and health status (e.g., Gruenewald & Kemeny, 2007; Penedo & Dahn, 2005). For example, as in Donna's case, the chronic stress of caregiving for an ill family member adversely affects cardiovascular, metabolic, and immune system functioning (Vitaliano, Zhang, & Scanlan, 2003) and also causes increases in depressive and anxiety symptoms, helplessness, social isolation, and perceived loss of control (Fortinsky, Tennen, Frank, & Affleck, 2007). In contrast, psychosocial interventions (e.g., cognitive restructuring, relaxation, hypnosis, exercise, etc.) can positively affect immune system functioning (Penedo & Dahn, 2005), and, perhaps, health. In short, the interaction of physical and mental well-being requires the clinician to work closely with the client's medical team.

In Mrs. C.'s case, for example, we may want to assess her current nutritional status, assure that the cancer treatments are undertaken, and coordinate with her doctor, upon whom she relies.

Summary and Conclusions

The stress and coping model is an important complement to the other models presented in this section of the book because, at some level, all mental health practitioners help their clients cope with whatever difficult experiences they are facing. This chapter reviewed the three key elements of the stress and coping process (strain; stressors; and transactions), and discussed the assessment and intervention approaches associated with the model, with applications to older adults.

The cases at the start of this chapter illustrate broader themes of the interaction of the individual and his or her ecology. The outcomes of coping will have positive or negative effects on physiological, psychological, social, and cultural functioning (Aldwin, 2007). In addition, increasing attention is focused on the "fundamental" causes of income inequality and its impacts (Hudson, 2016; Phelan, Link, & Tehranifar, 2010). We will return to these issues in Chapter 17.

For now, though, although excitement for this growing area of research and practice is understandable, caution is also necessary because our understanding of life stresses, coping, and aging is far from complete. Aldwin and Igarashi (2016) noted that the study of coping and aging is increasingly emphasizing a "self-regulation perspective," pointing out that older adults both respond to immediate stressors and also arrange their lives to minimize stressors and maximize positive affect. They link this capacity directly to resilience (Zautra & Reich, 2011), a framework we described in Chapter 3.

Aldwin and Igarashi (2016) provide a useful summary of the field and its growth:

> The field of coping and aging has come a long way in the past few decades: from early studies suggesting that older adults are more passive and "worse" copers, to the current recognition that coping processes and adaptive styles in later life are flexible, develop through experience, and result in complex patterns of changes in appraisal and self-regulation processes that vary by resource level and environmental demands. Older adults, barring cognitive impairment or long-standing mental illness, have learned self-regulation skills that minimize distress, and cope in ways that make the most efficient use of changing resources. They can become more adept at regulating their emotions, and focus on maintenance of meaningful close relationships. These skills may form the basis of resilience in later life." (Aldwin & Igarashi, 2016, p. 559)

Critical Thinking / Discussion Questions

1 Describe some of your common coping strategies for dealing with distress and difficult life circumstances. How might your self-awareness of your preferred strategies impact your clinical work with older adults, from the stress and coping perspective?
2 What approach would you take for an older adult client who has a hard time recognizing and describing her own typical coping strategies?
3 Coping can be conceptualized as reflecting either stable dispositional traits or situationally determined strategies. Which perspective resonates most clearly with you and why?

Website Resources

American Psychological Association Office on Aging: Coping with Stress and Anxiety
http://www.apa.org/pi/aging/09-33-coping-with-stress-fin.pdf
National Institute of Mental Health: Fact Sheet on Stress
https://www.nimh.nih.gov/health/publications/stress/index.shtml
American Psychological Association: How Stress Affects Your Health
http://www.apa.org/helpcenter/stress.aspx
The Mayo Clinic: Stress Symptoms—Effects on Your Body and Behavior
http://www.mayoclinic.org/healthy-lifestyle/stress-management/in-depth/stress-symptoms/art-20050987

References

Abramson, C. M. (2016). Unequal aging: Lessons from inequality's end game. *Public Policy & Aging Report, 26*(2), 68–72. doi: 10.1093/ppar/prw006

Ader, R. E. (Ed.) (2007). *Psychoneuroimmunology* (4th ed.). New York, NY: Academic Press/ Elsevier.

Adler, N., Pantell, M. S., O'Donovan, A., Blackburn, E., Cawthon, R., Koster, A., ...Epel, E. (2013). Educational attainment and late life telomere length in the Health, Aging, and Body Composition Study. *Brain Behavior & Immunology, 27*(1), 15–21.

Adler, N. E., & Prather, A. A. (2015). Determinants of health and longevity. In R. Kaplan, M. L. Spittel, & D. H. David (Eds.) *Population health: Behavioral and social science insights* (pp. 411–423). AHRQ Publication No. 15-0002. Rockville, MD: Agency for Healthcare Research and Quality and Office of Behavioral and Social Sciences Research, National Institutes of Health.

Aldwin, C. M. (1990). The Elders Life Stress Inventory: Egocentric and nonegocentric stress. In M. A. Parris Stephens, J. H. Crowther, S. E. Hobfoll, & D. L. Tennenbaum (Eds.), *Stress and coping in later-life families* (pp. 49–69). New York, NY: Hemisphere.

Aldwin, C. M. (2007). *Stress, coping, and development: An integrative perspective* (2nd ed.). New York, NY: Guilford.

Aldwin, C. M. (2011). Stress and coping across the lifespan. In S. Folkman (Ed.). *The Oxford handbook of stress, health and coping* (pp. 15–34). New York, NY: Oxford University Press.

Aldwin, C. M., & Igarashi, H. (2016). Coping, optimal aging, and resilience in a sociocultural context. In V. L. Bengtson & R. A. Settersten. Jr. (Eds.). *Handbook of the theories of aging* (3rd ed., pp. 551–576). New York, NY: Springer.

Aldwin, C. M., Park, C. L., & Spiro, A. (Eds.). (2007). *Handbook of health psychology and aging*. New York, NY: Guilford.

Aldwin, C. M., Yancura, L. A., & Boeninger, D. A. (2007). Coping, health, and aging. In C. M. Aldwin, C. L. Park, & A. Spiro (Eds.), *Handbook of health psychology and aging* (pp. 210–226). New York, NY: Guilford.

Bower, E. S., & Wetherell, J. L. (2015). Late-life anxiety disorders. In P. A. Lichtenberg & B. T. Mast (Eds.), *Handbook of clinical geropsychology. Vol 2: Assessment, treatment and issues of later life* (pp. 49–78). Washington, DC: American Psychological Association. doi: 10.1037/14459-002

Boyce, W. T. (2015). Epigenomics and the unheralded convergence of the biological and social sciences. In R. Kaplan, M. L. Spittel, & D. H. David (Eds.), *Population health: Behavioral and social science insights* (pp. 219–232). AHRQ Publication No. 15-0002. Rockville, MD: Agency for Healthcare Research and Quality and Office of Behavioral and Social Sciences Research, National Institutes of Health.

Burns, D. D., Shaw, B. F., & Crocker, W. (1987). Thinking styles and coping strategies of depressed women: An empirical investigation. *Behavioral Research and Therapy, 25*, 223–225.

Carroll, J. E., Diez-Roux, A. V., Adler, N. E., & Seeman, T. E. (2013). Socioeconomic factors and leukocyte telomere length in a multi-ethnic sample: Findings from the Multi-Ethnic Study of Atherosclerosis (MESA). *Brain Behavior & Immunology, 28*, 108–114.

Carver, C. S. (1997). You want to measure coping but your protocol's too long: Consider the Brief COPE. *International Journal of Behavioral Medicine, 4*, 92–100.

Carver, C. S., Scheier, M. F., & Weintraub, J. K. (1989). Assessing coping strategies: A theoretically based approach. *Journal of Personality and Social Psychology, 56*, 267–283.

Cohen, S., Kamarck, T., & Mermelstein, R. (1983). A global measure of perceived stress. *Journal of Health and Social Behavior, 24*, 385–396.

Crystal, S. (2016). Late-life inequality in the second gilded age: Policy choices in a new context. *Public Policy & Aging Report, 26*(2), 42–47. doi: 10.1093/ppar/prw005

Crystal, S., & Shea, D. (1990). Cumulative advantage, cumulative disadvantage, and inequality among elderly people. *The Gerontologist, 30*(4), 437–443.

Crystal, S., Shea, D., & Reyes, A. (2017). Cumulative advantage, cumulative disadvantage, and evolving patterns of late-life inequality. *Gerontologist, 57,* 910–920.

Daruna, J. H. (2012). *Introduction to psychoneuroimmunology* (2nd ed.). San Diego, CA: Elsevier Academic Press.

Davis, M. C., Zautra, A. J., Johnson, L. M., Murray, K. E., & Okvat, H. A. (2007). Psychosocial stress, emotion regulation, and resilience among older adults. In C. M. Aldwin, C. L. Park, & A. Spiro (Eds.), *Handbook of health psychology and aging* (pp. 250–266). New York, NY: Guilford.

Diehl, M., Coyle, N., & Labouvie-Vief, G. (1996). Age and sex differences in strategies of coping and defense across the life span. *Psychology and Aging, 11,* 127–139.

Folkman, S., & Lazarus, R. S. (1988). *Manual for the Ways of Coping Questionnaire.* Palo Alto, CA: Consulting Psychologists Press.

Folkman, S., Lazarus, R. S., Pimley, S., & Novacek, J. (1987). Age differences in stress and coping processes. *Psychology and Aging, 2,* 171–184.

Fortinsky, R. H., Tennen, H., Frank, N., & Affleck, G. (2007). Health and psychological consequences of caregiving. In C. M. Aldwin, C. L. Park, & A. Spiro (Eds.), *Handbook of health psychology and aging* (pp. 227–249). New York, NY: Guilford.

Gallagher-Thompson, D., & Thompson, L. W. (2010). *Treating late-life depression: A cognitive-behavioral therapy approach: Therapist guide.* New York, NY: Oxford University Press.

Garroway, A. M., & Rybarczyk, B. (2015). Aging, chronic disease and the biopsychosocial model. In P. A. Lichtenberg & B. T. Mast (Eds.), *Handbook of clinical geropsychology. Vol 1: History and status of the field and perspectives on aging* (pp. 563–586). Washington, DC: American Psychological Association. doi: 10.1037/14458-024

Gatz, M. (1992). Stress, control, and psychological interventions. In M. L. Wykle, E. Kahana, & J. Kowal (Eds.), *Stress and health among the elderly* (pp. 209–222). New York, NY: Springer.

Gatz, M., Kasl-Godley, J., & Karel, M. (1996). Aging and mental disorders. In J. E. Birren & K. W. Schaie (Eds.), *Handbook of the psychology of aging* (pp. 369–382). San Diego, CA: Academic Press.

Govia, I. O., Jackson, J. S., & Sellers, S. L. (2011). Social inequalities in K. L. Fingerman, C. A. Berg, J. Smith, & T. C. Antonucci (Eds.), *Handbook of life-span development* (pp. 727–744). New York, NY: Springer.

Gruenewald, T. L., & Kemeny, M. E. (2007). Psychoneuroimmunological processes in aging and health. In C. M. Aldwin, C. L. Park, & A. Spiro (Eds.), *Handbook of health psychology and aging* (pp. 97–118). New York, NY: Guilford.

Hardy, M. (2016). Societal legacies of risk and protection in the reproduction of health disparities. *Public Policy & Aging Report, 26*(2), 53–57. doi: 10.1093/ppar/prw004

Herbert, T. B., & Cohen, S. (1993). Stress and immunity in humans: A meta-analytic review. *Psychosomatic Medicine, 55,* 364–379.

Holmes, T., & Rahe, R. (1967). The social readjustment rating scale. *Journal of Psychosomatic Research, 11,* 213–218.

Hudson, R. B. (2016). Cumulative advantage and disadvantage: Across the life course, across generations. *Public Policy & Aging Report, 26*(2), 39–41. doi:10.1093/ppar/prw007

Jackson, J. S., Knight, K. M., & Rafferty, J. A. (2010). Race and unhealthy behaviors: Chronic stress, the HPA axis, and physical and mental health disparities over the life course. *American Journal of Public Health, 100*(5), 933–939. doi: 10.2105/AJPH.2008.143446

Johnson, C. J., & Johnson, F. A. (1992). Psychological distress among inner-city American elderly: Structural, developmental, and situational contexts. *Journal of Cross-Cultural Gerontology, 7,* 221–236.

Kiecolt-Glaser, J. K. (2009). Psychoneuroimmunology: Psychology's gateway to the biomedical future. *Perspectives on Psychological Science, 4,* 367–369.

Kim, J. H., & Knight, B. G. (2008). Effects of caregiver status, coping styles, and social support on the physical health of Korean American caregivers. *Gerontologist, 48,* 287–299. doi: 10.1093/geront/48.3.287

Kim, J. H., Knight, B. G., & Longmire, C. V. (2007). The role of familism in stress and coping processes among African American and White dementia caregivers: effects on mental and physical health. *Health Psychology, 26*(5), 564–576.

Krause, N. (1995a). Stress and well-being in later life: Using research findings to inform intervention design. In L. A. Bond, S. J. Cutler, & A. Grams (Eds.), *Promoting successful and productive aging* (pp. 203–219). Thousand Oaks, CA: Sage.

Krause, N. (1995b). Stress, alcohol use, and depressive symptoms in later life. *Gerontologist, 35,* 296–307.

Lawton, M. P. (1980). *Environment and aging.* Pacific Grove, CA: Brooks/Cole.

Lawton, M. P. (1982). Competence, environmental press, and the adaptation of old people. In M. P. Lawton, P. G. Windley, & T. O. Byerts (Eds.), *Aging and the environment: Theoretical approaches* (pp. 33–59). New York, NY: Springer.

Lazarus, R. S., & Folkman, S. (1984). *Stress, appraisal, and coping.* New York, NY: Springer.

Lewin, K. (1935). *A dynamic theory of personality: Selected papers of Kurt Lewin.* New York, NY: McGraw-Hill.

Lewinsohn, P. M., Munoz, R. F., Youngren, M. A., & Zeiss, M. A. (1992). *Control your depression* (Rev. ed.). New York, NY: Fireside.

Litt, M.D., Tennen, H., & Affleck, G. (2011). The dynamics of stress, coping, and health: Assessing processes in near real time. In S. Folkman (Ed.), *The Oxford handbook of stress, health and coping* (pp. 387–406). New York, NY: Oxford University Press.

Mace, N. L., & Rabins, P. V. (2001). *The 36 hour day: A family guide to caring for persons with Alzheimer Disease, related dementing illnesses, and memory loss in later life.* Baltimore, MD: The Johns Hopkins University Press.

McEwen, B. S. (1998). Protective and damaging effects of stress mediators. *New England Journal of Medicine, 338*(3), 171–179.

McEwen, B. S. (2015). The brain on stress: How behavior and the social environment "Get Under the Skin." In R. Kaplan, M. L. Spittel, & D. H. David (Eds.) *Population health: Behavioral and social science insights* (pp. 233–247). AHRQ Publication No. 15-0002. Rockville, MD: Agency for Healthcare Research and Quality and Office of Behavioral and Social Sciences Research, National Institutes of Health.

Molton, I. R., & Raichle, K. A. (2010). Psychophysiological disorders. In D. L. Segal, & M. Hersen (Eds.), *Diagnostic interviewing* (4th ed., pp. 343–369). New York, NY: Springer.

Moos, R. H., & Schaefer, J. A. (1984). The crisis of physical illness. In R. Moos (Ed.), *Coping with physical illness* (pp. 3–26). New York, NY: Plenum Press.

Murrell, S., Norris, F. H., & Hutchins, G. S. (1984). Distribution and desirability of life events in older adults: Population and policy implications. *Journal of Community Psychology, 12,* 301–311.

Needham, B. L., Carroll, J. E., Diez Roux, A.V., Fitzpatrick A. L., Moore K., Seeman, T. E. (2014). Neighborhood characteristics and leukocyte telomere length: The Multi-Ethnic Study of Atherosclerosis. *Health Place, 28*, 167–172.

Pargament, K. I. (2011). The spiritual dimension of coping: Implications for health and well-being. In S. Folkman (Ed.), *Oxford handbook of stress, health, and coping.* New York, NY: Oxford University Press.

Park, C. L. (2005). Religion as a meaning-making framework in coping with life stress. *Journal of Social Issues, 61*, 707–729.

Penedo, F. J., & Dahn, J. R. (2005). Psychoneuroimmunology and aging. In K. Vedhara & M. Irwin (Eds.), *Human psychoneuroimmunology* (pp. 81–106). New York, NY: Oxford University Press.

Phelan, J. C., Link, B. G., & Tehranifar, P. (2010). Social conditions as fundamental causes of health inequalities: Theory, evidence, and policy implications. *Journal of Health and Social Behavior, 51*(5), 528–540. doi: 10.1177/0022146510383498

Pruchno, R. A., Blow, F. C., & Smyer, M. A. (1984). Life events and interdependent lives: Implications for research and intervention. *Human Development, 27*, 31–41.

Qualls, S. H., & Benight, C. C. (2007). The role of clinical health geropsychology in the health care of older adults. In C. M. Aldwin, C. L. Park, & A. Spiro (Eds.), *Handbook of health psychology and aging* (pp. 367–389). New York, NY: Guilford.

Reich, J. W., & Zautra, A. J. (1989). A perceived control intervention for at-risk older adults. *Psychology and Aging, 4*, 415–424.

Reich, J. W., & Zautra, A. J. (1990). Dispositional control beliefs and the consequences of a control-enhancing intervention. *Journal of Gerontology: Psychological Sciences, 45*, P46–P51.

Segal, D. L., Hook, J. N., & Coolidge, F. L. (2001). Personality dysfunction, coping styles, and clinical symptoms in younger and older adults. *Journal of Clinical Geropsychology, 7*, 201–212.

Skaff, M. M. (2007). Sense of control and health: A dynamic duo in the aging process. In C. M. Aldwin, C. L. Park, & A. Spiro (Eds.), *Handbook of health psychology and aging* (pp. 186–209). New York, NY: Guilford.

Skinner, E., Edge, K., Altman, J., & Sherwood, H. (2003). Searching for the structure of coping: A review and critique of category systems for classifying ways of coping. *Psychological Bulletin, 129*, 216–269.

Smyer, M. A. (1995). Formal support in later life: Lessons for prevention. In L. A. Bond, S. J. Cutler, & A. Grams (Eds.), *Promoting successful and productive aging* (pp. 186–202). Thousand Oaks, CA: Sage.

Thompson, L. W., Dick-Siskin, L., Coon, D. W., Powers, D. V., & Gallagher-Thompson, D. (2010). *Treating late-life depression: A cognitive-behavioral therapy approach: Workbook.* New York, NY: Oxford University Press.

Uchino, B. N. (2009). Understanding the links between social support and physical health. *Perspectives on Psychological Science, 4*, 236–255.

Vedhara, K., & Irwin, M. (Eds.). (2005). *Human psychoneuroimmunology.* New York, NY: Oxford University Press.

Vitaliano, P. P., Zhang, J., & Scanlan, J. M. (2003). Is caregiving hazardous to one's physical health? A meta-analysis. *Psychological Bulletin, 129*, 946–972.

Wetherell, J. L., Afari, N., Rutledge, T., Sorrell J. T., Stoddard J.A., Petkus A. J., ...Atkinson J. H. (2011). A randomized, controlled trial of acceptance and commitment therapy and cognitive-behavioral therapy for chronic pain. *Pain, 152*(9), 2098–2107.

Zautra, A. J., Hoffman, J. M., & Reich, J. W. (1996). The role of two kinds of efficacy beliefs in maintaining the well-being of chronically stressed older adults. In B. H. Gottlieb (Ed.), *Coping with chronic stress* (pp. 269–290). New York, NY: Plenum Press.

Zautra, A. J., Reich, J. W., & Newsom, J. T. (1995). Autonomy and sense of control among older adults: An examination of their effects on mental health. In L. A. Bond, S. J. Cutler, & A. Grams (Eds.), *Promoting successful and productive aging* (pp. 153–170). Thousand Oaks, CA: Sage.

Zautra, A. J., & Reich, J. W. (2011). Resilience: The meanings, methods, and measures of a fundamental characteristic of human adaptation. In S. Folkman (Ed.). *The Oxford handbook of stress, health and coping* (pp. 173–185). New York, NY: Oxford University Press.

7

Family Systems Model

Why consider a family model of mental health and aging? Aren't older adults often abandoned by family members and left to live isolated, lonely lives in an institutional setting? We include a family systems model for conceptualizing mental health of older persons precisely because the myth of the isolated, abandoned elder is just that—a myth. Indeed, older adults nearly always are in frequent, close contact with their families (Shanas, 1979; Fingerman, Miller, & Seidel, 2009). Because of the close interrelatedness of older adults with their later-life families, it is important to consider how to support positive mental health of older persons by supporting family functioning, and also to explore the possibility that family dysfunction might deleteriously affect the mental health of older family members. The systems model for examining family relationships is a useful guide in those two endeavors, and will be described below. Before examining the conceptual model, however, a brief description of later-life families may help dispel a few other myths regarding relationships between older adults and their families. We will use the following two family situations to illustrate points throughout the chapter.

Jason Martinez, age 21, lives with Ruth and James Jones, his grandmother and her second husband, in the San Francisco Bay area. Jason's parents live by a rule that all of their children must move out on their own at age 18. Jason found it difficult to earn enough money to maintain an apartment and a car, and have a social life. After two failed roommate arrangements, he asked Ruth and James if he could live in their basement for a few months until he could get back on his feet. They agreed readily, hoping to be of some help to a grandson they viewed as floundering. Ruth and James have a long-standing conflict with Jason's parents, Nancy and Reuben, over what Ruth views as "mean rules that don't help the kids grow up." Although the entire family typically gathers for the major holidays, no one has initiated a gathering since Jason moved in with Ruth and James, a loss that Ruth mourns but

Aging and Mental Health, Third Edition. Daniel L. Segal, Sara Honn Qualls, and Michael A. Smyer.
© 2018 John Wiley & Sons, Inc. Published 2018 by John Wiley & Sons, Inc.

accepts because she believes they are just doing "what they have to do, and if Nancy can't understand that then it's her loss."

Jillian Jarvis insists vehemently that she will never leave the family farm in rural Nebraska. Last month when her daughter, Jean, came to visit from Chicago she was appalled to see the unkempt house, lack of food in the refrigerator, and Jillian's obvious dishevelment. Jean immediately drove her mother to a major medical center in a nearby city for a full evaluation. The initial evaluation showed that Jillian was malnourished and had significant bruising on several parts of her body, and that her vision and hearing were significantly impaired. Despite Jillian's protests, Jean made arrangements to place her mother in a nursing home in the city. Before the hospital social worker could accomplish the placement, John and JoAnn, Jean's brother and sister, arrived on the scene and insisted on taking Jillian back home "where she wants to be and where she belongs." They angrily demanded that the social worker produce evidence of their mother's incompetence "before she just goes and puts her away for all time." Jillian kept wringing her hands and saying she was sure that if Ed were only alive he would know what to do to keep the kids from fighting. The physician and social worker decided to hold Jillian in the hospital two more days to try to resolve the family disagreement, despite the fact that insurance was no longer paying for the hospital care.

Introduction to the Model: Aging Families

When you think of family, what do you picture? Do you picture children with parents whose task it is to rear them? Do you picture aunts, uncles, grandparents, and cousins? Family theorists traditionally have referred to the first kind of family as a *nuclear family* and the second set of relationships as *extended family* (Parsons, 1949). One implication is that the nuclear family is more important to individual development than is the extended family. Theory and data, however, suggest that the extended family is intimately involved with daily life functions of persons of all ages (Connidis, 2010) and maintains strong, solid bonds (Davey & Takagi, 2013). Sibling relationships are powerful relationships in adulthood just as they are in childhood. Parenting does not end when children go off to college or even when they create their own nuclear families. In essence, a model of family development, like models of individual development, cannot presume development ends when children enter adulthood. Family development is truly a life course phenomenon. Thus, the primacy of nuclear family relationships should not be presumed.

A second implication of the traditional image of nuclear and extended family as the context for aging is that the image is too simplistic for the complexities of modern families. Family structures now exhibit remarkable variability. Single parenting, cohabitation without marriage, step-relationships among divorced and blended families, and grandparents rearing grandchildren are a few of the variations in family life within which we age.

Marriage is an obvious form of daily family contact experienced by most older men (72%) and some older women (46%) over the age of 65 (Administration on Aging, 2014). The rates of widowhood are much higher for women (35%) than men (11%) over age 65. The rates of marriage decrease with advanced age, resulting in much lower rates of marriage for older women in particular. Other forms of intimate partnerships have increased in recent decades as social norms have shifted to acknowledge and value nonmarital intimate relationships. Generally, older persons report high rates of satisfaction with their later-life marriages (Umberson, Williams, Power, Chen, & Campbell, 2005), a phenomenon that appears to be at least partially a function of the tendency of the current older adult cohort to prize marital longevity, commitment, and contentment.

Contact with children occurs regularly for the vast majority of older persons. In contrast to the myth that our mobile society has limited face-to-face contact between adults and their aging parents, several studies report that regular weekly contact between older adults and their children is normative even among very old (85+) adults (Swartz, 2009). Even those living far away are involved in older person's lives through contacts, photographs, and memories. Family members view the frequency and nature of support differently, suggesting that reports of family connectedness are influenced by the reporter's position within the family (Kim, Zarit, Birditt, & Fingerman, 2014).

Sibling relationships are also highly valued by older adults despite the generally weaker ties of obligation than parent–child relationships (Bedford & Avioli, 2012). The sibling relationship evolves across the lifespan with lower rates of contact and investment in early adulthood that increase into old age. Siblings are not often the primary care providers, but maintain ties of mutual assistance and emotional connection that gain in meaning and salience across the lifespan.

Most older adults are grandparents (about 80%) and among older adults with adult children over age 40, 95% are grandparents (Szinovacz, 1998). Grandparents can be involved in the socialization of younger family members, in the exchange of goods and services within families, and in assisting their children in times of crisis (e.g., divorce, serious physical illness). Yet, these relationships are not all positive, reflecting variation in patterns within even the same family (Suitor, Gilligan, & Pillemer, 2016). Furthermore, the timing and sequencing of the transition to grandparenting is not in the older adult's control, and not surprisingly, the meaning of the grandparent role varies. For example, Kivnick (1985) describes five dimensions of meaning that mid-life and older adults may derive from the role: role centrality, valued eldership, immortality through clan, reinvolvement with personal past, and indulgence. As with other family relationships, the timing and sequencing of grandparenting within the life course and the broader social context of the relationship shapes the role definition and meaning (Suitor et al., 2016).

Other family ties certainly exist as well, but much less is known about them. Nieces and nephews, cousins, in-laws, and the variety of blended relationships that occur as a consequence of divorce and remarriage also are part of the relationship network of older adults. The structures of families vary across racial and ethnic groups, partnership structures (e.g., gay and straight), rural and urban, and social class. The size of families, the age at marriage or partnership, and patterns of divorce and remarriage are among the many family characteristics that are shaped by cultural identity and socialization.

What do people do in these relationships? A popular image is that of a frail older person being cared for by children and grandchildren. And this image is accurate—caregiving and care receiving is an important function of families of all ages, including later-life families (Qualls, 2016). However, the period of time when that image accurately characterizes later-life families is typically quite brief, and occurs at the very end of life. Of course, aging increases the probability that care recipients will be parents rather than children, but does not guarantee it. In contrast, a more accurate image would portray older adults as care providers because across the life course, including during old age, adults provide a significant amount of childcare services to their children, grandchildren, and great-grandchildren. They also give care to adult children who need assistance because of disability, injury, or illness. Caregiving occurs in all families, in multiple directions of caregiving and care receiving, with older adults participating most often as caregivers and only in advanced age as care recipients.

Families serve a variety of functions other than providing care for frail or disabled persons (Fingerman et al., 2009). As is true at any age, family relationships support the development of family members in a myriad of ways. Families often celebrate individual developmental milestones, provide mutual support in periods of stress, and share decision-making. Families are also the context in which values are socialized, a sense of personal lineage is created, and the most powerful individual developmental tasks are accomplished (Hagestad, 1986). For example, family relationships are the context within which individuals struggle with the dialectics between autonomy and dependency, connectedness and separateness, and continuity and change (Bengtson & Kuypers, 1984).

Individual developmental tasks and the events of later life often affect other family members. For example, three later-life transitions usually force a restructuring of family relationships: (1) the emptying and reemptying of the "nest," (2) retirement, and (3) onset of chronic physical illness. Individual life transitions such as these affect several key aspects of family relationships: time structure, roles, communication, power balance, and nurturance (Qualls, 1995). Families are primary components of the "life event web" in which the ripple effects of major life changes are felt (Pruchno, Blow, & Smyer, 1984).

Despite the familiar normative patterns of family contact among generations across the lifespan, families often find themselves organized in complex new structures. Recent decades have witnessed profound changes in the structure of Western populations that also affect family functioning. Among the demographic changes that alter family life are increased life expectancy, declining fertility, increased participation of women in the workforce, increased rates of cohabitation at all ages, increased rates of divorce, and ethnic diversification. The separate and cumulative effects of these shifts alter the structure and functioning of families into what is often referred to as a *beanpole family*. For example, families are far more likely to contain three or more generations. Family members tend to spend far more years in each relationship (e.g., perhaps 80–90 years as a sister and 60–70 years as a mother), but have fewer sisters or aunts or cousins from which to choose models or special relationships (Hagestad, 1988).

In summary, families are an active, powerful interpersonal context for older adults. Family contact is frequent and meaningful. Like younger persons, older adults meet many basic social needs within the family context and thus are vulnerable to the rippling effects of major life events in the lives of many family members. Deaths, divorces, marriages, births, retirement, illness, injury, misfortune—all occur in the families of older persons and alter the ways in which older persons' needs are met.

Family Dynamics: A Systems Model

How do families interact to accomplish their tasks? What causes conflict? Distress? Which family interactions might play a role in the development of mental disorders in older persons? What impact do mental disorders have on the families of older persons and on their efforts to provide care?

As applied to behavioral sciences, the systems model emphasizes the social context in which human beings live (Anderson, Sabatelli, & Kosutic, 2013). Problems are conceptualized as residing in the relationships among the elements of the social unit, rather than in the individual. Systems theory acknowledges that there are indeed organically based problems (e.g., Alzheimer's disease), but the problems are experienced as particularly distressing or problematic when the social unit cannot manage them effectively.

As a primary social unit, families constitute a system within which the mental health of older adults is created, experienced, and challenged. The family of an older adult is highly likely to be an idiosyncratically defined extended family constellation. In other words, it is not perfectly obvious who is "the family" that is relevant to a systems analysis. Spouses, adult children, nieces and nephews, siblings, and neighbors may be among those who are involved in significant ways in the life of the older person seeking assistance. The systems model would suggest beginning with those whose regular contact is important to the daily functioning of the older person. Other key persons may be included later if their interaction patterns are demonstrated to be significant to the functioning of the unit (e.g., in Jillian Jarvis's family the hospital social worker found that she was not dealing with all of the relevant members of the system). In the case of institutionalized older adults, the social unit might include key staff (e.g., the nurse aides who tend to the resident regularly, the charge nurse, the social worker, and perhaps a dietitian or administrator, depending on the nature of the problem) plus relevant members of the family (Norris, 2009).

The system is considered to be a complex interactive unit whose members are directly and indirectly affected by each other continually (Anderson et al., 2013). Each member of the unit is both actor and reactor. In traditional social science frameworks, cause and effect relationships are conceptualized as if they occur in linear sequences (e.g., A causes B; his remark made me angry). In contrast, systems theory argues that complex systems such as families are better conceptualized in terms of circular causality. Events are related through multiple interacting cycles in which it is arbitrary to identify one event as the cause and one as the consequence because if one interrupted the cycle at another moment those same events might be conceptualized differently. For example, a common scenario in which one person's angry remark provokes an angry response might be interpreted by those using linear causality as a two-point sequence in which the first angry remark caused the second. Systems theorists would point out that there was some preceding event that provoked the first angry remark that is just as relevant to understanding the sequence as either of the two recorded remarks. So Person A's perception that Person B put him down might be another point in the chain that warrants attention. Person B's quiet, leering look that preceded Person A's perception of the put-down might add further information. In other words, human interactions tend to consist of complex cycles of ongoing communication via behavior, expectations, and beliefs about behavior, and reactions to behavior. Thus, in families, every person's behavior is believed to be related directly or indirectly to every other person in the system.

Given the importance of understanding the circular causal sequences in human interactions, behaviors are observed carefully for their communication function (Watzlawick, Beavin, & Jackson, 1967). The vast majority of communication is accomplished nonverbally. In familiar social settings, an even greater percentage of communication occurs at the nonverbal level. Words are certainly used to communicate, but the context of the words creates the meaning of the communication. Actors make their living by learning the subtleties of communicating very different messages with the same text by altering tone of voice or body language. Relationship structures form an even more powerful context for communication.

Specific power dimensions and hierarchical linkages structure relationships. A faculty member's casual inquiry to a student, "So, did you go partying last night?" may elicit a defensive response simply because the student hears the question within the context of his or her salient awareness of the power differential in their relationship. A peer asking the same question may elicit a long excited description of the events of the previous evening. In the first family described above, the parents of Jason Martinez (Nancy and Reuben) may be withdrawing from contact with Ruth and James because the parents perceive the invitation for Jason to live with his grandparents as a direct insult. The previous relationship between Nancy and her mother and stepfather is the context in which Jason's living arrangement will be interpreted by all parties involved.

Family relationship structures are similarly powerful factors that influence family interactions. Generational hierarchies are among the most prominent structures, but gender roles, favorite son and daughter designations, or family scapegoat roles will also set the context for interpreting all interactions. The term "rules" is used to articulate the typically unspoken observations of behavior patterns that not only describe, but usually prescribe behavior. For example, "One must never show anger" is a family rule that will constrain behavior of family members. The very presence of this rule prescribes masking attempts, and establishes a family member as a rebel or a problem if he or she expresses overtly his or her anger. A family with such a rule may very well label a child as behaviorally disturbed if he acts out anger, even if the behavior would be considered appropriate by society at large or by mental health professionals. This example suggests that the child's "problem" may actually be a family system problem. In Jason Martinez's family the unspoken rule may be, "If you believe someone has insulted you, don't talk to that person."

Ironically, older family members who are identified as problems within a family may have invested considerable effort earlier in life enforcing family rules that they find unacceptable later in life. For example, an older person who decides to co-reside with a partner without marrying may find him or herself experiencing outrage from adult children who were taught by this elderly parent that such behavior was immoral. Even behavior that is caused by a cognitive or dementing disorder can be particularly upsetting to family members if it goes against the family rules (e.g., angry, combative behavior; sexual behavior). Any older person whose behavior changes from previously established family norms is particularly likely to elicit strong emotional responses from other family members because the elder him or herself had participated in generating or maintaining the very rules he or she is now breaking.

Boundaries are the rules that define who participates in what roles and which forms of participation are acceptable (Minuchin, 1974). The purpose of boundaries is to differentiate members within a family. For example, there are boundaries that define who makes financial decisions, who provides emotional support, and who disciplines children. Many systems theorists believe that the clearer the boundaries, the greater the probability that the family is healthy. However, family dysfunction may occur with boundaries that are either too rigid or too diffuse. Therapists refer to families with extremely rigid boundaries as *disengaged* (the boundaries keep them from being flexible in roles when adaptation is needed) and to families with diffuse boundaries as *enmeshed* (everyone engages in all possible roles). Most families are believed to fall somewhere between these polarities. Although formal measurement tools are available to assess these characteristics (e.g., Olson, 1996) clinicians commonly apply this framework from clinical observations.

Later-life families seldom share the same immediate household membership or residence as is characteristic of child-rearing nuclear families, but can nonetheless be conceptualized as functioning systems whose interaction patterns are governed by rules. Interactions consist of verbal and nonverbal behaviors that occur in repeating cycles. For example, when a decision must be made about the housing and medical care of Grandma, her oldest daughter and son-in-law typically decide what they believe is best and then call her other two children to get their approval. The rule in this case could be stated, "oldest daughter and son-in-law decide what is best, and inform other siblings who are expected to approve." If a brother were to disapprove, he might be labeled a troublemaker. Or, if the oldest daughter and son-in-law were to be gone on vacation when a crisis in care occurred, the family might be confused about how to proceed because the familiar rule could not be enacted. Think back to the conflict among Jillian Jarvis's children over how to decide about her care. The siblings probably have not ever had to negotiate explicitly their rules about how to make decisions about their mother. Neither has Jillian had experience letting her children decide, so her fantasy is to go back to the original nuclear structure in which her husband ruled over all of them.

Each member of the system carries a set of beliefs about what the rules are, why they are structured in that way, and what would be the consequences of breaking them. Attributions for the rules may be based on the personality of the persons involved (e.g., "she has to keep control over Grandma," or "he won't help so I don't bother asking"). Such personality-based attributions are focused on traits that appear to be unalterable and are likely not to generate task-focused problem-solving efforts. Indeed, many family difficulties arise from failed attempts to solve problems (Herr & Weakland, 1979). Personality-based attributions for family rules may generate attempts to change the personality of a person, an effort that is likely to be resisted by the target of the change efforts. The children of Jillian Jarvis are possibly locked in a personality-attribution model that undermines their ability to cooperate to address the task at hand effectively.

Members of systems can generate many more solution alternatives when they work from behavioral descriptions of the behavior sequences (e.g., "when a problem arises in Grandma's care I decide what to do, arrange for it, and then place telephone calls to my three siblings in which I describe what has been done; I do not expect or solicit any input and am surprised and insulted if my siblings want to participate in the decision with any communication except statements of approval"). Behavior descriptions offer multiple points for intervention and usually make it evident that a variety of interventions initiated by any one person in the sequence would alter its pattern and outcome.

The hospital social worker in the Jarvis case will need to help the adult children define the task at hand behaviorally. Rather than framing the question as, "Does Jean have a right to place her mother in a nursing home?" the family needs to work to meet Jillian's needs. Instead of focusing on the differences between the personalities of Jean, whose style is to "get the job done," and John, whose style is to "consider every option before acting," the siblings need to focus on the task. First, they need information. Exactly which of Jillian's capabilities are compromised? Which housing options are congruent with her level of functioning? The children's values and preferences about their mother's housing can be examined in the context of which options best serve her needs. Likely, all of the children want her to be safe and well cared for, yet as autonomous as possible. The task they need to accomplish is to identify the set of options that meet those values.

Family members are often bound to one another in particular kinds of ties that shape the dynamics of the family. Three kinds of relational ties that are often tracked in family systems are alliances, triangles, and coalitions. *Alliances* involve two persons who share a common interest not shared by a third person. In other words, two persons ally together "against" another. *Triangles* describe the relationship that occurs when two persons manage conflict by funneling it through a third person. *Coalitions* are like alliances, but are usually covert in nature and they create power blocks in families. The classic paradigm for triangles in child-rearing families shows a child with behavior problems (the "identified patient") who is triangulated between parents experiencing serious marital unhappiness or conflict. In aging families, the structure of the triangle is more variable (i.e., it is less likely to involve a married couple triangulating a child in their conflict). A prototypical scenario might involve two siblings with a long-standing conflicted relationship who enact their conflict by taking incompatible approaches to caring for a parent. The parent's care becomes a huge problem that deflects focus from the underlying sibling conflict, as appears to be the case in the Jarvis family. Many other family structures also can triangulate. A mother and daughter conflict can be deflected by their mutual concern over the father. In other words, triangles can cross generational lines and sibling, parent, cousin, aunt/uncle, and grandparent structures in diverse ways. Nancy and Reuben Martinez likely experience Jason's move into Nancy's mother and stepfather's home as indicative of a coalition being formed against them. In this case, Jason is triangulated between two couples—his parents and his grandparents.

Mental Health within a Systems Model

Systems that meet members' needs are considered functional and those that inhibit one or some members from meeting needs are considered problematic. Mental health, therefore, is not conceptualized as an individual-level construct. An older adult whose self-care capacity, social needs, or self-esteem needs are not met would not be labeled "mentally disordered." Rather, the systems model would argue it is more appropriate to examine the interpersonal context that elicits or supports this behavior. The specific interpersonal system relevant to an individual older person's problem would be examined to identify the circular causal loops that maintain the problematic behavior.

The current interpersonal interactions that are maintaining the problem behavior are the most important behavior sequences to track. Finding the historical cause of the behavior may help the members of the system understand how the circular loop evolved, but the immediate interpersonal interactions are far more important. Herr and Weakland (1979) point out that a family system's first attempts to solve a problem are often unsuccessful yet the same strategy may be maintained over time because the family cannot identify an alternative approach. The failed solution is likely to create another behavior problem (often the one for which help is sought) as a consequence of the ongoing failure experience. Thus, failed solutions are often functioning to maintain the current problem.

Systems with poorly functioning structures will encounter difficulties meeting members' needs throughout the lifespan, including later life. Families that are enmeshed or have poor boundaries around decision-making units (e.g., a marriage) are likely to encounter difficulty adjusting to both normative and non-normative life events. The structures themselves inhibit flexibility needed to adapt well or to communicate clearly about changing needs and preferences.

Even high-functioning families may be challenged by particular events if they lack knowledge about how to meet members' needs or choose a poor strategy for adapting. For example, families with a cognitively impaired member need a basic understanding of the impact of the disorder on the patient and family in order to make appropriate care decisions and to support caregivers adequately. Families who functioned well through previous life events but who lack knowledge of dementia may solve problems ineffectively, and may even become stuck in a failed solution that harms one or more family members. The underlying structure may be functioning well except in one problem area. As such, a limited psychoeducational intervention may be sufficient to solve the problem. Assume for the moment that Jillian Jarvis has a vascular dementia that renders her too confused to eat properly and unsteady in gait so she falls often. Jean's decision to place her in a nursing home may be appropriate. John and JoAnn may lack information about the diagnosis or nature of the cognitive disorder, and are primarily concerned to protect their mother's autonomy. A family meeting in which the cause and nature of the disorder is carefully described may be sufficient to engage the three children in shared problem-solving.

Some families bring to later life a long history of poor adaptation with poorly functioning family structures. Even an adequate knowledge base regarding dementia care is unlikely to engage the family in a collaborative care giving experience. If John and JoAnn have long-term unresolved conflicts with Jean that lead them to ally against her on any issue, then a common information base about their mother's needs may be only the first of several steps needed to resolve the family conflict that threatens Jillian's care.

Assessment

Assessment may be conducted with only one family member, or with many, depending upon who seeks services. Clinicians may only have the opportunity to work with the primary caregiver of an older adult or may ask that person to bring in other family members whose roles are important to the focus of concern. The care recipient may or may not participate in a family assessment or intervention. In cases of cognitive impairment that interferes with the person's ability to recognize the range or impact of cognitive deficits on daily functioning, participation in the room may be very limited. In other cases, the older adult is a key participant. Clinicians become skilled at deriving a relatively objective view of family functioning from careful interviews of individual family members using strategies described below. In cases of family conflict, however, engaging multiple members in the therapy room or even through email interchanges provides important clinical insight into the sequences of interaction.

What should be assessed? The answer to that question depends on the nature of the problem, of course. There are a few general categories of information a mental health worker would want to know if doing a family systems intervention.

Family structure

A graphic depiction of family structure, called a genogram, is a very useful way of organizing efficiently information about several generations of family members (McGoldrick, Gerson, & Petrie, 2008). Figure 7.1 shows an example of Jason Martinez's family.

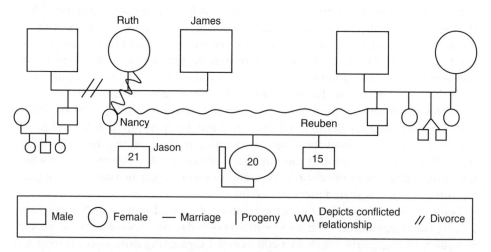

Figure 7.1   Genogram depicting Jason Martinez's family.

In addition to depicting the membership of the family according to generational lineage, a genogram can include information about the alliances, bonds, and conflicts in the family. The relationship between Jason and his grandmother is very strong, but his relationship with his mother and father is highly conflicted. The mild conflict between Nancy and Ruth in the past is blossoming into major warfare as they react to Jason's efforts to leave home.

Family development and life course

Another way to describe families is in terms of their stage in the family life cycle. A traditional model of the family life-cycle is shown in Figure 7.2 (Rodgers & White, 1993). The stages as sequenced in this figure illustrate a common pattern of family development stages in which stages are marked by the entry and exit of members from the nuclear family. Although entries and exits continue to mark major transitions in family life, many variations in family development shape the life course of a given family. Divorce, chronic illness, death of a child, and job loss are just a few of the life experiences that might alter the sequencing or meaning of various life stages (McGoldrick, Preto, & Carter, 2015). Young adults who exit the family home now

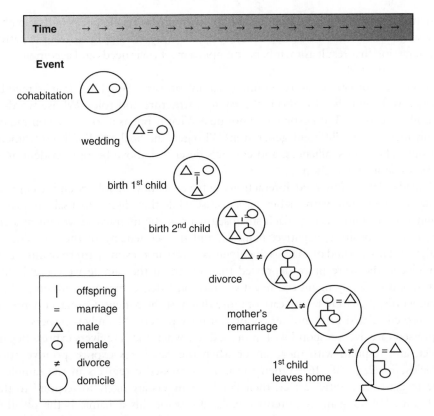

Figure 7.2 Family stages and events.
Source: Adapted from Rodgers & White (1993).

normatively return to it within a few years. Thus, the clarity of entries and exits that characterized the original concept of family life-cycle are now recognized to have far more variation than the traditional model would imply, and it needs to be mapped with appreciation of variations that individuals and families create, yielding a far more complex view of the life-cycle concept. Although childbearing occurs within a biologically constrained time period that places some constraints on the life-cycle, innovations in reproductive medicine, adoption policy, and grandparent parenting patterns push even those boundaries. In short, predictable sequencing of stages has declined, yielding increased variability that appears to work as well as more traditional views.

Mental health professionals can use the knowledge of each member's stage to identify ways in which the life tasks of various family members may be interfering with each other. For example, a young adult who is attempting to establish autonomy and independence may resist the desires of her grandmother to knit the family more closely. The family life-cycle is a method of identifying the developmental tasks appropriate to each family member that will inevitably affect the family's style of functioning.

Family functioning

Systems approaches want to understand how a family meets the needs of its members. The structure of the family often becomes apparent by examining closely the patterns of interaction that result as members attempt to meet their needs and accomplish their developmental tasks.

There are several ways to examine family process. Watching family members interact verbally tells a lot about the family's structure and roles. Whose words are heard by everyone? Who expresses emotions? What happens if someone contradicts a family member in a different generation? Who gets the final word? Who is blamed or left out? The bonds, alliances, and conflicts described above become evident as one observes family interactions.

Shields (1992) observed interactions between family members and a depressed caregiver to a patient with Alzheimer's disease while they discussed a salient issue the family was currently facing. Each small segment of the interaction was given a code for emotion (positive, negative, neutral), and the sequencing of the segments was analyzed. This method of analysis documented a very interesting pattern of interaction. Caregivers who were more depressed than others in the sample were highly likely to respond to family members' negative emotion-laden comments with empathy. In other words, they were taking care of more than just the patient. Caregiver depression was also correlated with another counterintuitive pattern. "Family members of more depressed caregivers respond with more sadness when the caregivers express negative affect, and respond with more anger when the caregivers express positive affect" (Shields, 1992, p. 25–26). When the most depressed caregivers in the sample are able to generate positive affect, their family members are likely to respond to them with anger! Among many potential explanations for this dynamic is the possibility that the anger or frustration that was not acceptable to unleash when depressed mood dominated may be communicated when the person appears more resilient to receive it. Obviously, the dynamics in these families are far more complex than is often acknowledged when we think of families as sources of support.

Another strategy for learning about family functioning is to identify the sequence of behaviors that family members use to accomplish a task. For example, when a physician calls a caregiver to inform her that the patient's lab tests show some disturbing information, what does that caregiver do? Whom does she call? Does everyone get the same amount of information? Who is involved in decisions? How do family members respond to the caregiver's distress? Which behaviors are experienced as supportive or interfering? Do those match the actor's intention? Herr and Weakland (1979, p. 103–112) describe a case that illustrates the ways in which behavior that is intended to be supportive may actually reinforce dependency. They describe a mid-life woman caring for her father in the home she shares with a husband and two boys. The father has become excessively dependent on the family to do tasks he could do for himself. She has tried several strategies to encourage him to perform activities on his own (e.g., pleading, cajoling, and demanding). When the family therapist began to elicit a detailed picture of the sequence of behavior interactions, it became evident that the daughter's behaviors were reinforcing her father's dependent demands. Her threats that she would not serve him were always met with efforts by her father to prove he needed help, to which she responded by "giving in" because it seemed cruel to let him suffer. Only by very carefully eliciting a detailed picture of behavior sequences could the clinician identify this pattern. This analysis is similar to that generated by a behaviorist because her "giving in" behavior is viewed as reinforcement in both models. However, a systems analysis emphasizes the reciprocal patterns of reinforcement rather than viewing the interaction as a linear Antecedent-Behavior-Consequence sequence that relates solely to the father's behavior.

A systems assessment also needs to examine outcomes of family activity: Are members' needs being met and are developmental tasks being accomplished? Families have a myriad of ways of structuring themselves to accomplish the task of supporting members' development. Thus, the methods of accomplishing tasks are primarily relevant to examine when some members' needs are not being met. For example, a family may be able to meet the needs of young children, but be unable to support the needs of adolescents to launch themselves. Or in later life, a family may adjust beautifully to the "empty nest," but be unable to adapt to the severe illness of an aging family member whose dependency needs exceed the children's skill or expectations. This functional deficit may become apparent through one member of the family whose behavior is problematic; this person is generally known as the *identified patient* (IP). The IP's abnormal functioning simply signals that the family is unable to meet all members' needs (rather than signaling some form of psychopathology in the IP), and thus a thorough assessment of the family would be useful.

Family history

Two aspects of family history may become relevant: how previous generations dealt with aging-related challenges, and how this particular family constellation adapted to previous life transitions. Systems theorists emphasize the importance of intergenerational transmission of family rules, values, interaction patterns, and even anxiety (Boszormenyi-Nagy & Spark, 1984; Bowen, 1978). A current systems problem may become simpler to solve when compared with the ways in which previous generations managed similar developmental tasks. Because previous generations were less likely to live until advanced old age, many families are struggling to manage current problems without the benefit of the experience of previous generations. Idealized images may be serving as a proxy for real family experiences with some of the particular challenges and events of old age. On the other hand, families with clear rules for handling aging-related problems may find that those rules do not work well when applied to the needs of a particular aging relative in a particular context.

Although families may experience aging-related challenges to be novel and unfamiliar, in many cases the family's strategies for adapting to previous life events will apply directly to the current difficulties. Families who successfully managed previous family transitions often have resources and strategies for interacting that would be useful to the current dilemma if they are reminded of their previous successes.

Intervention

When working with families, the first task for any professional is to join the family. A common role that families create for professional helpers is the "expert consultant." The consultant is expected to know something about aging and the adaptations required of families, and is expected to support the family as it adapts. Creating this role requires the family to acknowledge formally that there is a problem and also to open themselves somewhat to education. Professional helpers are obviously not members of the family so the process of joining and assessing the family is often an intervention itself. As such, the intervention process cannot be readily differentiated from assessment.

Systems models distinguish between interventions that are targeted at first-order change and those targeted at second-order change (Watzlawick, Weakland, & Fisch, 1974). *First-order change* is that which modifies behavior patterns without altering substantially the basic structures and functioning patterns of the family. *Second-order change* alters structures to create a new kind of system. Generally, the principle used by mental health professionals is to begin with interventions targeted at first-order change to see if they are sufficient to solve the problem, and proceed to second-order interventions only if the less intrusive interventions did not work.

Later-life families are often dealing with new challenges they simply do not understand. A common first-order intervention is education about the challenge (e.g., an illness, retirement, grief) and about the resources available to assist the family's adaptation and coping. Functionally, education about the problem takes the focus off the IP and onto the underlying problem. Education usually includes not only information about the life event or developmental task, but also about the importance of obtaining support, and the resources available in the community for assisting the family.

Second-order change efforts are explicitly targeted at altering the family's structure and familiar ways of functioning. One strategy commonly used is to reorganize the smaller units of the family system that are responsible for particular roles in the family. For example, a family therapist might direct the family to reorganize its decision-making structure if the current structure cannot function well. Or a therapist might encourage the family to break rules that make it taboo for adult children to tell a parent directly when they do not want to discuss a matter, for example, in a case where a widowed woman and her daughter appear to be engaging in constant conflicts primarily because they do not have any other ways of maintaining appropriate separateness.

Another strategy for accomplishing second order change is to alter the interaction patterns. Therapists may ask family members to alter where they sit in the therapy room in order to force an immediate restructuring of an alliance. Therapists also may direct the sequencing of an interaction, interrupting familiar and nonproductive patterns to allow new interaction patterns to form. In essence, systemic factors can create the stress experienced by later life families, including caregiving family members, and interventions that address family structures can be helpful (Mitrani et al., 2006).

One case that illustrates these principles is that of a 66-year-old woman who brought her 68-year-old husband and 42-year-old daughter to see a family therapist. The therapist immediately recognized a father–daughter alliance against the mother. An obvious enactment of the alliance against mother was evident in the very way the three members chose their chairs when they walked into the therapist's office: The father and daughter sat next to each other on the couch, leaving the mother the chair across the room next to the therapist. As the family explained to the therapist their reasons for coming, the mother suggested that she was worried about her daughter who seemed to lack initiative. The father interrupted her with, "That's crazy!" and immediately contradicted his wife by naming all of the activities the daughter did this week. The daughter sat silently, leaning against her father as if for support. The father and daughter were allied in their shared view that the daughter's inability to live independently is not a problem. However, the father–daughter alliance is interfering with the intimacy of the father and the mother in their marriage (a structure problem), and impeding the daughter from launching into independent adulthood (a developmental problem). Asking the father and mother to move their chairs close to one another and hold hands while discussing their perceptions of their daughter's strengths might force recognition of the marital bond that would be ignored if the father and daughter were allowed to enact their alliance.

Once the bond is made salient, the parents' discussion of their concerns about their daughter is much more likely to be productive. The therapist might alter the interaction sequences by creating first a conversation between the mother and the father that the daughter is not allowed to enter, then setting up a conversation between mother and daughter that the father is not allowed to enter. If the father's typical role is to deny the problem or run interference for the daughter, then the mother and the daughter will each feel anxious about interacting in a more direct and vulnerable way. This anxiety creates the opportunity for a new pattern of interaction to form, one that is more likely to handle directly the developmental tasks at hand. Families will attempt to maintain homeostasis, so therapists must engage actively and creatively with the family to create second-order change in the family structures (Qualls & Noecker, 2009).

Other approaches to work with aging families focus more at the level of family values, obligations, and balances in reciprocity (Hargrave & Anderson, 1992; Knight & Sayegh, 2010). Families pass across generations not only values statements about how it "should" be done (that may or may not be relevant to current social and familial conditions), but also pass along rules and obligations from the families' unique history and lineage (Boszormenyi-Nagy & Spark, 1984). Family conflict over parent care may be rooted in conflicted values or the sense of being trapped to fulfill obligations. Dialogue to increase awareness of the unspoken forces shaping the family members' interactions with each other is another intervention strategy.

The majority of published research on interventions with aging families has been conducted with one family member, the primary caregiver, for the purpose of assisting him or her in caring for another, ill older family member (Zarit, 2009). Researchers have now identified which interventions show the strongest effects (Burgio & Gaugler, 2016; Gallagher-Thompson & Coon, 2007; Pinquart & Sorensen, 2006).

The majority of interventions focus on first-order changes, such as education, support, and problem-solving about specific illness-generated difficulties. In addition growing evidence shows that analysis of the family system and interventions targeting the system are also helpful. Scharlach (1987) involved daughters who served as primary care providers to elderly mothers in one of two intervention conditions. Part of the sample was given information about caregiving and about community resources while encouraging the daughters to focus on meeting their mothers' needs for assistance. The other intervention group involved daughters in modifying unrealistic expectations of responsibility to their aging mothers, and encouraged them to promote self-reliance in their mothers while enhancing their own well-being. Daughters in the second group reported less burden and better relationship quality while their mothers report less loneliness than the first group (or a control group). Although only the daughters were involved in this intervention, this study could be interpreted as an intervention to teach daughters to set boundaries and take on different roles, thus altering family structure.

Flexible family interventions use a variety of intervention strategies and include whichever family members can be most helpful in creating the necessary change. Mittelman and colleagues, who have conducted the longest running family intervention in which they offered a combination of individual and family counseling to primary caregivers of relatives with dementia, delayed nursing home placement with their family intervention (Mittelman, Haley, Clay, & Roth, 2006). When compared with caregivers who received only support group interventions, the families receiving ongoing counseling reported more involvement from the family network in support of patient and caregiver, increased caregiver satisfaction with the support network, as well as delayed rate of institutionalization. Furthermore, the family intervention had beneficial effects even when placement ultimately had to occur (Gaugler, Roth, Haley, & Mittelman, 2008).

Technologies also have the potential to affect family functioning and well-being. Eisdorfer and colleagues (2003) found significant benefits to primary caregivers of persons with dementia from placing a conference-type telephone in the home. Other technologies are also used to help families remain supportive of one another, congruent in their approaches to care, and, quite simply, connected (Blechman, 2009; Williams & Lewis, 2009).

Unfortunately, the research base demonstrating the utility of the systems model with later-life families is limited. However, preliminary results of clinical cases (e.g., Auclair, Epstein, & Mittelman, 2009), clinical analysis (Qualls & Williams, 2013; Shields, King & Wynne, 1995), descriptive research (e.g., Shields, 1992), and outcome research (e.g., Mittelman et al., 2006; Gaugler et al., 2008) are promising. The need for both more theoretical and more empirical research is apparent, but the value of a model for mental health and aging that explicitly incorporates families as a system is also clear.

Summary and Conclusions

The mental well-being of older adults is often heavily influenced by characteristics of their families. Family systems theory offers a rich framework for examining the interpersonal environment of the family. The family systems model explains how the interpersonal context influences observable behavior as well as subjective well-being. Interventions with the family system can improve the well-being of older adults as well as their family members. Interventions can focus on family structures, processes, and dynamics that are as relevant in later life as during child-rearing years.

Critical Thinking / Discussion Questions

1 How can a family system influence mental health in an individual?
2 In what way is a family systems approach to assessment and intervention different from the other three theoretical approaches described in this book?
3 Compare and contrast the intervention approaches of a family systems therapist and a behavioral therapist to the case of the Martinez-Jones family at the beginning of the chapter.
4 What might a family systems theorist suggest would be a useful approach to resolving the conflict in the family of Jillian Jarvis, described at the beginning of the chapter?

Website Resources

American Psychological Association, Division 43: Society for Couple and Family Psychology
http://www.apa.org/about/division/div43.aspx
American Association for Marriage and Family Therapy
www.aamft.org
The Bowen Center
http://thebowencenter.org
Collaborative Family Healthcare Association
www.cfha.net

American Psychological Association: Family, Systems, and Health Journal
http://www.apa.org/pubs/journals/fsh
Family Systems Institute
http://www.thefsi.com.au

References

Administration on Aging. (2014). A profile of older Americans: 2014. Washington DC: US Department of Health and Human Services. Retrieved from http://aginginmarin.org/wp-content/uploads/2015/08/2014-Profile-Older-Amer-US-Dept-HHS.pdf

Anderson, S. A., Sabatelli, R. M., & Kosutic, I. (2013). Systemic and ecological qualities of families. In G. W. Peterson & K. R. Bush (Eds.), *Handbook of marriage and the family* (3rd ed., pp. 121–138). New York, NY: Springer. doi: 10.1007/978-1-4614-3987-5_6

Auclair, U., Epstein, C., & Mittelman, M. (2009). Couples counseling in Alzheimer's disease: Additional clinical findings from a novel intervention study. *Clinical Gerontologist, 32*, 130–46. doi:10.1080/07317110802676809

Bedford, V. H., & Avioli, P. S. (2012). Sibling relationships from midlife to old age. In R. Blieszner & V. H. Bedford (Eds.), *Handbook of families and aging* (2nd ed., pp. 125–151). Santa Barbara, CA: Praeger.

Bengtson, V. L., & Kuypers, J. A. (1984). The family support cycle: Psychosocial issues in the aging family. In J. M. A. Munnichs, P. Mussen, E. Olbrich, & P. G. Coleman (Eds.), *Life-span and change in a gerontological perspective* (pp. 257–273). Orlando, FL: Academic. doi: 10.1016/b978-0-12-510260-5.50020-7

Blechman, E. A. (2009). Personal health records for older adults with chronic conditions and their informal caregivers. In S. H. Qualls & S. H. Zarit (Eds.), *Aging families and caregiving* (pp. 287–310). Hoboken, NJ: Wiley.

Boszormenyi-Nagy, I., & Spark, G. M. (1984). *Invisible loyalties.* New York, NY: Brunner/Mazel.

Bowen, M. (1978). *Family therapy in clinical practice.* New York, NY: Aronson.

Burgio, L. D., & Gaugler, J. E. (2016). *The spectrum of family caregiving for adults and elders with chronic illness.* New York, NY: Oxford University Press.

Connidis, I.A. (2010). *Family ties and aging* (2nd ed.). Thousand Oaks, CA: Sage.

Davey, A., & Takagi, E. (2013). Adulthood and aging in families. In G. W. Peterson & K. R. Bush (Eds.), *Handbook of marriage and the family* (3rd ed., pp. 377–399). New York, NY: Springer. doi: 10.1007/978-1-4614-3987-5_17

Eisdorfer, C., Czaja, S. J., Loewenstein, D. A., Rubert, M. P., Arguelles, S., Mitrani, V. B., & Szapocznik, J. (2003). The effect of a family therapy and technology-based intervention on caregiver depression. *The Gerontologist, 43*, 521–531. doi: 10.1093/geront/43.4.521

Fingerman, K. L., Miller, L. M., & Seidel, A. J. (2009). Functions families serve in old age. In S. H. Qualls & S. H. Zarit (Eds.), *Aging families and caregiving* (pp. 19–44). Hoboken, NJ: Wiley.

Gallagher-Thompson, D., & Coon, D. W. (2007). Evidence-based psychological treatments for distress in family caregivers of older adults. *Psychology and Aging, 22*, 37–51. doi: 10.1037/0882-7974.22.1.37

Gaugler, J., Roth, D., Haley, W., & Mittelman, M. (2008). Can counseling and support reduce burden and depressive symptoms in caregivers of people with Alzheimer's disease during the transition to institutionalization? Results from the New York University Caregiver Intervention Study. *Journal of the American Geriatrics Society, 56*, 421–428. doi: 10.1111/j.1532-5415.2007.01593.x

Hagestad, G. O. (1986). The aging society as a context for family life. *Daedalus, 115*, 119–139.

Hagestad, G. O. (1988). Demographic change and the life course: Some emerging trends in the family realm. *Family Relations, 37*, 405–410.

Hargrave, T. D., & Anderson, W. T. (1992). *Finishing well: Aging and reparation in the inter-generational family.* New York, NY: Brunner/Mazel.

Herr, J. J., & Weakland, J. H. (1979). *Counseling elders and their families.* New York, NY: Springer.

Kim, K., Zarit, S. H., Birditt, K. S., & Fingerman, K. L. (2014). Discrepancy in reports of support exchanges between parents and adult offspring: Within- and between-family differences. *Journal of Family Psychology, 28*, 168–179. doi:10.1037/a0035735

Kivnick, H. Q. (1985). Grandparenthood and mental health. In V. L. Bengtson & J. F. Robertson (Eds.), *Grandparenthood* (pp. 211–224). Beverly Hills, CA: Sage.

Knight, B. G., & Sayegh, P. (2010). Cultural values and caregiving: The updated sociocultural stress and coping model. *The Journals of Gerontology: Series B: Psychological Sciences and Social Sciences, 65B*, 5–13. doi: 0.1093/geronb/gbp096

McGoldrick, M., Gerson, R., & Petrie, S. (2008). *Genograms: Assessment and intervention* (3rd ed.). New York, NY: Norton Professional Books.

McGoldrick, M., Preto, N. A. G., & Carter, B. A. (2015). *The expanding family life cycle: Individual, family, and social perspectives.* Boston, MA: Pearson.

Minuchin, S. (1974). *Families and family therapy.* Cambridge, MA: Harvard University Press.

Mitrani, V. B., Lewis, J. E., Feaster, D. J., Czaja, S. J., Eisdorfer, C., Schulz, R., & Szapocznik, J. (2006). The role of family functioning in the stress process of dementia caregivers: A structural family framework. *The Gerontologist, 46*, 97–105. doi: 10.1093/geront/46.1.97

Mittelman, M. S., Haley, W. E., Clay, O. J., & Roth, D. L. (2006). Improving caregiver well-being delays nursing home placement of patients with Alzheimer's disease. *Neurology, 67*(9), 1592–1599. doi:10.1212/01.wnl.0000242727.81172.91

Norris, M. P. (2009). Integrating families into long-term care psychology services: Orchestrating cacophonies and symphonies. In S. H. Qualls & S. H. Zarit (Eds.), *Aging families and caregiving* (pp. 189–208). Hoboken, NJ: Wiley.

Olson, D. (1996). Clinical assessment and treatment using the family circumplex model. In F. W. Kaslow (Ed.), *Handbook in relational diagnosis* (pp. 59–80). New York, NY: Wiley.

Parsons, T. (1949). The social structure of the family. In R. Anshen (Ed.), *The family: Its function and destiny* (pp. 173–201). New York, NY: Harper & Row.

Pinquart, M., & Sorensen, S. (2006). Helping caregivers of persons with dementia: Which interventions work and how large are their effects? *International Psychogeriatrics, 18*, 577–595. doi: 10.1017/s1041610206003462

Pruchno, R. A., Blow, F. C., & Smyer, M. A. (1984). Life events and interdependent lives. Implications for research and intervention. *Human Development, 27*, 31–41. doi: 10.1159/000272901

Qualls, S. H. (1995). Clinical interventions with later life families. In R. Blieszner & V. H. Bedford (Eds.), *Handbook on aging and the family* (pp. 474–487). Westport, CT: Greenwood Press.

Qualls, S. H. (2016). Caregiving families within the long-term services and support system for older adults. *American Psychologist, 71*, 283–293. doi: 10.1037/a0040252

Qualls S. H., & Noecker, T. L. (2009). Caregiver family therapy for conflicted families. In S. H. Qualls & S. H. Zarit (Eds.), *Aging families and caregiving* (pp. 1–27). Hoboken, NJ: Wiley.

Qualls, S. H., & Williams, A. A. (2013). *Caregiving family therapy.* Washington, DC: American Psychological Association.

Rodgers, R. H., & White, J. W. (1993). Family development theory. In P. G. Boss, W. J. Doherty, R. LaRossa, W. R. Schumm, & S. K. Steinmetz (Eds.), *Sourcebook of family theories and methods* (pp. 225–254). New York, NY: Plenum.

Scharlach, A. E. (1987). Relieving feelings of strain among women with elderly mothers. *Psychology and Aging, 2,* 9–13. doi: 10.1037/0882-7974.2.1.9

Shanas, E. (1979). Social myth as hypothesis: The case of the family relations of old people. *The Gerontologist, 19,* 3–9. doi: 10.1093/geront/19.1.3

Shields, C. G. (1992). Family interaction and caregivers of Alzheimer's disease patients: Correlates of depression. *Family Process, 31,* 19–33.

Shields, C. G., King, D. A., & Wynne, L. C. (1995). Interventions with later life families. In R. H. Mikesell, D. Lusterman, & S. H. McDaniel (Eds.), *Integrating family therapy: Handbook of family psychology and systems theory* (pp. 141–158). Washington, DC: American Psychological Association.

Suitor, J. J., Gillian, M., & Pillemer, K. (2016). Stability, change, and complexity in later-life families. In L. K. George & K. F. Ferraro (Eds.), *Handbook of aging and the social sciences* (pp. 205–226). San Diego, CA: Academic Press. doi: 10.1016/B978-0-12-417235-7.00010-x

Swartz, T. T. (2009). Intergenerational family relations in adulthood: Patterns, variations, and implications in the contemporary United States. *Annual Review of Sociology, 35,* 191–212. doi: 10.1146/annurev.soc.34.040507.134615

Szinovacz, M. (1998). Grandparents today: A demographic profile. *The Gerontologist, 38,* 37–52. doi: 10.1093/geront/38.1.37

Umberson, D., Williams, K., Power, D. A., Chen, M. D., & Campbell, A. M. (2005). As good as it gets? A life course perspective on marital quality. *Social Forces, 84,* 493–511.

Watzlawick, P., Beavin, J. H., & Jackson, D. D. (1967). *Pragmatics of human communication: A study of interactional patterns, pathologies, and paradoxes.* New York, NY: Norton.

Watzlawick, P., Weakland, J. H., & Fisch, R. (1974). *Change.* New York, NY: Norton.

Williams, M., & Lewis, C. (2009). A platform for intervention and research on family communication in elder care. In S. H. Qualls & S. H. Zarit (Eds.), *Aging families and caregiving* (pp. 269–286). Hoboken, NJ: Wiley.

Zarit, S. H. (2009). Empirically supported treatment for family caregivers. In S. H. Qualls & S. H. Zarit (Eds.), *Aging families and caregiving* (pp. 131–154). Hoboken, NJ: Wiley.

Part II
Summary and Commentary
Choosing Among Models of Mental Disorders in Later Life

In this section, we have described several different models of mental health and mental disorder. Before we consider the treatment of specific disorders in more detail in Part III, it may be useful to consider a simple question: How do you choose among the various models?

Let's begin to answer this question by reflecting on what we want from a model of mental health or mental disorder. Remember, a model is a representation, something like a map that draws our attention to certain aspects of the terrain while allowing us to find our way. Similarly, models cannot fully represent the complexity of an older adult's life situation. Instead, models focus our attention on the most salient elements of the older adult and his or her environment. In doing so, all models provide answers to several basic questions (see Table S1.1). Each model emphasizes certain elements for understanding mental health. By focusing our attention on certain aspects of the individual's functioning, the model explicitly and implicitly asserts that other elements are less important.

Similarly, the model's explanation of what changes in mental disorders and in aging implicitly alerts us to the potential targets of therapeutic intervention. For example, in psychodynamic perspectives, the focus of attention is on personality structures. As outlined in Chapter 4, structural change is often viewed as a desirable therapeutic goal, but is sometimes beyond the capacity of either the clinician or the client.

Models also differ in the *type* of change they predict for the older adult: quantitative (different in degree) or qualitative (different in kind). For example, the cognitive-behavioral models focus on differences in quantity of behaviors, behavioral excesses, or deficits. In contrast, systems perspectives focus on differences both in quantity and in quality of interactions among the system's components.

Aging and Mental Health, Third Edition. Daniel L. Segal, Sara Honn Qualls, and Michael A. Smyer.
© 2018 John Wiley & Sons, Inc. Published 2018 by John Wiley & Sons, Inc.

Table S1.1   Choosing among models

Model elements	Psychodynamic	Cognitive-behavioral	Stress and coping	Family systems
What is studied?	Motivation and personality	Thought patterns and overt behaviors	Strain, stressor, and interactions	Interactions among elements of the system
What changes with age or with mental disorder?	Personality structure	Cognitive and behavior patterns	Individual adaptability or stressors or their interaction	Developmental tasks and systems interactions
What kind of change occurs?	Qualitative change	Quantitative change (behaviors) and qualitative change (cognitions)	Qualitative and quantitative change	Qualitative and quantitative change
How is change explained?	Structure/functional relationships	Circular and interactive relationships between thoughts, behaviors, and feelings, although thought patterns and behaviors are targeted first	Interaction of the person and the environment	Interaction among the elements of the system

Finally, the models also differ in how they explain change. This set of assumptions provides the clearest set of suggestions for therapeutic intervention. For example, the cognitive-behavioral perspectives emphasize the chain of antecedents and consequences that develop and maintain specific behavior patterns. To alter behavior requires changing this chain by affecting either the antecedents or the consequences of behavior. Similarly, stress theorists focus on and assess the interaction of the individual's coping repertoire (including, perhaps, the immune system's stress reactivity) and the environmental stressors that confront him or her.

Applying Models to Individual Life Circumstances

With this understanding of models and their underlying assumptions, let's return to the cause that opened Part II, that of Mrs. Rankin.

Joan Rankin is a 74-year-old woman who lives in her home in a small rural community. Her husband, Jim, died two years ago, following a five-year bout with cancer. Now that she is alone, Joan is tempted to move closer to her children, but cannot quite make up her mind. Her house is paid for, and she is not sure she could buy a comparable house in a city with the proceeds from a sale of this house. She has a modest pension that will be sufficient unless she needs major medical care. Sometimes she worries about not having enough money to carry her through. She chooses to live frugally with an occasional indulgence.

Joan belongs to the local garden club, but is not a particularly active member. She does enjoy working in her own small flower garden during the nice weather seasons. She also attends church almost weekly. Joan has a few close friends, but many of those friendships were strained by the period of Jim's illness. Even two years after his death, she is not sure how to fill her days. Her nights are usually tolerable although sometimes she lies awake for long periods in the middle of the night. At those times she feels overwhelmingly alone and scared.

Joan is generally healthy, although she has high blood pressure and some difficulties with thyroid and arthritis. She takes ibuprofen for the arthritis, propranolol for blood pressure, and synthroid to regulate her thyroid.

Joan's two children live 300 miles away in major cities. Her daughter, Jeannie, is married, has three children (ages 4, 7, and 10), and teaches school. Her son, John, a very successful Realtor, is currently engaged to be remarried. He was divorced four years ago from his wife of 18 years, who has custody of their two children, ages 8 and 13. Jeannie and John have never been very close. Nor was John close to his father, although he confided his troubles and joys to his mother privately.

Joan has two younger sisters still living, and had two older brothers who died more than five years ago. Her sister Betty lives only two blocks away from Joan, and calls her daily. Sometimes Joan resents the call because Betty is so perky and enthusiastic about life. Betty insists that Joan get out to social events regardless of how tired or sick Joan is feeling. Betty has always been the cheerful one, encouraging all those around her to enjoy life. Recently she has hinted that she might like to move in with Joan to share expenses.

Her other sister Vivian lives with her husband 30 miles away on a farm. They stay busy with farm responsibilities, and with their children and grandchildren. Joan sees them only at family gatherings on holidays. Vivian has always been the quiet, solid one in the family. Joan would like to spend more time with her, but can see that she is too busy with daily responsibilities to socialize.

Her brothers, Elwood and Milt, were in business together in a city 150 miles from Joan's home. They died of heart attacks exactly one year apart. They left their families quite well off financially, and their children and grandchildren have continued their business. Joan only visits with her sisters-in-law or their offspring at the annual family reunion each summer.

How would each model approach Mrs. Rankin's life situation?

As outlined in Chapter 4, the psychodynamic perspective assumes that Mrs. Rankin's symptoms will resolve if she comes to terms with the normal developmental tasks of later life. Erikson and his colleagues, for example, argued that the primary conflict to be resolved in later life is between ego integrity versus despair (Erikson, Erikson, & Kivnick, 1986). Clearly, Mrs. Rankin has spent much time and energy in the earlier developmental conflict (generativity vs. self-absorption), providing care for her ailing husband. Within this perspective, much attention would initially focus on her beliefs and values and the meaning that she attributes to her life, and on the coherence of the personal narrative that she has developed in thinking about her life. A major goal of treatment within the dynamic perspective might be to provide supportive therapy for Mrs. Rankin as she reevaluates her experience in later life. In doing so, the clinician would begin with an assessment of Mrs. Rankin's capacity for insight, her ability to reflect upon her experiences, and her aptitude for engaging in the therapeutic process.

In contrast, a cognitive-behaviorally oriented clinician would not focus on the underlying structure of Mrs. Rankin's personality or the "coherence" of her personal narrative (see Chapter 5). Instead, someone working within the cognitive-behavioral perspective would focus on assessing specific thought patterns and problem behaviors including the context for the development and continuation of those behaviors. In Mrs. Rankin's case, for example, the focus might fall on her periods of sleeplessness at night. Exactly when and under what conditions does this occur? Conversely, are there conditions under which the sleeplessness does not occur? The clinician might ask Mrs. Rankin to keep an activity log or a record of her sleep pattern and context for several days, trying to identify the pattern of antecedents and consequences that affect the sleep disruption. The cognitive-behavioral treatment would focus on altering the contingencies within Mrs. Rankin's context. First, it would be important to identify the desired outcome, which in this case is uninterrupted sleep. Next, attention would focus on one of two strategies: expanding the conditions that have led to a full night's sleep in the past or eliminating the conditions that are associated with the current bouts of sleeplessness. For example, if it were found that Mrs. Rankin slept better on the days that she had talked with one of her children, the clinician might enlist the children in a schedule of calls or contact. Similarly, if it were discovered that Mrs. Rankin had disrupted sleep on days that Betty called after 4 p.m., the clinician might work with Betty to change the schedule of her contacts. In addition, the clinician might also focus on Mrs. Rankin's own thoughts regarding being alone (i.e., her report of feeling "alone and scared"). To what extent does she have catastrophic or hopeless thoughts about the future? Specific negative thought patterns would be identified and she would be helped to replace them with more adaptive thought patterns.

A clinician working in the stress and coping framework might try a variety of strategies targeting several key aspects of Mrs. Rankin's experience: chronic strains, social resources, Mrs. Rankin's own vulnerabilities and resources, and her physical well-being (see Chapter 6). For example, the clinician might begin by targeting assessment and treatment of two chronic strains that are currently affecting Mrs. Rankin: her concerns about her financial well-being and her coping with her chronic health problems (e.g., arthritis, high blood pressure, and thyroid problems). Another target for assessment and treatment might be Mrs. Rankin's social resources. Here, the emphasis might shift to first assessing her current levels of social involvement and then enlisting effective social support for her. A third element of assessment and treatment might emphasize Mrs. Rankin's own approach to appraising her situation and the attributions she makes about her current life circumstances. Again, an initial step might be an assessment of her current and previous coping strategies. What has she done previously that has been helpful? Treatment would then explore either application (and possible adjustment) of previously successful coping attempts or development of new coping skills to fit her current life context. Finally, a clinician working within the stress and coping framework might concentrate on improving Mrs. Rankin's health practices, perhaps by focusing on a relaxation training or meditation program to decrease her anxiety.

A mental health professional working within a family systems perspective would emphasize other aspects of Mrs. Rankin's situation: her family's structure and function (see Chapter 7). For example, a clinician working within a system's perspective might start by asking Mrs. Rankin to complete a family genogram, including information about the alliances and bonds among various members of the family. Similarly, the clinician might be interested in the family stages represented by the various members (e.g., her daughter's children are all 10 or under; her son's children are also in the school-age years, etc.). This information helps the clinician to be aware of other family members' developmental tasks that may be competing with Mrs. Rankin's own challenges. Another focus of assessment would be to understand how this particular family works: To whom does Mrs. Rankin turn in times of crisis? Whom does she call first for everyday help? For major assistance? Whom does she avoid? Treatment within this framework might require both "first-order" and "second-order" change. At the very least, the clinician should be clear whether the goal is to change the behavior patterns of the family or to alter the basic structure of the family. Either goal might require the active involvement of several family members in the treatment process.

In summary, each of the psychotherapeutic models offers directions for assessment and treatment. Each has explicit and implicit assumptions about the salient contributors to mental health and mental disorder in later life. Each focuses therapeutic attention and effort to specific aspects of Mrs. Rankin's life and circumstances.

If models differ substantially in their basic elements, how do we choose among them? Each of the four models presented in Part II is both precise and capable of explaining a wide scope of functioning in older adults. Each of the four models has also proven to be useful from clinical and research perspectives. The challenge for the clinician working with older adults is to assess which perspective will be more helpful in understanding and intervening on behalf of a particular older client. Another important factor is which perspective most closely matches the values, beliefs, and personal style of the clinician.

There are two different approaches that clinicians may follow: the single lens or the kaleidoscope. Some prefer to become an expert within a single framework, knowing its strengths and limitations in depth. For example, a clinician may focus on dynamic approaches exclusively or cognitive-behavioral strategies exclusively. The clinician comes to learn the precision afforded by the theoretical and practical aspects of the framework in extensive detail. He or she also comes to learn and respect the scope of clinical utility of the framework, respecting that it probably will not be adequate for all clients and all conditions.

Most clinicians, however, report that they are eclectic or integrative which means that they use techniques from a variety of perspectives, in a coherent and organized way. In contrast to someone who uses one framework exclusively, these clinicians may emphasize aspects of several different frameworks, as if turning the kaleidoscope to see different facets of the same scene.

In the end, the clinician must ask a differential diagnostic question: Which assessment and treatment approaches for which types of mental disorders among older people will produce which types of outcomes? Answering this question will force you to detail the precision and scope of your implicit or explicit frameworks, and we invite you to do so.

Reference

Erikson, E. H., Erikson, J. M., & Kivnick, H. Q. (1986). *Vital involvement in old age.* New York, NY: Norton.

Part III

Introduction to Mental Disorders

Consider the following letter Dr. Smyer once received from a client:

Dear Dr. Smyer:

I have toyed with the idea of writing you ever since I heard you speak at the Presbyterian Church a couple of years ago. The occasion was one of a series of brown-bag lunches sponsored, I think, by the Area Agency on Aging. You may remember me, since I'm sure you were embarrassed when I substituted one word for another in trying to ask a question about the part inheritance plays in senility. My question made no sense, and you tactfully said, "I don't believe I understand your question," and I repeated it, correctly, saying, "You can see I'm senile already." (I was trying to be funny, but I was not amused.)

The question I asked is one that has haunted me all my adult life (I've just turned 78), and I think I have always known the answer. My father's father, my father, and the three sisters who lived long enough were all senile. I am obviously following in their footsteps, and have discussed the matter with Dr. Klein, who became my physician last year. I have told him that I have never taken much medication and have been opposed to "pain-killers," tranquilizers, etc., but that the day may come when I will accept medical help as the lesser of two evils. He assures me that there are new drugs which may help.

My question, Dr. Smyer, is this: Since I'm sure there must be ongoing research into the problem of senility, would it be of any value to such research if I volunteered as a test subject? At this point my memory is failing so rapidly, and I suffer such frequent agonies of confusion, that I am at the point of calling on Dr. Klein for the help he has promised. But I don't want to do so yet if my experience can

Aging and Mental Health, Third Edition. Daniel L. Segal, Sara Honn Qualls, and Michael A. Smyer.
© 2018 John Wiley & Sons, Inc. Published 2018 by John Wiley & Sons, Inc.

be of value to someone else, and particularly to the nine daughters of my sisters, ranging in age from 58 to 70, and to my own daughter, 42, who must be wondering if they too are doomed.

Is there any merit to this proposal? I will be most grateful for any advice you can give me.

Sincerely,
Mrs. Rose

How would you respond? Immediately, you have to make a clinical judgment about the seriousness of this older woman's concerns. Are her complaints a part of normal aging? Are they part of a pattern of significant mental disorder? How do you make sense of her use of the term *senile,* which is no longer used clinically? Your answer implicitly combines information from developmental epidemiology, psychiatric epidemiology, clinical investigations, and the psychology of adult development and aging. If you decide that Mrs. Rose has a mental disorder, what would you do? Your answer reflects your assumptions regarding the cause of the disorder and how effective you can be in altering that cause.

The chapters in Part III are designed to describe the patterns of specific mental disorders along with effective methods for assessment and treatment. In preparing these chapters, we face the same dilemmas as clinicians: How do we know that specific symptoms are part of a picture of pathology? How can we identify specific treatments that are effective with older adults?

It is now apparent that the earlier models of psychology and psychiatry for describing patterns of disease, causation, and treatment were too simplistic. We would like to reduce the complexity of assessment and treatment to a simple focus on the individual, or perhaps even on one aspect of the individual (e.g., biological functioning). However, an effective understanding of mental disorders in later life requires an understanding of the ecology of interactions of several levels of influence—from the molecular to the molar, from genetic predispositions to the social environment—that either protect or exacerbate the older person's vulnerability.

At a summit sponsored by the Institute of Medicine (IoM) in 2009, health care leaders explored the challenges, opportunities, and imperatives for shifting to an integrative care approach to health care. The report from that summit, *Integrative Medicine and the Health of the Public* (2009), called for a broadening of the lens used by health care providers to encompass multiple domains of human lives. Rather than focusing on diseases, leaders called for patient-centered care that assessed the mental and behavioral health, environmental and social contexts, and beliefs and motivations as well as biomarkers and disease states. Over 20 years ago, the IoM developed a research agenda aimed at preventing mental disorders (Mrazek & Haggerty, 1994) by examining multiple points of possible intervention in a model that presaged the current call for integrative care. That IoM report on prevention suggested that we need to consider a new spectrum of mental health interventions for mental disorders. The spectrum includes three major classes of intervention: prevention, treatment, and maintenance. A central element in the scheme is the concept of risk for a disorder. Formerly, risk might be thought of as solely an individual characteristic, identified by individual indicators (e.g., genetic history, age, sex, socioeconomic status, etc.). However, recent work in epidemiology and clinical investigation suggests that risk for developing a disorder is an interaction of several systems and levels of influence, including aspects of the individual's setting, the individual's own characteristics, and characteristics of the broader culture. The multiple sources of risk suggest multiple options for intervention as well.

Susser and Susser (1996) put it this way:

> Systems also relate to one another; they do not exist in isolation. A metaphor may serve to illuminate this ecological perspective. We liken it to Chinese boxes—a conjurer's nest of boxes, each containing a succession of smaller ones. Thus, within localized structures, we envisage successive levels of organization, each of which encompasses the next and simpler level, all with intimate links between them.... The outer box might be the overarching physical environment which, in turn, contains societies and populations (the epidemiological terrain), single individuals, and individual physiological systems, tissues and cells, and finally (in biology) molecules. (pp. 675–676)

Gatz and her colleagues (1996) also emphasized the interaction of three types of influences on the development and presentation of mental disorders among older adults: the individual's level of vulnerability, which is a product of biological vulnerabilities and psychological factors affecting risk; stress, both environmental and social; and protective factors that can serve as psychological, biological, or social buffers. They argued that the combination of protective and risk factors affects the individual's susceptibility of developing a mental disorder.

To be effective, then, the clinician must understand the context of the individual and the patterns of interaction among several levels of influence (Qualls, 2005). This multilayered ecological perspective will affect how symptoms are labeled, how clinical syndromes are defined, and, ultimately, case identification. It will also affect strategies that are developed for assessment and treatment.

For example, consider Mrs. Rose's complaint about memory problems. If we look solely at her individual situation, we may miss important information about the social stresses that may be presenting a challenge for her. Optimally, we would like to place her current functioning in a larger context: Does she have a history of memory problems and complaints? Does she have a family history of such problems? Has she been treated for these difficulties in the past? What is the context of this most recent complaint (e.g., changes in her own functioning, her social context, her physical well-being, etc.)? Have her medications changed recently? Have there been any recent physical illnesses? In short, we would be assessing the three key elements of the scheme proposed by Gatz et al. (1996): individual vulnerability, stresses, and protective factors.

At the same time, we focus on two specific types of history: the history of the individual and the history of the disorder. Again, consider Mrs. Rose. We want to know much about her personal history and about the history of her memory complaint. Epidemiologists focus on incidence and prevalence rates: patterns of development of new episodes and rates of overall presence of the disorder, regardless of when it began. On the clinical level, we might envision different treatment strategies for two different patters: Some might grow old and get memory problems; others might develop memory problems and grow old (Kahn, 1975). These different life histories and different problem histories would suggest different approaches.

The chapters in Part III take the following elements as a starting point: an ecological perspective that acknowledges several layers of interacting influences that produce risk for the various mental disorders and the patterns of those disorders; individual life history and individual history of the specific mental disorder experienced by the person, both of which affect assessment and treatment of the disorder; and the necessity for an integrated approach to assessment and treatment of mental disorders that acknowledges individual vulnerability, assesses sources of stress, and builds upon current effective sources of social support. The chapters also emphasize effective case identification and treatment for older adults with specific mental disorders. In doing so, they draw from the models of mental health and mental disorder described in Part II. The assessment and treatment approaches outlined in Part III embody causal models of each disorder and, therefore, assumptions regarding effective clinical approaches.

References

Gatz, M., Kasl-Godley, J., & Karel, M. (1996). Aging and mental disorders. In J. E. Birren & K. W. Schaie (Eds.), *Handbook of the psychology of aging* (4th ed., pp. 365–382). San Diego, CA: Academic Press.

Institute of Medicine. (2009). *Integrative medicine and the health of the public.* Washington, DC: National Academies Press.

Kahn, R. L. (1975). The mental health system and the future aged. *The Gerontologist, 15*(2), 24–31.

Mrazek, P. J., & Haggerty, R. J. (Eds.) (1994). *Reducing risks for mental disorders: Frontiers for preventive intervention research.* Washington, DC: National Academy Press.

Qualls, S. H. (2005). Mental health in later life, ecology of. In C. B. Fisher & R. M. Lerner (Eds.), *Applied developmental science: An encyclopedia of research, policies, and programs.* Thousand Oaks, CA: Sage.

Susser, M. B., & Susser, E. (1996). Choosing a future for epidemiology, II: From black box to Chinese boxes and eco-epidemiology. *American Journal of Public Health, 86,* 674–677.

8

Cognitive Impairment and Neurocognitive Disorders

Neurocognitive disorders (NCDs) encompass a broad range of disorders indicating some degree of deterioration in cognitive function that alters daily functioning. The primary NCDs in the *Diagnostic and Statistical Manual of Mental Disorders*, fifth edition, (DSM-5) are delirium, mild NCD, and major NCD. The NCDs are not part of the typical process of adult development and aging and also must represent a change from the individual's previous level of functioning (American Psychiatric Association, 2013). Because of their devastating effect on the autonomy of older adults, NCDs warrant aggressive assessment and interventions to support the maximum possible level of functioning.

Anyone working with older adults must have some familiarity with the causes, consequences, and remedies for NCDs. In this chapter, we address the extent to which cognitive decline is a part of normal aging, apart from NCDs, and describe the clinical symptoms and presentations of delirium, mild NCD, and major NCD. We also discuss cognitive impairment due to depression, since this is a common concern for some older adults and is sometimes mistaken for a true NCD. We also describe strategies for assessing cognitive functioning and for designing interventions to enhance the functioning of cognitively impaired older persons. Consider the following three cases that describe some of the challenges faced by persons who are experiencing some degree of cognitive impairment.

> Jane Winthrop is an 85-year-old widow who is experiencing increasing difficulty living alone. Her daughter visits several times each week to write out bills, set up and monitor medication use in a pillbox, and take her shopping. Jane has trouble figuring out how much of her favorite foods to buy, and typically purchases prepared meals that can be heated in the microwave. Her daughter leaves reminder notes on the microwave about how to work it, and on the entry door to the apartment about the security measures that should be taken before bedtime. On the bathroom mirror is a reminder to brush teeth, and on the kitchen table is a

---

Aging and Mental Health, Third Edition. Daniel L. Segal, Sara Honn Qualls, and Michael A. Smyer.
© 2018 John Wiley & Sons, Inc. Published 2018 by John Wiley & Sons, Inc.

reminder to take medications after meals. Jane stays in her apartment most of the time because the hallways and elevator confuse her. She has recently gotten lost in her own building, where she has lived for over 20 years. Friends in the apartment complex check in on her daily.

Noni Smith's daughter was alarmed when she visited her mother last weekend. Within a week, her mother had changed! She had a vacant look in her eyes, was not interested in talking, was dressed in mismatched clothing, and her hair was dirty and uncombed. The neighbor shared the daughter's concern, indicating she had not seen Noni out walking this week as was her custom. The daughter called Noni's physician, who asked to see Noni immediately to check whether the new medications he initiated two weeks ago could be causing the problem.

Jim Hunt complains constantly about his poor memory. He is so disturbed by his inability to concentrate and remember things that he has quit two of his favorite hobbies—woodworking and reading about politics. Nothing gives him pleasure anymore and he feels very grumpy. He no longer has the showcase yard of the neighborhood because he seems able to do only the minimum. His family is growing concerned that he may have Alzheimer's disease.

What Jane, Noni, and Jim share in common is a perceived or real loss of abilities to think, remember, solve problems, and handle the affairs of everyday life. Indeed, having cognitive problems is among the most feared aspects of aging. Although there are changes in cognitive functioning that are normative with old age, these changes rarely affect daily functioning (Salthouse, 2012). However, the expectation for normative cognitive decline can keep some older people and those around them from seeking appropriate assessment. Family and friends often compensate for deficits in cognitive functioning by assisting with tasks, similarly to how they have done across the lifespan. Families and even professional staff often fail to recognize the extent of cognitive impairment (Nichols & Martindale-Adams, 2006).

The risks of cognitive impairment are well documented in both hospitalized and community-dwelling older adults. For example, the risk of hospitalization and a longer length of stay in the hospital are higher in older adults with impaired cognition than those with intact cognitive functioning. In 2015, for example, the total costs for health care, long-term care, and hospice care for people with Alzheimer's disease and other dementias were estimated to be a staggering $226 billion (Alzheimer's Association, 2015), making these disorders among the most expensive in the US. In addition, the costs of care provided by family members and friends are considerable: In 2014, for example, Americans provided nearly 18 billion hours of unpaid care to people with Alzheimer's disease or other dementias (Alzheimer's Association, 2015).

What is the range of cognitive functioning that is of interest to mental health providers? Cognition is usually examined within broad areas such as attention, language, visual-spatial skills, learning, memory, decision-making, social cognition, and executive functioning. Within each domain are many specific functions. Neuropsychologists organize their analyses of cognitive functioning within a hierarchy that ranges from the simplest functions (e.g., attention) to the most complex (e.g., executive functioning,

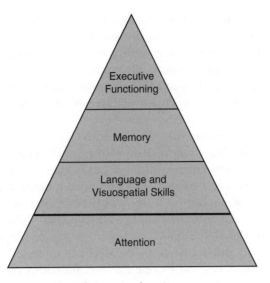

Figure 8.1   Conceptual hierarchy of cognitive functions.

including abstract reasoning and problem-solving), as illustrated in Figure 8.1. This hierarchical organization reflects the foundational role of the simpler functions for all complex cognitive activities that rank higher in the hierarchy. In other words, if basic processes like attention are impaired, all higher-order processes will be negatively affected. As a general rule, more complex functions are the most easily disrupted by illness, brain dysfunction, or potentially toxic agents like medications.

Is Cognitive Impairment Normal for Older Adults?

The answer to this question is actually a qualified, "clearly yes and no." On one hand, tests of cognitive functioning consistently show age-related decrements in many cognitive functions that begin during middle adulthood (Foster, Cornwell, Kisley, & Davis, 2006). On the other hand, the normative decrements in functioning that are evident in laboratory tests rarely make an impact on daily functioning (Salthouse, 2012).

Several factors make it possible for age decrements to be normative, but result in few effects of those changes in everyday life. First, laboratory tests of cognition push the limits of skills in ways that rarely occur in daily life. Age-related normative cognitive declines are relatively subtle, becoming visible primarily when functioning is pushed to its limits. Second, there is tremendous variability among older adults in the degree of decline experienced in any specific function. Thus, although mean scores may decline, the highest functioning older person may still be functioning above the average for younger adults. Third, humans are highly adaptive creatures who adjust their behavior to compensate for deficits (Salthouse, 2012). Decrements in cognitive impairment may not be evident in daily life because the individual is skilled at compensating for deficits with external aids (e.g., written grocery lists) or by drawing upon an intact skill to compensate (e.g., relying on a cognitive map to drive to a friend's house when verbal memory for directions is impaired). As per the DSM-5 nomenclature, *major NCDs* refer to impairments that are substantial enough to affect daily functioning, that is, those that are caused by some serious underlying disease or dysfunction that warrants intervention. In contrast, *mild NCDs* do not interfere with capacity for independence in daily activities although such functional deficits are often warded off by greater effort, compensatory strategies, or accommodation on the part of the person.

As a precursor to discussing major and mild NCDs, we first characterize some of the cognitive deficits that are normative with aging. Detailed summaries of findings on normative cognitive changes with age can be found elsewhere (Foster et al., 2006; Salthouse, 2012). In Chapter 2, we presented a figure depicting the typical longitudinal picture of cognitive changes with advancing age (see Figure 2.3), taken from the Seattle Longitudinal Study of Intellectual Abilities. Note that most abilities depicted in this figure remained stable or actually improved throughout middle adulthood. In one's 60s and 70s, declines in functioning begin to be apparent in some functions, and by one's 80s all functions show some degree of deterioration.

Although aging affects all of the skills in the pyramid in Figure 8.1, aging's greatest impacts are on the performance of complex skills illustrated at the top of the figure. Generally, simple attentional processes are maintained well into advanced old age. Language abilities are generally preserved intact until well into one's 70s, at which time some deficits are evident in semantic linguistic abilities (e.g., verbal meaning). Performances on complex laboratory tasks (e.g., selective attention) typically show some age-related decrements that ultimately relate to performance on complex tasks such as driving (Salthouse, 2012).

Researchers and clinicians have focused on the effects of aging on executive functions (EFs) because of their impact on complex behavior. Reuter-Lorenz, Festini, and Jantz (2016) provided a useful definition of EFs and their link to neurocognitive aging:

> EFs are multifaceted control processes that regulate thought and behavior...EFs typically refer to a family of general-purpose mechanisms (i.e., updating, inhibiting, switching, working memory, prioritizing, sequencing) largely mediated by the prefrontal cortex...that are critical to other higher cognitive abilities including planning, reasoning, long-term memory, decision making and problem solving. (Reuter-Lorenz et al., 2016, p. 246)

Despite the importance of EFs, there is still uncertainty over the role that age-related changes in the prefrontal cortex play in maintaining functioning in later life. The frontal lobes are vulnerable to the adverse effects of aging. However, on some tasks older adults "over-recruit" prefrontal regions to compensate for other losses and achieve better performance (Cabeza & Dennis, 2013; Reuter-Lorenz et al., 2016). In addition, there are individual differences in EF, as with other psychological functions. Finally, there has been only one lifespan, cross-sectional study of functional imaging and EF (Kennedy et al., 2015), suggesting that the over-recruitment process may begin in middle age. Because EFs are linked to many activities in daily life (e.g., driving and decision-making), it is important that they are fully assessed during any cognitive evaluation of older adults.

Memory functions have been the focus of more research than any other cognitive area. Lustig and Lin (2016) recently reviewed the memory and aging research from a neurocognitive perspective. They remind us that one summary of structural brain changes with age is a "front to back" or "last in, first out" pattern (Raz, 2000). Reducing a complex field to a broad summary, we can say that memory declines with age. Younger adults perform better than adults aged 50 years old and older on most memory tasks. By age 70, performance within several memory domains declines significantly. Of course, the extent of deficit is influenced by the method of assessment and the memory task (e.g., with and without cues, meaningful versus nonmeaningful stimuli, visual and verbal stimuli). Intervention research has demonstrated that some of the deficits seen in long-term memory can be ameliorated by providing additional structure to the memory tasks (e.g., providing cues, instructions in encoding strategies, or use of recognition rather than recall tasks), although memory skill remains lower, on average, for older adults than younger adults even under enhancement conditions. Not all memory processes are affected equally by age. Generally, sensory memory (e.g., very, very short-term memories of visual or auditory sensory data) and primary memory (or very short-term memory of a few seconds of duration) are least affected, whereas learning and retaining information over time (secondary memory) are where the greatest declines with aging are evident.

Memory tasks that rely on controlled or associative processes are the most vulnerable to declines with age (Lustig & Lin, 2016). Similarly, environmental cues that intentionally or unintentionally rely upon these processes may exacerbate aging-related declines. Abstract reasoning and complex problem-solving abilities also appear to decline by one's 60s and 70s (Foster et al., 2006). Tasks such as the Wisconsin Card Sort, the Block Design subtest on the Wechsler Adult Intelligence Scales, and explaining proverbs all elicit lower performances in older adults than in young adults. As is true of most cognitive functions, the method of assessment and the type of task produces variations in the results, although the picture that emerges is essentially consistent.

Knowledge of what is normative within healthy older adults is critical to the formation of appropriate expectations about performance on tests of cognitive functioning in clinical populations (American Psychological Association, 2012). The clinical assessment of cognitive impairment or NCDs requires either baseline data on the individual's previous functioning and/or normative data on older adults within an appropriate comparison group. The importance of age-appropriate norms will be discussed further in the section on assessment below.

Individual differences in memory and cognition across late adulthood make individual baselines even more valuable (Lustig & Lin, 2016). Nyberg and colleagues (2012), for example, reported longitudinal studies in which some older participants showed little or no memory decline. Following Stern (2002), they differentiate brain or cognitive *reserve* that allows continued good performance despite age-related pathology, and brain *maintenance* that focuses on protection from such pathology. (For a current debate in the field on the value of one maintenance factor—brain exercises—see Box 8.1).

Box 8.1   Is cognitive training an effective strategy for brain maintenance in later life?

You have probably heard the ads for Lumosity, an online brain training program. Online and on the airwaves, Lumosity promised to help older people avoid cognitive decline and keep their mental abilities sharp. They made those promises until the Federal Trade Commission (FTC) said that Lumosity could not back up its claims with scientific evidence. Lumosity agreed to a $50 million judgment and to stop making such unsupported claims (FTC, 2016).

Lumosity illustrates a broader issue: Is there compelling evidence that cognitive training helps either prevent or remediate cognitive decline? A group of more than 100 cognitive scientists, led by Laura Carstensen, issued a statement questioning the efficacy of these approaches (see Stanford Center on Longevity, 2014):

> The strong consensus of this group is that the scientific literature does not support claims that the use of software-based "brain games" alters neural functioning in ways that improve general cognitive performance in everyday life, or prevent cognitive slowing and brain disease.

Two of their concerns stand out: using a single assessment approach as a proxy for an entire domain, and the "transfer of training" effects from the computer games to real-life situations and across time. In response, another group of more than 100 cognitive scientists (Cognitive Training Data; CTD) issued their own assessment of the research and its implications:

> We fear that most readers would take this to mean there is little or no peer-reviewed evidence that certain brain exercises have been shown to drive cognitive improvements. There is, in fact, a large and growing body of such evidence. That evidence now includes dozens of randomized, controlled trials published in peer-reviewed journals that document specific benefits of defined types of cognitive training. Many of these studies show improvements that encompass a broad array of cognitive and everyday activities, show gains that persist for a reasonable amount of time, document positive changes in real-life indices of cognitive health, and employ control strategies designed to account for "placebo" effects. (CTD, 2014)

Clients and their family members may seek your guidance on the usefulness of these products and approaches. It will be important to clarify the specific cognitive function or functions that are of concern, the target of any preventive or remedial efforts, and the track record on transferring the training to the day-to-day settings and challenges that were the initial cause for concern.

Diagnostic Categories: A Time of Transition

For some time, there have been differences between research-based criteria and clinical criteria for diagnosing NCDs. In the last few years, some clarity has been provided by the new criteria for diagnosing cognitive disorders that were published in the DSM-5 (APA, 2013). Previously, the National Institute on Aging (NIA) and Alzheimer's Association (AA) appointed a task force to create criteria reflecting the continuum of impairments caused by neurodegenerative diseases (Jack et al., 2011). Their criteria used the term dementia, as did the previous editions of the DSM. The new DSM-5 acknowledges that the term dementia is consistent with Major Neurocognitive Disorder, but structures its discussion around major and mild NCDs. In contrast, the Patient Protection and Affordable Care Act (2010) requires use of the International Classification of Diseases (ICD-10) codes for billing diagnoses. As Castro and Smith (2015) point out, the ICD-10 structure for diagnosis of Alzheimer's disease and mild cognitive impairment follows DSM IV-TR more closely than DSM-5. (See Castro and Smith, 2015, for a very helpful discussion of the nomenclature changes.) For the clinician, the lessons are clear: One needs to understand the billing codes used in one's location, as well as the rationale and research behind them. We will use the DSM-5 framework in the following discussion.

Classifying neurocognitive disorders

The NCDs are disorders with a primary deficit in cognitive functioning. These disorders are not part of the normal, developmental aging process. Instead, they are diagnosed by focusing attention on three elements: an area of the brain affected, the severity and rapidity of onset, and the disruption to an individual's everyday functioning. Importantly, the NCDs represent a change in functioning from the individual's baseline functioning.

The DSM-5 summarizes the cognitive functions that are disrupted in NCDs, the type of everyday behavior affected, and assessment strategies used to assess these areas: complex attention, executive function, learning and memory, language, perceptual-motor abilities, and social cognition. DSM-5 also offers examples of symptoms and assessment approaches in each area.

Parkinson's disease (PD) illustrates many of the characteristics of NCDs. PD is the second most common neurodegenerative disorder, behind only Alzheimer's disease in prevalence. Approximately 1–2% of those 65 years and older and 4–5% of those 85 years and older have PD (Kowal, Dall, Chakrabarti, Storm, & Jain, 2013). To be considered within the NCDs, however, the cognitive dysfunction must follow the PD (APA, 2013). Among those with PD, up to 75% will develop a major NCD during the course of the disease (Aarsland, Zaccai, & Brayne, 2005). In addition to its hallmark motor dysfunctions (e.g., rigidity, tremor, bradykinesia, postural rigidity), PD also involves a number of behavioral symptoms that are challenging for patients with PD and their families, including apathy, anxiety, hallucinations, and delusions (Friedman, 2013).

Michael Kinsley (2014) has written a moving and perceptive autobiographical account of PD. For Kinsley, an editor and writer, the most harrowing part of the diagnosis was the impending cognitive decline, not the motor impairments. With a dark sense of humor, he describes the two forms of competition in the Boomer death-style Olympics: "There's dying last and there's dying lucid." Kinsley was diagnosed with PD at age 43, which represents an early onset since the highest incidence of initial diagnosis is in the 60s (APA, 2013). He agrees with neurologist Patrick McNamara (2011) that the neuropsychiatric elements of PD, especially deficits in executive functioning, can be as disabling as the motor symptoms. After the initial diagnosis, Kinsley explored the implications of cognitive changes with his neurologist:

> So I knew that thinking was involved. I asked my neurologist at the time, and he answered carefully. "Well, after a few years you may lose your edge." Lose my edge? Lose my edge? Oh Shit! I need my edge. My edge is how I make a living. More than that: My edge is my claim on the world. It's why people are my friends, why they invite me over for dinner, perhaps why they marry me. What am I worth to the world if I've lost my edge?

Kinsley's account also highlights two other aspects of PD as an NCD: the rate of change and the importance of individual baseline assessments. Kinsley was diagnosed over 20 years ago. Since then, he has observed changes in his motor functioning and in his cognition—slight changes from his perspective. Eight years ago, he had deep brain stimulation surgery. At that time, he also had pre- and post-operative cognitive assessments that provided a comparison for his functioning in 2014. Kinsley's wry and insightful account of neuropsychological testing concludes with the importance of understanding that intelligence is not a single number, but a complex interplay of many different abilities. In short, he did well in some areas and very poorly in other areas, a working definition of the process of losing one's edge.

Kinsley's account of PD is a reminder of several important lessons: The cognitive and behavioral aspects of an NCD like PD are important to consider. For Kinsley, a writer and public intellectual, the cognitive aspects are especially salient but for others (e.g., ski instructors, painters), the motor aspects may be more important. Individualized baseline measures and assessment of change allow us to tailor treatment. Finally, because Kinsley is such a good writer, he has provided us a rare glimpse into the experience of submitting to several hours of neuropsychological testing.

Delirium: A Common, Reversible Cause of Cognitive Impairment

A delirium is a disturbance of attention and awareness that is accompanied by a change in cognition that cannot be better accounted for by another preexisting NCD (APA, 2013). Delirium develops rapidly over the course of hours or days, and often fluctuates during the day. The case of Noni Smith described at the opening of this chapter is typical of a case of delirium. The onset is rapid, and the person's behavior

Table 8.1 Diagnostic features of delirium

- There is a disturbance in attention (i.e., diminished ability to direct, focus, sustain, and shift attention) and awareness (diminished orientation to the environment).
- The disturbance develops quickly (usually hours to a few days), marking a change from baseline attention and awareness, and the symptoms tend to fluctuate in severity throughout the day.
- There is an additional disturbance in other areas of cognition (e.g., memory deficit, disorientation, language, visuospatial ability, or perception).
- Another preexisting, established, or evolving neurocognitive disorder does not better explain the disturbance.
- The disturbance does not occur in the context of a severely reduced level of arousal (e.g., coma).
- The patient's medical history, physical examination, or laboratory findings indicate that the disturbance is a direct physiological consequence of another medical condition, substance intoxication or withdrawal (e.g., a drug of abuse or a medication), or exposure to a toxin, or is due to multiple etiologies.

Source: Adapted from American Psychiatric Association (2013).

is disorganized in ways that are not typical for her. By definition, the cognitive disturbance is caused by physiological factors.

The DSM-5 (APA, 2013) diagnostic features for all types of delirium, regardless of etiology, are outlined in Table 8.1. In addition to the criteria that require a disturbance in cognition, persons experiencing delirium are also likely to report a disturbed sleep–wake cycle and unpleasant affect (e.g., fear, depression, anger, apathy). People with delirium may shift from one emotional state to the other, sometimes quickly and unpredictably. Attentional processes are particularly disrupted, leading to impairment in higher-level cognitive functions (e.g., memory, problem-solving) (Choi et al., 2012). In addition, activity levels may be affected (e.g., hyperactive, hypoactive, or mixed levels of activity) (APA, 2013).

Older adults are especially at risk for delirium because of their increased likelihood of chronic illness and the increased use of medication to manage those illnesses. Within the full population, the prevalence of delirium is quite low, at approximately 1–2% (Inouye, 2006). Prevalence rates rise with age, however, reaching 14% among those 85 years of age and older. Common causes of delirium include the following:

- acute illnesses (e.g., urinary tract infections),
- medication / substance intoxication or withdrawal,
- central nervous system disorders (e.g., stroke),
- cardiovascular disorders,
- dehydration,
- metabolic disturbances.

As many as 30% of all hospitalized older adults, and from 15% to 53% of postoperative patients are diagnosable with delirium (Inouye, 2006; Noimark, 2009). Older adults show high rates of delirium during hospitalizations primarily due to factors related to the hospitalization (e.g., infection, medication changes, cardiovascular conditions), but risk is also increased among those with preexisting cognitive impairment. Similarly, high rates of delirium are found in intensive care settings and in post-acute care settings like nursing homes (APA, 2013). Although reversible, delirium is a serious risk factor for illness and mortality rates among older adults. Delirium also increases the risk of long-term care placement (Inouye, 2006; Saxena & Lawley, 2009).

Medications are among the first possible sources of delirium that need to be investigated. Almost any medication, including the most apparently innocuous over-the-counter medications, can cause delirium if the right conditions are present. One reason for vulnerability is that the process by which drugs are distributed, metabolized, and excreted are altered significantly with age (Hutchinson & O'Brien, 2007). Changes in several physiological systems contribute to the reduced capacity to metabolize, break down, and excrete drugs from the body. Thus, adverse drug reactions or drug toxicity are significant risk factors for older adults.

Older adults are also more vulnerable to medication-induced delirium because of their high rate of medication use. Results from a large study of community-dwelling older adults in the US showed that 81% used at least one prescription medicine, 29% used at least five prescription medications concurrently, and 49% used a dietary supplement (Qato et al., 2008). Among those using a prescription medicine, 46% concurrently used an over-the-counter medication and 52% concurrently used a dietary supplement. Not surprisingly, 4% of older adults were at risk for major drug–drug interactions (Qato et al., 2008). Because nursing home residents have a complex combination of physical and mental health problems, their use and over-use of medications is a major concern (Office of the Inspector General, 2001). A review of psychotropic drug use found that 8% of that usage was inappropriate for a variety of reasons, including duplicative therapies, unjustified chronic use, or too high a dose (Office of the Inspector General, 2001). Since this review, the Center for Medicare and Medicaid Studies (CMS) has focused on improving dementia care in nursing homes, including the reduction of antipsychotic drug use. The most recent data (CMS, 2014) indicate that 19% of long-stay nursing home residents were receiving antipsychotic medications, down from an earlier rate of 24%. Whether in the community or in a nursing home, older adults' potential for drug interactions is obviously extraordinarily high. Taken together, physiological changes result in altered responsiveness to medications such that even very small doses can produce delirium.

Finally, environmental conditions can also add to the probability of delirium, although delirium rarely results solely from environmental conditions. Psycho-social factors, sensory deprivation, and sleep deprivation may contribute to the development of delirium when other causal factors (e.g., toxic or metabolic factors) are present (APA, 2013). After a full medical assessment to identify the specific causes of a case of delirium, treatment aims to control or reverse the underlying causes. Prognosis for a full recovery is good, especially if the delirium and its causes are identified relatively quickly and treated aggressively. In some cases, it may take several weeks for the person's cognition and level of awareness to fully return to normal.

Mild Cognitive Impairment and Mild NCD

The past decade has witnessed increased interest in a milder form of cognitive impairment in older adults who do not meet the criteria for dementia but whose cognitive deficits are greater than would be produced by normal aging. Various categories for this construct have been proposed and evaluated, with Mild Cognitive Impairment (MCI) emerging as a term that is commonly used in clinical settings. The MCI category corresponds to the diagnosis of mild NCD in DSM-5's nomenclature.

The cognitive changes associated with normal aging overlap with those associated with MCI, suggesting a continuum of deterioration that may progress into a dementia for at least a portion of the population (Smith & Rush, 2006). Although evolving, the definition of MCI (and mild NCD) requires the presence of impairment in at least one domain of cognitive functioning, but the person's Instrumental Activities of Daily Living (including management of finances, transportation, telephone use) are basically intact. Two types of MCI have been identified (Alzheimer's Association, 2015), based on the type of thinking skills affected. *Amnestic MCI* is characterized by memory impairments, such as forgetting information that one previously would have easily recalled, for example appointments, conversations, or recent events. In contrast, *nonamnestic MCI* affects thinking skills other than memory, such as decision-making or visual perception.

Part of the interest in MCI is driven by the high prevalence rates (over 22% of persons over age 70 and rates as high as 13.7% in 60–64-year-olds), and high rates of conversion to dementia or major NCD (over 12% per year, with variability across subtypes) (Plassman et al., 2008). Causes of these MCIs include chronic medical conditions such as heart failure and diabetes as well as incipient dementia in very early predisease stages.

Do older people want to know if they are developing cognitive impairment at this mild level? Research makes it clear that older adults want to know about cognitive impairment in themselves or in a close family member (Dale, Hougham, Hill, & Sachs, 2006). Older adults also report being willing to be screened for MCI, although families anticipate resistance and anger at any suggestion that an evaluation is needed (Nichols & Martindale-Adams, 2006). Persons with MCI also appear more capable of accurately reporting their functional abilities than are persons with a dementia (Farias, Mungas, & Jagust, 2005).

Although families say they want to know about MCI, Whitehouse and Moody (2006) have voiced concern that very early clinical labeling of cognitive impairment can have deleterious effects on well-being. These researchers question the reliability and validity of the category that does not yet have strong predictive validity for diseases. Thus, very early medicalization of brain aging primarily may benefit the pharmaceutical industry, whose stake in early intervention is great. In contrast to medical frameworks for mild cognitive decline, social constructions of aging processes present powerful reasons not to use clinical language for a relatively ambiguous phenomenon. Among the negative effects of using clinical language for MCI is the establishment of an expectation of decline that can serve as a self-fulfilling and other-reinforcing prophecy. Very early diagnosis of cognitive decline prior to the time when its predictive validity is clear creates a medical framework that can easily dominate the meaning and structures of a person's life. Further research may render this debate moot, if cognitive testing improves in predictive validity. For today, however, Whitehouse and Moody remind us that the power of diagnostic labels to shape social construc- tions warrants thoughtful dialogue on the establishment of diagnostic criteria. (See Chapter 3 for more on the impact of negative stereotypes.)

The mainstream of care, however, reflects the belief that early detection of MCI has the same value as early detection of dementias of any type, including Alzheimer's disease. Patients have time to plan proactively for their future care, and families have time to anticipate future needs and care strategies. Many barriers exist to early detection, however, despite patients' and families' interests in obtaining it.

A recent Alzheimer's Association report focused on disclosure of a diagnosis of Alzheimer's disease or another dementia (Alzheimer's Association, 2015). The report framed disclosure within the ethical principles of assuring patient autonomy and truth-telling. (See Chapter 17 for a complete discussion of the ethics of diag- nosis and treatment.) A recent analysis of Medicare data found that less than half of patients with Alzheimer's disease or another dementia diagnosis reported being told the diagnosis. Higher rates of impairments in activities of daily living were associated with higher rates of disclosure: With greater impairment, patients or their proxies were more likely to report being told the diagnosis.

The Alzheimer's Association supports early disclosure to assist in better decision- making and planning by patients and their families. At the same time, it urges individ- ualized approaches to disclosure, accommodating different trajectories, personal and family histories, and resources. One patient advocate summed it up well:

> "Deliver the news in plain but sensitive language. This may be one of the most important things I ever hear. Please use language that I can understand and be sensitive to how this may make me feel." (Alzheimer's Association, 2015, p. 66)

As Castro and Smith (2015) point out, the annual well visit covered by Medicare under the Patient Protection and Affordable Care Act is required to include cognitive screening assessments. The Alzheimer's Association has provided a useful flow chart linked to this screening process to guide clinicians (Cordell et al., 2013). The avail- able screening tools detect difficulties in a limited set of domains, however, and are rarely able to predict transition from MCI to dementia (Lonie, Tierney, & Ebmeier, 2009). Until more effective screening tools, including those that require less labor (e.g., computerized screens), are developed for primary care and other settings where older adults routinely receive services, full neuropsychological evaluations are needed to produce a diagnosis.

Care for persons with MCI or mild NCD requires an appreciation for the experi- ence of the person with the condition (Lingler et al., 2006). The impairments caused by MCI or mild NCD are by definition mild in intensity and scope, and thus not readily discernible by others in surface level interaction. Thus, the person with the disorder lives suspended between his or her status as a normal, high-functioning-yet-impaired person and someone with deficits significant enough to be diagnosable with a dis- order. Those living with and caring for persons with MCI or a mild NCD observe subtle but important changes that alter their relationships (Blieszner, Roberto, Wilcox,

Barham, & Winston, 2007). Although not as overtly impairing as dementia, MCI or a mild NCD provides individuals and families with substantial challenges in daily life, and a likely prognosis for declining functioning in the future.

Major Neurocognitive Disorders

As noted earlier, the DSM-5 (APA, 2013) classifies NCDs into two broad categories: major and mild NCDs, differentiated by the extent of cognitive decline (Castro & Smith, 2015). Major NCD is characterized by significant cognitive decline from an earlier level of performance in one or more cognitive areas (e.g., complex attention, executive function, learning and memory, language, perceptual-motor abilities, social cognition). The deficits may be identified by the patient or key informants and confirmed by neuropsychological testing. Finally, to qualify as a major NCD, the deficits must interfere with the person's independent functioning.

Several elements are important to highlight in this definition. First is the importance of deviation from the individual's own baseline of previous functioning. Second is the key role of cognitive functioning broadly assessed, not solely memory complaints. Third is the essential role of neuropsychological testing in the diagnosis and treatment planning process.

Major neurocognitive disorder: Alzheimer's disease

Alzheimer's disease (AD) is a slowly progressing brain disease that begins before clinical symptoms emerge, with two neurological features: progressive accumulation of the protein fragment beta-amyloid (plaques) that form between neurons in the brain and twisted strands of the protein tau (tangles) that form inside neurons (Alzheimer's Association, 2015).

AD is the most common form of major NCD, with prevalence ranging from 11% of those 65 and older to 32% of those 85 and older (Alzheimer's Association, 2015). Within these general prevalence parameters, there are important demographic differences in prevalence rates by gender and by race/ethnic origin. For example, more women than men have AD or other dementias: Of the 5.1 million people 65 and older with AD in the United States, 3.2 million are women and 1.9 million are men (Alzheimer's Association, 2015).

Similarly, the risk for dementia, which is largely congruent with major NCD (from AD or other causes), varies by racial or ethnic group. Of those who reach age 65 without having dementia, the chances of developing dementia over the next 25 years reflects this variation: Blacks (38%); American Indians/Alaskan Natives (35%); Latinos (32%); Whites (30%); Asian Americans (28%); and Pacific Islanders (25%) (Mayeda, Glymour, Quesenberry, & Whitmer, 2016).

Persons with AD are usually aware of some degree of deficit (although not always), but they typically underestimate the level of deficit (Alzheimer's Association, 2015). Awareness is usually stronger in the early stages of the disease, and over time, the person begins to "forget she is forgetting." Family members are often the first to pick up on the problem. Yet even as they watch their loved one lose capacity to function at the level the person had previously enjoyed, families are slow to recognize the very early signs until a significant safety risk forces their attention to the amount of change that has already occurred (Nichols & Martindale-Adams, 2006). As discussed earlier, practice guidelines recommend the diagnosis be shared with the patient and family members (Alzheimer's Association, 2015).

Genetics plays a strong role in only a small number of cases (genetics appears more important in early-onset dementia, defined as onset before the age of 65 years, rather than late-onset dementia), although a genetic allele (apolipoprotein E-e4; APOE-e4) enhances risk of late-onset AD (Castro & Smith, 2015). Cardiovascular disease and the lifestyle patterns associated with risk for it (e.g., poor diet, limited exercise, obesity) are also risk factors for AD. Brain injuries and infections from earlier life also create risk for dementias, a fact of growing concern to athletes in high-contact sports (e.g., football, boxing, soccer) for whom concussions are relatively common. To date, no single cause has been identified that suggests a cure.

AD includes unusually high rates of neuronal cell loss, along with unusual concentrations of amyloid, and an increased prevalence of plaques and neurofibrillary tangles in the cortex, amygdala, and hippocampus areas of the brain. Park and Farrell (2016) recently reviewed the emerging data on amyloid and tau imaging. While there has been progress in imaging both, a paradox still remains: There is not a uniform mapping of level of either amyloid or tau and cognitive functioning. Decreased levels of acetylcholine, a neurotransmitter involved in learning and memory, as well as other neurotransmitters further compromise brain function.

AD usually progresses slowly and continuously, leading to declining functional capacities over time but without specific markers of decline. AD is accompanied by deficits in new learning and delayed recall with additional problems in language and semantic memory, abstract reasoning, executive functioning, and attention (Castro & Smith, 2015). There is some discussion about the earliest biomarkers of AD (Castro & Smith, 2015). Typically, indicators of accumulations of amyloid or tau were thought to be the earliest signs, predating clinically significant behavior change. However, a series of studies has documented that preclinical episodic memory changes are predictive of subsequent AD development (Jedynak et al., 2012), again reflecting the importance of baseline assessments and the importance of collaboration among the various disciplines on the health care team, as suggested in the American Psychological Association (2012) guidelines for diagnosis and assessment of Alzheimer's disease.

Major neurocognitive disorders with vascular involvement

Vascular dementias are caused by loss of neuronal tissue as a result of occlusions of vessels or small infarctions (i.e., hemorrhages) in the brain. Diagnosis of vascular dementia requires the presence of the cognitive signs of dementia or major NCD described above, as well as the documented presence of cerebrovascular disease or the presence of focal signs and symptoms that appear to be caused by localized damage to the brain (APA, 2013). Vascular NCDs can be either cortical or subcortical or mixed, depending upon location of the vascular damage (see Nyenhuis, 2015, for a helpful review.) Vascular dementia is the second most frequent cause of dementia confirmed by autopsy (Brunnstrom, Gustafson, Passant, & Englund, 2009).

Vascular dementias can present with a stepwise progression of small losses of functioning that result from the small infarcts, although those steps may be so small that observers describe the changes as continuous. Vascular dementias can follow a stroke, and alternatively, they share increased risk of stroke. The prognosis for vascular dementia is similar to that of AD: slow, progressive deterioration in a broad range of cognitive functions. Certainly, causes of dementias can copresent within a patient, such that, for example, vascular dementia and Alzheimer's dementia are both diagnosed.

Subcortical NCDs, a category containing many distinct diseases (e.g., Huntington's disease, Wilson's disease, Parkinson's disease, progressive supranuclear palsy), have effects on cognitive functioning that differ from other NCDs whose early, primary impact is in the cerebral cortex (Kaufer & Cummings, 2003). In contrast to the NCDs that attack the cerebral cortex early (e.g., Alzheimer's), subcortical NCDs tend to show memory retrieval deficits (not learning deficits), speech difficulties, and motor impairments. Similarities between cortical and subcortical dementias are in the areas of problem-solving deficits, and visual-perceptual and constructional deficits. The explosion of research in the neurosciences in recent years has made it possible to understand the finest of neurological distinctions among these diseases, and to discriminate often among these diseases premortem with the careful application of thorough assessment techniques. Knowledge of the specific diagnosis can be particularly helpful when designing behavior management interventions that need to draw upon the client's available cognitive abilities to compensate for deficits and behavior problems.

Ambrose (2016) recently argued that Alzheimer's disease and other dementias are examples of a larger process of reduced vascular capacity associated with aging. He suggests an *angiogenesis hypothesis*: Alzheimer's and dementia symptoms are due to a decline in formation of new blood vessels, leading to diminished blood flow, particularly in capillaries. Presently, this hypothesis awaits further data and confirmation.

Assessing Vascular Cognitive Impairment (VCI) can be a challenge because of the complexity of causes and the possible progression from vascular major NCD to AD (Nyenhuis, 2015). Consider, for example, the various sources of cardiovascular disease: hemorrhagic stroke, ischemic stroke, micro infarcts, microhemorrhages, transient ischemic attacks, atrophy, etc. The possible progression to AD adds to the complexity of assessment and diagnosis. The National Institute of Neurological Disorders and Stroke and the Canadian Stroke network recommended a 60-minute protocol focusing on five areas: executive function, language retrieval, visuospatial functioning, memory, and neuropsychiatric/depressive symptoms (Hachinski et al., 2006).

The impact of NCDs on daily life progresses from modest effects on self-management of daily affairs to nearly complete devastation of all self-care skills, as illustrated in the case of Jane Winthrop described at the beginning of this chapter. Independence is most threatened by the loss of ability to provide basic self-care functions that are usually measured as Activities of Daily Living (ADLs, including bathing, dressing, eating) and Instrumental Activities of Daily Living (IADLs, including managing money, shopping for groceries and clothing, preparing meals, taking medications as prescribed, transportation, telephone use). Early in the disease progression, IADLs become challenging for the person who may attempt to hide the level of difficulty experienced. Later, as the disease progresses, even the most basic ADLs require assistance as the person forgets how to eat or walk.

Problem behaviors also often occur, adding burden to the care of persons with NCDs. Common behavior problems include depression, sleep disturbances, wandering, and agitated behavior, each of which can be as disturbing of daily functioning and personal well-being for the person as the cognitive impairment itself. Severe behavioral disturbances are very disruptive to the individuals with NCD and their caregivers. A systematic approach to reducing the disturbance is required, often involving nonpharmacological interventions as well as medications (Salzman et al., 2008; Cohen-Mansfield, 2015). Not surprisingly, the costs of care for persons with NCDs accelerate with both the decline in cognitive functioning and the presence of clinical characteristics such as depression (Zhu et al., 2006).

Depression and Cognitive Impairment

Individuals with depression sometimes express concerns about their memory and/or actual functional deficits in daily cognitive functioning as reported by a family member or other informant. The negative cognitive set associated with depression produces excessively negative self-appraisals in many areas, including cognitive functioning. The case of Jim Hunt, offered at the beginning of the chapter, is a typical presentation of depression. He is very concerned about his own deficits and is withdrawing from activities that bring him pleasure. Obviously, a thorough evaluation is needed to rule out cognitive impairment, but the presentation is typical of a depressed person.

Although depressed adults complain about memory deficits even when no objective memory performance deficit is evident, depression is associated with actual cognitive deficits under two circumstances. First, depression is associated with deficits in actual cognitive performance, as is anxiety (Bierman, Comijs, Jonker, & Beekman, 2005). By definition, the cognitive impairment can be attributed to depression only if it remits with successful treatment of the depression. Cognitive impairment due to depression sufficiently mimics dementia that it was previously referred to as *pseudodementia*, a misnomer because the cognitive impairment is not false. Second, depression and dementia can, and often do, coexist. Approximately 30% to 50% of patients with dementia meet the criteria for diagnosis of depression, most often in the early stages of the disease (Edelstein, Bamonti, Gregg, & Gerolimatos, 2015; Steffens & Potter, 2008). Similarly, depression is commonly comorbid in MCI (Gabryelewicz et al., 2004). Other factors that are often present in older adults also can produce depression and dementia-like symptoms that further complicate matters. For example, disrupted sleep, anxiety, or physical illness can produce concentration deficits or personality changes that are common in either depression or dementia.

Summary of the Types of Cognitive Impairment

Differential diagnosis of delirium, depression, mild NCD, and major NCD, and other sources of cognitive impairment are common challenges to mental health providers working with older adults. The disorders present with similar symptoms; the symptoms can co-occur; and the symptoms can be misidentified (e.g., passivity in dementia may be described as depression; impaired attention due to delirium may be described as dementia). In addition, late-onset depression is often a predictor of the onset of dementia, suggesting that the disorders may actually present sequentially.

Assessment

To discriminate among the various potential causes of major and mild NCDs in older adults, multidisciplinary evaluations of medical, pharmacological, neuropsychological, and daily functioning are necessary. Multiple disciplines must be involved to gather a picture of the full range of functional abilities and deficits, and to examine all possible causes of deficits. The medical evaluation includes a thorough physical and history of all the current and medical problems, and a review of current medications. Social workers provide a social history that includes occupational, social, and family history and functioning. Psychologists evaluate cognitive, emotional, and personality functioning, and neuropsychologists provide an in-depth examination of cognitive and memory functioning. Pharmacy consultants and psychiatrists often contribute to the evaluation of the effects of illnesses and medications on psychological functioning (cognitive as well as mood). Other health professions such as physical therapy, dentistry, or occupational therapy may be involved in the evaluation if problems in posture, range of motion, movement safety, oral health, or functional capacity to fulfill daily tasks are in question.

The medical aspects of the evaluation are particularly critical because reversible causes of delirium and major and mild NCDs must be ruled out immediately. Left untreated, reversible causes can produce permanent deficits. The functional components of the examination (e.g., evaluation of ADLs and IADLs) are key to determining the level of independent functioning that is possible and safe. In the case of patients with dementia, evaluation of family functioning is also important. Family caregivers maintain responsibility for patient well-being and are often highly distressed.

Neuropsychological examinations often begin with screening tools that evaluate mental status and depression, and proceed to a full evaluation only when needed (i.e., when a person flags as potentially impaired on the screening measure). The Folstein Mini-Mental State Examination (FMMSE; Folstein, Folstein, & McHugh, 1975) is among the most the commonly used screening measure for cognition, although newer screening tools are now recommended based on their greater effectiveness and improved psychometric properties. Two good examples are the Montreal Cognitive Assessment (MoCA) which is designed to detect mild cognitive impairment (see the MoCA website for further details: www.mocatest.org) and the Saint Louis University Mental Status (SLUMS) Examination. Each screening tool assesses functioning in several domains, but with little depth of examination in each area. Any indication of deficit leads to more rigorous examination of cognitive functioning. Diagnosis cannot be made on the basis of any screening measure!

A full neuropsychological examination often takes between three and six hours, and includes tests of specific domains of functioning that can portray a rich picture of the strengths and the deficits of the functioning of a particular patient. Test data are compared with norms from age-matched older adults living in a similar setting (e.g., community dwelling, nursing home) to determine whether one individual's performance varies from what would be normative for a person that age in that setting.

A neuropsychological assessment report provides detailed information on the patient's performance on each test, compared to national norms for healthy older adults. Test performances are interpreted within the context of the patient's past educational and occupational experiences. In highly educated persons, an average score may not appear to be deficient if compared against national norms, but may be well below that person's historical capacity to function. The report concludes by addressing any specific questions (e.g., capacity to function safely within current living environment or decision-making capacity) and summarizing cognitive strengths that can be used to compensate for any deficits. Many neuropsychologists provide personalized feedback to patients and families in a face-to-face session, or clinicians may provide a written report that translates the neuropsychological findings into practical advice for family adaptation (Qualls & Noecker, 2009).

Recent developments in the field of assessment of NCDs have focused on "person-centered" assessment and intervention (Mast, Shouse, & Camp, 2015). Here, the focus is not solely on the underlying NCD, but on the person behind the diagnosis, with a personal past, personal preferences, and strengths. Mast and his colleagues, for example, suggest shifting from a disease to a disability framing of NCDs or dementia. Within this framing, persons with dementia (PWDs) might be considered disabled and discriminated against under the Americans with Disabilities Act of 1990. As Mast et al. put it: "Where are the cognitive ramps for PWDs?" (p. 321). Within a person-centered approach, areas for assessment might include assessment of values and preferences (Whitlatch, Feinberg, & Tucke, 2005), fear of Alzheimer's disease (French, Floyd, Wilkins, & Osato, 2012), as well as mood (Tappen & Williams, 2008).

In addition to diagnostic evaluations, assessments are also conducted to evaluate the existence of distress in persons with dementia and in their caregivers, and to determine the extent of problem behaviors (Cohen-Mansfield, 2015). In people with dementia, common forms of distress are depression and anxiety, often comorbid in this population just as they are in the general population. Assessment of depression in dementia is effective. In addition, anxiety assessment tools are available to use with persons with dementia (Snow et al., 2012).

A thorough evaluation should include assessment of family stress due to the burdens of managing care and the behavior problems that often accompany major and mild NCDs (Zarit & Heid, 2015). (See Chapter 16 for a fuller discussion of caregiver issues.) The Revised Memory and Behavior Problems Checklist (Teri et al., 1992) is a commonly used tool that identifies significant behavior problems, and the degree of distress each problem evokes in the caregiver. Family members should also be evaluated for depression, a distressingly common consequence for caregivers whose sources of pleasure are usually disrupted at the same time that they are dealing with the PWD's challenging health and behavior problems.

Assessment of problem behaviors often engages the caregiver in recording behaviors, including the time, location, and social context of the behavior. Behavioral observations may be used to gather accurate records of behavior, especially in long-term-care settings, but informant reports are generally accurate enough to suggest reliance on their more efficient approach (Cohen-Mansfield, 2015).

Finally, an especially important field of assessment of persons with dementia focuses specifically on their decision-making capacity (Lichtenberg, Qualls, & Smyer, 2015; Moye & Marson, 2007). Critically important legal and ethical issues arise as a person's cognitive abilities decline, especially when one's awareness of the decline is absent. Persons may be at substantial risk of self-neglect or abuse, or exploitation and fraud, if their capacities are lower than required to remain safe within their environments. Often, these assessments focus not only on memory but also on executive functions. The American Psychological Association and American Bar Association have collaborated on a series of handbooks to guide lawyers, judges, and psychologists through the process of evaluating a person's capacity for decision-making in a variety of contexts (e.g., health, financial, and legal contexts) (ABA/APA, 2008). (See Chapter 17 for a fuller discussion of the capacity issues.)

Interventions

A thorough assessment can be considered the first and most important intervention for cognitive impairment or NCDs. If the cause of the cognitive impairment is reversible (e.g., delirium or depression), then the evaluation should lead to aggressive treatment of the underlying condition, which will partially or completely resolve the problem. When the NCD is determined to be caused by a nonreversible etiology, such as Alzheimer's disease, the focus of intervention turns toward management of the disease, with the goal of preventing excess disability and rapid decline. Planning, environmental interventions, behavioral interventions, and education and support for those who will provide care for the impaired person are all useful management strategies. Direct intervention to improve cognitive functioning may be beneficial in certain cases.

Families of persons with dementia have too often lamented that they were told by their physician something like, "I'm sorry, but your husband has Alzheimer's disease and there's nothing that can be done." The hopelessness and despair produced by such pronouncements of doom are substantial, and truly unnecessary. Furthermore, the statement is only true in the sense that no treatment reverses the damage caused by the disease. Indeed, many interventions can be useful.

Management of progressive, intractable NCDs focuses on maximizing independent functioning while anticipating the consequences of current and future levels of impairment on the patient and the caregivers. The case of Jane Winthrop, with which the chapter opened, is an example of intensive management to maintain independence in her living environment. Early in a dementing process, families often begin to

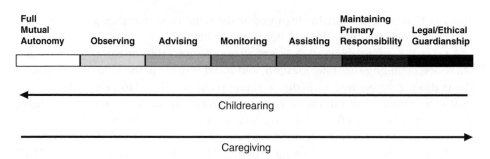

Figure 8.2   Continuum of family roles for childrearing and caregiving.

implement small supportive interventions that allow the person with dementia to maintain independence in his or her own home. For example, a son or daughter may initially "check in" on a mother to make sure she is okay. Later, the adult child may handle complex financial transactions such as taxes, even though the person with dementia continues to manage the monthly budget. Later, the checkbook may be handled by an adult child, and eventually even routine grocery shopping may have to be done by a caregiver. In Jane Winthrop's case, the family was using external memory aids so Jane could maintain basic safety in her own home. The implied sequence of increasing care services is illustrated in Figure 8.2, which shows the continuum of family roles vis-à-vis a person with dementia.

Planning

Ideally, a person with a mild or major NCD has the opportunity to make significant decisions about how legal, financial, housing, and health care decisions will be made prior to significant cognitive impairment, when there are sufficient cognitive abilities intact to make sound decisions. Whitlatch and her colleagues (2006), for example, developed a dyadic intervention focused on the 19 tasks that someone with dementia may need help with. The seven sessions were provided in the couple's home and focused on both the value preferences of caregiver and care recipient and the practical solving of current and anticipated problems. Similarly, adults with early stage dementia are encouraged to work with an attorney and family members to determine appropriate financial, legal, and health care decision-making arrangements for the future when the impairment will disable their decision-making capacity (Lichtenberg et al., 2015) (see Chapter 17).

In recent years, several legal tools have been developed to help adults state their intentions for handling their affairs once they are no longer capable. For example, a *durable healthcare power of attorney* identifies and sanctions a legal decision-maker to handle health care decisions once an individual is incapacitated. A *living will* identifies the level of medical intervention desired by the individual when he or she is both incapable of stating his or her own needs and when heroic measures might be used to sustain life in the face of death. Housing options, such as life-care communities that guarantee provision of the level of care needed by the older adult who purchased the life care services ahead of time, allow an individual to select the housing for the future. Advanced planning for finances and other needs ensures that the individual's own desires will be the basis for decisions once capacity to decide is compromised.

When individuals with cognitive impairment have not legally stated their wishes for how things should be handled after they are incapacitated, surrogate decision-makers are called upon to make the key decisions. State statutes define who is the surrogate decision-maker of choice for health care decisions, with a sequence of alternative persons in a specific order. Typically, a spouse is the first person of choice, followed by a parent or an adult child, with specific assignments of priority thereafter. For other decisions (e.g., housing or finances), a similar strategy is typically supported by the legal system even though it may not be defined by statute.

Even an individual with cognitive impairment is his or her own legal decision-maker, except when decisions would generate a threat to someone's welfare, or the court appoints a guardian. Guardianship is a dramatic step that strips an individual of basic rights and liberties. The decision to appoint a guardian is made by a judge, based upon evidence that relates to the specific state statutes that define the basis for incompetency. No national standard has been established for competency determinations—neither a standard definition of competence and incompetence, nor a standard procedure for determining competency—but consensus has grown as to the appropriateness of assessing functional abilities for specific capacity domains (Lichtenberg et al., 2015). In most states, partial or limited guardianships can be granted to cover only domains in which the individual's incapacity is sufficient to warrant an alternative decision-maker (e.g., finances but not housing). Indeed, the determination of competency is a highly complex legal process that rests upon significantly complex psychological and legal constructs (Qualls & Smyer, 2007).

Legal and health professionals consistently encourage adults to plan ahead for the event of their cognitive incapacity so the individual's wishes guide subsequent decisions, regardless of the decision-maker. Planning typically involves the selection of a proxy decision-maker to step in at the point at which the person loses cognitive capacity for particular types of decision, as well as a statement of values regarding the types of care preferred under particular conditions.

Considerable evidence shows that interventions can reduce stress and burden on family caregivers whose roles will often span many years for persons with dementia (Zarit & Heid, 2015). The point at which families seek help will shape the selection of interventions from a wide range of options, making assessment a critical component in caregiver interventions (Zarit, 2009). Almost all interventions include education, problem-solving, and efforts to increase social support for the caregiver. In addition, caregiving interventions need to take into account the variability of caregiver's resources and circumstances, the variability of the care recipient's physical and mental health challenges, and the contexts of caring available for the caregiver and care recipient (Zarit & Heid, 2015).

For example, two large multisite studies that were funded by the National Institute on Aging demonstrate that multiple interventions may be effective if selected for caregivers based on assessment results. These studies, referred to as REACH 1 and REACH 2 (Resources for Enhancing Alzheimer's Caregiver Health), generated a diverse set of approaches that were tested in multiple regions of the country with multiple culturally diverse populations (Belle et al., 2006; Wisniewski et al., 2003).

Interventions with caregiving families are powerful tools for reducing the burden and stress on the caregivers, improving the care for the care recipients, and delaying the need for intensive institutional care. (See Chapter 16 for more on working with caregivers.)

Environmental interventions

Individuals with NCDs are more vulnerable to the impact of the environment on their capacity to function than are non-impaired individuals (Lawton & Nahemow, 1973). As illustrated in Figure 8.3, lower levels of competence limit the range of environments in which the individual can competently function. Thus, the selection of an appropriate environment can profoundly affect, positively or negatively, an individual's capacity for independent functioning. Effective management of individuals with cognitive impairment requires that caregivers identify the level of environmental prosthesis that will support independent functioning maximally, by providing sufficient challenge to require the individual to use available cognitive capacities without generating frustration or excess disability.

Persons with mild cognitive impairment may be able to live alone in a familiar home or apartment with minimal support. However, substantial cognitive impairment usually requires at least one move from independent living to a more supportive level of housing. Meals, janitorial, maintenance, and housekeeping services may be sufficient to maintain a state of relative independence. Nursing homes provide the most intensive levels of health-supportive services, including medication dispensing, nutrition monitoring, and skilled nursing services. The high rate of NCDs in nursing homes, noted earlier in this chapter, reflects the negative effects of institutional life as well as the increased likelihood of needing the full array of support services once one is experiencing significant cognitively impairment.

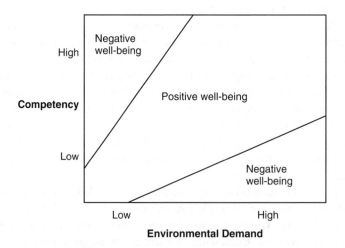

Figure 8.3   Relationship between environmental press, competency, and well-being.
Source: Adapted from Lawton & Nahemow (1973).

Architectural features of a living environment can profoundly impact behavior, especially among those with cognitive impairment, and are thus appropriate targets for intervention. Among the numerous environmental characteristics that affect the behavior of normal as well as impaired older adults are factors such as privacy, availability of small group spaces, opportunities to facilitate family–resident interactions, support for way-finding, and focused and appropriate stimulation (Cutler, 2007). The arrangement of public and private spaces can affect the frequency and value of social interaction to residents of senior housing. Environmental richness (sounds, sights, and tactile stimulation) affects rate of activity and socializing. For persons with dementia and depressed individuals with NCDs, environmental interventions that increase the rate of stimulation without requiring initiation on the part of the impaired individual can produce significant improvements in functioning as long as the stimuli are paced in frequency and intensity.

Facilities designed for persons with Alzheimer's disease use creative design features to foster desired behavior. For example, colored blocks inlaid into the surface of a table to look like a placemat have been used to help people with dementia identify the territory within which their food is served. Pictures of a resident as a young person as well as a current picture of the aging person may be used instead of a name or number outside the door to enhance the likelihood that the resident can identify his or her own room.

Environmental technology to support independence is another area of rapid development. Technologies now exist for monitoring and prompting, structuring tasks, and simplifying access to computers. Technologies targeted at caregivers offer assistive devices to assist with practical care (e.g., bathing) as well as communication technologies that facilitate interaction. Not surprisingly, the use of technology in dementia care is garnering increasing attention (Topo, 2009). For example, the European Union sponsored an effort to apply artificial intelligence algorithms in analyzing motion monitor data to predict changes in the capacity of persons with dementia to perform activities of daily living (Gonzalez-Diaz et al., 2015). (See www.demcare.eu for more information.)

Behavior management

Cognitive impairment and NCDs can limit the range of behavior as well as produce problematic behaviors that can benefit from behavior management. Handling behavior problems is one of the most stressful aspects of providing care to a person with dementia. Behavior management strategies are available to help manage wandering, incontinence, disruptive vocalizations (e.g., screaming), and inappropriate sexual behaviors, as well as to enhance independent self-care behaviors such as grooming, ambulation, and eating (Logsdon, McCurry, & Teri, 2007). Agitated behaviors are some of the more complex behaviors to manage (Cohen-Mansfield & Libin, 2004) but several strategies have been demonstrated to be effective (Kong, Evans, & Guevera, 2009; Logsdon et al., 2007). Daily care providers such as family members or Certified Nurse Aids in nursing homes must be trained to implement evidence-based behavior management protocols to achieve successful results. In contrast to medications that are sometimes used to sedate individuals whose agitation is extremely disruptive to their environment, behavior management programs rarely produce side effects. Physicians generally prefer nonpharmacological interventions and federal regulations discourage use of antipsychotic and other sedating medications unless used in the presence of psychiatric diagnosis, but physicians often view lack of resources and knowledge as a barrier to using behavioral interventions in long-term-care settings (Cohen-Mansfield & Jensen, 2008). Ethical concerns about altering the behaviors of persons who are not capable of consenting to treatment always warrant careful consideration.

Cohen-Mansfield (2015), for example, suggests that many disruptive behaviors associated with dementia in institutional settings may stem from a lack of social contact, a lack of engagement, or from physical discomfort. She suggests careful assessment of the underlying cause and she outlines a variety of nonpharmacological interventions aimed at these underlying causes.

The burden of caring for cognitively impaired individuals falls heavily upon family members. Problem behaviors associated with cognitive impairment provoke the most adverse emotional and physical consequences for caregivers (see reviews by Pinquart & Sörensen, 2007, and Zarit & Heid, 2015). The disruptive and odd behaviors that often accompany NCDs can significantly interfere with sleep, daily routines, and social contact. However, the burden of care tasks and social loss also falls on families. Interventions for families usually focus on education about the disease, problem-solving assistance, encouragement to maintain strong social support, and, when needed, family therapy to resolve serious family dysfunction (Qualls & Noecker, 2009; Zarit & Heid, 2015).

Interventions to enhance cognitive functioning

Efforts to reverse or slow deterioration in the NCDs include pharmacological inter-ventions and cognitive retraining. Medications to enhance cognitive functioning in patients with dementia (especially Alzheimer's disease) show short-term benefits (6–12 months) in about half of individuals (Alzheimer's Association, 2015). These effects are primarily produced by increasing the concentration of specific neurotrans-mitters in the brain. Unfortunately, currently available medications can neither cure nor stop the development of NCDs.

In laboratory settings, older adults have been demonstrated to be capable of benefiting from training to use memory aids, and strategies such as spaced retrieval (Camp, 2006; Unverzagt et al., 2007). Rarely does that training generalize to behaviors outside the behaviors that were targeted in the training, which limits its utility. Hyer, Mullen, and McKenzie (2015) recently summarized their review of cognitive training (CT):

> In sum, cognitive decline is the result of dynamic tension between a progressive disease and the brain's limited ability to adapt, react, and regenerate. There is a complex interaction between cognitive reserve factors (e.g., education) and biomarkers of neuronal injury and neurodegeneration that moderates the benefits of cognitive interventions....the exact CT technique applicable for a particular person has yet to be identified. Unfortunately, only moderate evidence suggests that CT can generalize to untrained cognitive abilities, but the complexity of the program of CT as well as individual factors play a large role. (p. 346)

Summary and Conclusions

The major NCDs are among the most dreaded changes associated with aging because of their profound negative impact on autonomy and the very identity of the person experiencing the disorder. Reversible causes of NCDs are sufficiently prevalent among older adults to warrant aggressive evaluation. Irreversible causes of mild and major NCDs in older adults are primarily caused by underlying brain disorders which produce devastating, progressive, and long-term effects on cognition and one's functioning. A thorough assessment requires the involvement of multiple disciplines in a coordinated effort to identify a multidimensional picture of the person's physical, psychological, social, and self-care functioning. Based on the assessment, many interventions are possible to assist the impaired person and those caring for him or her.

Critical Thinking / Discussion Questions

1   A neighbor asks for your help. She is worried that her husband is more forgetful and may be in the early stages of Alzheimer's disease. What course of action would you recommend to her and why?
2   An alumni group at your university has asked you to speak to the 25th reunion class about "keeping your cognitive edge." What would you recommend to them and why?
3   A student affairs staff member at your college has invited you to meet with a group of graduating seniors, as part of the college's "packing for the next steps on your journey" series. What would you recommend to the graduating seniors as actions they can take in their 20s to assure ongoing cognitive health?
4   A woman in her early 50s contacts you, concerned for herself and her twin brother. Their parents had both been diagnosed with Alzheimer's disease when they were in their 60s. The woman had been having cognitive testing on a regular basis to establish a baseline of functioning, but her brother refused to discuss the issue. Recently, she was diagnosed with Mild Cognitive Impairment. She wants advice: Should she tell her brother? If so, what should she tell him?

Website Resources

National Parkinson Foundation
www.parkinson.org
The Michael J. Fox Foundation for Parkinson's Research
www.michaeljfox.org
The Alzheimer's Association
www.alz.org
National Institute on Aging Alzheimer's Disease Education and Referral Center
https://www.nia.nih.gov/alzheimers/publication/alzheimers-disease-fact-sheet

Dem@Care: Dementia Ambient Care—Multi-Sensing Monitoring For Intelligent Remote Management and Decision Support
www.demcare.eu
Fraying at the Edges by N. R. Kleinfield, *The New York Times,* May 1, 2016. An in-depth description of the process of living with a diagnosis of Alzheimer's disease
http://www.nytimes.com/interactive/2016/05/01/nyregion/living-with-alzheimers. html?_r=0

References

Aarsland, D., Zaccai, J., & Brayne, C. (2005). A systematic review of prevalence studies of dementia in Parkinson's disease. *Movement Disorders, 20*(10), 1255–1263.

Alzheimer's Association (2015). *2015 Alzheimer's disease facts and figures.* Available from https://www.alz.org/facts/downloads/facts_figures_2015.pdf

Ambrose, C. T. (2016). Angiogenesis, aging, and Alzheimer's disease. *American Scientist, 104*(3), 82–85.

American Bar Association Commission on Law and Aging & American Psychological Association. (2008). *Assessment of older adults with diminished capacity: A handbook for psychologists.* Washington, DC: American Bar Association and American Psychological Association.

American Psychiatric Association. (2013). *Diagnostic and statistical manual of mental disorders* (5th ed.). Arlington, VA: Author.

American Psychological Association. (2012). Guidelines for the evaluation of dementia and age-related cognitive change. *American Psychologist, 67*(1), 1–9.

Belle, S. H., Burgio, L., Burns, R., Coon, D., Czaja, S. J., Gallagher-Thompson, D., …Zhang, S. (2006). Enhancing the quality of life of dementia caregivers from different ethnic or racial groups: A randomized, controlled trial. *Annals of Internal Medicine, 145,* 727–738.

Bierman, E. J. M., Comijs, H. C., Jonker, C., & Beekman, A. T. F. (2005). Effects of anxiety versus depression on cognition in later life. *American Journal of Geriatric Psychiatry, 13,* 686–693.

Blieszner, R., Roberto, K., Wilcox, K., Barham, E., & Winston, B. (2007). Dimensions of ambiguous loss in couples coping with mild cognitive impairment. *Family Relations, 56,* 196–209.

Brunnstrom, H., Gustafson, L. Passant, U., & Englund, E. (2009). Prevalence of dementia by subtype: A 30-year retrospective survey of neuropathological reports. *Archives of Gerontology and Geriatrics, 49,* 146–149. doi:10.1016/.archger.2008.06.005

Cabeza, R., & Dennis, N. A. (2013). Frontal lobes and aging: Deterioration and compensation. In D. T. Stuss & R. T. Knight (Eds.), *Principles of frontal lobe function* (2nd ed., pp. 628–655). New York, NY: Oxford University Press.

Camp, C. (2006). Spaced retrieval: A model for dissemination of a cognitive intervention for persons with dementia. *Geriatric neuropsychology: Assessment and intervention* (pp. 275–292). New York, NY: Guilford.

Castro, M., & Smith, G. E. (2015). Mild cognitive impairment and Alzheimer's disease. In P. A. Lichtenberg & B. T. Mast (Eds.), *APA handbook of clinical geropsychology. Vol 2: Assessment, treatment, and issues of later life* (pp. 173–207). Washington, DC: American Psychological Association.

Center for Medicare and Medicaid Studies (CMS), Department of Health and Human Services (2014). *Partnership to improve dementia care in nursing homes antipsychotic drug use in nursing homes trend update.* Available at https://www.cms.gov/Outreach-and-Education/Outreach/NPC/Downloads/2014-10-27-Trends.pdf

Choi, S. H., Lee, H., Chung, T. S., Park, K. M., Jung, Y. C., Kim, S. I., & Kim, J. J. (2012). Neural network functional connectivity during and after an episode of delirium. *American Journal of Psychiatry, 169*(5), 498–507.

Cognitive Training Data (2014). Response letter. Retrieved from http://www.cognitivetraining data.org/the-controversy-does-brain-training-work/response-letter/

Cohen-Mansfield, J. (2015). Behavioral and psychological symptoms of dementia. In P. A. Lichtenberg & B.T. Mast (Eds.). *APA handbook of clinical geropsychology. Vol 2: Assessment, treatment, and issues of later life* (pp. 271–317). Washington, DC: American Psychological Association.

Cohen-Mansfield, J., & Jensen, B. (2008). Nursing home physicians' knowledge of and attitudes toward nonpharmacological interventions for treatment of behavioral disturbances associated with dementia. *Journal of American Medical Directors Association, 9*, 491–498.

Cohen-Mansfield, J., & Libin, A. (2004). Assessment of agitation in elderly patients with dementia: Correlations between informant rating and direct observation. *International Journal of Geriatric Psychiatry, 19*, 881–891.

Cordell, C. B., Borson, S., Boustani, M., Chodosh, J., Reuben, D., Verghese, J...the Medicare Detection of Cognitive Impairment Workgroup (2013). Alzheimer's association recommendations for operationalizing the detection of cognitive impairment during the Medicare Annual Wellness Visit in a primary care setting. *Alzheimer's and Dementia, 9*, 141–150. doi:10.1016/j.jalz.2012.09.011

Cutler, L. (2007). Physical environments of assisted living: Research needs and challenges. *Gerontologist, 47*, 68–82.

Dale, W., Hougham, G. W., Hill, E. K., & Sachs, G. A. (2006). High interest in screening and treatment for mild cognitive impairment in older adults: A pilot study. *Journal of American Geriatrics Society, 54*, 1388–1394.

Edelstein, B. A., Bamonti, P. M., Gregg, J. J., & Gerolimatos, L. A. (2015). Depression in later life. In P. A. Lichtenberg & B.T. Mast (Eds.), *APA handbook of clinical geropsychology: Vol 2. Assessment, treatment, and issues of later life* (pp. 3–47). Washington, DC: American Psychological Association.

Farias, S. T., Mungas, D., & Jagust, W. (2005). Degree of discrepancy between self and other-reported everyday functioning by cognitive status: Dementia, mild cognitive impairment, and healthy elders. *International Journal of Geriatric Psychiatry, 20*, 827–834.

Federal Trade Commission (2016, January 5). Lumosity to pay $2 million to settle FTC deceptive advertising charges for its "brain training" program. Retrieved from https://www.ftc.gov/news-events/press-releases/2016/01/lumosity-pay-2-million-settle-ftc-deceptive-advertising-charges

Folstein, M. F., Folstein, S. E., & McHugh, P. R. (1975). "Mini-Mental State": A practical method for grading the cognitive state of patients for the clinician. *Journal of Psychiatric Research, 12*, 189–198.

Foster, S. M., Cornwell, R. E., Kisley, M. A., & Davis, H. P. (2006). Cognitive changes across the lifespan. In S. H. Qualls & M. A. Smyer (Eds.), *Changes in decision-making capacity: Assessment and intervention* (pp. 25–60). Hoboken, NJ: Wiley.

French, S. L., Floyd, M., Wilkins, S., & Osato, S. (2012). The fear of Alzheimer's disease scale: A new measure designed to assess anticipatory dementia in older adults. *International Journal of Geriatric Psychiatry, 27*, 521–528. doi: 10.1002/gps/2747

Friedman, J. H. (2013). *Making the connection between brain and behavior: Coping with Parkinson's disease* (2nd ed.). New York, NY: Demos Health.

Gabryelewicz, T., Styczynska, M., Pfeffer, A., Wasiak, B., Barczak, A., Luczywek, E.,...
Barcikowska, M. (2004). Prevalence of major and minor depression in elderly persons with
mild cognitive impairment – MADRS factor analysis. *International Journal of Geriatric Psychiatry, 19*, 1168–1172.

Gonzalez-Diaz, I., Buso, V., Benois-Pineau, J., Bourmaud, G., Usseglio, G., Mégret, R.,...
Dartigues, J-F. (2015). Recognition of instrumental activities of daily living in egocentric
video for activity monitoring of patients with dementia. In A. Briassouli, J. Benois-Pineau,
& A. Hauptmann (Eds.), *Health monitoring and personalized feedback using multimedia
data* (pp 161–178). New York, NY: Springer.

Hachinski, V., Iadecola, C., Petersen R. C., Breteler, M. M., Nyenhuis, D. L., Black, S. E.,...
Leblanc, G. G. (2006). National Institute of Neurological Disorders and Stroke-Canadian
Stroke Network vascular cognitive impairment harmonization standards. *Stroke, 37*, 2220–
2241. doi:10.1161/01.STR.0000237236.88823.47

Hutchinson, L. C., & O'Brien, C. E. (2007). Changes in pharmacokinetics and pharmacody-
namics in the elderly patient. *Journal of Pharmacy Practice, 20*, 4–12.

Hyer, L. Mullen, C., & McKenzie, L. (2015). Cognitive training for mildly impaired older
adults. In P. A. Lichtenberg & B. T. Mast (Eds.), *APA handbook of clinical geropsychology. Vol 2: Assessment, treatment, and issues of later life* (pp. 341–368). Washington, DC:
American Psychological Association.

Inouye, S.K. (2006). Delirium in older persons. *New England Journal of Medicine, 354*(11),
1157–1165.

Jack, C. R., Albert, M. S., Knopman, D. S., McKhann, G. M., Sperling, R. A., Carrillo,
M. C., ... Phelps, C. H. (2011). Introduction to the recommendations from the National
Institute on Aging–Alzheimer's Association workgroups on diagnostic guidelines for
Alzheimer's disease. *Alzheimer's & Dementia: The Journal of the Alzheimer Association,
7*(3), 257–262.

Jedynak, B. M., Lang, A., Liu, B., Katz, E., Zhang, Y., Wyman, B. T., ...Prince, J. L. (2012).
A computational neurodegenerative disease progression score: method and results with
the Alzheimer's disease Neuroimaging Initiative cohort. *Neuroimage, 63*, 1478–1486.

Kaufer, D. I., & Cummings, J. L. (2003). Delirium and dementia: An overview. In T.
E. Feinberg & M. J. Farah (Eds.), *Behavioral neurology and neuropsychology* (2nd ed.,
pp. 495–500). New York, NY: McGraw-Hill.

Kennedy, K. M., Rodrigue, K. M., Bischof, G. N., Hebrank, A. C., Reuter-Lorenz, P. A., &
Park, D. C. (2015). Age trajectories of functional activation under conditions of low and
high processing demands: An adult lifespan fMRI study of the aging brain. *Neuroimage,
104*, 21–34.

Kinsley, M. (2014, April 28). Have you lost your mind? More bad news for Boomers. *The
New Yorker.* Available from http://www.newyorker.com/magazine/2014/04/28/
have-you-lost-your-mind

Kong, E., Evans, L., & Guevara, J. (2009). Nonpharmacological intervention for agitation in dementia: A systematic review and meta-analysis. *Aging & Mental Health, 13*,
512–520.

Kowal, S. L., Dall, T. M., Chakrabarti, R., Storm, M. V., & Jain, A. (2013). The current
and projected economic burden of Parkinson's disease in the United States. *Movement
Disorders, 28*, 311–318. doi:10.1002/mds.25292

Lawton, M. P., & Nahemow, L. (1973). Ecology and the aging process. In C. Eisdorfer & M. P.
Lawton (Eds.), *The psychology of adult development and aging* (pp. 619–673). Washington,
DC: American Psychological Association.

Lichtenberg, P. A., Qualls, S. H., & Smyer, M. A. (2015). Competency and decision-making
capacity: Negotiating health and financial decision making. In P. A. Lichtenberg & B. T.

Mast (Eds.), *APA handbook of clinical geropsychology. Vol 2: Assessment, treatment, and issues of later life* (pp. 553–578). Washington, DC: American Psychological Association.

Lingler, J. H., Nightendale, M. C., Erlen, J. A., Kane, A. L., Reynolds, C. F., Schulz, R., & DeKosky, S. T. (2006). Making sense of Mild Cognitive Impairment: A qualitative exploration of the patient's experience. *The Gerontologist, 46*, 791–800.

Logsdon, R. G., McCurry, S. M., & Teri, L. (2007). Evidence-based psychological treatments for disruptive behaviors in individuals with dementia. *Psychology and Aging, 22*, 28–36.

Lonie, J. A., Tierney, K. M., & Ebmeier, K. P. (2009). Screening for mild cognitive impairment: A systematic review. *International Journal of Geriatric Psychiatry, 24*, 902–915.

Lustig, C., & Lin, Z. (2016). Memory: Behavior and neural basis. In K. W. Schaie & S. L. Willis (Eds.), *Handbook of the psychology of aging* (8th ed., pp. 147–163). San Diego, CA: Academic Press.

Mast, B. T., Shouse, J., & Camp, C. J. (2015). Person-centered assessment and intervention for people with dementia. In P. A. Lichtenberg & B. T. Mast (Eds.), *APA handbook of clinical geropsychology. Vol 2: Assessment, treatment, and issues of later life* (pp. 319–339). Washington, DC: American Psychological Association.

Mayeda, E. R., Glymour, M. M., Quesenberry, C. P., & Whitmer, R. A. (2016). Inequalities in dementia incidence between six racial and ethnic groups over 14 years. *Alzheimer's & Dementia, 12*(3), 216–224.

McNamara, P. (2011). *The cognitive neuropsychiatry of Parkinson's disease.* Cambridge, MA: The MIT Press.

Moye, J., & Marson, D. C. (2007). Assessment of decision-making capacity in older adults: An emerging area of practice. *Journals of Gerontology: Psychological Sciences, 62B*, P3–P11.

Nichols, L. O., & Martindale-Adams, J. (2006). The decisive moment: Caregivers' recognition of dementia. *Clinical Gerontologist, 30*, 39–52.

Noimark, D. (2009). Predicting the onset of delirium in the post-operative patient. *Age and Ageing, 38*, 368–373.

Nyberg, L., Lovden, M., Riklund, K., Lindenberger, U., & Backman, L. (2012). Memory aging and brain maintenance. *Trends in Cognitive Sciences, 16*(5), 292–305.

Nyenhuis, D. (2015). Vascular cognitive impairment. In P. A. Lichtenberg & B. T. Mast (Eds.), *APA handbook of clinical geropsychology: Vol 2: Assessment, treatment, and issues of later life* (pp. 209–226). Washington, DC: American Psychological Association.

Office of the Inspector General, Department of Health and Human Services (2001). *Psychotropic drug use in nursing homes.* Washington, DC: US Government Printing Office. Available from http://oig.hhs.gov/oei/reports/oei-02-00-00490.pdf

Park, D. C., & Farrell, M. E. (2016). The aging mind in transition: Amyloid deposition and progression toward Alzheimer's disease. In K. W. Schaie & S. L. Willis (Eds.), *Handbook of the psychology of aging* (8th ed., pp. 87–103). San Diego, CA: Academic Press.

Patient Protection and Affordable Care Act (2010). Public Law, No. 111–148. Washington, DC.

Pinquart, M., & Sörensen, S. (2007). Correlates of physical health of informal caregivers: A meta-analysis. *The Journals of Gerontology: Series B: Psychological Sciences and Social Sciences, 62*(2), P126–P137.

Plassman, B. L., Langa, K. M., Fisher, G. G., Heeringa, S. G., Weir, D. R., Ofstedal, M. B., ... Wallace, R. B. (2008). Prevalence of cognitive impairment without dementia in the United States. *Annals of Internal Medicine, 148*, 427–434.

Qato, D. M., Alexander, G. C., Conti, R. M., Johnson, M., Schumm, P., & Lindau, S. T. (2008). Use of prescription and over-the-counter medications and dietary supplements among older adults in the United States. *Journal of the American Medical Association, 300*(24), 2867–2878. doi:10.1001/jama.2008.892

Qualls, S. H., & Noecker, T. L. (2009). Caregiver family therapy for conflicted families. In S. H. Qualls & S. H. Zarit (Eds.), *Aging families and caregiving: A clinician's guide to research, practice, and technology* (pp. 155–188). Hoboken, NJ: Wiley.

Qualls, S. H., & Smyer, M. A. (Eds.). (2007). *Changes in decision-making capacity in older adults; Assessment and intervention*. Hoboken, NJ: Wiley.

Raz, N. (2000). Aging of the brain and its impact on cognitive performance: Integration of structural and functional findings. In F. I. M. Craik & T. A. Salthouse (Eds.), *Handbook of aging and cognition-II* (pp. 1–90). Mahwah, NJ: Erlbaum.

Reuter-Lorenz, P. A., Festini, S. B., & Jantz, T. K. (2016). Executive functions and neurocognitive aging. In K.W. Schaie & S. Willis (Eds.), *Handbook of the psychology of aging* (pp. 245–262). San Diego, CA: Academic Press.

Salthouse, T. (2012). Consequences of age-related cognitive declines. *Annual Review of Psychology, 63*, 201–26.

Salzman, C., Jeste, D. V., Meyer, R. E., Cohen-Mansfield, J, Cummings, J., Grossberg, G. T., … Zubenko, G.S. (2008). Elderly patients with dementia-related symptoms of severe agitation and aggression: Consensus statement on treatment options, clinical trials methodology, and policy. *Journal of Clinical Psychiatry. 69*, 889–98.

Saxena, S., & Lawley, D. (2009). Delirium in the elderly: A clinical review. *Postgraduate Medicine Journal, 85*, 405–13.

Smith, G., & Rush, B. K. (2006). Normal aging and mild cognitive impairment. In D. K. Attix & K. A. Welch-Bohmer (Eds.), *Geriatric neuropsychology: Assessment and intervention* (pp. 27–55). New York, NY: Guilford.

Snow, A. L. Huddleston, C., Robinson, C., Kunik, M. E., Bush, A. L., Wilson, N., … Stanley, M. A. (2012). Psychometric properties of a structured interview guide for the rating for anxiety in dementia. *Aging & Mental Health, 16*, 592–602. doi:10.1080/13607863.2011.644518

Stanford Center on Longevity (2014, October 20). A consensus on the brain training industry from the scientific community. Retrieved from http://longevity3.stanford.edu/blog/2014/10/15/the-consensus-on-the-brain-training-industry-from-the-scientific-community/

Steffens, D. C., & Potter, G. G. (2008). Geriatric depression and cognitive impairment. *Psychological Medicine, 38*, 163–175. doi:10.1017/S003329170700102X

Stern, Y. (2002). What is cognitive reserve? Theory and research application of the reserve concept. *Journal of the International Neuropsychological Society, 8*(03), 448–460.

Tappen, R. M., & Williams, C. L. (2008). Development and testing of the Alzheimer's Disease and Related Dementias Mood Scale. *Nursing Research, 57*, 426–435. doi: 10.1097/NNR.0b013e31818c3dcc

Teri, L., Truax, P., Logsdon, R., Uomoto, J., Zarit, S., & Vitaliano, P. P. (1992). Assessment of behavioral problems in dementia: The revised memory and behavior problem checklist. *Psychology and Aging, 7*, 622–631.

Topo, P. (2009). Technology studies to meet the needs of people with dementia and their caregivers: A literature review. *Journal of Applied Gerontology, 28*(1), 5–37.

Unverzagt, F., Kasten, L., Johnson, K., Rebok, G., Marsiske, M., Koepke, K., …Tennstedt, S. L. (2007). Effect of memory impairment on training outcomes in ACTIVE. *Journal of the International Neuropsychological Society, 13*, 953–960.

Whitehouse, P. J., & Moody, H. R. (2006). Mild cognitive impairment: A "hardening of the categories"? *Dementia: The International Journal of Social Research and Practice, 5*, 11–25.

Whitlatch, C. J., Feinberg, L. F., & Tucke, S. S. (2005). Measuring the values and preferences for every-day care of persons with cognitive impairment and their family caregivers. *The Gerontologist, 45*, 370–380.

Whitlatch, C. J., Judge, K., Zarit, S. H., & Femia, E. E. (2006). A dyadic intervention for family caregivers and care receivers in early stage dementia. *The Gerontologist, 46,* 688–694. doi:10.1093/geront/46.5.688

Wisniewski, S. R., Belle, S. H., Coon, D. W., Marcus, S. M., Ory, M. G., Burgio, L. D., … Schulz, R. (2003). The Resources for Enhancing Alzheimer's Caregiver Health (REACH): Project design and baseline characteristics. *Psychology and Aging, 18,* 375–384.

Zarit, S. H. (2009). Empirically supported treatment for family caregivers. In S. H. Qualls & S. H. Zarit (Eds.), *Aging families and caregiving* (pp. 131–153). Hoboken, NJ: Wiley.

Zarit, S. H., & Heid, A. R. (2015). Assessment and treatment of family caregivers. In P. A. Lichtenberg & B. T. Mast (Eds.), *APA handbook of clinical geropsychology. Vol 2: Assessment, treatment, and issues of later life* (pp. 521–551). Washington, DC: American Psychological Association.

Zhu, C. W., Scarmeas, N., Torgan, R., Albert, M., Brandt, J., Blacker, D., …Stern, Y. (2006). Clinical features associated with costs in early AD: Baseline data from the Predictors Study. *Neurology, 66,* 1021–1028.

9

Major Depression and Bipolar Disorder

In this chapter, we focus on two of the most serious mood disorders listed in the *Diagnostic and Statistical Manual of Mental Disorders*, 5th edition (DSM-5; American Psychiatric Association, 2013): Major Depressive Disorder and Bipolar Disorder. Both of these disorders involve disruptions in one's subjective mood (or how one typically feels) along with diverse behavioral symptoms. A primary distinction is that in major depression, one's mood is unusually dysphoric, low, or "down in the dumps," whereas in bipolar disorder we see the opposite pattern, in which one's mood is abnormally elevated, euphoric, or "on top of the world." For both of these disorders, we characterize the primary symptoms and causes and describe how clinicians and researchers assess and treat individuals suffering from these potentially debilitating and serious conditions. Let's start with major depression.

Jenny Miller's husband of 46 years died three years ago from a sudden heart attack. She keeps thinking she will get over it and get on with life, but she somehow can't seem to figure out what life is anymore. Her children call her every week, and each one flies out to visit a couple of times each year, but they haven't been able to help her get over her grief. Unfortunately, she feels like she has no energy to handle daily routines, let alone try new things. Every morning she wakes up about 4 a.m. and is unable to get back to sleep. Her lack of sleep is frustrating for her and she feels irritable much of the time. She is sure that other people won't want to be around her these days. She rarely calls her friends, and complains that most of her "couple" friends obviously don't want to see her now that she is a widow. Although she has enjoyed sewing and needlework all of her life, she hasn't started a project in a couple of years because she just doesn't care that much about them anymore, and frankly doesn't believe she has the mental capacity to pursue them. She also gave up on pleasure reading, due to difficulty focusing. She is convinced that her memory is failing and complains that she can't concentrate on anything. Much of her day is spent watching the soap operas and game shows, dozing off occasionally because she is so tired and unmotivated.

Aging and Mental Health, Third Edition. Daniel L. Segal, Sara Honn Qualls, and Michael A. Smyer.
© 2018 John Wiley & Sons, Inc. Published 2018 by John Wiley & Sons, Inc.

Jenny Miller is experiencing what clinicians define as a Major Depressive Disorder (MDD), sometimes simply called major depression, clinical depression, or unipolar depression. As described below in more detail, Jenny reports many characteristic symptoms of depression, including insomnia, fatigue, irritability, social withdrawal, difficulty concentrating, memory difficulties, and a lack of interest in almost all aspects of her life. She is not particularly dysphoric or sad, nor does she cry excessively, so some people might think she is not depressed. Unfortunately, her experience is what some people imagine is normal for later life, leading the general public and even some health professionals to believe that depression is so common among older adults that it is almost expected. Although depression is indeed among the more common mental disorders experienced by older adults, it is also the case that fewer older adults than young adults suffer from diagnosable depression.

Definition of Depression

The DSM-5 (American Psychiatric Association, 2013) classifies depression within a new diagnostic category called *Depressive Disorders*, which includes four disorders that vary by intensity and duration. The most intense depressions are classified as Major Depressive Disorder (MDD), whereas the most chronic are termed Persistent Depressive Disorder (also called Dysthymic Disorder). The third depressive disorder is called Disruptive Mood Dysregulation Disorder, which is characterized by severe and recurrent temper outbursts that are out of proportion in intensity or duration to the situation. This disorder is usually diagnosed in children who have severe temper tantrums. The fourth depressive disorder is Premenstrual Dysphoric Disorder, which is a severe form of premenstrual syndrome involving physical and behavioral symptoms (e.g., bloating, joint pain, extreme sadness and crying, mood swings, irritability, and fatigue) that usually resolve with the onset of menstruation. It is uncommon among older adults. Table 9.1 shows the DSM-5 classifications for Major Depressive Disorder and Persistent Depressive Disorder, including the general diagnostic features for each. Two other disorders involving dysphoric mood should also be included as part of one's thinking about differential diagnosis. These include Adjustment Disorder with Depressed Mood, which is classified under the Trauma- and Stressor-Related Disorders category, and Persistent Complex Bereavement Disorder, which was added to the appendix of DSM-5 for further study.

In addition to the depressive disorders recognized by the DSM-5, minor or sub-syndromal depression is currently being espoused as a major clinical concern for older adults that may warrant its own diagnostic code. Epidemiological studies consistently find high rates of depressive symptoms in older adults (about 15–20%) compared to the relatively low rates of diagnosable MDD. That is, there are high rates of symptoms that do not meet the diagnostic threshold for one of the formal depressive disorders in the DSM. These *minor depressions* are receiving increasing attention because of their clinical importance to physical health as well as mental health. Minor depression is technically diagnosed as Other Specified Depressive Disorder within the DSM-5 classification system, but it is increasingly recognized as distinctive within the research literature.

Table 9.1 Diagnostic features for major depressive disorder and persistent depressive disorder (dysthymic disorder)

Type of depression	Diagnostic features
Major Depressive Disorder	A. Five or more of the following symptoms have been present during the same 2-week period and represent a change from previous functioning: At least one of the symptoms is either (1) depressed mood or (2) loss of interest or pleasure.
	(1) depressed or sad mood experienced most of the day, nearly every day
	(2) diminished interest or pleasure in activities
	(3) meaningful unintended weight loss or weight gain, or meaningful decrease or increase in appetite
	(4) sleep disturbance (too little or too much)
	(5) psychomotor restlessness or slowing
	(6) low energy or fatigue
	(7) feelings of worthlessness or excessive guilt
	(8) reduced ability to make decisions or impaired concentration
	(9) recurrent thoughts of death, suicidal ideation, a plan for completing suicide, or a suicide attempt
	B. The cluster of symptoms cause meaningful personal distress or an impairment in social, occupational, or other areas of functioning.
	C. The symptoms are not attributable to direct physiological effects of a substance or to a medical condition.
	D. The symptoms are not due to schizoaffective disorder, schizophrenia, or other psychotic disorders, and there has never been a manic or hypomanic episode.
Persistent Depressive Disorder	A. Depressed or sad mood for most of the day, for more days than not, lasting at least 2 years.
	B. Presence, while depressed, of at least two of the following:
	(1) poor appetite or overeating
	(2) sleep disturbance (too little or too much)
	(3) low energy or fatigue
	(4) low self-esteem
	(5) reduced ability to make decisions or impaired concentration
	(6) having feelings or hopelessness
	C. During the 2-year period of the disturbance, the person has never been without significant symptoms for more than 2 months at a time.

Source: Adapted from the American Psychiatric Association (2013).

There appear to be some consistent differences in the presentation of depressed older adults compared to depressed younger adults, with depressed older adults typically (but not always) showing fewer affective symptoms (e.g., feelings of sadness or guilt) but more cognitive symptoms (e.g., complaints about memory; executive functions deficits), somatic symptoms (e.g., fatigue, sleep disruption), and loss of interest in activities and living. Note these are general patterns and do not apply to all cases. In a study directly comparing symptom profiles among depressed older adults and middle-aged adults, the older patients were more likely to endorse reduced appetite and loss of interest in sex, but less likely to endorse feeling sad, frequent crying, feeling fearful, enjoying life, feeling as good as others, feeling useless, and having suicidal thoughts (Hybels, Landerman, & Blazer, 2012). The latter finding regarding lower reports of suicidal thinking is particularly provocative and alarming given the elevated suicide rates among older adults (discussed later in this chapter).

Note that having a sad or dysphoric mood is not required for a diagnosis of MDD, as long as several other characteristic signs and symptoms are present. Many people who are, in fact, clinically depressed recognize having the disorder and view themselves as depressed. However, some individuals who are clinically depressed do not recognize their symptoms, which typically limits their ability to seek out appropriate assessment and intervention. It has been our clinical experience that older men in the current cohort, especially those 80+ years of age, are less likely to perceive themselves as being depressed, instead seeing themselves as crabby, grouchy, irritable, or simply apathetic. Increased education and awareness are indicated in these situations.

Prevalence of Depression in Older Adults

Recall from the introductory comments to this section that prevalence rates for mental disorders are reported in a variety of ways. One way of examining population patterns of disorders is in terms of the rates of disorder among a specific population within the past year, referred to as 1-year prevalence rates. Lifetime prevalence rates describe the percentage of a population who have ever experienced the disorder. The prevalence rates reported in this section are drawn from reviews of the literature written by Fiske, Wetherell, and Gatz (2009) and Blazer and Hybels (2014), who describe the epidemiological literature in considerable detail.

Community-dwelling older adults living in the United States as well as around the world show generally low rates of diagnosable MDD, with rates ranging from 2% to 11%. Figure 9.1 presents 30-day, 12-month, and lifetime prevalence estimates by age for major depressive episode (MDE), which is essentially the symptoms of MDD with the exception of ruling out substances and medical conditions. As can be seen in the figure, 12-month prevalence rates for MDE are highest in the 18–34-year-old group, the rates are slightly lower for the 35–49-year-old group and the 50–64-year-old group, and are the lowest for the 65+ group, at only 2.6%. Lifetime rates for MDE show a slightly different picture, with rates peaking in the 35-49-year-old group. Note, however, that for all three time periods (30-day, 12-month, and lifetime), older adults show the lowest rates of MDE, despite the fact that their advanced age has afforded many more years in which a disorder could develop (Kessler et al., 2010). These data speak to the resiliency developed by many older adults who are able to ward off clinical depression despite many of the challenges posed by growing older. Other explanations for the pattern include differential mortality rates for persons with depressive disorders or differences in recollections of depressive episodes.

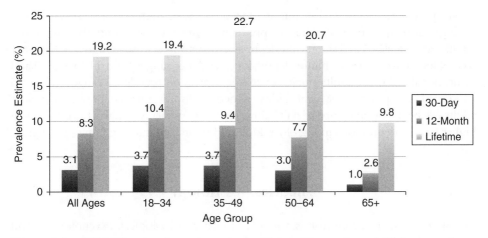

Figure 9.1 DSM-IV major depressive episode 30-day, 12-month, and lifetime prevalence estimates by age.
Source: Adapted from Kessler et al. (2010).

In contrast to the low rates for MDE and MDD, prevalence rates for subsyndromal depressions are quite high among community-dwelling older adults at about 15–20%, depending on the measures used and the cutoff for significance. In a large study, subsyndromal depression among older adults was a strong risk factor for subsequent development of full-blown MDD and anxiety disorders (Laborde-Lahoz et al., 2015). Women consistently report more depressive symptoms than men throughout the full adult lifespan (at about a 2:1 ratio) although the gender gap appears to narrow some-what in later life. The reasons for this narrowing remain unclear (Fiske et al., 2009). There are no differences in depressive symptoms with increasing age when confound-ing variables such as gender and functional status are controlled. About half of older adults with depression have the first onset of depression in later life (60 years old or older), called *late-onset depression*. The remaining half of older adults with depression had experienced prior episodes of depression, called *early-onset depression*, in some cases maintaining the disorder as they entered the later life stage (Fiske et al., 2009). When depression becomes especially severe, sufferers may experience psychotic symptoms (for example, hallucinations and delusions) that are part of the depressive disorder and typically remit when the depression is treated. This presentation is often called *psychotic depression*.

Rates for Persistent Depressive Disorder are less than 2% for community-dwelling older adults. Persistent Depressive Disorder rarely begins in later life but may persist from midlife into later life (Blazer & Hybels, 2014). Because Persistent Depressive Disorder can begin early in life and last for many years, some older adults with the disorder fail to recognize it, perceiving their chronic, low-level misery to be "normal" for them. Think of Eeyore the donkey, from the *Winnie-the-Pooh* books. Eeyore is characteristically and chronically gloomy and pessimistic, hardly ever enjoying life in his corner of the Hundred Acre Wood, but his problems do not seem to rise to the level of diagnosable MDD. It is more likely that Eeyore's symptom pattern is consis-tent with Persistent Depressive Disorder.

The prevalence of depression among older adults varies significantly across different settings. In sharp contrast to the low prevalence rates for community-dwelling older adults, rates of MDD and significant depressive symptoms are much higher in hospitalized older adults (major or minor depression prevalence ranges from 11% to 23%) and institutionalized older adults (major or minor depression prevalence ranges from 14% to 31%). The importance of comorbidity of medical disorders with depression for older adults will be discussed in more detail below. What is particularly noteworthy is the much higher rates of depression among older adults in hospital and nursing homes settings.

Theories of Etiology

Across the lifespan, depression is a mental disorder of biological, psychological, and social etiology. These three factors typically *interact* to cause depression in an older person, at least in the majority of cases. Typically, some degree of biological and/or psychological vulnerability to depression is present, and then an environmental stressor (e.g., loss of loved one; physical illness or disability; conflict within a close relationship) precipitates development of the depressive episode. In this section, biological, psychological, and social aspects will be discussed; approaches to assessment and treatment will be described in the following sections.

Biological factors

Biological models of the etiology of depression focus on genetics and on the chemical deficiencies of particular neurotransmitters. Studies of aging twins in the Swedish Twin Registry indicate that genetic heritability for lifetime major depression was moderate overall, but stronger for women (42%) than men (29%) (Kendler, Gatz, Gardner, & Pedersen, 2006). Several hypotheses regarding the structural and chemical mechanisms through which biological changes might create or enact depression have been offered and examined closely. The profile of neurotransmitters in the brains of adults with depression, and specifically older adults with depression, are different from those in adults without depression. The presence of higher or lower concentrations of particular neurotransmitters in persons with depression than without, along with the effectiveness of antidepressant medications that are intended to alter the concentrations of those same neurotransmitters, led some researchers to conclude that depression has a biological etiology. However, the biochemical markers that characterize the brains of adults with depression are also found in other disorders, and thus lack the specificity to serve either as an assessment tool or as a clear causal link at this time. It is also difficult to determine if the neurotransmitter changes are the *cause* of depression or a biological *effect* of being clinically depressed. These biological factors (i.e., a genetic propensity toward depression; neurotransmitter changes) are probably best considered as risk factors for depression in later life but are likely not direct causes of depression. In other words, these factors are correlates of depression, not causes.

In older adults, depression is often associated with medical illnesses, medications taken to treat medical conditions, and other psychoactive substances that alter brain

Table 9.2 Medical conditions and medications associated with depression

Medical conditions
Neurological disorders
Stroke, Huntington's disease, Parkinson's disease, multiple sclerosis, traumatic brain injury
Coronary artery disease
Hypertension, myocardial infarction, coronary artery bypass surgery, congestive heart failure
Metabolic disturbances
Hypothyroidism or hyperthyroidism, Cushing's disease, Diabetes mellitus
Other conditions
Chronic obstructive pulmonary disease, rheumatoid arthritis, deafness, chronic pain, sexual dysfunction, renal dialysis
Medications
antiviral agents; cardiovascular agents (primarily antihypertensive medications); retinoic acid derivatives; psychotropic medications (including antidepressants and antipsychotics); anticonvulsants; antimigraine agents; hormonal agents (including oral contraceptives); smoking cessation agents; immunological agents

Source: Adapted from the American Psychiatric Association (2013).

chemistry through various mechanisms, producing depression as a side effect. In cases where depression is a direct physiological result of a medical condition or of ingesting a psychoactive substance (whether legal or illegal in nature), the formal diagnoses, respectively, would be Depressive Disorder Due to a General Medical Condition or Substance-Induced Depressive Disorder. Table 9.2 provides a list of medical conditions and medications that commonly produce depressive symptoms among adults and older adults. A thorough evaluation of depression in older adults should therefore include a detailed assessment of current medical conditions and current medications, whether prescribed or over-the-counter.

Psychological factors

Each model of mental health and aging generates its own theory of depression. As described in Chapter 4, the psychodynamic model of depression in older adults describes several mechanisms through which an older adult may become depressed. One central theme revolves around the high rate of losses in later life that challenge the individual's ego functioning (Newton, Brauer, Gutmann, & Grunes, 1986). Losses of social roles, friends, family members, spouse or partner, and physical vitality and functioning, all must be grieved. The grief itself is a risk factor for depression, and the fact that the losses are often cumulative in a short period of time yields particular vulnerability to depression. Additional complications of loss may occur if the person experienced a highly significant loss in childhood (e.g., the loss of an attachment figure) that may establish a particular vulnerability for reexperiencing the highly intense grief as it was experienced when a child. Immature defense mechanisms always leave a person vulnerable to complications during significant life transitions because immature defenses offer less flexibility to adapt. Thus, individuals with lifelong patterns of immature coping are particularly vulnerable to poor adaptation to the many losses of later life (Vaillant, 2002).

Since a major theme of later life is decline of physical strength and, in some, cognitive abilities, this diminished capacity is also viewed as a risk factor for depression by psychodynamic theorists. Such losses drain the strength of the ego to structure internal and external adaptation, thus leaving the individual vulnerable to feeling out of control, inadequate, and ultimately, depressed. Finally, psychodynamic theorists describe the importance of integrating later-life losses into one's personal narrative in a manner that creates meaning and a coherent life story (Cohler & Hostetler, 2003). Narratives that cannot integrate loss themes in ways that sustain a strong sense of personal meaning can lead to despair and depression.

Behavioral theories relate depression to a loss of reinforcers. Depressed individuals tend to engage in lower rates of behavior in general and thus receive lower levels of positive reinforcement in their environments (Gallagher-Thompson & Thompson, 2010; Laidlaw, 2015; Laidlaw, Thompson, Dick-Siskin, & Gallagher-Thompson, 2003; Zarit & Zarit, 2007). A vicious cycle develops in which the person, who may feel apathetic or blue, begins to isolate himself. This isolation leads to less contact with things/persons/events that were previously pleasurable, and serves to maintain or worsen the depression.

A related premise is that there are *decreased positive interactions* between the person and his or her environment. There is a well-known and strong contingent relationship between pleasant activities and depression among adults and older adults. Persons with depression engage in fewer pleasant activities and receive less pleasure from them than do persons without depression. Interventions have further demonstrated the causal relationships between activities and mood. For example, reducing the frequency of pleasant events in a nondepressed person's life increases the risk of negative mood, whereas increasing the rate and pleasurableness of pleasant activities also reduces the rate of depression. Some depressed older individuals experience a loss of ability to engage in previously enjoyed activities, either through physical challenges or social losses (e.g., one's golfing buddy dies or relocates). The loss of significant others due to death or withdrawal can lead to a palpable reduction in reinforcers, particularly if the significant other was one on whom the person relied to maintain activities.

Finally, from a behavioral perspective, increased aversive interactions between the older person and his or her environment can also lead to the development of depressive symptoms. Especially noteworthy are interpersonal conflicts and social stressors (for example, conflict with one's spouse or partner, with adult children, or with other residents in congregate living settings) that serve as important risk factors for depression in older adults (Hinrichsen & Emery, 2005). Overall, in the behavioral model, behaviors and contingent relationships between behavior and reinforcers are viewed as causal agents for depressive disorders. Behavioral treatment, focusing on improving relationship skills, reducing aversive interactions, and increasing engagement with positive and valued activities, is quite powerful and effective.

Cognitive theories of depression implicate unhelpful or maladaptive thought patterns as being causal, emphasizing the role of negative thinking in developing and maintaining depression. Think of the famous metaphor of a pessimistic person who "sees the glass as half empty, rather than half full." Although cognitions are given primary importance in the development of mood states, the model is best thought of as being more circular in nature, in which the effects of mood states on thought patterns are also important. Several specific cognitive distortions (or irrational beliefs) are common among depressed persons, including catastrophizing, all-or-nothing reasoning, jumping to conclusions without first checking the evidence, using their emotional state to explain causal sequences, and the use of "should" statements (Laidlaw, 2015; Laidlaw, Thompson, Dick-Siskin, & Gallagher-Thompson, 2003). As has been demonstrated with adults of all ages, specific cognitive distortions create depressed feelings (Beck, Rush, Shaw, & Emery, 1979). Depression, on the other hand, also maintains cognitively distorted and negative perceptions of the self, the world, and the future, commonly called the "cognitive triad" for depression. In practice, the cognitive and behavioral models are typically blended into the cognitive behavioral therapy (CBT) perspective.

Social factors

Social factors (that is, psychosocial stressors) are almost always involved in the onset of depression or in the deterioration of a person currently experiencing depression. People with depression can typically identify several stressors that are negatively affecting their mood, and sometimes the stressor is the precipitating event for treatment (e.g., retirement, death of spouse, divorce, diagnosis of a chronic illness, relocation to a care facility). A small minority of people with depression cannot seem to easily identify any specific stressor, but during a thorough clinical interview with the person, some relevant stressors typically can be uncovered. The point we are emphasizing is that depression usually does not occur "in a vacuum" outside of the context of a particular person's psychological and social environments.

George (1994) organized psychosocial factors that affect risk for depression among older adults into six categories that progress from distal to proximal factors (see Table 9.3). Demographic variables (category 1) such as age, gender, and race/ethnicity affect prevalence rates of depression although the correlation of these variables with depression is often weaker for older than younger adults. Category 2, events and achievements from childhood, such as deprivations (e.g., poverty or parental separation and divorce) and poor educational attainment, predict depression throughout adulthood. Later events and achievements such as work and marital experiences also predict depression (category 3). For older adults, these characteristics often reflect past lifestyles more than current experiences, again offering less predictive power. Social integration (category 4) encompasses both individual level characteristics (e.g., social networks) and aggregate level characteristics (e.g., neighborhood disintegration).

The fifth and sixth categories of this model include the factors that have been studied most extensively in older adults. Category 5 includes factors related to chronic stress that either render a person vulnerable or are protective over time. Chronic financial problems, chronic physical illness, and persistent and onerous caregiving responsibilities have all been shown to have negative effects upon mental health, and depression in particular. Social support is recognized to have very positive, protective effects against the impact of chronic stress. Three types of social support have been demonstrated to affect mental health: (1) social network (size and structure of network of significant persons); (2) tangible support (e.g., instrumental and emotional services); and (3) perceptions of social support (George, 1994). One's *perception* of

Table 9.3 Social antecedents of depression

Category	Name	Illustrative indicators
1	Demographic variables	Age, sex, race, ethnicity
2	Early events and achievements	Education, childhood traumas
3	Later events and achievements	Occupation, income, marital status
4	Social integration	Religious affiliation, voluntary organization participation, neighborhood stability
5	Vulnerability and protective factors	Chronic stressors, social support versus isolation
6	Provoking agents and coping efforts	Life events, coping styles and strategies

Source: Adapted from George (1994).

available support appears to be a more powerful buffer of stress than any objective characteristics of the network. As such, the understanding of perceptions of support systems is an important topic in clinical interviews with older adults with depression.

Category 6 includes the factors that are current and salient: life events and coping strategies. Several events are recognized to provoke adaptive behavior in the lives of older adults, including retirement, widowhood, death of friends, and onset of physical illness. Life events show a consistent relationship to depression, although it is a modest one. Clearly, most older adults experience the events of later life without becoming depressed. That is, most older individuals are generally able to cope effectively with the challenges of aging. When one's coping resources are either chronically inadequate or become overwhelmed by stressors, then symptoms of distress typically develop.

Other risk factors for depression

One of the life events most widely believed to be associated with depression in later life is the death of a loved one and the consequent bereavement and grief. Perhaps because social losses are common in later life, grief is an intuitively compelling predictor. Indeed, in some cases the grief process produces emotions, thoughts, and behaviors that are similar to those evoked by depression, a pattern called *complicated grief*. The loss of a relationship that in many cases is life-long (exceeding 50 or 60 years together) can leave survivors with a deep sense of despair, loneliness, and other mood symptoms. The case of Jenny Miller described above illustrates the depression that can result from an unresolved or complicated grief process. Prigerson and her colleagues (e.g., Prigerson et al., 2009) have argued that the symptoms of complicated grief are associated with enduring functional impairments and appear to define a unique problem that is deserving of specialized diagnosis and treatment. As we noted earlier, Persistent Complex Bereavement Disorder was included in the DSM-5 as a condition deserving further empirical scrutiny and perhaps validation.

Grief, however, typically proceeds forward to resolve the symptoms without the persistent, pervasive effects of depression. Indeed, from his series of well-designed studies, Bonanno (2004, 2009) concluded that most people are naturally resilient in the face of bereavement and other traumatic losses and that in many cases people cope with grief and loss in ways that seem at first blush to be counterintuitive, such as by experiencing joy, laughter, and a deepening of connections to others. Again, it is important to recognize that although loss, bereavement, and grief are normative in later life, depression is not.

Coping strategies may be one mediating variable that buffers individuals from the deleterious effects of negative life events. Two types of coping appear to be useful: problem-focused or instrumental coping, and emotion-focused or accommodative coping (Lazarus & Folkman, 1987). People use problem-focused coping to try to change the circumstances that produced the impact of the negative event. Emotion-focused coping, on the other hand, directs people to accommodate to the circumstances by reducing the emotional impact of the stressor. In contrast to the benefits of problem-focused coping and emotion-focused coping, it appears that a ruminative coping style, in which one repeatedly but passively thinks about one's distress, is associated with depression among older adults (Fiske et al., 2009). Note that we discussed coping strategies and their impacts on mental health more thoroughly in Chapter 3.

Personality variables may also place a person at risk for depression, especially the trait of neuroticism which is robustly related to depression among adults and older adults. Furthermore, the clinical evidence of comorbidity between personality disorders (discussed fully in Chapter 13) and depression, estimated to be about 50%, also suggests an important role for personality pathology as a risk factor for depression in older people. Whether personality disorder features are risk factors, are simply comorbid, or are even consequences of depression is unclear, but the risk of coexisting personality disorder traits in depressed older adults is substantial. Conversely, more adaptive personality traits (e.g., optimism, extraversion) can also serve as buffers against depression.

Physical illness is a major risk factor for depression in older adults. Indeed, depression and medical problems commonly coexist among older adults, and the causal pathways are bidirectional (Blazer & Hybels, 2014). A good example is diabetes, which is known to be a risk for depression, and depression is also known to be a risk factor for developing diabetes (Renn, Feliciano, & Segal, 2011). At any age, effective coping with significant medical problems is difficult, especially if the problems cause functional impairments or disability. It is no wonder that patients in medical settings commonly experience high levels of depression. A key factor is the degree of *medical burden*: as burden increases, so does the risk for depressive symptoms. Unfortunately, depression also can complicate healing and rehabilitation because persons with depression are far more likely to report "excess disability" or disability beyond their actual limitations. Excess disability reporting can lead to noncompliance with rehabilitative efforts that leaves the person vulnerable to reduced functional capacity and further illness.

Institutionalization is another risk factor for depression. A high rate of nursing home residents experience depressive symptoms or MDD, as described earlier. Apparently, institutionalization itself places people at risk, in addition to the risks produced by their physical illnesses. The mechanism for this tendency for residents to become depressed is likely a combination of the increased disability produced by physical illnesses, isolation from personally meaningful relationships, decreased engagement in meaningful activities, reduced sense of control, and the tendency for staff to support dependent rather than independent behavior. Due to the high rates of depression in these settings, an expert interdisciplinary panel led by the American Geriatrics Society and the American Association for Geriatric Psychiatry (2003) recommended routine and regular screening for depression in every nursing home resident. Sadly, assessment and appropriate treatment of depression among long-term-care residents remain poor in many institutions, and the most vulnerable residents are often unable to advocate effectively for their own care.

Vascular Depression and its Link to Dementia

In addition to the biopsychosocial etiological factors for depression, a growing literature has documented an important connection between cardiovascular disease and depression in some older adults. Specifically, the *vascular depression hypothesis* suggests that cardiovascular disease can *predispose, precipitate, or perpetuate* a depressive episode in many older adults with underlying neurologic brain disorders (Taylor, Aizenstein, & Alexopoulos, 2013). This hypothesis is supported by the high frequency of depression in older adults with coronary artery disease, hypertension, diabetes, and stroke. The progression over time of cognitive deficits and cerebral hyperintensities (which are the radiological hallmarks of vascular depression) predicts a poor course of the depression and likely reflects the underlying worsening of vascular disease (Taylor et al., 2013).

A related issue is that the emergence of depressive symptoms in late life appears, in most cases, to be associated with greater cognitive impairments, especially executive function deficits such as impaired planning, judgment, and organizing behavior. This particular manifestation is sometimes referred to as the *depression-executive dysfunction syndrome*. Typically, depressed older adults who present with significant executive function deficits lack awareness of the problems, which complicates treatment. Discovering the exact causes of this syndrome is an active area of investigation. Finally, older adults with late-onset depression are also more likely to subsequently develop a neurocognitive disorder. This is particularly true for those with accompanying cognitive impairment or evidence of structural brain changes (e.g., from an MRI exam), suggesting that some types of late-onset depressions represent the prodromal or early precursor phase of dementia (Fiske et al., 2009).

Assessment

Assessment of depression serves four major purposes: screening for the presence of the problem or disorder; identifying the general classification of the problem; establishing baseline levels of symptoms, which is useful for planning interventions; and assessing the outcomes of the interventions in a standardized manner.

Assessment tools are chosen to meet a specific purpose because each type of tool has its strengths and limitations. Generally, *self-report scales* are very useful for identifying clinical levels of depression, although they do not provide a diagnosis. *Structured and semistructured interviews* are more useful for creating a reliable and valid diagnosis, although they typically take at least one to two hours to fully administer. Neither of those strategies is sufficient to serve as a basis for guiding intervention planning or measuring progress toward treatment goals. Treatment planning and evaluation require measurement of the specific domains of functioning targeted by the treatment (e.g., cognition or behavior).

Refer back to the case of Jenny Miller at the beginning of the chapter. How would you proceed with an evaluation of Jenny? Although there are obvious psychosocial factors we might suspect to be involved in her depression, other factors such as medical illness, pharmacological agents, and substance abuse must be ruled out before proceeding with a psychologically focused intervention for depression.

Self-report measures are used primarily for screening purposes, and as a quick indicator of the intensity of clinical symptoms during treatment process. Several short depression screening instruments are readily available for clinical and research use:

- The Geriatric Depression Scale (GDS; Yesavage et al., 1983) is a 30-item self-report measure designed specifically for use with older adults, making it by far the most popular screening inventory for clinical and research purposes with older adults. As shown in Figure 5.2 (in Chapter 5), all of the items of the GDS are appropriate for use with older adults. The GDS focuses on cognitive and behavioral aspects of depression, whereas somatic items are generally excluded which prevents the possible spurious elevation in screening measure scores obtained by medically ill but not depressed older adults. Another useful feature of the GDS is the very simple "yes/no" response format for each item. In 20 of the 30 items, the answer "yes" indicates depression; in the remaining 10, the answer "no" indicates depression. The total GDS score consists of the sum of all items. The recommended cutoffs for the GDS include 0–10 for minimal to mild depression, 11–20 for mild to moderate depression, and 21–30 for severe depression. Several modified versions of the GDS are available, including short versions containing either 5 or 15 items, which have been validated for use as screening measures. Potential drawbacks to the GDS include its reduced validity for use with some ethnic minority older adult groups and its lowered effectiveness among older adults with cognitive impairment (Marty, Pepin, June, & Segal, 2011).
- The Center for Epidemiologic Studies—Depression Scale (CES-D; Radloff, 1977) consists of 20 self-report items that tap depressive symptoms experienced over the past week. Each item is rated on a four-point Likert-type scale ranging from 0 (rarely/none) to 3 (most of the time). Traditionally, a total score is calculated by adding the ratings for all items. The possible range of total scores is from 0 to 60, with higher scores reflecting greater levels of depression. The CES-D was developed primarily as a research instrument for studies with adolescents and adults, although it has been used successfully with older adults due to its relatively low emphasis on somatic symptoms.
- The Beck Depression Inventory—Second edition (BDI-II; Beck, Steer, & Brown, 1996) is a 21-item self-report questionnaire that is widely used in clinical research and practice as a screening measure. Each item describes a specific manifestation of depressive symptoms, and the respondent reads four evaluative statements and

indicates his/her current severity level for that item. Thirteen items assess psychological symptoms of depression, whereas eight items assess somatic symptoms. Potential scores range from 0 to 63, with higher scores corresponding to higher levels of depression. According to the BDI-II manual, scores of 0–13 denote minimal depression, scores of 14–19 denote mild depression, scores of 20–28 denote moderate depression, and scores of 29–63 denote severe depression. The main criticisms of the BDI-II are that it has many somatic items, which may not be reflective of depression in some older adults and that the response format is not as simple as the other popular self-report measures, a particular detriment when working with individuals with cognitive impairment. A recent study reported excellent psychometric properties of the BDI-II among community-dwelling older adults (Segal, Coolidge, Cahill, & O'Riley, 2008), suggesting that the BDI-II has adequate support for its use with older adults.

For more detailed reviews of the various tools available for the screening of depression, see Edelstein et al. (2008), Fairchild and Scogin (2008), and Feliciano, Segal, and Vair (2011).

Despite popularity of the self-report measures described previously, it should be noted that a definitive diagnosis of depression (or any mental disorder for that matter) should never be made on the basis of self-report inventories alone, which can be subject to response biases (e.g., social desirability) and generally can be easily faked. In practice, a two-step process is typical whereby elevated self-reported scores on the screening instrument are followed up by a clinical or structured interview to confirm presence or absence of the disorder.

A clinical interview is the most common method of assessing depression in everyday clinical practice, typically in unstructured format. During the interview, the clinician gathers information about the person's current symptoms of depression, including a history of the depression, attempts at coping with the depression, and psychosocial stressors impacting the depression. Other topics are typically pursued to place the experiences with depression in the context of overall functioning, including an in-depth personal history (including information about responses to life transitions and major life events); mental health history (including interventions); medical history; marital, family, social, and work history; substance use and misuse; and a mental status examination. Collateral interviews with concerned family members or caregivers are a common and usually informative component of the depression assessment. To facilitate rapport, clinicians should explain clearly the purposes and procedures of the assessment, address any concerns the person may have about the evaluation, and be especially flexible when engaging older persons and their family members (Segal, Coolidge, & Hersen, 1998). Clinicians should also be generous with warmth, support, reassurance, and genuine caring as these help with rapport. During the interview it is important for clinicians to screen for cognitive disorders to rule out cognitive impairments that could be causing some or all of the depressive symptoms. Likewise, a screening for substance misuse, especially alcohol misuse, is particularly salient for older adults with depressive symptoms, due to the depressant nature of alcohol.

In contrast to an unstructured clinical interview, structured interviews provide increased clinical accuracy by structuring questions to elicit details about frequency and intensity of symptoms. Structured interviews are known to increase reliability and validity of diagnosis, but they are not panaceas (Segal & Williams, 2014). One of the most popular structured interviews used for clinical research and training which has a full module for depressive disorders is the *Structured Clinical Interview for DSM-5 Disorders* (SCID-5; First, Williams, Karg, & Spitzer, 2016). The SCID has been demonstrated to be useful for adults and older adults.

The focus and strategies of assessment for the purpose of treatment planning is shaped significantly by the theoretical model from which the therapist works. A cognitive-behavioral therapist may focus on assessing the frequency of participating in pleasant and unpleasant activities as well as the nature of the client's thought patterns, whereas a psychodynamic therapist may evaluate in detail the client's interpersonal relationship style in engaging the therapist and the client's use of a range of defenses. Treatment goals such as reducing depressogenic cognitive distortions require specific assessment of the types and frequency of cognitive distortions. Only by documenting the specific, operationalized instances of the distortions can a therapist design an appropriate intervention or measure the impact of the intervention on that specific problem.

Our original point about assessment bears repeating: Assessment tools need to be selected to be appropriate for the task at hand. For example, a screening instrument is insufficient to determine a diagnosis but useful for detecting problematic symptoms, and a clinical interview is insufficient to guide treatment planning but appropriate for diagnosis. Referring back again to the Jenny Miller case, an appropriate assessment strategy might begin with administering a self-report screening instrument such as the Geriatric Depression Scale to determine the intensity and range of symptoms experienced, followed by a clinical interview to identify the appropriate diagnosis. If she is indeed clinically depressed, assessment of her specific concerns may be used to formulate a treatment plan. Further assessment of her grieving process, family and friend relationships, daily activity schedule, cognitive framework, coping strategies, and mental abilities are all needed before treatment can be planned.

Interventions

More research and clinical case studies have focused on interventions with depressed older adults than any other older clinical population, highlighting clearly that various psychotherapeutic approaches and biological interventions *are effective* for late-life depression.

Biological/somatic approaches

The two main categories of biological treatments for depression include antidepressant medications and electroconvulsive therapy (ECT).

Most older adults seek treatment for depression from their primary care provider rather than from a mental health specialist. Thus, it is not surprising that a high percentage of mental health treatment for older adults is pharmacological. The vast majority of medications used to treat depression fall into one of four categories: tricyclic antidepressants (TCAs), monoamine oxidase (MAO) inhibitors, selective serotonin reuptake inhibitors (SSRIs), and serotonin norepinephrine reuptake inhibitors (SNRIs). These classes of medications work on somewhat different aspects of the neurotransmitter systems of the brain (American Psychiatric Association, 2010). The general effectiveness of antidepressant medications is generally comparable between classes and within classes of medications, with about 50% to 75% of clients showing meaningful improvements. It takes time for these medications to begin working, usually four to six weeks, although side effects often begin much earlier. As such, a common challenge is to maintain adherence. Continuation of medication may be needed for many months and even years in severe cases.

Medications are typically chosen according to the following criteria: side effect profile, prior history of response to medication, history of first-degree relatives' response to medication, concurrent medications and illnesses that may render one choice more risky than another, likelihood of adherence to the medical regimen, degree of interference with life style, cost, and preference of patient or prescriber. The tricyclic antidepressants show the same effectiveness in older adults as in young adults. Their primary disadvantage is the high probability of unpleasant side effects (e.g., dry mouth, constipation, weight gain, sedation, cardiovascular effects, postural hypotension, and confusion). MAO inhibitors are used as a last resort because their usage is complicated by the necessity of dietary and medication restrictions, but they are also effective with older adults. SSRIs and SNRIs represent the newest types of antidepressant medications. They have the fewest side effects, and thus represent a first line medication choice for many older adults (Blazer & Hybels, 2014; Shanmugham, Karp, Drayer, Reynolds, & Alexopoulos, 2005).

ECT has been a controversial intervention used primarily for severe recalcitrant depression that has not responded to either pharmacotherapy or psychotherapy and has life-threatening complications, for example, incapacitating psychotic symptoms or severe suicidal potential. The literature on ECT suggests it is an effective, evidence-based form of treatment that is used disproportionately with older adults (Kelly & Zisselman, 2000). Improvement is seen in about 80% of patients (although relapse can be a problem) and evidence that it is used effectively with patients for whom other treatments have failed lends further credence to claims of its effectiveness (Kelly & Zisselman, 2000; Wilkinson, 2011). Treatments are generally administered three times a week on nonconsecutive days for several weeks. Most patients reach a therapeutic plateau within 6 to 12 treatment sessions. During ECT sessions, the patient's heart rate, respiration, blood pressure, and pulse oximetry are closely monitored before and after the electrical stimulus is applied. Due to high relapse rates associated with ECT as a stand-alone intervention, follow-up treatments are almost always needed, which can include maintenance ECT sessions, antidepressant medications, and/or psychotherapy.

At present the exact mechanisms by which ECT creates therapeutic improvements are not fully understood. Potential complications for ECT among older adults include cardiac problems, confusion, memory loss (which is usually temporary), and transient delirium, suggesting that caution to this approach is advised (Fiske et al., 2009), particularly among individuals with preexisting cognitive impairment. Some modifications to the standard ECT procedure for use with older adults, designed to reduce neuro-cognitive impacts, include using unilateral (rather than bilateral) electrode placement, lower electrical stimulus, and less frequent treatments. Especially among medically ill older adults, discussions weighing the pros and cons of ECT should be thoughtfully pursued with the treatment team and informed consent must necessarily be obtained.

Less-studied biological approaches for depression include transcranial magnetic stimulation and vagus nerve stimulation. At present, there is insufficient evidence to classify these approaches as effective for treating MDD in older adults, and they are not first choice options.

Psychotherapeutic approaches

The effectiveness of psychological interventions for clinical levels as well as subclin-ical levels of depression among older adults is quite high, indicating that several types of psychotherapy meet the benchmark for an effective evidence-based interven-tion. These interventions include behavioral therapy, cognitive-behavioral therapy, cognitive bibliotherapy, problem-solving therapy, brief psychodynamic therapy, and reminiscence therapy (Shah, Scogin, & Floyd, 2012; Scogin, Welsh, Hanson, Stump, & Coates, 2005).

Psychotherapy outcome studies find that pharmacotherapy and psychotherapy of various types are approximately equally effective, treating successfully between 50% and 70% of older adults with major depressive disorder within 12–20 sessions. A meta-analysis comparing psychological and pharmacological interventions for depression indicated that effect sizes may even favor psychotherapy (Pinquart, Duberstein, & Lyness, 2006). The presence of personality disorder features in the older client often reduces the success rate of psychotherapies and generally makes treatment longer and more turbulent (Segal, Zweig, & Molinari, 2012).

The conceptual and statistical analyses comparing the effectiveness of different therapies (including pharmacotherapy and the range of empirically tested psychother-apies) yields a consistent conclusion: No one empirically supported therapy is clearly superior to all others, but all of the empirically supported therapies are superior to no intervention or placebo. This pattern is helpful to clinicians who typically draw upon a variety of frameworks and techniques to effect change with a wide variety of clients. Of course, the full range of clients who are depressed is not included in research outcome studies, many of which are notably lacking in their inclusion of nursing home residents, ethnic minority older adults, and the very old (over 85 years of age). Researchers find it most useful to narrow the possible confounding variables in psychotherapy outcome studies by limiting participation to older adults without other physical and mental health problems. Clinical work in other settings requires more flexibility in working with depression of many varieties combined with various other physical or mental health problems (e.g., arthritis, anxiety, or substance abuse). Thus, the therapy outcome studies provide very useful guidance, but the treatment protocols often must be adapted to meet the needs of clients with complex situations.

CBT is the most thoroughly tested psychotherapy used with depressed older adults. CBT attempts to alter the cognitive frameworks of clients to eliminate depressogenic thought patterns and to change behavior patterns to include a higher rate of pleasant activities (Feliciano et al., 2011; Gallagher-Thompson & Thompson, 2010; Laidlaw, 2015; Laidlaw et al., 2003). The essence of this treatment model is to help clients learn to monitor and then alter their thought patterns and behavior simultaneously by engaging in structured therapy sessions including substantial homework activity between sessions. Therapists help clients to identify, plan, and increase pleasant events and to learn the connections between thoughts and feelings, identify cognitive distortions, and change negative thought patterns. To help clients increase pleasant events, the behaviorally based interventions involve identifying enjoyable activities through behavioral self-observations using an activity diary and a mood-rating scale. Once mood-enhancing activities have been identified, the procedure entails increasing involvement in enjoyable activities that are realistic given the older person's current physical and cognitive abilities. These interventions may also include a component aimed at decreasing behaviors that lead to or maintain depressive symptoms (e.g., overdependence, passivity) (Laidlaw, 2015; Laidlaw et al., 2003).

CBT for older adults is generally similar to CBT for adults, with some typical modifications, namely to understand the context of later life as part of the case formulation, understanding and adapting the treatment to accommodate sensory and physical challenges (when present), and appreciating that ageism on the part of clinician or client may be barriers to change (Feliciano et al., 2011; Laidlaw, 2015). Other common modifications are needed if the older client has cognitive impairment. In such cases, more repetition of core concepts is needed, a slower pace is expected, and in-session memory aids, such as cue cards and recording of sessions, may be helpful (Shah et al., 2012).

Methodologically rigorous outcome studies suggest that CBT shows efficacy rates that are maintained over a two-year period, similar to the success rates of pharmacological treatments and psychodynamic psychotherapy (Pinquart et al., 2006). CBT has been used effectively with depressed caregivers of ill older adults, with depressed Alzheimer's patients, and with older adults experiencing MDD (Gallagher-Thompson & Thompson, 2010; Laidlaw, 2015; Laidlaw et al., 2003).

Cognitive bibliotherapy involves participants learning the principles and techniques of CBT by reading books about the topic, such as the classic book *Feeling Good* by David Burns (1999). In essence, cognitive bibliotherapy is self-administered CBT. Its educative and self-paced structure may be ideal for older adults, and the outcome data show it is an effective form of treatment (Floyd, Scogin, McKendree-Smith, Floyd, & Rokke, 2004).

Problem-solving therapy (PST) has at its core a step-by-step process that clients learn in order to identify and implement solutions to problems they are experiencing (see Chapter 5 for a more thorough description of the PST model and specific problem-solving steps). PST therapy is known to be effective for a wide range of depressed older adults including outpatients, frail homebound older adults, primary care patients, and older adults with executive dysfunction problems (see Chapter 5).

Psychodynamic psychotherapy has been shown to be effective with depressed older adults. As we discussed in Chapter 4, psychodynamic therapies focus on working through grief and loss concerns that generate sufficient anxiety to impede the maturation of functioning. By addressing the anxiety directly, clients are able to proceed with their development, toward more mature styles of coping and defense (see Chapter 4 for a more thorough discussion of this model). A brief form of psychodynamic therapy showed the same success rate as CBT in treating MDD in depressed older adult caregivers (Gallagher-Thompson & Steffan, 1994), and psychodynamic psychotherapy provided to older adults at a large community mental health center was also effective (Roseborough, Luptak, McLeod, & Bradshaw, 2013).

Another model that has generated considerable interest in its use with older people is interpersonal therapy (IPT; Weissman, Markowitz, & Klerman, 2000), a practical, brief, diagnosis-targeted, present-focused psychotherapy that has been adapted successfully for older adults (Hinrichsen, 2008; Hinrichsen & Clougherty, 2006). IPT focuses on disturbances in current relationships by addressing four themes considered core to the development or maintenance of depression: grief (e.g., the death of a loved one); interpersonal disputes (e.g., conflict with peers or children); role transitions (e.g., retirement); and interpersonal deficits (e.g., lack of communication or assertiveness skills). Using a semistructured, time-limited approach (12–20 sessions), IPT uses a range of eclectic psychotherapeutic techniques intended to improve interpersonal communication, clarify emotional states, express affect, and support renegotiated role relationships. Due to the many social changes and losses endemic to later life, IPT is ideally suited to the older population. Indeed, IPT has been shown to be an effective treatment for depression in older adults, both in the acute phase and also for relapse prevention (Hinrichsen, 2008).

Reminiscence therapy is another empirically supported therapy approach for depression in older adults. As one of the few therapeutic modalities that has arisen specifically from clinical work with older adults, it warrants attention. Building on the theories of Erik Erikson, Butler (1974) proposed that conducting a life review is a normal developmental task of later life. The life review requires older adults to integrate the disparate themes, especially successes and failures, of a given life. Persons who do not integrate their lives successfully are vulnerable to despair and depression, whereas those who are successful often feel a greater sense of meaning and satisfaction in life. Several different forms of reminiscence therapy have been developed, ranging in degree of structure offered to the reminiscence. The most widely studied variant is a highly structured version called life review therapy. Clinical applications tend to structure the reminiscence around the themes Erikson believed to be salient (e.g., past accomplishments and failures, interpersonal conflicts, meaning). There is ample support for reminiscence therapy as an evidence-based treatment (Serrano, Latorre, Gatz, & Montanes, 2004). Although not specific to depression, a meta-analysis (Bohlmeijer, Roemer, Cuijpers, & Smit, 2007) indicated that life review is a worthwhile intervention for enhancing psychological well-being in older adults with effect sizes comparable to CBT.

With the plethora of useful approaches available for treating depression in older adults, how does one decide which to use and for how long? Early algorithms for treatment decisions initially recommended medications as the first line of attack, but more recent evidence resulted in the recommendation of either medications, psychotherapy, or their combination depending on the clinical presentation and patient preferences (American Psychiatric Association, 2010). In cases of severe depression, medication is often indicated early in the process to boost mood and energy, which can help clients participate more effectively in psychotherapy. Interestingly, when given a choice, older primary care patients seem to prefer psychotherapy approaches over medication (Gum et al., 2006). Sadly, despite the effectiveness of many treatments, depression in older adults is often not assessed thoroughly (if at all), not adequately identified, and thus significantly undertreated across multiple settings (Barry, Abou, Simen, & Gill, 2012). Some reasons for this problem include: biases of clinicians and older adults themselves (e.g., assuming it is normal to become depressed in later life; assuming that there are no appropriate treatments); misattribution of symptoms; the difficulty detecting depression due to the age-differences in presentation described earlier; and the true complexity of diagnosing depression in medically ill or neurologically impaired older adults (Fiske et al., 2009; Karel, Ogland-Hand, Gatz, & Unützer, 2002).

We will conclude this section on interventions for later-life depression with a brief mention of three programs that have a strong evidence base:

- Improving Mood-Promoting Access to Collaborative Treatment (IMPACT; Unützer et al., 2002);
- Identifying Depression, Empowering Activities for Seniors (Healthy IDEAS; Quijano et al., 2007);
- Program to Encourage Active Rewarding Lives for Seniors (PEARLS; Ciechanowski et al., 2004).

These programs were designed to treat older adults with depressive symptoms (either MDD, minor depression, or dysthymia). They share several commonalities, most notably that they all follow the *depression care management model*, which is an interdisciplinary team-based approach to treating depression. Care teams typically involve the patient, a primary care physician, a depression care manager, and a psychiatric consultant, who all work together to deliver evidence-based psychological and pharmacological interventions delivered either in the medical clinic or at the older person's home. Each of these programs has a solid evidence base for effectiveness (e.g., reduced depression and increased quality of life), across multiple sites, and can save costs in the long-run. Consultations and implementation toolkits are available for each program. Despite strong evidence of effectiveness, wide implementation across the US has been lagging.

Prevention of Depression

We have just provided an overview of treatments for depression in older adults, highlighting the point that several biological and psychological treatments for depression are evidence-based, empirically supported, and as such known to be effective for older adults. However, one may wonder: What do we know about the *prevention* of depression in late life?

Prevention efforts for depression in later life may be aimed at three goals: to avoid a first onset of depression in later life, to prevent the recurrence of depression in older individuals with a prior history of MDD, and to prevent relapse after successful treatment for depression (Fiske et al., 2009). Targeting older adults who are at high risk for developing depression is an important and effective strategy. For example, treating older adults with subsyndromal levels of depression (before it becomes a full-fledged diagnosable mental disorder—i.e., secondary prevention) could prevent almost 25% of new cases in later life. Because insomnia is a known risk factor for depression in later life, treatment for insomnia (discussed in more detail in Chapter 12) may be another avenue to prevent the development of depression in older adults (Fiske et al., 2009).

Other preventive efforts may also be directed at older adults at risk for depression due to physical illness and its consequences, bereavement, caregiving responsibilities for an ill person, and loneliness. Finally, educational efforts directed at physicians, senior service professionals, and older adults in the community to help them recognize the signs and symptoms of depression and understand that depression is *not* a normal part of aging may also help with early detection and intervention (Fiske et al., 2009).

Suicide

Among the most devastating consequences of depression is suicide. Worldwide, it is estimated that about 1 million people die each year by suicide. In the US, 42,773 people died by suicide in 2014, making suicide the 10th leading cause of death, with a national suicide death rate of 13.4 per 100,000 people (Drapeau & McIntosh, 2015). Suicide in later life warrants special attention because of the elevated suicide rates among older adults in many populations across the globe. In the US, for example, 7,693 people aged 65 years old and older died by suicide in 2014, indicating a suicide rate of 16.6 per 100,000 people. This rate is almost 24% greater than the national rate. On average, one older adult dies by suicide in the US every 1 hour and 8 minutes.

Suicide is indeed disproportionate among older adults as they comprise about 14.5% of the population but complete about 18% of all suicides, reflecting a greatly elevated risk in later life. Suicide attempts are much more common among women than men (at about a ratio of 3:1), but suicide deaths are much more common among men than women (at a ratio of 3.4:1), due to more immediately lethal means used, especially firearms, among men and to premorbid physical frailties (Drapeau & McIntosh, 2015). Suicide rates are particularly high among older men, especially older White men, with rates higher than any other group. In contrast, some populations, especially African-American women, have remarkably low suicide rates across the lifespan, indicating a tremendous resiliency that should be studied closely.

Older adults are more likely than younger adults to die by suicide during an attempt, due to more lethal methods of suicide attempt and lowered communications about their suicidal intent. Suicide among older adults is associated with diagnosable psychopathology (especially major depression) in 71% to 97% of cases (Conwell, Van Orden, & Caine, 2011; Fiske, Smith, & Price, 2015). Sadly, the majority of older adults who died by suicide had seen their primary care physician within the month prior to suicide (Conwell et al., 2011; Luoma, Martin, & Pearson, 2002). It is unclear exactly what these individuals wanted, but what is clear is that they did not get the relief they were seeking. Thus, there is a serious need for better preparation of physicians for screening and treatment of geriatric depression, and for screening and prevention of older adults at risk for suicide (Raue, Ghesquiere, & Bruce, 2014). "Double suicides" involving spouses or partners occur most frequently among older adults. The typical scenario is an older person who first kills his or her partner, who usually is suffering greatly from a serious, chronic, and debilitating disease (e.g., severe dementia, Amyotrophic Lateral Sclerosis), and then subsequently kills him or herself.

It is likely that there are multiple, complex, and interrelated causes to any death by suicide. Much has been learned in the past two decades about robust risk and resiliency factors for later-life suicide. The most prominent risk and protective factors are listed in Table 9.4. We highlight a few points here. The strongest risk factor is having a current mental disorder, most notably MDD. A systematic review of social factors and suicidal behavior among older people revealed that limited social connectedness to friends, family members, or other communities was strongly related to suicide (Fässberg et al., 2012). Relatedly, a recent review found associations between suicidal behavior and a number of specific physical illnesses, including malignant diseases, neurological disorders, pain, male genital disorders, pulmonary disease, liver disease, and arthritis (Fässberg et al., 2016). Regarding institutionalization, this process is especially painful if it is against the wishes of the older person, who may or may not have the capacity to understand such placement. Additionally, residents of nursing homes tend to use more subtle forms of self-harm that, when resulting in death, may not be labeled officially as suicide, due to stigma to the setting and to the surviving family members. Important current research is trying to elucidate how cultural scripts, such as increased permissibility or acceptability of suicide, might be operating to explain the vulnerability of certain groups, such as older men (Canetto, 2017; Winterrowd, Canetto, & Benoit, 2017).

Table 9.4 Key risk and protective factors for suicide among older adults

Risk factors	*Protective factors*
Mental disorders, particularly major depression	Receiving care for mental and physical health problems
Substance use problems (including abuse of prescription medications)	Social connectedness and social support
Physical illness, disability, and pain; Institutionalization	A sense of purpose or meaning in life
Maladaptive personality traits	Skills in coping and adapting to change
Social isolation; Limited social connectedness	Cultural or religious beliefs that discourage suicide
Cognitive deficits, especially deficits in executive functions	
Stressful life events and social losses	
Perceived burdensomeness and thwarted belongingness	
Hopelessness	
Access to lethal means	

Source: Adapted from Conwell, Van Orden, & Caine (2011) and from Fiske, Smith, & Price (2015).

As with any age group, suicidal thoughts and intent must be assessed in any depressed older adult. General queries about suicidal ideation should be followed up with probes about specific plans and intent. This information should be considered in the context of chronic and acute stressors that may be impinging on the older person's ability to effectively cope now and in the immediate future. Fortunately, there are formal assessment measures for suicide-related ideation or suicidal risk including:

- The Geriatric Suicide Ideation Scale (GSIS; Heisel & Flett, 2006) is an elder-specific, 31-item self-report multidimensional measure of suicidal ideation in older adults. Each item is rated on a five-point Likert-type scale. The GSIS provides a total score as well as scores on four subscales: Suicide Ideation (e.g., "I want to end my life."); Death Ideation (e.g., "I welcome the thought of drifting off to sleep and never waking up."); Loss of Personal and Social Worth (e.g., "I generally feel pretty worthless."); and Perceived Meaning in Life (e.g., "I am certain that I have something to live for."). This latter subscale is reverse-scored so that higher scores indicate lowered meaning in life. A wealth of data support the construct validity of the use of the GSIS for a wide range of older adults in clinical and research settings (Heisel & Flett, 2016).
- The Scale for Suicidal Ideation (SSI; Beck, Kovacs, & Weissman, 1979) is a 21-item scale that is completed by a clinician following a semistructured interview. The SSI is not an elder-specific measure but it has been used effectively with older adults.

There are a few other popular assessment instruments that do not measure suicidal ideation per se, but rather measure important factors that are related to suicide:

- The Geriatric Hopelessness Scale (GHS; Fry, 1986) is a 30-item self-report scale with a simple "yes/no" response format designed to assess pessimism and cognitions of hopelessness in older adults, which are theoretically related to suicidal behavior in Beck's model of depression.
- The Reasons for Living Inventory (RFL; Linehan, Goodstein, Nielsen, & Chiles, 1983) is a 48-item self-report measure that assesses a range of beliefs thought to be important in differentiating suicidal from nonsuicidal individuals. The RFL contains six subscales: Survival and Coping Beliefs, Responsibility to Family, Child-Related Concerns, Fear of Suicide, Fear of Social Disapproval, and Moral Objections. The RFL has a solid theoretical base, is extensively used in research, and has abundant evidence of reliability and validity for use with older adults. For example, older adults rated Child-Related Concerns and Moral Objections as stronger reasons for living compared to younger adults (Miller, Segal, & Coolidge, 2001) and overall reasons for living was positively associated with perceived physical well-being (Segal, Lebenson, & Coolidge, 2008) and problem- and emotion-focused coping strategies (Marty, Segal, & Coolidge, 2010).
- The Reasons for Living Scale Older Adult version (RFL-OA; Edelstein et al., 2009) is an adapted, elder-specific version of the RFL. The measure includes 69 self-report items that are all content valid for older adults, representing a true strength of this measure. The measure is accumulating solid evidence for validity as an effective assessment tool, especially in research settings (Heisel, Neufeld, & Flett, 2016).

Clearly, if the assessment reveals that the older client is currently at risk for self-harm, the clinician must act to protect the client. This could involve having the client agree to a realistic safety plan, having the client notify others in his or her family of the crisis situation and arrange for more support and monitoring, and certainly removing lethal means of suicide such as guns and stockpiles of pills. If the client is in immediate and imminent danger of suicide and less restrictive treatments or strategies are not sufficient, the clinician is required to hospitalize the client for the client's own safety. It is best if such hospitalization can be done collaboratively and with the older person's consent by explaining the benefits that may result from a hospital stay (e.g., stabilization with medications, and increased access to a team of helping professionals, including social work services). In some cases, hospitalization needs to be done without the consent of the older person, and this process is called *involuntary commitment.* This is often stressful for the older person and mental health professional alike. Complications that can arise from involuntary commitments include the hospitalized patient's anger at the clinician and subsequent termination of therapy once released, and the incurred and unwanted financial costs for the hospitalization. As such, involuntary hospitalization is only considered after all other reasonable approaches are exhausted to keep the suicidal older person safe, and must be followed up by other interventions (Fiske et al., 2015). A main point to highlight is that suicide is largely preventable, and the key first steps are thorough screening and assessment for those older adults most at risk, followed by appropriate psychological and pharmacological interventions to support health and safety.

Bipolar Disorder

William West, a 61-year-old, divorced former substitute teacher, has been down in the dumps for most of the past month. For reasons he does not understand, he has been feeling better lately, euphoric actually, with great energy and enthusiasm, believing that he has discovered a way to predict and, in fact, control weather patterns across the nation. He began furiously charting the weather, writing almost 600 pages in a journal over a 48-hour period, foregoing eating and showering. He excitedly believed he had found a way to "weaponize the weather" which would most surely make him a celebrity and very valuable to federal authorities. After four days of frenzied activity, having barely slept during this time, the episode came to an abrupt (and painful conclusion) when William tossed a small TV and most of his clothes off his apartment balcony, thinking that the FBI was "spying" on him through the TV and tracking his location through "transistors implanted in his clothes." William was taken to a psychiatric hospital by the apartment manager, where William was sedated and stabilized. He reported to his clinician later that he does not remember many details of the past few days, but he does recall having a few similar periods in his past when he would get "high without drugs" and behave erratically. Having been evicted from his current apartment, William is anxious to speak to his social worker in the hopes he can get help to find a new place to live.

The DSM-5 category of *Bipolar and Related Disorders* is thought to represent a bridge between the depressive disorders and the psychotic disorders. The prominent disorders included in this category include bipolar I disorder, bipolar II disorder, and cyclothymic disorder. Bipolar I disorder is the most well-known and represents what historically was called manic-depression. For diagnosis of bipolar I, the person must experience a full-fledged *manic episode* that may be preceded or followed by hypomanic or depressive episodes. Note that depressive episodes are common in bipolar I but are not required for a diagnosis. Some people report cycling from one mood state to the other, while others have periods of relatively normal mood in between mood episodes. Manic episodes tend to have rapid onset (within hours or days) but may evolve over several weeks.

The essential feature of a manic episode is an abnormally persistent euphoric, expansive, or irritable mood and abnormally persistent increased activity or energy present most of the time for at least one week, with at least three other symptoms from the following: (1) inflated self-esteem or grandiosity; (2) decreased need for sleep; (3) being more talkative than usual or feeling pressure to keep talking (often referred to as pressured speech); (4) flight of ideas or racing thoughts; (5) distractibility; (6) increase in goal-directed activity (either socially, at work or school, or sexually) or psychomotor agitation; and (7) excessive involvement in pleasurable activities that have high potential for painful consequences. People in a manic episode often exhibit impaired judgment and engage in reckless behaviors such as unrestrained buying sprees, compulsive gambling, reckless driving, foolish business investment, and sexual indiscretions. Several days of lack of sleep can bring about or worsen psychotic symptoms, which are more common in bipolar disorder than in MDD. In the case example above, William shows several characteristic signs of being in a manic state, including paranoid thinking, that were not present before he cycled upward. Delusions of persecution and grandiosity (e.g., believing one is a deity or possessed by a deity, or that one has special powers or abilities) are common during manic states.

Although bipolar I disorder requires presence of at least one lifetime manic episode (with or without depression), bipolar II disorder is characterized by at least one lifetime episode of MDE and one hypomanic episode, which is essentially a milder version of mania, lasting at least four days but is not severe enough to cause substantial impairment in social or occupational functioning or psychotic symptoms. Cyclothymic disorder is characterized by a chronic, fluctuating mood disturbance, lasting at least two years, involving numerous periods of hypomanic symptoms (that do not meet criteria for a hypomanic episode) and depressive symptoms (that do not meet criteria for an MDE).

For all of the bipolar-related disorders, as part of differential diagnosis, one must ensure that symptoms are not attributable to the physiological effects of an ingested substance or another medical condition. Several substances are known to precipitate manic symptoms in adults and older adults, including the stimulant class of drugs (e.g., cocaine, amphetamines), phencyclidine (PCP), and steroids. We are also aware of cases in which initiation of an antidepressant medication regimen seemed to trigger a manic episode. Medical conditions known to cause hypomanic or manic symptoms include cardiovascular disease, stroke, multiple sclerosis, traumatic brain injury, hyperthyroidism, hypothyroidism, Cushing's disease, Addison's disease, and infections (Brooks, Sommer, & Ketter, 2010).

Prevalence of Bipolar Disorder in Older Adults

According to the DSM-5, bipolar I disorder is relatively rare in the general adult US population with a 12-month prevalence estimate of 0.6%. There is an almost equal male-to-female ratio of 1.1:1. Bipolar disorder is associated with an elevated suicide risk, at least 15 times higher than in the general population. In general, the course of bipolar disorder is not as favorable as MDD. For many people, bipolar disorder is a chronic mood condition that requires lifelong management. We often use the example or analogy of diabetes, which also must be managed on a daily basis for better outcomes to ensue.

Bipolar disorder is understudied among older adults but a small literature has emerged. Among older adults, bipolar disorder is much less common than MDD, affecting only 0.1% to 0.5% of older adults in the general community (Marino & Sirey, 2013). As would be expected, rates are higher in clinical settings, as bipolar disorder is diagnosed in 3% to 9.7% of nursing home residents, in 2% to 8% of older adults receiving outpatient mental health services, in 5% to 18% of older adults admitted to inpatient psychiatric units, and in 17% of older adults presenting to a psychiatric emergency room (see reviews by Depp & Jeste, 2004; Sajatovic et al., 2015).

The presentation of geriatric bipolar disorder is quite variable, which is believed to delay appropriate identification and treatment (Sajatovic & Chen, 2011). Bipolar disorder in older adults includes those who became symptomatic in younger life and aged with the disorder and a much smaller minority (about 10%) who experience mania for the first time after age 50 (called late-onset bipolar disorder). The late-onset type appears to have higher medical and neurological comorbidity, which can cause diagnostic confusion. Longitudinal assessment of older patients with bipolar disorder often reveals significant cognitive deterioration, worse than is seen in age-matched peers without the disorder. Bipolar disorder appears to increase the risk for having a stroke and developing diagnosable dementia in later life. The mechanisms for these relationships are unclear. Substance abuse is a common comorbidity across the adult lifespan, often with people using substances to self-medicate their symptoms of mania or depression.

There is some evidence that symptoms of mania present somewhat differently in older people compared to younger people. For example, mood may be more irritable than happy, and anger may dominate the presentation (Blazer & Hybels, 2014). The mixture of manic and depressive symptoms may be more severe in older adults (Marino & Sirey, 2013). Additionally, it is likely that the behavioral manifestation of some symptoms of mania will be different (possibly attenuated) in older adults, due to normal aspects of aging, such as reduced energy and stamina, which might make physically reckless behaviors less likely and sexual acting out less common, especially if fewer partners are readily available. Cognitive symptoms (such as distractibility or racing thoughts) may be misattributed to memory problems or cognitive impairment. It is unclear whether psychotic symptoms are more or less common in older versus younger adults with bipolar disorder.

Etiology, Assessment, and Interventions

Bipolar disorder has a strong biological component to etiology, across the adult lifespan. From twin studies, the concordance rates for bipolar disorder in mono-zygotic (identical) and dizygotic (fraternal) twins were 79% and 24%, respectively, which suggests a strong genetic component but also indicates the disorder is not caused by genetics alone. Bipolar disorder often runs in families, with a high familial presence of mood disorder (about 50–80%) in first-degree relatives (Sajatovic & Chen, 2011). There are no accepted psychological theories to explain the occur-rence of mania, but that does not mean psychological factors are unimportant. How one manages stress and copes with adversity is linked to the development or main-tenance of the depressive and bipolar disorders. Social factors, especially stressors, are almost always implicated in the onset of manic episodes. In the case example, during a subsequent assessment William revealed that a few days before the onset of his manic symptoms he received news that one of his few friends was diagnosed with terminal lung cancer. One could infer that the stress from this news was partly responsible for the mania onset.

Clinicians are advised to regularly conduct screening and follow-up assessment of mania in older adults, especially those who present with mood symptoms or agi-tation. A popular self-report screening assessment instrument is the Mood Disorder Questionnaire (Hirschfeld et al., 2000), which takes about five minutes to complete. Respondents are asked about 13 specific symptoms of mania, whether the symptoms co-occurred, and the extent to which the symptoms caused impairment in functioning. Another self-report screening instrument for mania is the Altman Self-Rating Mania Scale, which is included as one of the cross-cutting symptom measures in the DSM-5. A clinician-administered rating scale is the Young Mania Rating Scale, which includes 11 symptoms whose ratings are based on client's subjective report and behavioral observation. As such, this measure requires significant training to complete. There are no elder-specific assessment instruments for bipolar disorder. Positive screens for symptoms of mania should be followed up with a full evaluation. Clinical interview assessment often involves a full history of depressive and manic symptoms, triggers to mood episodes (whether depressive or manic), patterns of mood cycling, social functioning, current stressors, substance abuse, suicide risk, and strategies or coping efforts to manage mood symptoms. For DSM-5 diagnosis, the SCID-5 has a helpful module on bipolar disorders with questions that are directly tied to DSM-5 criteria.

Because new onset mania in later life is often directly related to medications (e.g., corticosteroids and dopamine-related drugs) and medical conditions (called *secondary mania*), clinicians should take a thorough medical history and they often need to communicate with the client's physician to address possible medical causes of mania. It is unclear whether recovery rates are different for younger or older adults with bipolar disorder. The presence of comorbid medical problems, common among older adults with bipolar disorder, appears to complicate the course and outcome of the disorder (Sajatovic & Chen, 2011).

Another important diagnostic issue is that mania must be distinguished from neu-rocognitive disorders. For example, agitation, impulsivity, poor decision-making, and disinhibition characteristic of some types of dementia may be mistaken for signs of mania. Mania may also be confused with agitation and distractibility associated with delirium, although patients with delirium have a greater fluctuation in consciousness and orientation.

Once diagnosed, management of bipolar disorder is similar among adults and older adults. Because bipolar disorder is a recurrent illness, long-term preventive treatment is recommended, with psychiatric medication as the cornerstone of treatment (Blazer & Hybels, 2014). The most common medications are mood-stabilizing agents, including lithium carbonate, valproic acid, lamotrigine, and clonazepam. For lithium, regular monitoring of serum lithium levels is required. Antipsychotic agents are also commonly used to treat acute symptoms of mania (especially psychosis), and antidepressant medications are sometimes used to treat individuals in the depressive phase. Older adults are at risk for experiencing unpleasant side effects from medication regimens for bipolar disorder, as well as medication toxicity due to comorbid diseases and multiple medications, all of which can adversely affect adherence and outcome. If medication is ineffective or not tolerated well, and the mania is severe and intractable, ECT may be an option (Sajatovic et al., 2015), although outcome data are somewhat limited for older adults.

Psychosocial treatments are always indicated in conjunction with medication. In fact, the combination of medication and psychosocial interventions is optimal. The psychosocial approach typically consists of education of the client (and family members, if available) about the disorder, promoting adherence to medication, lifestyle management, effective stress management, and improving early identification of deterioration or new episodes to prevent hospitalization (Reiser, Reddy, Parkins, Thompson, & Gallagher-Thompson, 2011). It is important to help clients understand their cycling history, whether fast or slow or anywhere in between, and possible triggers, as part of the psychoeducational package. Indeed, education and awareness are critical for the older person to effectively manage his or her bipolar symptoms.

Cognitive behavioral therapy has utility, especially when clients are in the depressed phase. CBT strategies usually focus on maintaining medication adherence and regular activity and sleep levels, detecting early warning signs of relapse, improving relationships, improving problem-solving, and helping clients to develop coping plans to reduce relapse (Reiser et al., 2011). Family-focused treatment may help the client maintain or restore functional family relationships, and reduce the level of negative interactions and emotions expressed toward the client, with the goal of increasing positive support available to the older person with the disorder. Family members may also be helpful in monitoring medication compliance and detecting early signs of deterioration or relapse. Interpersonal social rhythm therapy (IPSRT) emphasizes importance of interpersonal events on the client's social and circadian rhythms. In IPSRT, clients are expected to keep a daily log of sleep/wake times, level of social stimulation, timing of daily routines, and daily mood. Resolution of interpersonal problems and having a regular daily routine and regular sleep are thought to help clients keep their mood stabilized. IPSRT also focuses on adherence to medication. IPSRT has not been adequately studied in older adults. Overall, psychosocial interventions are important and often lead to increased mood stability, fewer hospitalizations, and improved functioning for the client. With comprehensive treatment (and compliance), there is hope for many older adults with bipolar disorder to have symptomatic relief and to function effectively. Even with the best available treatments, however, some people with bipolar disorder develop chronicity and have a high degree of disability.

Summary and Conclusions

Although depression is a disorder commonly believed to be nearly normative with aging, the rates of clinical depressive disorders in older adults is generally lower than are found in younger adults. However, depression must be taken seriously when it is encountered in older adults, particularly in light of the higher risks of suicide and high degree of excess disability associated with depression. We know more about depression in later life than almost any other mental disorder experienced by older people. Unfortunately, the knowledge base about bipolar disorder in later life is much more incomplete. Methods of assessing and treating older adults with depressive or bipolar disorders are similar to what is used with younger adults, with minimal alterations required, resulting in similar rates of effectiveness. Despite solid evidence of treatment efficacy for depression, a significant problem is that many older adults with depression do not receive adequate diagnosis and treatment. Due to the high emotional and physical costs of depression, our understanding and increased effectiveness in preventing depression in later life are top priorities for researchers and clinicians.

Critical Thinking / Discussion Questions

1   You encounter an aging family member who has become clearly depressed, subsequent to the death of her spouse, relocation to an assisted living facility, and some worsening physical limitations due to arthritis. She tells you that she has a "chemical imbalance and just needs some medication." What would you tell her to correct some of her misperceptions? What assessment and treatment approaches would you recommend?
2   Your friend tells you that her 80-year-old grandfather is actively suicidal. What advice and resources would you offer to your friend?

Website Resources

American Association of Suicidology
http://www.suicidology.org
American Foundation for Suicide Prevention
www.afsp.org
Depression and Bipolar Support Alliance
http://www.dbsalliance.org

National Institute of Mental Health: Depression
http://www.nimh.nih.gov/health/topics/depression/index.shtml
Program to Encourage Active Rewarding Lives for Seniors (PEARLS)
http://www.pearlsprogram.org

References

American Geriatrics Society and American Association for Geriatric Psychiatry. (2003). Consensus statement on improving the quality of mental health care in US nursing homes: Management of depression and behavioral symptoms associated with dementia. *Journal of the American Geriatrics Society, 51,* 1287–98.

American Psychiatric Association. (2010). *Practice guideline for the treatment of patients with major depressive disorder* (3rd ed.). Arlington, VA: Author.

American Psychiatric Association. (2013). *Diagnostic and statistical manual of mental disorders* (5th ed.). Arlington, VA: Author.

Barry, L. C., Abou, J. J., Simen, A. A., & Gill, T. M (2012). Under-treatment of depression in older persons. *Journal of Affective Disorders, 136,* 789–796.

Beck, A. T., Kovacs, M., & Weissman, A. (1979). Assessment of suicidal ideation: The Scale for Suicidal Ideation. *Journal of Consulting and Clinical Psychology, 47,* 343–352.

Beck, A. T., Rush, A. J., Shaw, B. F., & Emery, G. (1979). *Cognitive therapy of depression.* New York, NY: Guilford.

Beck, A. T., Steer, R. A., & Brown, G. K. (1996). *Manual for the Beck Depression Inventory-II.* San Antonio, TX: Psychological Corporation.

Blazer, D. G., & Hybels, C. F. (2014). Depression in later life: Epidemiology, assessment, impact, and treatment. In I. H. Gotlib & C. L. Hammen (Eds.), *Handbook of depression* (3rd ed., pp. 429–447). New York, NY: Guilford Press.

Bohlmeijer, E., Roemer, M., Cuijpers, P., & Smit, F. (2007). The effects of reminiscence on psychological well-being in older adults: A meta-analysis. *Aging & Mental Health, 11,* 291–300.

Bonanno, G. A. (2004). Loss, trauma, and human resilience: Have we underestimated the human capacity to thrive after extremely adverse events? *American Psychologist, 59,* 20–28.

Bonanno, G. A. (2009). *The other side of sadness: What the new science of bereavement tells us about life after loss.* New York, NY: Basic Books.

Brooks, J. O., Sommer, B. R., & Ketter, T. A. (2010). Management of bipolar disorder in older adults. In T. A. Ketter (Ed.), *Handbook of diagnosis and treatment of bipolar disorders* (pp. 453–497). Washington, DC: American Psychiatric Publishing.

Burns, D. (1999). *Feeling good: The new mood therapy.* New York, NY: Harper Collins.

Butler, R. (1974). Successful aging and the role of life review. *Journal of the American Geriatric Society, 22,* 529–535.

Canetto, S. S. (2017). Suicide: Why are older men so vulnerable? *Men and Masculinities, 20*(1), 49–70. doi: 10.1177/1097184X15613832

Ciechanowski, P., Wagner, E., Schmaling, K., Schwartz, S., Williams, B., Diehr, P.,…LoGerfo, J. (2004). Community-integrated home-based depression treatment in older adults: A randomized controlled trial. *Journal of the American Medical Association, 291,* 1569–1577.

Cohler, B. J., & Hostetler, A. J. (2003). Linking life course and life story: Social change and the narrative study of lives. In J. Mortimer & R. Shanahan (Eds.), *Handbook of the life course* (pp. 555–578). New York, NY: Kluwer Academic/Plenum Publishing Company.

Conwell, Y., Van Orden, K., & Caine, E. D. (2011). Suicide in older adults. *Psychiatric Clinics of North America, 34,* 451–468.

Depp, C. A., & Jeste, D. V. (2004). Bipolar disorder in older adults: A critical review. *Bipolar Disorders, 6*, 343–367.

Drapeau, C. W., & McIntosh, J. L. (for the American Association of Suicidology) (2015, December 22). *U.S.A. suicide 2014: Official final data.* Washington, DC: American Association of Suicidology. Available from http://www.suicidology.org

Edelstein, B. A., Heisel, M. J., McKee, D. R., Martin, R. R., Koven, L. P., Duberstein, P. R., & Britton, P. C. (2009). Development and psychometric evaluation of the Reasons for Living-Older Adults Scale: A suicide risk assessment inventory. *The Gerontologist, 49*, 736–745.

Edelstein, B. A., Woodhead, E. L., Segal, D. L., Heisel, M. J., Bower, E. H., Lowery, A. J., & Stoner, S. A. (2008). Older adult psychological assessment: Current instrument status and related considerations. *Clinical Gerontologist, 31*(3), 1–35.

Fairchild, K., & Scogin, F. (2008). Assessment and treatment of depression. In K. Laidlaw & B. G. Knight (Eds.), *Handbook of emotional disorders in later life: Assessment and treatment* (pp. 213–231). New York, NY: Oxford University Press.

Fässberg, M. M., Cheung, G., Canetto, S. S., Erlangsen, A., Lapierre, S., Reinhart, L., … Waern, M. (2016). A systematic review of physical illness, functional disability and suicidal behavior in later life. *Aging & Mental Health, 20*, 166–194.

Fässberg, M. M., van Orden, K. A., Duberstein, P., Erlangsen, A., Lapierre, S., Bodner, E., … Waern, M. (2012). A systematic review of social factors and suicidal behavior in older adulthood. *International Journal of Environmental Research and Public Health, 9*, 722–745.

Feliciano, L., Segal, D. L., & Vair, C. L. (2011). Major depressive disorder. In K. H. Sorocco & S. Lauderdale (Eds.), *Cognitive behavioral therapy with older adults: Innovations across care settings* (pp. 31–64). New York, NY: Springer.

First, M. B., Williams, J. B. W., Karg, R. S., & Spitzer, R. L. (2016). *Structured clinical interview for DSM-5 disorders: Clinician version (SCID-5-CV).* Arlington, VA: American Psychiatric Association.

Fiske, A., Smith, M. D., & Price, E. C. (2015). Suicidal behavior in older adults. In P. A. Lichtenberg & B. T. Mast (Eds.), *APA handbook of clinical geropsychology. Vol 2: Assessment, treatment, and issues of later life* (pp. 145–172). Washington, DC: American Psychological Association.

Fiske, A., Wetherell, J. L., & Gatz, M. (2009). Depression in older adults. *Annual Review of Clinical Psychology, 5*, 363–389.

Floyd, M., Scogin, F., McKendree-Smith, N. L., Floyd, D. L., & Rokke, P. D. (2004). Cognitive therapy for depression: A comparison of individual psychotherapy and bibliotherapy for depressed older adults. *Behavior Modification, 28*, 297–318.

Fry, P. S. (1986). Assessment of pessimism and despair in the elderly: A Geriatric Scale of Hopelessness. *Clinical Gerontologist, 5*, 193–201.

Gallagher-Thompson, D. E., & Steffan, A. M. (1994). Comparative effects of cognitive-behavioral and brief psychodynamic psychotherapies for depressed family caregivers. *Journal of Consulting and Clinical Psychology, 62*, 543–549.

Gallagher-Thompson, D., & Thompson, L. W. (2010). *Treating late-life depression: A cognitive-behavioral therapy approach: Therapist guide.* New York, NY: Oxford University Press.

George, L. K. (1994). Social factors and depression in late life. In L. S. Schneider, C. F. Reynolds, B. D. Lebowitz, & A. J. Friedhoff (Eds.), *Diagnosis and treatment of depression in late life: Results of the NIH consensus development conference* (pp. 131–153). Washington, DC: American Psychiatric Press.

Gum, A. M., Areán, P. A., Hunkeler, E., Tang, L., Katon, W., & Hitchcock, P., …Unützer, J. (2006). Depression treatment preferences in older primary care patients. *The Gerontologist, 46*, 14–22.

Heisel, M. J., & Flett, G. L. (2006). The development and initial validation of the Geriatric Suicide Ideation Scale. *The American Journal of Geriatric Psychiatry, 14,* 742–751.

Heisel, M. J., & Flett, G. L. (2016). Investigating the psychometric properties of the Geriatric Suicide Ideation Scale (GSIS) among community-residing older adults. *Aging & Mental Health, 20,* 208–221. doi: 10.1080/13607863.2015.1072798

Heisel, M. J., Neufeld, E., & Flett, G. L. (2016). Reasons for living, meaning in life, and suicide ideation: Investigating the roles of key positive psychological factors in reducing suicide risk in community-residing older adults. *Aging & Mental Health, 20,* 195–207. doi: 10.1080/13607863.2015.1078279

Hinrichsen, G. A. (2008). Interpersonal psychotherapy as a treatment for depression in later life. *Professional Psychology: Research and Practice, 39,* 306–312.

Hinrichsen, G. A., & Clougherty, K. F. (2006). *Interpersonal psychotherapy for depressed older adults.* Washington, DC: American Psychological Association.

Hinrichsen, G. A., & Emery, E. (2005). Interpersonal factors and late life depression. *Clinical Psychology: Science and Practice, 12,* 264–275.

Hirschfeld, R. M. A., Williams, J. B. W., Spitzer, R. L., Calabrese, J. R., Flynn, L., Keck, P. E.,…Zajecka, J. (2000). Development and validation of a screening instrument for bipolar spectrum disorder: The Mood Disorder Questionnaire. *American Journal of Psychiatry, 157,* 1873–1875.

Hybels, C. F., Landerman, L. R., & Blazer, D. G. (2012). Age differences in symptom expression in patients with major depression. *International Journal of Geriatric Psychiatry, 27,* 601–611.

Karel, M. J., Ogland-Hand, S., Gatz, M., & Unützer, J. (2002). *Assessing and treating late-life depression: A casebook and resource guide.* New York, NY: Basic Books.

Kelly, K. G., & Zisselman, M. (2000). Update on electroconvulsive therapy (ECT) in older adults. *Journal of the American Geriatrics Society, 48,* 560–566.

Kendler, K. S., Gatz, M., Gardner, C. O., & Pedersen, N. L. (2006). A Swedish national twin study of lifetime major depression. *American Journal of Psychiatry, 163,* 109–14.

Kessler, R. C., Birnbaum, H., Bromet, E, Hwang, I., Sampson, N., & Shahly, V. (2010). Age differences in major depression: Results from the National Comorbidity Survey Replication (NCS-R). *Psychological Medicine, 40,* 225–237.

Laborde-Lahoz, P., El-Gabalawy, R., Kinley, J., Kirwin, P. D., Sareen, J., & Pietrzak, R. H. (2015). Subsyndromal depression among older adults in the USA: Prevalence, comorbidity, and risk for new-onset psychiatric disorders in late life. *International Journal of Geriatric Psychiatry, 30,* 677–685.

Laidlaw, K. (2015). *CBT for older people: An introduction.* Thousand Oaks, CA: Sage.

Laidlaw, K., Thompson, L. W., Dick-Siskin, L., & Gallagher-Thompson, D. (2003). *Cognitive behaviour therapy with older people.* New York, NY: Wiley.

Lazarus, R. S., & Folkman, S. (1987). Coping and adaptation. In W. D. Gentry (Ed.), *Handbook of behavioral medicine* (pp. 282–325). New York, NY: Guilford.

Linehan, M. M., Goodstein, J. L., Nielsen, S. L., & Chiles, J. A. (1983). Reasons for staying alive when you are thinking of killing yourself: The Reasons for Living Inventory. *Journal of Consulting and Clinical Psychology, 51,* 276–286.

Luoma, J. B., Martin, C. E., & Pearson, J. L. (2002). Contact with mental health and primary care providers before suicide: A review of the evidence. *American Journal of Psychiatry, 159,* 909–916.

Marino, P., & Sirey, J. (2013). Epidemiology of late-life mood disorders. In H. Lavretsky, M. Sajatovic, & C. F. Reynolds III (Eds.), *Late-life mood disorders* (pp. 32–41). New York, NY: Oxford University Press.

Marty, M. A., Pepin, R., June, A., & Segal, D. L. (2011). Geriatric depression scale. In M. Abou-Saleh, C. Katona, & A. Kumar (Eds.), *Principles and practice of geriatric psychiatry* (3rd ed., pp. 152–156). New York, NY: Wiley.

Marty, M. A., Segal, D. L., & Coolidge, F. (2010). Relationships among dispositional coping strategies, suicidal ideation, and protective factors against suicide in older adults. *Aging & Mental Health, 14,* 1015–1023.

Miller, J. S., Segal, D. L., & Coolidge, F. L. (2001). A comparison of suicidal thinking and reasons for living among younger and older adults. *Death Studies, 25,* 357–365.

Newton, N., Brauer, D., Gutmann, D. L., & Grunes, J. (1986). Psychodynamic therapy with the aged: A review. *Clinical Gerontologist, 5,* 205–229.

Pinquart, M., Duberstein, P. R., & Lyness, J. M. (2006). Treatments for later-life depressive conditions: A meta-analytic comparison of pharmacotherapy and psychotherapy. *American Journal of Psychiatry, 163,* 1493–1501.

Prigerson, H. G., Horowitz, M. J., Jacobs, S. C., Parkes, C. M., Aslan, M., Goodkin, K., … Maciejewski, P. K. (2009). Prolonged grief disorder: Psychometric validation of criteria proposed for *DSM-V* and *ICD-11.* *PLoS Medicine, 6*(8): e1000121. doi:10.1371/journal.pmed.1000121

Quijano, L. M., Stanley, M. A., Petersen, N. J., Casado, B. L., Steinberg, E. H., Cully, J. A., & Wilson, N. L. (2007). Healthy IDEAS: A depression intervention delivered by community based case managers serving older adults. *Journal of Applied Gerontology, 26,* 139–156.

Radloff, L. S. (1977). The CES-D scale: A self-report depression scale for research in the general population. *Applied Psychological Measurement, 1,* 385–401.

Raue, P. J., Ghesquiere, A. R., & Bruce, M. L. (2014). Suicide risk in primary care: Identification and management in older adults. *Current Psychiatry Reports, 16*(9), 466. doi: 10.1007/s11920-014-0466-8

Reiser, R., Reddy, S., Parkins, M. M., Thompson, L. W., & Gallagher-Thompson, D. (2011). Psychosocial treatment of bipolar disorder in older adults. In K. H. Sorocco & S. Lauderdale (Eds.), *Cognitive behavioral therapy with older adults: Innovations across care settings* (pp. 65–93). New York, NY: Springer.

Renn, B. N., Feliciano, L., & Segal, D. L. (2011). The bidirectional relationship of depression and diabetes: A systematic review. *Clinical Psychology Review, 31,* 1239–1246.

Roseborough, D., Luptak, M., McLeod, J., & Bradshaw, W. (2013). Effectiveness of psychodynamic psychotherapy with older adults: A longitudinal study. *Clinical Gerontologist, 36,* 1–16.

Sajatovic, M., & Chen, P. (2011). Geriatric bipolar disorder. *Psychiatric Clinics of North America, 34,* 319–333.

Sajatovic, M., Strejilevich, S. A., Gildengers, A. G., Dols, A., Al-Jurdi, R. K., Forester, … Shulman, K. I. (2015). A report on older-age bipolar disorder from the International Society for Bipolar Disorders Task Force. *Bipolar Disorders, 17,* 689–704.

Scogin, F. R., Welsh, D., Hanson, A., Stump, J., & Coates, A. (2005). Evidence-based psychotherapies for depression in older adults. *Clinical Psychology: Science and Practice, 12,* 222–237.

Segal, D. L., Coolidge, F. L., Cahill, B. S., & O'Riley, A. A. (2008). Psychometric properties of the Beck Depression Inventory-II (BDI-II) among community-dwelling older adults. *Behavior Modification, 32,* 3–20.

Segal, D. L., Coolidge, F. L., & Hersen, M. (1998). Psychological testing of older people. In I. H. Nordhus, G. R. VandenBos, S. Berg, & P. Fromholt (Eds.), *Clinical geropsychology* (pp. 231–257). Washington, DC: American Psychological Association.

Segal, D. L., Lebenson, S., & Coolidge, F. L. (2008). Global self-rated health status predicts reasons for living among older adults. *Clinical Gerontologist, 31,* 122–132.

Segal, D. L., & Williams, K. N. (2014). Structured and semistructured interviews for differential diagnosis: Fundamental issues, applications, and features. In D. C. Beidel, B. C. Frueh, & M. Hersen (Eds.), *Adult psychopathology and diagnosis* (7th ed., pp. 103–129). Hoboken, NJ: Wiley.

Segal, D. L., Zweig, R., & Molinari, V. (2012). Personality disorders in later life. In S. K. Whitbourne & M. Sliwinski (Eds.), *Wiley-Blackwell handbook of adulthood and aging* (pp. 312–330). Malden, MA: Wiley-Blackwell.

Serrano, J. P., Latorre, J. M., Gatz, M., & Montanes, J. (2004). Life review therapy using auto-biographical retrieval practice for older adults with depressive symptomatology. *Psychology and Aging, 19*, 272–277.

Shah, A., Scogin, F., & Floyd, M. (2012). Evidence-based psychological treatments for geriatric depression. In F. Scogin & A. Shah (Eds.), *Making evidence-based psychological treatments work with older adults* (pp. 87–130). Washington, DC: APA Books.

Shanmugham, B., Karp, J., Drayer, R., Reynolds, C. F. III, & Alexopoulos, G. (2005). Evidence-based pharmacologic interventions for geriatric depression. *Psychiatric Clinics of North America, 28*, 821–835.

Taylor, W. D., Aizenstein, H. J., & Alexopoulos, G. S. (2013). The vascular depression hypothesis: Mechanisms linking vascular disease with depression. *Molecular Psychiatry 18*, 963–974.

Unützer, J., Katon, W., Callahan, C. M., Williams, J. W., Jr, Hunkeler, E., Harpole, L., ... Langston, C. (2002). Collaborative care management of late-life depression in the primary care setting. *Journal of the American Medical Association, 288*, 2836–2845.

Vaillant, G. E. (2002). *Aging well: Surprising guideposts to a happier life from the landmark Harvard study of adult development.* Boston, MA: Little, Brown & Co.

Weissman, M. M., Markowitz, J. C., & Klerman, G. L. (2000). *Comprehensive guide to interpersonal psychotherapy.* New York, NY: Basic Books.

Wilkinson, D. G. (2011). Electroconvulsive therapy (ECT). In M. Abou-Saleh, C. Katona, & A. Kumar (Eds.), *Principles and practice of geriatric psychiatry* (3rd ed., pp. 529–536). New York, NY: Wiley.

Winterrowd, E., Canetto, S. S., & Benoit, K. (2017). Permissive beliefs and attitudes about older adult suicide: A suicide enabling script? *Aging & Mental Health, 21(2)*. doi: 10.1080/13607863.2015.1099609

Yesavage, J. A., Brink, T. L., Rose, T. L., Lum, O., Huang, V., Adey, M. B., & Leirer, V. O. (1983). Development and validation of a geriatric depression screening scale: A preliminary report. *Journal of Psychiatric Research, 17*, 37–49.

Zarit, S. H., & Zarit, J. M. (2007). *Mental disorders in older adults* (2nd ed.). New York, NY: Guilford Press.

10

Serious Mental Disorders in Older Adults
Schizophrenia and Other Late-Life Psychoses

Stephen J. Bartels MD, MS[1], Karen L. Fortuna PhD[2] and John A. Naslund MPH[3]

Mr. A. is a 63-year-old man who lives alone in his house. He does not have any children, and after a long history of behavioral disturbances, his brother and sister no longer speak with him. He was perceived as odd at times, yet he never had any psychiatric hospitalizations or a history of mental health treatment.

After his good friend died from HIV/AIDS, Mr. A. became increasingly concerned about his personal health. He believed that the HIV/AIDS virus could be transmitted through touching objects such as tables, chairs, or countertops. He decided that not touching anything and incessantly washing his hands would protect him from the virus. He began to ask people if there was HIV/AIDS on surfaces (i.e., on countertops) or in canned or packaged food products. Mr. A. was able to function well, he could go grocery shopping, but couldn't eat the food unless someone inspected it for HIV/AIDS. His speech and thinking appeared entirely normal, except when discussions turned to issues having to do with health. While his family was not around, his friends dealt with the problem by avoiding conversation about these issues altogether yet continued to pretend to check his food for him for HIV/AIDS.

Mr. A. was at the primary care office and asked if there was HIV on the doctor's hands. This odd behavior prompted the doctor to refer Mr. A. for a psychiatric evaluation at another clinic across town. Since Mr. A. does not own a car or drive,

1 Director, Dartmouth Centers for Health and Aging; Professor of Psychiatry, Community and Family Medicine, and The Dartmouth Institute for Health Policy and Clinical Practice
2 Post-Doctoral Fellow, Dartmouth Centers for Health and Aging; CDC Health Promotion Research Center at Dartmouth; Geisel School of Medicine at Dartmouth—Department of Psychiatry
3 PhD Candidate, The Dartmouth Institute for Health Policy and Clinical Practice, Dartmouth College; Dartmouth Centers for Health and Aging; CDC Health Promotion Research Center at Dartmouth

Aging and Mental Health, Third Edition. Daniel L. Segal, Sara Honn Qualls, and Michael A. Smyer.
© 2018 John Wiley & Sons, Inc. Published 2018 by John Wiley & Sons, Inc.

he decided he did not want to take the bus to his psychiatric appointment and never received a psychiatric evaluation or psychiatric medications.

Mr. A.'s paranoia increased and turned his attention to protecting himself from the Mafia, which he believed was engaged in a plot to kill him by planting the HIV/AIDS virus in his house and in his food. He made repeated telephone calls to the police to ask them for protection from the Mafia. His concerns escalated when he began to believe that the Mafia was monitoring his phone calls. He believed that the Mafia was disguised as normal people watching his every move, waiting to kill him. He would stay up at night and watch out the window for any sign he was in danger. This really affected his sleep.

Eventually, after repeated telephone calls, the police visited Mr. A. and after a brief psychiatric evaluation he was involuntarily hospitalized. During his stay he was diagnosed with late-onset schizophrenia and he was placed on an antipsychotic medication. Over the course of several weeks, his delusions gradually resolved and he became less fearful. Following discharge, he had a social worker and a nurse regularly visit him in his home. Within one month, he reported no further delusions and was less paranoid. Within several months, he reported that he no longer believed that he was at risk from the Mafia or HIV/AIDS.

As the number of older adults dramatically increases over the coming decades, the nation's capacity to adequately care for an aging population with schizophrenia will be significantly challenged. Schizophrenia is among the most serious mental disorders, affecting nearly 1% of the population (Meeks & Jeste, 2008). Schizophrenia spectrum disorder is associated with health care costs of approximately $40,000 per person per year (Curto, Masters, Girardi, Baldessarini, & Centorrino, 2016), and these costs increase with age (Bartels, Clark, Peacock, Dums, & Pratt, 2003). In the broader context of improved health-care services and extended life expectancy, the treatment of older adults with schizophrenia poses a serious health challenge as the population is expected to grow significantly in the coming decades.

Schizophrenia is a serious mental disorder that has a dramatic and debilitating effect on most aspects of life functioning, behavior, and personal experience. Early views of schizophrenia maintained the illness always began in young adulthood and inevitably resulted in a progressive deterioration of function, thinking, and cognition. This perspective was reflected in the name "dementia praecox," first introduced by Kraepelin (1919/1971) to describe the disorder of schizophrenia (Reeves & Brister, 2008). This term reflected a belief that people affected by the illness had permanent and progressive mental deterioration beginning at an early age.

Since the original description of dementia praecox, studies of schizophrenia and aging have challenged this view of the illness. Studies of older populations have found that schizophrenia can begin in middle or old age (Reeves & Brister, 2008). More importantly, longitudinal research on schizophrenia over the lifespan has shown considerable variation in long-term outcomes. In contrast to the view that schizophrenia results in inevitable cognitive and functional decline, many individuals with schizophrenia experience substantial improvement in symptoms and function as they age (Cohen, Izediuno, Yadack, Ghosh, & Garrett, 2013; Folsom et al., 2009; Jeste et al., 2003), including some who have full remission of the disorder.

More commonly, schizophrenia consists of persistent symptoms and functional challenges throughout the lifespan (Jeste, Wolkowitz, & Palmer, 2011). Frequent factors that complicate the course of schizophrenia in older age include medical comorbidity (e.g., obesity, diabetes, hypertension, heart disease, chronic obstructive pulmonary disease, hepatitis, and HIV/AIDS), depression, substance abuse, cognitive impairment, and premature nursing home admission and institutionalization (Andrews, Bartels, Xie, & Peacock, 2009; Bartels, 2004; Felmet, Zisook, & Kasckow, 2011; Rystedt & Bartels, 2008). Advancements in the treatment of schizophrenia have affected the course and outcome of the disorder for many individuals. Modern treatment options include pharmacological therapy, psychosocial rehabilitation, vocational rehabilitation, and models of support for community-dwelling individuals, including relapse prevention through mobile health technology and automated self-management telehealth interventions. These treatment options have resulted in more individuals with schizophrenia surviving into old age (Reeves & Brister, 2008; Cohen, 2000).

This chapter contains an overview of schizophrenia over the lifespan, including a description of symptoms, gender differences, course, and outcomes. The chapter first provides an overview of the difference between early-onset and late-onset schizophrenia, in conjunction with considerations in the assessment and treatment process, and concludes with a discussion of future challenges and areas of focus to advance treatment options for older adults with schizophrenia.

Overview of Schizophrenia Throughout the Lifespan

Schizophrenia is a syndrome characterized by disordered perceptions, thinking, and behavior that has a pervasive effect on personal, social, and vocational functioning. For some individuals, the earliest signs of the disorder may include problems in premorbid (pre-illness) functioning such as difficulties in social adjustment and interpersonal relationships (Folsom et al., 2009). For others, there may be no signs of significant psychological problems until the onset of psychosis. The onset of schizophrenia generally develops over a period of months. Early signs typically consist of social withdrawal, unusual perceptions or thoughts, and declining interest and spontaneity. For example, a person may fail to show up for work or school and spend long hours in seclusion. Contacts with friends or family may be punctuated by hostile, paranoid, or bizarre comments.

There are a variety of symptoms that make up the syndrome of schizophrenia once it has fully emerged, including positive, negative, and affective symptoms. *Positive symptoms* consist of the primary active symptoms of psychosis. The most common positive symptoms include delusions and hallucinations. Examples of other positive symptoms include severe problems in thought processes such as illogical or poorly related thoughts or illogical or "loose" associations. Behavioral problems include bizarre behaviors, repetitive or ritualistic behaviors, and posturing. Exacerbations of positive symptoms are the most common signs of acute relapse and may require acute hospitalization.

Negative symptoms, or psychomotor poverty symptoms, consist of deficit symptoms including a lack of active or spontaneous behaviors, emotions, or thoughts. Negative symptoms were first used to describe the appearance of neurologically impaired patients who had traumatic brain injuries involving the frontal lobes of the brain

(Jackson, 1984). These victims of traumatic brain injury were often passive, spoke few words, and lacked emotional responsiveness. This concept was subsequently applied to the subgroup of individuals with schizophrenia who often lacked prominent active positive symptoms of psychosis, but had severe deficits in social, emotional, and cognitive functioning. Common negative symptoms include the "five As" of negative symptoms in schizophrenia:

- blunted or flat affect (lack of emotional expression),
- alogia (reduced amount of speech or poverty of content),
- asociality (social withdrawal),
- apathy (lack of interest or spontaneity or psychomotor retardation),
- attentional impairment (difficulty concentrating or performing sequential tasks).

Severe negative symptoms are strongly associated with poor social functioning (Herbener & Harrow, 2004) and are relatively stable over time (Jeste et al., 2011).

In addition to positive and negative symptoms, *affective symptoms* such as depression, are common in schizophrenia. Approximately 60% of adults with schizophrenia experience major depressive disorder during the course of the illness, with postpsychotic depression occurring after 25% of acute schizophrenic episodes. Contrary to early clinical descriptions suggesting better prognosis, depression is associated with poorer outcomes, including increased rate of relapse, longer duration of hospitalization, poorer response to pharmacological treatments, chronicity, and suicide. Three broad subtypes have been described within depression in schizophrenia: depressive symptoms secondary to organic factors (e.g., medication side effects, alcohol and substance abuse, medical disorders); depressive symptoms associated with acute psychosis; and depressive symptoms in chronic states, including secondary major depression, negative symptoms, and chronic demoralization, and early signs of acute psychotic episodes (Bartels & Drake, 1988). Appropriate and effective treatment of depression in schizophrenia is dependent on identifying the subtype and implementing the appropriate treatment or intervention (Bartels & Drake, 1989).

Schizophrenia is a heterogeneous disorder with considerable variation in severity of symptoms and functioning across different individuals. However, a hallmark of the syndrome consists of impaired functioning in basic living skills, including initiating and maintaining meaningful interpersonal relationships, fulfilling major roles in society (e.g., education, employment), or engaging in basic self-care or community-living skills (e.g., grooming, hygiene, managing finances, etc.). Many people with schizophrenia experience problems obtaining basic needs such as medical care (Olfson, Gerhard, Huang, Crystal, & Stroup, 2015).

Distinguishing Schizophrenia from Other Psychotic Disorders

Schizophrenia must be distinguished from several other related psychotic disorders in the *Diagnostic and Statistical Manual of Mental Disorders*, 5th edition (DSM-5). Schizoaffective disorder is a psychiatric disorder that shares psychotic features commonly associated with schizophrenia, while also presenting with significant mood (affective) symptoms. Schizoaffective disorder is a psychotic disorder that is character-ized by the co-occurrence of features of schizophrenia, including psychotic symptoms such as hallucinations, delusions, and symptoms of bipolar disorder, including persis-tent episodes of mania or depression (American Psychiatric Association [APA], 2013). Schizoaffective disorder can be subclassified into depressive type, characterized by persistent episodes of depression, or bipolar type, in which both persistent episodes of mania *and* episodes of depression occur (APA, 2013). The DSM-5 indicates the presentation of schizoaffective disorder varies with age, with the depressive type more prevalent in older adults and the bipolar type more prevalent in younger adults (APA, 2013).

In addition to these differences in affective symptoms, there are significant differences between schizophrenia and schizoaffective disorder with respect to functioning and course of the disorder. Individuals with schizoaffective disorder have less cognitive impairment compared to individuals with schizophrenia (DeRosse, Burdick, Lencz, Siris, & Malhotra, 2013; Studentkowski et al., 2010; Torniainen et al., 2012). Schizoaffective disorder is also associated with higher vocational functioning, better quality of life, and better physical health compared to individuals with schizophrenia (Birindelli, Montemagni, Crivelli, Bava, Mancini, & Rocca, 2014; Lake & Hurwitz, 2006; Wiffen, Rabinowitz, Fleischhacker, & David, 2010). However, individuals with schizoaffective disorder have higher rates of hospitalizations compared to individuals with schizophrenia (Birindelli et al., 2014). These differences persist throughout the lifespan. Compared to middle-aged and older adults with schizophrenia, individuals with schizoaffective disorder have less functional impairment as related to community-living skills; however, they experience more hospital admissions and higher rates of depression (Rolin, Aschbrenner, Whiteman, Scherer, & Bartels, 2017).

Schizophrenia can be distinguished from several other related psychotic disorders in the DSM-5 (APA, 2013):

- Schizotypal personality disorder is characterized by social and interpersonal con-flicts. In contrast to schizophrenia, schizotypal personality disorder does not include psychotic symptoms such as delusions and hallucinations symptoms.
- Schizophreniform disorder is typified by the presentation of symptoms of schizo-phrenia; however, it presents for a shorter duration (i.e., at least one month but less than six months).
- Delusional disorder is characterized by the presence of a minimum of one month of delusions but without other psychotic features of schizophrenia.

Differences in the Onset, Course, and Outcome of Schizophrenia

Age

The onset of schizophrenia most commonly occurs in late adolescence or early adulthood, between the ages of 16 and 30 years old. However, for a minority of individuals schizophrenia can first occur in middle age and, less commonly, in old age (Jeste & Nasrallah, 2003). In a review of the literature, Harris and Jeste (1988) found that 23% of all individuals with schizophrenia have onset of the illness after the age of 40. A population-based study by Castle and Murray (1993) found similar rates of late-onset schizophrenia, reporting that one-quarter (28%) of the new cases of schizophrenia in the Camberwell (London, UK) catchment area from 1965 to 1984 occurred after age 44, and 12% occurred after age 64. Overall, the annual incidence rate for late-onset schizophrenia was 12.6/100,000, approximately half that for those aged 16–25.

Gender

Gender differences have been found in both age of onset and the outcome of schizophrenia. The mean age of onset of schizophrenia in women is approximately five years later than in men (Moriarty et al., 2001). Women with schizophrenia are more likely to marry (Aleman, Kahn, & Selten, 2003), are more likely to maintain contact with their children (Aleman et al., 2003), and tend to have better social support systems compared to men with schizophrenia (Grossman et al., 2006). Higher levels of social skills have been found in women with schizophrenia (Mueser, Pratt, Bartels, Forester, Wolfe, & Cather, 2010), perhaps due to older age before illness onset among women where they may have greater opportunities for psychosocial experiences and development of these skills (Grossman, Harrow, Rosen, & Faull, 2006). This may result in less social isolation and better function in the community among women. Male gender, by itself, may represent a risk factor to poorer outcomes in schizophrenia (McGrath, Saha, Chant, & Welham, 2008). This increased risk may be due to biological causes such as structural differences in male and female brains (Cosgrove, Mazure, & Staley, 2007) or differences in protective hormonal levels, such as estrogen (Häfner, 2003).

Alternatively, secondary complications of schizophrenia that dramatically affect function and outcome may be less prevalent in women. For example, women with schizophrenia report significantly less substance and alcohol abuse than men (Drake, Osher, & Wallach1989; Galderisi, Bucci, Üçok, & Peuskens, 2012). Such abuse has been associated with a variety of poor outcomes, including increased use of hospitalization and emergency services (Sayers et al., 2005), incarceration (Munetz, Grande, & Chambers, 2001), and housing instability and homelessness (Winklbaur, Ebner, Sachs, Thau, & Fischer, 2006).

Factors Complicating the Course and Outcomes of Schizophrenia

Medical comorbidity

As many as 75% of persons with schizophrenia have a co-occurring medical disorder (Rystedt & Bartels, 2008). Oftentimes these co-occurring disorders complicate the course and outcome of the illness over the lifespan. As mentioned earlier, several factors that complicate the course and outcomes of persons with schizophrenia include medical comorbidity, early nursing home admission, and substance abuse. Collectively, these factors are associated with increased disability, diminished quality of life, and early mortality. This section reviews each of the complicating factors associated with schizophrenia and explores the impact they have on individuals over the lifespan.

Medical comorbidity, including diabetes and cardiovascular disease, chronic obstructive pulmonary disease (COPD), HIV/AIDS, and Hepatitis B and C, is more common among persons with schizophrenia compared to the general population (Folsom et al., 2002; Morden, Mistler, Weeks, & Bartels, 2009; Rystedt & Bartels, 2008). Some prevalence estimates indicate that one in six people with schizophrenia has diabetes and one in four has hypertension. Estimates also indicate that one in eight has cardiovascular disease while almost a quarter of persons with serious mental disorder have COPD. Hepatitis B and C infections, and HIV, are more common in persons with schizophrenia than the general population.

Higher rates of medical comorbidity experienced by persons with schizophrenia are in part due to a lack of preventive health care over the lifespan and health behaviors associated with chronic illness, including lack of exercise, poor diet, smoking, alcohol and drug abuse, and unsafe sexual activity. An important approach to reducing the risk of serious medical conditions resulting in disability and early mortality for persons with schizophrenia focuses on helping individuals implement healthy lifestyle changes.

At the same time, many of the antipsychotic medications used to treat the core symptoms of schizophrenia are associated with weight gain, diabetes, and increased cardiovascular risk factors. Switching to alternative antipsychotic medications with a lower likelihood of causing weight gain can sometimes help to reduce the risk of medical disorders associated with obesity. Finally, improving health outcomes for persons with schizophrenia will be supported by efforts aimed at the addressing poorer quality of health care experienced by many persons with psychiatric disabilities.

Early mortality

A recent systematic review and meta-analysis found that individuals with serious mental disorders die up to 32 years earlier than individuals without serious mental disorders (median of 10.1 years) (Walker, McGee, & Druss, 2015). Of major significance, longevity for individuals with serious mental disorders has actually declined over the past three decades (Saha, Chant, & McGrath, 2007) at the same time that overall longevity has increased to the longest average lifespan ever: approximately 79 years on average. Among major psychiatric disorders, schizophrenia is associated with among the highest risks of premature death (Brown, Inskip, & Barraclough, 2000). Mortality rates for persons with schizophrenia have been estimated at two to four times the rate in the general population (Cohen, 2000) and include both natural and unnatural mortality. According to a national sample of consumers with schizophrenia enrolled in the Medicaid program (aged 20–64 years old), the most common cause of early mortality is cardiovascular disease (Olfson, Gerhard, Huang, Crystal, & Stroup, 2015).

Overall, increased mortality is largely due to heart disease, diabetes, and respiratory disorders, as well as unrecognized medical disease (Olfson et al., 2015). Other factors associated with poor health outcomes include alcohol and substance abuse

(Olfson et al., 2015) and poor treatment compliance for medical issues, including problems with health care coverage, lack of transportation, and other financial limitations (Rystedt & Bartels, 2008). There is also a slightly increased mortality rate associated with antipsychotic treatment, especially second-generation antipsychotic medications (Saha et al., 2007).

Policy reforms have focused on the integration of medical and psychiatric health care as a means to address the prevalence of chronic health conditions among this population. Traditionally, the community mental health system of care has been physically, financially, and organizationally separate from general health care. For example, mental health services have been financially "carved out" in health insurance plans. Fortunately, the Patient Protection and Affordable Care Act of 2010 included a provision supporting the development of integrated models of medical and psychiatric services for people with serious mental disorders through Medicaid specialty health homes (Bartels, Gill, & Naslund, 2015). Medicaid specialty health homes offer primary health care within a community-based mental health or behavioral health facility or enhanced referral to a designated primary care provider (Bartels, Gill, & Naslund, 2015). This provision is especially important for improving the care of middle-aged and older adults with serious mental disorders who characteristically have high rates of medical comorbidities and are particularly likely to benefit from colocation primary health care services within community-based mental health and behavioral health organizations (Bao, Casalino, & Pincus, 2013).

Under this provision in the Patient Protection and Affordable Care Act, national and state initiatives have stimulated the development of Medicaid specialty health homes tailored to meet the special needs of persons with serious mental disorders. For example, the Substance Abuse and Mental Health Administration (SAMHSA) is engaged in a large-scale, time-limited national demonstration, the Primary Care and Behavioral Health Care Integration program, involving over 100 integrated health homes for people with serious mental disorders (SAMHSA-HRSA Center for Integrated Health Solutions, n.d.). An early evaluation of outcomes for 56 integrated health homes reported improvements in indicators of early mortality risk and cardiovascular disease risk (i.e., diastolic blood pressure, total cholesterol, LDL cholesterol, and plasma glucose) (Scharf et al., 2013).

Evidence-based lifestyle interventions aimed at addressing the risk factors associated with early mortality are a critical strategy in advancing healthy aging in persons with serious mental disorders. In addition to provisions in the Patient Protection and Affordable Care Act supporting the integration of medical and physical health care, provisions under Medicaid waiver programs (1115 and 1915i waivers) can be leveraged by states to promote healthy behaviors that specifically address smoking, alcohol use, diet and other mitigating lifestyle factors at the community level for persons with schizophrenia (Brown, Inskip, & Barraclough, 2000). For example, In SHAPE is a health promotion intervention designed to foster community integration and address the diet and exercise needs of individuals with serious mental disorders who are obese. As part of the intervention, In SHAPE offers a gym membership and individualized meetings with a fitness trainer. In SHAPE fitness trainers meet with individuals with serious mental disorders each week for one hour at a gym. They provide exercise coaching, encouragement, and reminders to continue to exercise and eat healthy foods. In two different randomized control trials, the In SHAPE program has shown a clinically significant reduction in cardiovascular disease risk factors in half of participants (Bartels et al., 2013; Bartels et al., 2015).

Premature nursing home admission

Middle-aged and older adults with serious mental disorders are not only at high risk for early mortality, but they are also at significantly increased risk of inappropriate and disproportionately high rates of placement in nursing homes. In study tracking nursing home admissions over a 10-year period, persons with schizophrenia were more likely to enter a nursing home earlier (median age 65) than persons without mental disorders (median age 80) (Andrews et al., 2009). Most importantly, the greatest disparity in nursing home placement was found in middle-aged adults with serious mental disorders. Adults with schizophrenia between the ages of 40 and 64 were three and one-half times more likely to be admitted to nursing homes than other individuals enrolled in Medicaid who did not have a mental health diagnosis (Andrews et al., 2009).

Nursing home admission for persons with schizophrenia may significantly diminish quality of life, including hindering opportunities to interact with family and friends, to engage in meaningful work, and to build a fulfilling life. In the 1999 Olmstead decision, the United States Supreme Court determined that unnecessary or avoidable nursing home admissions for persons with mental disorders and other disabilities violated the fundamental right to participate in meaningful and productive activities in the community. Specifically, this ruling determined that preventable residence in a nursing home for persons with disabilities is a violation of the Americans with Disabilities Act when a community-based alternative is preferred (Bartels, Miles, Dums, & Levine, 2003; Bartels & Van Citters, 2005). In addition to diminished opportunities that result from being segregated from community living, premature admission increases overall health-care costs due to the expense of skilled nursing home care compared to less intensive community-based options. Overall, the costs of medical and psychiatric care for individuals with schizophrenia is among the highest of any single group, with a substantial cause of Medicare and Medicaid expenditures due to nursing home care (Bartels, Clark, et al., 2003).

The Aging Person with Schizophrenia: Early-Onset Schizophrenia (EOS)

Historical overview

Schizophrenia is a heterogeneous disorder with a variety of clinical presentations and outcomes. The term early-onset schizophrenia (EOS) commonly refers to individuals who first manifest the symptoms of schizophrenia in adolescence or early adulthood, although "early onset" is technically defined as occurring any time before the age of 45 (Jeste et al., 1995). EOS is characterized by positive symptoms (e.g., hallucinations, delusions), negative symptoms (e.g., apathy and deficiencies in emotional responses), and significant psychosocial functional impairment (Reeves & Brister, 2008). Of note, the long-term course of schizophrenia over the lifespan has been marked by considerable debate and controversy.

The earliest descriptions addressing the life course of schizophrenia assumed a persistent, chronic, and gradual deterioration of psychosocial and cognitive functioning. As we saw earlier, Kraepelin's (1919/1971) term *dementia praecox* underscored the assumption that early onset of schizophrenia was associated with an inevitable progressive decline in functioning and premature syndrome of dementia (Palmer et al., 1999). However, early treatment methods for schizophrenia were limited to chronic institutionalization, which was highly correlated with a decrease in functioning over time. Despite this pessimistic view of the illness, longitudinal outcomes studies have found half or more individuals with schizophrenia experience substantial remission of symptoms in older age, including for some, complete recovery (Harding, Brooks, Ashikaga, Strauss, & Breier, 1987a, 1987b; Jeste et al., 2011).

In general, the process of aging with schizophrenia is associated with improved psychosocial function, reduced substance use (Jeste et al., 2011), reduced risk of psychiatric hospitalization, improved quality of life (Folsom et al., 2009), and remission of symptoms in more than half of individuals with the disorder (Harding et al., 1987a, 1987b; Jeste et al., 2011). This suggests that some older individuals may be spared the risks of continued exposure to antipsychotic medications. Jeste and colleagues (1993) reviewed six double blind studies of antipsychotic drug withdrawal that included older adults with schizophrenia followed for a mean of six months and found an average relapse rate of 40%, compared to a relapse rate of 11% for those who continued on medication. The authors concluded that stable, chronic outpatients without a history of antipsychotic discontinuation should be considered for a carefully monitored trial of antipsychotic withdrawal.

It is likely that better long-term outcomes can be attributed to treatment methods that have improved over the years, emphasizing community integration, psychosocial rehabilitation, supported employment, and integrated treatment of substance use disorders and medical care. At the same time, a subgroup of older adults with schizophrenia have persistent impairment of functioning and suffer from significant cognitive impairment in older age, including those who have experienced long-term residence in institutions (Harvey, Loewenstein, & Czaja, 2013). The following sections provide an overview of these two cohorts of individuals with schizophrenia, including the oldest-old subgroup of adults with EOS who lived in an era marked by extensive long-term institutional care, and a younger-old subgroup of individuals with schizophrenia who lived during a time of deinstitutionalization with an emphasis on community-based integration and services.

The oldest-old with EOS and long-term institution-based care

A subgroup of the oldest-old with EOS developed the disorder prior to the introduction of antipsychotic medication, at a time when long-term institutionalization was the rule for psychotic disorders. This cohort had significant exposure to living in institution-based settings, including state mental health hospitals and nursing homes. In general, individuals in this subgroup have impaired independent living skills, have poor social skills, and depend on a structured supervised setting to meet their needs. Older individuals with extensive histories of institutional care represent a specific age and treatment cohort with substantially different exposure to rehabilitative treatments and limited opportunities for developing independent living skills. As a cohort they also have different risk factors for adverse outcomes. Following the first wave of deinstitutionalization in the 1960s there has been a progressive closure of state-funded institutions, including long-term psychiatric hospital settings and nursing homes dedicated to caring for persons with psychiatric disorders. Unfortunately, early infusions of funding for home and community-based alternatives have eroded. These concurrent trends over the last two decades have been associated with alarming increases of homelessness for persons with serious mental disorders (Folsom et al., 2002), exposure to crime and victimization (Eisenberg, 2005), institutionalization in the criminal justice system (Fazel & Danesh, 2002), exposure to public health epidemics such as HIV infection (Baillargeon et al., 2008), and high rates of substance use disorder (Olfson et al., 2015).

The following case study describes an older adult with EOS who spent over three decades residing in a state psychiatric hospital with minimal exposure to contemporary models of community-based psychosocial rehabilitation. In addition, this case study describes physical health complications that can occur with psychiatric medication treatment that require ongoing health care management that is integrated into the overall delivery of mental health services. The case study highlights the risk factors associated with EOS and illustrates the importance of assessment and treatment with regard to positive outcomes.

Mr. K. is a 78-year-old man with a long history of multiple hospitalizations dating back to his early 20s. As a teen he was somewhat isolated and had few friends. At the age of 19 he became withdrawn and reclusive, quitting his job as a factory worker based on a belief that his foreman had tried to poison him. Thereafter, he began to report to his family that voices were telling him that Satan had placed a "spell" on the family. During a gathering over the Christmas holiday, he became acutely agitated, screaming at his parents that they were "doomed" and ran out of the house partially clothed. He was picked up by the local police authorities, who brought him to the local hospital. After a brief evaluation, he was mandated to the State hospital, where he was hospitalized for most of the following 30 years. He was placed on a variety of trials of "first-generation" antipsychotic medications, including chlorpromazine and haloperidol, and his delusions and hallucinations decreased. However he remained withdrawn and lacked basic self-care skills. He also developed neurological side effects, including tremors due to antipsychotic-induced Parkinson's syndrome. Attempts to reduce his antipsychotic medication to a lower dose were not pursued due to concerns that he would experience a symptomatic relapse. At the age of 50, he was transferred to a board and care home when the long-term care unit at the State hospital was closed. For the following decade he resided in the board and care home, spending most of his time in his room with little involvement in the surrounding community.

At the age of 65 he was moved to a different room when the board and care home was remodeled. He became acutely agitated and paranoid, refusing to take his medications. After being hospitalized, he was started on olanzapine with the goal of treating his psychosis with a second-generation antipsychotic medication with fewer neurological side effects. He subsequently became less withdrawn and began to voluntarily take his medications once again. He returned to the board and care home, where he continued to need supervision and assistance with basic living and self-care skills. His tremors dramatically decreased on olanzapine, but he also began to gain weight. In addition, he continued to smoke two packs of cigarettes per day.

Over the subsequent five years, Mr. K.'s weight increased from 190 to 255 pounds. More recently (over the past year), Mr. K. complained that Satan had put a snake in his abdomen, creating intermittent pain and cramping. He complained that the snake in his stomach was constantly thirsty and consumed large amounts of fluids. The manager of the board and care home attributed these symptoms to his long-standing religious delusions, and his antipsychotic medication was increased by his local physician by an order given over the phone. His physical status continued to decline until he eventually stopped eating altogether and was admitted to the hospital acutely dehydrated, weak, and acutely confused. On admission, Mr. K. was found to have dangerously high blood glucose levels and a diagnosis was made of adult onset diabetes. He was also found to have high blood pressure and high blood lipid levels. With medical treatment, his blood glucose levels and blood pressure decreased, and his pain and dehydration were addressed. His confusion resolved, and he was discharged back to his board and care home with orders for a visiting nurse to monitor his medications (including insulin treatment, glucose testing, and lipid-lowering medications required by his medical physician) as well as diabetes education. His psychiatrist successfully switched Mr. K. to an alternative antipsychotic with less likelihood of causing weight gain and increased blood lipids. Once his diabetes had stabilized, the case manager and visiting nurse collaborated on supporting a plan for physical exercise and worked with the group home to provide a balanced diabetic diet. Finally, a smoking cessation program was initiated.

This case illustrates several key points in the assessment and treatment of the aging person with schizophrenia. First, Mr. K. has an extremely severe disorder with persistent negative symptoms and limited functional abilities, and he belongs to a generation of individuals who were chronically institutionalized. He is representative of the oldest and most severely ill individuals with EOS who first became ill before the development of antipsychotic medication, at a time when treatment generally consisted of long-term institutionalization. Like many, he remained in institutions for most of his adult life, first residing in a state psychiatric hospital, followed by discharge to a board and care home, and then finally, admission to a nursing home. The years of institutional care have left Mr. K with few (if any) social supports outside of the institutional setting, poor social skills, and severe limits in functional abilities. Without adequate independent living skills, he is largely dependent on care providers for basic needs. Due to these limitations, Mr. K. initially experienced his transfer to a board and care home as a disorienting and traumatic event, resulting in an acute depression and decompensation.

This case also illustrates the significant interaction of psychiatric illness and medical illness in the older adult with a serious mental disorder: the psychiatric illness affecting medical symptoms, and the medical disorder affecting psychiatric symptoms. In the first instance, Mr. K.'s psychiatric illness was associated with worsening of his physical health. In a state of depression and agitation following his transfer to a board and care home he stopped taking medications that were essential to his physical and mental health. His anticonvulsant medications had controlled his seizure disorder for years, yet on stopping these medications he once again suffered from uncontrolled seizures. After resuming his medications in the hospital he recovered. Several years later he developed another medical disorder, insulin-dependent diabetes, yet this time this severe condition went undiagnosed. In this instance, his medical condition directly influenced his psychiatric status causing severe confusion, withdrawal, and physical symptoms that were mistaken for delusions.

Co-occurring medical disorders are a common complication of the aging process and are often undiagnosed and undertreated in individuals with serious mental disorders. Factors which may contribute to this poor physical health include a high prevalence of health-damaging behaviors such as smoking (Brown, Birtwistle, Roe, & Thompson, 1999) and substance abuse (Olfson et al., 2015), limited access to good health care (Leucht, Burkard, Henderson, Maj, & Sartorius, 2007), and a delay in seeking medical treatment as a result of the high pain threshold found in many persons with schizophrenia (Dworkin, 1994). The physical health of individuals with schizophrenia in late middle age or early old age may be more typical of the health status of individuals without mental disorders who are much older (Bartels, 2004; Rystedt & Bartels, 2008). The high rate of medical comorbidity in persons with schizophrenia underscores the need to include a thorough medical evaluation and ongoing general health care services as an integrated component of comprehensive psychiatric services to older persons with serious mental disorders (Morden et al., 2009).

This case also illustrates the development of co-occurring cognitive impairment. In addition to the complication of medical illnesses that often accompanies the aging process, older individuals with serious mental disorders are also vulnerable to the development of comorbid cognitive impairment. Older adults with EOS and late-onset schizophrenia both have global cognitive deficits when compared to normal controls, although these deficits are stable in most individuals, and have been described as a static encephalopathy following the initial onset of the disorder (Goldberg, Hyde, Kleinman, & Weinberger, 1993; Heaton et al., 1994). However, several studies suggest that a subset of individuals with schizophrenia progresses to states of dementia (Davidson et al., 1995; Lesser et al., 1993). For individuals like Mr. K., the symptoms of dementia can overshadow the psychosis and become the primary source of functional impairment in late life. At this point a supportive, supervised setting becomes even more of a necessity and nursing home care may be unavoidable. Comorbid cognitive impairment is one of the most significant differences between older adults with serious mental disorders in nursing homes compared to those living in the community (Bartels, Mueser, & Miles, 1997b). In a study that included older adults with schizophrenia residing in nursing homes and the community, the factors most associated with nursing home status (after adjusting for age). Overall, degree of cognitive impairment may be one of the most important clinical factors associated with level of care and level of function among older persons with schizophrenia (Bartels, Mueser, & Miles, 1997a).

Overall, the case of Mr. K. illustrates an era of institution-based treatment that is coming to an end. A growing number of aging individuals with serious mental disorders have received much of their treatment in the community following dein-stitutionalization and have different levels of functional ability and treatment needs.

The younger old with EOS and community-based services

In contrast to the chronically institutionalized cohort of individuals with EOS, a more recent and younger group of aging individuals with serious mental disorders have spent most of their adult life in community treatment settings following the deinstitu-tionalization movement of the 1960s. This group of individuals with schizophrenia is known as the community-dwelling cohort. Community-dwelling individuals are more likely to have social supports in the community, to have used community resources, to have developed community-living skills associated with more favorable outcomes, and to have been treated earlier in their illness with newer (and more effective) antipsychotic agents. At the same time, however, this group is also more likely to have experienced the negative consequences of declining public funds for community mental health services over the last two decades (Druss et al., 2008).

The following case describes an older person with schizophrenia who has benefited from a community support program and medication management.

> Mrs. M. is a 62-year-old woman with schizophrenia who resides with a companion in a senior housing apartment in the community. She was married at the age of 19 and had her first psychotic episode at age 20. She then underwent a series of psychiatric hospitalizations, at first returning to live with her husband, until her husband eventually became overwhelmed by her recurrent paranoid episodes and pursued a divorce. Thereafter, she moved in with her parents, and received outpa-tient treatment at the local community mental health center.
>
> Mrs. M. continued to have severe paranoid symptoms over the early years of her illness, requiring episodic hospitalizations. Her parents worked closely with the mental health case managers to develop the needed supports and monitoring of symptoms to keep Mrs. M. in the community as much as possible. This included notifying treatment providers of the early symptoms of relapse, as well as assuring that Mrs. M. regularly took the appropriate dose of her antipsychotic medication. During periods of relative remission of symptoms, Mrs. M. was able to hold down a part-time job and regularly went out for dinner and to cultural events with her parents. Although her psychiatric symptoms were relatively well controlled with her antipsychotic medication (haloperidol), Mrs. M. had long-standing side effects. These included episodes of muscle stiffness and slowed movement (drug-induced Parkinson's syndrome) and tardive dyskinesia manifested by significant abnormal involuntary movements (twitching and writhing movements) of her face, arms, fingers, and trunk. Attempts to substantially reduce her dose of medication to min-imize side effects resulted in psychotic relapse.

When Mrs. M. turned 55, her father had a stroke and was placed in a nursing home. Shortly thereafter Mrs. M.'s mother had a sudden heart attack and died. Mrs. M. stopped taking her medication, became acutely psychotic, and was admitted to a psychiatric hospital. Due to her long-standing difficulties with neurological side effects to the haloperidol, Mrs. M. was started on a second-generation anti-psychotic medication, clozapine. Mrs. M. improved and returned to her former level of function. In addition, she no longer had medication-induced Parkinson's symptoms and had a decrease in her symptoms of tardive dyskinesia. The discharge planning team recognized her reliance on others for social support and monitoring of medications and symptoms, and recommended that Mrs. M. be discharged to a senior housing apartment with a roommate, complemented by frequent visits by her case manager from the geriatric mental health outreach team. With active support by the mental health team, Mrs. M. made this transition without major difficulties and resumed many of her former activities. She has successfully switched to an alternative antipsychotic medication (aripiprazole) that is easier to monitor and has fewer side effects. Over time, she joined the local senior center and is engaged in volunteer work at the local hospital.

This case illustrates several important points. First, Mrs. M. belongs to a different treatment cohort than Mr. K. Most of her treatment occurred in community-based programs with episodic acute hospitalizations. Thus, she was able to reside in the community and developed community living skills. Older adults with serious mental disorders residing in the community have substantial difficulties in many areas of functioning compared to disorders such as depression (Bartels et al., 1997a). However, comprehensive support services can overcome many of these problems and facilitate living in the community. Her treatment included services that sought to minimize institutional dependence (unlike Mr. K.) and to maximize her ability to live in the least restrictive setting. She was able to develop and maintain social skills and supports. Unfortunately, the severity of her illness resulted in substantial stress to her marriage, leading to an eventual divorce. Although this was a significant loss, she was able to fall back on the support of her family of origin, moving back to live with her parents.

Secondly, this anecdote illustrates the importance of social supports. One of the major differences between older individuals with serious mental disorders residing in the community compared to nursing homes and other institutions is the presence of family members who are able (and willing) to provide assistance with daily activities and needs. Compared to individuals without a psychiatric disorder, individuals with schizophrenia are less likely to marry, less likely to have children, and less likely to work. In the community, their social support networks are often constrained to members of their families of origin, and a few friends. In this respect, family supports are especially crucial to community tenure. The family members who provided a stable and supportive environment helped to facilitate Mrs. M.'s ability to remain in the community. This aspect underscores a vulnerability of the individual with serious mental disorders who is aging. Many individuals with serious mental disorders reside with family members (often parents). The aging, illness, and eventual death of parents who are key supports places these individuals at risk for loss of ability to continue to reside in individual placement in the community. When the parent becomes ill or dies, the child, then frequently in his/her 40s, is left to cope with the emotional impact of losing a parent and a primary source of social contact and support. At the same time, the individual must quickly adjust to a dramatic reduction in financial and social support, which may also coincide with a loss of residence.

This case also illustrates that older persons are especially sensitive to the adverse side effects of medications, and thoughtful attention to choosing the appropriate type and dose of medication can be extremely important. Mrs. M. had medication-induced Parkinson's syndrome caused by extrapyramidal nervous system side effects (EPS) from haloperidol. Aging is associated with an increased prevalence of EPS due to biological changes in neuroreceptor sensitivity and a declining amount of dopamine occurring with age. Clozapine and other second generation or "atypical" antipsychotic agents are associated with little or no EPS. However, agents such as clozapine may require particularly close monitoring of potential side effects that may impair function, such as sedation and weight gain.

Finally, this case illustrates the different characteristics of older individuals with EOS from different age and treatment cohorts or groups. Many of the oldest individuals with EOS have spent most of their lives in institutional settings, as illustrated in the first case example. More recently, a different group of EOS older individuals has emerged. These individuals are the young-old (in their 60s) and are among the first wave of seriously mentally ill individuals who became ill when states were closing their long-term wards and shifting treatment into the community. This historical cohort of younger individuals with schizophrenia includes individuals who have developed independent-living skills and are more likely to continue to live independently in the community in late life.

Course and outcomes of early-onset schizophrenia

The long-term course of early-onset schizophrenia is highly variable. A minority of individuals experience poor outcomes and marked impairment. Factors associated with worse outcomes include preadolescent onset, poor premorbid adjustment, poor cognitive functioning, cerebral asymmetry, and negative symptoms during prodromal and post-onset phases (Malla & Payne, 2005). For example, individuals with these risk factors are more likely to experience high rates of occupational impairment of at least moderate severity (44%), financial dependence on parents (52%) or public assistance (31%), or low rates of independent living (17%) (Malla & Payne, 2005).

However, many individuals experience gradual improvement, and in some cases, total remission, later in life (Harding et al., 1987a, 1987b; Jeste et al., 2011). Neuropsychological studies of individuals with schizophrenia in their third, fourth, fifth, sixth, and seventh decades of life do not suggest progressive dementia or deterioration (Goldberg et al., 1993). Long-term studies of the natural history of schizophrenia suggest that the first 10 years of the illness are marked by exacerbations and remissions, but symptoms substantially remit in over half of the individuals with schizophrenia in later life. This improvement is likely a result of many factors. For example, biological changes such as age-related decreases in the neurotransmitter dopamine may result in symptom reductions. This model posits that many of the symptoms of schizophrenia result from an imbalance in opposing neurotransmitter systems, such as a relative excess of dopamine (as well as norepinephrine and serotonin) compared to acetylcholine (and the inhibitory neurotransmitter GABA). Hence, psychotic symptoms may remit with age due to a restoration of the balance between dopaminergic and cholinergic neurotransmitter systems caused by generalized reduction of dopamine (and relative maintenance of acetylcholine) that normally occurs with aging (Finch & Morgan, 1987).

Other factors that may contribute to improvement of symptoms with aging for some individuals with EOS include learned coping and symptom management skills. In addition, individuals may learn over time to avoid the use of alcohol and street drugs that are associated with symptom exacerbation and poorer functioning (Zisook et al., 1992). Older adults with schizophrenia may also experience greater stability and fewer symptoms because they represent a resilient group of individuals who were able to avoid early mortality during young adulthood. This is known as the "survivor effect" because these individuals may have avoided death due to the hardships and challenges of living in poverty, increased risk of suicide and substance use, or acute illness (Jeste et., 2011). Overall, there is greater optimism for favorable long-term outcomes for many individuals afflicted with schizophrenia, though a subgroup remains that continues to require intensive treatment and supervision in late life.

Assessment and treatment

Early intervention is now considered a priority in the treatment of EOS with the goal of improving long-term outcomes. There is a critical period of three to five years after the onset of psychosis in which interventions are most likely to be effective and have the maximum impact on recovery. Contemporary treatment for EOS individuals includes both pharmacological therapy and psychosocial rehabilitation with the goal of improving functional outcome and quality of life for young individuals. Specific areas of emphasis include community and social functioning, employment and education, and financial and housing independence (Malla & Payne, 2005). The following section provides an overview of pharmacological and psychosocial treatment options for individuals with EOS.

Pharmacological Pharmacological treatment for EOS is comprised of two tiers of medication, including first-generation antipsychotics (FGAs) and second-generation antipsychotics (SGAs). First-generation antipsychotics (e.g., haloperidol, perphenazine, and thioridazine) are associated with neurological side effects, including tardive dyskinesia, neuroleptic malignant syndrome, and arrhythmia (Palmer, Heaton, & Jeste, 1999). Second-generation antipsychotics (e.g., clozapine, risperidone, olanzapine, aripiprazole) are associated with fewer neurological side effects, yet are much more likely to result in metabolic side effects including weight gain, high cholesterol, high blood sugar and resistance to insulin (resulting in type 2 diabetes), and related cardiovascular disease (Vitiello et al., 2009). It is important to note, whether individuals take first- or second-generation antipsychotics, individuals with schizophrenia who take antipsychotics into older adulthood are at an increased risk for side effects (i.e., Parkinson's symptoms, falls, and metabolic syndrome) (Jeste & Maglione, 2013; Jin et al., 2013). Despite early claims of substantially greater efficacy of SGAs compared to FGAs, a large-scale comparative effectiveness trial (i.e., CATIE: Clinical Antipsychotic Trials of Intervention Effectiveness) found no major differences in alleviating the primary symptoms of schizophrenia between the older and newer agents (Carpenter & Buchanan, 2008; Swartz et al., 2008).

Psychosocial rehabilitation   Psychosocial rehabilitation refers to of the range of social, educational, occupational, behavioral and cognitive interventions designed to improve functioning and enhance recovery for persons with serious mental disorders (Bartels & Mueser, 2008; Bartels & Pratt, 2009; Pratt, Bartels, Mueser, & Forester, 2008; Pratt, Van Citters, Mueser, & Bartels, 2008). Effective psychosocial rehabilitation models developed for young adults with serious mental disorders include assertive community treatment, social skills training, cognitive behavioral therapy and cognitive remediation therapy, integrated dual diagnosis treatment of mental disorders and substance abuse disorders, family psychoeducation, illness self-management, and supported employment. Psychosocial rehabilitation for older adults with serious mental disorders is focused on enhancing independent living skills, self-management of both psychiatric and medical problems, engaging in meaningful and fulfilling activities, improving quality of life, and living independently in the community.

Several promising skills training interventions for older adults with serious mental disorders have been systematically evaluated and reviewed (Pratt, Van Citters et al., 2008). These include Functional Adaptation Skills Training (FAST) (Patterson et al., 2003) and Cognitive-Behavioral Social Skills Training (CBSST). FAST is a social skills training program for middle-aged and older adults with chronic psychotic disorders (Patterson et al., 2003). CBSST is a combined skills training and cognitive behavioral treatment program for older adults with schizophrenia (Granholm et al., 2005). CBSST consists of an integrated treatment program for older adults with schizophrenia that combines cognitive behavioral therapy and social skills training.

Further, several promising integrated medical and psychiatric self-management interventions for adults with serious mental disorders have been systematically reviewed (Whiteman, Naslund, Di Napoli, Bruce, & Bartels, 2016). Of which, two interventions were identified for middle-aged and older adults with serious mental disorders and chronic health conditions. These include Integrated Illness Management and Recovery (I-IMR) (Bartels, Pratt, Mueser, Naslund, et al., 2014; Mueser, Bartels, Santos, Pratt, & Riera, 2012); and Helping Older People Experience Success (HOPES) (Bartels, Pratt, Mueser, Forester, et al., 2014; Mueser, Pratt, Bartels, Swain et al., 2010; Pratt, Bartels et al., 2008). These two programs are described in greater detail below.

Integrated Illness Management And Recovery   I-IMR aims to improve the ability of people with serious mental disorders to manage their medical and psychiatric illness, minimize symptoms and their disruptive effects, and avoid hospitalizations. For each psychiatric self-management skill module, there is a corresponding medical illness self-management training component (see Table 10.1).

I-IMR combines four evidence-based psychosocial interventions shown to be effective among people with serious mental disorders: (1) *psychoeducation*, which

Table 10.1 Integrated medical and psychiatric modules in Integrated Illness Management and Recovery (I-IMR)

I-IMR for psychiatric illness	*I-IMR for medical illness management and wellness*
Recovery: Setting personal recovery goals and strategies to achieve goals to maximize functioning	**Wellness:** Setting health promotion goals and strategies to achieve goals to maximize health and functioning
Psychoeducation on mental disorders: Psychoeducation on SMI	**Education on medical illness:** Education on common medical disorders
Stress vulnerability and mental disorders: causes of mental disorders and factors that affect its course and actively engage in treatment	**Stress-vulnerability and medical illness:** interaction between psychiatric and medical illness leading to worse health outcomes
Building social supports and recovery: how to build social supports to improve well-being & stability	**Building social supports and wellness:** how to build social supports helpful in achieving and sustaining wellness
Psychiatric medication adherence strategies: behavioral tailoring and motivational techniques for psychiatric medication adherence	**Medical medication adherence strategies:** behavioral tailoring, and motivational techniques for medical medication adherence
Psychiatric relapse prevention: identify warning signs and develop a psychiatric relapse prevention plan for psychiatric symptoms	**Medical relapse prevention:** identify warning signs/medical symptoms and develop a relapse prevention plan for medical symptoms
Coping with psychiatric symptoms: establish a step-by-step method managing psychiatric symptoms and problem solving	**Coping with health-related stress and solving problems:** stressors that exacerbate medical symptoms and strategies to cope with stress
Coping with stress and solving problems: identifying stressors that exacerbate symptoms and strategies to cope with stress	**Coping with chronic pain and medical symptoms:** establish a step-by-step approach for pain management and problem-solving
Substance abuse: overcoming substance abuse and the effects on psychiatric symptoms and functioning	**Medication misuse:** the consequences of unsafe medication use and strategies for using medications safety
A guide to navigating the mental health system: accessing mental health services and insurance benefits, making informed decisions	**A guide to navigating the medical health care system:** accessing medical care and insurance benefits, making informed decisions

improves knowledge about mental illness management; (2) *behavioral tailoring*, which improves medication adherence; (3) *relapse prevention training*, which decreases relapses and rehospitalizations; and (4) *coping skills training*, which reduces distress related to symptoms. In I-IMR, skills training is provided by a specialist guided by modules. Skills training is complemented by health care management offered by a registered nurse. In a randomized pilot study comparing I-IMR ($n = 36$) to usual care ($n = 35$) (Bartels, Pratt, Mueser, Naslund et al., 2014), I-IMR was associated with improved psychiatric illness self-management and diabetes self-management and decreased hospitalizations.

The Aging Person with Schizophrenia: Late-Onset Schizophrenia (LOS)

Historical overview

A second group is composed of older adults who have the onset of their illness in middle or old age, or late-onset schizophrenia (LOS). The following section contains an in-depth overview of LOS. The diagnosis of late-onset schizophrenia evolved from early descriptions of a disorder called paraphrenia. Kraepelin (1919/1971) used the term "paraphrenia" to describe a group of individuals, frequently older in age, with symptoms similar to dementia praecox, but with fewer negative and cognitive symptoms. Kay and Roth (1961) later described "late paraphrenia" as a paranoid syndrome occurring in late life that was not accompanied by co-occurring dementia. Late paraphrenia was characterized by onset after age 45 of a well-organized paranoid delusional system, with or without auditory hallucinations, and often occurred with preserved personality. Late paraphrenia was more common among women than men. More recently, psychiatric diagnostic criteria have been revised to reclassify most individuals formally diagnosed with late paraphrenia as late-onset schizophrenia. For example, DSM-5 (APA, 2013) allowed for a diagnosis of schizophrenia with the first onset of symptoms after age 45.

Course and outcomes of late-onset schizophrenia

The following clinical anecdote illustrates many of the characteristics of late-onset schizophrenia in an older individual.

> Mrs. W. is a 63-year-old widowed woman who lives alone in her house. She has two children who live in the next town. During much of her life, she worked as a librarian until she retired at the age of 60. She was seen by many as somewhat odd and eccentric, yet never had any psychiatric hospitalizations or mental health treatment history during her younger years. Her husband died five years earlier from a myocardial infarction. Her own health is quite good, though her hearing has substantially deteriorated. Over the last two years, Mrs. W. has become increasingly concerned for her safety. She initially believed that there were prowlers or burglars trying to get into her house at night due to strange noises that she heard in the yard. She made repeated calls to the local police department, who inspected the grounds and found no signs of intruders. Her concerns escalated when she began to believe that a group of men were constantly monitoring her every move with the plan to torture and murder her. She believed that these men regularly entered her

bedroom at night and attempted to physically accost her as she slept. She resolved this problem by sitting up most of the night in her living room, and falling asleep in her chair—avoiding her bedroom at night.

Attempts to involve mental health professionals in her treatment were unsuccessful. Mrs. W. insisted that her problems were due to a group of "criminals and rapists" who had targeted her house and complained that she only needed better police protection. She refused a psychiatric evaluation or psychiatric medications. By day Mrs. W. functioned relatively well. She went out for lunch with her daughters on a regular basis and played cards one night a week with a small group of women friends. Her speech and thinking appeared entirely normal, except when discussion turned to issues having to do with crime or her personal safety. Family and friends dealt with the problem by avoiding conversation about these issues altogether.

At the age of 70, Mrs. W. began to have unexplained episodes of losing consciousness, followed by transient weakness on her right side. Though she was convinced this was due to the group of men who were trying to kill her, an astute mental health case manager insisted on taking Mrs. W. to her medical physician, who quickly diagnosed transient ischemic attacks (TIAs) and placed her on anticoagulant medication, preventing subsequent attacks. During the hospitalization, her physician was able to convince her to attempt a trial of low-dose risperidone. In addition, she was evaluated by audiology and was fitted for a hearing aid that substantially improved her hearing. Following discharge, her case manager and a visiting nurse regularly visited her in her home and ensured that Mrs. W. continued to take her medications as prescribed. Within one month, she reported no further auditory hallucinations and was significantly less paranoid. Within several months, she reported that she no longer believed that she was at risk, as the men had left the neighborhood.

This case example demonstrates several key points about the assessment and treatment of older adults with LOS. First, Mrs. W. had the onset of her psychiatric symptoms in late life (age 63) and in the absence of any significant signs of cognitive impairment or neurological illness. As noted earlier, approximately 20% of individuals with schizophrenia have the onset of their disorder after age 40 (Harris & Jeste, 1988; Jeste & Maglione, 2013). Consistent with early descriptions of paraphrenia, her premorbid personality was generally preserved, so that she maintained many of the appearances of her daily social routine and function. Hence, she did not seek or receive treatment for her psychiatric illness until she was medically hospitalized for an unrelated disorder.

Second, this case typifies LOS since women are overrepresented among those affected by the disorder (Folsom et al., 2006). In contrast, most studies of EOS report similar proportions of women to men. Several explanations for this difference have been proposed. One view suggests that EOS and LOS are different forms of schizophrenia with different characteristics, including different rates among men and women. An alternative view suggests that biological factors are responsible for a later onset of schizophrenia in women, resulting in the overrepresentation of women compared to men for LOS. In a community study which included EOS and LOS, Castle and Murray (1993) found that 16% of males had the onset of schizophrenia after age 45, compared to 38% of females. Speculation about the difference in age of onset between men and women includes a possible protective effect of estrogens or a precipitating effect of androgens (Häfner, 2003).

Third, this case illustrates the symptoms of LOS which typically include relatively well-circumscribed, non-bizarre delusions, in the absence of a formal disorder in thought processes. Non-bizarre delusions involve situations that may occur in real life include being poisoned, afflicted with an incurable disease, stalked, attacked, or deceived by a spouse or lover. In contrast, bizarre delusions involve phenomena that are considered totally implausible within one's culture (APA, 2013). Mrs. W.'s delusions and hallucinations are relatively clearly defined and involve the psychotic (though theoretically possible) belief that she is in danger of being attacked by a group of criminals who are stalking her. In addition, her thinking processes remain well organized. When she is not focusing on her delusions, her speech and function are almost indistinguishable from that of her friends who do not have a major mental illness. This is in marked contrast to the examples of EOS where thought disorder and difficulties in basic living skills were prominent. Delusions and hallucinations are common symptoms in late-onset schizophrenia and occur at a rate comparable to those found in young adults with early-onset schizophrenia. Delusions are often paranoid and systematized (Almeida, Howard, Levy, & David, 1995; Howard, Castle, Wessely, & Murray, 1993; Kay & Roth, 1961). Auditory hallucinations are substantially more common than visual or somatic hallucinations, similar to young adults with EOS (Almeida et al., 1995). In contrast to EOS, LOS is significantly less likely to manifest formal thought disorder, negative symptoms, or inappropriate affect (Almeida et al., 1995; Howard et al., 1993; Kay & Roth, 1961; Pearlson & Rabins, 1988; Pearlson et al., 1989).

The fourth point demonstrated by the case of Mrs. W. relates to her premorbid (pre-illness) level of functioning and subsequent ability to continue to function at a relatively good level during the course of her illness. Compared to EOS, individuals with LOS are more likely to show better premorbid occupational adjustment (Post, 1966) and higher marriage rates. However, compared to normal comparison groups, individuals with LOS are frequently socially isolated and often have schizoid, schizotypal, or paranoid premorbid personalities (Harris & Jeste, 1988; Kay & Roth, 1961). Mrs. W.'s reputation for being "odd and eccentric" is consistent with this view of her personality. Nonetheless, her abilities to function independently and engage in some social relationships continued even after the onset of her illness.

Mrs. W.'s case also illustrates the presence of sensory impairment that appears to predate the onset of the disorder. Mrs. W. has marked sensory (hearing) impairment, a risk factor for LOS. In a review of 27 articles that assess visual and hearing abilities in older adults with late-onset disorders, Prager and Jeste (1993) concluded that sensory deficits are overrepresented in older adults with late-onset psychotic disorders. An association between visual impairment and visual hallucinations is suggested by the literature, although a specific relationship between visual impairment and late-onset paranoid psychosis remains controversial. On the other hand, the majority of studies reviewed support a specific association between hearing deficits and late-onset paranoid psychosis. Moderate to severe hearing deficits have been reported in approximately 40% of those with late-onset paranoid psychoses (Kay & Roth, 1961). As in Mrs. W.'s case, significant reductions in psychotic symptoms have been reported for some individuals who have late-onset paranoid disorders after being fitted with a hearing aid, suggesting that deafness may precipitate or worsen symptoms (Almeida, Förstl, Howard, & David, 1993).

Clinically, the strong association between sensory impairments, psychotic symptoms, and LOS suggests that these individuals may benefit from systematic instruction in coping strategies for the management of positive symptoms. In recent years, growing evidence has emerged that younger individuals with schizophrenia employ a wide range of different strategies for coping with positive symptoms (Holubova et al., 2015). Methods for managing positive symptoms typically involve either disattention or relaxation, with coping efficacy strongly related to the number of coping strategies employed by the individual. The Helping Older People Experience Success (HOPES) intervention consisted of health management and skills training modules that addressed living a healthy lifestyle, developing social supports, health self-advocacy, developing communication skills, making the most of leisure time, medication self-management, and residential independence (Pratt, Bartels et al., 2008). Two-year psychosocial outcomes of a large randomized trial of the HOPES intervention found that this intervention was effective in improving self-efficacy, social skills, and community functioning (Mueser, Pratt, Bartels, Swain et al., 2010). Three-year outcomes found continued support for community functioning, and self-efficacy (Bartels, Pratt, Mueser, Forester et al., 2014). Additional outcomes included lower overall psychiatric and negative symptoms, greater acquisition of preventive health care, and greater completed advance directives (Bartels, Pratt, Mueser, Forester, et al., 2014). This encouraging study suggests that older persons with schizophrenia characterized by persistent psychotic symptoms benefit from skills training and other psychosocial rehabilitative interventions.

Finally, Mrs. W. eventually showed significant improvement when treated with a combination of mental health outreach support services and antipsychotic medications. Older adults with LOS have been shown to be as responsive to antipsychotic medications as young individuals with schizophrenia when treated with appropriate agents and dosages. For example, response rates of late-onset schizophrenia to antipsychotic medications range from 62% (Post, 1966) to 86% (Rabins, Pauker, & Thomas, 1984).

In general, the assessment and treatment of late-onset schizophrenia parallels the principles and practices used in the treatment of early-onset schizophrenia incorporating a biopsychosocial perspective. This perspective assumes that optimal assessment and treatment addresses the biological, psychological, and social aspects of the person. For the older person with a serious mental disorder, this broad spectrum approach is particularly critical. Aging is associated with substantial biological changes that directly affect medication metabolism and side effects. Furthermore, the presence of multiple medical problems and other medical medications must be considered in treatment. The psychological impact of mental disorders and the effects of aging must also be carefully weighed in designing a program of treatment. The individual's cognitive abilities must be comprehensively assessed in order to inform the choice of intervention. Finally, social supports and stressors are a major consideration in assessing needed services. One of the most important factors determining whether an older person remains in the community or permanently resides in a nursing home is the presence of social and instrumental supports. In summary, the biopsychosocial perspective should be the foundation to assure a comprehensive clinical assessment and effective plan of treatment.

Future Directions and Opportunities

The aging of the population of adults with schizophrenia and other serious mental disorders presents numerous challenges to the system of care for mental health, physical health, and long-term care in the United States. Recent studies suggest that the fifth decade of life for people with serious mental disorders is a period of especially high vulnerability and risk. Between the ages of 50 and 65, adults with serious mental disorders are three and a half times more likely to be admitted to nursing homes compared to other disabled or financially challenged adults who are Medicaid beneficiaries. At the same time, as mentioned earlier in this chapter, individuals with serious mental disorders die up to 32 years earlier than individuals without mental disorders (median of 10.1 years) (Walker, McGee, & Druss, 2015). This reflects a dramatic health disparity largely due to greater rates of cardiovascular disease and diabetes that translates to an average life expectancy of approximately 54 years of age for people with serious mental disorders. At the same time, the aging of the current Baby Boomer generation will result in a substantial increase in the numbers of adults with serious mental disorders reaching middle and old age over the coming decade.

Implementing new models of integrated care and psychosocial rehabilitation

These converging trends will require new models of care and services that are specifically tailored for the needs of the older adult with serious mental disorders. Home and community-based alternatives to nursing homes will need to be developed that respond to the special psychiatric, rehabilitative, and medical needs of the aging person with serious mental disorders. Integrated medical and psychiatric self-management, health promotion, and prevention, will need to become a core component of the future mental health service delivery system for middle-aged and older adults. Psychiatric and medical needs will need to be considered coequal priorities for future models of mental health care that explicitly recognize interdependence of physical and mental health. This will require the development of competency in primary health care and prevention as a central mission for publicly funded mental health services.

Future models of psychosocial rehabilitation will need to incorporate strategies to enhance cognition or to compensate for cognitive and physical limitations associated with the aging process. In addition to cognitive remediation and pharmacological agents developed to enhance cognition, novel applications of technology may have the potential to assist individuals with physical and cognitive limitations to remain in the community. New models of vocational rehabilitation, supported employment, and skill development will need to be developed to respond to the desires of older adults to engage in meaningful activities in late life. Consistent with the goals of older adults, future services should emphasize not simply "adding more years to life," but instead "adding more life to years."

Self-management and older adults with serious mental disorders

Integrated medical and psychiatric self-management interventions have been developed to address the high rates of multimorbidity and premature mortality among individuals with serious mental disorders. Self-management interventions commonly put emphasis on three areas of focus: medical management, role management, and emotional management (Corbin & Strauss, 1988). The most recent systematic review found nine interventions that addressed the medical and psychiatric needs of adults with serious mental disorders (Whiteman et al., 2016), two of which were developed specifically for middle-aged and older adults (i.e., I-IMR and HOPES). While these interventions have high promise for middle-aged and older adults, there has been limited adoption and dissemination (Whiteman et al., 2016). However, the length of these interventions (12 months+) and associated cost may deter wide-scale implementation (Whiteman et al., 2016). As described in detail below, the inclusion of lay providers (e.g., peer providers) and technology may promote uptake and reach in real-world settings (Whiteman et al., 2016).

Peer support

Peers are individuals who have a mental health disorder and who are providing services to other people with mental health disorders (Solomon, 2004). Since the 1970s, peers have provided effective recovery services (Wexler, Davidson, & Styron, 2008). Peers can quickly develop a strong working alliance with patients since peers are viewed as role models who have more credibility than providers because they have experienced similar life circumstances as consumers (Solomon, 2004). For adults with serious mental disorders and chronic health conditions, peer-supported self-management and health promotion programs have demonstrated increased patient engagement, positive medical outcomes, increased patient activation, and increased self-management techniques (Whiteman et al., 2016) and preliminary clinical effectiveness as related to reducing cardiovascular disease risk (i.e., weight loss) (Aschbrenner, Naslund, Barre, Mueser, Kinney, & Bartels, 2015). Peer delivered services may be just as effective as services delivered by professional staff (Chinman et al., 2014) and may offset costs of traditional providers (Whiteman et al., 2016).

The future community-based mental health workforce: Reverse innovation

By 2030, the Institute of Medicine estimates that there will be upwards of 15 million older Americans with mental health or substance use disorders (Eden, Maslow, Le, & Blazer, 2012). This represents a substantial increase from the 5–8 million reported in 2012. As a result, demand for mental health services will continue to grow at unprecedented rates. Clinicians, policymakers, and healthcare administrators must acknowledge that status quo solutions that emphasize training more mental health providers, including psychiatrists or nurses specializing in geriatric mental health, and renewed investment in costly hospital-based practices and mental health infrastructure will likely never adequately meet this burgeoning demand (Bartels, Pepin, & Gill, 2014). For the community mental health workforce to meet the growing needs of older adults with mental health disorders, it is critical that innovative and unconventional approaches are explored (Bartels & Naslund, 2013). This section provides an overview of three important areas that may play an essential role in driving future efforts to treat mental health and substance use disorders among older adults.

First, it is necessary to consider the complexities involved in providing effective and high quality care to older adults with mental health disorders. As highlighted throughout this chapter, there are numerous challenges in addressing serious mental disorders such as schizophrenia in old age, including the need to consider co-occurring chronic medical illness and psychiatric conditions. It is unrealistic to expect that any single professional discipline can meaningfully advance efforts to meet the growing care demands of older adults with serious mental disorders. Collaboration across multiple disciplines will be instrumental toward identifying new strategies to care for older adults with mental health disorders. To effectively facilitate interdisciplinary collaboration, more is required than simply bringing together people from different disciplines. Efforts are needed to allow individuals from different disciplines to openly share their own views and opinions toward solving specific problems (Witteman & Stahl, 2013). This is referred to as an interdisciplinary framework to problem solving, and techniques can be employed to facilitate teamwork across disciplines by encouraging communication and interaction (Witteman & Stahl, 2013). For example, multidisciplinary teams comprised of physicians and mental health care workers, as well as economists, designers, social workers, and engineers, will be essential for considering complex problems from diverse perspectives in order to develop, pilot test, and implement the next line of innovative approaches for treating and preventing mental disorders among older adults.

Second, the growing demand for mental health care imposed by an aging population is not unique to high-income countries such as the United States. Globally, mental health disorders represent the leading cause of disability (Vigo, Thornicroft, & Atun, 2016) and account for about 8 million deaths each year (Walker, McGee, & Druss, 2015). In low-income and middle-income countries, where populations are also aging, the gap in treatment between individuals with mental disorders in need of care and available providers is extreme. It is estimated that as many as 90% of people with mental disorders have no access to care in the lowest resource settings (Patel, 2009). In many low-income countries, there is less than one psychiatrist per 100,000 people, and in some countries there may only be one or two psychiatrists for the entire population (Saxena, Thornicroft, Knapp, & Whiteford, 2007). Such extreme scarcity of mental health care providers has prompted the development and implementation of innovative approaches aimed at mobilizing community resources for the treatment and prevention of mental disorders (Patel et al., 2007). A robust body of evidence supports the use of community health workers, volunteers, and lay providers to support individuals with mental disorders in settings where conventional mental health care is not available (Patel et al., 2007). Trials of community programs delivered in rural and urban areas of countries such as India, Uganda, Pakistan, and China support the feasibility, acceptability, and effectiveness of these approaches (Patel et al., 2007). With mental disorders representing a major global health concern, researchers, clinicians and policymakers must collaborate internationally to identify best practices for addressing mental disorders when services and resources are limited. In a concept described as "reverse innovation," evidence-based practices developed in low-income countries may offer important insight for informing care efforts in high-income countries (Govindarajan & Trimble, 2013). For example, it is possible that effective approaches for treating geriatric mental health disorders in settings in the United States and other high-income countries could be modeled after evidence-based community efforts developed and implemented in rural settings in countries such as India, South Africa, China, or Brazil (Bartels & Naslund, 2013). Given the complexity of geriatric mental health disorders, country-specific efforts may be limited, and the role of international collaboration must be considered as an approach for developing innovative care models transferable across settings.

Lastly, patients and families likely represent the greatest untapped resource for advancing geriatric mental health care. Patients and families must be considered central to efforts aimed at addressing mental health disorders among older adults. The voices of patients and families can help to inform the development of interventions that are both highly relevant to the target population and potentially sustainable over time. For example, prior studies have shown that programs can help to empower patients with schizophrenia to communicate more effectively with their mental health clinicians (Steinwachs et al., 2011), support shared decision-making and patient-centered care surrounding medication management within community mental health settings (Stein et al., 2013), and promote more collaborative primary care visits among middle-aged and older adults with serious mental disorders (Bartels, Aschbrenner et al., 2013). A prior study also found that family members are highly involved in the care of an older relative with serious mental disorders, but rarely play an active role in medical visits (Aschbrenner et al., 2014). This highlights an important area of future potential, where older adults with serious mental disorders and their family members are empowered to play a more active role in decisions related to both medical and mental health care. The involvement of patients and families will be critical to extending the reach of interventions beyond clinical settings and for supporting recovery and long-term illness self-management in the community. Future efforts must involve patients and families as active members of development teams, as significant contributors to interdisciplinary efforts aimed at providing care to the increasing number of older adults with serious mental disorders. These three approaches described here represent only a selection of the many important approaches needed to advance geriatric mental health care. In the next section, the highly promising role of technology for advancing these efforts is discussed in greater detail.

Technology, aging, and mental health

For older adults with serious mental disorders there are many promising opportunities for mobile, online, and remote technologies to advance treatment efforts, facilitate symptom monitoring and tracking, support illness self-management, and coordinate care among mental health and primary care providers. As diverse technologies become an increasingly important part of the daily lives of people with mental disorders, these platforms will be key toward supporting the care of the high-risk group of older adults with serious mental disorders. Several studies have shown the increasing rates of ownership and use of mobile devices among people with serious mental disorders (Ben-Zeev, Davis, Kaiser, Krzsos, & Drake, 2013; Firth et al., 2016). In a community sample of middle-aged adults with serious mental disorders, use of mobile devices and the Internet was similar to rates of use observed in the general population (Naslund, Aschbrenner, & Bartels, 2016b). There is also mounting evidence to support the use of different technology-based interventions among people with serious mental disorders. For example, several recent systematic reviews offer strong support for the feasibility, acceptability, and potential effectiveness of diverse mobile and online technologies for supporting psychiatric illness management and treatment among people with serious mental disorders (Alvarez-Jimenez et al., 2014; Naslund, Marsch, McHugo, & Bartels, 2015; van der Krieke, Wunderink, Emerencia, de Jonge, & Sytema, 2014).

Mobile and online technologies can be used to address a number of different medical and psychiatric health care concerns. For example, telehealth has emerged as a potentially effective approach for supporting the complex clinical care of older patients with psychiatric and chronic medical conditions. A telehealth intervention can contribute to improved self-efficacy for managing mental and physical health concerns among middle age adults with serious mental disorders (Pratt et al., 2013). A similar telehealth intervention appeared effective for managing psychiatric instability and contributed to reduced acute care utilization among adults with serious mental disorders (Pratt, Naslund, Wolfe, Santos, & Bartels, 2015). There are also opportunities for multicomponent technology interventions to support the clinical management of complex cases. The Health Technology Program is a comprehensive technology-based intervention aimed at preventing relapse after hospitalization for psychosis (Brunette et al., 2016). The program is in the developmental stages and is currently being evaluated in community mental health settings (Brunette et al., 2016). The program consists of multiple components including in-person relapse prevention planning, technology-based cognitive-behavioral therapy tailored to individuals with psychosis, family psychoeducation for schizophrenia, and online decision support for mental health providers (Brunette et al., 2016). This highly novel multicomponent approach to care management may be particularly valuable for older adults with serious mental disorders who experience complex care needs. Future research should explore opportunities to adapt a similar program for geriatric mental health care.

Mobile technologies specifically afford opportunities to target individuals with serious mental disorders in their homes or community settings. For example, the carefully developed FOCUS smartphone application appears highly promising for promoting self-management of psychiatric symptoms among individuals with schizophrenia (Ben-Zeev, Brenner, et al., 2014; Ben-Zeev, Kaiser, et al., 2013). Short Message Service (SMS) text messaging programs appear effective for supporting medication adherence, promoting treatment engagement, and monitoring symptoms among people with serious mental disorders (Granholm, Ben-Zeev, Link,

Bradshaw, & Holden, 2011; Montes, Medina, Gomez-Beneyto, & Maurino, 2012; Spaniel et al., 2012). Similar programs have also been used to provide encouragement, support goal setting and functioning, and reinforce coping skills in this high-risk group (Pijnenborg et al., 2010). Regular text messages from a mobile interventionist can also be used to support symptom monitoring and medication reminders, and to provide daily support and encouragement to individuals with serious mental disorders and co-occurring substance use disorders living in the community (Aschbrenner, Naslund, Gill, Bartels, & Ben-Zeev, 2016; Ben-Zeev, Kaiser, & Krzos, 2014). There may also be opportunities to use technology to support health promotion efforts among people with serious mental disorders given recent studies that have shown the feasibility and acceptability of using wearable devices or smartphones for activity tracking among people with serious mental disorders (Ben-Zeev et al., 2016; Macias et al., 2015; Naslund, Aschbrenner, Barre, & Bartels, 2015; Naslund, Aschbrenner, & Bartels, 2016a). There is also promising evidence that mobile technologies can support community-based lifestyle interventions among middle-aged adults with serious mental disorders, as seen in a series of pilot studies that have demonstrated the feasibility and acceptability of using wearable devices, smartphone applications, and social media to promote physical activity and healthy eating among middle-age adults with serious mental disorders (Aschbrenner, Naslund, Barre, et al., 2015; Aschbrenner, Naslund, & Bartels, 2016; Aschbrenner, Naslund, Shevenell, Kinney, & Bartels, 2016; Aschbrenner, Naslund, Shevenell, Mueser, & Bartels, 2015; Naslund, Aschbrenner, Marsch, & Bartels, 2016).

It may also be possible to use popular online platforms such as social media to reach older adults with serious mental disorders. Several studies have documented the increasing use of online support networks and social media among people with serious mental disorders (Miller, Stewart, Schrimsher, Peeples, & Buckley, 2015), as well as the potential to deliver effective psychosocial support interventions to individuals with serious mental disorders through online platforms (Alvarez-Jimenez et al., 2013; Naslund, Aschbrenner, Marsch, McHugo, & Bartels, 2015). While no studies have specifically surveyed or targeted older adults with serious mental disorders, a study of a community sample of middle-aged adults with serious mental disorders found that use of social media such as Facebook was comparable to rates of use in the general population (Naslund, Aschbrenner, & Bartels, 2016b). Additionally, evidence from the general population suggests that adults over age 65 represent one of the fastest-growing demographics beginning to use popular social media (Perrin, 2015). Popular platforms may afford important opportunities to connect older adults who have serious mental disorders with others who share similar health conditions. This form of online peer-to-peer support may be beneficial for individuals with serious mental disorders as there are potentially important opportunities to share information and tips or strategies for coping with mental disorders, and also for feeling less alone and finding a supportive community of peers online (Naslund, Aschbrenner, Marsch, & Bartels, 2016; Naslund, Grande, Aschbrenner, & Elwyn, 2014). Few studies have evaluated the use of popular social media among people with serious mental disorders given that this is a nascent field of research. In an effort to identify highly scalable and unconventional approaches for supporting older adults with serious mental disorders, the role of social media and its wide-reaching influence should not be overlooked.

Future studies are needed to explore the acceptability of using social media to support or extend care efforts targeting this high-risk group, while also evaluating the safety, potential risks, and preliminary effectiveness of such novel approaches.

To date the evidence on the use of various technologies for supporting people with serious mental disorders is compelling, yet many of these studies are in the early stages and only preliminary findings have been reported. It is clear that future efforts and rigorous effectiveness studies are needed to assess the role that technology can play in supporting aging in place, delivering patient-centered interventions, and reaching individuals at their own convenience through on-demand services. Mobile and online technologies may be effective for overcoming the requirement for costly in-person care or direct contact with mental health clinicians and providers, and will likely play a key role in extending mental health services to reach the high-risk group of older adults with serious mental disorders. It is also highly promising that components of the Affordable Care Act can support the development, evaluation, and implementation of technology-based interventions (Bartels, Gill, & Naslund, 2015), which likely will further contribute to the future success of these important efforts. With new collaborations across disciplines locally and abroad, greater involvement of patients and their families, and an emphasis on the potential for technology to support care and illness self-management, there is great potential to address the growing needs of the aging population of people with serious mental disorders.

Summary and Conclusions

Despite recent advances, remarkably little is known about factors affecting the course or outcome of schizophrenia in older age. Schizophrenia can continue to manifest in late life as part of a life long illness (early-onset schizophrenia), or first appear in older age (late-onset schizophrenia). Important factors that may affect the clinical presentation and treatment needs of the older person with schizophrenia (regardless of age of onset) include past history of treatment and cohort effects, comorbid medical illness, cognitive impairment, and the availability of social supports. Late-onset schizophrenia is less common than early-onset schizophrenia and is characterized by several distinct differences. Individuals with LOS compared to EOS are more likely to be women and to have better premorbid functioning, including better occupational history and a greater likelihood of having been married. The clinical presentation of LOS is more likely to include a predominance of positive symptoms such as paranoid delusions and auditory hallucinations and less likely to have negative symptoms. Formal thought disorder is rare in LOS, but common in EOS. Among those with EOS who have the onset of their disorder after age 60, there is a greater incidence of hearing loss compared to the general population. Finally, the limited data on treatment suggests that response to antipsychotic medication among individuals with LOS is comparable to EOS.

In general, there remains a paucity of research on treatments and services for older persons with serious mental disorders, particularly in the area of psychosocial treatment. In particular, little attention has focused on the individual with life long early-onset schizophrenia who is now in late-middle age or old age. Further research is needed to determine the most effective and appropriate pharmacological and psychosocial interventions for the older person with schizophrenia. Important future directions include the effective application and dissemination of effective health promotion, prevention, and self-management interventions, in conjunction with fully integrated models of care. Finally, there is a rapidly developing field consisting of the applied use of technologies that are the most promising advances supporting "aging in community" for older adults with serious mental disorders.

Critical Thinking / Discussion Questions

1   Use a biopsychosocial perspective to identify and discuss differences in risk and protective factors that change for individuals with schizophrenia over the lifespan.
2   Discuss the potential limitations and opportunities of using technology to deliver interventions with middle-aged and older adults with schizophrenia.
3   Is schizoaffective disorder most accurately categorized as a psychotic mood disorder or as a type of schizophrenia?
4   Design an intervention to address the early mortality rate among individuals with schizophrenia.

Website Resources

Implementing Health Promotion Activities Within a Mental Health Center
https://www.youtube.com/watch?v=He4Tihk8SXA
National Institute of Mental Health: Schizophrenia
https://www.nimh.nih.gov/health/topics/schizophrenia/index.shtml

References

Aleman, A., Kahn, R. S., & Selten, J. P. (2003). Sex differences in the risk of schizophrenia: Evidence from meta-analysis. *Archives of General Psychiatry, 60*, 565–571.
Almeida, O. P., Förstl, H., Howard, R., & David, A. S. (1993). Unilateral auditory hallucinations. *British Journal of Psychiatry, 162*, 262–264.
Almeida, O. P., Howard, R. J., Levy, R., & David, A. (1995). Psychotic states arising in late life (late paraphrenia): The role of risk factors. *British Journal of Psychiatry, 166*, 215–228.
Alvarez-Jimenez, M., Alcazar-Corcoles, M., Gonzalez-Blanch, C., Bendall, S., McGorry, P., & Gleeson, J. (2014). Online, social media and mobile technologies for psychosis treatment: A systematic review on novel user-led interventions. *Schizophrenia Research, 156*(1), 96–106.
Alvarez-Jimenez, M., Bendall, S., Lederman, R., Wadley, G., Chinnery, G., Vargas, S., … Gleeson, J. (2013). On the HORYZON: Moderated online social therapy for long-term recovery in first episode psychosis. *Schizophrenia Research, 143*(1), 143–149.

American Psychiatric Association. (2013). *Diagnostic and statistical manual of mental disorders* (5th ed.). Arlington, VA: Author.

Andrews, A.O., Bartels, S. J., Xie, H., & Peacock, W. J. (2009). Increased risk of nursing home admission among middle aged and older adults with schizophrenia. *American Journal of Geriatric Psychiatry, 17*, 697–705.

Aschbrenner, K. A., Naslund, J. A., Barre, L. K., Mueser, K. T., Kinney, A., & Bartels, S. J. (2015). Peer health coaching for overweight and obese individuals with serious mental illness: Intervention development and initial feasibility study. *Translational Behavioral Medicine, 5*(3), 277–284.

Aschbrenner, K. A., Naslund, J. A., & Bartels, S. J. (2016). Peer-to-peer support in a hybrid face-to-face and online social networking lifestyle intervention for adults with serious mental illness. *Psychiatric Rehabilitation Journal, 39*, 328–334. doi: 10.1037/prj0000219

Aschbrenner, K. A., Naslund, J. A., Gill, L. E., Bartels, S. J., & Ben-Zeev, D. (2016). A qualitative study of client-clinician text exchanges in a mobile health intervention for individuals with psychotic disorders and substance use. *Journal of Dual Diagnosis, 12*(1), 63–71. doi:10.1080/15504263.2016.1145312

Aschbrenner, K. A., Naslund, J. A., Shevenell, M., Kinney, E. C., & Bartels, S. J. (2016). A pilot study of a peer-group lifestyle intervention enhanced with mHealth technology and social media for adults with serious mental illness. *Journal of Nervous and Mental Disease, 204*(6), 483–486. doi: 10.1097/NMD.0000000000000530

Aschbrenner, K. A., Naslund, J. A., Shevenell, M., Mueser, K. T., & Bartels, S. J. (2015). Feasibility of behavioral weight loss treatment enhanced with peer support and mobile health technology for individuals with serious mental illness. *Psychiatric Quarterly, 87*(3), 401–415.

Aschbrenner, K. A., Pepin, R., Mueser, K. T., Naslund, J. A., Rolin, S. A., Faber, M. J., & Bartels, S. J. (2014). A mixed methods exploration of family involvement in medical care for older adults with serious mental illness. *The International Journal of Psychiatry in Medicine, 48*(2), 121–133.

Baillargeon, J.G., Paar, D. P., Wu, H., Giordano, T. P., Murray, O., Raimer, B. G., ... Pulvino, J. S (2008). Psychiatric disorders, HIV infection and HIV/hepatitis co-infection in the correctional setting. *AIDS Care, 20*(1), 124–129.

Bao, Y., Casalino, L. P., & Pincus, H. A. (2013). Behavioral health and health care reform models: patient-centered medical home, health home, and accountable care organization. *Journal of Behavioral Health Services and Research, 40*, 121–32.

Bartels, S. J. (2004). Caring for the whole person. Integrated health care for older adults with severe mental illness and medical comorbidity. *Journal of the American Geriatrics Society, 52*, S249–S257.

Bartels, S. J., Aschbrenner, K. A., Rolin, S. A., Hendrick, D. C., Naslund, J. A., & Faber, M. J. (2013). Activating older adults with serious mental illness for collaborative primary care visits. *Psychiatric Rehabilitation Journal, 36*(4), 278.

Bartels, S. J., Clark, R. E., Peacock, W. J., Dums, A. R., & Pratt S. I. (2003). Medicare and Medicaid costs for schizophrenia patients by age cohort compared with depression, dementia, and medically ill patients. *American Journal of Geriatric Psychiatry, 11*, 648–657.

Bartels, S. J., & Drake, R. E. (1988). Depressive symptoms in schizophrenia: Comprehensive differential diagnosis. *Comprehensive Psychiatry, 29*, 467–483.

Bartels, S. J., & Drake, R. E. (1989). Depression in schizophrenia: Current guidelines to treatment. *Psychiatric Quarterly, 60*, 333–345.

Bartels, S. J., Gill, L., & Naslund, J. A. (2015). The Affordable Care Act, accountable care organizations, and mental health care for older adults: Implications and opportunities. *Harvard Review of Psychiatry, 23*(5), 304–319.

Bartels, S. J., Miles, K. M., Dums, A. R., & Levine, K. J. (2003). Are nursing homes appropriate for older adults with severe mental illness? Conflicting consumer and clinician views and implications for the Olmstead decision. *Journal of the American Geriatrics Society, 51,* 1571–1579.

Bartels, S. J., Mueser, K. T., & Miles, K. M. (1997a). Functional impairments in elderly with schizophrenia and major affective disorder living in the community: Social skills, living skills, and behavior problems. *Behavior Therapy, 28,* 43–63.

Bartels, S. J., Mueser, K. T., & Miles, K. M. (1997b). A comparative study of elderly patients with schizophrenia and bipolar disorder in nursing homes and the community. *Schizophrenia Research, 27*(2–3), 181–90.

Bartels, S. J., & Mueser, K. T. (2008). Psychosocial rehabilitation for older adults with serious mental illness: Introduction to special series. *American Journal of Psychiatric Rehabilitation, 11*(1), 1–6.

Bartels, S. J., & Naslund, J. A. (2013). The underside of the silver tsunami – older adults and mental health care. *New England Journal of Medicine, 368*(6), 493–496.

Bartels, S. J., Pepin, R., & Gill, L. E. (2014). The paradox of scarcity in a land of plenty: Meeting the needs of older adults with mental health and substance use disorders. *Generations, 38*(3), 6.

Bartels, S. J., & Pratt, S. I. (2009). Psychosocial rehabilitation and quality of life for older adults with serious mental illness: Recent findings and future research directions. *Current Opinion in Psychiatry, 22,* 381–385.

Bartels, S. J., Pratt, S. I., Aschbrenner, K., Barre, L., Jue, K., Wolfe, R., ...Mueser, K. (2013). Clinically significant improved fitness and weight loss among overweight persons with serious mental illness. *Psychiatric Services, 64*(8), 729–736.

Bartels, S. J., Pratt, S. I., Aschbrenner, K., Barre, L., Naslund, J., Wolfe, R., Bird, B. (2015). Pragmatic replication trial of health promotion coaching for obesity in serious mental illness and maintenance of outcomes. *American Journal of Psychiatry, 172*(4), 344–352.

Bartels, S. J., Pratt, S. I., Mueser, K., Forester, B., Wolfe, R., Cather, C., ...Feldman J. (2014). Long-term outcomes of a randomized trial of integrated skills training and preventive healthcare for older adults with serious mental illness. *American Journal of Geriatric Psychiatry, 22,* 1251–61.

Bartels, S. J., Pratt, S. I., Mueser, K., Naslund, J., Wolfe, R., Santos, M., ...Riera, E. (2014). Integrated IMR for psychiatric and general medical illness for adults aged 50 or older with serious mental illness. *Psychiatric Services, 65,* 330–337.

Bartels, S. J., & Van Citters, A. D. (2005). Community-based alternatives for older adults with serious mental illness: The Olmstead decision and deinstitutionalization of nursing homes. *Ethics, Law, and Aging Review, 11,* 3–22.

Ben-Zeev, D., Brenner, C. J., Begale, M., Duffecy, J., Mohr, D. C., & Mueser, K. T. (2014). Feasibility, acceptability, and preliminary efficacy of a smartphone intervention for schizophrenia. *Schizophrenia Bulletin, 40*(6): 1244–53.

Ben-Zeev, D., Davis, K. E., Kaiser, S., Krzsos, I., & Drake, R. E. (2013). Mobile technologies among people with serious mental illness: opportunities for future services. *Administration and Policy in Mental Health and Mental Health Services Research, 40*(4), 340–343.

Ben-Zeev, D., Kaiser, S. M., Brenner, C. J., Begale, M., Duffecy, J., & Mohr, D. C. (2013). Development and usability testing of FOCUS: A smartphone system for self-management of schizophrenia. *Psychiatric Rehabilitation Journal, 36*(4), 289.

Ben-Zeev, D., Kaiser, S. M., & Krzos, I. (2014). Remote "hovering" with individuals with psychotic disorders and substance use: Feasibility, engagement, and therapeutic alliance with a text-messaging mobile interventionist. *Journal of Dual Diagnosis, 10*(4), 197–203.

Ben-Zeev, D., Wang, R., Abdullah, S., Brian, R., Scherer, E. A., Mistler, L. A., …Choudhury, T. (2016). Mobile behavioral sensing for outpatients and inpatients with schizophrenia. *Psychiatric Services, 67*(5), 558–561. doi: 10.1176/appi.ps.201500130

Birindelli, N., Montemagni, C., Crivelli, B., Bava, I., Mancini, I., & Rocca, P. (2014). Cognitive functioning and insight in schizophrenia and in schizoaffective disorder. *Rivista di Psichiatria, 49,* 77–83.

Brown, S., Birtwistle, J., Roe. L., Thompson, C. (1999). The unhealthy lifestyle of people with schizophrenia. *Psychological Medicine, 29*(3): 697–701.

Brown, S., Inskip, H., & Barraclough, B. (2000). Causes of the excess mortality of schizophrenia. *British Journal of Psychiatry, 177,* 212–217.

Brunette, M. F., Rotondi, A. J., Ben-Zeev, D., Gottlieb, J. D., Mueser, K. T., Robinson, D. G.,… Schooler, N. R. (2016). Coordinated technology-delivered treatment to prevent rehospitalization in schizophrenia: A novel model of care. *Psychiatric Services, 67*(4), 444–447.

Carpenter, W. T., & Buchanan, R. W. (2008). Lessons to take home from CATIE. *Psychiatric Services, 59,* 523–525.

Castle, D. J., & Murray, R. M. (1993). The epidemiology of late-onset schizophrenia. *Schizophrenia Bulletin, 19,* 691–700.

Chinman, M., George, P., Dougherty, R., Daniels, A., Ghose, S., Swift, A., & Delphin-Rittmon, M. (2014). Peer support services for individuals with serious mental illnesses: Assessing the evidence. *Psychiatric Services, 65*(4), 429–441.

Cohen, C. I. (2000). Practical geriatrics: Directions for research and policy on schizophrenia and older adults: Summary of the GAP committee report. *Psychiatric Services, 51,* 299–302.

Cohen, C., Izediuno, I., Yadack, A., Ghosh, B., & Garrett, M. (2013). Characteristics of auditory hallucinations and associated factors in older adults with schizophrenia. *American Journal of Geriatric Psychiatry, 22*(5), 442–449.

Corbin, J., & Strauss, J. (1988). *Unending work and care: Managing chronic illness at home.* San Francisco, CA, Jossey-Bass.

Cosgrove, K. P., Mazure, C. M., & Staley, J. K. (2007). Evolving knowledge of sex differences in brain structure, function and chemistry. *Biological Psychiatry, 62*(8), 847–855.

Curto, M., Masters, G. A., Girardi, P., Baldessarini, R. J., & Centorrino, F. (2016). Factors associated with costs of hospitalization of severely mentally ill patients. *Bipolar Disorder, 2,* 103. doi:10.4172/2472-1077.1000103

Davidson, M., Harvey, P. D., Powchick, P., Parrella, M., White, L., Knobler, H. Y., …Frecska, E. (1995). Severity of symptoms in chronically institutionalized geriatric schizophrenic patients. *American Journal of Psychiatry, 152,* 197–207.

DeRosse, P., Burdick, K. E., Lencz, T., Siris, S., & Malhotra, A. (2013). Empirical support for DSM-IV schizoaffective disorder: Clinical and cognitive validators from a large patient sample. *PloS One, 8,* e63734.

Drake, R. E., Osher, F. C., & Wallach, M. A. (1989). Alcohol use and abuse in schizophrenia: A prospective community study. *Journal of Nervous and Mental Disease, 177,* 408–414.

Druss, B. G., Marcus, S. C., Campbell, J., Cuffel, B., Harnett, J., Ingoglia, C., & Mauer, B. (2008). Medical services for clients in community mental health centers: Results from a national survey. *Psychiatric Services, 59,* 917–20.

Dworkin, R. H. (1994). Pain insensitivity in schizophrenia: A neglected phenomenon and some implications. *Schizophrenia Bulletin, 20,* 235–248.

Eden, J., Maslow, K., Le, M., & Blazer, D. (2012). *The mental health and substance use workforce for older adults: in whose hands?* Washington, DC: National Academies Press.

Eisenberg, L. (2005). Violence and the mentally ill: Victims, not perpetrators. *Archives of General Psychiatry, 62*, 825–8236.

Fazel, S., & Danesh, J. (2002). Serious mental disorder in 23,000 prisoners: A systematic review of 62 surveys. *The Lancet, 359*(9306), 545–550.

Felmet, K., Zisook, S., & Kasckow, J. W. (2011). Elderly patients with schizophrenia and depression: Diagnosis and treatment. *Clinical Schizophrenia & Related Psychoses, 4*(4), 239–250.

Finch, C. E., & Morgan, D. (1987). Aging and schizophrenia: A hypothesis relating to asynchrony in neural aging processes to the manifestations of schizophrenia and other neurologic diseases with age. In N. E. Miller & G. Cohen (Eds.), *Schizophrenia and aging* (pp. 97–108). New York: Guilford.

Firth, J., Cotter, J., Torous, J., Bucci, S., Firth, J. A., & Yung, A. R. (2015). Mobile phone ownership and endorsement of "mHealth" among people with psychosis: A meta-analysis of cross-sectional studies. *Schizophrenia Bulletin, 42*(2): 448–455.

Folsom, D. P., Depp, C., Palmer, B. W., Mausbach, B. T., Golshan, S., Fellows, I., ...Jeste, D.V. (2009). Physical and mental health-related quality of life among older people with schizophrenia. *Schizophrenia Research, 108*, 207–213.

Folsom, D. P., Lebowitz, B. D., Lindamer, L. A., Palmer, B. W., Patterson, T. L., & Jeste, D. V. (2006). Schizophrenia in late life: Emerging issues. *Dialogues in Clinical Neuroscience, 8*(1), 45–52.

Folsom, D. P., McCahill, M., Bartels, S. J., Lindamer, L. A., Ganiats, T. G., & Jeste, D. V. (2002). Medical comorbidity and receipt of medical care by older homeless people with schizophrenia or depression. *Psychiatric Services, 53*, 1456–1460.

Galderisi, S., Bucci, P., Üçok, A., & Peuskens, J. (2012). No gender differences in social outcome in patients suffering from schizophrenia. *European Psychiatry, 27*(6), 406–8.

Goldberg, T. E., Hyde, T. M., Kleinman, J. E., & Weinberger, D. R. (1993). Course of schizophrenia: Neuropsychological evidence for a static encephalopathy. *Schizophrenia Bulletin, 19*, 797–804.

Govindarajan, V., & Trimble, C. (2013). *Reverse innovation: Create far from home, win everywhere*: Boston, MA: Harvard Business Press.

Granholm, E., Ben-Zeev, D., Link, P. C., Bradshaw, K. R., & Holden, J. L. (2011). Mobile Assessment and Treatment for Schizophrenia (MATS): A pilot trial of an interactive text-messaging intervention for medication adherence, socialization, and auditory hallucinations. *Schizophrenia Bulletin, 38*(3), 414–425.

Granholm, E., McQuaid, J. R., McClure, F. S., Auslander, L. A., Perivoliotis, D., Pedrelli, P., ... Jeste, D. V. (2005). A randomized, controlled trial of cognitive behavioral social skills training for middle-aged and older outpatients with chronic schizophrenia. *American Journal of Psychiatry, 162*, 520–529.

Grossman, L.S., Harrow, M., Rosen, C., & Faull, R. (2006). Sex differences in outcome and recovery for schizophrenia and other psychotic and nonpsychotic disorders. *Psychiatric Services, 57*, 844–850.

Häfner, H. (2003). Gender differences in schizophrenia. *Psychoneuroendocrinology, 28*, 17–54.

Harding, C. M., Brooks, G. W., Ashikaga, T., Strauss, J. S., & Breier, A. (1987a). The Vermont longitudinal study of persons with severe mental illness, I: Methodology, study sample, and overall status 32 years later. *American Journal of Psychiatry, 144*, 718–726.

Harding, C. M., Brooks, G. W., Ashikaga, T., Strauss, J. S., & Breier, A. (1987b). The Vermont longitudinal study of persons with severe mental illness, II: Long-term outcome of subjects who retrospectively met DSM-III criteria for schizophrenia. *American Journal of Psychiatry, 144*, 727–735.

Harris, M., & Jeste, D. (1988). Late-onset schizophrenia: An overview. *Schizophrenia Bulletin,* *14*, 39–55.

Harvey, P. D., Loewenstein, D. A., & Czaja, S. J. (2013). Hospitalization and psychosis: Influences on the course of cognition and everyday functioning in people with schizophrenia. *Neurobiology of Disease, 53*, 18–25.

Heaton, R., Paulsen, J. S., McAdams, L. A., Kuck, J., Zisook, S., Braff, D., ...Jeste, D. V. (1994). Neuropsychological deficits in schizophrenics: Relationship to age, chronicity, and dementia. *Archives of General Psychiatry, 51*, 469–476.

Herbener, E., & Harrow, M. (2004). Are negative symptoms associated with functioning deficits in both schizophrenia and nonschizophrenia patients? A 10-year longitudinal analysis. *Schizophrenia Bulletin, 30* (4).

Holubova, M., Prasko, J., Hruby, R., Kamaradova, D., Ociskova, M., Latalova, K., & Grambal, A. (2015). Coping strategies and quality of life in schizophrenia: cross-sectional study. *Neuropsychiatric Disease and Treatment, 11*, 3041–3048.

Howard, R., Castle, D., Wessely, S., & Murray, R. (1993). A comparative study of 470 cases of early- and late-onset schizophrenia. *British Journal of Psychiatry, 163*, 352–357.

Jackson, J. H. (1984). Remarks on the evolution and dissolution of the nervous system. *Journal of Mental Science, 33*, 25–48.

Jeste, D. V., Harris, M. J., Krull, A., Kuck, J., McAdams, L. A., & Heaton, R. (1995). Clinical and neuropsychological characteristics of patients with late-onset schizophrenia. *American Journal of Psychiatry, 152*, 722–730.

Jeste, D. V., Lacro, J. P., Gilbert, P. L., Kline, J., & Kline, N. (1993). Treatment of late-life schizophrenia with neuroleptics. *Schizophrenia Bulletin, 19*, 817–830.

Jeste, D. V., & Maglione, J. E. (2013). Treating older adults with schizophrenia: Challenges and opportunities. *Schizophrenia Bulletin, 39*(5): 966–968.

Jeste, D. V., & Nasrallah, H. A. (2003). Schizophrenia and aging: No more dearth of data? *American Journal of Geriatric Psychiatry, 11*, 584–587.

Jeste, D. V., Twamley, E. W., Eyler Zorrilla, L. T., Golshan, S., Patterson, T. L., & Palmer, B. W. (2003). Aging and outcome in schizophrenia. *Acta Psychiatrica Scandinavica, 107*, 336–343.

Jeste, D. V., Wolkowitz, O. M., & Palmer, B. W. (2011). Divergent trajectories of physical, cognitive, and psychosocial aging in schizophrenia. *Schizophrenia Bulletin, 37*, 451–455.

Jin, H., Shih, P. A., Golshan, S., Mudaliar, S., Henry, R., Glorioso, D. K., ...Jeste, D. V. (2013). Comparison of longer-term safety and effectiveness of 4 atypical antipsychotics in patients over age 40: A trial using equipoise-stratified randomization. *Journal of Clinical Psychiatry, 74*, 10–18.

Kay, D., & Roth, M. (1961). Environmental and hereditary factors in the schizophrenias of old age ("late paraphrenia") and their bearing on the general problem of causation in schizophrenia. *Journal of Mental Science, 107*, 649–686.

Kraepelin, E. (1971). *Dementia praecox and paraphrenia* (R. M. Barclay, Trans.). Huntington, NY: Rovert E. Kreiger. (Original work published in 1919.)

Lake, C. R., & Hurwitz, N. (2006). Schizoaffective disorders are psychotic mood disorders; there are no schizoaffective disorders. *Psychiatry Research, 143*, 255–287.

Lesser, I., Miller, B., Swartz, R., Boone, K., Mehringer, C., & Mena, I. (1993). Brain imaging in late-life schizophrenia and related psychoses. *Schizophrenia Bulletin, 19*, 773–782.

Leucht, S., Burkard, T., Henderson, J. H., Maj, M., & Sartorius, N. (2007). *Physical illness and schizophrenia.* Cambridge, England: Cambridge Press.

Macias, C., Panch, T., Hicks, Y. M., Scolnick, J. S., Weene, D. L., Öngür, D., & Cohen, B. M. (2015). Using smartphone apps to promote psychiatric and physical well-being. *Psychiatric Quarterly, 86*(4), 505–519.

Malla, A., & Payne, J. (2005). First-episode psychosis: Psychopathology, quality of life, and functional outcome. *Schizophrenia Bulletin, 31,* 650–657.

McGrath J., Saha S., Chant D., Welham J. (2008). Schizophrenia: A concise overview of incidence, prevalence, and mortality. *Epidemiologic Reviews, 30*(1), 67–76.

Meeks, W., & Jeste, D.V. (2008). Older individuals. In K. T. Mueser & D. V. Jeste (Eds.) *Clinical handbook of schizophrenia* (pp 390–398). New York: Guilford.

Miller, B. J., Stewart, A., Schrimsher, J., Peeples, D., & Buckley, P. F. (2015). How connected are people with schizophrenia? Cell phone, computer, email, and social media use. *Psychiatry Research, 225*(3), 458–463.

Montes, J. M., Medina, E., Gomez-Beneyto, M., & Maurino, J. (2012). A short message service (SMS)-based strategy for enhancing adherence to antipsychotic medication in schizophrenia. *Psychiatry Research, 200*(2), 89–95.

Morden, N. E., Mistler, L. A., Weeks, W. B., & Bartels, S. J. (2009). Health care for patients with serious mental illness: Family medicine's role. *Journal of the American Board of Family Medicine, 22,* 187–195.

Moriarty, P. J., Lieber, D., Bennett, A., White, L., Parrella, M., Harvey, P. D., & Davis, K. L. (2001). Gender differences in poor outcome patients with lifelong schizophrenia. *Schizophrenia Bulletin, 27,* 103–113.

Mueser, K., Bartels, S., Santos, M., Pratt, S., & Riera, E. (2012). Integrated illness management and recovery: A program for integrating physical and psychiatric illness self-management in older persons with severe mental illness. *American Journal of Psychiatric Rehabilitation, 15,* 131–156.

Mueser, K., Pratt, S., Bartels, S., Swain, K., Forester, B., Cather, C., & Feldman, J. (2010). Randomized trial of social rehabilitation and integrated health care for older people with severe mental illness. *Journal of Consulting and Clinical Psychology, 78,* 561–73.

Mueser, K. T., Pratt, S. I., Bartels, S. J., Forester, B., Wolfe, R., & Cather, C. (2010). Neurocognition and social skill in older persons with schizophrenia and major mood disorders: An analysis of gender and diagnosis effects. *Journal of Neurolinguistics, 23*(3), 297–317.

Munetz, M. R., Grande, T. P., Chambers, M. R. (2001). The incarceration of individuals with severe mental disorders. *Community Mental Health Journal, 37*(4), 361–72.

Naslund, J. A., Aschbrenner, K., Marsch, L., & Bartels, S. (2016). The future of mental health care: Peer-to-peer support and social media. *Epidemiology and Psychiatric Sciences, 25*(2), 113–122.

Naslund, J. A., Aschbrenner, K. A., Barre, L. K., & Bartels, S. J. (2015). Feasibility of popular m-health technologies for activity tracking among individuals with serious mental illness. *Telemedicine and e-Health, 21*(3), 213–216.

Naslund, J. A., Aschbrenner, K. A., & Bartels, S. J. (2016a). Wearable devices and smartphones for activity tracking among people with serious mental illness. *Mental Health and Physical Activity, 10,* 10–17.

Naslund, J. A., Aschbrenner, K. A., & Bartels, S. J. (2016b). How people living with serious mental illness use smartphones, mobile apps, and social media. *Psychiatric Rehabilitation Journal, 39*(4), 364–367. doi: 10.1037/prj0000207

Naslund, J. A., Aschbrenner, K. A., Marsch, L. A., & Bartels, S. J. (2016). Feasibility and acceptability of facebook for health promotion among people with serious mental illness. *Digital Health.* doi: 10.1177/2055207616654822

Naslund, J. A., Aschbrenner, K. A., Marsch, L. A., McHugo, G. J., & Bartels, S. J. (2015). Crowdsourcing for conducting randomized trials of internet delivered interventions in people with serious mental illness: A systematic review. *Contemporary Clinical Trials, 44,* 77–88.

Naslund, J. A., Grande, S. W., Aschbrenner, K. A., & Elwyn, G. (2014). Naturally occurring peer support through social media: the experiences of individuals with severe mental illness using YouTube. *PloS One, 9*(10), e110171.

Naslund, J. A., Marsch, L. A., McHugo, G. J., & Bartels, S. J. (2015). Emerging mHealth and eHealth interventions for serious mental illness: A review of the literature. *Journal of Mental Health, 24*(5), 321–332.

Olfson, M., Gerhard, T., Huang, C., Crystal, S., & Stroup, T. (2015). Premature mortality among adults with schizophrenia in the United States. *JAMA Psychiatry, 72*(12), 1172–1181.

Palmer, B. W., Heaton, S. C., & Jeste, D. V. (1999). Older patients with schizophrenia: Challenges in the coming decades. *Psychiatric Services, 50*, 1178–1183.

Patel, V. (2009). The future of psychiatry in low-and middle-income countries. *Psychological Medicine, 39*(11), 1759–1762.

Patel, V., Araya, R., Chatterjee, S., Chisholm, D., Cohen, A., De Silva, M., ...van Ommeren, M. (2007). Treatment and prevention of mental disorders in low-income and middle-income countries. *The Lancet, 370*(9591), 991–1005.

Patterson, T. L., McKibbin, C., Taylor, M., Goldman, S., Davila-Fraga, W., Bucardo, J., & Jeste, D.V. (2003). Functional adaptation skills training (FAST): A pilot psychosocial intervention study in middle-aged and older patients with chronic psychotic disorders. *American Journal of Geriatric Psychiatry, 11*, 17–23.

Pearlson, G. D., Kreger, L., Rabins, P. V., Chase, G. A., Cohen, B., Wirth, J. B., ...Tune, L. E. (1989). A chart review study of late-onset and early-onset schizophrenia. *American Journal of Psychiatry, 146*, 1568–1574.

Pearlson, G. D., & Rabins, P. V. (1988). The late onset psychoses: Possible risk factors. *Psychiatric Clinics of North America, 11*, 15–33.

Perrin, A. (2015). Social media usage: 2005–2015. Retrieved from http://www.pewinternet.org/2015/10/08/social-networking-usage-2005-2015

Pijnenborg, G., Withaar, F., Brouwer, W. H., Timmerman, M., Bosch, R., & Evans, J. (2010). The efficacy of SMS text messages to compensate for the effects of cognitive impairments in schizophrenia. *British Journal of Clinical Psychology, 49*(2), 259–274.

Post, F. (1966). *Persistent persecutory states of the elderly*. London, England: Pergamon Press.

Prager, S., & Jeste, D. V. (1993). Sensory impairment in late-life schizophrenia. *Schizophrenia Bulletin, 19*, 755–772.

Pratt, S. I., Van Citters, A. D., Mueser, K. T., & Bartels, S. J. (2008). Psychosocial rehabilitation in older adults with serious mental illness: A review of the research literature and recommendations for development of rehabilitative approaches. *American Journal of Psychiatric Rehabilitation, 11*, 7–40.

Pratt, S., Bartels, S. J., Mueser, K. T., & Forester, B. (2008). Helping older people experience success: An integrated model of psychosocial rehabilitation and health care management for older adults with serious mental illness. *American Journal of Psychiatric Rehabilitation, 11*, 41–60.

Pratt, S. I., Bartels, S. J., Mueser, K. T., Naslund, J. A., Wolfe, R., Pixley, H. S., & Josephson, L. (2013). Feasibility and effectiveness of an automated telehealth intervention to improve illness self-management in people with serious psychiatric and medical disorders. *Psychiatric Rehabilitation Journal, 36*(4), 297.

Pratt, S. I., Naslund, J. A., Wolfe, R. S., Santos, M., & Bartels, S. J. (2015). Automated telehealth for managing psychiatric instability in people with serious mental illness. *Journal of Mental Health, 24*(5), 261–265.

Rabins, P. V., Pauker, S., & Thomas, J. (1984). Can schizophrenia begin after age 44? *Comprehensive Psychiatry, 25*, 290–293.

Reeves, R. R., & Brister, J. C. (2008). Psychosis in late life: Emerging issues. *Journal of Psychosocial Nursing and Mental Health Services, 46,* 45–52.

Rolin, S., Aschbrenner, K., Whiteman, K. L., Scherer, E., & Bartels, S. J. (2017). Characteristics and service use of older adults with schizoaffective disorder versus older adults with schizo-phrenia and bipolar disorder. *American Journal of Geriatric Psychiatry.* doi: 10.1016/j. jagp.2017.03.014

Rystedt, I. B., & Bartels, S. J. (2008). Medical comorbidity. In K. T. Mueser & D. V. Jeste (Eds.), *Clinical handbook of schizophrenia* (pp. 424–436). New York: Guilford.

Saha, S., Chant, D., & McGrath, J. (2007). A systematic review of mortality in schizophrenia: Is the differential mortality gap worsening over time? *Archives of General Psychiatry, 64,* 1123–1131.

SAMHSA-HRSA Center for Integrated Health Solutions. (n.d.). Primary care in behavioral health. Retrieved from http://www.integration.samhsa.gov/integrated-care-models/ primary-care-in-behavioral-health

Sayers, S. L., Campbell, E. C., Kondrich, J., Mann, S. C., Cornish, J., O'Brien, C., & Caroff, S. N. (2005). Cocaine abuse in schizophrenic patients treated with olanzapine versus haloperidol. *Journal of Nervous and Mental Disorders, 193*(6), 379–86.

Saxena, S., Thornicroft, G., Knapp, M., & Whiteford, H. (2007). Resources for mental health: Scarcity, inequity, and inefficiency. *The Lancet, 370*(9590), 878–889.

Scharf, D., Eberhart, N., Hackbarth, N., Horvitz-Lennon, M., Beckman, R., Han, B., … Burnam M. A. (2013). *Evaluation of the SAMHSA primary behavioral health care integration (PBHCI) grant program: Final report.* Washington, DC: Office of Disability, Aging and Long-Term Care Policy; Office of the Assistant Secretary for Planning and Evaluation; US Department of Health and Human Services.

Solomon P. (2004). Peer support/peer provided services underlying processes, benefits, and critical ingredients. *Psychiatric Rehabilitation Journal, 27*(4): 392–401.

Spaniel, F., Hrdlicka, J., Novak, T., Kozeny, J., Hoeschl, C., Mohr, P., & Motlova, L. B. (2012). Effectiveness of the information technology-aided program of relapse prevention in schizophrenia (ITAREPS): A randomized, controlled, double-blind study. *Journal of Psychiatric Practice, 18*(4), 269–280.

Stein, B. D., Kogan, J. N., Mihalyo, M. J., Schuster, J., Deegan, P. E., Sorbero, M. J., & Drake, R. E. (2013). Use of a computerized medication shared decision making tool in community mental health settings: impact on psychotropic medication adherence. *Community Mental Health Journal, 49*(2), 185–192.

Steinwachs, D. M., Roter, D. L., Skinner, E. A., Lehman, A. F., Fahey, M., Cullen, B., … Gallucci, G. (2011). A web-based program to empower patients who have schizophrenia to discuss quality of care with mental health providers. *Psychiatric Services, 62,* 1296–1302.

Studentkowski, G., Scheele, D., Calabrese, P., Balkau, F., Höffler, J., Aubel, T., … Assion, H. J. (2010). Cognitive impairment in patients with a schizoaffective dis-order: A comparison with bipolar patients in euthymia. *European Journal of Medical Reseasrch, 15,* 70–78.

Swartz, M. S., Stroup, T. S., McEvoy, J. P., Davis, S. M., Rosenheck, R. A., Keefe, R. S., … Lieberman, J.A. (2008). What CATIE found: Results from the schizophrenia trial. *Psychiatric Services, 59,* 500–506.

Torniainen, M., Suvisaari, J., Partonen, T., Castaneda, A. E., Kuha, A., Suokas, J., …Tuulio-Henriksson A. (2012). Cognitive impairments in schizophrenia and schizoaffective dis-order: Relationship with clinical characteristics. *Journal of Nervous and Mental Disorders, 200,* 316–322.

Van der Krieke, L., Wunderink, L., Emerencia, A. C., de Jonge, P., & Sytema, S. (2014). E–mental health self-management for psychotic disorders: State of the art and future per-spectives. *Psychiatric Services, 65*(1), 33–49.

Vigo, D., Thornicroft, G., & Atun, R. (2016). Estimating the true global burden of mental illness. *The Lancet Psychiatry, 3*(2), 171–178.

Vitiello, B., Correll, C., van Zwieten-Boot, B., Zuddas, A., Parellada, M., & Arango, C. (2009). Antipsychotics in children and adolescents: Increasing use, evidence for efficacy and safety concerns. *European Neuropsychopharmacology, 19,* 629–635.

Walker, E. R., McGee, R. E., & Druss, B. G. (2015). Mortality in mental disorders and global disease burden implications: a systematic review and meta-analysis. *JAMA Psychiatry, 72*(4), 334–341.

Winklbaur, B., Ebner, N., Sachs, G., Thau, K., & Fischer, G. (2006). Substance abuse in patients with schizophrenia. *Dialogues in Clinical Neuroscience, 8*(1), 37–43.

Witteman, H. O., & Stahl, J. E. (2013). Facilitating interdisciplinary collaboration to tackle complex problems in health care: Report from an exploratory workshop. *Health Systems, 2*(3), 162–170.

Wexler, B., Davidson, L., & Styron T. (2008). Severe and persistent mental illness. In S. Jacobs & E. Griffith (Eds.), *40 years of academic public psychiatry.* London, England: Wiley.

Wiffen, B., Rabinowitz, J., Fleischhacker, W. W., & David, A. S. (2010). Insight: Demographic differences and associations with one-year outcome in schizophrenia and schizoaffective disorder. *Clinical Schizophrenia & Related Psychoses, 4,* 169–175.

Whiteman, K. L., Naslund, J., Di Napoli, E., Bruce, M. L., & Bartels, S. J. (2016). Systematic review of integrated medical and psychiatric self-management interventions for adults with serious mental illness. *Psychiatric Services, 67*(11), 1213–1225. doi: 10.1176/appi. ps.201500521

Zisook, S., Heaton, R., Moranville, J., Kuck, J., Jernigan, T., & Braff, D. (1992). Past substance abuse and clinical course of schizophrenia. *American Journal of Psychiatry, 149,* 552–553.

11

Anxiety Disorders, Hoarding Disorder, and Post-Traumatic Stress Disorder

Every day, Genevieve struggles to make herself do the daily routine. She is so shaky all of the time; if she could just feel safe. The neighborhood is deteriorating, and her fear of what the kids will do to her is growing. She imagines all kinds of torture they could inflict if they decided to, and no one would know. The worst part is the terror she feels when her heart speeds up, she feels faint, and her face and neck become uncomfortably red, hot, and clammy. She is sure that this is the final curtain call. If her heart acts up when she is out and about, she gets particularly scared. So recently, she has prevailed upon her son and daughter-in-law to bring her groceries and supplies into the house, which she rarely leaves anymore.

Morris has always been a pack rat. In fact, he considers himself a "collector" of knick knacks and goes to garage sales several days a week to find more treasures. For many years, he kept his collection manageable, often at the insistence of his wife to declutter the house. But since she died three years ago, Morris has been bringing more and more stuff in and nothing has gone out, including the trash and several years of newspapers, magazines, and stacked mail. The entire house (and his backyard) are filled to the brim. Besides caring for eight or nine cats, his only social contact is with a daughter whom he sees infrequently. In fact, Morris doesn't want her to visit because all she does is argue with him about his living conditions. Morris thinks it is manageable, but his clutter is making his home unsafe. He can barely move around in his house and the odor is becoming toxic. He hasn't seen three of his cats in months and he fears the worst.

George still remembers the horror of World War II on a daily basis, although he never talks about it. One by one his buddies went down when their ship was sunk. How he survived he'll never quite know, but he prays daily for help living with the memories and the guilt. He thinks to himself "I'm nothing special. Why did I live

Aging and Mental Health, Third Edition. Daniel L. Segal, Sara Honn Qualls, and Michael A. Smyer.
© 2018 John Wiley & Sons, Inc. Published 2018 by John Wiley & Sons, Inc.

and my friends died?" For many years, George gets drunk and passes out at night. This is the only way he has discovered to limit the impact of nightmares of gruesome events he witnessed during his tour of duty.

Anxiety disorders, hoarding disorder, and post-traumatic stress disorder (PTSD) are increasingly well-researched disorders in clinical geropsychology. Although the choice to combine the three in one chapter is primarily an organizational convenience, there is also a logical reason for linking them: Each of these disorders has excessive fear or anxiety as a central feature. In fact, in prior editions of the *Diagnostic and Statistical Manual of Mental Disorders* (DSM), PTSD was included in the anxiety disorders module and hoarding was a variant of obsessive-compulsive disorder, which was also formerly included in the anxiety disorders module. The vignettes presented above depict serious problems that are producing functional shifts in life patterns and declines in overall well-being. For the disorders in this chapter, we discuss classification and epidemiology, followed by a description of how they are experienced by older adults. Then, we discuss theories that explain the disorders and conclude with a review of approaches to assessment and treatment among older adults. Let's begin with the anxiety disorders.

Anxiety

Imagine you are hiking in beautiful Cheyenne Canyon, Colorado, and come across a mountain lion. Should you be anxious? Of course you should! Normal anxiety is experienced by most people and is very useful. Anxiety warns us about possible threats in the environment (e.g., dangerous animals present, or a looming exam at school) and motivates us to be safe by engaging in adaptive behaviors that reduce anxiety (e.g., slowly backing away from predators; studying to reduce worry about the upcoming exam). However, when anxiety gets out of control or is excessive, then an anxiety disorder may be possible. The disorders that make up the anxiety category bring significant distress and functional disability to adults of any age.

The hallmarks of anxiety are the combination of symptoms that may be characterized in three domains:

- cognitive symptoms, such as ruminative thinking and distractibility;
- affective symptoms, such as worry, fearfulness, low mood, or irritability;
- and somatic symptoms, such as a racing heart, sweating, stomach distress, or other signs of physical arousal.

To apply this to yourself, ponder the following: When you are really anxious or stressed, how does the anxiety hit you? Can you identify cognitive, somatic, and affective aspects of your experience? People experience anxiety in a multitude of different ways, so it is likely your experience is at least somewhat different than that of your peers and may represent different ratios of cognitive, somatic, and affective symptoms. Regardless of how it manifests, the cost of excessive anxiety to the individual is high. Not surprisingly, anxious individuals seek medical services at high rates, thus generating large health care costs (Deacon, Lickel, & Abramowitz, 2008). Given the serious impact of excessive anxiety among older adults, the recent surge of research on the nature of anxiety disorders as well as on strategies to assess and treat them effectively in later life are welcome occurrences.

Types of anxiety disorders

The classification of anxiety disorders within the DSM-5 includes several diverse disorders that are listed in Table 11.1, along with their essential features (American Psychiatric Association [APA], 2013).

Table 11.1 Diagnostic features for anxiety disorders

Specific phobia

Marked and persistent fear that is excessive or unreasonable, cued by the presence or anticipated presence of a specific object or situation (e.g., animals, flying, heights, seeing blood).

Exposure to the feared stimulus almost invariably provokes an immediate anxiety response.

The fear or anxiety is out of proportion to the actual danger posed by the object or situation.

The object or situation is avoided or endured with intense anxiety or distress.

The fear or avoidance is persistent, and causes either distress or impairments in one's daily functioning.

Social anxiety disorder (social phobia)

A marked and persistent fear of social or performance situations in which the person is exposed to unfamiliar people or to possible scrutiny by others.

The person fears that he or she will act in a way that will be humiliating, embarrassing, or offensive.

Exposure to the feared social situation usually provokes immediate anxiety.

The social situations are avoided or endured with intense anxiety or distress.

The fear or anxiety is out of proportion to the actual danger posed by the situation and context.

The fear or avoidance is persistent, and causes either distress or impairments in one's daily functioning.

Generalized anxiety disorder

Excessive anxiety or worry, occurring more days than not for at least six months, about multiple events or activities.

The person finds it difficult to control the worry.

The anxiety and worry are associated with three or more of the following six symptoms:

- Restlessness or feeling keyed up or on edge
- Fatigued easily
- Difficulty concentrating
- Irritability
- Muscle tension
- Sleep disturbance

The anxiety or worry causes either distress or impairments in one's daily functioning.

(Continued)

Table 11.1   (Continued)

Panic disorder

Recurrent panic attacks (defined as surges of intense anxiety, that peak within minutes),
during which four or more of the following symptoms are present:

- Racing heart or palpitations
- Sweating
- Physical trembling
- Shortness of breath
- Feelings of choking
- Having chest discomfort
- Feeling nauseous
- Having chills or hot flashes
- Having numbness or tingling sensations
- Having feeling of unreality or of being detached from oneself
- Fear of losing control
- Fear of dying

The panic attacks are followed by either persistent concerns about having additional attacks
or maladaptive behavior changes due to the attacks, such as avoiding places and activities
associated with attacks.

Agoraphobia

Significant anxiety or fear about two or more of the following agoraphobic situations:

- Being in open spaces
- Being in enclosed spaces
- Using transportation, such as riding in cars, buses, boats, planes, or trains
- Being in a crowd or standing in line
- Being out of one's home alone

The person fears or avoids the situations due to concerns that he or she might not be able to
escape or find help should panic-like symptoms develop.

Exposure to the agoraphobic situations usually provokes immediate anxiety.

The situations are avoided, endured with intense anxiety or distress, or require the presence
of a companion.

The fear or anxiety is out of proportion to the actual danger posed by the situation and
context.

The fear or avoidance is persistent, and causes either distress or impairments in one's daily
functioning.

Source: Adapted from the DSM-5 (APA, 2013).

Specific phobia is characterized by persistent fears and avoidance of a particular
object or situation, for example, animals, heights, flying, and seeing blood. *Social
anxiety disorder* (also called social phobia) is characterized by excessive fears about
social situations in which the person is fearful of being scrutinized and evaluated
negatively. *Generalized anxiety disorder* (GAD) is the descriptor for the broadest set
of anxiety symptoms that includes excessive or unrealistic worry on most days for six
months or longer. *Panic disorder* is characterized by recurrent panic attacks, which
are abrupt surges of intense fear, peaking within a few minutes, with a host of physical
and cognitive symptoms (e.g., shortness of breath, increased heart rate, sweating, tingling in hands and feet, fear of dying, fear of losing control, or fear of going crazy).

Panic attacks may be unexpected, in which there are no obvious cues or triggers at the time of occurrence, or expected, in which there are salient cues or triggers, for example, only occurring in an elevator, at a specific family member's house, or in a grocery store line. A common characteristic of the setting in which panic attacks tend to occur is that escape is perceived as difficult. As a strategy for coping with the fear of panic, some individuals restrict their activities to safe areas and become fearful of leaving their home, thus developing *agoraphobia*, which is coded as a distinct anxiety disorder. In the case example presented earlier, Genevieve is at risk for developing serious agoraphobia due to her desire to avoid uncomfortable situations, feelings, and symptoms.

Prevalence

Researchers reported the worldwide prevalence of anxiety disorders among adults through a meta-analysis of data from 87 studies across 44 countries (Baxter, Scott, Vos, & Whiteford, 2013). These researchers found that anxiety disorders among adults were common across cultures. The current global prevalence was 7.3%, ranging from 5.3% in African cultures to 10.4% in Euro/Anglo cultures, representing a high worldwide burden of disease. Left untreated, the anxiety disorders contribute to billions of dollars each year in health care costs and lost worker productivity.

Among older adults specifically, anxiety is a widespread problem and a cause for major clinical concern. Whereas there is a large amount of literature on depression in later life, the knowledge base about anxiety in the older adult populations is much less developed. This is unfortunate especially since anxiety disorders are, in fact, more common than depression in older adults. This finding frankly surprised the clinical community from the earliest community epidemiological studies in the US that included older adults. Based on a comprehensive review of the major epidemiology studies, prevalence estimates of anxiety disorders in later life ranged from 3.2% to 14.2% (Wolitzky-Taylor, Castriotta, Lenze, Stanley, & Craske, 2010). The rate is much higher in psychiatric samples of older adults, ranging from 15% to 56% (Bryant, Jackson, & Ames, 2008). Figure 11.1 depicts prevalence variation across the most common anxiety disorders in late adulthood and older age, and shows the powerful effects of age and gender on prevalence of all of these disorders. Note that the younger age group (55–64) had higher rates than the later age groups and that women had higher rates than men for almost all data points (Reynolds, Pietrzak, El-Gabalawy, Mackenzie, & Sareen, 2015).

Anxiety in later life is associated with many challenges, including decreased physical activity, poor self-perceptions of health, decreased life satisfaction, increased loneliness, and worse health-related quality of life compared to asymptomatic individuals (Fuentes & Cox, 2000; Wetherell et al., 2004). Although anxiety disorders are common among older adults, anxiety disorders are still less common among older adults than younger adults (Wolitzky-Taylor et al., 2010). Similar to depression, many older adults who do not reach the full threshold for a diagnosable anxiety disorder report disturbingly high rates of symptoms that are now identified as subsyndromal or subthreshold anxiety, which is estimated to affect approximately 25% of older adults (Grenier, Preville, & Boyer, 2011).

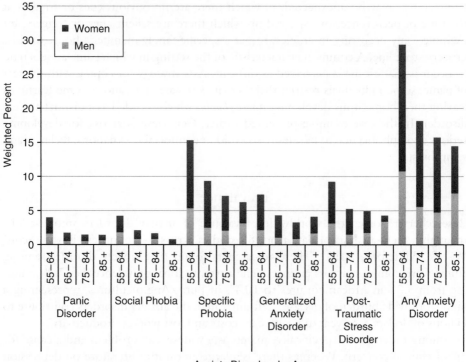

Figure 11.1 Past-year prevalence of DSM-IV anxiety disorders by gender and age among 12,312 US adults aged 55 years and older.

Source: Adapted from Reynolds et al. (2015).

Note: PTSD was removed from the anxiety disorders category in DSM-5 and placed into a new category called Trauma- and Stressor-Related Disorders.

Although the onset of anxiety among the population 60-years-old and older is lower than at earlier points in adulthood, anxiety can occur for the first time even in advanced old age (Streiner, Cairney, & Veldhuizen, 2006). According to the National Comorbidity Survey Replication study in the US (Kessler et al., 2005), the lifetime prevalence rate for any anxiety disorder was almost 29%, suggesting that anxiety has affected the life experience of a substantial portion of the population, typically beginning in youth or early adulthood. Anxiety disorders appear to be relatively stable over time. A six-year longitudinal study in Amsterdam that followed 112 persons diagnosed with anxiety disorders found that 23% maintained their diagnosis six years later, and another 47% showed subclinical levels of anxiety disorders (Schuurmans et al., 2005).

Presentation in older adults

The presence of comorbid medical illnesses that produce symptoms similar to anxiety disorders creates a challenging differential diagnosis for many health providers. Effective means of assessing anxiety exist, as described below, but primary care providers who are the first source of help-seeking for many older adults often rely on patient self-report to identify anxiety. The symptoms reported by older adults may be somatic, overlapping symptoms of existing medical illnesses, or may be affective, overlapping with depression. Cognitive symptoms such as worry may lead the older adult as well as the health providers to focus on the content of the worry (e.g., racing heart, shortness of breath) rather than the pattern of excessive worry that exemplifies anxiety. To complicate matters further, anxiety can also be a contributing factor to a variety of medical illnesses (e.g., gastrointestinal disorders), and anxiety symptoms are commonly present in older adults who are not diagnosable with an anxiety disorder. Sleep difficulties provide a good example, because aging adults often experience insomnia but not with the frequency, intensity, or impact as is the case for persons with GAD, for example (Wetherell, LeRoux, & Gatz 2003).

Other mental disorders present with symptoms that overlap anxiety symptoms and anxiety disorders. For example, depression has a high rate of comorbidity with anxiety (Beekman et al., 2000), and is hypothesized to share certain psychological and perhaps neurological underpinnings with anxiety (Teachman, Siedlecki, & Magee, 2007). Other mental disorders are also commonly comorbid with anxiety. Personality disorder traits are more prevalent in persons with elevated levels of anxiety (Coolidge, Segal, Hook, & Stewart, 2000). Neurocognitive disorders or dementia (and in some cases, milder forms of cognitive impairment) produce high rates of anxiety symptoms, particularly agitation and restlessness. However, the relationship between anxiety and agitation in persons with neurocognitive disorders is difficult to disentangle (Seignourel, Kunik, Snow, Wilson, & Stanley, 2008). In some cases, the agitation is due to an underlying anxiety, but in other cases agitation may be due to environmental factors, such as lack of stimulation, excessive noise, lack of privacy, or changes in caregiver arrangements. Yet in other cases, agitation may be due to comorbid medical conditions, medication side effects, or untreated pain. In older adults with dementia, anxiety has been associated with reduced quality of life (Seignourel et al., 2008), suggesting the need for aggressive identification and treatment. However, it can be difficult to accurately assess levels of anxiety in people with dementia, especially in cases where language and communication deficits are present.

The relationship between cognition and anxiety is emerging as an interesting area for research. Certainly, the content of thought is influenced by anxiety. The worries of the oldest-old focus on health and memory, but considerable variation exists in the worry pattern over time (Jeon, Dunkle, & Roberts, 2006). Anxiety creates hypervigilance to threat in older adults as in younger adults (Fox & Knight, 2005), suggesting that age does not fully influence the content of worry. The anxiety disorders shape the cognitive processes involved in worry, as evidenced by data showing that the worry of older adults with GAD is distinct from that of other older adults in frequency, uncontrollability, distress, and content (Wetherell et al., 2003). Anxiety is also associated with loss of inhibitory control, suggesting that age-related brain changes may be another source of important investigation in anxiety research (Price & Mohlman, 2007). It is likely that the relationship between anxiety and impaired cognition is bidirectional. That is, anxiety symptoms can cause cognitive problems (or worsen existing cognitive difficulties) and having cognitive problems can lead the person to become anxious or fearful.

What is the effect of anxiety on health and disability? Certainly, anxiety is associated with high rates of medical service utilization, especially among persons suffering from panic attacks (Deacon et al., 2008). Medical help-seeking occurs for both the anxiety symptoms as well as for comorbid medical symptoms that generate more worry among persons with anxiety. Anxiety actually increases mortality and risk of disease, including coronary artery disease in men (Van Hout et al., 2004). Anxiety also has been investigated as having a role in the development of functional disability. For example, in a study of rates of decline in the ability to manage activities of daily living, anxiety was associated with significant declines in functioning (Brenes et al., 2005).

Theories of etiology

Several models for conceptualizing anxiety in older adults inform research and clinical work. From a biological perspective, the current consensus is that people inherit vulnerabilities for anxiety and panic symptoms but not for anxiety disorders per se. Stress and unfortunate life circumstances activate one's vulnerability, along with prior learning and experiences, within the classic diathesis–stress model.

The cognitive-behavioral model of anxiety characterizes anxiety as having three interrelated components, namely cognitive, emotional, and behavioral aspects. Regarding the cognitive aspect, people predisposed to anxiety problems are likely to *perceive threats* in the environment, even in situations that most other people would not see as frightening. Specifically, they hold strong beliefs that they cannot manage stress effectively or cope with adversity, which leads them to see most situations as threatening. Then, in response to the perceived threats, the person experiences physiological arousal, commonly referred to as the *fight or flight response*, character-ized by increased sweating, heart rate, and blood pressure, along with hypervigilance. The individual then begins to become fearful, afraid, or apprehensive (the emotional aspect), and responds behaviorally by trying to reduce or cope with the threat, for example, by running away, hiding, fighting, or freezing.

Another variant of the cognitive behavioral model views anxiety behaviors as reflecting an absence of effective skills, distortions in thinking, and/or behavior patterns that avoid or circumvent more useful ways of addressing fearful thoughts about threat. The cognitive aspects of this model emphasize thought processes as the mechanisms by which difficult situations are turned into anxiety symptoms (Beck, 2011; Laidlaw, 2015). Specifically, anxiety symptoms are viewed as a natural consequence of a number of unhelpful beliefs, and their variants, that are known to be anxiety-inducing. Some examples include the following:

- Bad things are going to happen to me.
- This situation is horrible and I can't cope with it.
- The world is a scary place and I'm powerless to protect myself.
- I have no control over what's happening to me.
- I'm inept and others will reject me.
- I'm responsible for taking care of everybody, despite not having any control over them.

Especially relevant to anxiety and related disorders is *catastrophic thinking*, which magnifies both the immediate and future consequences of perceived threats in the environment (Gellatly & Beck, 2016). Specifically, excessively anxious individuals are likely to misinterpret and magnify external threats (such as accidents, attacks, and motivations of other people) and are also prone to misinterpret and magnify perceived internal threats and bodily signs of arousal (Gellatly & Beck, 2016).

In recent years, an overarching model has been developed that focuses on broad emotion regulation deficits as the core problem (Borkovec, Alcaine, & Behar, 2004). Worry may be a strategy used to try to reduce arousal that is poorly tolerated by a subset of persons. The poor tolerance of arousal or negative emotional states may be the core problem rather than worry itself. This model would address other anxious behaviors as similar manifestations of coping strategies intended to reduce the undesirable negative affect or arousal. Poor interpersonal functioning, such as social isolation or conflict, is a common negative outcome of the coping strategies used by highly anxious persons that can perpetuate negative thought patterns and arousal that are characteristic of anxiety.

The high rate of comorbidity of anxiety with depression has led to efforts to conceptualize the common and distinct characteristics of these two disorders. A tripartite model suggests that anxiety shares with depression a higher-order factor of negative affect, along with lower-order factors of low positive affect (primary relevant to depression) and arousal (primarily relevant to anxiety) (Teachman et al., 2007).

Risk factors for anxiety in later life are plentiful (Wolitzky-Taylor et al., 2010), including chronic illness, poor coping, neuroticism, external locus of control, loneliness, lack of social support, stressful life events, lower educational levels, and being female. A recent study in this area (Mahoney, Segal, & Coolidge, 2015) found that anxiety sensitivity, experiential avoidance, and low mindfulness were strong correlates of anxiety symptoms in older adults, suggesting their possible role as risk factors, pending verification from prospective or longitudinal studies.

Assessment

Several barriers hamper the accurate screening and assessment of anxiety among older adults, most notably the high rates of medical comorbidity and cognitive impairment among older adults, and changes in life circumstances not faced by younger adults (Wolitzky-Taylor et al., 2010). The issue of the medical comorbidity is especially problematic because anxiety is often predominantly experienced, and presented, as physical symptoms among older adults. Indeed, some older adults may incorrectly attribute physical symptoms of anxiety to medical problems, including muscle tension, hypervigilance, and difficulties related to sleep (Kogan, Edelstein, & McKee, 2000). In turn, many physical conditions (e.g., cardiovascular disease, respiratory disease, hyperthyroidism, and pulmonary difficulties) can mimic symptoms of anxiety, making it difficult to disentangle the symptoms of anxiety from the symptoms of medical illnesses (Kogan et al., 2000).

Yet another problem in the assessment and diagnosis of anxiety in older adults is the high rate of comorbidity of anxiety and other psychiatric problems, including depression (Beekman et al., 2000; King-Kallimanis, Gum, & Kohn, 2009), personality disorders (Coolidge et al., 2000), and substance abuse (Fingerhood, 2000). Moreover, anxiety symptoms are known to be particularly difficult for older adults to identify correctly compared to younger adults (Wetherell et al., 2009).

Despite these challenges, assessment of anxiety is typically accomplished through self-report measures, clinical interviews, and semistructured interviews. Self-report scales are used for screening for anxiety, yielding scores that are not informative for diagnosis, but provide an indicator of the presence and intensity of anxiety as a problem. Two popular self-report measures for anxiety developed for adults (not older adults) are the Beck Anxiety Inventory (Beck, Epstein, Brown, & Steer, 1988) and the State-Trait Anxiety Inventory (Spielberger et al., 1983). However, both of these measures have some limitations for use with older adults for whom physical illness symptoms can artificially inflate anxiety scores due to the inclusion of several somatic items on both of these scales (Wetherell & Gatz, 2005). Another popular self-report measure designed for the general adult population is the Penn State Worry Questionnaire (PSWQ; Meyer, Miller, Metzger, & Borkovec, 1990). The PSWQ is a cognitively focused 16-item measure that emphasizes trait pathological worry. The measure has been successfully used to measure worry severity among clinical and non-clinical populations of older adults (Wuthrich, Johnco, & Knight, 2014), but because it focuses on trait worry, it is not sensitive to changes over time that are important when using self-report scales as indicators of treatment progress.

Two elder-specific self-report assessment measures have been developed and extensively validated in recent years. These include the Geriatric Anxiety Inventory and the Geriatric Anxiety Scale. The Geriatric Anxiety Inventory (GAI; Pachana et al., 2007) includes 20 self-report items. Participants are asked to respond "yes" or "no" to statements regarding their experience with anxiety in the past week. Possible scores range from 0 to 20, with higher scores indicating greater anxiety. The internal consistency of the GAI scores is high, $\alpha = .91$, as is its convergent validity with other measures (Pachana et al., 2007). A short version of the GAI has been developed, and the full measure has been translated into 20 languages. The GAI is available under license from the following website: http://gai.net.au.

The Geriatric Anxiety Scale (GAS; Segal, June, Payne, Coolidge, & Yochim, 2010) is a 30-item self-report measure used to assess anxiety symptoms among older adults. Individuals are asked to indicate how often they have experienced each symptom during the last week, answering on a four-point Likert scale ranging from "Not at all" (0) to "All the time" (3). GAS items were derived from the broad range of anxiety disorder symptoms in the *DSM-IV-TR*. Scoring provides a total score and three subscales (somatic symptoms, cognitive symptoms, and affective symptoms) for which normative and interpretive guidelines are available. The GAS total score is based on the first 25 items and ranges from 0 to 75. The additional five content items assess areas of anxiety commonly reported to be of concern for older adults: concern about finances, concern about one's health, concern about children, fear of dying, and fear of becoming a burden to others. These content items are used clinically and they do not load on the total score. The GAS demonstrated high internal consistency of scale scores and strong evidence of validity for the quantitative assessment of anxiety symptoms in diverse community and clinical samples of older adults (Gould et al., 2014; Segal et al., 2010; Yochim, Mueller, June, & Segal, 2011; Yochim, Mueller, & Segal, 2013). A 10-item short version, called the GAS-10, is available and has strong psychometric properties as a screening instrument in diverse samples of older adults (Mueller et al., 2015). The GAS has been successfully translated—and preliminarily evaluated—into several languages, including German (Gottschling, Segal, Häusele, Spinath, & Stoll, 2016), Chinese (Xiao-Ling, Lu, Gottschling, Segal, & Tang, 2017), Persian (Bolghan-Abadi, Segal, Coolidge, & Gottschling, 2013), and Italian (Gatti et al., in press). Several other linguistic adaptations and psychometric evaluations are currently underway, including the Dutch, Spanish, and Turkish languages.

In clinical settings, elevated scores on screening measures usually trigger a more thorough clinical interview regarding anxiety symptoms and experiences. Clinicians should evaluate the onset, frequency, intensity, and duration of anxiety symptoms in order to facilitate differential diagnosis of the anxiety disorders, many of which share some common features. In most cases, the clinical evaluation is rather straightforward because many older adults who have significant anxiety symptoms recognize their symptoms as problematic. This pattern is most true for those experiencing phobias, agoraphobia, panic attacks, and social anxiety. In contrast, some older adults with GAD or obsessive-compulsive disorder (OCD) fail to recognize their symptoms as part of a mental disorder, because the early-onset (sometimes in childhood) and long-standing nature of the problems has made them ego-syntonic. Limited insight, or the complete lack of insight, hampers the assessment process, so clinicians are advised to gently probe about chronic worry, obsessions, and compulsions as part of their screening for anxiety problems. A variation on this theme we have observed is among older adults with long-standing OCD who do not disclose their symptoms due to shame and secrecy, despite knowing that their obsessions and compulsions are not typical.

Due to the high comorbidity between the anxiety disorders with depression and substance abuse, a thorough evaluation of mood symptoms and substance use is recommended among older adults who present with anxiety problems. Regarding substance use, a common pattern is one of self-medication of anxiety symptoms with depressant substances, most commonly alcohol, which reduces self-focus and social anxiety. When comorbid disorders are present, the clinician should try to determine which of the disorders came first (or which one diagnostically is the principal diagnosis), although this can be challenging when comorbidities have been present for many years.

To facilitate formal diagnosis in clinical and research settings, semistructured interviews may be used. The *Structured Clinical Interview for DSM-5 Disorders* (SCID-5; First, Williams, Karg, & Spitzer, 2016) has a full anxiety disorders module linked to DSM-5 diagnostic criteria, whereas the *Anxiety and Related Disorders Interview Schedule for DSM-5* (ADIS-5; Brown & Barlow, 2014) is designed to aid in diagnosis of current and past anxiety, mood, obsessive-compulsive, trauma, and related disorders (e.g., somatic symptom, substance use), with significant depth, based on DSM-5 criteria. Both the SCID-5 and the ADIS-5 generate specific diagnoses by asking about presence, intensity, longevity, and impact on daily life of particular anxiety symptoms. As mentioned earlier, in research studies, diagnoses from structured or semistructured interviews are considered the gold standard.

Interventions for anxiety disorders

A recent upsurge in psychotherapy outcome research testing psychosocial interventions for various anxiety disorders has produced an array of options for reasonably effective treatment, as highlighted in a number of major reviews (Ayers, Sorrell,

Thorp, & Wetherell, 2007; Bower & Wetherell, 2015; Mohlman, 2004; Nordhus & Pallesen, 2003; Wetherell, Lenze, & Stanley, 2005; Wetherell, Sorrell, Thorp, & Patterson, 2005; Wolitzky-Taylor et al., 2010). According to Ayers et al. (2007), four psychotherapy approaches were found to meet standards for evidence-based treatment for anxiety disorders in older adults in a limited number of studies: relaxation training, cognitive-behavioral therapy (CBT), supportive therapy, and cognitive therapy. These four treatments were applied to a mix of specific anxiety disorders, although their patient samples were primarily suffering from GAD, or having subjective distress over anxiety symptoms across diagnostic categories.

Although a variety of research methodologies have been used, in general, the approaches with the strongest evidence base include CBT (for anxiety disorders) and relaxation training (for anxiety symptoms). Indeed, CBT effectiveness studies are the most numerous, and the strongest support was found for CBT use with older adults experiencing GAD. The typical intervention protocol was short-term (8–15 sessions) of individual or group intervention. Some studies experimented effectively with between-session prompts to complete homework (e.g., Mohlman et al., 2003). Improvement across diverse studies was found in anxiety symptom reduction, in overall quality of life improvement, and on measures of depression.

From a behavioral perspective, anxiety is incompatible with relaxation. As such, relaxation training as a behavioral intervention is commonly used for anxiety symptoms across the lifespan. There are many different strategies for relaxation, with progressive muscle relaxation training and diaphragmatic breathing exercises among the most popular (Segal & Feliciano, 2011). Relaxation training is especially useful because it can be conducted in a few sessions of training in a variety of settings and it shows lasting benefits. A recent review of relaxation interventions among older adults (Klainin-Yobas, Oo, Yew, & Lau, 2015) supported the beneficial effects of relaxation on both anxiety and depression.

Whereas meaningful effectiveness can be claimed for various interventions, especially CBT and relaxation training, less encouraging are data suggesting that the overall effect size of psychotherapy is somewhat lower for older adults with anxiety disorders compared to younger and middle-aged adults with anxiety disorders (Gould, Coulson, & Howard, 2012). Moreover, few studies have examined the mechanisms by which interventions achieve desired outcomes, and few studies have followed the samples over a period of years to study long-term effectiveness, suggesting important areas for further research.

Pharmacological interventions continue to be the most commonly used approach for anxiety, at least in part because primary care is a common site for help-seeking. In particular, the benzodiazepines (e.g., diazepam, alprazolam, lorazepam) are the most commonly prescribed medications for the treatment of anxiety symptoms and disorders. Their calming effect occurs because of decrease in central nervous system activity, placing users at serious risk for adverse consequences such as loss of alertness and balance, impaired cognitive functioning, falls, and hip fractures (Wolitzky-Taylor et al., 2010). The benzodiazepines are also typically addictive. As such, we advise against benzodiazepine use for older adults, with the exceptions of the most brief and short-term use. Antidepressants, particularly the selective serotonin reuptake inhibitors (SSRIs) and the serotonin and norepinephrine reuptake inhibitors (SNRIs), are also commonly prescribed to manage anxiety symptoms, with lower safety risks and greater effectiveness. The SSRIs and SNRIs appear to be equally efficacious and tolerable for older adults as compared to younger adults (Wolitzky-Taylor et al., 2010). However, a significant minority of both younger and older adults discontinue the antidepressant medication regimen due to unpleasant side effects or limited effectiveness. In these cases, psychotherapy may be most optimal.

Hoarding Disorder

Hoarding disorder was officially included for the first time as a distinct mental disorder in the DSM-5 (APA, 2013). It is included in a new diagnostic category called Obsessive-Compulsive and Related Disorders, which contains several linked disorders characterized by anxiety symptoms and behaviors that appear out of control. Besides hoarding disorder, the other disorders in this category include:

- Obsessive-compulsive disorder (OCD), characterized by recurring obsessions (which are persistent thoughts, images, or urges that are experienced as unwanted and intrusive) and/or compulsions (which are repetitive behaviors or mental acts that the person feels driven to perform, usually in response to obsessive thoughts or to prevent some calamity from occurring). Most people with OCD have both obsessions and compulsions. The 12-month prevalence for OCD in the US is quite low, at 1.2% (APA, 2013). Onset of OCD after age 35 is unusual although the course of OCD is usually chronic, especially without treatment, and can persist across the lifespan.
- Body dysmorphic disorder (BDD), characterized by a preoccupation with one or more perceived defects or flaws in one's physical appearance, coupled with repetitive behaviors (for example, excessive grooming or repeated mirror checking) in response to the perceived defect. The point prevalence for BDD among adults in the US is 2.4%, with higher rates among dermatology patients and cosmetic surgery patients (APA, 2013). The majority of individuals with BDD had an onset before age 18. Like OCD, BDD generally has a chronic course, especially without treatment, with a waxing and waning of symptoms across the lifespan.
- Excoriation (skin-picking) disorder, characterized by the repeated urge to pick at one's own skin, often to the extent that skin damage is caused by this disorder, coupled with attempts to decrease or stop the skin picking. The lifetime month prevalence for excoriation disorder in adults is around 1.4%, with the majority of those with the disorder being female (APA, 2013). This disorder is sometimes referred to as dermatillomania or pathologic skin picking. It has a typical onset during adolescence and a generally chronic course.
- Trichotillomania (hair-pulling disorder), characterized by recurrent hair pulling resulting in hair loss, coupled with attempts to decrease or stop hair pulling. The 12-month prevalence estimate for trichotillomania in adults and adolescents in the US is 1–2%, with females much more likely than males to be diagnosed at a ratio of 10:1 (APA, 2013). Like excoriation, its onset is typically during adolescence and it has a generally chronic course.

Overview of hoarding disorder

Hoarding disorder is characterized by a chronic difficulty parting with possessions, regardless of their actual value, a concomitant strong perceived need to save the items, and the experience of distress associated with discarding of the items. Over time, these symptoms result in the accumulation of a large number of items that can eventually overwhelm the person's living space. Nationally representative studies of the prevalence of hoarding disorder are not available, because the formal criteria for the disorder are relatively new (codified in DSM-5). However, community studies suggest a prevalence rate for clinically significant hoarding (not hoarding disorder per se) to be between 2% and 6% (APA, 2013). Hoarding behaviors usually begin early in life and commonly span well into later life (Dozier, Porter, & Ayers, 2015). In fact, the severity of hoarding usually increases with each decade of life (APA, 2013). The course of hoarding is typically chronic with remission being highly unlikely without intensive intervention.

There is an endless variety of objects that become the focus of individuals who hoard, including dolls, newspapers, books, clothes, cans, bicycles, action figures, and almost any object regardless of actual use or value. A minority of people with hoarding disorder include animals in their hoard, which often overrun the person's living space. Cats and dogs are the most common animals hoarded, but other animals may be involved as well, including rabbits, birds, pigs, chickens, snakes, and rodents. In some case, hundreds of animals have been discovered, with many of them being sick, diseased, malnourished, or dead. Animal feces and urine are commonly accumulated throughout the person's living space, including in his or her bed. Indeed, animal hoarding is most likely to result in squalor and extremely unsanitary and unsafe living conditions for the animals and for the person with hoarding disorder. Despite the clear inhumane and unsanitary conditions, animal hoarders typically do not recognize that they are not effectively taking care of their pets, and resist receiving help from others.

Presentation in older adults

While precise prevalence estimates of hoarding disorder among older adults are lacking, clinically significant hoarding behaviors are known to be high in certain older adult populations, including 25% of senior day-care residents and 15% of nursing home residents (see review by Ayers, Najmi, Mayes, & Dozier, 2015). Across the lifespan, individuals with hoarding disorder infrequently recognize the severity and impact of their hoarding behaviors, despite the negative effects being obvious to those who observe the person's living conditions.

Because the disorder generally has a chronic course without treatment, hoarding behavior usually worsens with advancing age. As the disorder persists over time, older adults with hoarding disorder usually amass larger and larger collections of "stuff" that increasingly make their living environment unsafe and unmanageable. Adults may also "normalize" their hoarding symptoms with advancing age, which makes accurate detection a challenge (Ayers et al., 2015). Aging has other synergistic effects on hoarding. From a qualitative study of 22 older adults with hoarding behaviors,

Eckfield and Wallhagen (2013) identified three themes that made the hoarding symptoms worse with advancing age:

- Declining health, strength, and mobility served as barriers to cleaning one's home and discarding items.
- Social losses, such as the death of a spouse, made hoarding worse especially in cases when the spouse was relied on to make decisions about what to keep or discard and to actually get rid of unwanted items. Having received inherited items from friends or family members who passed away also contributed to the worsening of hoarding in some cases, as the sheer amount of new possessions overwhelmed the person's ability to effectively dispose of the items.
- Moving to a new home or apartment made the situation worse in cases when all of the person's possessions were moved with him or her and placed into boxes that were never unpacked following the move.

Hoarding often has serious adverse health and functional consequences among older adults. It has been linked to social isolation, falls, poor hygiene, poor nutrition, food contamination, increased fire hazard, and increased risk for eviction and homelessness (Ayers et al., 2015). Emerging evidence strongly implicates impaired executive functioning among many older adults with hoarding problems (Ayers et al., 2015). As such, they are at risk of mismanaging both diet and medications, which can contribute to a worsening of coexisting medical problems. They are also at risk for other likely consequences of impaired executive functioning, including poor planning, organization, and decision-making. Older adults with hoarding disorder report having significantly more medical conditions than older adults without hoarding disorder. Hoarding severity also predicted the total number of medical conditions (Ayers, Iqbal, & Strickland, 2014). Yet sadly, many older adults with hoarding disorder do not receive adequate medical care. Many older adults with a long history of hoarding are also likely to have lost supportive relationships with friends and family members over the years, due to conflicts about the ongoing hoarding. This social aspect was illustrated in the case of Morris, presented at the beginning of the chapter. Many family members give up on older relatives with hoarding due to their own frustrations and inability to effectively intervene.

Theories of etiology

The etiology of hoarding disorder is multifaceted and complex. Hoarding behavior runs in families and likely has some genetic underpinnings. Psychological aspects include having excessive emotional attachments to the possessions, for example, reminding the person of a happier time in her life or of a specific person or relationship that is no longer present. As the individual focuses on the possessions, and avoids experiencing upsetting emotions, the hoarding behaviors become negatively reinforced. Hoarding behaviors are also positively reinforced when the person feels safe or comforted in possessing objects that she believes she needs to have. Impaired executive functioning is also implicated, which may lead to the person being unable to make decisions about how to effectively sort and discard his or her saved items. In the absence of decisions about what to keep or discard, items simply accumulate more and more over time. Yet another psychological factor is that some individuals hoard items because of concerns about financial insecurity. They believe the items may be of some monetary value in the future (for example, they could possibly sell the items) and worry that if they got rid of the items, they would not be able to afford to buy them again if needed.

Assessment

Assessment of hoarding is often challenging in the clinical setting with adults and older adults. A primary reason for this is that most adults and older adults do not spontaneously report their hoarding symptoms or behaviors (APA, 2013), because they view their collecting or saving behaviors as comforting and intentional, at least in many cases. In contrast, individuals with hoarding disorder often present clinically with signs and symptoms of other mental disorders as the stated reason for seeking treatment. In fact, comorbidity is the rule rather than the exception for hoarding disorder. About 75% of individuals with hoarding disorder have a comorbid anxiety or mood disorder. The most common comorbid disorders include major depression, social anxiety disorder, and generalized anxiety disorder (APA, 2013). Home visits are extremely valuable, if possible, to see the conditions first-hand. In addition, inclusion of family members, caregivers, and any involved social service agencies usually provides valuable information that may not be provided by the person with the disorder, and ensures different professionals are working in concert to help the individual who has hoarding problems.

An important differential diagnosis process for hoarding disorder is to discriminate it from OCD. About 20% of those with hoarding disorder also have OCD (APA, 2013). Another issue relates to neurocognitive disorders or dementia. Late-onset hoarding behaviors are known to sometimes emerge during the course of dementia (Ayers, Najmi, Howard, & Maddox, 2014). Likewise, individuals with hoarding disorder can, and do, develop dementia, which complicates the assessment.

There are no elder-specific measures for hoarding, but several general adult measures seem to be effective with older adults. The Saving Inventory-Revised (Frost, Steketee, & Grisham, 2004) includes 23 self-report items that assess hoarding severity in three domains: clutter, acquisition, and problems discarding items. This measure has demonstrated strong psychometric properties for use with older adults (Ayers, Dozier, & Mayes, 2017). The Hoarding Rating Scale (Tolin, Frost, & Steketee, 2010) is an even shorter measure, with only five items (administered either by an interviewer or self-report), used for brief screening. A more thorough clinician-administered questionnaire is the UCLA Hoarding Severity Scale (Saxena, Ayers, Dozier, & Maidment, 2015), which contains 10 items that tap core features of hoarding disorder and associated features of indecisiveness, perfectionism, procrastination, and task prolongation. The Clutter Image Rating (Frost, Steketee, Tolin, & Renaud, 2008) includes distinct pictures that represent varying levels of clutter in one's home. The respondent simply picks out the pictures that most closely resemble the clutter in distinct rooms (specifically, the living room, kitchen, bedroom) in his or her home. This particular measure may be useful for older adults with limited insight into the hoarding or cognitive impairment, and the measure has been specifically validated for use with older adults (Dozier & Ayers, 2015). Regarding cognitive impairment, cognitive screens should always be administered as part of a formal assessment of geriatric hoarding. In cases where impairment is suspected from a screen, formal neuropsychological assessment is warranted.

Interventions for hoarding disorder

Due to a recent upsurge in research on treatment of hoarding in older adults, several approaches appear to be modestly effective, at least preliminarily. The most common form of psychotherapy involves CBT-aligned exposure-based strategies, in which the person with hoarding problems learns to systematically sort and decide to give away items cluttering his or her living space. The general goal is for the older adult with hoarding to learn skills to continue to manage his or her home after the formal treatment ends. Exposure strategies seem more effective and preferred by older clients than traditional cognitive restructuring strategies in the classic CBT approach. In an open trial of manualized CBT for compulsive hoarding among older adults (N = 12), researchers found a meaningful reduction in hoarding symptom severity, although hoarding symptoms remained elevated and only 25% of the sample were classified as treatment responders (Ayers, Wetherell, Golshan, & Saxena, 2011).

To address the possible limiting effects of neurocognitive weaknesses among older adults with hoarding disorder, a novel approach called Cognitive Rehabilitation and Exposure/Sorting Therapy (CREST) has recently been developed and tested. CREST pairs cognitive rehabilitation strategies to improve executive functioning with traditional behavior therapy strategies that focus on exposure to the distress of discarding items and not acquiring new items. In an open trial of CREST among 11 older adults with hoarding disorder (Ayers, Saxena, et al., 2014), treatment resulted in decreased severity of hoarding symptoms at posttreatment, with large treatment effects. In fact, 8 of the participants (73%) were classified as treatment responders. This focus on neurocognitive deficits in behavioral therapy improved outcomes compared to the standard CBT trial. Most recently, in a randomized control trial with 58 older adults diagnosed with hoarding disorder (Ayers, Dozier, Twamley, et al., 2017), participants in the CREST condition showed greater decreases in hoarding behaviors compared to those receiving traditional case management (CM) services. Moreover, a greater proportion of CREST participants (78%) were classified as treatment responders compared to the case management group (28%). Despite some clear advantages for CREST, both treatments resulted in meaningful benefits and both had low attrition rates (70% of CM participants and 80% of CREST participants completed the six-month follow-up). We are enthused to see further evaluations of CREST and its derivatives and more widespread dissemination into diverse clinical and community settings. Adults and older adults who hoard animals are poorly represented in treatment studies (Ung, Dozier, Bratiotis, & Ayers, 2016). Thus, current knowledge is limited about the effectiveness of psychosocial interventions for this subset of individuals with hoarding disorder.

Medications are widely used to treat hoarding disorder in adults and older adults, although evidence for their effectiveness is mixed (Ayers et al., 2015) and medications are not considered a stand-alone approach. Antidepressants are the most common type of medications, especially the SSRIs. In most cases, medications are used as part of a larger approach, including psychotherapy.

A recent trend has been the creation of multiagency hoarding teams in cities in which multiple public groups work together to address hoarding, especially in cases when the hoarding poses a threat to the health of the individual or to the safety of the community. The common players include social service agencies, health departments, and fire departments. Animal control agencies may also become involved in cases of animal hoarding. Such interagency coordination takes resources, which is a major barrier to widespread implementation. Relatedly, an entire private industry has blossomed in recent years in which companies offer decluttering and clean-up services targeted toward those with problematic hoarding. As noted earlier, it can be challenging for many people with hoarding behaviors to willingly accept help from such services because of limited awareness of the problematic nature of the hoarding behaviors. In many cases, concerned family members or social service workers dictate that the older adults receive such cleaning services. However, in the absence of any psychological or behavioral changes, many people with hoarding disorder simply begin collecting items again after the forced clean-up is completed, as emotional factors are not addressed by this service. A definite problem is engaging older adults with hoarding in treatment (whether psychotherapeutic, pharmacological, or clean-up services) due their limited awareness, but in other cases older adults with hoarding shy away from treatment due to embarrassment, shame, and fear of being reported to authorities (Ayers, Najmi, et al., 2014), presumably due to the unsanitary or dangerous living conditions.

Post-Traumatic Stress Disorder (PTSD)

Although prior editions of the DSM included Post-Traumatic Stress Disorder (PTSD) as an anxiety disorder, the DSM-5 included PTSD in a new category called Trauma- and Stressor-Related Disorders, along with several other disorders, all linked by the exposure to traumatic or stressful events in one's environment. These disorders reflect the heterogeneity in maladaptive responses to traumatic events. Besides PTSD, the other disorders in the category include:

- Reactive attachment disorder, which is diagnosed in young children who do not form healthy emotional attachments with their primary caregivers, due to a history of being severely neglected or abused.
- Disinhibited social engagement disorder, which is also diagnosed in children who have experienced severe neglect, and is characterized by overly friendly social behavior with strangers and a lack of fearfulness when interacting with unfamiliar people, reflecting excessive social disinhibition.
- Acute stress disorder (ASD), characterized by similar symptoms to PTSD and must occur within one month of the traumatic event and resolve within that same one-month period. Should the symptoms persist for more than one month, the diagnosis is changed from ASD to PTSD.
- Adjustment disorders, characterized by clinically significant emotional or behaviors symptoms that develop in response to an identifiable stressor (not necessarily defined as a traumatic event).

Overview of PTSD

PTSD also occurs following exposure to a traumatic event, and is diagnosed when the individual experiences a broad range of upsetting and impairing symptoms. The disorder was significantly reconceptualized in the DSM-5, with some new diagnostic features. In the DSM-5, the symptoms of PTSD are grouped into four important clusters: intrusion symptoms, persistent avoidance, negative shifts in cognitions and mood, and alterations in arousal and reactivity. The essential features of PTSD are provided in Table 11.2. In addition to these major symptoms, formal diagnosis requires that the duration of symptoms is more than one month, that the

Table 11.2 Diagnostic features for Post-Traumatic Stress Disorder

1. Person was exposed to a traumatic event characterized as actual or threatened death, serious injury, or sexual violence, experienced in one of the following ways:
   * Direct experience
   * In-person witnessing
   * Learning about such exposure to close family member of friend
   * Repeated exposure to the details of the traumatic experience
2. Intrusion symptoms associated with the traumatic event, characterized by one or more of the following:
   * Intrusive recollections or memories of the event
   * Distressing dreams of the event
   * Acting or feeling as if the event was happening again
   * Intense psychological distress at reminders of the event
   * Physiological reactivity to exposure to reminders of the event
3. Persistent avoidance of stimuli associated with the traumatic event, characterized by one or more of the following:
   * Avoidance of memories, thoughts, or feelings associated with the traumatic event
   * Avoidance of external reminders of the traumatic event, for example, activities, places, or people associated with the event
4. Negative thoughts and mood associated with the traumatic event, characterized by two or more of the following:
   * Poorly recalled memories for important aspects of the event
   * Negative thoughts about oneself, other people, or the world
   * Faulty beliefs about the cause or sequelae of the traumatic event
   * Persistent emotional distress
   * Diminished interest in significant activities
   * Feeling detached or estranged from others
   * Inability to experience positive emotions
5. Arousal or reactivity associated with the traumatic event, characterized by two or more of the following:
   * Irritability or outbursts of anger
   * Reckless behaviors
   * Hypervigilance
   * Exaggerated startle response
   * Difficulty concentrating
   * Difficulty falling or staying asleep

Source: Adapted from the DSM-5 (APA, 2013).

symptoms cause significant distress or impairment, and that the symptoms are not attributable to the effects of a substances or a known medical condition.

During the diagnostic process, the clinician can specify whether dissociative symptoms are present or not. Additionally, although some symptoms of PTSD usually begin immediately after exposure to the event, it is possible that a full clinical picture is delayed for six months or longer. In this case, the clinician can use the diagnostic specifier of *delayed expression*.

In the US, the projected *lifetime* prevalence for adults (using DSM-IV criteria) is 8.7%. (APA, 2013). PTSD is more prevalent among women than men, across the lifespan, primarily due to greater exposure to sexual assault and interpersonal violence among women. Rates of PTSD are also elevated in individuals whose jobs or vocations place them at greater risk for exposure to traumatic events, including veterans, police officers, firefighters, paramedics, and other first responders (APA, 2013). Symptoms of PTSD typically fluctuate over time: About 50% of people with PTSD recover within the first three months. However, for a minority of individuals, PTSD becomes a chronic condition, lasting more than 50 years in some cases (APA, 2013). Comorbidity of PTSD with other mental disorders is common, most notably substance use disorders, depression, bipolar disorder, and anxiety disorders. PTSD is also with increased risk for suicidal ideation and suicide attempts (APA, 2013).

Recent data from a large national survey among adults in the US showed that there is a strong correlation between exposure to traumatic events and a host of negative physical health and mental health outcomes (Forman-Hoffman et al., 2016). Specifically, adults exposed to potentially traumatic events (PTEs) tended to be older, veterans, and non-Hispanic white, and they were more likely to have certain health conditions, such as asthma, high blood pressure, sinusitis, ulcer, and doctor-diagnosed anxiety and depression. Furthermore, adults exposed to one or more PTEs were more likely to engage in illicit drug use, binge drinking, and heavy drinking, and to have suicidal thoughts compared to adults without exposure to PTEs. Similarly, adults who had experienced PTEs were more likely to suffer from PTSD and major depression than those not exposed. As such, trauma exposure and PTSD are associated with significant personal and social costs.

Presentation in older adults

Across several studies, the prevalence of diagnosable PTSD appears to be lower in older adults than in younger adults. For example, data from a large, representative study of PTSD across the adult lifespan in the US showed that the overall prevalence of past-year PTSD was lower among older adults (2.6%) compared to younger adults (4.3%). Additionally, older adults reported experiencing fewer traumatic events and fewer symptoms of PTSD, and had lower odds of psychiatric comorbidity than younger adults (Reynolds, Pietrzak, Mackenzie, Chou, & Sareen, 2016).

In a large study of the past-year prevalence of PTSD across older adulthood (Reynolds et al., 2015), a similar pattern emerged (see data presented in Figure 11.1). As can be seen, rates of PTSD among were highest in the 55-64-year-old group and were much lower in the 65-74 group, the 75-84 group, and the 85+

group. Women had higher rates in each of these age-groupings with the exception of the oldest group (85+).

PTSD can develop at any point in the lifespan, subject to exposure to severe and harrowing trauma(s). However, not everyone (whether young or old) who experiences a traumatic event subsequently develops PTSD. Many people are remarkably resilient in the face of extreme duress and catastrophe. In fact, in a study of older veterans in the US, about 70% of the veterans who endured a significant number of traumatic events in their lives (average of 5.5 traumas) were classified as psychologically *resilient* (Pietrzak & Cook, 2013). Across the lifespan, the strongest predictors of PTSD are the severity of the traumatic event and a lack of social support, both before and after the event.

According to the DSM-5 (APA, 2013), PTSD symptoms among older adults may be exacerbated by worsening health problems, social isolation, and cognitive decline. The DSM-5 also notes that, among older adults, subthreshold presentations are more likely than full PTSD, although these subthreshold symptoms confer significant functional impairment, and thus should be taken seriously.

In older adults, one can differentiate three kinds of onset of PTSD. First, PTSD can develop after exposure to traumatic experience in the recent past. Second, in chronic PTSD, the symptoms are present from the time of the traumatic exposure, which can be decades ago. Third, PTSD symptoms can become reactivated by a new traumatic event, after a long period of time without active symptoms (Van Zelst, De Beurs, Beekman, Deeg, & Van Dyck, 2003). Some evidence suggests that one's age at trauma exposure may play a role in subsequent symptomatology. For example, older adults who experienced their most distressing traumatic event during childhood exhibited more severe PTSD symptoms and lower subjective happiness compared with older adults who experienced their traumatic event after transition to adulthood (Ogle, Rubin, & Siegler, 2013).

PTSD symptoms in older people have many known adverse consequences including impaired cognitive functioning across a broad range of domains compared to older adults without PTSD (Schuitevoerder et al., 2013), and lower life satisfaction, greater disability, and greater dissatisfaction with their health care compared to older persons drawn from the general population (Van Zelst, De Beurs, Beekman, Deeg, & Van Dyck, 2006). PTSD symptoms are also associated with poorer physical functioning and increased risk for several diseases. According to Pietrzak, Goldstein, Southwick, and Grant (2012), older adults with PTSD were more likely to have been diagnosed with hypertension, angina pectoris, tachycardia, other heart disease, stomach ulcer, gastritis, and arthritis, compared to respondents who experienced one or more traumatic life events but who did not meet lifetime criteria for full or subclinical PTSD.

Although women have higher rates of PTSD than men across much of the adult lifespan, studies specifically focusing on the unique experiences of older women with PTSD are notably sparse. In one of the few large studies in this area (including a representative sample of over 3,300 community-residing older women), 7% of the women reported a lifetime history of physical assault, 3.6% reported a history of sexual assault, and 2.6% reported a history of both physical and sexual assaults (Cook, Pilver, Dinnen, Schnurr, & Hoff, 2013). Although many of these interpersonal assaults were reported to have occurred many decades ago, many of these women reported the persistence of high levels of PTSD symptoms, and other mental health problems, into later life.

Theories of etiology

PTSD is often conceptualized as a normal response to a traumatic event that continues over an extended time period, beyond its usefulness. The two most prominent psychosocial theories of PTSD are the *cognitive model of PTSD* (Ehlers & Clark, 2000) and the *emotional processing theory of PTSD* (Foa, Hembree, & Rothbaum, 2007).

In the cognitive model, PTSD symptoms are believed to become persistent when individuals process the traumatic event and/or its sequelae in a way that leads to a sense of serious, current threat. According to the model, two key processes are believed to lead to this sense of current threat. First, people with chronic PTSD show idiosyncratic, often very negative and pessimistic, personal meanings or appraisals of the trauma, for example, believing that "bad things always happen to me," "I'll forever be damaged by the trauma," and "nobody will be able to help me." Second, the nature of the traumatic memories explains the occurrence of reexperiencing symptoms, in that the memories are poorly elaborated and inadequately integrated into an appropriate context (Ehlers & Clark, 2000). Furthermore, when individuals with PTSD perceive a significant current threat and their accompanying symptoms, they tend to engage in a series of behaviors that have positive short-term effects, but in the long term are actually maladaptive in that they directly produce more PTSD symptoms or they prevent individuals from changing their appraisals about the traumatic event and its consequences. Examples of some maladaptive responses include thought suppression, selective attention to threat cues, ruminating about the event, avoiding reminders of the trauma, using alcohol and drugs to numb one's feelings, giving up or avoiding positive activities, and engaging in excessive safety-seeking behaviors, for example, by being hypervigilant.

According to the emotional processing model (Foa et al., 2007), PTSD develops due to fear conditioning. Specifically, PTSD develops from deficits in extinction of a learned response. Moreover, an overgeneralized fear response to perceived threats maintains the trauma symptoms. Avoidance also maintains the fear response and prevents appropriate emotional processing. For example, a Marine who felt scared of debris on the side of a road (representing a possible explosive device) in a war zone in Iraq has a completely justifiable fear. However, if this Marine experiences the same fear when driving on a road in rural Colorado (where roadside bombs are exceptionally rare), the fear would be characterized as unrealistic and excessive. In this example, to the extent that the Marine subsequently avoids driving on roads in the US (and outside of dangerous areas), the fear response would be strengthened due to negative reinforcement. As we describe later in this chapter, both of these influential etiological models of PTSD suggest a number of psychotherapeutic strategies to reduce symptoms and distress associated with PTSD.

Assessment

Several solid screening and assessment measures for PTSD are available, including some that have been updated to be consistent with DSM-5. Although the measures discussed in this section are widely (and effectively) used with older adults, there are no elder-specific assessment measures for PTSD or trauma symptoms. Among the most widely used measures is the PTSD Checklist for DSM-5 (PCL-5; Weathers, Litz, et al., 2013), which is available from the National Center for PTSD. The PCL-5 includes 20 self-report items that each tap a specific DSM-5 symptom of PTSD. Respondents rate the extent to which each symptom has been bothering them in the past month, answering on a five-point Likert-type response format (0 = "Not at all," 2 = "Moderately," and 4 = "Extremely"). The total score for the measure is calculated as the sum of the scores for the 20 items, and thus ranges from 0 to 80. Scale scores can also be computed for each of the four major symptom clusters. It is possible that lower cut scores on the PCL-5, and other PTSD screening instruments, may be needed to help identify probable PTSD in older adults.

Should a respondent flag as having significant symptoms on the PCL-5, a more thorough assessment is warranted to finalize the diagnostic process. The gold standard structured interview for diagnosis of PTSD is the Clinician-Administered PTSD Scale for DSM-5 (CAPS-5, Weathers, Blake, et al., 2013), also available from the National Center for PTSD. Both the PCL-5 and the CAPS-5 are widely used in the Veterans Affairs (VA) health care system, with a wealth of evidence for their clinical utility with older adults. Another structured interview option is the SCID-5, which has a full PTSD module based on DSM-5 criteria.

A potential complication of assessment of PTSD with older adults is that some older adults who have experienced significant trauma do not recognize the adverse physical or psychological consequences of the trauma and often do not proactively disclose these experiences to their health care providers (Cook & Simiola, 2017). As such, routine and sensitive screening is advised in clinical settings. Another potential complication is that some symptoms of PTSD may be misattributed or misinterpreted by the client and/or the clinician. For example, sleep problems (actually due to PTSD) could be misattributed to somatic disease, and problems with concentration, attention, and memory (actually due to PTSD) could be incorrectly attributed to cognitive impairment. Finally, during the assessment of PTSD and trauma symptoms among older adults, a routine screening for suicidality should always be included, since elevated risk of self-harm is evident in adults and older adults with significant symptoms of PTSD.

Interventions for PTSD

To date, there are no large, randomized controlled trials published on the efficacy of PTSD treatment specifically with older adults (see review by Dinnen, Simiola, & Cook, 2015), although some case reports, case series, pilot studies, and small randomized studies have appeared in recent literature. The clinical literature suggests that currently well-validated treatments for PTSD among adults can be adapted to meet the needs of older adults in treatment. Indeed, in recent years, the field has come a long way in developing several CBT-based, exposure-oriented psychological treatments that are known to be evidence-based and effective for PTSD (see Schnyder & Cloitre, 2015; also see Böttche, Kuwert, & Knaevelsrud, 2012). These treatments are sometimes collectively grouped under a larger rubric termed *trauma-focused cognitive-behavioral therapy* (TF-CBT).

Two of the most common TF-CBT approaches are Prolonged Exposure (PE) and Cognitive Processing Therapy (CPT). PE is a psychotherapy based on the emotional processing theory of PTSD, described earlier in this chapter. Emotional processing refers to the modification of memory structures that underlie emotions. Effective emotional processing requires the activation of the traumatic memories and the learning of corrective information. Typical components of PE include breathing retraining, basic psychoeducation about trauma and its impacts, imaginal exposure to the traumatic memories, and in vivo exposure to cues or triggers of the trauma, often conducted in between sessions. In a pilot study among older veterans, Thorp, Stein, Jeste, and Wetherell (2012) reported that conducting PE was feasible and efficacious. In contrast, CPT focuses on cognitive interventions, for example, Socratic questioning to help the client learn to identify and challenge distorted or unhelpful beliefs about the traumatic event and its aftermath, in conjunction with typical exposure-based strategies.

Both PE and CPT require exposure to one's traumatic memories. As such, clinicians using these modalities are highly aware that avoidance contributes to the problem. Thus, avoidance is targeted as a behavior to be reduced or eliminated. George, in the case example presented at the beginning of this chapter, has been using alcohol (and likely other means) to avoid his thoughts and feelings about his traumatic experiences that happened decades ago. Indeed, for some older individuals with PTSD, the index traumatic event(s) may have occurred 50 or 60 years earlier in life.

One challenge associated with these exposure-based treatments is keeping the clients engaged in the treatment and preventing premature dropout. As you can imagine, for those who have spent years, in some cases decades, avoiding their thoughts and feelings about their traumatic experiences, exposure treatments are often very painful, scary, and threatening. It is critically important that the clients learn and practice self-soothing and self-care skills to help them manage their distress during the early stages of emotional processing in psychotherapy. Psychoeducation is also important to help the client understand that avoidance of painful thoughts and feelings feels good in the short run, but it contributes to unresolved trauma symptoms in the long run. According to Schnyder and Cloitre (2015), the evidence-based psychotherapies for PTSD have several features in common, including:

- psychoeducation,
- teaching emotion regulation and coping skills,
- imaginal exposure to traumatic memories,
- cognitive processing and restructuring,
- a focus on emotions common among trauma sufferers (e.g., fear, shame, guilt, anger, grief, and sadness),
- enhanced memory processes, including creation of a consistent trauma narrative.

Treatment considerations among older adults may also focus on the presence of cognitive decline, such as impairments in memory, learning, attention, and concentration. To deal with the presence of cognitive impairments, one can modify treatment by slowing the pace of treatment, repeating the material, presenting information in various ways, and focusing on one topic at a time to optimize results (O'Connor & Elklit, 2015). Caregivers can also play an important role in the treatment for an older adult with cognitive or physical impairments; caregivers can provide collateral information, and help with a wide range of activities, for example, to assist in treatment appointments or to take care of transportation (Cook & O'Donnell, 2005). Despite several psychotherapeutic approaches that are likely effective, not all older adults with PTSD receive appropriate services. For example, among older veterans recently diagnosed with PTSD in the US VA health care system, the oldest veterans (80-years-old and older) were at increased risk of not receiving timely and appropriate help (Smith, Cook, Pietrzak, Hoff, & Harpaz-Rotem, 2016). Although the extant psychotherapy studies generally show promise among older adults with PTSD, noticeable gaps in this emerging literature exist—namely, few studies with cultural and ethnic minority older adults, women, those with significant cognitive impairments, and those in the oldest-old age group (85+) (Dinnen et al., 2015).

Finally, antidepressant medications (including SSRIs and SNRIs) have moderate effects in some adults with PTSD, but most do not have full recovery with medications alone. Moreover, studies in which these medications have been tested have infrequently included older adults, so the generalization of these findings is unknown. Although clinical use of these medications with older adults is not uncommon, we recommend psychotherapy as the first-line treatment either alone or in combination with medication.

Summary and Conclusions

Three categories of disorders were addressed in this chapter. Anxiety disorders are the most common type of mental disorders found in older adults. A variety of assessment tools are now available, including two elder-specific measures, which can be used to effectively identify anxiety in older adults and to track treatment. Researchers have generated empirically supported treatments for a wide range of anxiety disorders among older adults, and research in this area continues to progress rapidly. Likewise, research on hoarding disorder and on PTSD in older adults is also growing rapidly, generating strategies for assessment and intervention that are promising but require validation from larger randomized clinical trials that include diverse types of older adults.

Critical Thinking / Discussion Questions

1   In your clinical practice, you encounter a 75-year-old man with a lifelong history of severe social anxiety. For years, he has coped with this anxiety by drinking heavily when in social situations. But recently he has been experiencing physical problems due to his long-term drinking and his doctor has advised him that he must stop drinking. He's seriously thinking about going to detox. What strategies and approaches would you use the support this client's emerging sobriety and help him manage his intense anxiety?

2   Your older client with hoarding disorder tells you her children are "forcing" her to have her house cleaned up by a local cleaning crew. She tearfully admits that she

needs some help to reduce clutter in her home, but she also says that her children have no right to force a clean-up on her and she won't be home when the cleaners come: "They will have to do it without me." What would be your plan of action to intervene in this situation, with the client and with her children?

3 An older family member who has served on the battlefield in the Gulf War has hinted to you, over time, that he witnessed horrible events that still plague him. However, he refuses to talk about his wartime experiences with you, or with anyone else in the family, becoming angry when the topic is broached. Based on what you know about the problems associated with avoidance, and the many promising treatments for PTSD, what advice would you offer to your family member to help him engage in treatment?

Website Resources

Anxiety and Depression Association of America
http://www.adaa.org
National Center for PTSD
http://www.ptsd.va.gov
National Child Traumatic Stress Network
http://www.nctsn.org

References

American Psychiatric Association. (2013). *Diagnostic and statistical manual of mental disorders* (5th ed.). Arlington, VA: Author.

Ayers, C. R., Dozier, M. E., & Mayes, T. L. (2017). Psychometric evaluation of the Saving Inventory-Revised in older adults. *Clinical Gerontologist, 40*(3), 191–196. 10.1080/07317115.2016.1267056

Ayers, C. R, Dozier, M. E., Twamley, E. T., Granholm, E., Saxena, S., Mayes, T. L., & Wetherell, J. L. (2017). Cognitive rehabilitation and exposure/sorting therapy for hoarding disorder among older adults: A randomized controlled trial. *The Journal of Clinical Psychiatry.* Advance online publication. doi: 10.4088/JCP.16m11072

Ayers, C. R., Iqbal, Y., & Strickland, K. (2014). Medical conditions in geriatric hoarding disorder patients. *Aging & Mental Health, 18*, 148–151.

Ayers, C. R., Najmi, S., Howard, I., & Maddox, M. (2014). Hoarding in older adults. In R. O. Frost & G. Steketee (Eds.), *The Oxford handbook of hoarding and acquiring* (pp. 341–352). New York, NY: Oxford University Press.

Ayers, C. R., Najmi, S., Mayes, T. L., & Dozier, M. E. (2015). Hoarding disorder in older adulthood. *American Journal of Geriatric Psychiatry, 23*, 416–422.

Ayers, C. R., Saxena, S., Espejo, E., Twamley, E. W., Granholm, E., & Wetherell, J. L. (2014). Novel treatment for geriatric hoarding disorder: An open trial of cognitive rehabilitation paired with behavior therapy. *American Journal of Geriatric Psychiatry, 22*, 248–252.

Ayers, C., Sorrell, J., Thorp, S., & Wetherell, J. (2007). Evidence-based psychological treatments for late-life anxiety. *Psychology and Aging, 22*(1), 8–17.

Ayers, C. R., Wetherell, J. L., Golshan, S., & Saxena, S. (2011). Cognitive-behavioral therapy for geriatric compulsive hoarding. *Behavioral Research and Therapy, 49*, 689–694.

Baxter, A. J., Scott, K. M., Vos, T., & Whiteford, H. A. (2013). Global prevalence of anxiety disorders: a systematic review and meta-regression. *Psychological Medicine, 43,* 897–910.

Beck, J. S. (2011). *Cognitive behavior therapy: Basics and beyond* (2nd ed.). New York, NY: Guilford Press.

Beck, A. T., Epstein, N., Brown, G., & Steer, R. (1988). An inventory for measuring clinical anxiety: Psychometric properties. *Journal of Consulting and Clinical Psychology, 56,* 893–897.

Beekman, A. T. F., De Beurs, E., Van Balkom, A. J. L. M., Deeg, D. J. H., Van Dyck, R., & Van Tilburg, W. (2000). Anxiety and depression in later life: Co-occurrence and communality of risk factors. *American Journal of Psychiatry, 157,* 89–95.

Bolghan-Abadi, M., Segal, D. L., Coolidge, F. L., & Gottschling, J. (2013). Persian version of the Geriatric Anxiety Scale: Translation and preliminary psychometric properties among Iranian older adults. *Aging & Mental Health, 17,* 896–900.

Borkovec, T. D., Alcaine, O., & Behar, E. (2004). Avoidance theory of worry and generalized anxiety disorder. In R. G. Turk, C. L. Turk, & D. S. Mennin (Eds.), *Generalized anxiety disorder* (pp. 77–108). New York, NY: Guilford.

Böttche, M., Kuwert, P., & Knaevelsrud, C. (2012). Posttraumatic stress disorder in older adults: An overview of characteristics and treatment approaches. *International Journal of Geriatric Psychiatry, 27,* 230–239. doi:10.1002/gps.2725

Bower, E. S., & Wetherell, J. L. (2015). Late-life anxiety disorders. In P. A. Lichtenberg & B. T. Mast (Eds.), *APA handbook of clinical geropsychology. Vol. 2: Assessment, treatment, and issues of later life* (pp. 49–77). Washington, DC: American Psychological Association.

Brenes, G. A., Guralnik, J. A., Williamson, J. D., Friend, L. P., Simpson, C., Simonsick, E. M., & Penninx, B. W. J. H. (2005). The influence of anxiety on progression of disability. *Journal of the American Geriatrics Society, 53,* 34–39.

Brown, T. A., & Barlow, D. H. (2014). *Anxiety and related disorders interview schedule for DSM-5 (ADIS-5), Clinician manual.* New York, NY: Oxford University Press.

Bryant, C., Jackson, H., & Ames, D. (2008). The prevalence of anxiety in older adults: Methodological issues and a review of the literature. *Journal of Affective Disorders, 109,* 233–250.

Cook, J. M., & O'Donnell, C. (2005). Assessment and psychological treatment of posttraumatic stress disorder in older adults. *Journal of Geriatric Psychiatry and Neurology, 18*(2), 61–71.

Cook, J. M., Pilver, C., Dinnen, S., Schnurr, P. P., & Hoff, R. (2013). Prevalence of physical and sexual assault and mental health disorders in older women: Findings from a nationally representative sample. *American Journal of Geriatric Psychiatry, 21,* 877–886.

Cook, J. M., & Simiola, V. (2017). Trauma and PTSD in older adults: Prevalence, course, concomitants and clinical considerations. *Current Opinion in Psychology, 14,* 1–4.

Coolidge, F. L., Segal, D. L., Hook, J. N., & Stewart, S. (2000). Personality disorders and coping among anxious older adults. *Journal of Anxiety Disorders, 14,* 157–172.

Deacon, B., Lickel, J., & Abramowitz, J. S. (2008). Medical utilization across the anxiety disorders. *Journal of Anxiety Disorders, 22,* 344–350.

Dinnen, S., Simiola, V., & Cook, J. M. (2015). Post-traumatic stress disorder in older adults: a systematic review of the psychotherapy treatment literature. *Aging & Mental Health, 19,* 144–150.

Dozier, M. E., & Ayers, C. R. (2015). Validation of the Clutter Image Rating in older adults with hoarding disorder. *International Psychogeriatrics, 27,* 769–776. doi: 10.1017/S1041610214002403

Dozier, M. E., Porter, B., & Ayers, C. R. (2015). Age of onset and progression of hoarding symptoms in older adults with hoarding disorder. *Aging & Mental Health, 20,* 736–742.

Eckfield, M. B., & Wallhagen, M. I. (2013). The synergistic effect of growing older with hoarding behaviors. *Clinical Nursing Research, 22,* 475–491.

Ehlers, A., & Clark, D. M. (2000). A cognitive model of posttraumatic stress disorder. *Behaviour Research and Therapy, 38*, 319–345.

Fingerhood, M. (2000). Substance abuse in older people. *Journal of the American Geriatrics Society, 48*, 985–995.

First, M. B., Williams, J. B. W., Karg, R. S., & Spitzer, R. L. (2016). *Structured Clinical Interview for DSM-5 Disorders: Clinician Version (SCID-5-CV)*. Arlington, VA: American Psychiatric Association.

Foa, E. B., Hembree, E. A., & Rothbaum, B. O. (2007). *Prolonged exposure therapy for PTSD*. Oxford, England: Oxford University Press.

Forman-Hoffman, V. L., Bose, J., Batts, K. R., Glasheen, C., Hirsch, E., Karg, R. S., ... Hedden, S. L. (2016). *Correlates of lifetime exposure to one or more potentially traumatic events and subsequent posttraumatic stress among adults in the United States: Results from the Mental Health Surveillance Study, 2008–2012* (Data Review). Center for Behavioral Health Statistics and Quality. Retrieved from: http://www.samhsa.gov/data/sites/default/files/CBHSQ-DR-PTSDtrauma-2016/CBHSQ-DR-PTSDtrauma-2016.htm

Fox, L. S., & Knight, B. G. (2005). The effects of anxiety on attentional processes in older adults. *Aging & Mental Health, 9*, 585–593.

Frost, R. O., Steketee, G., & Grisham, J. (2004). Measurement of compulsive hoarding: Saving Inventory-revised. *Behaviour Research and Therapy, 42*, 1163–1182.

Frost, R. O., Steketee, G., Tolin, D. F, & Renaud, S. (2008). Development and validation of the Clutter Image Rating. *Journal of Psychopathology and Behavioral Assessment, 30*, 193–203.

Fuentes, K., & Cox, B. J. (2000). Assessment of anxiety in older adults: A community-based survey and comparison with younger adults. *Behaviour Research and Therapy, 38*, 297–309.

Gatti, A., Gottschling, J., Brugnera, A., Adorni, R., Zarbo, C., Compare, A., & Segal, D. L. (in press). An investigation of the psychometric properties of the Geriatric Anxiety Scale (GAS) in an Italian sample of community-dwelling older adults. *Aging & Mental Health*.

Gellatly, R., & Beck, A. T. (2016). Catastrophic thinking: A transdiagnostic process across psychiatric disorders. *Cognitive Therapy and Research, 40*, 441–452.

Gottschling, J., Segal, D. L., Häusele, C., Spinath, F. M., & Stoll, G. (2016). Assessment of anxiety in older adults: Translation and psychometric evaluation of the German version of the Geriatric Anxiety Scale (GAS). *Journal of Psychopathology and Behavioral Assessment, 38*, 136–148.

Gould, R. L., Coulson, M. C., & Howard, R. J. (2012). Efficacy of cognitive behavioral therapy for anxiety disorders in older people: A meta-analysis and meta-regression of randomized controlled trials. *Journal of the American Geriatrics Society, 60*, 218–229.

Gould, C., Segal, D. L., Yochim, B. P., Pachana, N. A., Byrne, G. J., & Beaudreau, S. A. (2014). Measuring anxiety in late life: A psychometric examination of the Geriatric Anxiety Inventory and Geriatric Anxiety Scale. *Journal of Anxiety Disorders, 28*, 804–811.

Grenier, S., Preville, M., & Boyer, R. (2011). The impact of DSM-IV symptom and clinical significant criteria on the prevalence estimates of subthreshold and threshold anxiety in the older adult population. *American Journal of Geriatric Psychiatry, 19*, 316–326.

Jeon, H-S., Dunkle, R., & Roberts, B. L. (2006). Worries of the oldest old. *Health and Social Work, 31*, 256–265.

Kessler, R. C., Berglund, P., Demler, O., Jin, R., Merikangas, K. R., & Walters, E. E. (2005). Lifetime prevalence and age-of-onset distributions of DSM-IV disorders in the National Comorbidity Survey Replication (NCS-R). *Archives of General Psychiatry, 62*, 593–602.

King-Kallimanis, B., Gum, A., & Kohn, R. (2009). Comorbidity of depressive and anxiety disorders for older Americans in the National Comorbidity Survey-Replication. *American Journal of Geriatric Psychiatry, 17*, 782–792.

Klainin-Yobas, P., Oo, W. N., Yew, P. Y. S., & Lau, Y (2015). Effects of relaxation interventions on depression and anxiety among older adults: a systematic review. *Aging & Mental Health, 19*, 1043–1055.

Kogan, J. N., Edelstein, B. A., & McKee, D. R. (2000). Assessment of anxiety in older adults: current status. *Journal of Anxiety Disorders, 14*, 109–132.

Laidlaw, K. (2015). *CBT for older people: An introduction.* Thousand Oaks, CA: Sage.

Mahoney, C. T., Segal, D. L., & Coolidge, F. L. (2015). Anxiety sensitivity, experiential avoidance, and mindfulness among younger and older adults: Age differences in risk factors for anxiety symptoms. *International Journal of Aging and Human Development, 81*, 217–240.

Meyer, T. J., Miller, M. L., Metzger, R. L., & Borkovec, T. D. (1990). Development and validation of the Penn State Worry Questionnaire. *Behavior Research and Therapy, 28*, 487–495.

Mohlman, J. (2004). Psychosocial treatment of late-life generalized anxiety disorder: Current status and future directions. *Clinical Psychology Review, 24*, 149–169.

Mohlman, J., Gorenstein, E. E., Kleber, M., DeJesus, M., Gorman, J. M., & Papp, L. A. (2003). Standard and enhanced cognitive-behavioral therapy for late-life generalized anxiety disorder. *American Journal of Geriatric Psychiatry, 11*, 24–32.

Mueller, A. E., Segal, D. L., Gavett, B., Marty, M. A., Yochim, B., June, A., & Coolidge, F. L. (2015). Geriatric Anxiety Scale: Item response theory analysis, differential item functioning, and creation of a ten-item short form (GAS-10). *International Psychogeriatrics, 27*, 1099–1111.

Nordhus, I. H., & Pallesen, S. (2003). Psychological treatment of late-life anxiety: An empirical review. *Journal of Consulting and Clinical Psychology, 71*, 643–651.

O'Connor, M., & Elklit, A. (2015). Treating PTSD symptoms in older adults. In U. Schnyder & M. Cloitre (Eds.), *Evidence based treatments for trauma-related psychological disorders* (pp. 381–397). Geneva, Switzerland: Springer.

Ogle, C. M., Rubin, D., & Siegler, I. C. (2013). The impact of the developmental timing of trauma exposure on PTSD symptoms and psychosocial functioning among older adults. *Developmental Psychology, 49*, 2191–2200. doi: 10.1037/a0031985

Pachana, N., Byrne, G., Siddle, H., Koloski, N., Harley, E., & Arnold, E. (2007). Development and validation of the Geriatric Anxiety Inventory. *International Psychogeriatrics, 19*, 103–114.

Pietrzak, R. H., & Cook, J. M. (2013). Psychological resilience in older U.S. veterans: Results from the National Health and Resilience in Veterans Study. *Depression and Anxiety, 30*, 432–443.

Pietrzak, R. H., Goldstein, R. B., Southwick, S. M., & Grant, B. F. (2012). Physical health conditions associated with posttraumatic stress disorder in U.S. older adults: Results from wave 2 of the National Epidemiologic Survey on Alcohol and Related Conditions. *American Journal of Geriatric Psychiatry, 60*, 296–303.

Price, R. B., & Mohlman, J. (2007). Inhibitory control and symptom severity in late life generalized anxiety disorder. *Behaviour Research and Therapy, 45*, 2628–2639.

Reynolds, K., Pietrzak, R. H., El-Gabalawy, R., Mackenzie, C. S., & Sareen, J. (2015). Prevalence of psychiatric disorders in US older adults: Findings from a nationally representative survey. *World Psychiatry, 14*(1), 74–81.

Reynolds, K., Pietrzak, R. H., Mackenzie, C. S., Chou, K. L., & Sareen, J. (2016). Post-traumatic stress disorder across the adult lifespan: Findings from a nationally representative survey. *American Journal of Geriatric Psychiatry, 24*, 81–93.

Saxena, S., Ayers, C. R., Dozier, M. E., & Maidment, K. M. (2015). The UCLA Hoarding Severity Scale: Development and validation. *Journal of Affective Disorders, 175*, 488–493.

Schnyder, U., & Cloitre, M. (Eds.) (2015). *Evidence based treatments for trauma-related psychological disorders.* Geneva, Switzerland: Springer.

Schuitevoerder, S., Rosen, J. W., Twamley, E. W., Ayers, C. R., Sones, H., Lohr, J. B., ... Thorp, S. R. (2013). A meta-analysis of cognitive functioning in older adults with PTSD. *Journal of Anxiety Disorders, 27*, 550–558.

Schuurmans, J., Comijs, H. C., Beekman, A. T. F., Deeg, D. J. H., Emmelkamp, P. M. G., & Van Dyke, R. (2005). The outcome of anxiety disorders in older people at 6-year follow-up: results from the Longitudinal Aging Study Amsterdam. *Acta Psychiatrica Scandinavica, 111*, 420–428.

Segal, D. L. & Feliciano, L. (2011). Relaxation training. In Kreutzer, J. S., DeLuca, J., & Caplan, B. (Eds.), *Encyclopedia of clinical neuropsychology* (pp. 2149–2150). New York, NY: Springer.

Segal, D. L., June, A., Payne, M., Coolidge, F. L., & Yochim, B. (2010). Development and initial validation of a self-report assessment tool for anxiety among older adults: The Geriatric Anxiety Scale. *Journal of Anxiety Disorders, 24*, 709–714.

Seignourel, P. J., Kunik, M. E., Snow, L., Wilson, N., & Stanley, M. (2008). Anxiety in dementia: A critical review. *Clinical Psychology Review, 28*, 1071–1082.

Smith, N. B., Cook, J. M., Pietrzak, R., Hoff, R., & Harpaz-Rotem, I. (2016). Mental health treatment for older veterans recently diagnosed with PTSD. *American Journal of Geriatric Psychiatry, 24*, 201–212.

Spielberger, C., Gorsuch, R., Lushene, R., Vagg, P. R. & Jacobs, G. A. (1983). *Manual of the State-Trait Anxiety Inventory.* Palo Alto, CA: Consulting Psychologists Press.

Streiner, D. L., Cairney, J., & Veldhuizen, S. (2006). The epidemiology of psychological problems in the elderly. *Canadian Journal of Psychiatry, 51*, 185–191.

Teachman, B. A., Siedlecki, K. L., & Magee, J. C. (2007). Aging and symptoms of anxiety and depression: Structural invariance of the tripartite model. *Psychology and Aging, 22*, 160–170.

Thorp, S. R., Stein, M. B., Jeste, D. V., & Wetherell, J. L. (2012). Prolonged Exposure therapy for older Veterans with posttraumatic stress disorder: A pilot study. *American Journal of Geriatric Psychiatry, 20*, 276–280.

Tolin, D. F., Frost, R. O., & Steketee, G. (2010). A brief interview for assessing compulsive hoarding: The Hoarding Rating Scale-Interview. *Psychiatry Research, 178*, 147–152.

Ung, J., Dozier, M. E., Bratiotis, C., & Ayers, C. R. (2016). An exploratory investigation of animal hoarding symptoms in a sample of adults diagnosed with hoarding disorder. *Journal of Clinical Psychology.* Advance online publication. doi: 10.1002/jclp.22417

Van Hout, H. P., Beekman, A. F., De Beurs, E. Comijs, H., Van Marwijk, H., De Haan, M., & Deeg, D. J. (2004). Anxiety and the risk of death in older men and women. *British Journal of Psychiatry, 185*, 399–404.

Van Zelst, W. H., De Beurs, E., Beekman, A. T. F., Deeg, D. J. H., & Van Dyck, R. (2003). Prevalence and risk factors of Posttraumatic Stress Disorder in older adults. *Psychotherapy and Psychosomatics, 72*, 333–342.

Van Zelst, W. H., De Beurs, E., Beekman, A. T. F., Deeg, D. J. H., & Van Dyck, R. (2006). Well-being, physical functioning, and use of health services in the elderly with PTSD and subthreshold PTSD. *International Journal of Geriatric Psychiatry, 21*, 180–188.

Weathers, F. W., Blake, D. D., Schnurr, P. P., Kaloupek, D. G., Marx, B. P., & Keane, T. M. (2013). *The Clinician-Administered PTSD Scale for DSM-5 (CAPS-5).* Interview available from the National Center for PTSD at www.ptsd.va.gov.

Weathers, F. W., Litz, B. T., Keane, T. M., Palmieri, P. A., Marx, B. P., & Schnurr, P. P. (2013). *The PTSD Checklist for DSM-5 (PCL-5)*. Scale available from the National Center for PTSD at www.ptsd.va.gov.

Wetherell, J. L., & Gatz, M. (2005). The Beck Anxiety Inventory in older adults with generalized anxiety disorder. *Journal of Psychopathology and Behavioral Assessment, 27*, 17–24.

Wetherell, J. L., Lenze, E. J., & Stanley, M. A. (2005). Evidence-based treatment of geriatric anxiety disorders. *Psychiatric Clinics of North America, 28*, 871–896.

Wetherell, J. L., LeRoux, H., & Gatz, M. (2003). *DSM-IV* criteria for Generalized Anxiety Disorder in older adults: Distinguishing the worried from the well. *Psychology and Aging, 18*, 622–627.

Wetherell, J. L., Petkus, A. J., McChesney, K., Stein, M. B., Judd, P. H., Rockwell, E., ... Patterson, T. L. (2009). Older adults are less accurate than younger adults at identifying symptoms of anxiety and depression. *Journal of Nervous and Mental Disease, 197*, 623–626.

Wetherell, J. L., Sorrell, J. T., Thorp, S. R., & Patterson, T. L. (2005). Psychological interventions for late-life anxiety: A review and early lessons from the CALM Study. *Journal of Geriatric Psychiatry and Neurology, 18*, 72–82.

Wetherell, J. L., Thorp, S. R., Patterson, T. L., Golshan, S., Jeste, D. V., & Gatz, M. (2004). Quality of life in geriatric generalized anxiety disorder: A preliminary investigation. *Journal of Psychiatric Research, 38*, 305–312.

Wolitzky-Taylor, K. B., Castriotta, N., Lenze, E. J., Stanley, M. A., & Craske, M. G. (2010). Anxiety disorders in older adults: A comprehensive review. *Depression and Anxiety, 27*, 190–211.

Wuthrich, V. M., Johnco, C., & Knight, A. (2014). Comparison of the Penn State Worry Questionnaire (PSWQ) and abbreviated version (PSWQ-A) in a clinical and non-clinical population of older adults. *Journal of Anxiety Disorders, 28*, 657–663.

Xiao-Ling, L., Lu, D., Gottschling, J., Segal, D. L., & Tang, S. (2017). Validation of a Chinese version of the Geriatric Anxiety Scale among community-dwelling older adults in mainland China. *Journal of Cross-Cultural Gerontology, 32*, 57–70.

Yochim, B. P., Mueller, A. E., June, A., & Segal, D. L. (2011). Psychometric properties of the Geriatric Anxiety Scale: Comparison to the Beck Anxiety Inventory and Geriatric Anxiety Inventory. *Clinical Gerontologist, 34*, 21–33.

Yochim, B. P., Mueller, A., & Segal, D. L. (2013). Late life anxiety is associated with decreased memory and executive functioning in community dwelling older adults. *Journal of Anxiety Disorders, 27*, 567–575.

12

Sexual Disorders, Sleep Disorders, and Chronic Pain

John's diabetes has created erectile dysfunction that has undermined the sexual satisfaction that has always been an important part of his relationship with Morris. He avoids physical touch now, fearing that Morris will want it to "lead somewhere" that John can no longer go. Losing sex has brought a devastating loss of intimacy to a relationship that was remarkable for its decades of closeness.

Marion is awakened at least four or five times each night when Stephen gets up to wander around trying to figure out whether it is night or day. She has tried to sleep through his wanderings, but is just too afraid he will walk out the door or do something else unsafe. Recently, Marion has begun to have trouble falling asleep and she has become so exhausted from lack of sleep that she can barely function. She feels like an emotional and a physical wreck. In her mind, she can't go on like this for much longer.

Bob, now 73 years old, was a football player in high school and college. He enjoyed his time as a player, but as he got older he suffered with joint pain and especially severe pain in his neck and back. His doctors told him his pain was probably caused by injuries sustained earlier in life, possibly from his recurrent trauma while playing football. Managing Bob's pain has become a major focus for Bob and his wife, Ellen. "Pain is part of the uniform" now has a different meaning for Bob.

Sex and sleep are normal aspects of life, but dysfunctions in either area can occur and can be devastating. Chronic pain is not typical with aging but represents another challenge for some in later life. In some cases, these problems may become intertwined. For example, pain may be a major cause of disruption of normal sleep and sexual functioning. As noted in the opening vignettes, problems with sex, sleep, or pain often produce functional declines and lowered well-being. For each of the three areas, the classifications and epidemiology of the disorders or difficulties will be

Aging and Mental Health, Third Edition. Daniel L. Segal, Sara Honn Qualls, and Michael A. Smyer.
© 2018 John Wiley & Sons, Inc. Published 2018 by John Wiley & Sons, Inc.

presented, followed by a description of problems experienced by older adults, theories that explain the disorders or problems, and approaches to assessment and treatment in older adults.

Sexual Disorders

Cultural images that promote definitions of what is normative and desirable influence heavily one's definitions of sexuality. Historically, older adults were portrayed as asexual beings with neither interest nor ability to give or receive pleasure through sexual interactions. More recently, intensive marketing of pharmaceuticals designed to assist men in achieving and maintaining erections is affecting our images of aging to include not only the opportunity, but the social imperative to maintain a particular type of sexual functioning (Potts, Grace, Vares, & Gavey, 2006). A more holistic view of sexuality in later life, however, considers the biological, psychological, social, and cultural aspects that affect sexual satisfaction, expression, and expectations (Syme, Cordes, Cameron, & Mona, 2015).

Reduced rates of sexual activity with advancing age are normative, for a very diverse set of reasons (outlined below) that do not necessarily relate to sexual disorders. Starting in late midlife, sexual activity rates drop dramatically across late adulthood (Lindau et al., 2007). Sex differences also influence rates of sexual activity. For example, data from the National Social Life, Health and Aging Study indicated that 39.5% of women and 67% of men through the age of 74 years reported having "any sex." Comparable figures between the ages of 75 and 84 years of age reflected both a decline and a continuing gender difference: 16.7% of women and 38.5% of men (Waite, Laumann, Das, & Schumm, 2009). The decline in rate of sexual behavior is not necessarily an indicator of sexual disorder or difficulty, because loss of partners and onset of medical conditions and disabilities also affect access and opportunity.

Definitions

Sexual disorders are diagnosed using the same categories in the *Diagnostic and Statistical Manual of Mental Disorders,* Fifth Edition (DSM-5; APA, 2013) for persons of all ages. The DSM-5 reflects a recent conceptualization of sexual desire. Female sexual arousal disorder includes the inability to achieve vaginal lubrication and swelling—common problems for older women. Even if subjectively aroused, women may have a sexual arousal disorder if they do not achieve genital arousal without lubrication (Galinsky, 2012). For women, sexual pain disorders include vaginismus (discomfort and inability to achieve vaginal penetration) and dyspareunia (persistent pain before, during, or after sexual intercourse) (Syme et al., 2015). For men, arousal problems are reflected in the inability to have and sustain an erection during sexual activity (i.e., erectile dysfunction, commonly called ED). Men and women are also vulnerable to sexual dysfunction due to another general medical condition that interferes with sexual responses.

Recent approaches reflect broader definitions of sexual fulfillment, acknowledging the diversity of sexual experiences beyond sexual intercourse (Syme et al., 2015).

For example, the Complete State of Sexual Health uses a two-dimensional approach, asking the clinician to assess both the client's sexual well-being (satisfaction, pleasure, emotional intimacy) and sexual dysfunction (e.g., pain) (Mona, Syme, Goldwaser, et al., 2011).

A unique set of problems arises when the onset of cognitive impairment introduces difficulties with intimacy into the lives of its victims and their caregivers. Over time, affection and sexual functioning both decline more rapidly for couples including a person with dementia than same-age couples without dementia. Caregiving partners may be confused about the ethics of continuing to be sexually active with a partner who is so dependent on the caregiver that the person may be unwilling to risk displeasing the caregiver by declining sexual activity. On the other hand, sexual intimacy between a person with any disability and the caregiving partner may be a powerful validation of relationship endurance in the face of permanent disability. Although persons with dementia can become less inhibited sexually, the probability of inappropriate sexual behaviors is quite low. Inquiry about sexual activity invites care partners to discuss what is often a hidden set of challenges because they hesitate to initiate the conversation.

Sexual behavior in the face of cognitive impairment provides challenges at the intersection of clinical, legal, and ethical frameworks (Syme et al., 2015). Although legal definitions of capacity to consent vary from state to state, the American Bar Association and the American Psychological Association (ABA/APA, 2008) have provided guidance for legal and psychology practitioners. They emphasize three elements for assessment: knowledge, reasoned understanding, and the voluntariness

---

Box 12.1 Sexuality and changing cognitive capacity

Jack and Ramona enjoy cuddling in the public spaces of the memory care unit where they reside, and are observed to enter each other's rooms for periods of sexual activity. Ramona's son is angry at the facility for allowing this to happen to his mother. Jack's daughters are grateful that their father has a source of pleasure in his life.

Careful assessment of capacity was accomplished and shared with the medical decision-makers for Jack and Ramona. Both members of the couple were found to have capacity to make this decision and both reported finding only pleasure and joy in the relationship. Jack's son reluctantly admitted that he had his own personal values challenged with the relationship but he was trying to become more flexible.

Select staff were educated about how to identify signs of distress in either participant, just in case the sexual activity produced pain or discomfort that the participant would be unable to report verbally. In an in-service education session, a geropsychologist invited staff to think about the impact of labeling the loving behavior as "cute" or "racy" and were provided more normalizing frames and language for sexual activity in older adults, even in long-term-care settings.

of the activity. (See Chapter 8 for a broader discussion of assessing decision-making capacity.) Complexities arise when family members of the couple question the appropriateness of the sexual activity based on the participants' historical values and preferences.

Prevalence

Prevalence of sexual activity and sexual satisfaction decline with advancing age in both men and women (Hillman, 2011), although patterns may vary by region of the globe. Almost one-half of a national probability sample of adults age 57–85 report having a bothersome problem with their sexuality (Lindau et al., 2007).

Variability in prevalence of dissatisfaction varies by gender and culture. A large, international study of sexual attitudes and behaviors in 29 diverse countries indicated that women report less physical pleasure, emotional pleasure, satisfaction with sexual functioning, and importance of sex compared with men (Laumann et al., 2005). Substantial cross-national variation was also evident in this study, with Western countries reporting more satisfaction overall, and Asian countries reporting the lowest levels of satisfaction by both men and women.

The sexual experience of older lesbian, gay, bisexual, and transgender persons (LGBT) is poorly researched (Kimmel, Rose, & David, 2006). In addition, there is a serious paucity of data on sexual disorders in this group. The current cohort of LGBT older adults experienced their sexuality in a context of powerful stigma that often made it impossible to be open about their sexuality if they wanted to be socially engaged (Knauer, 2011). Such cohort experience is one of the more powerful factors in understanding what may be viewed as normal or disordered about sexual functioning among LGBT older adults. For persons who early in life found that they experienced other than exclusively opposite-sex attraction were highly unlikely to have received appropriate education within which to interpret their own sexual experiences. This absence of developmental support is particularly powerful for all non-heterosexuals because it so profoundly influences identity development that is shaped by a person's understanding of his or her sexual orientation, gender, and gender identity. Thus, the current cohort of older adults who identify as LGBT is likely to have had particularly challenging identity and intimacy paths through life, often maintaining separate public and private identities, or experiencing significant social marginalization when claiming their own sexual identity. Calzo and colleagues (Calzo, Antonucci, Mays, & Cochran, 2011) found that older and younger generations of LGBT individuals showed similar patterns of timing of sexual orientation and same-sex experience. Additional research is needed to assess the impact of early sexual orientation, the contexts of support, and development across the lifespan.

The aging experience of sexuality is shaped by changes in one's body and psychological representations of one's body identity or image, regardless of sexual orientation. Because sexual identity is usually expressed interpersonally, persons who identify as LGBT often face unique challenges because of internalized stigma as well as social stigmas that can interfere with normal sexual exploration. For some older adults, receipt of professional or personal care reveals aspects of their sexual identity that they had not previously revealed or prefer not to reveal (e.g., a transgendered person being bathed in a nursing home no longer has an option of choosing who knows what) (Hinchliff & Gott, 2011). Additionally, there may be big differences in the value structure of care staff and residents so one is revealing to strangers who may readily show their disapproval or delight in knowing the secret. Mental health among older persons who identify as LGBT is shaped by the same myriad factors as those for heterosexual adults, with a strong overlay of cohort-bound experiences that shaped identity and interpersonal relationship formation.

Risk factors

Risk factors for sexual disorders and difficulties again follow the biopsychosocial model, falling into physiological factors, psychological factors, and social factors, with high likelihood of interactions among the categories of risk.

Normal aging is associated with physiological changes in the sexual response cycle (outlined in Table 12.1) that create risk for sexual disorders and difficulties.

Menopause in women is associated with reduced estrogen production, which can reduce desire and arousal, along with reduced production of lubrication that creates discomfort. Thinning of the vaginal wall also creates risk of discomfort during intercourse (Hillman, 2011). A survey of postmenopausal women (Ambler, Bieber, & Diamond, 2012) found that the majority expressed sexual concerns, including low libido, problems with arousal, decreased intensity or absence of orgasm, painful intercourse, and concerns about body image or attractiveness. Not surprisingly, marital problems, as well as physiological changes, are also strongly associated with sexual difficulties in women.

In late midlife, men report reduced frequency of sexual thoughts and decreased sexual enjoyment, along with decreased erectile and orgasmic functioning, with a majority of men over the age of 75 reporting concerns related to erectile dysfunction (Albersen, Orabi, & Lue, 2012). The functional decline is evident in slower response time in the earlier stages of the cycle, and reduced penile circumference during arousal. Although erectile problems result from these physiological changes, sensation may not be affected. Those affected by ED currently have pharmaceuticals available that can create an erection, and implants are available as well. Some persons choose to focus less on the erection and more on the sensation and pleasuring, however. Just as young adults with anxiety may experience premature ejaculation, that problem can extend into later life. Despite these declines in the intensity and frequency of sexual

Table 12.1 The sexual response cycle

The sexual response cycle is typically divided into the following phases:

1 Desire—fantasies about, and desire for, sexual activity
2 Excitement—subjective sense of sexual pleasure; physiological changes characteristic of sexual arousal
3 Orgasm—the peak of sexual pleasure; release of sexual tension; rhythmic contractions
4 Resolution—muscular relaxation and a sense of general well-being

responses, most people describe their sexuality as satisfying. Thus, as in other aspects of life, most people adapt to the changes of aging without identifying themselves as experiencing disorder or difficulty.

Sexual disorders and difficulties can occur as secondary effects of chronic illnesses and the medications used to treat them. Erectile dysfunction is commonly comorbid with diabetes mellitus, hypertension, coronary artery disease, radical prostatectomy, or pelvic trauma. Medications that increase risk for erectile dysfunction include antihypertensive, antiepileptic, antianxiety, or antidepressant agents. As explained below, the impact of these diseases and medications on sexual functioning is due to the fact that sexual responses are essentially vascular responses, thus decline in cardiovascular functioning almost always has a negative effect on sexual responsiveness. Alcohol use is an additional risk factor (Rowland, van Diest, Incrocci, & Slob, 2005).

Theories of etiology

Physical aging and age-related illness, medications, and over-the-counter agents are all primary causes of the onset of sexual dysfunction in later life. Each specific category of sexual dysfunction represents a descriptive category of some component of the sexual response cycle that is not working well. The mechanics of the sexual response cycle are complex, involving every major organ system of the body so almost any physiological difficulty can contribute to sexual dysfunctions.

Ageism and stereotypes of aging also contribute to sexual dysfunction in later life by shaping expectations for what is normal or even possible (Hillman, 2011). Indeed, attitudes are stronger predictors of sexual desire than biomedical factors (DeLamater, 2012). Negative biases about the appropriateness of desiring sexual intimacy inhibit relationship exploration. Whereas a younger person might seek alternative strategies for remaining sexually active even after disability, an older person with beliefs that sexual desire is abnormal or unnecessary in later life may not even investigate the information or strategies available to adapt to the disability. Ageism in care providers can also exert powerful influence on older adults as well (Pangman & Seguire, 2000) (see Box 12.1).

Social causes are also significant factors as age increases the probability that women, in particular, will lose their husbands as sexual partners due to serious illness or death. The gender imbalance in later life poses a serious barrier for heterosexual women who might wish to partner again (Syme et al., 2015) and influences sexual desire (DeLamater & Sill, 2005), as well as for gay men who may face fewer options after losing a partner in later life. LGBT partners may also lose the privacy that afforded them social safety if either member of the couple requires assistance of formal service providers or residential placement.

Finally, anxiety about performance has deleterious effects on sexual functioning in both men and women, across adulthood. Often, anxiety about changes in sexual functioning can exacerbate the negative impact of what otherwise would have been a mild change. The compounding effect of anxiety often leads to avoidance of the intimacy that leads to satisfying sexual experiences or to poorly organized or structured sexual behaviors that are not satisfying.

Assessment

Sexual functioning should be assessed regularly in primary care as well as in mental health and relationship counseling. Physicians are less likely to ask older persons about their sexual well-being although the question would be welcomed by their patients (Hinchliff & Gott, 2011). Screening assessment can be as simple as a single question; questions simply need to be asked. Once a problem has been disclosed, assessment typically engages multiple disciplines, ideally in the context of an interprofessional team (Zeiss, Zeiss, & Davies, 1999).

Clinical interview is the first step in the assessment of sexual disorders and difficulties. Initially, a broad lens is cast on the life circumstance of the client to look for causal factors in all spheres of biopsychosocial functioning. Physical health is an obvious area to research, with detailed assessment of illness history, current health status, use of medications, substance abuse, and medicinal uses of nontraditional health substances (e.g., herbs) or over-the-counter medications (e.g., laxatives). Psychological well-being is also evaluated with particular attention to the presence of anxiety, depression, and cognitive impairment. Characteristics of intimate social relationships are assessed along with the aspects of the broader social environment that might influence accessibility or comfort with sexual activity.

If a problem has been identified, the interview also includes detailed assessment of the sexual functioning of the client using questions that elicit very specific descriptions of sexual behavior sequences. Disorders or difficulties may result from misunderstanding of normal age-related changes in physiological functioning (e.g., decreased lubrication) or to inadequate adaptation to physical disabilities that interfere with familiar ways of interacting sexually. General attitudes about sexuality, values, and language used to discuss sexual activity need to be documented because they shape the choice of interventions. The client's view of the problem is also detailed, along with previous efforts to address the problem and their results.

Based on assessment findings, the goal of the intervention needs to be developed explicitly. Syme and her colleagues (2015) outline a thorough semistructured interview format, building on the earlier work of Zeiss et al. (1999). When partners are interviewed together, the interview detailed above would elicit information from both persons with follow-up assessment of discrepancies in viewpoint, experience, attitude, and previous solution attempts. Partners may discover during a joint interview that their efforts have been conflicted enough to actually undermine the potential efficacy of either person's approach. Joint interviews provide rich relationship information available only when observing two people who are seeking help for a particularly intimate aspect of their relationship. The assessment interview affords the opportunity to intervene in small ways by offering permission to state one's own view or experience without judgment, or to ask questions of a partner in nonjudgmental ways that reduce shame or defensiveness. Of course, the clinical interview may or may not include partner(s), depending on their availability and the intervention goals.

Standardized instruments can also supplement the clinical interview. For example, the European Male Aging Study Sexual Function Questionnaire (O'Connor et al., 2008) and the McCoy Female Sexuality Questionnaire (McCoy, 2000) have been developed and validated for use with older adults.

Older adults experiencing sexual dysfunction should be examined carefully by a physician to determine whether the difficulty is primary or secondary to a chronic illness or medication. Because the sexual response cycle is particularly sensitive to functional losses in the cardiovascular or neurological systems due to illness or medication, the physical exam is of particular importance to older clients.

Interventions for sexual disorders

Sex therapy focuses on problems identified in a thorough multidisciplinary assessment (Syme et al., 2015). Therapy may be undertaken with an individual or couple, and may focus heavily on sexual functioning or more broadly address intimacy and other social aspects of primary relationships. In general, psychotherapy interventions for sexual dysfunctions have not been well researched; the clinical literature relies on case studies primarily.

Cognitive behavior therapy offers an organized basis for treatment of sexual disorders in older adults (Crowther & Zeiss, 1999). The Permission, Limited Information, Specific Suggestions, Intensive Therapy (PLISSIT) model creates a framework for starting with the least necessary intervention and progressing toward more intensive treatment only as needed (Annon, 1974). Starting with Permission, the interventions proceed through sharing Limited Information, Specific Suggestions, and, when necessary, Intensive Therapy. Permission addresses sexual problems created by attitudinal factors as well as with poor adjustment to disability or illness that interrupted familiar ways of being sexually active. The opposite focus of permission is also relevant—permission *not* to demand hyperperformance from oneself just because pharmaceutical companies use media advertising to raise expectations (Potts et al., 2006). Informational interventions often address the particular educational needs of the individual, although they can also be offered in a group context. Specific suggestions may be particularly useful to older adults seeking to adapt to age-related physiological changes in sexual responsiveness. Intensive Therapy would engage an individual or couple in extensive changes in the relationship, sexual behaviors, or in adjusting to the impact of loss of particular types of sexual functioning. Emerging therapies, such as values clarification and sensual mindfulness, are other psychosocial interventions that are being used increasingly with older adults (Syme et al., 2015).

Pharmacological and prosthetic interventions are also available to restore sexual functioning. In women, the focus of these interventions is on hormonal enhancement of desire or genital arousal via enhancement of vascular functioning in the clitoral area. Topical application of vaginal estrogen decreases dryness and discomfort, and mechanical devices such as vibrators and vacuum systems stimulate clitoral engorgement (Potter, 2007). Recent public marketing of erectile dysfunction medications for men (e.g., Viagra) have generated remarkable sales, but effects on satisfaction with sexual functioning and relationship well-being have not yet been fully evaluated. Penile prostheses are available that create rigidity in the penis sufficient to engage in intercourse, with positive benefits documented for sexual as well as psychological and relationship well-being. The biopsychosocial context influences intervention choice. For example, pharmacological agents are the preferred treatment method (compared to other approaches), despite possible problems with compliance to the drug regimen (Porst, 2016).

Education and training of health providers are obviously needed to enhance their comfort and skill in assessing and treating sexual problems in older adults. Staff in long-term-care facilities are somewhat knowledgeable about sexual functioning but tend to deny interest in sexual behavior among residents (Syme et al., 2015). Administrators in institutional settings particularly need to be proactive in formulating policies for protection of resident rights to be sexually active along with appropriate resources to assess capacity to consent to sexual behavior among persons with cognitive impairments (Lyden, 2007). An excellent set of resources to support education about aging and sexuality is available on the American Psychological Association's Office on Aging website at http://www.apa.org/pi/aging/resources/guides/sexuality.aspx.

Sleep Disorders

Complaints of sleep difficulties are more common in older adults than in any other age group, occurring in approximately half of all older adults at any moment in time (Neikrug & Ancoli-Israel, 2010; Ohayon, 2002). The consequences of sleep disorders are significant: greater risk of physical and mental health comorbidities, higher health service utilization, greater functional disability, reduced quality of life, and indeed, mortality (Dew et al., 2003). Obviously, healthy sleep is a significant component of mental health as well as a predictor of well-being that warrants attention in later life.

Before examining disorders of sleep, the normal effects of aging on sleep patterns need to be understood. Sleep is divided into rapid eye movement (REM) sleep and four stages of non-REM sleep. The non-REM stages are simply numbered 1–4, with each larger number indicating a deeper stage of sleep characterized by slower brain waves. The percentage of slow-wave sleep decreases linearly by approximately 2% per decade in adulthood, up to age 60, after which the decline levels off (Neikrug & Ancoli-Israel, 2010; Ohayon, Carskadon, Guilleminault, & Vitiello, 2004). However, these changes are insufficient to account for the sleep complaints of older adults, which primarily focus on decreased ability to maintain sleep (Ancoli-Israel & Ayalon, 2006).

Definitions and prevalence

Sleep disorders include various types of disrupted sleep patterns and various causes of those disruptions. In other words, sleep disorders are categorized according to descriptions of a disordered pattern (e.g., sleep initiation problems), an etiology (e.g., sleep apnea), or a behavioral consequence (e.g., excessive daytime sleepiness). The 10 major categories of sleep–wake disorders included in the DSM-5 are listed in Table 12.2. Due to disturbed sleep patterns caused by these disorders, people who experience them commonly experience distress about lack of quality sleep, the timing and amount of sleep, daytime sleepiness, and significant functional impairment. However, the majority of sleep change in adult sleep patterns occurs before the age of 60 and changes after age 60 are less variable compared to earlier in the lifespan (Neikrug & Ancoli-Israel, 2010; Ohayon, Carskadon, Guilleminault, & Vitiello, 2004).

Table 12.2   Major sleep–wake disorders in the DSM-5

Insomnia Disorder
Hypersomnolence Disorder
Narcolepsy
Breathing-Related Sleep Disorders, including:
    obstructive sleep apnea hypopnea
    central sleep apnea
    sleep-related hypoventilation
Circadian-Rhythm Sleep–Wake Disorders, including Advanced Sleep Phase Disorder
Non-Rapid Eye Movement Sleep Arousal Disorders
Nightmare Disorder
Rapid Eye Movement Sleep Behavior Disorder
Restless Legs Syndrome
Substance/Medication-Induced Sleep Disorder

Source: Adapted from the DSM-5 (APA, 2013).

Following the lead of McCrae, Roth, Zamora, Dautovich, and Lichstein (2015), we will concentrate on three areas of sleep disorders from Table 12.2 that clinicians who are serving older adults are most likely to encounter: Advanced Sleep Phase Disorder—a type of Circadian-Rhythm Sleep Disorder; Insomnia; and Breathing-Related Sleep Disorders. We will then look briefly at three of the table's other types of sleep disorders.

Advanced Sleep Phase Disorder is a type of circadian-rhythm disorder that reflects a misalignment of the client's sleep pattern with societal norms for the timing of sleeping and waking (Thorpy, 2012). Typically, this disorder reflects sleeping and waking more than three hours earlier than typical patterns. Along with earlier bedtimes, advanced sleep phase disorders may be associated with early evening fatigue or sleepiness and early morning awakening (Reid & Zee, 2011). These patterns of sleep and waking tend to interfere with social and work functioning, often a source of clients' complaints.

Insomnia Disorder is characterized by dissatisfaction with sleep quantity or quality with difficulties initiating or maintaining normal sleep. Such nonrestorative sleep leaves the person functioning poorly the next day. Patterns may include trouble falling asleep, difficulty falling back to sleep after nighttime awakening, or very early morning wakening without ability to fall back to sleep. Rybarczyk and his colleagues (2013) report that insomnia rates in the general population range from 6% to 10% using the most precise definition of insomnia, to approximately 30% of adults reporting some insomnia symptoms (Morin, LeBlanc, Daley, Gregoire, & Merette, 2006; Ohayon, 2002). Among community-dwelling older adults, prevalence rates are 15–45% for difficulties initiating sleep, 20–65% for disrupted sleep, and 15–54% for terminal insomnia, while nonrestorative sleep is reported by 10% of older persons (Ohayon, 2002). Advancing age does not predict significant increases in these rates, but women report more sleep disruption than men.

Primary Insomnia is a sleep disturbance with three characteristics: It lasts at least one month; it causes significant distress or functional impairment; and it is not attributable to medical or psychiatric causes (Rybarczyk et al., 2013). If no medical or psychiatric cause is established, the insomnia is labeled comorbid insomnia. The duration of the insomnia is another differentiator (Rybarczyk et al., 2013). Acute insomnia may last from a few days to several weeks. Intermittent insomnia reflects recurring short-term sleep disturbances. Chronic insomnia last longer, at least several nights a week for more than a month.

Breathing-Related Sleep Disorders. Sleep-disordered breathing (SDB) problems involve either partial or full disruption of respiration 10–15 or more times per hour during sleep, conditions commonly called hypopneas or apneas. SDB prevalence increases dramatically from middle age (4–9%) to older adults (age 60+) for whom 45–62% meet criteria for diagnosis (Ancoli-Israel et al., 1991; Neikrug & Ancoli-Israel, 2010; Young et al., 1993).

In addition to these three disorders, older adults also experience other types of sleep disorders:

Restless Legs Syndrome (RLS) describes the patient's leg movements that are the only relief available to deal with the unpleasant sensation of "pins and needles" or "creepy, crawly feelings." RLS increases with age, with almost twice the prevalence in women as in men (Ohayon & Roth, 2002).

Another movement disorder, *Rapid Eye Movement Sleep Behavior Disorder* (RBD), results in complex motor movements and actions that may even harm the patient or others, apparently caused by lack of muscle inhibition during dream states. The highest prevalence of RBD is in older men although it occurs in persons of all ages (Montplaisir, 2004).

Hypersomnolence Disorder (HD) is a consequence of other sleep disorders or may be caused by other physiological, psychological, or social factors that disrupt sleep. HD is associated with a myriad of risks, including driving accidents, mortality from cardiovascular accidents, psychiatric disorders, falls, and cognitive deficits. Daily functioning is also impaired in areas such as social functioning, activity level, general productivity, and vigilance, especially in those with multiple medical conditions or multiple medications (Gooneratne et al., 2003).

Risk factors

Although age-related changes in the sleep cycle are often lamented as disruptive of good restfulness, aging per se is not the cause of sleep disturbances although it may be a risk factor (Rybarczyk et al., 2013). Multiple biopsychosocial factors that are age-related are implicated, however, and they should be evaluated carefully when older adults complain of sleep problems (Ancoli-Israel & Ayalon, 2006). Risk for almost all of the sleep disorders increases with diagnosis of multiple chronic illnesses, use of multiple medications, and presence of mental disorders (especially depression and anxiety), as well as changes in the timing and chronicity of sleep. Ironically, any sleep disorder also increases risk for other sleep problems.

Demographic characteristics are differentially associated with specific sleep disorders. For example, women report higher rates of insomnia than men, across all ages; similarly, women self-report sleep disturbances and tiredness at higher rates than men at all ages. In contrast, sleep apnea is more common among men than women across the lifespan, but the gap narrows after menopause (McCrae et al., 2015). When sleep patterns of African Americans and Caucasians are compared, African Americans evidence higher rates of sleep problems as reflected in a number of outcome measures: sleep onset latency, total sleep time, rated sleep quality, and less slow-wave sleep (McCrae et al., 2015; Song et al., 2011). In addition, lower socioeconomic status is associated with a greater prevalence of sleep problems (e.g., less sleep and restless sleep patterns) (Piccolo, Yang, Bliwise, Yaggi, & Araujo, 2013).

Theories of etiology

Sleep disorders are best explained within the biopsychosocial model because their etiology can be purely physiological, as occurs with medication-induced insomnia, or may occur because of significant psychological factors (e.g., depression) or social factors (e.g., disruption due to household activity).

Physiological sources of sleep disorders are particularly common in later life when aging itself reduces the robustness and satisfaction of sleep at the same time that chronic illnesses that disrupt sleep become normative. As described above, aging-induced changes in the brain reduce the amount of time spent in deeper stages of sleep. With less available deep sleep time, all other interruptions of sleep have greater disruptive impacts on sleep. For example, RLS creates behavioral disruptions that lead to frequent wakening, which has a disproportionately interruptive impact on sleep in older persons.

Chronic illnesses and medications have direct negative effects on sleep. A remarkably wide range of physical illnesses add to risk of sleep problems (Ancoli-Israel & Ayalon, 2006). Two illnesses that have particularly high rates of sleep disorders associated with them are Parkinson's disease and Alzheimer's disease, both of which are increasingly prevalent in later life (Friedman, 2013). The medications prescribed for these and other conditions can also contribute to sleep problems. Additionally, medications can have diuretic effects that increase urinary frequency during the night, resulting in multiple trips to the bathroom that also interrupt the sleep cycle.

Aging reduces synchronization of circadian rhythms with external cues of the time of day or behavior patterns that structure day/night behavior sequences. These biological dysregulations lead older adults to experience Advanced Sleep Phase Disorder, sleeping off-time with the social norms for sleep cycles, often with the urge to sleep early in the evening followed by middle of the night wakening for the "day" (McCrae et al., 2015). The causes of circadian disruption range from genetics to decreased light exposure, core body temperature cycle changes, and a range of environmental and behavioral factors (Rybarczyk et al., 2013).

Sleep apneas and other breathing-related sleep disorders are caused by temporary collapse of the airway that is often accompanied by loud snoring and breathing cessation. The impact on sleep has multiple pathways, including reduced oxygen intake (intermittent nighttime hypoxemia), self-awakening from the sounds of snoring, and the sudden awakening that terminates the cessation of breathing.

Psychological causes of sleep disruption include worry, anxiety, loneliness, and especially depression (McCrae et al., 2015). To the extent people ruminate and worry, their sleep is often negatively affected. Additionally, wakefulness rather than sleep-induction may be promoted psychologically if the sleep environment stimulates mental activation. Anxiety disorders and depressive disorders are also possible con-tributors to poor sleep, and anxiety and depressive disorders also include sleep distur-bance within the constellation of symptoms within several disorders.

Social causes are also potential factors in sleep disorders in older adults. Any activity in the environment that forces awakening will also disrupt the sleep cycle and put the person more at risk for sleep disorder. Research on spousal caregivers, for example, has shown that sleep disruption is one of their most common and problematic sources of distress (McCurry, Logsdon, Vitiello, & Terry, 1998). A cognitively impaired spouse who wanders in the night not only makes noise that awakens the caregiver, but also poses a safety risk that renders the caregiver too vigilant to sleep well. Nursing home residents who spend large proportions of their day in bed also have unusual sleep–wake patterns that disrupt successful sleep.

Assessment

With the etiological complexity of sleep disorders, assessment of sleep problems requires a multidisciplinary approach to evaluation (McCrae et al., 2015). In addition, assessment often requires distinguishing among: normal age-related changes in sleep; the most likely treatable causes (among many, potentially), including psychiatric dis-orders such as depression; and long-term sleep difficulties that have been present prior to older age (Kay & Dzierzewski, 2015).

Schutte-Rodin and her colleagues (Schutte-Rodin, Broch, Buysse, Dorsey, & Sateia, 2008) advise that general clinicians who do not specialize in sleep disorders should include several elements in an assessment: a general medical questionnaire, a daytime sleepiness questionnaire (e.g., Epworth Sleepiness Scale; Johns, 1991), and two weeks of sleep diaries. As part of a treatment team, the psychologist can also draw on a thorough medical examination, including both history and physical, including current use of prescription and over-the-counter medications.

Self-report questionnaires are also useful in identifying potential clinical disorders as well as for reporting of subjective perceptions of sleep cycle disruption and distress (McCrae et al., 2003). For example, self-reported daytime sleepiness or chronic tired-ness in patients willing to undergo a sleep evaluation produced high prevalence of diagnosable disorders (77% of women and 98% of men were diagnosed in one study; Bailes, Baltzan, Alapin, Fichten, & Libman, 2005).

A sleep diary is a useful starting point for assessment, because it is cost- and time-efficient (Lichstein, Durrence, Riedel, Taylor, & Bush, 2004). Although several versions are available online through the American Academy of Sleep Medicine, Carney and her colleagues (2012) developed a consensus sleep diary to provide some standardization for research and clinical purposes. Sleep diaries track sleep–wake patterns in detail repeatedly over a period of days or weeks to identify the variation in sleep patterns that help identify social as well as psychological sources of disruption. Multiple measures can be attained in diaries, including perceived sleep latency, number of nighttime awakenings, amount of time spent awake, sleep time, sleep efficiency (percentage of in-bed time spent asleep), nap patterns, and sleep quality ratings. Depression and anxiety questionnaires also are used consistently by clinicians and researchers studying sleep, due to the high comorbidity among sleep disorders with depression and anxiety.

Psychosocial interviews are used to obtain diagnostic information as well as detailed descriptions of thoughts and behaviors prior to and during difficult sleep periods, food/drink ingestion patterns, and nighttime awakening patterns. Sleep management strategies also are assessed to determine what the older person already uses successfully or without benefit. Finally, assessment of consequences of sleep disturbances can examine effects as diverse as daytime sleepiness, cognitive functioning, and activity rate.

Although not recommended routinely in primary care, polysomnography provides the gold standard of sleep cycle patterns and is available in specialty sleep clinics. Physiological sleep assessments typically involve nighttime monitoring of breathing, physiological measurement of brain activity using electroencephalograph (EEG) readings, and urine analysis during the night.

Many older adults now have available a less technology-intensive approach to monitoring sleep patterns: Personal devices such as a Fitbit provide a record of the total time of sleep, number of awakenings, and periods of disruption. While not as detailed as polysomnography, they can provide a starting point for assessing the gap between self-report and actual sleep patterns. A successful assessment produces a detailed description of the sleep pattern, subjective perceptions of sleep problems, subjective distress about sleep problems, and data that assist with diagnosis of the etiology of the disorder(s) as well as treatment planning.

Interventions for sleep disorders

Consistent with the assessment model described above, interventions begin with treatment of any primary condition that produces sleep disorders as a secondary consequence. Careful review of medication alternatives can sometimes produce options for treating chronic conditions that do not produce adverse sleep effects.

The American Academy of Sleep Medicine developed consensus treatment protocols for various sleep disorders, including insomnia (Morgenthaler et al., 2015). The guidelines reflect the importance of sleep diaries as both an assessment and treatment element. The diaries serve several functions: a baseline of functioning prior to treatment; a monitor of changing sleep regimens, contexts, and conditions; and an outcome measure of change.

Pharmacological interventions are commonly prescribed when sleep problems are reported in primary care settings. Benzodiazepines are among the most commonly prescribed and recommended pharmacological sleep agents despite limited evidence of their effectiveness (Bain, 2006; Simon & Ludman, 2006). A newer set of medications are classified as nonbenzodiazepine sedative-hypnotics for example, zolpidem (Ambien) and eszopiclone (Lunesta). These medications work quickly, usually within 15–30 minutes, and are effective in initiating sleep but not in maintaining sleep. None of these medications are recommended for long-term use. In addition, the benzodiazepines and the sedative-hypnotics can have dangerous side effects or consequences, especially among older adults, including cognitive impairment, daytime sleepiness, and falls. In general, comparative research shows poorer outcomes from these sleep medications than cognitive behavior therapies (Rybarczyk et al., 2013), which should be the cornerstone of any long-term treatment approach.

Nonpharmacological approaches to intervention offer fewer potential medical complications and better evidence of long-term efficacy than pharmacological approaches (Bain, 2006; Rybarczyk et al., 2013). Controlled clinical trials document the impact of cognitive-behavioral therapies (CBT) for older adults on several aspects of sleep quality and quantity, primarily on self-report measures but with growing evidence of physiological impact as well (Rybarczyk et al., 2013; Sivertsen, Omvik, & Pallesen, 2006). Sivertsen and colleagues (2006) demonstrated the impact of CBT on sleep efficiency (percentage of time asleep) and on increased time in slow-wave sleep (stages 3 and 4). Impressively, maintenance of gains has generally extended months or years beyond the end of treatment (Rybarczyk et al., 2013).

Multicomponent cognitive-behavioral therapy techniques included in outcome studies showing positive benefits include sleep hygiene, sleep restriction, stimulus control, cognitive therapy, sleep compression, and relaxation (McCrae et al., 2015; Rybarczyk et al., 2013). Rybarczyk and his colleagues (2013) note that the relaxation component often is omitted, because many older adults do not continue this element on their own. However, controlling the setting, timing, and conditions of sleep has significant, positive effects.

Some evidence suggests that patient characteristics predict which type of intervention helps most. For example, Lichstein, Riedel, Wilson, Lester, and Aguillard (2001) found that patients with high daytime fatigue responded best to interventions that extended sleep whereas others responded best to interventions focused on sleep compression.

These approaches are also successful in challenging populations such as caregivers of persons with dementia who still experience the demands of providing care (McCrae, Tierney, & McNamara, 2005). People with dementia also benefit from behavioral interventions (McCurry et al., 1998) to improve sleep.

Chronic Pain

According to the International Association for the Study of Pain (IASP), pain is "an unpleasant sensory and emotional experience associated with actual or potential tissue damage, or described in terms of such damage" (IASP, 2017; Merskey & Bogduk, 1994). This definition highlights the combination of biological and psychological factors that affect reports of chronic pain (IASP, 2017; Hadjistavropoulos, 2015). As with sexual disorders and sleep disorders, an integrated biopsychosocial approach will frame our discussion of chronic pain.

Definitions and prevalence

The DSM-5 (APA, 2013) recognizes the interaction of psychological and physical factors in pain (Hadjistavropoulos, 2015). The *somatic symptom* disorder is evidenced in "somatic symptoms that cause significant disruption, excessive thoughts and feelings, and behaviors associated with such symptoms and chronicity" (Hadjistavropoulos, 2015, p. 414).

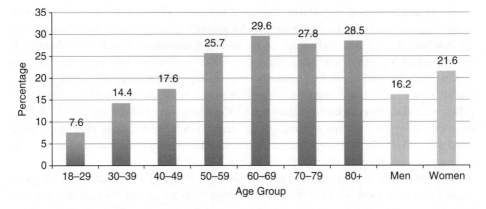

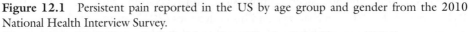

Figure 12.1   Persistent pain reported in the US by age group and gender from the 2010 National Health Interview Survey.
Source: Adapted from Kennedy, Roll, Schraudner, Murphy, & McPherson (2014).

Persistent pain is an especially problematic and debilitating type of pain, characterized as constant pain lasting longer than three months. About 19% of adults in the US report persistent pain, and rates generally increase with advancing age (Kennedy, Roll, Schraudner, Murphy, & McPherson, 2014). As can be seen in Figure 12.1, the prevalence of persistent pain increases steadily from young adulthood through mid-life and peaks in the 60–69-year-old group, at which point it generally levels out. Figure 12.1 also reflects that women report having higher rates of persistent pain than men.

Pain intensity follows a different pattern. Whereas pain prevalence increases with age, the incidence of severe pain is highest in midlife (45–65 years) (Langley, 2011; Molton & Terrill, 2014). Survey data indicate that when older adults acknowledge pain, most (60%) report it as moderate, while approximately 25% describe it as "severe" (Langley, 2011; Molton &Terrill, 2014).

Among older adults, persistent pain limits activities because engaging in the activity increases pain or the older person is afraid of injuring herself further and exacerbating the pain (Molton & Terrill, 2014). Although an initial reduction of activity may make sense in response to acute pain, ongoing activity reduction in the face of persistent pain may have both physical and social impacts. Physically, activity reduction may lead to increased weight and, in some case, obesity, which further limits activities and increases pain in knees, hips, and lower back (Molton & Terrill, 2014). Similarly, decreased activity may erode sources of social support and contact.

Persistent pain can also affect an older adult's pattern of sleep—both getting to sleep and staying asleep (Chen, Hayman, Shmerling, Bean, & Leveille, 2011), especially for older adults with pain at multiple sites. As a result, almost half of middle-aged and older adults with persistent pain also report chronic sleep deprivation (Artner et al., 2013). Sleep deprivation can also contribute to decreased activity and greater disability over time (Molton & Terrill, 2014).

Persistent pain may also affect older adults' mood, in particular clinically relevant depression. Among older adults with persistent pain, approximately one-fourth experience major depression (Gleicher, Croxford, Hochman, & Hawker, 2011; Molton &

Terrill, 2014). In addition, persistent pain is associated with increased rates of suicidal ideation among older adults (Almeida et al., 2012). Older adults who have both chronic pain and depression often experience an overlap of both somatic symptoms and depressive symptoms (Parmelee, Harralson, McPherron, & Schumacher, 2013), making assessment a challenge—a theme we will return to later in this chapter.

Risk factors

An estimated 60–75% of older adults (65 and over) report at least some persistent pain (Tsang et al., 2008). Pain is often associated with chronic medical conditions that occur in later life. For example, older adults with osteoarthritis report high rates of low back or neck pain (65%). Older adults also report significant rates of musculoskeletal pain (approximately 40%), peripheral neuropathic pain (35%, often associated with diabetes), and chronic joint pain (15–25%) (Molton & Terrill, 2014). Not surprisingly, residents in long-term-care settings, who have higher rates of chronic illness, also report higher rates of persistent pain than community-dwelling older adults. While rates of persistent pain may range from 25–65% of community older adults, these rates may reach as high as 80% in long-term-care settings (Charlton, 2005).

Of special concern for clients with chronic pain is the risk of prescription opioid abuse. Recent national attention has focused on the economic and clinical impact of abuse, in the light of very real possibility for abuse by chronic pain sufferers (Institute of Medicine, 2011). Despite public concern, however, there are few evidence-based treatment approaches to guide the use of opioid treatment in general and for older adults in particular. Chou and his colleagues (Chou et al., 2015) conducted a meta-analysis of the effectiveness and risks of long-term (more than one year) opioid therapy for chronic pain. They found that, despite widespread use of opioid therapy and increasing risks for adverse outcomes (e.g., opioid-related overdose, falls, fractures), there is such a dearth of research that we cannot reliably assess the effectiveness of long-term opioid therapy for chronic pain. The US Department of Health and Human Services (2016) has outlined a plan for developing a national pain strategy, including additional outcomes research and prescriber education. For the moment, though, the best advice on opioid prescribing for older adults with chronic pain may be to start low and go slow.

Theories of etiology

Similar to the sexual and sleep disorders covered earlier in this chapter, the etiology of pain is also best conceptualized as having biopsychosocial elements. From a neurological perspective, changes associated with normal aging (e.g., reduction in brain volume in the prefrontal cortex and the hypothalamus) may contribute to increasing perceptions and reporting of pain with increasing age (Molton & Terrill, 2014). In a comprehensive review of theories of etiology, Hadjistavropoulos (2015) emphasized three models that highlight the role of psychological factors in pain: the operant model, the fear avoidance model, and the cognitive-behavioral theory of pain.

As introduced in Chapter 5, the operant model focuses our attention on the consequences of pain behavior, including how those consequences might maintain and increase the pain behavior (e.g., Fordyce, Shelton, & Dundore, 1982). This model draws our attention to the interpersonal and behavioral context of an individual's pain. For example, a widow who complains of chronic pain may find that she gets more visits and social support from her friends than when she had no such complaints. One aspect that the operant model does not encompass is the important role of the individual's appraisal as part of the pain experience (Sharp, 2001).

The fear avoidance model of pain views pain through the lenses of classical conditioning (Vlaeyen & Linton, 2000). Within this perspective, an older adult's movement that is associated with pain (e.g., walking down stairs) may become a conditioned stimulus for fear of pain. Similarly, if avoiding that activity reduces pain, the immobility becomes reinforced. If avoiding the stairs reduces pain, eventually this might lead to less ability to navigate the stairs or more.

The focus here is on assessing what established the avoidance in the first place and what maintains it. The following example illustrates the cycle of avoidance and immobility in some cases of chronic pain:

> Mary Ellen had almost died from a brain aneurysm. Now, seven months after rehabilitation in a long-term-care setting, she was back home. Her physician urged her to walk every day, but she still moved slowly, in part because she was worried about falling on the uneven paths near her home in the country. As the months went by, she walked less and less.
>
> Meanwhile, she began to "reward" herself with comfort food whenever she felt depressed or in pain; her favorite reward was ice cream. Over the next year, Mary Ellen gained almost 100 pounds. The added weight made it hard for her to walk; her knees ached and she became more concerned about falling.

The underlying assumptions of the cognitive-behavioral theory of pain are outlined in Table 12.3. This model assumes a much more active role for the individual in forming a perception of pain and in developing and maintaining reactions to pain. One area of emphasis, for example, is the interaction between the individual and her environment—not only the behavioral antecedents and consequences, but the person's thoughts and perceptions—the cognitive portion of the cognitive behavioral model. Not surprisingly, these different theories and models focus our attention on different aspects of assessment and intervention. We turn to these next.

Table 12.3 Basic assumptions of the cognitive-behavioral model of pain

1	People actively interpret their experiences.
2	Beliefs and perceptions can affect psychological states, physical functioning, and behavior.
3	Behavior is a function of the person and the environment and their interaction.
4	Maladaptive ways of feeling, thinking, and behaving may have been learned.
5	People contribute to developing and maintaining maladaptive thoughts and can be agents in changing these thoughts.

Source: Adapted from Hadjistavropoulos (2015) and Skinner, Wilson, & Turk (2012).

Assessment

Hadjistavropoulos (2015) outlined the central areas of a clinical interview assessment of an older adult's pain experience. He emphasized the importance of involving an interdisciplinary team in the assessment process, including a physician to provide a comprehensive physical examination and a psychologist to assess the emotional and psychological contributors to pain.

History   A starting point for the assessment is the client's description of the pain and its effects on daily functioning, including the timing of onset and fluctuations. Simple numeric rating scales (0–10) or simple verbal ratings (mild, severe, very severe) offer an initial assessment (Hadjistavropoulos, 2015). Detailed history of changes in the intensity or frequency of pain may be key to identifying etiology.

Another approach focuses on brief assessment measures with proven psychometric properties for use with older adults. Hadjistavropoulos (2015) recommends two instruments: the Brief Pain Inventory (BPI) (Cleeland & Ryan, 1994) along with the Short-Form of the McGill Pain Questionnaire (MPQ-SF) (Melzack, 1975). The BPI includes self-reported pain intensity and the self-reported extent to which pain interferes with functioning. The MPQ-SF has 15 pain quality words that are scored on a Likert scale for severity.

The client's expectations about pain and aging are also key components of the assessment (Molton & Terrill, 2014). For example, do they underreport pain because they expect that increasing pain comes with increasing age? Do they compare this current pain pattern with pain or disruption caused by another medical problem, leading to underreporting or affecting the clinician's accurate understanding of the course, severity, and impact of the pain? Do they compare their situation to friends' experiences? Another key element is the client's social support system (Molton &Terrill, 2014). Are there close friends to turn to for physical and psychological support? What is the client's history with the give-and-take of social support?

Antecedents   It is useful to assess the physical and psychological antecedent of the pain. What is the context for the current situation? Consider the following incident:

> Ida had always led an active life. Her diagnosis of Parkinson's disease hit her hard. Recently, she had curtailed her active exercise program, because of pain. Today, she called for an appointment for a painful episode of sciatica. It turns out that she had walked eight miles the day before, because she was feeling very good. In conversation with her physician, it was clear that the physical strain of overdoing her return to exercise was a key element in Ida's sciatica. Another contributor, though, was her ongoing resistance to limit her activities because of her Parkinson's diagnosis.

Consequences   Another assessment area is the set of consequences of pain for the client, both physical and psychological. In Ida's case, she could barely move because of the sciatica, leaving her temporarily housebound and depressed.

Comorbidities   What are the other physical and psychological conditions that challenge the coping capacity of the client? Optimally, these will emerge in a comprehensive physical and in the clinical interview. This area includes the client's current and previous treatment history for these conditions.

Goals   What are the client's expectations, concerns, and goals for treatment? Are they realistic, given the client's own history and lifestyle? What are the expectations for ownership of the goals? Does he expect a medication to restore a pain-free life? Does she believe she must create goals for changing her lifestyle behaviors in order to minimize pain?

Special concerns in assessment in the presence of dementia   Most of the pain assessment processes described above rely upon self-report. Depending on the extent of cognitive deterioration, this is problematic when the client has a dementing illness. As Hadjistavropoulos (2015) points out, there is a danger of undertreatment of pain in clients with dementia. In contrast, 30–50% of people with dementia experience persistent pain (Corbett et al., 2012; McAuliffe, Brown, & Fetherstonhaugh, 2012). Thus, it is important to assure assessment strategies are available for all clients.

An initial approach is to use a screening tool to assess for cognitive impairment. For example, Hadjistavropoulos (2005) suggested that clients with scores of 18 or more on the Mini-Mental Status Examination (MMSE) (Folstein, Folstein, & McHugh, 1975) usually can self-report pain, while those with scores of 13 or less have difficulty. (See Chapter 8 for a fuller discussion of assessing cognitive impairment.) Those whose score falls between 13 and 18 may be prime candidates for a fuller assessment beyond the screening tool.

Some simple self-report approaches (e.g., a simple number rating or a simple verbal descriptor) may work with clients with a neurocognitive disorder. Another approach is the colored visual analogue scale (CAS; McGrath et al., 1996). Hadjistavropoulos (2015) described the CAS:

> The CAS typically is made of plastic and has rectangular shape (like ruler). The front of the scale shows the words *most pain* at the top and *no pain* at the bottom. Moreover, the color of the scale starts as a white to light pink at the bottom and becomes progressively more red as it approaches the top of the scale. The patient uses a plastic glide, that moves along the scale, to indicate his or her level of pain. The back of the scale includes numbers (0–10) that can be recorded by the clinician and signify pain intensity (10 = glide at the stop of the scale...) (p. 419).

The CAS has proven reliable in assessing clients with dementia. As a first step, it is important to assure that the client can point out the scale, and can anchor the glide in the "no pain" position.

Another approach is an observational scale, focused on pain-related behaviors (Hadjistavropoulos, 2015). For example, a 31-item version of the Pain Assessment Checklist for Seniors with Limited Ability to Communicate includes behaviors that are useful for pain assessment (e.g., facial expressions, vocalizations, body movements, changes in activity patterns, interpersonal interactions) (Chan, Hadjistavropoulos,

Williams, & Lints-Martindale, 2014). Hadjistavropoulos (2015) cautions, however, that individual differences are important in assessing an older adult with a cognitive disorder. Thus, individual baselines and observations or reports on deviations from that baseline are important.

Interventions for chronic pain

A starting point for an effective intervention plan for an older adult coping with chronic pain is understanding her own assumptions and expectations about pain and about the clinician's ability to intervene. For example, older adults tend to minimize or underreport their pain, compared to younger adults (Molton & Terrell, 2014). This pattern may stem from a self-statement like the following: "Of course I have pain; I'm old. And the older I get, the more I'll be in pain." In her mind, equating chronic pain with advanced age leaves little room for intervention (other than age-reversal schemes!).

Fear may be another element in the client's approach to assessment and intervention. Especially if the cause of the pain is uncertain, an older client may choose to "not know": "What I don't know can't hurt me." This fear may also keep older clients away from earlier assessment and treatment activities. Generational differences may also affect what is disclosed and what is considered an appropriate intervention topic. A 90-year-old woman, for example, reported to her daughter that she did not feel comfortable talking to her physician (whom she'd seen for 35+ years) about a painful urinary tract infection because "you just don't talk to doctors about those things."

For all of these reasons, the first step of the intervention process may need to be an educational one, focusing in a more detailed way on the links between the assessment findings and the intervention strategies, while also assessing the client's internal and external barriers to treatment. With this context, we will consider several intervention approaches and conclude with comments on the contexts of interventions and providers.

Pharmacological approaches Although older adults are generally more adherent to prescription use than younger populations, this trend does not hold when it comes to medications prescribed particularly for pain. With these medications, they may self-manage their regimen: taking lower doses and/or taking them less frequently than directed by the prescriber (e.g., Chang, Wray, Sessanna, & Peng, 2011); stockpiling unused pills (e.g., Ellis, Mullan, & Worsley, 2011); or sharing "pain pills" with friends in need.

Thus, an initial starting point for the intervention effort is often a "brown bag" exercise, asking the client to bring in the prescription and over-the-counter medications that he or she currently has available to help manage the pain. This allows the clinician to compare the prescriber's intent on the label (frequency and dose) with the client's self-report of use.

We have discussed the risks of polypharmacy in treating older adults in Chapter 13. In treating chronic pain, a starting assumption is the importance of integrating pharmacotherapy and its adherence into a broader treatment plan for the older client.

Nonpharmacological approaches Hadjistavropoulos (2015) provided a useful distinction among several distinct non-pharmacological approaches.

Cognitive-behavioral therapy Skinner and her colleagues (Skinner et al., 2012) outlined four broad areas of therapeutic techniques that might be useful for people with chronic pain: (1) cognitive techniques, including approaches such as cognitive restructuring and problem solving; (2) behavioral techniques, such as relaxation approaches and behavioral activation; (3) supportive techniques, such as psychoeducational approaches focused on the client's self-statements; and (4) complementary approaches, such as hypnosis or biofeedback. (See Hadjistavropoulos, 2015) for a fuller discussion of these approaches.)

One meta-analysis of the effectiveness of CBT for older adults with chronic pain (Lunde, Nordhus, & Pallesen, 2009) found a moderate effect of CBT on self-reported pain, but not on other areas such as physical function, depression, and medication use. The long-term efficacy of CBT for chronic pain in older adults remains to be determined.

Mindfulness approaches This range of approaches encompasses attention to mediation, a focus on breathing, and nonjudgmental attention to the body. Among them are acceptance and commitment therapy (ACT). ACT focuses on the client's emotions and thoughts, using them as targets for exposure. Efficacy comparisons have been made between ACT and relaxation approaches (Thorsell et al., 2011) and between ACT and CBT (Wetherell et al., 2011). However, relatively little research has been done on ACT with older adults experiencing chronic pain. One exception is work by McCracken and Jones (2012) that offers preliminary support for using ACT with clients over 60. Clearly, this is another area ripe for further study.

Self-management of pain A final approach to intervention is to work with the client in implementing self-management strategies, either alone, with professional supervision, or in a group (Hadjistavropoulos, 2012). This approach capitalizes upon the individual's unique history of chronic pain perception and presentation, and unique ecosystem of support. However, it also faces challenges of lower compliance and fidelity to the treatment plan. Although there have been reports of success in managing pain and disability among those with arthritis (e.g., Du et al., 2011), other results have been mixed (Hadjistavropoulos, 2015). Since "self-management" encompasses a range of approaches and can include both the presence and absence of professional assistance, this is an area that needs standardized approaches to be used across a variety of settings and populations to establish more robust efficacy information.

Barriers to treatment Some of the issues that arise in self-management apply more broadly to all potential interventions. Older adults have usually developed a history of coping with pain prior to the current consultation. This may include both limiting activities (reducing social contacts, not going out) as well as pacing themselves if they are not feeling well. We include this under barriers, because the client's history of coping with pain may frame her expectations and involvement with any intervention plan.

Another set of barriers may be on the other side of the consultation desk: If care providers expect that chronic pain is part of the aging process, they may contribute to the pattern of underinvestigation and undertreatment (Molton & Terrell, 2014).

It is important to assess the team's individual and collective expectations and how these frame success for treating chronic pain.

Finally, as with any other condition, the client's social and cultural context may affect treatment outcomes. Chronic pain may be more difficult to treat effectively in settings or communities that have fewer resources (e.g., rural, under-resourced). The following case report, drawn from our experience, illustrates the impact of cultural context on the client's expectations and the therapist's response:

> Mrs. Davis came to the rural mental health clinic complaining of chronic back pain. She knew the source of the pain which she'd had for a couple of years: Her neighbor had put a curse on her because of a disagreement about trash in the yard. Mrs. Davis was convinced that it was the neighbor's curse that was the cause; she was at the clinic to get the cause reversed.
>
> The therapist conducted a clinical interview and assessment process, ruling out a variety of other causes. With her permission, he had also reviewed Mrs. Davis's electronic medical records, which were available online. Her primary care physician had found no physical cause for her pain.
>
> After the assessment and consultation, the therapist asked Mrs. Davis to wait for a few moments. He came back with a mask on, carrying a rattle with feathers. Mrs. Davis said, "What are you doing?" The therapist replied, "I am breaking the spell." After a couple of minutes of chanting and circling Mrs. Davis, the therapist told her that the spell had been broken and the pain would slowly recede over the next 24 hours. Mrs. Davis reported three days later that the pain was gone.

Summary and Conclusions

Three categories of disorders were addressed in this chapter: sexual disorders, sleep disorders, and chronic pain disorders. Research on sexual disorders in older adults is growing rapidly, generating effective strategies for assessment and intervention of the most common disorders. Sleep disorders are common in older adults and produce a wide range of deleterious effects. Strategies to improve sleep quantity and quality have been demonstrated to have benefits for older adults. Chronic pain is another common concern for older adults. This area has seen progress in assessment strategies and initial intervention work. All three areas warrant additional research to develop a sufficient evidence-base to treat the full range of disorders that are known to affect older adults.

Critical Thinking / Discussion Questions

1 At a family reunion, your grandmother asks you for advice: She complains that she is not sleeping well—waking early, feeling sleepy throughout the day. She is considering taking an over-the-counter sleep medication. What would you recommend for her?

2   You have been asked to consult with a continuing care retirement community regarding "sex after 60." Staff members are not sure what is appropriate among residents in independent living and among those in long-term-care settings. Outline the offerings you would include in workshops for both residents and staff members.
3   The pain clinic at the local hospital is concerned about the increase of opioid addiction in the region. They ask you for advice on chronic pain approaches for their geriatric patients. What would you recommend?

Website Resources

American Psychological Association Office on Aging (2007): Aging and Human Sexuality Resource Guide
http://www.apa.org/pi/aging/resources/guides/sexuality.aspx
The National Institute on Aging: Sexuality in Later Life
https://www.nia.nih.gov/health/publication/sexuality-later-life
The AARP: Sex & Intimacy
http://www.aarp.org/home-family/sex-intimacy
The American Academy of Sleep Medicine: Sleep Education
http://www.sleepeducation.org/home
National Sleep Foundation: Aging and Sleep
https://sleepfoundation.org/sleep-topics/aging-and-sleep
American Psychological Association: Older Adults and Insomnia Resource Guide
http://www.apa.org/pi/aging/resources/guides/insomnia.aspx
The Institute of Medicine (2011): Relieving Pain in America—A Blueprint for Transforming Prevention, Education, Care and Research
https://www.ncbi.nlm.nih.gov/pubmed/22553896
US Department of Health and Human Services (2016): HHS National Pain Strategy
https://iprcc.nih.gov/docs/HHSNational_Pain_Strategy.pdf

References

Albersen, M., Orabi, H., & Lue, T.F. (2012). Evaluation and treatment of erectile dysfunction in the aging male: A mini-review. *Gerontology, 58*, 3–14. doi: 10.1159/000329598

Almeida, O. P., Draper, B., Snowdon, J., Lautenschlager, N.T., Pirkis, J., Byrne, G., ... Pfaff, J. J. (2012). Factors associated with suicidal thoughts in a large community sample of older adults. *The British Journal of Psychiatry, 201*, 466–472. doi:10.1192/bjp.bp.112.110130

Ambler, D. R., Bieber, E. J., & Diamond, M. P. (2012). Sexual function in elderly women: A review of current literature. *Reviews in Obstetrics and Gynecology, 5*, 16–27.

American Bar Association/American Psychological Association. (2008). *Assessment of older adults with diminished capacity: A handbook for psychologists.* Washington, DC: Author.

American Psychiatric Association. (2013). *Diagnostic and statistical manual of mental disorders* (5th ed.). Arlington, VA: Author.

Ancoli-Israel, S., & Ayalon, L. (2006). Diagnosis and treatment of sleep disorders in older adults. *American Journal of Geriatric Psychiatry, 14*, 95–103.

Ancoli-Israel, S., Kripke, D. F., Klauber, M. R., Fell, R., & Kaplan, O. (1991). Sleep-disordered breathing in community-dwelling elderly. *Sleep, 14,* 486–495.

Annon, J. F. (1974). *The behavioral treatment of sexual problems.* Honolulu, HI: Enabling Systems.

Artner, J., Cakir, B., Spiekermann, J., Kurz, S., Leucht, F., Reichel, H., & Lettig, F. (2013). Prevalence of sleep deprivation in patients with chronic neck and back pain: A retrospective evaluation of 1,016 patients. *Journal of Pain Research, 6,* 1–6. doi:10.2147/JPR.S36386

Bailes, S., Baltzan, M., Alapin, I, Fichten, C. S., & Libman, E. (2005). Diagnostic indicators of sleep apnea in older women and men: A prospective study. *Journal of Psychosomatic Research, 59,* 365–373.

Bain, K. T. (2006). Management of chronic insomnia in elderly persons. *The American Journal of Geriatric Pharmacotherapy, 4,* 168–192.

Calzo, J. P., Antonucci, T. C., Mays, V. M., & Cochran, S. D. (2011). Retrospective recall of sexual orientation identity development among gay, lesbian, and bisexual adults. *Developmental Psychology, 47*(6), 1658–1673. doi: 10.1037/a0025508

Carney, C. E., Buysse, D. J., Ancoli-Israel, S., Edinger, J. D., Krystal, A. D., Lichstein, K. L., & Morin, C.M. (2012). The consensus sleep diary: Standardizing prospective sleep self-monitoring. *Sleep, 35*(2), 287–302. doi.org/10.5665/sleep 1642

Chan, S., Hadjistavropoulos, T., Williams, J., & Lints-Martindale, A. (2014). Evidence-based development and initial validation of the Pain Assessment Check List for Seniors with Limited Ability to Communicate–II. *Clinical Journal of Pain, 30,* 816–824. doi: 10.1097/AJP 0000000000000039

Chang, Y., Wray, L. O., Sessanna, L., & Peng, H. (2011). Use of prescription opioid medication among community-dwelling older adults with noncancer persistent pain. *Journal of Addictions Nursing, 22,* 19–24. doi:10.3109/10884602.2010.545088

Charlton, J. E. (2005). *Core curriculum for professional education in pain* (3rd ed.). Seattle, WA: IASP Press.

Chen, Q., Hayman, L. L., Shmerling, R. G., Bean, J. F., & Leveille, S. G. (2011). Characteristics of persistent pain associated with sleep difficulty in older adults: The Maintenance of Balance, Independent Living, Intellect, and Zest in the Elderly (MOBILIZE) Boston study. *Journal of the American Geriatrics Society, 59,* 1385–1392. doi:10.1111/j.1532-5415.2011.03544.x

Chou, R., Turner, J. A., Devine, E. B., Hansen, R. N., Sullivan, S. D., Blazina, I., …Deyo, R. A. (2015). The effectiveness and risks of long-term opioid therapy for chronic pain: A systematic review for a National Institutes of Health pathways to prevention workshop. *Annals of Internal Medicine, 162,* 276–286. doi: 10.7326/M14-2559

Cleeland, C. S., & Ryan, K. M. (1994) Pain assessment: Global use of the Brief Pain Inventory. *Annals of the Academy of Medicine Singapore, 23,* 129–138.

Corbett, A., Husebo, B., Malcangio, M., Staniland, A., Cohen-Mansfield, J., Aarsland, D., & Ballard, C. (2012). Assessment and treatment of pain in people with dementia. *Nature Reviews Neurology, 8*(5), 264–274. doi:10.1038/nrneurol.2012.53

Crowther, M. R., & Zeiss, A. M. (1999). Cognitive-behavior therapy in older adults: A case involving sexual functioning. *In Session: Psychotherapy in Practice, 55,* 961–975.

DeLamater, J. (2012). Sexual expression in later life: A review and synthesis. *Journal of Sex Research, 49,* 125–141. doi: 10.1080/00224499.2011.603168

DeLamater, J. D., & Sill, M. (2005). Sexual desire in later life. *Journal of Sex Research, 42,* 138–149.

Dew, M. A., Hoch, C. C., Buysse, D. J., Monk, T. H., Begley, A. E., Houck, P. R., …Reynolds, C. F. (2003). Healthy older adults' sleep predicts all-cause mortality at 4 to 19 years of follow-up. *Psychosomatic Medicine, 65,* 63–72.

Du, S., Yaun, C., Xiao, X., Chu, J., Qiu, Y., & Qian, H. (2011). Self-management programs for chronic musculoskeletal pain conditions: A systematic review and meta-analysis. *Patient Education and Counseling, 85,* e299–e310.

Ellis, J. C., Mullan, J., & Worsley, T. (2011). Prescription medication hoarding and borrowing or sharing behaviours in older residents in the Illawarra, New South Wales, Australia. *Australasian Journal of Ageing, 30*, 119–123. doi:10.1111/j.1741-6612.2010.00457.x

Folstein, M. L., Folstein, S. E., & McHugh, P. R. (1975). Mini-mental state: A practical method for grading the cognitive status of patients for the clinician. *Journal of Psychiatric Research, 12*, 189–198.

Fordyce, W. E., Shelton, J. L., & Dundore, D. E. (1982). The modification of avoidance learning pain behaviors. *Journal of Behavioral Medicine, 5*, 405–414. doi:10.1007/BF00845370

Friedman, J. H. (2013). *Making the connection between brain and behavior: Coping with Parkinson's disease* (2nd ed.). New York, NY: Demos Health.

Galinsky, A. M. (2012). Sexual touching and difficulties with sexual arousal and orgasm among U.S. older adults. *Archives of Sexual Behavior, 41*, 875–890. doi: 10.1007/s10508-011-9873-7

Gleicher, Y., Croxford, R., Hochman, J., & Hawker, G. (2011). A prospective study of mental health care for comorbid depressed mood in older adults with painful osteoarthritis. *BMC Psychiatry, 11*, 147–157. doi:10.1186/1471-244X-11-147

Gooneratne, N. S., Weaver, T. E., Cater, J. R., Pack, F. M., Arner, H. M., Greenberg, A. S., & Pack, A. I. (2003). Functional outcomes of excessive daytime sleepiness in older adults. *Journal of the American Geriatrics Society, 51*, 642–649.

Hadjistavropoulos, T. (2015). Pain assessment and management in older adults. In P. A. Lichtenberg & B. T. Mast (Eds.), *APA handbook of clinical geropsychology. Vol. 2: Assessment, treatment, and issues of later life* (pp. 413–439). doi: 10.1037/14459-016

Hadjistavropoulos, T. (2012). Self-management of pain in older persons: Helping people help themselves. *Pain Medicine, 13*, S67–S71. doi: 10.1111/j.1526-4637.2011.01272.x

Hadjistavropoulos, T. (2005). Assessing pain in older persons with severe limitations in ability to communicate. In S. Gibson & D. Weiner (Eds.), *Pain in older persons* (pp. 135–151). Seattle, WA: IASP Press.

Hillman, J. (2011). *Sexuality and aging: Clinical perspectives.* New York, NY: Springer.

Hinchliff, S., & Gott, M. (2011). Seeking medical help for sexual concerns in mid-and later-life: A review of the literature. *Journal of Sex Research, 48*, 106–117. doi:10.1080/0022 4499.2010.548610

Institute of Medicine (2011). *Relieving pain in America: A blueprint for transforming prevention, education, care and research.* Washington, DC: National Academies Press.

International Association for the Study of Pain (2017). *IASP taxonomy.* Retrieved from http://www.iasp-pain.org/Taxonomy

Johns, M. W. (1991). A new method for measuring daytime sleepiness: The Epworth sleepiness scale. *Sleep, 14*, 540–545.

Kay, D. B., & Dzierzewski, J. M. (2015). Sleep in the context of healthy aging and psychiatric syndromes. *Sleep Medicine Clinics, 10*(1), 11–15. doi: 10.1016/j.jsmc.2014.11.012

Kennedy, J., Roll, J. M., Schraudner, T., Murphy, S., & McPherson, S. (2014). Prevalence of persistent pain in the US adult population: New data from the 2010 National Health Interview Survey. *Journal of Pain, 15*(10), 979–984.

Kimmel, D., Rose, T., & David, S. (Eds.) (2006). *Lesbian, gay, bisexual and transgender aging: Research and clinical perspectives.* New York, NY: Columbia University Press.

Knauer, N. (2011). "Gen Silent": Advocating for LGBT elders. *Elder Law Journal, 19*, 101–161.

Langley, P. C. (2011). The prevalence, correlates, and treatment of pain in the European Union. *Current Medical Research and Opinion, 27*, 463–480. doi:10.1185/03007995.2010.542136

Laumann, E. O., Nicolosi, A., Glasser, D. B., Paik, A., Gingell, C., Moreira, E., Wang, T., & GSSAB Investigator's Group (2005). Sexual problems among women and men aged 40–80 years: Prevalence and correlates identified in the Global Study of Sexual Attitudes and Behaviors. *International Journal of Impotence Research, 17,* 39–57.

Lichstein, K. L., Durrence, H. H., Riedel, B. W., Taylor, D. J., & Bush, A. J. (2004). *Epidemiology of sleep: Age, gender, and ethnicity.* Mahwah, NJ: Erlbaum.

Lichstein, K. L., Riedel, B. W., Wilson, N. M., Lester, K. W., & Aguillard, R. N. (2001). Relaxation and sleep compression for late-life insomnia: A placebo-controlled trial. *Journal of Consulting and Clinical Psychology, 69,* 227–239.

Lindau S. T, Schumm, L. P., Laumann, E. O., Levinson, W., O'Muircheartaigh, C. A., Waite, L. J. (2007). A study of sexuality and health among older adults in the United States. *New England Journal of Medicine, 357,* 762–774.

Lunde, I., Nordhus, I. H., & Pallesen, S. (2009). The effectiveness of cognitive and behavioural treatment of chronic pain in the elderly: A quantitative review. *Journal of Clinical Psychology in Medical Settings, 16,* 254–262. doi: 10.1007/s10880-009-9162-y

Lyden, M. (2007). Assessment of consent capacity. *Sexuality and Disability, 25,* 3–20. doi:10.1007/s11195-006-9028-2

McAuliffe, L., Brown, D., & Fetherstonhaugh, D. (2012). Pain and dementia: An overview of the literature. *International Journal of Older People Nursing, 7*(3), 219–226. doi:10.1111/j.1748-3743.2012.00331.x

McCoy, N. (2000). The McCoy Female Sexuality Questionnaire. *Quality of Life Research, 9,* 739–745.

McCracken, L. M., & Jones, R. (2012). Treatment for chronic pain for adults in the seventh and eighth decades of life: A preliminary study of Acceptance and Commitment Therapy (ACT). *Pain Medicine, 13,* 860–867. doi: 10.1111/j.1526-4637.2012.01407.x

McCrae, C. S., Roth, A. J., Zamora, R., Dautovich, N. D., & Lichstein, K. L. (2015). Late-life sleep and sleep disorders. In P. A. Lichtenberg & B. T. Mast (Eds.), *APA handbook of clinical geropsychology. Vol. 2: Assessment, treatment, and issues of later life* (pp. 369–394). doi:10.1037/14459-014

McCrae, C. S., Tierney, C. G., & McNamara, J. P. H. (2005). Behavioral intervention for insomnia: Future directions for nontraditional caregivers at various stages of care. *Clinical Gerontologist, 29,* 95–114.

McCurry, S. M., Logsdon, R. G., Vitiello, M. V., & Teri, L. (1998). Successful behavioral treatment for reported sleep problems in elderly caregivers of dementia patients: A controlled study. *Journal of Gerontology B: Psychological and Social Sciences, 53,* 122–129.

McGrath, P. A., Seifert, C., Speechley, K. N., Booth, B., Stitt, L., & Gibson, M. C. (1996). A new analogue scale for assessing children's pain: an initial validation study. *Pain, 64,* 435–443.

Melzack, R. (1975). The McGill Pain Questionnaire: Major properties and scoring methods. *Pain, 1,* 277–299. doi: 10.106/0304-3959(75)90044-5

Merskey, H., & Bogduk, N. (Eds.) (1994). *Classification of chronic pain: Descriptions of chronic pain syndromes and definitions of pain terms.* Seattle, WA: IASP Press.

Molton, I. R., & Terrill, A. L. (2014). Overview of persistent pain in older adults. *American Psychologist, 69,* 197–207. doi: 10.1037/a0035794

Mona, L. R., Syme, M. L., Goldwaser, G., Cameron, R. P., Chen, S., & Clemency, C., … Lemos, L. (2011). Sexual health in older adults: Conceptualization and treatment. In K. Sorocco & S. Lauderdale (Eds.), *Cognitive behavioral therapy with older adults: Innovations across care settings* (pp. 261–285). New York, NY: Springer.

Montplaisir, J. (2004). Abnormal motor behavior during sleep. *Sleep Medicine, 5,* S31–S24.

Morgenthaler, T. I., Aronsky, A. J., Carden, K. A., Chervin, R. D., Thomas, S. M., & Watson, N.F. (2015). Measurement of quality to improve care in sleep medicine. *Journal of Clinical Sleep Medicine, 11*(3), 279–291. doi.:10.5664/jcsm.4548

Morin, C. M., LeBlanc, M., Daley, M., Gregoire, J. P, & Merette, C. (2006). Epidemiology of insomnia: Prevalence, self-help treatments, consultations, and determinants of help-seeking behaviors. *Sleep Medicine, 7*, 123–130.

Neikrug, A. B., & Ancoli-Israel, S. (2010). Sleep disorders in the older adult: A mini-review. *Gerontology, 56*(2), 181–189. doi: 10.1159/000236900

O'Connor, D. B., Corona, G., Forti, G., Tajar, A., Lee, D. M., Finn, J. D., ...Wu, F.C. (2008). Assessment of sexual health in aging men in Europe: Development and validation of the European Male Ageing Study Sexual Function Questionnaire. *Journal of Sexual Medicine, 5*, 1374–1385. doi:10.1111/j.1743-6109.2008.00781.x

Ohayon, M. M. (2002). Epidemiology of insomnia: What we know and what we still need to learn. *Sleep Medicine Reviews, 6*, 97–111.

Ohayon, M. M., Carskadon, M. A., Guilleminault, C., & Vitiello, M.V. (2004). Meta-analysis of quantitative sleep parameters from childhood to old age in healthy individuals: Developing normative sleep values across the human lifespan. *Sleep, 27*, 1255–1273.

Ohayon, M. M., & Roth, T. (2002). Prevalence of restless legs syndrome and periodic limb movement disorder in the general population. *Journal of Psychosomatic Research, 53*, 547–554.

Pangman, V. C., & Seguire, M. (2000). Sexuality and the chronically ill older adult: A social justice issue. *Sexuality and Disability, 18*(1), 49–59.

Parmelee, P. A., Harralson, T. L., McPherron, J. A., & Schumacher, H. R. (2013). The structure of affective symptomatology in older adults with osteoarthritis. *International Journal of Geriatric Psychiatry, 28*, 393– 401. doi:10.1002/gps.3837

Piccolo, R. S., Yang, M., Bliwise, D. L., Yaggi, H. K., & Araujo, A. B. (2013). Racial and socioeconomic disparities in sleep and chronic disease: results of a longitudinal investigation. *Ethnicity & Disease, 23*(4), 499–507.

Porst, H. (2016). Patient insight and treatment expectations in erectile dysfunction. *European Medical Journal, 1*(2), 34–41.

Potter, J. E. (2007). A 60-year-old woman with sexual difficulties. *JAMA, 297*(6), 620–633. doi: 10.1001/jama.297.6.620

Potts, A., Grace, V. M., Vares, T., & Gavey, N. (2006). "Sex for life"? Men's counter-stories on "erectile dysfunction," male sexuality and ageing. *Sociology of Health and Illness, 28*, 306–329.

Reid, K. J., & Zee, P. C. (2011). Circadian disorders of the sleep–wake cycle. In M. H. Kryger, T. Roth, & W.C. Dement (Eds.), *Principles and practice of sleep medicine* (5th ed., pp. 470–482). St. Louis, MO: Elsevier Saunders. doi: 10.1016/B978-1-4160-6645-3.00041-4

Rowland, D., van Diest, S., Incrocci, L., & Slob, A. K. (2005). Psychosexual factors that differentiate men with inhibited ejaculation from men with no dysfunction or another sexual dysfunction. *Journal of Sexual Medicine, 2*(3), 383–389.

Rybarczyk, B., Lund, H. G., Garroway, A. M., & Mack, L. (2013). Cognitive behavioral therapy for insomnia in older adults: Background, evidence, and overview of treatment protocol. *Clinical Gerontologist, 36*, 70–93. doi: 10.1080/07317115.2012.731478

Schutte-Rodin, S., Broch, L., Buysse, D., Dorsey, C., & Sateia, M. (2008). Clinical guideline for the evaluation and management of chronic insomnia in adults. *Journal of Clinical Sleep Medicine, 4*, 487–504.

Sharp, T. J. (2001). Chronic pain: A reformulation of the cognitive-behavioural model. *Behaviour Research and Therapy, 39*, 787–800. doi:10.1016/S0005-7967 (00)00061-9

Sivertsen, B., Omvik, S., & Pallesen, S. (2006). Cognitive behavioral therapy vs. zopiclone for treatment of chronic primary insomnia in older adults: a randomized controlled trial. *JAMA, 295*, 2851–2858. doi:10.1001/jama.295.24.2851

Simon, G. E., & Ludman, E. J. (2006). Outcome of new benzodiazepine prescriptions to older adults in primary care. *General Hospital Psychiatry, 28*, 374–378.

Skinner, M., Wilson, H. D., & Turk, D. C. (2012). Cognitive-behavioral perspective and cognitive-behavioral therapy for people with chronic pain: Distinctions, outcomes, and innovations. *Journal of Cognitive Psychotherapy, 26*, 93–113.

Song, Y., Ancoli-Israel. S., Lewis, C. E., Redline, S., Harrison S. L., Stone, K. L. (2011). The association of race/ethnicity with objectively measured sleep characteristics in older men. *Behavioral Sleep Medicine, 10*(1), 54–69.

Syme, M. L., Cordes, C. C., Cameron, R. P., & Mona, L. R. (2015). Sexual health and well-being in the context of aging. In P. A. Lichtenberg & B. T. Mast (Eds.), *APA handbook of clinical geropsychology. Vol 2: Assessment, treatment, and issues of later life.* (pp. 395–412). doi: 10.1037/14459-015

Thorsell, J., Finnes, A., Dahl, J., Lundgren, T., Gybrant, M., Gordh, T., & Buhrman, M. (2011). A comparative study of 2 manual-based self-help interventions, acceptance, and commitment therapy and applied relaxation, for persons with chronic pain. *Clinical Journal of Pain, 27*, 716–723. doi: 10.1097/AJP.0b013e318219a933

Thorpy, M. J. (2012). Classification of sleep disorders. *Neurotherapeutics, 9*(4), 687–701. doi: 10.1007/s13311-012-0145-6

Tsang, A., Von Korff, M., Lee, S., Alonso, J., Karam, E., Angermeyer, M. C., …Watanabe, M. (2008). Common chronic pain conditions in developed and developing countries: Gender and age differences and comorbidity with depression-anxiety disorders. *Journal of Pain, 9*, 883–891. doi:10.1016/j.jpain.2008.05.005

US Department of Health and Human Services (2016). *HHS National Pain Strategy.* Washington, DC. Retrieved from https://iprcc.nih.gov/docs/HHSNational_Pain_Strategy.pdf

Vlaeyen, J. W. S., & Linton, S. J. (2000). Fear-avoidance and its consequences in chronic musculo-skeletal pain: A state of the art. *Pain, 85*, 317–332. doi: 10.1016/S0304-3959(99)00242-0

Waite, L. J., Laumann, E. O., Das. A., & Schumm, L. P. (2009). Sexuality: Measures of part-nerships, practices, attitudes, and problems in the National Social Life, Health, and Aging Study. *The Journals of Gerontology. Series B: Psychological Sciences and Social Sciences, 64* (Suppl. 1), 56–66. doi:10.1093/geronb/gbp038

Wetherell, J. L., Afari, N., Rutledge, T., Sorrell, J. T., Stoddard, J. A., Petkus, A. J., …Hampton Atkinson, J. (2011). A randomized controlled trial of acceptance and commitment therapy and cognitive-behavioral therapy for chronic pain. *Pain, 152*, 2098–2107. doi: 10.1016/jpain.2011.05.016

Young, T., Palta, M., Dempsey, J., Skatrud, J., Weber, S., & Badr, S. (1993). The occurrence of sleep-disordered breathing among middle-aged adults. *New England Journal of Medicine, 328*, 1230–1235.

Zeiss, A. M., Zeiss, R. A., & Davies, H. M. (1999). Assessment of sexual function and dysfunction in older adults. In P. Lichtenberg (Ed.), *Handbook of assessment in clinical gerontology* (pp. 270–296). New York, NY: Wiley.

13

Substance-Related Disorders and Personality Disorders

Substance-related disorders and personality disorders are often *hidden* problems in later life because either mental health professionals may not detect older adults with difficulties in these areas or older adults themselves do not fully recognize or understand the symptoms of these disorders. The vignettes described below depict the challenging nature of these types of problems because none of the cases show a clear route to appropriate mental health assessment and treatment. For both the substance-related disorders and the personality disorders, we describe epidemiology, presentation in later life, theories of etiology, and approaches to assessment and treatment in older adults. We begin with the substance-related disorders.

Substance-Related Disorders

Lincoln and Lois rarely fought until after his retirement, although their marriage has always been filled with tension. She rarely misses a chance now to let him know just how unhappy she is with his drinking. He tells her to shut up, that there is no problem, and that she should quit trying to take away one of the peaceful pleasures of his retirement. Lincoln doesn't miss the pressure of work but he does miss the peaceful hours of driving that were a daily occurrence in his job as a salesman. Lois used to think she couldn't wait until Lincoln retired, but now is frustrated every afternoon when she hears the whiskey decanter rattle about 3 o'clock. She knows that by dinner he will be pretty out of it, and he will fall asleep by 7 p.m. What kind of retirement is this?

Jim never was much of a drinker throughout his adult years, although he enjoyed a beer or two here or there. But after his wife Ella died from cancer a couple of years ago, he has become increasingly lonely and isolated. After all, it was Ella who

---

Aging and Mental Health, Third Edition. Daniel L. Segal, Sara Honn Qualls, and Michael A. Smyer.
© 2018 John Wiley & Sons, Inc. Published 2018 by John Wiley & Sons, Inc.

was the "social planner" for the couple, and it seems as if Jim's friends have slowly disappeared from his life. Now, in the evenings, Jim finds himself drinking more and more, thinking to himself that he does not have anything else to do to "pass the time." He has also been doubling up on his prescription pain medication, because he likes the way it relaxes him. Recently, he has fallen down a couple of times during periods of intoxication, breaking his arm the last time, but his doctors do not know about his drinking and increased pill popping, and Jim certainly does not want to bring it up.

In the DSM-5 (American Psychiatric Association [APA], 2013), the category of Substance-Related Disorders is divided into two groups: substance use disorders and substance-induced disorders. In essence, the substance-induced disorders refer to substance intoxication and to withdrawal of the various substances of abuse.

In the substance use disorders, the person shows a problematic pattern of use of at least one psychoactive substance. A *psychoactive substance* is one that meaningfully impacts the way one thinks, feels, or behaves. As you can imagine, many different kinds of psychoactive substances can be used and abused, including legal and illegal substances, and they vary tremendously in their psychoactive effects, often dependent on the route of administration (e.g., ingested orally, smoked, injected, snorted) and the amount taken. All substances of abuse directly activate the brain's reward system (APA, 2013), which produces pleasurable effects or a "high" that is emotionally reinforcing. The DSM-5 lists nine specific classes of substances for which one can be diagnosed with a substance use disorder: alcohol; cannabis; hallucinogens (including phencyclidine [PCP] and other hallucinogens, like LSD and mescaline); inhalants (e.g., nitrous oxide); opioids; sedatives, hypnotics, and anxiolytics; stimulants (e.g., cocaine, amphetamines); tobacco; and other (or unknown) substances. Alcohol is, by far, the most commonly abused substance among adults and older adults. Note that caffeine is included as a psychoactive substance in the DSM-5. Caffeine is implicated in two possible diagnoses (caffeine intoxication and caffeine withdrawal), but there is no caffeine use disorder.

Prior editions of the DSM divided substance use disorders into two categories (substance abuse or substance dependence), but this artificial distinction was removed in DSM-5. As a single unified category, a substance use disorder is defined as "a cluster of cognitive, behavioral, and physiological symptoms indicating that the individual continues using the substance despite significant substance-related problems" (APA, 2013, p. 483). Note that the criteria (provided next) focus on *consequences* of the substance use and not on the amount used per se, and that the criteria are the same for each of the nine classes of substance.

According to DSM-5, the diagnosis requires the person to show a problematic pattern of use leading to clinically significant impairment or distress, as manifested by at least two of the following criteria, occurring within a 12-month period:

- The substance is taken in larger amounts or over a longer period than was intended (e.g., the person can't control his use of alcohol, continuing to drink until severely intoxicated despite having set a limit of only one drink).
- There is a persistent desire or unsuccessful efforts to cut down or control substance use. Often, there have been many unsuccessful efforts to decrease or discontinue use.

- A great deal of time is spent in activities necessary to obtain the substance, use the substance, or recover from its effects. In some cases, virtually all of the person's daily activities revolve around substance use.
- Having cravings or strong urges to use the substance.
- Recurrent substance use resulting in failure to fulfill major role obligations at work, school, or home.
- Continued substance use despite having persistent social problems caused or exacerbated by the effects of the substance.
- Important social, occupational, or recreational activities are given up or reduced because of substance use. In some case, the individual may withdraw from family activities and hobbies in order to use the substance in private or to spend more time with substance-using friends.
- Recurrent substance use in situations in which it is physically hazardous (e.g., drunk or buzzed driving).
- Continued substance use despite knowledge of having a persistent physical or psychological problem that is likely to have been caused or exacerbated by the substance (e.g., continuing to drink alcohol despite an awareness that the alcohol worsens the person's feelings of depression or worsens the person's liver problems).
- Tolerance, defined by either a need for markedly increased amounts of the substance to achieve intoxication or a markedly diminished effect with continued use of the same amount of the substance. The degree to which tolerance develops varies greatly across substances. Individuals with heavy use of alcohol, opioids (morphine), and stimulants (cocaine) can develop substantial (e.g., tenfold) levels of tolerance, often to a dosage that would be lethal to a nonuser.
- Withdrawal, as manifested by either the characteristic withdrawal syndrome for the substance or the substance (or related substance) is taken to relieve or avoid withdrawal symptoms. The withdrawal syndrome includes negative physical and psychological reactions evidenced when a person suddenly stops taking a substance to which the person is addicted. Withdrawal occurs when blood or tissue concentrations of a substance decline in an individual who had maintained prolonged heavy use of the substance. Although withdrawal symptoms vary somewhat across the various classes of substances, some common symptoms include: sweating, cramping, nausea or vomiting, anxiety, agitation, insomnia, shaking, and in more severe cases having hallucinations, delusions, and seizures.

As an organizational expedient, the criteria for substance use disorder (mentioned above) may be grouped into four categories: impaired control (criteria 1–4); social impairment (criteria 5–7); risky use (criteria 8–9); and pharmacological (or biological) impacts (criteria 10–11) (APA, 2013). Regarding this latter group, tolerance and withdrawal represent physical signs of substance use, sometimes called physical signs of addiction. Note, however, that the DSM does not use the word addiction as a diagnostic term. Some people unwittingly do develop tolerance to an addictive substance when they are in fact not abusing or misusing the substance. For example, one of our former psychotherapy clients was an older woman who had been taking a morning and nighttime dose of valium, as prescribed, for many years. Over time she developed tolerance to the usual dosing and she became concerned because she did not want to increase her dose. In contrast, the majority of people who develop a large tolerance to an addictive substance are in fact abusing the substance. Let's use alcohol as an illustrative example. Most social drinkers (e.g., having a beer or glass of wine with dinner) do not develop tolerance to alcohol. In contrast, we know some heavy drinkers of alcohol who can drink a case of beer or a 750 ml bottle of vodka in an evening, yet they do not usually appear to be highly intoxicated. This level of tolerance almost certainly indicates a problem.

Withdrawal causes other problems. Most if not all people who begin using a psychoactive substance do so because use of the substance makes them feel good. However, many people who become addicted to a substance find themselves, over time, using it to *avoid feeling bad*. In essence, they are now using to avoid experiencing unpleasant symptoms of withdrawal. Similar to the development of significant tolerance, using to avoid withdrawal is a sign of abuse or misuse of a substance, in most cases.

Due to the dimensional nature of substance use disorders, severity specifiers are included in the DSM-5. As part of the diagnosis, the person's pattern of use may be specified as mild (presence of two or three symptoms), moderate (four or five symptoms), or severe (six symptoms or more). These same severity specifiers may be used for all nine classes of substances.

Polysubstance abuse, which refers to use of different substances at the same time, can be exceptionally dangerous, and even deadly, due to the interactions among the substances. For example, combinations of alcohol and sedatives can lead to respiratory arrest since both substances are central nervous system depressants and slow bodily functions. When clients admit to misuse or abuse of any psychoactive substance, the clinician should do a thorough assessment of polysubstance abuse.

Substance abuse in older adults tends to focus on a different set of psychoactive substances than those abused by younger adults, with the exception of alcohol, which is commonly abused across the adult lifespan. Compared with younger adults, older adults are far less likely to abuse illegal drugs (e.g., heroin, cocaine, LSD), but they are far more likely to misuse or abuse psychoactive prescription medications and over-the-counter (OTC) medications (Blow & Barry, 2012). The consequences of this "legal" drug abuse can be as serious as illegal drug use, but has generated far less attention from substance abuse intervention programs.

Prevalence

In the United States, substance abuse is a pervasive and costly problem. According to the 2014 National Survey on Drug Use and Health (Center for Behavioral Health Statistics and Quality, 2015), approximately 21.5 million people aged 12 and older (representing about 8% of the people aged 12 and over in the US) met criteria for substance use disorder in the past year (see Figure 13.1). The vast majority of those diagnosed had an alcohol use disorder (17 million people).

The substance abuse problem among older adults is serious as well, although definitive prevalence data for community-dwelling older adults are lacking for many specific substances. We know the most about alcohol use disorder. In 2013, 41.7% of older adults (ages 65+) reported current alcohol use within the past month, 9.1%

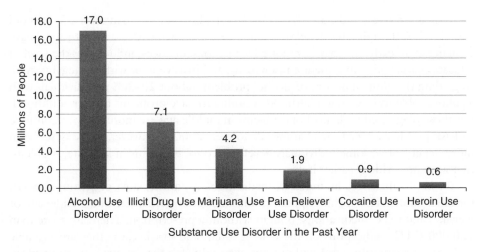

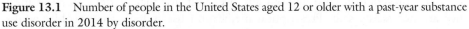
Substance Use Disorder in the Past Year

Figure 13.1   Number of people in the United States aged 12 or older with a past-year substance use disorder in 2014 by disorder.
Source: Adapted from Center for Behavioral Health Statistics and Quality (2015).
Note: People may be diagnosed with more than one disorder.

reported binge drinking (defined as having five or more drinks on the same occasion on at least one day in the past month), and 2.1% reported heavy use (defined as having five or more drinks on the same occasion on each of five or more days in the past month) (Substance Abuse and Mental Health Services Administration, 2014). In general, older adults consume less alcohol and have fewer alcohol-related problems than younger adults. In fact, the rates peak in the 21–25-year-old age group for current alcohol use (69.3%), binge drinking (43.3%), and heavy use of alcohol (13.1%) (Substance Abuse and Mental Health Services Administration, 2014).

However, it appears that drinking patterns remain relatively stable with age (Wang & Andrade, 2013), likely reflecting the social and cultural norms that prevailed when the person began drinking, and indicating that the negative effects of alcohol misuse among older adults remain substantial. Rates for alcohol problems among older adults are especially elevated, as high as 22%, in specific groups such as medical inpatients, outpatient psychiatric patients, and emergency department admits (Kuerbis & Sacco, 2013). Despite these high rates, substance abuse is likely underdiagnosed and underreported in the older adult population, due to the tendency among older adults toward denial, inadequate screening and case-finding strategies, and limited relevance of some diagnostic criteria for substance abuse (Blow & Barry, 2012; King, Van Hasselt, Segal, & Hersen, 1994). Unfortunately, lack of accurate detection and diagnosis is a major barrier to adequate intervention.

Young adulthood is the life period associated with the highest rates of alcohol use and misuse. The 2013 National Survey on Drug Use and Health (Substance Abuse and Mental Health Services Administration, 2014) revealed that 21–25-year-olds reported the highest levels of current alcohol use (69.3%). Rates of current alcohol use generally declined with advancing age, but were still significant in older age groups (69% in 26–29-year-olds; 63.6% in 30–34-year-olds, 60.2% in 35–39-year-olds, 60.7% in 40–44-year-olds, 58.9% in 45–49-year-olds; 59.9% in 50–54-year-olds,

52.5% in 55–59-year-olds, 53.6% in 60–64-year-olds, and 41.7% in those 65 years old and older). Although rates of heavy alcohol use are known to decrease with age, heavy drinking at an early age may have long-lasting consequences, influencing the level of education attained, subsequent employment, and involvement with the legal system. Regarding the lifespan history of alcohol problems, about 20–30% of individuals with alcohol problems in young adulthood continue to have problems in later adulthood, but those diagnosed with alcohol problems in middle age are more likely to continue to have problems over time (Larimer & Kilmer, 2000). However, as we describe in more detail below, some individuals develop alcohol problems in later life, problems that were not evident earlier in life.

Abuse of substances intended as medications is another area of serious concern for older adults. This includes prescription medications (whether obtained legally or illegally) and OTC medications, bought without a prescription. There are more than 100,000 OTC medications on the market today, and just because they are available without a prescription (and without any oversight, for that matter) does not mean they are necessarily safe. Prescription medication use is high among older adults. According to the National Center for Health Statistics (2016), 89.8% of older adults (65+) took at least one prescription medication in the past 30 days, 64.8% took three or more medications, and 39.1% took five or more medications (aggregated data from 2009–2012). Put another way, it is normative for older adults to be on multiple medications. Table 13.1 lists the most common prescribed medications consumed by older adults. Older adults are also high users of OTC medications, accounting for around 30% of all nonprescription and OTC medication use (National Council on Patient Information and Education, 2010), a percentage far greater than their proportion of the population (around 13%).

Table 13.1   Prescription medications used in past 30 days, among older adults

Prescription drug class	Total	Men	Women
Antihyperlipidemic agents (high cholesterol)	46.8	51.9	42.8
Beta-adrenergic blocking agents (high blood pressure, heart disease)	31.2	32.6	30.0
ACE inhibitors (high blood pressure, heart disease)	23.3	28.8	19.0
Diuretics (high blood pressure, heart disease, kidney disease)	21.6	19.4	23.3
Proton pump inhibitors or H2 antagonists (gastric reflux, ulcers)	21.6	18.9	23.8
Antidiabetic agents (diabetes)	19.0	22.0	16.7
Calcium channel blocking agents (high blood pressure, heart disease)	17.3	16.6	17.8
Anticoagulants or antiplatelet agents (blood clot prevention)	16.3	20.3	13.0
Analgesics (pain relief)	15.8	14.5	16.9
Thyroid hormones (hypothyroidism)	15.6	9.2	20.8
Antidepressants (depression and related disorders)	15.0	10.3	18.7
Antihypertensive combinations (high blood pressure)	13.1	9.2	16.3
Angiotensin II inhibitors (high blood pressure, heart disease)	12.0	11.6	12.3
Antiarrhythmic agents (heart rhythm irregularities)	9.3	9.1	9.5

Note: The table shows the percentage of population with at least one prescription drug in drug class in past 30 days in the United States among older adults aged 65+ by sex.
Source: Adapted from the National Center for Health Statistics (2016).

Rates of medication misuse appear to be increasing among older adults (Schonfeld et al., 2010). From a large survey, social services providers working with older adults reported that 18–41% of their clients misused prescribed medication, depending on the particular sample (Schonfeld et al., 2010). Polypharmacy, which is the use of multiple medications, is common among older adults. Because older adults commonly take numerous medications prescribed by multiple providers and metabolize medications more slowly than younger adults, older adults are at a much greater risk for both adverse reactions to a prescription or OTC medication and to adverse drug–drug interactions than younger adults. Although not necessarily involved in abuse or misuse patterns, these high rates of usage combined with physiological changes render older adults vulnerable to a variety of substance-induced symptoms and disorders, as exemplified by the falls experienced by Jim, described at the beginning of this chapter. In contrast, illicit drug use among older adults is less common, as only 1.5% of older adults (65+) reported illicit drug use in the past month (Substance Abuse and Mental Health Services Administration, 2014). However, illicit drug usage patterns in older adults are expected to become more widespread in the future as the current cohorts of young adults and middle-aged adults with much greater illicit drug experiences reach later life (Arndt, Clayton, & Schultz, 2011; Wang & Andrade, 2013). Overall, it is clear that the incidence of substance use disorders among older adults in the US is increasing, representing a major public health challenge (Blow & Barry, 2012).

Presentation in Older Adults

Two patterns of onset are evident in older adult alcohol abusers: early- and late-onset alcohol abuse (Fingerhood, 2000). About two-thirds of older adult alcohol abusers fall into the early onset group, with alcohol problems evident earlier in life. This group is more likely to have been in alcohol treatment, more likely to have serious financial, legal, and occupational consequences of drinking, more likely to have chronic health problems and impaired cognition, and less likely to have a solid support system in place. Among many early onset problem drinkers, aging appears not to lead to resolution of the problem. Whereas rates of alcohol abuse appear to be relatively stable over the lifespan, the current cohorts of older adults have been less intensive users of alcohol than current young adults. In other words, there is a cohort effect with later-born cohorts using significantly more alcohol than earlier-born cohorts, but all evidence points to stability over time for each cohort.

Late-onset alcohol abuse is defined as beginning after the age of 60. Late-onset abusers usually enter treatment in a state of crisis and they are more likely to report feelings of depression, more likely to deny they have a problem with alcohol, and are more likely to have a supportive network in place (Fingerhood, 2000). Regardless of the time of onset, substance abuse by older adults usually develops as a mechanism for coping. Among older adults, alcohol use is commonly associated with efforts to reduce social anxiety, to enhance socialization, to cope with isolation due to widowhood or other social losses, to manage the loss of esteem associated with retirement, to cope with financial or health problems, and to avoid problems.

The two cases presented at the beginning of this chapter illustrate the late-onset pattern. Lincoln increased his rate of drinking following retirement because he lacked sufficiently compelling alternative activities to fill his time and to avoid conflict with his wife, whereas Jim increased his drinking and pain medication use in response to the loneliness that followed the death of his spouse. Regarding prescribed pain medications (usually opioids, such as oxycodone, codeine, fentanyl, morphine, methadone, hydrocodone, and tramadol), older adults typically begin to use these medications as prescribed, to help manage chronic and debilitating physical pain (West, Severtson, Green, & Dart, 2015). However, some older adults begin to enjoy the "numbed-out" feelings provided by these medications, and begin to misuse the medications to help them drown out negative mood states, like depression, anxiety, or loneliness, as shown in Jim's case. Of course, drowning out or ignoring problems does not make them go away, but the temporary avoidance due to substance misuse can be a powerful reinforcer.

A key factor in substance abuse patterns is the different physiological responses of aging bodies to chemical substances. Due to changes in the efficiency with which substances are processed in the body, older adults are more susceptible to adverse drug reactions, drug interactions, and drug toxicity as compared to younger adults. Mental health professionals must be aware of the vulnerability of aging bodies to even the most innocent-appearing substances (e.g., aspirin) in altering the psychological functioning of older persons (for a review of what professionals should know about psychopharmacology and polypharmacy, see Arnold 2015).

Regardless of age of onset, alcohol use disorder among older adults is strongly associated with other medical complications (APA, 2013) and makes many existing medical conditions worse, including diabetes, high blood pressure, congestive heart failure, liver problems, and memory problems. Alcohol misuse also increases one's risk for car crashes, accidents, falls, and violence. In addition, age-related changes among older adults result in increased brain susceptibility to the depressant effects of alcohol and reduced liver functioning. Together, these changes make older adults susceptible to greater intoxication and greater complications of intoxication at lower levels of consumption (APA, 2013). Due to a decrease in the amount of water in the body as one ages, there is less water in one's body to dilute the alcohol that is ingested. As such, older adults have higher blood alcohol concentrations than younger adults, after consuming the same amount of alcohol. Thus, older adults may increasingly experience problems due to alcohol without a change in their drinking habits.

Theories of Etiology

A theme we hope you will come to recognize throughout this book is that the vast majority of mental disorders are complex and multidetermined, within the bio-psychosocial model, and substance-related disorders are no exception. Regarding psychological factors, the behavioral theory of substance abuse suggests that people use substances to increase positive moods, decrease negative moods, or both. When the desired psychological effect of the ingested substance is achieved, the substance use is reinforced. The behavioral model also suggests that many people begin using a psychoactive substance by modeling peers or family members who use or abuse substances. The cognitive model emphasizes the role of thought processes in initiating and maintaining substance use behavior. In particular, thoughts may include *expectancies* about intoxication. To the extent the person holds positive beliefs about the effects of the substance (e.g., "A few drinks will help me relax and cope with my problems"), then the person will be more likely to use the substance. Conversely, to the extent the person holds negative beliefs about his or her ability to abstain from substance use (e.g., "I can't control myself"), then the person will also be more likely to use the substance.

There is also a strong biological basis to the development of substance abuse problems. Specifically, a great deal of research has sought to determine the genetic contributions of substance abuse, with the vast amount of this research focusing on alcohol problems. The risk of developing serious alcohol problems is about 15% for daughters of people with alcohol abuse and 30% for sons of people with alcohol abuse. The overall heritability of alcohol dependence is estimated to be at about 50–60%, meaning that at least half of the tendency to develop severe alcohol problems can be attributed to one's genetics (see review by Dick & Bierut, 2006). It is presently unclear, however, exactly how many specific genes are implicated, their locations, and the exact mechanisms by which genes exert their influence on the development of substance problems.

Social and cultural factors are also strongly related to the development (and prevention) of substance problems. We know this to be true due to the vast cross-cultural differences in rates of abuse of certain substances. For example in parts of the world where there are strong social and legal prohibitions against casual use of psychoactive substances, we see relatively low rates of use and low rates of misuse. Conversely, in parts of the world where there are very tolerant attitudes about substance use (for example, drinking vodka in parts of Russia), we see relatively higher rates of use and abuse. As such, during a clinical evaluation, it is important to understand the specific cultural, subcultural, and social factors that are impinging on the client's substance use.

Assessment of Substance Use and Abuse

Inquiring about substance use and misuse should be a standard part of *any* mental health evaluation with older adult clients. Assessment of substance use disorders is often complicated and challenging because of the tendency among older substance abusers to fail to recognize their substance use as problematic or to fail to fully appreciate the negative impacts of the substance use, despite ample evidence to the contrary. Health care providers may also tend to overlook alcohol problems and medication mismanagement or endorse negative stereotypes of older adults with substance use problems. Even families may not be willing to address a substance use disorder in an older family member, trivializing it due to ageism (e.g., "Grandpa only has a few years left. So what if he takes an extra drink here or there."). In addition, the symptoms or expressions of substance abuse problems among older adults may be mistaken for those of other problems associated with later life, such as depression or dementia.

Finally, relatives of older adults with a substance abuse problem may be ashamed of the problem and choose to ignore it.

Another challenge to assessment is the poor match between older adult substance abuse patterns and some diagnostic criteria for substance use disorder in the DSM-5 (APA, 2013). Specifically, the DSM criteria emphasize impact of the substance use on occupation and social relationships and responsibilities that may not be as readily recognized in older adults as in young adults who fulfill multiple roles publicly. Also, mental health professionals who rely on traditional criteria are unlikely to recognize the patterns of substance abuse most problematic among older adults whose substances are far more likely to be OTC or prescribed medications.

Clinicians typically try to draw out information about substance use in the course of clinical interviews. As rapport is established, clients have a greater likelihood of sharing accurate information. Asking a broad, nonjudgmental, open-ended prompt such as "Please tell me a little bit about your use of alcohol or drugs" in a matter-of-fact way may serve to create an open dialogue about the person's substance use patterns rather than using a more punitive style such as "How often do you get drunk?" During the assessment, it is also important to gather details, in a sensitive nonjudgmental way, about the frequency, quantity, and patterns of consumption for psychoactive substances the client admits using. During the assessment, clinicians should also inquire about any family history of substance abuse and carefully assess common complications associated with substance misuse such as falls, impaired judgment, legal problems, and social problems.

Similarly, when an older adult reports a history of falls, accidents, poor psychosocial functioning, depression, insomnia, cognitive changes, disorientation, poor nutrition, or self-neglect, substance abuse should certainly be assessed to rule out the possibility of substance abuse either causing the problem or making an existing problem worse. During the assessment, clinicians should gather information about all medications taken by the client and be aware of possible adverse effects caused by the interactions between medications and psychoactive substances, especially alcohol. Finally, clinicians should be aware that most adults and older adults who do not have a substance use problem give accurate answers about their use of psychoactive substances, but those with substance use problems may minimize their use. A helpful strategy is to embed questions about substance use within a larger context of assessment of other health behaviors, such as smoking, weight, and exercise (Blow & Barry, 2012).

Three brief self-report measures of alcohol are available to aid in the screening and detection of alcohol problems. The CAGE (Mayfield, McLeod, & Hall, 1974) is a mnemonic for four non-incriminating questions with good validity as a gross screening instrument for alcohol abuse among adults and older adults:

- Have you ever felt you needed to *Cut* down on drinking?
- Have people *Annoyed* you by criticizing your drinking?
- Have you ever felt *Guilty* about drinking?
- Have you ever had a drink first thing in the morning (*Eye-opener*) to steady your nerves or to get rid of a hangover?

Due to its simplicity, the CAGE is easy to use but it lacks specificity, and false positives are not uncommon. As such, a positive (yes) response to even one CAGE item warrants further evaluation in a clinical interview. A total score of two or greater usually indicates a clinically significant problem with alcohol.

The Michigan Alcoholism Screening Test (MAST) has a geriatric version (MAST-G; Blow et al., 1992), which is the most widely and successfully used measure in clinical practice. The MAST-G is presented in Table 13.2. As can be seen in the table, the measure contains 24 simple Yes/No items unique to older problem

Table 13.2   Michigan Alcoholism Screening Test—Geriatric Version (MAST-G)

	Yes (1)	No (0)
1. After drinking have you ever noticed an increase in your heart rate or beating in your chest?	1. ____	____
2. When talking with others, do you ever underestimate how much you actually drink?	2. ____	____
3. Does alcohol make you sleepy so that you often fall asleep in your chair?	3. ____	____
4. After a few drinks, have you sometimes not eaten or been able to skip a meal because you didn't feel hungry?	4. ____	____
5. Does having a few drinks help decrease your shakiness or tremors?	5. ____	____
6. Does alcohol sometimes make it hard for you to remember parts of the day or night?	6. ____	____
7. Do you have rules for yourself that you won't drink before a certain time of the day?	7. ____	____
8. Have you lost interest in hobbies or activities you used to enjoy?	8. ____	____
9. When you wake up in the morning, do you ever have trouble remembering part of the night before?	9. ____	____
10. Does having a drink help you sleep?	10. ____	____
11. Do you hide your alcohol bottles from family members?	11. ____	____
12. After a social gathering, have you ever felt embarrassed because you drank too much?	12. ____	____
13. Have you ever been concerned that drinking might be harmful to your health?	13. ____	____
14. Do you like to end an evening with a night cap?	14. ____	____
15. Did you find your drinking increased after someone close to you died?	15. ____	____
16. In general, would you prefer to have a few drinks at home rather than go out to social events?	16. ____	____
17. Are you drinking more now than in the past?	17. ____	____
18. Do you usually take a drink to relax or calm your nerves?	18. ____	____
19. Do you drink to take your mind off your problems?	19. ____	____
20. Have you ever increased your drinking after experiencing a loss in your life?	20. ____	____
21. Do you sometimes drive when you have had too much to drink?	21. ____	____
22. Has a doctor or nurse ever said they were worried or concerned about your drinking?	22. ____	____
23. Have you ever made rules to manage your drinking?	23. ____	____
24. When you feel lonely does having a drink help?	24. ____	____

Scoring: 5 or more "Yes" responses indicative of alcohol problem.

For further information, contact Frederic C. Blow, Ph.D., at the UM Addiction Center and Substance Abuse Section, Department of Psychiatry, University of Michigan, Ann Arbor, Michigan; email fredblow@umich.edu

Source: © The Regents of the University of Michigan, 1991.

drinkers. In all cases, "yes" is the pathological response and a cutoff of five positive responses indicates an alcohol problem (Blow et al., 1992). The MAST-G has excellent psychometric properties. For example, the MAST-G was found to have a sensitivity of 94% and specificity of 78% when the DSM diagnosis of alcohol dependence was used as the validation criteria. Factor analysis of the MAST-G has indicated five dimensions: loss and loneliness, relaxation, dependence, loss of control with drinking, and rule-making. A short version of the MAST-G (SMAST-G), with 10 Yes/No items, is also commonly used, and has a cut-score of two or more positive responses.

The third screening measure for alcohol is the Alcohol Use Disorders Identification Test (AUDIT), which is designed to detect persons with harmful or hazardous patterns of alcohol use. The AUDIT was developed and validated by the World Health Organization and is designed for international use (Babor, Higgins-Biddle, Saunders, & Monteiro, 2001). It is freely available. It consists of 10 self-report items that focus on alcohol use in the previous year. Each item is rated on 0–4 point scale (with higher scores indicating greater problems associated with alcohol use). In adult populations, the recommended cut-score for clinical significance is eight points, although a cut-score of seven is recommended for older adults (Babor et al., 2001). The AUDIT is also recommended for screening among ethnic minority adults and older adults. An interview version of the AUDIT contains the same 10 questions and response format but allows for clarification of ambiguous responses and can be administered to those with low reading ability (Babor et al., 2001). The AUDIT has some psychometric support for use with older adults, especially in hospital and primary care settings (Powell & McInness, 1994).

A tool recommended for the screening of drug use, including prescription medication, is the ASSIST, which was developed by the US National Institute on Drug Abuse (available at https://www.drugabuse.gov). Several adapted versions of the ASSIST are available, but they all essentially assess the pure domains of prescription medicine and illicit substance use in adults age 18 and older, focusing on the past two weeks.

Clearly, a thorough evaluation of substance abuse should be a part of any standard clinical evaluation with older adults because a substance use disorder can be severe and debilitating in its own right, but it can also worsen other comorbid conditions such as anxiety and depression, and make treatment for those conditions more complicated. In addition, substance use disorders are linked to increased rates of suicide attempts and suicide deaths. Routine screening is recommended in primary care settings and senior service settings, in addition to traditional and specialty mental health settings, to more effectively identify those in need of help and services. Positive screens on any of the assessment measures described above should be followed by a thorough clinical or diagnostic interview. For those who prefer structured interview assessments, the *Structured Clinical Interview for DSM-5 Disorders* (SCID-5-CV; First, Williams, Karg, & Spitzer) has a thorough substance use module that is linked to DSM-5 criteria.

Interventions for Substance Abuse

The number of older adults in need of substance abuse treatment is projected to increase from 1.7 million in 2000/2001 to 4.4 million in 2020 (Gfroerer, Penne, Pemberton, & Folsom, 2003), which will surely strain the capacity and resources of health care and mental health care agencies and providers, many of whom do not have adequate or specialized training for working with older adults with substance abuse problems. Substance abuse treatments typically focus on three goals: stabilization and reduction of substance consumption, treatment of coexisting problems, and arrangement of appropriate psychosocial interventions. With older adults, education rather than confrontation is usually used to reduce minimization or denial of the abuse pattern. For example, education about the changes in drug metabolism, the interaction of medications, and the importance of compliance with physician instructions can lead to increased compliance. Research demonstrates the role of cognitive factors in determining medication compliance (Gould, 2004). Evidence from laboratory experimentation suggests that altering the presentation of drug usage information can increase understanding and compliance with medication instructions, thus reducing the opportunity for substance misuse.

Education of physicians is an important component of a treatment plan for prescription and OTC drug abuse. Physicians may not recognize the potential for medication interactions to produce psychological symptoms. Physicians also may be unaware of all of the prescribed medications a patient is using if the patient is obtaining prescriptions from more than one physician. Thus, engaging physician cooperation is critical when attempting to intervene with prescription or OTC misuse.

Treatment of coexisting problems (e.g., depression, anxiety, insomnia, pain, or social isolation) can reduce the motivation for using substances inappropriately. This strategy is similar to that used with younger adult substance abusers, although the specific problems that need to be addressed may vary with age. In the case of Lincoln, marital therapy and, possibly, treatment of depression, would be critical elements of the treatment plan. As long as home life is stressful, and Lincoln lacks a sense of purpose or skill for creating separateness from Lois, then he is likely to try to avoid conflict and unpleasant feelings in a familiar way—alcohol. Jim needs help with social skills so that he can begin to reconnect with old friends and develop new relationships to reduce his isolation.

The CBT approach to treatment focuses on behavioral interventions to help the client learn new, healthier patterns of behavior to replace substance use, and cognitive restructuring to reduce positive expectancies and to increase negative expectancies regarding the effects of substance use. Some specific behavioral interventions include the following: identification of antecedents (situations, thoughts, feelings, and cues) that provoke the substance misuse; explication of short-term and long-term consequences of substance misuse, including benefits of use (e.g., reducing social anxiety) as well as detrimental effects; assertion training, especially for those who use substances to dull their emotions in relationship conflicts, in contrast to assertive expression of one's needs; self-monitoring of substance use (as part of ongoing data collection strategies); behavior contracting (agreeing to specific, lower levels of substance use);

and implementing reinforcement for progress toward treatment goals. Finally, training in self-management skills is often used to help the client generate more effective coping skills, again reducing the urge to use psychoactive substances to manage (or avoid) problem situations.

Treatment outcome studies suggest that older patients generally stay in treatment longer and respond equally as well to alcohol interventions as do younger patients (Kuerbis & Sacco, 2013). In essence, treatment generally works for those who seek help. As could be expected, the outcomes are more favorable among persons with shorter histories of problem drinking (i.e., late onset). Although the data are not definitive, it appears that outcomes may be improved somewhat by treating older patients in age-segregated settings, that is separate from younger adults. These effects are believed to be due to greater treatment engagement in age-specific programs (Kuerbis & Sacco, 2013). Among older adults, it is possible that aging Baby Boomers who seek treatment will want or need separate programs from their older counterparts, in their 70s and 80s (the World War II cohorts), although data are needed regarding this growing issue.

The Florida Brief Intervention and Treatment for Elders (BRITE) Project is a well-documented and successful screening and brief intervention program for older adults who are misusing or abusing substances (Schonfeld et al., 2010). Screening results indicated that prescription medication misuse was the most prevalent substance use problem (26.4%), followed by alcohol (9.7%), OTC medications (7.8%), and illicit substances (1.1%). Older adults who received the BRITE intervention showed many benefits, including improvements in alcohol, medication misuse, and depression measures. An expanded version of the BRITE Project, in 75 sites across 18 Florida counties, showed that screening, brief intervention, and referral to treatment services can be successfully implemented in diverse service settings, including general medical, mental health, substance abuse, and aging services settings (Schonfeld et al., 2015). Another large-scale effectiveness study, called the Primary Care Research in Substance Abuse and Mental Health for the Elderly study (PRISM-E; Oslin et al., 2006), found similarly positive findings for screening and brief intervention in two care models: integrated care and enhanced specialty referral. Both were equally effective at reducing alcohol use among older adults in primary care. Despite the wealth of data from BRITE and PRISM-E, wide-scale implementation of these models has been limited, primarily due to poor funding for these services.

Although there have been good success rates for those older adults who enter treatment, the vast majority of older adults with a substance use disorder either do not receive adequate treatment or do not adequately perceive the need for treatment (Choi, DiNitto, & Marti, 2014; Schonfeld et al., 2010). Additionally, we know very little about the effectiveness of treatments for minority older adults, who are very underrepresented in treatment studies and treatment settings. Treatment needs are expected to increase greatly in the coming years due to the large population of Baby Boomers who have higher rates of substance misuse and abuse than the current cohort of older adults. In particular, as we have seen earlier in this chapter, the rate of illicit drug use among older adults is expected to greatly increase as younger cohorts with greater illicit drug problems enter later life.

Personality Disorders

Alice has had relationship problems most of her adult life. Nobody ever seemed to be good enough for her or to appreciate her talents. But her life and relationships were manageable when she was able to throw herself into her work, having had a successful career as an attorney in a prestigious firm. Things began to crumble when she retired one year ago and now she is having an especially hard time adjusting to life in the rehabilitation facility after having heart surgery. She refuses to participate in the physical rehab exercises, thinking that "the doctors are ignorant" and that they don't understand how hard it is for her to be ill. Alice also is having problems with her roommate—"she is so rude talking to her family and friends on the phone several times a day and not paying any attention to me." She also dislikes most staff and becomes enraged when they request that she attempt to do some care activities herself like feeding herself and bathing—"Don't these fools understand who I am? I expect good service and will not put up with their attempts to get out of taking care of me. Instead of being the patient here, I should be running this whole place. I'd fire them all and get a top-notch staff to replace them." The staff dread having to take care of Alice.

The DSM-5 (APA, 2013) defines a personality disorder as "an enduring pattern of inner experience and behavior that deviates markedly from the expectations of the individual's culture, is pervasive and inflexible, has an onset in adolescence or early adulthood, is stable over time, and leads to distress or impairment" (p. 645). Essentially, a personality disorder (PD) is diagnosed when one's own personality traits (defined as characteristic ways of thinking, feeling, perceiving, and behaving) become inflexible, maladaptive, and pervasive across a broad range of situations. There is a dimensionality inherent in understanding PDs, as the symptoms reflect exaggerations of more adaptive traits. Patterns of inner experiences and behaviors that represent expectable or typical reactions to particular life experiences or represent a normal part of a developmental stage are not considered part of a PD. The DSM-5 defines 10 prototypical and categorically defined PDs which are described in Table 13.3. Four PDs that were listed in prior editions of the DSM (namely, depressive, passive-aggressive, sadistic, and self-defeating PDs) are also included in the table, because they still have clinical and heuristic value and describe important aspects of personality pathology that have no equivalent in the remaining disorders (Millon, Millon, Grossman, Meagher, & Ramnath, 2004). As is sadly true for many disorders classified in the DSM-5, younger adults were considered as the prototypes for all of the PDs.

As an organizational tool, the DSM-5 groups the 10 prototypical PDs into three superordinate clusters based on presumed descriptive commonalities. Cluster A groups three disorders in which individuals often appear odd, eccentric, or withdrawn: paranoid, schizoid, and schizotypal PDs. Cluster B includes four disorders in which individuals appear to be impulsive, dramatic, emotional, or erratic, often with intense interpersonal conflicts: antisocial, borderline, histrionic, and narcissistic PDs. Cluster C contains three disorders in which individuals often appear fearful or anxious: avoidant, dependent, and obsessive-compulsive PDs. Most individuals

Table 13.3   Description of the 10 DSM-5 personality disorders and four personality disorders from prior editions of the DSM

	DSM-5 personality disorders
Antisocial	A pervasive pattern of disregard for, and violation of, societal norms and the rights of others, as well as lack of empathy.
Avoidant	A pervasive pattern of social inhibition, low self-esteem, and hypersensitivity to negative evaluation.
Borderline	A pervasive pattern of instability in interpersonal relationships, self-image, and emotions, as well as marked impulsivity.
Dependent	A pervasive and excessive need to be taken care of and a perception of being unable to function without the help of others leading to submissive and clinging behaviors.
Histrionic	A pervasive pattern of excessive emotionality and attention-seeking behavior, with superficiality.
Narcissistic	A pervasive pattern of grandiosity, need for admiration, and lack of empathy and compassion for others.
Obsessive-compulsive	A pervasive pattern of preoccupation with orderliness, perfection, and control at the expense of flexibility, openness, and efficiency.
Paranoid	A pattern of pervasive distrust and suspicion of others such that their motives are perceived as malevolent.
Schizoid	A pervasive pattern of detachment from social relationships and a restricted range of emotional expression.
Schizotypal	A pervasive pattern of social deficits marked by acute discomfort with close relationships, as well as eccentric behavior and cognitive and perceptual distortions.

	Personality disorders from prior editions of DSM
Depressive	A pervasive pattern of depressive, pessimistic, and gloomy cognitions and behaviors occurring in a variety of contexts (from DSM-IV-TR, Appendix B).
Passive-aggressive	A pervasive pattern of negativistic attitudes, stubbornness, and passive resistance to demands for adequate performance in diverse contexts (from DSM-IV-TR, Appendix B).
Sadistic	A pervasive pattern of cruel, aggressive, and demeaning behavior directed toward others and deriving pleasure from harming others (from DSM-III-R).
Self-defeating	A pervasive pattern of self-defeating behavior, which may include avoiding or undermining pleasurable experiences, being drawn to situations or relationships in which they will suffer, and preventing others from helping them (from DSM-III-R). An apt metaphor for this type is one who characteristically "snatches defeat from the jaws of victory."

Source: Adapted from DSM-5 (APA, 2013), DSM-IV-TR (APA, 2000), and DSM-III-R (APA, 1987).

with PDs do not fit neatly into one of these categories. As such, a common diagnosis is what was previously called PD Not Otherwise Specified (renamed in DSM-5 to be either *Other Specified Personality Disorder* or *Unspecified Personality Disorder*). In essence, these diagnoses are used when a client has prominent traits of several different PDs but fails to meet the diagnostic threshold for any specific PD. Yet another diagnostic option in DSM-5 is *Personality Change Due to Another Medical*

Condition, which is a persistent personality disturbance that is judged to be due to the direct physiological effects of a medical condition. For example, a person who experiences aggression, emotional lability, disinhibition, and apathy subsequent to a traumatic brain injury would be diagnosed with this disorder. In addition to head trauma, other medical conditions known to cause personality changes include brain tumors, cerebrovascular disease (including stoke), epilepsy, Huntington's disease, and lupus (APA, 2013).

Although the knowledge base about PDs in older adults has grown significantly in recent years, including publication of two books solely devoted to this topic (Rosowsky, Abrams, & Zweig, 1999; Segal, Coolidge, & Rosowsky, 2006), PDs in older adults remain a relatively understudied area for several reasons. Changing definitions of PDs across the various editions of the DSM have hampered longitudinal studies. The field of personality psychology has also struggled with the extent to which personality should be conceptualized as a set of enduring traits versus situationally influenced behaviors, especially patterns of coping with stress. Apparently, personality traits (including adaptive and maladaptive ones) are both stable and adaptable across the lifespan (Clark, 2009; Vaillant, 2002). Obviously, models of personality serve as a backdrop for models of PDs. Thus, stability in personality traits could be construed as a backdrop for PDs that are also considered generally stable but not immutable, with shifting amounts of distress and dysfunction depending on contextual variables, especially stressors. Although the formal definition of PD requires an onset of the PD no later than early adulthood, in some cases a PD is not diagnosed or treated until later life, often when the stressors associated with later life prompt an exacerbation of the person's maladaptive behaviors (Molinari & Segal, 2011; Segal, Zweig, & Molinari, 2012).

Despite methodological and conceptual challenges, it is clinically important to understand PDs in older adults for a number of reasons. First, because PDs affect the way a person copes with the vicissitudes of life, older individuals with a PD are likely to have less success in negotiating age-related losses (Molinari & Segal, 2011; Sadavoy, 2014). Consider for example a histrionic person who has characteristically relied on her physical attractiveness and sexual seductiveness to acquire attention for herself. With advancing age, such a person may feel increasingly neglected, dejected, and angry as she loses some of her seductiveness and its attendant attention from others. As another example, a narcissistic person may feel a particularly painful loss of esteem and prestige when faced with retirement from a high-powered position, becoming exceptionally angry and depressed. This was the case for Alice, who was also having difficulty coping with physical illness.

Second, because PD affects one's social functioning, older individuals with a PD are likely to be less effective in managing the social and interpersonal compromises necessary for peaceful institutional living (Molinari & Segal, 2011). For example, an avoidant older adult may dread the increased social "opportunities" provided by living at an assisted living facility, instead perceiving such occurrences as "more opportunities for rejection." Third, PDs typically influence or distort the presentation of diverse clinical disorders, such as anxiety, depression, and substance abuse, thus hampering diagnosis and treatment and leading to a poorer prognosis. Molinari and Segal (2011) provide the example of disruptive behavior in a nursing home resident that camouflages the fact that the resident is suffering from severe depression that is exacerbating premorbid antisocial PD features. In general, the presence of PDs that are comorbid with other clinical disorders makes treatment more difficult and makes the therapeutic alliance more difficulty to maintain and prone to more frequent ruptures. As such, presence of comorbid PD often results in a worse prognosis for the older individual seeking services (Molinari & Segal, 2011; Segal et al., 2006).

Fourth, there is a strong relationship between PD features and suicidal behaviors among older adults, highlighting potential dangerousness among older adults with personality deficits. In a study of relationships between the 10 standard PDs in the DSM-IV/DSM-5 and suicidal ideation (as measured by the Geriatric Suicide Ideation Scale; Heisel & Flett, 2006), the PD dimensions explained a majority (55%) of the variance in suicidal ideation. Two significant predictors emerged: Borderline PD was a significant positive predictor, whereas histrionic PD was a significant negative predictor (Segal, Marty, Meyer, & Coolidge, 2012). In a follow-up study that examined the four PDs that were included in prior editions of the DSM (namely, depressive, passive-aggressive, sadistic, and self-defeating PDs), findings indicated that these PD dimensions explained almost half (48%) of the variance in suicidal ideation, which was attributable to the high positive predictive power of depressive PD (Segal, Gottschling, Marty, Meyer, & Coolidge, 2015). These findings are consistent with previous studies which indicated that PD features increase risk for suicidal thinking, suicide attempts, and death by suicide among older people (e.g., Duberstein et al., 2000). One could argue that the deficits in coping skills and impaired social functioning commonly experienced by older adults with PDs or PD features might make them especially vulnerable to the full spectrum of suicidal behaviors. Fifth, and finally, PDs adversely affect the morale and functioning of diverse health care providers (Sadavoy, 2014), because older adults with PD have an impaired capacity to trust and rely on others for care without inviting conflict.

Prevalence

The prevalence of PDs in the general adult population is estimated to be about 10% (Lenzenweger, 2008), indicating that PDs are actually quite common. However, the true prevalence among the older population is presently unknown and reflects a source of considerable debate in the literature. In an attempt to lend clarity to this issue, Abrams and Horowitz (1996) conducted a meta-analysis of the most methodologically sophisticated epidemiological studies among older adults, reporting an overall PD prevalence rate of 10% (with a range of 6–33%), neither confirming nor disputing an age effect on prevalence. However, Abrams and Horowitz concluded that the bulk of the evidence supports a modest decline in the frequency and intensity with age, at least for certain PDs. The exact cause for this decline is unknown, and is a current source of controversy and debate (Molinari & Segal, 2011).

Changing definitions and conceptualizations of PDs, poorly normed assessment devices, and the limited number of large studies among older adults all make prevalence estimates confusing and of limited value. Most studies have been conducted on inpatient units, examining the comorbidity of PDs with other clinical disorders. PDs are believed to be much more common than is generally recognized by outpatient mental health professionals. For example, among older outpatients with a depression diagnosis, 33% were diagnosed with PD (Thompson, Gallagher, & Czirr, 1988), most commonly avoidant and dependent PDs. Much higher rates of PD prevalence (e.g., 56%) are found in studies of older psychiatric inpatients (e.g., Molinari, Ames, & Essa, 1994). Coolidge et al. (2000) found similarly high PD rates among young (66%) and old (58%) chronically mentally ill patients, but the younger group was more likely to be specifically diagnosed with antisocial, borderline, and schizotypal PD. A combined inpatient and outpatient sample of depressed older adults yielded a prevalence rate of 63% (Molinari & Marmion, 1995).

The question of how PDs are affected by aging has been debated, but has lacked a research base on which to anchor a definitive answer. Some evidence points to a decline in expression of the symptoms associated with the cluster of PDs labeled *dramatic and erratic* (including borderline, histrionic, and narcissistic PDs) in midlife with an increase in symptoms again in later life (Reich, Nduaguba, & Yates, 1988). Others suggest that the decline in dramatic PDs relates to increased mortality rates among impulsive and erratic individuals, a decrease in energy and stamina needed to maintain the high energy symptoms (e.g., brawling with others), and the poor fit of the DSM diagnostic criteria to accurately detect geriatric variants of the PDs (Segal et al., 2006).

Presentation in Older Adults

The stresses of old age are believed to produce personality regressions that mimic PDs and to exacerbate the expression of PD symptoms in some older adults (Segal et al., 2006; Rosowsky & Molinari, 2014). Loss of control of the environment that is characteristic of the increasing dependency that comes with loss of mobility and declining resources can provoke anxiety that generates PD symptoms. However, the symptom criteria used by the *DSM* system include life circumstances that may be irrelevant to older adults. For example, difficulties in the work environment and with residential family life may be less relevant because of the lower rate of participation in the work force and the tendency not to co-reside with family members. Thus, the behavioral expressions of PDs in older adults may not match the template typically used to identify PDs in younger adults.

In some cases, there is an emergence of PD symptoms that were "hidden" earlier in life (Segal et al., 2006). Consider for example a highly dependent woman who married young and was essentially nurtured along and taken care of by her more dominant spouse throughout their marriage. In such a case, it would only be after her husband's death that her struggles to take care of herself and the extent of her "disorder" would be recognized and perhaps diagnosed. Regarding this issue, Rosowsky and Molinari (2014) wisely observed that:

> Many older adults with personality disorders have had a partner or someone in their life who protected them or run adaptive interference for them, to ward off the disorder's more florid manifestations. Often, the older adult with a personality disorder will come to clinical attention when this personal support is no longer present or when a "protector" is now unable to "do the job." (p. 38)

Thus, it is fair to say that PDs can and do change with aging. A theorized pattern or "geriatric variant" for each of the PDs is depicted in Table 13.4. Note that in most

Table 13.4   Theorized patterns or geriatric variants for the personality disorders in later life

Antisocial	For this type, there is a diminished chance of surviving into later life due to a lifestyle of recklessness, impulsivity, and risky behaviors. The underlying trait of psychopathy does not seem to change with age but there is a reduction of impulsive and physically aggressive behaviors due to physiological declines associated with aging. Physical disability, sensory decline, and cognitive impairment can be particularly problematic for older antisocial individuals who are incarcerated because their limitations make them especially vulnerable to exploitation from other prisoners.
Avoidant	This type commonly arrives at later life lonely, inhibited, and disconnected from others having missed out on the normal developmental pathway to social confidence experienced by others. They are particularly vulnerable to the social losses that are commonly a part of later life (e.g., death of family members; migration of children) because their networks are generally constricted to begin with and they typically have great trouble replacing relationships that have been lost. Avoidant individuals can easily become more alone and frightened as their limited networks inevitably shrink.
Borderline	Physical fights, substance abuse, sexual acting out, self-mutilation, and other impulsive and physically taxing behaviors will typically become muted in later life. Geriatric variants of self-harming behaviors may include intentional anorexia, self-prescribed polypharmacy, refusal of needed medical attention, or sabotage of medical care. Aging typically has little impact on the chronic feelings of emptiness and unstable and intense interpersonal relationships. This type is especially likely to cause havoc upon their move to assisted living facilities, rehabilitation hospitals, or nursing facilities. They may intensely attach themselves to unsuspecting residents and staff only to turn against them in a brief period.
Dependent	This type experiences extreme difficulty with widowhood, leaving the person in the threatening and unfamiliar position of having to depend on him or herself. After such a loss, dependent older adults commonly appear helpless, unable to perform the most mundane of functions after decades of relying excessively on their partners. Feeling lost and vulnerable, these older adults often turn to their adult children to fill the void left by the deceased spouse. In many cases, their excessive neediness quickly becomes burdensome, frequently leading to their children feeling overwhelmed.
Histrionic	This type is particularly intolerant of the physical declines that come with age (e.g., wrinkles, hair loss) because their self-worth is based largely on superficial characteristics such as physical appearance. Due to their lifelong reliance on their physical attributes to attract attention, many older people with this disorder respond to normal physical changes by becoming excessive users of plastic surgery and other anti-aging techniques. They also become depressed or angry when their flirtatious and seductive style becomes less rewarded.

(Continued)

Table 13.4   (Continued)

Narcissistic	One pattern is for the narcissistic type to come to old age alone, isolated, and bitter about their lack of success. Another pattern is for them to come to old age with great histories of accomplishment, although they often can no longer maintain that success. "Narcissistic injuries" due to the loss of power and prestige and general ageism in society often lead to depression, anxiety, and anger. The aging narcissist typically has trouble coping with age-related physical declines (e.g., hair loss, wrinkles, shrinking muscle mass) because they perceive these signs as detracting from their superiority over others. When older people with this disorder need care and support from others due to illness, rageful reactions are common resulting in increased negative feedback and further blows to the narcissist's sense of self.
Obsessive-compulsive	Increased dependency on others is likely to be a difficult stressor for this type because their lifelong pattern of "doing things their own way" makes them resistant to change and unable to tolerate needing help from others. Believing there is only one way to accomplish tasks, they typically have great difficulty being flexible with lost or reduced physical and cognitive functions. Older adults with this disorder may feel resentful or be offended when offered help, which is interpreted by them as a statement that they are not in complete control. When having to receive help becomes inevitable, obsessive-compulsive older adults may react with catastrophic depression.
Paranoid	Sensory impairments (e.g., declines in hearing and vision) are likely to make the underlying paranoia more pronounced. The emergence of cognitive dysfunction due to a cognitive disorder may also worsen premorbid paranoid traits. Dealing with increased dependency on others will also likely be problematic because people with this disorder are not used to and are uncomfortable with accepting help from others. The paranoid type will have a particularly difficult time with aging due to the loss of the few relationships they may have developed earlier in life and the subsequent increasing isolation.
Schizoid	Increased dependency on others will be especially difficult for the schizoid older adult to manage. Because the person's disconnected style is ego-syntonic, it will likely cause marked distress when the person must by necessity depend on relationships with others for their care (e.g., as a resident in an assisted living facility or nursing home). A typical pattern is that of the lifelong recluse becoming more reclusive with advancing age, usually lasting for as long as the person can manage being alone until changes with aging require increased contact with others.
Schizotypal	This type responds particularly poorly to increased dependency on others due to the older schizotypal person's acute social anxiety. People with this disorder are likely to become agitated if physical infirmities force them to endure relationships with health care professionals, staff, and residents in congregate living settings. Their unusual and bizarre behaviors also make them an easy target for rejection in communal social settings. Some schizotypal adults become increasingly reclusive and isolated with advancing age, frequently becoming even more bizarre due to the complete or near complete lack of social contact.

Source: Adapted from Segal, Coolidge, & Rosowsky (2006).

cases, the challenges of growing older overwhelm the person's fragile and limited coping mechanisms and result in symptoms of distress that often precipitate clinical attention and diagnosis. Some common stressors to which older adults with PD respond poorly include having to rely on others for care; relocating to a new environment (e.g., a congregate living facility); loss of social supports (e.g., death of a protective spouse); and loss or declines of power, prestige, control, and physical attractiveness (Rosowsky & Molinari, 2014).

Theories of Etiology

Because PDs and PD features begin relatively early in life and generally persist across adulthood and later life, it can be assumed that the etiology of PDs includes significant psychosocial and biological factors.

Psychosocial factors

From his psychoanalytic perspective, Sigmund Freud embedded the idea of personality within his psychosexual stages (i.e., oral, anal, oedipal, latency, and genital stages). Freud suggested that inborn temperamental traits combine with parental influences during these psychosexual periods to shape one's personality. How early figures react to the growing child's needs forges a rigid template that is operative throughout the person's life. These templates reflect whether a person will satisfy his or her psychological and social needs in an adaptive manner or in an exaggerated, repetitious, maladaptive manner that is a hallmark of PDs. Acute symptomatology erupts when current stressors intersect with the psychosocial dynamics and interpersonal sensitivities laid out early in life that forge a hard bedrock of personality traits (Molinari & Segal, 2011).

The cognitive model of psychopathology suggests that PDs are characterized by *cognitive distortions* which are derived from biases in information processing and dysfunctional *schemas* or core beliefs that influence people's perceptions and thoughts at the conscious level (Beck, Freeman, Davis, & Associates, 2003). As described in Chapter 5, some cognitive distortions include all-or-none thinking, catastrophizing, magnification and minimization, and personalization. Examples of cognitive distortions and schemas relevant to each of the 10 PDs are as follows:

- An individual with antisocial PD perceives the rules of society as not pertaining to him, and as such, he feels free to violate the rights of others and to engage in criminal-type behavior with little or no remorse or guilt.
- An individual with avoidant PD sees himself as socially inept and others as superior or threatening. He perceives himself as unable to tolerate feelings associated with being rejected by others, and thus avoids evaluative situations.
- An individual with borderline PD is prone to sort people into categories of either "all good" or "all bad" and is further preoccupied with feelings of abandonment and emptiness.

- An individual with dependent PD sees herself as weak, incompetent, and inadequate, requiring constant reassurance, nurturance, and direction from others.
- An individual with histrionic PD perceives herself as glamorous and seductive while seeing others as potential admirers. She believes it is acceptable to use all means necessary to garner the affection and attention she thinks she deserves.
- An individual with narcissistic PD chronically perceives himself as being special and others as being inferior, so much so that he believes that the standard rules do not apply to him and that he deserves special treatment from others.
- An individual with obsessive-compulsive PD tends to be a slave to the belief that he must be perfect and always in control.
- An individual with paranoid PD is prone to habitually and chronically perceive others as deceitful, abusive, and malicious. He is further prone to accuse others of being harmful and may counterattack in response to perceived slights.
- An individual with schizoid PD sees himself as self-sufficient and others as intrusive. The main strategy is to stay away from others, believing that relationships are messy and undesirable.
- An individual with schizotypal PD holds odd, superstitious, and idiosyncratic beliefs about him or herself and others, and thus believes it is safer to be isolated from others than to reveal one's inner weirdness.

Note that in the cognitive model, each PD may be characterized by a set of core beliefs the person holds about him or herself and about others, and these beliefs often drive stable and predictable cognitively based strategies for how to negotiate interpersonal relationships.

Developmental theorists assert that PDs begin to develop in response to adverse early life experiences, such as disruptions in attachments to parents or other important caregivers. Through this lens, the child's abnormal personality develops over time as he or she learns to relate to others and the world in disturbed and maladaptive ways. Consider, for example, the paranoid person who was devastatingly hurt and betrayed by his primary caregivers and therefore has (reasonably) become distrustful of others, or the histrionic person who was neglected as a child and only received attention when she displayed dramatic outbursts or outlandish behaviors. Sadly, although these coping strategies are usually relatively adaptive in the child's early environment, or at least reflect the child's best efforts to cope with uncaring, unkind, cruel, or otherwise distressing or unfortunate circumstances, they often persist into adulthood and across different contexts. In these ways, early life experiences, especially early experiences with significant adversity, leave marks on the individual that often persist throughout the lifespan.

Biological factors

The biological factor most extensively studied for the PDs is that of genetics. In an early study, Jang, Livesley, Vernon, and Jackson (1996) studied 483 adult twin pairs, reporting a median heritability coefficient estimate of .44 for 66 of 69 PD facet traits. A related twin study by Jang, Livesley, and Vernon (1996) found that genetic contributions to PD traits actually increase with age. Torgersen et al. (2000) used a structured interview to diagnose the full range of PDs among 221 adult twin pairs, finding an overall heritability estimate of .60. In an interesting study of 112 child and adolescent twins aged 4–15 years old, Coolidge, Thede, and Jang (2001) reported a median heritability coefficient of .75 for 12 specific PDs. This study suggests that the genetic component of PDs becomes evident relatively early in childhood and adolescence. Most recently, Kendler et al. (2008) studied 2,794 adult twins in Norway. The results indicated that one genetic factor reflected a broad vulnerability to PD pathology and negative emotionality, whereas two other genetic factors more specifically reflected high impulsivity/low agreeableness and introversion. To summarize this genetic data, heritable traits certainly play a significant role in the formation of PDs but heritability alone does not directly cause an individual to develop a specific PD. In a sense, genetics may prime the proverbial pump, but adverse early environments and psychological factors almost always play a major role.

Assessment of Personality Disorders

The assessment of PDs is known to be particularly challenging across the lifespan. Specifically, it is generally difficult to distinguish one PD from another (Coolidge & Segal, 1998) since most people have a mix of diverse PD features and rarely present with all the prototypical features of one specific PD without features of other PDs. In essence, comorbidity is the rule not the exception. The context of aging and later life further complicates the assessment of PDs because most of the standardized instruments used to screen for and measure specific PDs were developed for younger populations and thus do not adequately consider the context of later life (Balsis, Segal, & Donahue, 2009; Oltmanns & Balsis, 2011; Rossi, van den Broeck, Dierckx, Segal, & van Alphen, 2014; Segal et al., 2006).

PDs are commonly seen in diverse mental health settings yet are seldom formally diagnosed. It is possible that some mental health professionals are reluctant to diagnose PDs in older adults due to mistaken beliefs that PDs are rare in older adults, to pessimistic beliefs about the prospects of therapeutic change for older individuals with a PD, or to concerns over pejorative, stigmatizing biases associated with a PD diagnosis (Segal, Zweig, et al., 2012). It is also possible that some professionals tend to focus their assessments on other disorders that are more easily identified, such as anxiety, depression, and cognitive disorders (Molinari & Segal, 2011).

Zweig (2008) thoughtfully articulated three special challenges in the assessment of older adults with PD. First, differentiating PD from co-occurring clinical disorders (e.g., the state versus trait problem) can be an arduous task, particularly when heightened irritability and interpersonal dysfunction are related at least in part to a mood change due to a recent loss. Second, differentiating PD from context-dependent roles and behaviors can pose a major diagnostic undertaking. For example, poor adaptation to a changing role such as becoming overwhelmed after the death of a spouse may reflect the anxiety of an acute adjustment disorder rather than the emergence of a dependent PD. A key point is that situational maladjustment must be disentangled from personality pathology. This task becomes complicated when disruptions in life contexts are ongoing or when stressors are chronic. Third, differentiating PD from personality change due to a neurological or medical condition can require an exhaustive medical work-up. Indeed, in a geriatric setting, somatic presentations of PD are common, which can complicate teasing out true comorbid medical/cognitive problems from personality dysfunction.

A final assessment challenge is that the diagnostic criteria sets do not fit older adults as well as they do younger adults (Balsis, Segal, & Donahue, 2009; Segal et al., 2006; van Alphen, Rossi, Segal, & Rosowsky, 2013). In an empirical investigation of potential age-bias using item analysis, Balsis, Gleason, Woods, and Oltmanns (2007) found evidence of age-bias in 29% of the criteria for seven PDs. In this study, some diagnostic criteria were differentially endorsed by younger and older adults with equivalent PD pathology, suggesting a bias. Self-report personality inventories, which are widely used in clinical research, are helpful to assess PD dimensions but they have some inherent limitations, especially those that were not developed specifically for older adults. When available, informant reports often provide valuable supplements to self-report inventories (Rossi et al., 2014). Perceptions of significant others can be especially useful for assessment of PDs since those with PDs usually have pronounced impairments in the interpersonal sphere, although insight into those problems may be limited, if not completely absent.

To aid in the screening of general PD pathology (not specific PDs) in later life, a brief specialized self-report measure called the Gerontological Personality Disorders Scale (GPDS; van Alphen, Engelen, Kuin, Hoijtink, & Derksen, 2006) has been developed and preliminarily examined. Items on the GPDS are based on the General Diagnostic Criteria for PDs, and as a consequence the measure does not assess specific PDs. The GPDS includes two subscales (habitual behavior and biographical information). In the validation study, the sensitivity and specificity of the GPDS as compared to a clinical diagnosis were both 69%, which suggests the measure has moderate diagnostic accuracy. Although this measure is promising, it does not fill the important need for a broad screening measure for specific PDs in later life.

An excellent structured interview for the assessment of PDs is the SCID-5-PD (First, Williams, Benjamin, & Spitzer, 2016) which faithfully adheres to the diagnostic criteria for PDs in the DSM-5 and can be used to make PD diagnoses, either categorically (present or absent) or dimensionally. The SCID-5-PD includes a self-report screening questionnaire that can be used before the full interview assessment. Advantages of the SCID-5-PD are that it ensures assessment of all specific diagnostic criteria for the PDs of interest, and its modular, disorder-by-disorder format enables efficient assessment of those PDs of interest in clinical or research settings. The primary disadvantage is that some DSM-5 criteria are known to be age-biased, as discussed earlier. At present there is no "gold standard" of diagnosis for PDs in older adults.

Interventions for Personality Disorders

Persons with PD primarily seek treatment when their familiar methods of coping and meeting their own needs can no longer be enacted or are distressing someone else, who then demands that treatment occur. For example, upon widowhood, they might be on their own for the first time in their lives. They might find themselves entering a new community, needing to make new friends and establish a social network for the first time in many years. As they come to experience that their lifelong ways of coping are no longer working for them, they become even more distressed, function even less well, and their behavior worsens. This vicious cycle is one component of treatment that typically makes intervention challenging (Segal et al., 2006).

Older adults with PD who seek professional help generally present for symptom relief or to address a specific problem, typically related to interpersonal conflicts. They frequently come to treatment secondary to the loss of autonomy and control, or upon the strong suggestion of another person on whom they need to depend, for example an adult child, a housing manager, or a primary care physician. They do not generally self-refer for psychotherapy, as their psychopathology is typically experienced as ego-syntonic (Segal et al., 2006). Indeed, we have observed in our clinical work that, among older adults, some PD features appear to have become even more ego-syntonic with advancing age, simply as a function of the PD symptoms being present for a longer duration, in some cases well over 50 or 60 years. This ego-syntonic nature of the PDs hampers assessment as well as treatment.

According to Livesley (2004), a guiding principle to treatment is the recognition of a PD as being chronic and as defining the essence of the individual. Thus, the aim of treatment is not to cure but rather to reduce distress and improve function. Livesley has proposed four "principles" as inherent to PDs, each of which needs be considered in the treatment plan.

- A PD is central and involves all aspects of the personality structure. Therefore, an effective treatment plan must incorporate a range of interventions, and not just be a response to a specific problem. An implication of this is that the treatment indicated is typically more long-term than brief.
- There exist core features common to all PDs as well as other features common to specific PDs. Therefore, treatment needs to incorporate strategies to manage the PD as a general psychopathology, as well as to offer customized strategies to address the more specific and idiosyncratic manifestations of specific PDs.
- Because PDs reflect a biopsychosocial etiology, interventions must reflect multiple contributing factors with the overarching goals of reducing distress and facilitating adaptation and functionality.
- Because those with PDs are especially vulnerable to poor reactions to stressors common to later life, interventions also must address the consequences of the particular stressors impacting the person.

Perhaps the most clearly articulated model of treatment for PDs specific to later-life is the Goodness of Fit Model (Segal et al., 2006), which describes the relationships between the older person with a PD and their mental health clinician, care provider, or the context of care. This model includes four primary tenets which are used to guide understanding of the older client with PD and to suggest routes for intervention.

- Each PD trait lies along a continuum where it can be, by its point on this continuum, identified as suggesting either personality "style" or a "disorder."
- The composite of these traits establishes a personality trait profile, or template, which can be identified as suggesting a personality "style" or a "disorder."
- The clinician or care provider, or context of care, favors certain personality traits and devalues certain others. Those that are valued are moved along the continuum toward the "style" pole, whereas those that are devalued, or negatively regarded, are moved toward the "disorder" pole.
- The "goodness of fit" between the individual and the provider or context of care affects whether a person is diagnosed with a PD and impacts the type of treatment offered.

As is evident, PD complicates treatment across the lifespan. As such, goals of treatment should be modest and directed more at management of the PD rather than at full remission. In other words, the goal is to help the older individual move from person-ality *disorder* to personality *style* (Rosowsky & Segal, 2011; Segal et al., 2006). This implies that, in some cases, changes in the environment may be what are indicated rather than directing treatment toward changes in the behavior of the older person with PD. Although the individual's dominant personality traits will remain generally constant, how these traits mesh with the later-life context or with what is being asked of the person can make these traits be identified as either pathological (as a PD) or as idiosyncratic (as a personality style). In cases where environmental contingencies can offer some flexibility, such changes may benefit the older person with PD, who by definition is pathologically inflexible.

As can be imagined, development of the therapeutic alliance between the older adult with PD and the mental health professional is usually fraught with difficulty but is nonetheless a therapeutic priority. Wise clinicians should expect challenges to the development of rapport and threatened ruptures to the alliance over the course of treatment. Ruptures are especially likely with Cluster B (antisocial, borderline, histri-onic, and narcissistic) PDs. The clinician should expect that the client will relate to her in a similarly dysfunctional manner as that with which the client relates to other people in his or her life. While this pattern can be frustrating, it can also be informative. We advise clinicians to pay close attention to the emotional reactions engendered in them by the older client with PD. To do so often provides valuable insights into the types of reactions that other people likely have in response to the client and can inform diag-nostic hypotheses and therapeutic interventions. Finally, although no medications are specifically approved for treating PDs, medications can be used to target symptoms that resemble clinical problems such as agitation, anxiety, depression, and loose thinking.

Summary and Conclusions

Although less thoroughly studied, the disorders and difficulties described in this chapter obviously also challenge some later-life individuals and families. It may well turn out to be the case that substance abuse and PDs are each as impactful and deleterious as other difficulties more commonly associated with aging (e.g., depression, anxiety). Much more research is needed to determine the true prevalence and nature of these difficulties with older adults. Assessments and treatments, similarly, are areas in which considerable research is needed.

Critical Thinking / Discussion Questions

1   Describe why substance abuse problems are likely to increase as the current cohort of Baby Boomers reach later life. What should be done about this growing problem?
2   Think about the kind of "difficult personalities" you have encountered in your life. Describe the types of personality disorders which you have encountered most frequently and then describe your emotional reactions to the individuals with those disorders. How would your prior experiences impact your work with an older adult with a personality disorder?
3   Describe and discuss some diagnostic and intervention challenges associated with treating an older adult who has a substance abuse problem and a comorbid personality disorder.

Website Resources

National Institute on Drug Abuse
https://www.drugabuse.gov
Alcoholics Anonymous
http://www.aa.org
BRITE—Implementing Florida's BRITE Project
https://www.youtube.com/watch?v=eOusOcBOxgA
PsychCentral: Personality Disorders
http://psychcentral.com/personality

References

Abrams, R. C., & Horowitz, S. V. (1996). Personality disorders after age 50: A meta-analysis. *Journal of Personality Disorders, 10*, 271–281.

American Psychiatric Association. (1987). *Diagnostic and statistical manual of mental disorders* (DSM-III-R; 3rd ed., rev.). Washington, DC: Author.

American Psychiatric Association. (2000). *Diagnostic and statistical manual of mental disorders* (DSM-IV-TR; 4th ed., text revision). Washington, DC: Author.

American Psychiatric Association. (2013). *Diagnostic and statistical manual of mental disorders* (5th ed.). Arlington, VA: Author.

Arndt, S., Clayton, R., & Schultz, S. K. (2011). Trends in substance abuse treatment 1998–2008: Increasing older adult first-time admissions for illicit drugs. *American Journal of Geriatric Psychiatry, 19*, 704–711.

Arnold, M. (2015). Psychopharmacology and polypharmacy. In P. A. Lichtenberg & B. T. Mast (Eds.), *APA handbook of clinical geropsychology. Vol.1: History and status of the field and perspectives on aging* (pp. 587–605). Washington, DC: American Psychological Association.

Babor, T. F., Higgins-Biddle, J. C., Saunders, J. B., & Monteiro, M. G. (2001). *The Alcohol Use Disorders Identification Test: Guidelines for use in primary care* (2nd ed.). Geneva, Switzerland: World Health Organization.

Balsis, S., Gleason, M. E. J., Woods, C. M., & Oltmanns, T. F. (2007). An item response theory analysis of DSM-IV personality disorder criteria across younger and older age groups. *Psychology and Aging, 22*, 171–185.

Balsis, S., Segal, D. L., & Donahue, C. (2009). Revising the personality disorder diagnostic criteria for the *Diagnostic and Statistical Manual of Mental Disorders – Fifth Edition (DSM-V)*: Consider the later life context. *American Journal of Orthopsychiatry, 79*, 452–460.

Beck, A. T., Freeman, A., Davis, D. D., & Associates. (2003). *Cognitive therapy of personality disorders* (2nd ed.). New York, NY: Guilford.

Blow, F. C., & Barry, K. L. (2012). Alcohol and substance misuse in older adults. *Current Psychiatry Reports, 14*, 310–319.

Blow, F. C., Brower, K. J., Schulenberg, J. E., Demo-Dananberg, L. M., Young, J. P., & Beresford, T. P. (1992). The Michigan Alcoholism Screening Test – Geriatric Version (MAST-G): A new elderly-specific screening instrument. *Alcoholism, 16*, 372.

Center for Behavioral Health Statistics and Quality. (2015). Behavioral health trends in the United States: Results from the 2014 National Survey on Drug Use and Health (HHS Publication No. SMA 15-4927, NSDUH Series H-50). Retrieved from http://www.samhsa.gov/data

Choi, N. G., DiNitto, D. M., & Marti, C. N. (2014). Treatment use, perceived need, and barriers to seeking treatment for substance abuse and mental health problems among older adults compared to younger adults. *Drug and Alcohol Dependence, 145*, 113–120.

Clark, L. A. (2009). Stability and change in personality disorder. *Current Directions in Psychological Science, 18*, 27–31.

Coolidge, F. L., & Segal, D. L. (1998). Evolution of the personality disorder diagnosis in the *Diagnostic and Statistical Manual of Mental Disorders. Clinical Psychology Review, 18*, 585–599.

Coolidge, F. L., Segal, D. L., Pointer, J. C., Knaus, E. A., Yamazaki, T. G., & Silberman, C. S. (2000). Personality disorders in older adult inpatients with chronic mental illness. *Journal of Clinical Geropsychology, 6*, 63–72.

Coolidge, F. L., Thede, L. L., & Jang, K. L. (2001). Heritability of personality disorders in childhood: A preliminary investigation. *Journal of Personality Disorders, 15*, 33–40.

Dick, D. M., & Bierut, L. J. (2006). The genetics of alcohol dependence. *Current Psychiatry Reports, 8*, 151–157.

Duberstein, P. R., Conwell, Y., Seidlitz, L., Denning, D. G., Cox, C., & Caine, E. D. (2000). Personality traits and suicidal behavior and ideation in depressed inpatients 50 years of age and older. *The Journals of Gerontology, Series B: Psychological Sciences and Social Sciences, 55*, 18–26.

Fingerhood, M. (2000). Substance abuse in older people. *Journal of the American Geriatrics Society, 48*, 985–995.

First, M. B., Williams, J. B. W., Benjamin, L. S., & Spitzer, R. L. (2016). *Structured clinical interview for DSM-5-personality disorders (SCID-5-PD)*. Arlington, VA: American Psychiatric Association Publishing.

First, M. B., Williams, J. B. W., Karg, R. S., & Spitzer, R. L. (2016). *Structured clinical interview for DSM-5 disorders: Clinician version (SCID-5-CV)*. Arlington, VA: American Psychiatric Association.

Gfroerer, J., Penne, M., Pemberton, M., & Folsom, R. (2003). Substance abuse treatment need among older adults in 2020: The impact of the aging baby-boom cohort. *Drug and Alcohol Dependence, 69*, 127–135.

Gould, O. N. (2004). Aging, cognition, and medication adherence. In C. Spielberger (Ed.-in-Chief.), *Encyclopedia of applied psychology* (pp. 111–116). New York, NY: Elsevier.

Heisel, M. J., & Flett, G. L. (2006). The development and initial validation of the Geriatric Suicide Ideation Scale. *American Journal of Geriatric Psychiatry, 14*, 742–751.

Jang, K. L., Livesley, W. J., & Vernon, P. A. (1996a). The genetic basis of personality at different ages: A cross-sectional twin study. *Personality and Individual Differences, 21*, 299–301.

Jang, K. L., Livesley, W. J., Vernon, P. A., & Jackson, D. N. (1996b). Heritability of personality disorder traits: A twin study. *Acta Psychiatrica Scandinavica, 94*, 438–444.

Kendler, K. S., Aggen, S. H., Czajkowski, N., Røysamb, E., Tambs, K., Torgersen, S., … Reichborn-Kjennerud, T. (2008). The structure of genetic and environmental risk factors for *DSM-IV* personality disorders: A multivariate twin study. *Archives of General Psychiatry, 65*, 1438–1446.

King, C., Van Hasselt, V. B., Segal, D. L., & Hersen, M. (1994). Diagnosis and assessment of substance abuse in older adults: Current strategies and issues. *Addictive Behaviors, 19*, 41–55.

Kuerbis, A., & Sacco, P. (2013). A review of existing treatments for substance abuse among the elderly and recommendations for future directions. *Substance Abuse: Research and Treatment, 7*, 13–37.

Larimer, M. E., & Kilmer, J. R. (2000). Natural history. In G. Zernig, A. Saria, M. Kurz, & S. O'Malley (Eds.), *Handbook of alcoholism* (pp. 13–28). Boca Raton, FL: CRC Press.

Lenzenweger, M. F. (2008). Epidemiology of personality disorders. *Psychiatric Clinics of North America, 31*, 395–403.

Livesley, W. J. (2004). A framework for an integrated approach to treatment. In J. Livesley (Ed.), *Handbook of personality disorders: Theory, research, and treatment.* New York, NY: Guilford.

Mayfield, D., McLeod, G., & Hall, P. (1974). The CAGE questionnaire: Validation of a new alcoholism screening instrument. *American Journal of Psychiatry, 131*, 1121–1123.

Millon, T., Millon, C. M., Grossman, S., Meagher, S., & Ramnath, R. (2004). *Personality disorders in modern life* (2nd ed.). New York, NY: Wiley.

Molinari, V., Ames, A., & Essa, M. (1994). Prevalence of personality disorders in two geropsychiatric inpatient units. *Journal of Geriatric Psychiatry and Neurology, 7*, 209–215.

Molinari, V., & Marmion, J. (1995). Relationship between affective disorders and Axis II diagnoses in geropsychiatric patients. *Journal of Geriatric Psychiatry and Neurology, 8*, 61–64.

Molinari, V., & Segal, D. L. (2011). Personality disorders: Description, aetiology, and epidemiology. In M. Abou-Saleh, C. Katona, & A. Kumar (Eds.), *Principles and practice of geriatric psychiatry* (3rd ed., pp. 649–654). New York, NY: Wiley.

National Center for Health Statistics. (2016). *Health, United States, 2015: With special feature on racial and ethnic health disparities.* Hyattsville, MD: Author

National Council on Patient Information and Education. (2010). *Fact sheet: Medicine use and older adults.* Retrieved from http://www.bemedwise.org/documents/must_factsheet.pdf

Oltmanns, T. F., & Balsis, S. (2011). Personality disorder in later life: Questions about the measurement, course, and impact of disorders. *Annual Review of Clinical Psychology, 7*, 321–349.

Oslin, D. W., Grantham, S., Coakley, E., Maxwell, J., Miles, K., Ware, J., …Zubritsky, C. (2006). PRISM-E: Comparison of integrated care and enhanced specialty referral in managing at-risk alcohol use. *Psychiatric Services, 57*(7), 954–958. doi: 10.1176/appi. ps.57.7.954

Powell, J. E., & McInness, E. (1994). Alcohol use among older hospital patients: Findings from an Australian study. *Drug and Alcohol Review, 13*, 5–12.

Reich, J., Nduaguba, M., & Yates, W. (1988). Age and sex distribution of DSM-III personality cluster traits in a community population. *Comprehensive Psychiatry, 29*, 298–303.

Rosowsky, E., Abrams, R. C., & Zweig, R. A. (Eds.) (1999). *Personality disorders in older adults: Emerging issues in diagnosis and treatment*. Mahwah, NJ: Erlbaum.

Rosowsky, E., & Molinari, V. (2014). Personality disorders in later life. *Generations, 38*, 37–44.

Rosowsky, E., & Segal, D. L. (2011). Personality disorders. In N. A. Pachana, K. Laidlaw, & B. G. Knight (Eds.), *Casebook of clinical geropsychology: International perspectives on practice* (pp. 195–209). New York, NY: Oxford University Press.

Rossi, G., van den Broeck, J., Dierckx, E., Segal, D. L., & van Alphen, S. P. J. (2014). Personality assessment among older adults: The value of personality questionnaires unraveled. *Aging and Mental Health, 8*, 936–940.

Sadavoy, J. (2014). Disorders of personality in later-life. In N. A. Pachana & K. Laidlaw (Eds.), *Oxford handbook of clinical geropsychology* (pp. 504–525). New York, NY: Oxford University Press.

Schonfeld, L., Hazlett, R. W., Hedgecock, D. K., Duchene, D. M., Burns, L. V., & Gum, A. M. (2015). Screening, brief intervention, and referral to treatment for older adults with substance misuse. *American Journal of Public Health, 105*, 205–211.

Schonfeld, L., King-Kallimanis, B. L., Duchene, D. M., Etheridge, R. L., Herrera, J. R., Barry, K. L., & Lynn, N. (2010). Screening and brief intervention for substance misuse among older adults: The Florida BRITE Project. *American Journal of Public Health, 100*, 108–114.

Segal, D. L., Coolidge, F. L., & Rosowsky, E. (2006). *Personality disorders and older adults: Diagnosis, assessment, and treatment*. Hoboken, NJ: Wiley.

Segal, D. L., Gottschling, J., Marty, M., Meyer, W. J., & Coolidge, F. L. (2015). Relationships among depressive, passive-aggressive, sadistic and self-defeating personality disorder features with suicidal ideation and reasons for living among older adults. *Aging and Mental Health, 19*, 1071–1077.

Segal, D. L., Marty, M. A., Meyer, W. J., & Coolidge, F. L. (2012). Personality, suicidal ideation, and reasons for living among older adults. *Journal of Gerontology: Psychological Sciences and Social Sciences, 67*, 159–166.

Segal, D. L., Zweig, R., & Molinari, V. (2012). Personality disorders in later life. In S. K. Whitbourne & M. Sliwinski (Eds.), *Wiley-Blackwell handbook of adulthood and aging* (pp. 312–330). Malden, MA: Wiley-Blackwell.

Substance Abuse and Mental Health Services Administration. (2014). *Results from the 2013 National Survey on Drug Use and Health: Summary of National Findings (NSDUH Series H-48, HHS Publication No. (SMA) 14-4863)*. Rockville, MD: Author.

Thompson, L. W., Gallagher, D., & Czirr, R. (1988). Personality disorder and outcome in the treatment of late-life depression. *Journal of Geriatric Psychiatry, 21*, 133–146.

Torgersen, S., Lygren, S., Øien, P. A., Skre, I., Onstad, S., Edvardsen, J., ... Kringlen, E. (2000). A twin study of personality disorders. *Comprehensive Psychiatry, 41*, 416–425.

Vaillant, G. E. (2002). *Aging well*. Boston: Little, Brown and Company.

Van Alphen, S. P. J., Engelen, G. J. J. A., Kuin, Y., Hoijtink, H. J. A., & Derksen, J. J. L. (2006). A preliminary study of the diagnostic accuracy of the Gerontological Personality disorders Scale (GPS). *International Journal of Geriatric Psychiatry, 21*, 862–868.

Van Alphen, S. P. J., Rossi, G., Segal, D. L., & Rosowsky, E. (2013). Issues regarding the proposed DSM-5 personality disorders in geriatric psychology and psychiatry. *International Psychogeriatrics, 25*, 1–5.

Wang, Y., & Andrade, L. H. (2013). Epidemiology of alcohol and drug use in the elderly. *Current Opinion in Psychiatry, 26*, 343–348.

West, N. A., Severtson, S. G., Green, J. L., & Dart, R. C. (2015). Trends in abuse and misuse of prescription opioids among older adults. *Drug and Alcohol Dependence, 149*, 117–121.

Zweig, R. A. (2008). Personality disorder in older adults: Assessment challenges and strategies. *Professional Psychology: Research and Practice, 3*, 298–305.

Part IV
Settings and Contexts of Mental Health

The previous section on mental disorders emphasized a social ecological approach to definitions and expressions of mental disorders. This section takes that framework one step farther by providing overviews of key contexts that influence mental health and disorders, and in which they are experienced. Books on mental health rarely address in detail the contexts in which mental health and mental disorders exist, or how those contexts relate to the disorders. The last chapters in this book provide information about key contexts for mental health and disorders in later life, with a heavy emphasis on the formal service systems available to support mental health or address mental disorders in later life.

Service providers to older adults who want to support positive mental health must become familiar with the contexts of mental health in order to provide effective care and support. Researchers obviously must look beyond a score on a test or a description of a person in order to study mental health in older adults. When an older person relocates from a long-term home in a suburban neighborhood to a senior residence, who does what to support or undermine adaptation and adjustment? An 85-year-old woman tripped on an uneven sidewalk and fell, resulting in a broken hip from which she never recovered her full functioning. Will she now move into a nursing home or her daughter's home? With what consequences to her mental health? Obviously, multiple environments have been, and will be, key factors in her mental well-being.

An overview of the health services system in the US is presented in Chapter 14. The health care industry is one of the most complex in the US, combining public and private service systems and payers in a complex delivery system that is the focus of considerable angst and distress for consumers and policymakers alike. Aging almost universally brings people into more frequent contact with the health care system. A key question that runs through this chapter is how mental health can be supported more effectively by these service systems.

Aging and Mental Health, Third Edition. Daniel L. Segal, Sara Honn Qualls, and Michael A. Smyer.
© 2018 John Wiley & Sons, Inc. Published 2018 by John Wiley & Sons, Inc.

The housing and social services industries are described in Chapter 15. The vast majority of older adults live in community housing similar to other adults, where social services and community resources can serve as key supports for well-being. Transportation, home-delivered meals, and homemaker services can make the difference between human connection and social isolation that easily results in loneliness and anxiety, for example. The likelihood of spending at least some time in a long-term-care setting for short-stay rehabilitation or longer-stay residence is quite high at some point in later life. Housing is now a very complex industry with a rich continuum of services, but also with complex regulatory realities. It is also challenging in matching individuals with the environment that will best support mental and physical health. Public policy is of intense importance in housing and social services, industries with which service providers must have familiarity.

The family is the key caregiving context in later life, positioning critical care services inside an interpersonal system that is complex and typically decades old in its structures, as described in Chapter 16. Families often struggle as they transition from providing everyday care for members similar to what has been done throughout the life span, to providing extraordinary levels of service that we refer to as caregiving. The health, housing, and social service systems described in previous chapters are unfamiliar territory when families first encounter them. Family dynamics are overfamiliar territory to members, but mysteries to the provider systems they encounter. Chapter 16 introduces readers to the challenges families face as they navigate the transitions of later life.

We end the section by noting some key ethical and legal contexts for mental health in later life in Chapter 17. Basic ethical challenges are faced daily by families, professionals, and direct care workers, with consequences for the mental health of older adults. The legal challenges of supporting human rights of frail and vulnerable older persons often bring together the mental health and legal service systems. Readers interested in positive mental health as well as mental disorders will find the information in this chapter provocative.

The chapters in Part IV are new to this edition, representing our growing understanding and appreciation of services contexts as critical factors in supporting mental health and addressing mental disorders. Integration of mental health services into primary care is occurring rapidly within US health care. Yet too often mental health research and services continue in a person-focused way that decontextualizes the experience. We invite you to embrace the opportunity to question the ways in which mental health is experienced and addressed across multiple sectors of our society.

14

Health Services Delivery Systems

Liz realizes her mother can't manage in the big family home alone any longer. But she wants to stay there, so Liz was shocked to discover that Medicare does not pay for home health services except for rehabilitation following hospital stay. Who can help?

Tanner is training to become a geropsychologist. She hears from colleagues that the new model of care might open job opportunities for her inside primary care but she will need to work differently. What exactly does that mean?

Dr. Martinez has joined faculty from medicine, nursing, and pharmacy to develop an Interprofessional Education (IPE) program at his university, and wonders how to change psychology and social work curriculum to prepare students to participate. He also wonders how IPE will work differently for older patients and clients of service delivery systems.

The health care industry is a powerful context for identifying and addressing mental health needs of older adults, investigating the mutual impact of mental health and physical health on well-being, and exploring the intersection of health services with other service systems such as long-term care residential settings and social services. Yet linkages of physical and mental health services, research, and education are in their infancy and face substantial barriers to development due to the complexities of the industry. Persons interested in mental health of older adults need to become familiar with what appears to be an overwhelmingly complex industry. This chapter is intended to serve as an introductory roadmap, providing an overview of the major components of the health care system, linkage between physical and mental health, and models for working with mental health inside primary care and long-term care.

Aging and Mental Health, Third Edition. Daniel L. Segal, Sara Honn Qualls, and Michael A. Smyer.
© 2018 John Wiley & Sons, Inc. Published 2018 by John Wiley & Sons, Inc.

Integration of behavioral health into traditional physical health care systems is one of many transformative changes happening within the health industry today. The magnitude of this transition is not yet in view, because the transformation is in its early stages. Yet compelling evidence of the deep linkages of physical and mental health point to the inevitability of delivering services through integrated models across the entire health care system. Three significant transitions in service delivery since 2000 propel the move toward integration of mental and physical health services.

The first transition relates to funding. After decades of efforts to achieve parity of reimbursement for mental health with physical health services, policy changes in government programs such as Medicare finally established that co-payments should be set at an equal percentage for the two sets of services. Prior to 2010, mental health services were reimbursed at only 50% of the allowable rate, requiring a far more burdensome co-payment than for physical health services that were reimbursed at the 80% level. Since the phase-in of parity was completed in 2014, Medicare has reimbursed mental and physical health at the same level: 80% of allowable costs. Insurance companies quickly followed suit, making it more attractive to health organizations to incorporate mental health services.

A second substantial factor was the introduction of screening tools to identify the presence of mental disorders within various health care settings. Once it became evident that mental disorders were easy to detect and prevalent at rates that warranted substantial services, the idea of integrating mental health services into primary care and other settings became obvious. The larger health care system could identify mental disorders in persons who were not already seeking evaluation from mental health specialists, in the same way that lab tests often identify physical health problems that were not previously identified.

A third push toward integration came from the policy change in Medicare that allowed reimbursement for behavioral health interventions that address physical health conditions and functioning. For the first time in 2002, psychologists could deliver services for medical conditions that required behavior change as part of their treatment, even when mental disorders were not present. Thus, psychologists are now eligible to contribute to teams that treat chronic diseases such as diabetes or cardiovascular disease, billing under Health and Behavior codes (Qualls & Benight, 2007). Lifestyle change is often a key component of chronic disease management, requiring significant behavior changes that are not simple to accomplish (Newsom et al., 2012). These policy changes positioned psychologists to participate in the mainstream health care delivery system in ways that were simply impossible previously.

Health Service Delivery Systems 101

Health care is perhaps the most complex industry in most industrialized countries. The US system is particularly complicated because of the diversity of payors and providers of services. In many countries, the government is the sole payor and provider. However, in the US, a myriad of private and nonprofit insurers join the government as payors of services. The US government primarily funds health care through Medicare,

Medicaid, and military and veteran services. The US government also operates two of the largest health service delivery systems in the world through its military and Veterans Administration networks. Yet most citizens access services through nongovernment agencies, even if the source of payment for services is government funding (e.g., Medicare, Medicaid). The complexity for consumers and providers is daunting as millions of providers participate in a massive system with layers of organizational structures operating within a morass of laws, regulations, and rules governing their operations.

Health care industry overview

Health care can be viewed as a continuum of services, ranging from most intense to least intense. Acute care hospitals provide emergency, surgical, and in-patient services for a very wide range of serious illnesses and injuries that also vary in intensity. Physicians and nurses are joined by a myriad of other providers that range from technicians to specialized professionals. During recovery from illness or injury, rehabilitation services are offered in inpatient and outpatient settings to assist people with regaining strength, skills, and functional health. Rehabilitation teams include physical and occupational therapists as well as speech therapists, specialty physicians, nurses, and psychologists.

Outpatient services are available from providers of many specializations, typically coordinated by a primary care provider. The range of outpatient providers is vast, addressing every organ system and functional domain of health. Generally, outpatient services are scheduled one at a time, in separate locations, so a person with regular appointments with multiple providers may have many separate trips to various locations during a month. Day programs or partial hospitalization programs offer transitional services between hospital and outpatient services, with a few hours of services per day. These programs target particular populations (e.g., cardiac rehabilitation, mental health) for whom they provide multiple services, sometimes in a half-day visit.

Home health is a large industry that includes medical services as well as nonmedical services to support home-based living. Home health is paid by government and private insurers primarily when a person is recovering from an illness or injury that required several days in the hospital. Nonmedical home health includes light housekeeping, food preparation, and support with basic self-care, whereas medical home health care assists with medication management, wound care, and other medical services. Some states offer a package of home health services as an alternative to nursing home placement under long-term-care waiver programs, but otherwise, home health services are quite costly when paid privately.

The pharmaceutical industry and pharmacy professionals are other powerful participants in the health service system. The cost of medications is a common target of media attention that raises public awareness of ethical concerns about balancing corporate profit and public access to services. The research and development arm of the pharmaceutical industry is a critical component of the health industry because it conducts the translational research that is the basis for government's decisions to approve or disapprove a medication as safe and useful.

Long-term-care services are health services that are delivered over long time periods, with a focus on day-to-day care support. Residential services for older adults may be for relatively brief stays for posthospitalization rehabilitation or permanent residency for persons with stable care needs. Long-term care includes homes and apartments in senior housing complexes as well as assisted living facilities, skilled nursing facilities, and memory care residences (the housing industry is the focus of Chapter 15). The key variation among those types of housing is in the amount of support services that are available, with accompanying variations in cost. Cost is also affected by factors such as location, amenities, amount of space, and staff. Higher-end facilities offer amenities that cannot be offered in low-income housing. Furthermore, the geographic structure of senior housing varies from isolated campuses to facilities that are integrated into neighborhoods, and from single-level housing to campuses that include multiple levels of housing.

An array of medical specialties provides expert care for particular organ systems or disease types, so oncology, radiology, cardiology, nephrology, neurology, and a long list of other "–ologies" are also linked to services across the health care continuum from acute care to outpatient care. Increasingly, hospital-based care is overseen by physicians who specialize in care within that setting, often known as hospitalists. Specialty providers may move among outpatient, inpatient, and sometimes surgical settings to provide services.

Mental health specialty services represent a relatively small portion of this massive system, a portion which is dropping. The Substance Abuse and Mental Health Services Administration (SAMHSA) predicts that mental health and substance abuse spending will drop from approximately 11.8% of Medicaid spending on health care overall in 2010 to 8.2% in 2020 (SAMHSA, 2014). Shrinking spending, however, should not be confused with shrinking need. As we have echoed throughout this book, the mental health service needs of older adults are generally growing, not declining.

Operating primarily in a silo separate from the rest of health care, a wide range of mental health services is available in specialty settings, including assessment, intervention, and well-being support. Mirroring the array of services for physical health care, mental health uses inpatient hospitals and crisis stabilization units to provide the most acute care, and supportive community-based services for the least intensive service needs. In between those poles is an array of services that include partial hospitalization or day programs, rehabilitation programs, residential care (e.g., for brain injury or memory care), pharmacotherapy, and a wide range of intervention services focused on behavior change. Assessment services cross that full continuum of mental health specialty services as well, ranging from screening, clinical interviews, psychological and neuropsychological testing, and capacity evaluations to inform legal decisions.

Wellness and public health

Almost completely disconnected from the health care industry are two related industries: wellness and public health. The disconnect is both cultural and systemic. Culturally, health care has focused on those who are sick, with the most intensive services targeted at the sickest. Wellness has focused on those motivated to improve health through behavior change or practices often referenced as complementary and alternative health care. The payment sources for wellness services are primarily private, from individuals or employer programs, whereas mainstream health care is funded through private or public insurance.

As a rapidly growing industry, the wellness industry includes gyms and fitness centers, nutrition counselors and retail shops, outdoor space and trails planners, recreation centers, etc. Health insurance rarely pays for the services from the wellness industry, although that may change in the future. Currently health systems are in a state of flux as companies merge to compete in the marketplace, often aggregating hospitals, specialty practices, primary care, and occasionally, wellness programming. Industry realignment is incentivized by payment structures that reward evidence of accomplishing what has been called the "triple aim" of achieving fiscal value, high-quality services, and positive health outcomes (Berwick, Nolan, & Whittington, 2008). Engagement in wellness services may pay off sufficiently in reducing usage rates for costlier services such that private and public insurance payors may increase funding for components of the wellness industry. Examples that are now emerging with increased frequency are innovative partnerships that colocate primary care in buildings with physical activities programs or organizations (e.g., YMCA), mental health, and nutritional counselors.

> George and Velma are shocked at the difference in their lives compared to a year ago when George had a heart attack. His rehabilitation team convinced them to go together to the YMCA and find a class to continue the exercise routines he had developed while recovering from the heart attack. Wow—what a difference a year makes. They love the classes at the YMCA—yoga, spinning, weights—and have found new friends who really care about their health. Last week they even went on a hike in a local park. Not only are their bodies stronger and healthier, they are simply happier with a lot less bickering, better moods, and a wider range of activities.

Public health has a community-wide focus that includes the monitoring of indicators of the population's health and well-being, ensuring that food services and health facilities are safe, and initiating community policies and practices that will improve health. International (e.g., World Health Organization) and national organizations (e.g., Centers for Disease Control, Institute of Medicine) establish priorities for policymakers and practitioners to address issues of public concern, conduct research, and define best practices. Local public health officials have responsibility for managing local environmental risks such as water, and health practices in restaurants, health services, and public places. Linkages of public health activities with health care providers' activities is progressing, but still limited.

Payment for health services

Perhaps the most complicating factor in the health system in the US is the complex payment structures. Consumers and providers alike struggle to understand which services can be accessed from which providers under which health payment plans. Other countries with a centralized government payor and provider system operate somewhat more like the military or government health service system in the US. Once enrolled in the government program, the provider system is well defined. Access occurs through a centralized process that manages workflow, timing, and access to services. A major challenge in these systems is the allocation of resources in a timely way to the consumers. A major advantage is the linkage of providers in a common record-keeping system that allows providers to know and communicate about their treatments, which is fundamental to coordinated care.

After age 65, most people in the US are enrolled in the Medicare government payment system along with adults of all ages living with disabilities. Medicare is divided into Parts that cover acute hospital services (A), outpatient services (B), capitated payment plans (C), and pharmacy (D). Consumers choose the parts in which they wish to enroll, and may be surprised at the absence of covered benefits when needed. Consumers also may choose to allocate their Medicare benefits to a private insurer in programs that are often referred to as Medicare Advantage plans that require lower or no co-payments in exchange for more payor control over the range of providers.

Medicaid is the US payment system for persons whose income is below a threshold, usually defined as a percentage of the poverty rate. For example, in 2016, the federal poverty guideline defines a single-person household as living in poverty if income is less than $11,880, or less than $24,300 for a family of four (ASPE, n.d.).

Older persons living on low incomes are often enrolled in both Medicare and Medicaid. Medicare is the first payor for health services, with Medicaid picking up remaining costs that fall within its policies and regulations. Providers usually receive only a very small portion of the allowed co-payment from Medicaid, however, so they experience a substantial loss of revenue on persons who use that combination of government insurance. Furthermore, state governments establish the payment rates even though Medicaid is jointly funded by federal and state governments, producing variation in service options across states due to variability in funding.

Medicaid is the only government-funded payor for long-term care. Medicare offers no long-term-care benefit, paying for skilled nursing *only* during a rehabilitation stay posthospitalization. Medicaid pays only for persons of low income, so the de facto long-term-care payment insurance in the US is private payment until resources are expended after which the consumer may become eligible for Medicaid. Private long-term-care insurance is another potential source of payment for long-term care. Long-term-care insurance policies pay a per diem rate for a range of services defined in each policy, and are fully separate from health insurance policies. The per diem payment is often lower than the full cost of care. Long-term-care insurance may provide consumers selecting facilities and programs with a choice that is broader than the options for persons whose payment source is Medicaid.

> George has about $10,000 in his savings account and owns his home. Now that he needs to live in a nursing home for the long term, he will likely need to sell his home and use the proceeds along with his savings to pay privately for care that costs approximately $7,000 per month. Once he has spent his assets down to the Medicaid eligibility level (approximately $2,000), he will qualify for the government to pay for his nursing home through Medicaid. George hates that he will have no money to leave to his children, and the process for getting approved for Medicaid is neither fast nor easy.

Summary

This very broad view of the complicated health services system is truly a 50,000-foot view of systems for which the devil is in the details. Mental health professionals are often shocked to encounter older adults whose government-funded insurance restricts them from using Medicare or Medicaid to pay the provider for services. For example, older adults who have not enrolled in Medicare Part B or who have enrolled in a Medicare Advantage plan (Part C) that includes few mental health providers may have great difficulty accessing services. Medicaid policies in many states exclude reimbursement for neuropsychological evaluations. Families may assume they can access home health care, but are shocked to discover that Medicare only pays for a limited time period posthospitalization, not for the long term. The learning curve for providers, older consumers, and families is steep on the array of services, the structures within which they are organized, and the payment systems for them.

Mental Health Services Industry

All service delivery systems deal with mental health across all types of services in all settings, so integration of mental health providers seems logical. However, mental health also exists as a specialty care service system. Older adults may now encounter mental health services within the larger physical health care system, by referral from a provider of physical health services to a provider of mental health services, or directly from a mental health service provider.

Mental health services delivery system

The mental health services system is dominated by traditional outpatient services but also offers a continuum of care that includes partial hospitalization or day programs and inpatient hospital services. Rarely does one organization provide the full continuum of services. Thus, the industry functions more as a cottage industry with a few organizational participants than a full mental health system. In the second half of the 20th century, the public mental health institutes or hospitals that housed hundreds of severely mentally ill individuals either have closed, or operate at a fraction of their former size. This transition was fueled by the advent of medications that made it possible for persons with severe mental disorders to live safely in the community, along with a public health initiative to deinstitutionalize in favor of community-based living and services. Community mental health service systems emerged in the 1960s and 1970s to address the growing need for outpatient service models, but older adults rarely accessed services there. Drastic funding cuts in the 1980s and 1990s have functionally dismantled that system so that only fee-for-service models paid by private or government (primarily Medicaid) payors now dominate community mental health.

For older adults, skilled nursing facilities/homes (SNFs) became the de facto inpatient setting for persons with serious mental illness during the period of deinstitutionalization. However, federal legislation in the late 1980s that is commonly referenced as OBRA

(Omnibus Budget Reconciliation Act) changed that pattern by requiring mental health screening upon admission to SNFs. As a result, access to SNFs was restricted for persons whose primary reason for needing residential care was mental health. Unfortunately, alternative housing is not readily available for individuals whose primary need for residential services is mental health. Persons with secondary mental illnesses living in SNFs are required to be provided active treatment of those mental illnesses along with other health services appropriately to their other health problems.

A critical failure of the deinstitutionalization movement was the lack of development of residential alternatives. Adults of all ages found themselves in the community with limited practical supports for handling the challenges of daily life (e.g., case management services). They also face a dearth of supportive living residential environments in almost all communities. In the US, this fact combined with escalation of housing costs compared to wages has resulted in a growing homeless population of persons with severe mental illness.

Inpatient psychiatric services have also switched from a longer-term model to short stays, from a few days to at most a few weeks. Rarely do patients remain in the facility for more than 10 days. The focus has shifted to stabilization and triage back into the community rather than the former focus on active treatment during the inpatient stay. Inpatient care is increasingly provided by a specialty company that operates psychiatric inpatient units in multiple sites, and less often as a unit within a larger hospital of a large health care system. For older adults, this can result in isolation of mental health acute care from physical health acute care.

> Toni Tenet was transferred from her SNF home to an inpatient psychiatric facility when her behavior outbursts grew so disruptive that neither staff nor residents could manage them. Before she could be admitted, however, she needed medical clearance, so she was shuttled to the nearest hospital emergency department where multiple tests were run. By the time she was cleared for admission to the inpatient psychiatric facility, she was exhausted and even further disoriented. The psychiatrist who evaluated her the next day found her difficult to interview. The initial choice of medication focused on the current symptoms, which were now quite different from those exhibited in her typical living environment.

> James requires complex medical support from nursing staff, so he cannot be managed in a psychiatric inpatient unit that lacks those services. When his mental health is dysregulated, the only option for more acute care is a medical unit in the local hospital where his behavior problems will require a 24-hour sitter to manage. The staff on the medical unit are confused about how to manage his behavior challenges within their protocols and workflow.

> Dr. Sprouse is medical director of a geriatric medical-psychiatric unit within a larger hospital. The patients she oversees have complex medical problems combined with challenging mental health issues. It is not uncommon for a patient to have a serious medical issue, dementia, and a lifelong history of bipolar disorder. The intersection of those care needs requires specialized staff who understand aging, mental disorders, physical illnesses, and neurocognitive disorders. They also need to know

how to prepare their older patients, their families, and the residential environment for post-discharge care. Dr. Sprouse knows how precious this resource is to the community; rarely do communities have this type of unit.

Outpatient services are provided by multiple professions, including psychologists, social workers, professional counselors, care managers, psychiatrists, psychiatric nurses, marriage and family therapists, and alcohol and substance abuse counselors. Each profession has a scope of practice defined by its state's licensure or certifications. Only some have authority to conduct certain types of evaluations or tests, provide diagnosis or treatment plan, or prescribe medications. Substantial overlap also exists among their roles, especially in the area of psychotherapy or counseling.

Outpatient services may be provided in a private practice setting, within a larger health or mental health organization, or in a hospital-based setting. Outpatient sessions typically last one hour or less, with more time allocated for group or family sessions. The standards set for public spaces to meet the needs of persons with disabilities has had a very important impact on access for older adults with mobility or sensory deficits. Previously, outpatient mental health settings rarely accommodated older adults who represented very small portions of outpatient practices. Older adults continue to be less likely than younger adults to seek help for mental health problems such as depression (Van Citters & Bartels, 2004), but the sheer volume of demographic growth and expected increase in openness among cohorts of older adults will raise their visibility in mental health service systems. Mental health practices can expect to serve older adults and need to have a physical environment that can accommodate their physical and sensory needs.

Models linking mental and physical health

Like many women in their 70s, Candace expects her primary care provider will tell her to lose weight at every appointment. She is well aware that she is obese, and that her weight has negative effects on her diabetes and heart condition. She also knows that she is ashamed of her body and dreads the conversation. After 40 years of intermittent dieting, she's accepted her failure to get control of her body. "Telling me to lose weight is not only useless, it makes me avoid going to the doctor. I would rather go to the emergency room when I really need something."

Trent is pretty sure he is having heart problems, but frankly doesn't care. Joining his wife in heaven is the happiest thought he can come up with these days. He's going for his physical only because his daughter insisted. He certainly doesn't see anyone else these days.

Older adults like many other populations report their mental health problems primarily in primary care (Petterson, Miller, Payne-Murphy, & Phillips, 2014). As the main provider of mental health services to older adults, primary care is a site where mental health challenges can be identified if proper screening is used. Social and resource challenges can also be identified and addressed there, especially with the emergence of Patient Navigators who guide people to useful resources they often did not know were available. The benefits of integrating mental and social health into physical health care are based on a model of well-being that is now driving services models.

The biopsychosocial model of health (Frankel, Quill, & McDaniel, 2003), outlined in Chapter 1, guides all disciplines to focus on the intersection of the three domains (and some would add other domains such as spiritual) in preparing future health providers, researchers, educators, and policymakers. The model focuses on identifying three dimensions of health and their intersections: biological, psychological, and social. Biological factors have been the historic focus of health care, although even the physical health domain continues to broaden to areas like wellness and prevention. Whereas medicine historically focused on disease, injury, and biological treatments (e.g., surgery, medications), this model also points to health promotion activities such as exercise and nutrition as critical components of health care. Psychological factors similarly encompass resilience and personality, schemas and motivation, as well as traditional mental disorders. Social determinants of health are highlighted often as disparities in health conditions, services access, and quality. Disparities have been documented across social locations such as race and ethnicity, geography (rural/urban, neighborhood), income, gender, and social support. When health is conceptualized as multidimensional, the health care industry must figure out how to integrate dimensions that have historically been missing in services structures, including mental health.

Looking to the Future: Integration of Health Services

Why integrate mental health into health care?

Mental disorders complicate essentially all aspects of health care services, and we note a few examples next. Persons living with mood disorders may struggle with motivation for physical self-care if they lack hope for a brighter future. Older persons living with cognitive impairment may be incapable of managing complex daily health routines. Health behaviors related to management of chronic disease (e.g., medication management, adherence to recommended physical activity routines) are more challenging for persons living with anxiety, dementia, or insomnia, for example. Paying for health care is harder for persons whose mental disorders lead to lower income or unemployment. Regular attendance at health appointments or wellness activities suffers when mental disorders are active, yet overall health services costs go up in persons with mental disorders (Simning et al., 2010). Substance abuse adds risk for falls, exploitation, social dislocation, and physical and cognitive disability.

Physical illnesses negatively impact mental health. Adjustment to acute or chronic illness requires active effective coping with mental health symptoms such as anxiety, low mood, and in more substantial cases, delirium. Various illnesses and the medications or processes used to treat them often create depression, anxiety, agitation, confusion, or irritability. Illnesses (e.g., urinary tract infections) and medications are the most common cause of delirium in long-term-care settings. Fatigue from illness can be a significant challenge for people who maintain their psychological well-being through activities that require stamina. In short, feeling poorly makes people cranky. A long series of acute illnesses or elongated periods of recovery from influenza, a broken hip, or pneumonia can tee up a mental disorder.

Living long term with chronic disease is stressful, adding burden to the mental health of the person living with the disease. The initial response to learning that one must live with a disease such as Parkinson's disease or diabetes for the rest of one's life can elicit a strong psychological reaction in a person with the disease and his or her family. Many chronic diseases impact daily functioning through deficits in mobility, strength, stamina, or reorganization of daily life routines. Any of these can interfere with previously meaningful activities or social interaction, and thus add to the risk of mental disorders such as depression or anxiety. Furthermore, chronic diseases often flare in acute episodes that must be managed medically with more intensive intervention that may require a hospitalization or home-bound period. Those interruptions in normal functioning often have a reverberating effect on the physical and mental health of the person.

Alan lives with Chronic Obstructive Pulmonary Disease (COPD), often referred to as emphysema. He carries portable oxygen with him at all times, but is still out of breath by the time he walks from the parking lot to the grocery store. Last winter his cold turned into pneumonia that laid him up for several weeks, after which it was still a long, slow process to regain anything like a normal routine. Meanwhile he had missed months of contact with his men's breakfast group, church, and even short walks with his dog. Before he was back into the groove of normal life, he also had to battle his way out of an anxious depression.

Further complicating the picture is that many physical health problems in later life affect either the cardiovascular or neurological system which can have direct negative impact on brain functioning. An accumulation of factors, that limit blood flow to the brain, or that reduce the presence and effectiveness of neurotransmitters in the brain, will likely produce some negative impact on cognitive functioning and/or mood regulation. Higher cortical functioning is critical to self-management of daily life patterns, mood, and emotional reactivity. Thus, loss of executive functioning abilities can have both direct and indirect impact on ability to function independently with positive mental health.

Based on the sheer prevalence of chronic disease in later life, older adults who live with mental disorders are often also living with a growing array of chronic diseases. More than 25% of Americans have multiple chronic conditions, which disproportionately affect the elderly and minorities (Institute of Medicine, 2012). For older adults, approximately 92% have at least one chronic disease, and 77% have at least two. Four chronic diseases—heart disease, cancer, stroke, and diabetes—cause almost two-thirds of all deaths each year (National Council on Aging, 2014). Consider the added burden of self-care with multiple chronic diseases and the treatments of them, the periods of exacerbation into an acute condition as Alan faced, and the struggle to keep life "normal" enough to support mental well-being.

Bill has lived on the streets for 25 years off and on, interrupted by inpatient hospitalizations where he starts on psychotropic medications that reduce the rate and intensity of hallucinations. Once released to the community, Bill's pattern is to cut off contact with his therapist and psychiatrist, quit taking his medication, and move back into the familiar pattern on the streets. He can usually hustle enough money to get high on marijuana when the voices are too annoying. In the past five years, Bill has developed significant arthritis that makes the hard earth feel harder. He notices that his ankles are swollen and red much of the time now. Bill is building up the same chronic diseases that are common in men considerably older than him, but he has no regular physical health care, nor would he take medications regularly if they were administered.

Solutions: Changing service structures

The integration of mental health into primary care is proceeding with accelerating speed. Multiple benefits accrue from integration of mental health services within physical health care service systems. Integrating behavioral health into primary care saves overall health care costs in addition to the other benefits noted above (Blount et al., 2007). By addressing both mental health and behavioral chronic disease self-management issues, symptoms are managed better overall, leading to fewer high-cost emergencies or even acute episodes of illness. Furthermore, medical providers generally hold positive views of behavioral health clinicians in integrated care. In a study of medical providers in primary care (Torrence et al., 2014), the medical personnel perceived the behavioral health clinicians as being valuable members of the integrated health care team who helped the medical providers to improve their abilities to provide care and to address their patients' physical and behavioral health problems.

Within the next decade, government payment systems will be providing single contracts for physical and mental health rather than carving out behavioral health for separate contracts. Health systems will be managing both aspects of health, and will be interested in how the service delivery systems intersect from a cost containment viewpoint. They will also be rewarded for improving overall health outcomes through high quality of care.

The proliferation of integrated care programs has led to innovation at the grass roots level. To date, no single model for integrating behavioral health into primary care has emerged as superior or even feasible (Sieber et al., 2012). Pragmatic issues within the particular practice setting often dictate the model adopted. Factors such as space, payor sources, provider readiness to embrace, administrative investment, and population served all influence the selection of models.

Providers of behavioral health services within family medicine clinics have decades of experience from which to offer guidance and strategies for offering behavioral health services in patterns that work within the specific constraints and opportunities of primary care clinics (Burg & Oyama, 2016; Hunter, Goodie, Oordt, & Dobmeyer, 2009). Family medicine draws on mental health providers' skills in working with family systems and the broader health care systems within which they receive care (McDaniel, Doherty, & Hepworth, 2014; Rolland, 1994).

A variant on integrated care that is relevant to frail older adults is the Program for All-Inclusive Care for the Elderly (PACE) model. Developed as an alternative to nursing home placement, PACE combines home care with an adult day health model to offer a remarkable array of services. A triangle of integration wraps primary care, rehabilitation services, and residential/home-care into a single service system for low-resourced frail older adults who need significant assistance with the basic activities of daily living that would otherwise force them into a nursing home. Funded through Medicare and state-approved Medicaid waiver programs, PACE is now available in over 100 locations across a majority of the states in the United States.

Preparing the workforce

The complexities of these settings require professionals to develop new skills and strategies for effective service delivery. Guidelines for practice and for training in gero-psychology emphasize the importance of preparing to work with other professionals in a variety of health settings (Knight, Karel, Hinrichsen, Qualls, & Duffy, 2009; Qualls, 2015). Guidelines for practice by psychologists in primary care are now available (McDaniel, Grus, et al., 2014).

Many academic health centers now offer explicit training in IPE to prepare professionals in all disciplines for the future of health service delivery that will inevitably increase interprofessional approaches to care. Core competencies for interprofessional collaborative practice have been established to guide training in all health disciplines (Interprofessional Education Collaborative Expert Panel, 2011). Learning to work effectively in different types of teams of health professionals is viewed as key to mental health service delivery for older adults (Carney, Gum, & Zeiss, 2015).

Mental health services are structured around briefer encounters than is typical in specialty care that uses 45–60 sessions as the norm. Screening tools are often used to identify needs, including screens for depression, anxiety, or cognitive functioning. The screening tool may be implemented routinely in the intake packet for the primary care practice, or may be administered by a staff person. *Co-visits* are used in some clinics, with a medical provider drawing a mental health provider into the exam room when mental health problems are introduced by the patient. Some systems use *flow visits* to introduce behavioral health providers as core members of the team to every new patient in the initial meeting in the clinic.

Generally, the integrated models used in health care emphasize short-term treatment (one to six sessions) of briefer visits (20–30 minutes) within the primary care examination rooms. Brief models such as Problem-Solving Therapy or Brief Solution-Focused Therapy lend themselves to this style of work. Many programs use Motivational Interviewing to enhance engagement. The primary care setting is not used for longer-term mental health treatment, but those fuller therapeutic approaches may be launched from primary care. The services within primary care focus on enhancing motivation to engage in needed behavior change or additional services. Triage to additional mental health services may be facilitated with a warm handoff (actual introduction to the mental health provider in a nearby clinic). In short, mental health services delivered in primary care (and most other health settings) must follow very different approaches from those used in mental health specialty care.

Summary and Conclusions

The massive health care industry is in a period of rapid transition as it reshapes itself to address serious challenges related to quality of care that were identified toward the end of the 20th century. At the level of business structures and service delivery models, integration is accelerating as leaders focus on the triple aim of improving quality of health services and health outcomes while containing costs. Mental health has been identified as a critical component of the overall health care system, and thus is now being integrated into health care in new ways. Although mental health services for older adults are still available in specialty care settings, they will increasingly be integrated into and collaborate with other service systems. Mental health providers now have guidelines for practice to support effective participation in new settings. Integrated care is also producing new opportunities for older adults to access behavioral health services in settings where they receive other services.

Critical Thinking / Discussion Questions

1 In a period of rapid change within the health care industry, what opportunities are there for mental health integration to improve access to services for older adults? How would you feel about working in an integrated setting?
2 How will training in mental health services for older adults need to change as mental health providers prepare to work across health care settings?

Website Resources

Collaborative Family Health Care Network
www.cfhc.net
Integrated Care Models
http://www.integration.samhsa.gov/integrated-care-models
Interprofessional Education Collaborative
www.ipecollaborative.org
Programs for All-Inclusive Care for the Elderly (PACE)
https://www.medicare.gov/your-medicare-costs/help-paying-costs/pace/pace.html
Psychologists in Integrated Health Care
http://www.apa.org/health/integrated-health-care.aspx

References

ASPE. (n.d.). *Poverty guidelines.* Washington, DC: US Department of Health and Human Services. Retrieved from https://aspe.hhs.gov/poverty-guidelines.
Berwick, D. M., Nolan, T. W., & Whittington, J. (2008). The triple aim: Care, health, and cost. *Health Affairs, 27,* 759–769.

Blount, A., Kathol, R., Thomas, M., Schoenbaum, M., Rollman, B. L., O'Donohue, W., & Peek, C. J. (2007). The economics of behavioral health services in medical settings: A summary of the evidence. *Professional Psychology: Research and Practice, 38,* 290–297.

Burg, M. A., & Oyama, O. (2016). *The behavioral health specialist in primary care.* New York, NY: Springer.

Carney, K. O., Gum, A. M., & Zeiss, A. M. (2015). Geropsychology in interprofessional teams across different practice settings. In P. A. Lichtenberg & B. Mast (Eds.), *APA handbook of clinical geropsychology.* Vol. *1,* pp. 72–100. Washington, DC: American Psychological Association.

Frankel, R. M., Quill, T. E., & McDaniel, S. H. (Eds.) (2003). *The biopsychosocial approach: Past, present, and future.* Rochester, NY: University of Rochester Press.

Hunter, C. L., Goodie, J. L., Oordt, M. S., & Dobmeyer, A. C. (2009). *Integrated behavioral health in primary care: Step-by-step guidance for assessment and intervention.* Washington, DC: American Psychological Association.

Institute of Medicine. (2012). *Living well with chronic illness: A call for public health action.* Washington, DC: The National Academies Press.

Interprofessional Education Collaborative Expert Panel. (2011). *Core competencies for interprofessional collaborative practice: Report of an expert panel.* Washington, DC: Interprofessional Education Collaborative.

Knight, B., Karel, M., Hinrichsen, G., Qualls, S. H., & Duffy, M. (2009). Pikes Peak model for training in professional geropsychology. *American Psychologist, 64,* 205–214. doi: 10.1037/a0015059

McDaniel, S. H., Grus, C. L., Cubic, B. A., Hunter, C. L., Kearney, L. K., Schuman, C. C., ... Johnson, S. B. (2014). Competencies for practice in primary care. *American Psychologist, 69,* 409–429. doi: 10.1037/a0036072

McDaniel, S. H., Doherty, W. J., & Hepworth, J. (2014). *Medical family therapy and integrated care.* Washington, DC: American Psychological Association.

National Council on Aging (NCOA). (2014). *Fact sheet: Healthy aging.* Retrieved from https://www.ncoa.org/resources/fact-sheet-healthy-aging

Newsom, J. T., Huguet, N., McCarthy, M. J., Ramage-Morin, P., Kaplan, M. S., Bernier, J., & Oderkirk, J. (2012). Health behavior change following chronic illness in middle and later life. *The Journal of Gerontology, Series B: Psychological Sciences and Social Sciences, 67,* 279–288. doi:10.1093/geronb/gbr103

Petterson, S., Miller, B. F., Payne-Murphy, J. C., & Phillips, R. J. (2014). Mental health treatment in the primary care setting: Patterns and pathways. *Families, Systems, & Health, 32*(2), 157–166. doi:10.1037/fsh0000036

Qualls, S. H. (2015). Building competencies in professional geropsychology: Guidelines, training model, and strategies for professional development. In P. Arean (Ed.), *Treatment of late life depression, anxiety, trauma, and substance abuse* (pp. 11–48). Washington, DC: American Psychological Association. doi:10.1037/14524-002

Qualls, S. H., & Benight, C. C. (2007). The role of clinical health geropsychology in the health care of older adults. In C. M. Aldwin, C. L. Park, & A. I. Spiro (Eds.), *Handbook of health psychology and aging* (pp. 367–389). New York, NY: Guilford.

Rolland, J. S. (1994). *Families, illness, and disability: An integrative treatment model.* New York, NY: Basic Books.

Sieber, W. J., Miller, B. F., Kessler, R. S., Patterson, J. E., Kallenberg, G. A., Edwards, T. M., & Lister, Z. D. (2012). Establishing the Collaborative Care Research Network (CCRN): A description of initial participating sites. *Families, Systems, & Health, 30*(3), 210–223. doi:10.1037/a0029637

Simning, A., Richardson, T. M., Friedman, B., Boyle, L. L., Podgorski, C., & Conwell, Y. (2010). Mental distress and service utilization among help-seeking, community-dwelling older adults. *International Psychogeriatrics, 22*(5), 739–749. doi:10.1017/S104161021000058X

Substance Abuse and Mental Health Services Administration. (2014). *Projections of National Expenditures for Treatment of Mental and Substance Use Disorders, 2010–2020 (HHS Publication No. SMA-14-4883)*. Rockville, MD: Author.

Torrence, N. D., Mueller, A. E., Ilem, A. A., Renn, B. N., DeSantis, B., & Segal, D. L. (2014). Medical provider attitudes about behavioral health consultants in integrated primary care: A preliminary study. *Families, Systems, & Health, 32*, 426–432.

Van Citters, A. D., & Bartels, S. J. (2004). A systematic review of the effectiveness of community-based mental health outreach services for older adults. *Psychiatric Services, 55*, 1237–1249. doi: 10.1176/appi.ps.55.11.1237

15

Housing, Social Services, and Mental Health

Mental well-being requires a sense of safety, belonging, and support for identity and other dimensions of the self, all of which are intensively affected by place and resources. Consider how your sense of safety, belonging, and identity is linked to people, place, and resources in your current world. You live in a residence that you can access with your level of mobility and vision. You read and listen to lectures that your hearing and cognition support. Yet a substantial change in one domain in functioning can impact safety and autonomy, even in familiar environments.

This chapter invites you to consider how mental well-being is influenced by residential environments and social services designed to support independence as we age. You will be introduced to the conceptual frameworks that help us understand how and why environments are so potent to our well-being, at all points in the lifespan but especially so in later life. An overview of senior housing options will introduce you to characteristics of the various options, and some of the ways in which mental well-being is supported and challenged within them. Many services are available to older adults for the purpose of improving safety and supporting autonomy. In this chapter, we provide an overview of services options and information about how to access them. We also identify some key policy issues related to housing and social services that are likely to be the focus of considerable debate in coming decades as the US wrestles with policy choices to support its burgeoning aging population.

Person–Environment Fit: A Key Principle That Shapes Housing Choices and Challenges

The notion that well-being is a function of both the person and the environment has roots as far back as Lewin (1935), who postulated that behavior was a product of both person and environment. Applying that principal to older adults, Lawton expanded

Aging and Mental Health, Third Edition. Daniel L. Segal, Sara Honn Qualls, and Michael A. Smyer.
© 2018 John Wiley & Sons, Inc. Published 2018 by John Wiley & Sons, Inc.

it beyond the two factors of person and environment to examine a third factor, the *interaction* between person and environment, as a predictor of a sense of well-being. In a series of testable hypotheses, Lawton and colleagues proposed a variety of ways that the interaction between person and environment influences well-being (summarized in Lawton, 1998). For example, the environmental docility hypothesis states that persons with lower levels of competency (e.g., in cognition or physical functioning) require more environmental supports to maintain their well-being. Persons with higher levels of competence will proactively seek more complexity in their environments according to the principle of environmental proactivity.

The term *environment* is not limited to characteristics of the physical environment; the social world is also a salient aspect of one's environment. Social ties are often linked to the places most important to us. Social capital, defined here as the benefits of social relationships, can be an embedded characteristic of particular activity settings. Social capital can be particularly important for ethnic minority populations, as found in a study of Korean older adults living in Chicago, for example (Shin, 2014). In short, the term *environment* inevitably incorporates both physical characteristics and social components of the physical space. Even more complicated to characterize are the adaptive strategies used over time to manage changes in either person or environment in later life that are likely to influence well-being. Older adults must use both short-term and long-term adaptation strategies to maintain their well-being.

> Larry refuses to move from his home of 70 years. Now in his 90s, he limits his driving to the neighborhood grocery and barbershop. He refuses to discuss giving his car to his great-granddaughter as his son suggests. He would be "stuck here all day every day with arthritis that makes it hard to move." The stairs at home have become a major chore. He's grateful for both the food and the chance for some friendly conversation.

Almost universally, older adults report a strong preference to age in their own home, yet homes that provided a perfect person–environment fit for persons in their 40s or 50s are often poorly matched to the biopsychosocial functioning of persons in their 80s and 90s. Researchers have identified two dimensions of well-being that are important in the study of person–environment fit: belonging and agency (Oswald & Wahl, 2013). At all ages, humans need to feel a sense of belonging within their living spaces. Agency refers to the perception that we have the ability to act to maintain our well-being by acting with effectiveness within our spaces. A major challenge for older adults is how to support these ongoing needs for belonging and agency in the context of changing self and changing environment.

Risks of continuing to live in a mismatched environment include social isolation, loneliness, depression, anxiety, falls, and reduced physical functioning if safety concerns constrain exercise or nutrition access. Risks of moving from a familiar environment to one with more supports include grief, social discontinuity, increased anxiety, fatigue from the demands of adaptation, and loss of identity.

Viewed with a focus on benefits rather than risks, advantages to remaining in a long-term home or moving into a more supportive environment are also compelling. Congregate living environments are attractive to individuals at many points in the lifespan (e.g., college students, young professionals, older adults) because of social advantages. The density of people within the housing environment increases the likelihood of social interaction and supports the viability of activity programming that is accessible and relevant. Compared with a suburban lifestyle designed for nuclear families that requires car transportation to services and amenities, senior housing campuses or urban complexes offer high access within the community or neighborhood. Higher likelihood of social interaction offsets risks of isolation and associated problems such as loneliness and depression while reducing the chance that problems with daily functioning will go unnoticed. In short, there is no universally right or wrong approach, so a more nuanced understanding of the opportunities and challenges and the individual's weighting of each is usually helpful.

One such approach is to focus on the potential ways in which functional needs can be met in various environments. A functional approach to well-being (described in Chapter 3) focuses on how the activities of daily living can be supported by the environment in which a person lives. Architectural features of homes that support a wide range of functioning are often referred to as universal design. Common examples of universal design are doorways that can accommodate wheelchairs and doorknobs that can be used by persons with limited mobility. Although changes in some regional building codes enforce some aspects of universal design in new construction, the majority of residential environments are built to support optimal physical and cognitive functioning.

A wide range of strategies can be used to adapt environments to support changes in function that are common with age (Lawlor & Thomas, 2008). Changes in lighting, addition of handrails and grab-bars, and flooring updates to reduce risks of trips and falls are among the most common adaptations. More elaborate changes can make kitchens fully accessible to persons who use wheelchairs for mobility, who are blind, or who have cognitive impairment. Chair-lifts can reduce the impact of stairs as a barrier to living safely at home.

Sophisticated electronic systems often called "smart homes" can prompt behaviors using various types of auditory, tactile, or visual signals while monitoring activities that are key to health and safety (Czaja, 2016). Beds and chairs can be outfitted with weight-sensing technologies to monitor both nighttime movement and daily weight changes that are useful in monitoring frailty risk. Signals can warn the occupant that the stove is still on if the kitchen has not been occupied for a few minutes. Tablets can prompt and remind a person with memory impairment how to complete tasks that are no longer easily recalled, to take medications at a particular time, or to make a phone call to a friend. Many options exist to use technology to connect the person living alone with many members of his/her network on a regular basis and more options are likely to proliferate as these technologies continue to improve and become more widespread in use.

In-home services can support people living at home even when living with substantial disability in functioning. Home and community based services (HCBS) are now used by more Medicaid-funded consumers in many states than are nursing homes (Eiken, Sredl, Burwell, & Saucier, 2016). Consider, for example, the impact of a twice-weekly house cleaning and personal bathing assistance for a person who needs only those resources to remain safely at home. Transportation services or grocery-delivery services may be the critical supports. More detailed accounts of in-home services are provided below.

> Jorge's family is devoted to keeping him at home despite his dementia. Increasingly, he has difficulty managing the tasks of daily living. Recently, he forgot how to use the microwave. His hygiene is declining as he avoids baths that he finds annoying (and confusing?). His oldest daughter visits daily, and is thinking that a family member is going to need to start staying with him overnight soon. With everyone working full-time, it is not clear how long the family can sustain this level of commitment.

Family and friends may offer practical as well as emotional support that enhances well-being. Indeed, families often begin taking on the instrumental activities of daily living gradually, with little fanfare or even recognition of the transition. Although families offer a viable source of support for many older adults who require additional help, others lack that resource. Emotional support similarly is a complicated and multifaceted aspect of family relationships at all ages, including later life. A more detailed analysis of family caregiving roles is discussed in Chapter 16. For the purposes of this chapter, it is valuable to note that the desire to remain at home can be sustained by family or, alternatively, family may lack capacity to facilitate that desire. Furthermore, some states that promote person-centered and self-directed care allow older adults to choose family members to be paid as their in-home caregivers as an alternative to either institutional- or agency-chosen staff.

The meaning of place

Researchers within the field of environmental gerontology seek to understand how people turn spaces into places over the life course, and the meaning of places to older adults (Rowles & Bernard, 2013). The process of transforming a generic space (e.g., dorm room, apartment, empty house) into a place called home, for example, requires an effortful investment over time. Repeated patterns of behavior, or dwelling, in one's living space add familiarity and routine to a space that may eventually be defined as home. Once it becomes home, the living space is usually experienced as "centering," offering a sense of permanence and reflection of the self (Rowles & Bernard, 2013).

Public spaces also become personalized as we engage in meaningful activities that support a sense of familiarity and may be coded as emotionally laden memories. Simply consider the time it takes to find a "favorite" coffee shop, restaurant, and grocery store after moving to a new neighborhood or city. The characteristics of public places influence participation by all generations, including older adults, and thus influence the meaning of place (Peace, 2013).

Older adults spend increased amounts of time in the home, often more than 80% (Baltes, Maas, Wilms, & Borschelt, 1999). With advancing frailty, *life space* shrinks as fatigue and functional limitations in mobility or sensation renders the one or two rooms in which most activities are conducted to be the most relevant to daily life (Baker, Bodner, & Allman, 2003). The shrinkage of life space has been associated with declines in physical and mental health (Bentley et al., 2013; Rantakokko et al., 2016), perhaps as cause but also as consequence.

Obviously, *home* is a very loaded term because of the meanings associated with personally meaningful places. Yet functional decline forces adaptation of person–environment fit either within the same space, or in a new space that requires effort and time to become home. Not surprisingly, most older adults do not want to leave their long-term homes, yet advancing frailty shrinks the usable life space within the home, and can bring safety risks or burdens that require substantial support from others to sustain. The need for simpler, smaller spaces in which to create home has generated a myriad of senior housing options as well as in-home supports through social services. The remainder of the chapter will familiarize you with the types of senior housing and social services that can be used in the service of enhancing mental health in later life.

The Continuum of Senior Housing

Senior housing is a burgeoning industry that includes residential options for independent living and supportive living. The latter industry is referenced as "long-term care," including assisted living and skilled nursing facilities (SNFs) where diverse services are readily available.

Far more older adults live in residential settings that are designed for independent living among age-similar peers than in SNFs, and there appears to be no slow down in new development in this industry. The 45,654 facilities within the $63.3 billion senior housing industry are almost evenly divided between assisted living and other supportive senior housing and multilevel or continuing care retirement communities (48.8% and 51.2%, respectively; Diment, 2016). Middle- and upper-income individuals now can choose to move into patio homes on a multilevel campus, enjoying amenities offered in the independent apartment complex, long before they need "care." In contrast, low-income housing is a serious challenge that is nearly universal. Since the minimum Social Security income level is under $800 per month, many older adults face the necessity of living in subsidized housing because adequate low-income housing is simply not available at the scale that is needed.

Marketing of senior living campuses often presents a lifestyle of healthy, socially active individuals, similar to the approach that might be used for marketing resorts or hotels. The juxtaposition of marketing images of the permanent cruise lifestyle, the desire for home, and the reality of a future trajectory of health challenges is an interesting conundrum for the industry and the older adults and families who are consumers.

High rates of chronic disease including cognitive impairment are found in residents of independent senior living facilities, just as they are in the community. As noted in Chapter 8, rates of dementia in persons over age 85 are estimated to be at least one-third. Since the average age at entry to independent living is in the early 80s, it is apparent that even independent apartments for older adults will house many persons with significant needs for support. The marketed image of a resort lifestyle is aspirational but not feasible for many because it does not address the common challenges of being around persons with significant impairment. In some facilities, for example, residents have revolted against the "walker brigade" outside the restaurant. In contrast, residents helping other residents can be a meaningful social structure, much as it is in neighborhoods. The density of older adults can make senior housing less attractive for some, however, who prefer not to deal with others' age-related challenges so intimately.

> Wanda hates the fact that she lost her home and has to live in this small apartment in assisted living. "Life is over." Everyone here already has friends with no apparent interest in her. She doesn't like the activities they offer, so she only leaves her apartment for meals, often dining alone.

Facilities face serious challenges when a resident's health declines to such an extent that the current level of housing is no longer sufficiently supportive yet the resident refuses to move to a more supportive environment, such as assisted living. Navigating transitions across living levels is a serious challenge to the industry, families, and residents.

Long-term care (LTC) is an umbrella term that includes assisted living, SNFs, home health, and adult day programs. These categories differ in the amount and intensity of support provided. People move into residential care or accept services in home when they can no longer care for themselves independently because of sensory, cognitive, or physical challenges. All LTC programs support people with certain activities of daily living (ADLs). Often, ADLs are divided into two categories: (1) basic self-care ADLs, and (2) instrumental ADLs (IADLs) that include skills needed to live independently in the community (see Table 15.1).

As aging processes affect their sensory, cognitive, or physical functioning, older adults may need LTC resources to support either category of the ADLs as well as their mental well-being. The percentages of persons needing assistance with ADLs who are using different types of long-term care services are presented in Figure 15.1.

Across the spectrum of LTC, approximately nine million people were served in 2014 (Harris-Kojetin et al., 2016). Approximately 67,000 paid, regulated service organizations served older adults, including 30,200 assisted living facilities, 15,600 nursing homes, 12,400 home health agencies, 4,800 adult day service centers, and 4,000 hospices. With nine million people served by these various agencies in a single year,

Table 15.1 Activities of daily living

Basic	Instrumental
Feeding	Finances
Bathing	Appointments
Dressing	Transportation
Transferring	Shopping
Ambulating	Medications
Toileting	Food preparation
	Laundry
	Telephone

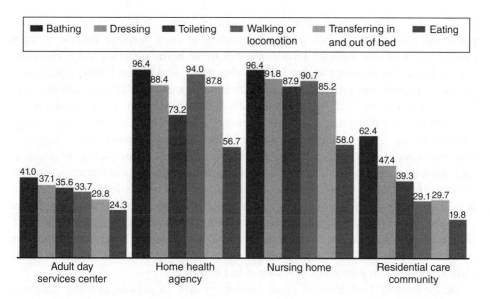

Figure 15.1 Percentage of long-term-care services users by sector and activity, in the US 2013 and 2014.
Source: CDC/NCHS (2016).

it is clear that many of us will experience LTC. Indeed, among people who reach age 65, over two-thirds will need long-term-care services at some point (Kemper, Komisar, & Alecxih, 2005-2006), including a 46% chance of spending at least some time in a nursing home (Spillman & Lubitz, 2002). The financial estimate for the average cost of LTC for a person over the lifetime is $138,000 in future services costs (Favreault & Dey, 2015).

> Melvin and Viola decided to move into a senior residence now, while the choice is theirs and while they can realistically build new friendships. They refuse to have their children burdened with clearing out their home of 40 years, so they are painstakingly sorting and discarding, giving away, and sharing with family the artifacts of their lives. The task is almost overwhelming, but they are determined to downsize their "things" in order to upsize their lives in a simpler, smaller, less demanding condominium environment. They keep thinking back to the transition to college when the simplicity of a dorm room left them free to live life on the campus as a whole. That's the current dream: build a life in the community with the time and effort they previously spent on their own home. They are also comforted by the fact that as they age, the supports they need are available on site, whether in-home services or assisted living, or even skilled nursing care.

Mental health factors often influence the decision to move into senior residences. Some residents seek the positive psychosocial benefits of living with fewer maintenance demands and more opportunities for engagement in meaningful social activity. Some people prefer to move before they *need* to, choosing to move while their functional health is good so they have time to adapt and enjoy the lifestyle rather than wait until they cannot manage the maintenance and upkeep demands of life in their previous residence. Others move when they feel burdened by their previous lifestyle, perhaps due to vision loss or mobility limitations that make home upkeep harder, especially if their home has far more square footage than they need or can handle. Death of a spouse or partner can provoke a decision to move nearer to children or siblings, creating an opportunity to downsize from a stand-alone house into a senior residence.

Cognitive impairment is the most common cause of moves into assisted living. Assisted Living (AL) handles many of the IADLs, such as housekeeping, shopping, and meal preparation, and can offer far more intensive services such as medication and appointment management, bathing and dressing support, and incontinence care (often with additional costs for these services). Even if an older adult's physical health is positive, neurocognitive disorders or dementia can undermine her ability to live in a community or even independent senior housing. Not surprisingly, assisted living, including specialized assisted living memory care, is a choice for many who cannot live safely in the community. The percentage of persons living with dementia who access different long-term-care services is shown in Figure 15.2.

Skilled nursing facilities offer either long-term care for persons needing assistance with multiple basic ADLs due to illness or disability, or short-term rehabilitation therapies to support recovery from illness or surgery, post-hospitalization. Some facilities offer both types of services, often accommodating transfer from short-term rehabilitation stay into longer-term placement if the recovery is not sufficient to allow safe return home. Rarely does someone return home from a long-term placement.

SNFs operate on a medical model, with priority placed on medical care needs. A medical chart is maintained and medical personnel are always available on site. The staff are labeled with medical names (e.g., nurses, nursing assistants), and medical processes dictate schedules (e.g., medication administration, physical therapy, bathing). In the past two decades, a "culture change" movement has emerged to attempt to shift the

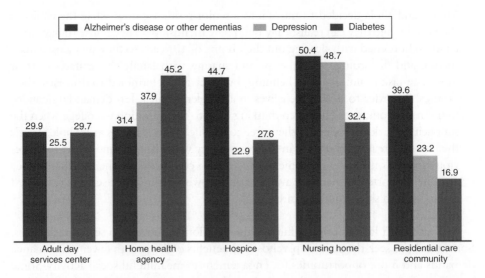

Figure 15.2 Percentage of long-term services care users across sectors, in the US 2013 and 2014. *Source*: CDC/NCHS (2016).

focus to quality of life in a home like environment, with person-centered care focusing staff onto the resident's definition of care. One visible example of the implementation of this model is the Green House model developed and promoted by Dr. William (Bill) Thomas, and recently subjected to a large-scale evaluation of impact (Cohen et al., 2016). The model promotes small units (10–12 residents) with a psychosocial model of care rather than a medical model, engaging residents in everyday behaviors within the shared residence that is laid out more like a home than an institution (Rabig, Thomas, Kane, Cutler, & McAlilly, 2006). Now implemented across the US, the Green House model has been examined closely for its impact with generally positive outcomes for residents and staff (e.g., Miller, Mor, & Burgess, 2016).

Although policies are in place to deter the use of SNFs as the default long-term psychiatric inpatient hospitals as occurred in previous decades, the rates of mental disorders in SNFs remain high. The Nursing Home Reform Act of 1987 created a psychiatric screening process prior to admission to SNFs to identify mental disorders at the time of admission, and require either alternative placement if the disorder is the primary reason for placement or active treatment if other factors require SNF placement for persons living with mental disorder. The process was intended to: (a) divert potential nursing home residents to psychiatric settings if intensive treatment was needed; (b) divert them to less restrictive environments if mental health problems were the reason for SNF placement; (c) to reduce the use of physical and chemical restraints that were nontherapeutic; and (d) to provide access to active treatments, both pharmacological and nonpharmacological, that would improve the level of mental health. Although reasonably successful in achieving its aims, two factors undermine the overall success of the approach: lack of alternative housing for persons living with a serious mental disorder and high rates of comorbid mental disorders in older adults requiring skilled nursing care for physical disabilities. Nursing homes continue to be a setting with serious challenges to the mental well-being of residents where mental health services are needed (Carney & Norris, 2017).

In conclusion, senior housing can be viewed as a continuum of residential services, with multiple options for supporting individuals at various levels of functioning. A functional approach to matching everyday living skills with environments offers a basis for identifying and selecting relevant options. Older adults often emphasize the value and importance of home, resisting change in residence until absolutely necessary. Although the senior housing industry appears poised for continued growth, home-based services and technologies are also expected to grow rapidly, offering more options for self-directed care. Mental health clinicians have key roles in senior housing, including assessment of functional abilities and the capacity for independent living, as well as assisting families with housing transitions in addition to treatment of mental disorders, as described in other chapters.

Social Services

A network of social services for older adults was founded in 1965 with the passage of the Older Americans Act (OAA) at roughly the same time that Medicare was created. The OAA created an Administration on Aging in the US government and authorized

Table 15.2   Funding for the Titles of the Older Americans Act (2012)

Title II	Administration on Aging	40.1 million
Title III	Supportive Services, Nutrition Services, and Family Caregiver Services	1.4 billion
Title IV	Health, Independence, Longevity	16.7 million
Title V	Community Service Employment	434.4 million
Title VI	Grants to Native Americans	38.7 million
Title VII	Elder Rights Protection	20.7 million
	TOTAL	$1.9 billion

Source: Adapted from Colello & Napili (2016).

state units on aging, and subsequently, regional units called Area Agencies on Aging (AAA). Each AAA contracts with local providers to serve older adults in the region with social, nutritional, transportation, legal, in-home, health education and illness prevention programs, and other services targeted to the protection of vulnerable populations (e.g., ombudsman program for long-term care, elder abuse prevention programs). Each AAA must identify service providers capable of implementing the services according to federal and state guidelines; thus each region's service system is unique, yielding a system with significant variation in structures across regions.

The network of aging services provides basic services that are an infrastructure for mental well-being. The sections of the legislation that authorize aging services describe the categories of services included in the OAA, as shown in Table 15.2, along with the financial allocations for each category from the government (Colello & Napili, 2016). Although funding has not kept pace with growth of the older population or inflation of services cost, this network of aging services continues to provide services that are often critical to maintain many older adults in their homes.

Among the many services provided by the AAAs directly or through contracts for services are Information and Assistance resources that are typically available online, by telephone, and in printed directories of local resources. Providers and families seeking services can access significant amounts of information at this single resource site. Examples include listings of all local residential facilities by category, along with details for each facility about cost, Medicaid reimbursement eligibility, pet-friendliness, number of beds, and many other variables of interest to a particular person seeking services. Local AAAs are easy to find at www.eldercare.gov, where users enter a zip code in order to find the contact information for the nearest AAA.

Each weekday morning Lois drops Eugene at the day program where he "meets with the guys." Although he said he hated it at first, he now looks forward to seeing his friends each day, and Lois and Eugene enjoy discussing their separate activities over dinner each evening. Lois is so relieved to have time to take care of their business, meet with friends, and even do some volunteer work. The day program has been a lifesaver, keeping her stress level in check, and making it possible to care for Eugene at home longer. She is keenly aware that when Eugene can no longer move about their home safely, she will have to move him to a dementia unit.

Box 15.1 Developing trend

Uber and Lyft offer new models for transporting older adults that are relatively low cost. The personalized transportation cuts the time commitment of the more traditional multiuser van rides. Both companies have partnerships with aging services providers in some regions.

The initial model for the AAAs was focused on enhancing socialization, so early funding helped establish senior centers where recreational and social activities take place (Hudson, 2016). Recent decades have witnessed a focus on more vulnerable older adults, with funds targeted to persons in need of basic services such as transportation, home-delivered meals, healthy congregate meals at central sites, and case management to identify and access critical services. Additionally, the aging services network has become more involved in long-term care, offering critical services such as the ombudsman program that assists residents, families, and facilities in resolving conflicts within LTC facilities. Funds for elder abuse prevention can be used to educate communities, older adults, and families, about what constitutes abuse and how to report it. Caregiver support services include counseling, public information, and respite care (in-home or in-facility). This substantial range of services has become critical to community support for older adults, but services vary across states and regions.

Mental health providers need deep familiarity with the aging services systems in order to maximize their impact on older adult clients. Older adults often have difficulty with transportation, which, outside the largest metropolitan areas, is primarily a personal rather than public industry.

Thus, any interruption of driving can strand a person without access to food, health services, or social contact. Age-related declines in mobility or sensory functioning, or increased fatigue can be as devastating as cognitive decline in limiting access to needed resources and supports. Knowledge of how to access core aging services can empower older adults to live in less isolation, with more support, and thus with better safety, belonging, and identity.

Mental health providers find it critical to have strong liaisons with the local social services network. Although not necessarily social workers by profession, mental health counselors and therapists must know more about the services network than would be typical for their roles with other populations. Clients who are malnourished or unable to be transported to health appointments need help from their clinicians to identify resources for food or transportation before the clients can participate consistently in mental health services.

In the past decade, the Administration on Aging was merged with the Administration on Disabilities into a new Administration on Community Living (ACL) in response to growing awareness of the overlapping array of services needed by vulnerable older adults and other persons living with disabilities. The ACL is moving toward person-centered planning approaches that emphasize individual needs and preferences rather than population-based planning (Hudson, 2016). The disability community

Box 15.2 Hot issue

Medicaid funding represents a major portion of state budgets, and is expected to grow as the population ages. Reliance on Medicaid to fund long-term-care services effectively places the primary burden on state governments that are heavily stretched to meet mandated priorities such as prisons and courts, transportation, and education. Strategies that reduce use of residential care in favor of community-based services offer a cost containment option yet require state-by-state policy changes and local investment in community support services.

has advocated for self-directed services, which is a different policy model from the need-based approach to funding services within the aging services network. Melding these two approaches and populations has generated some confusion in paradigms for services as well as prioritization. For example, disability advocates view the services as a fundamental right for participation in society, while aging service providers focus on filling gaps for persons in need. Added to the policy mix are the pressures to provide the least restrictive level of housing, a priority since the Olmstead Act, and the pressures to reduce financial burdens on the states for long-term-care residential care funded by Medicaid. Clearly, government policies to support older adults living in the community in their own homes are becoming a priority, but the policies are currently a complex set of silos of aging services, disability services, health care, and legal services that is not simple to navigate.

In sum, social services are critical to sustaining many older adults in their homes, or in the least restrictive environment. They are organized within the aging services network, the disabilities network, and health care systems, often operating invisibly to persons who have not yet investigated what is available. The mental well-being of older adults often rests on access to fundamental supports that sustain independence and social integration. Thus, mental health providers need a working understanding of the services networks, eligibility for services, and skill in incorporating use of services that support autonomy and safety within any mental health interventions.

Summary and Conclusions

The balance of personal abilities and community resources needed to remain independent shifts across late adulthood, especially in advanced old age. Mental health practitioners play important roles in assessing older adults' capacities for self-care and independent living, in facilitating decision-making by older adults and their families, and in coordinating care among public and private resources available in the local community. Playing these roles requires an understanding of the processes of physical and mental health in later life, as well as the ecologies of care that are shaped by both public policy and private enterprise. With the aging of our society, issues of where and how to care for older adults will be increasingly important.

Critical Thinking / Discussion Questions

1 Senior housing administrators often face the unpleasant task of telling a resident that he or she must move from an independent apartment to assisted living. What do housing staff need to consider before broaching that subject? How can mental health providers assist?

2 Are community resources to support independent living a *right* that states and regions simply must fund?

3 How can rural communities effectively support aging-in-place, given the challenges of delivering services over large geographic regions?

4 How might ethnic and racial variations need to be considered in housing policies?

Website Resources

Administration for Community Living: Aging and Disabilities programs
https://acl.gov/programs
Eldercare Locator (find local Area Agency on Aging by entering postal zip code)
www.eldercare.gov
Centers for Disease Control and Prevention: Long-term care health information
https://www.cdc.gov/longtermcare/index.html
LeadingAge (national trade association of aging-related nonprofit organizations, including senior housing)
www.leadingage.org
American Health Care Association (national trade association for long-term care organizations)
www.ahcancal.org

References

Baltes, M. M., Maas, L., Wilms, H.-U., & Borchelt, M. (1999). Everyday competence in old and very old age: Theoretical considerations and empirical findings. In P. B. Baltes & K. U. Mayer (Eds.), *The Berlin aging study* (pp. 384–402). Cambridge, England: Cambridge University Press.

Bentley, J. P., Brown, C. J., McGwin, G., Sawyer, P., Allman, R. M., & Roth, D. L. (2013). Functional status, life-space mobility, and quality of life: A longitudinal mediation analysis. *Quality of Life Research, 22*, 1621–1632. doi:10.1007/s11136-012-0315-3

Carney, K. O., & Norris, M. P. (2017). *Transforming long-term care: Expanded roles for mental health professionals.* Washington, DC: APA.

Centers for Disease Control / National Center for Health Statistics [CDC/NCHS] (2016). *National Study of Long-Term Care Providers.* Retrieved from https://www.cdc.gov/nchs/nsltcp

Cohen, L. W., Zimmerman, S., Reed, D., Brown, P., Bowers, B. J., Nolet, K., ...Horn, S. (2016). The Green House model of nursing home care in design and implementation. *Health Services Research, 51*(Suppl. 1), 352–377. doi:10.1111/14756773.12418

Colello, K. J., & Napili, A. (March 15, 2016). *Older Americans Act: Background and overview.* Washington, DC: Congressional Research Service.

Czaja, S. (2016). Long term care service and support systems for older adults: The role of technology. *American Psychologist, 71*, 294–301.

Diment, D. (2016). *Retirement communities in the U.S.* IBISWorld Industry Report 62331.

Eiken, S., Sredl, K., Burwell, B., & Saucier, P. (2016). *Medicaid expenditures for long-term services and supports (LTSS) in FY 2014.* Boston, MA: Truven Health Analytics.

Favreault, M., & Dey, J. (2015). *Long-term services and supports for older Americans: Risks and financing* (ASPE Research Brief). Retrieved from https://aspe.hhs.gov/basic-report/ long-term-services-and-supports-older-americans-risks-and-financing-research-brief

Harris-Kojetin, L., Sengupta, M., Park-Lee, E., Valverde., R., Caffrey, C., Rome, V., & Lendon, J. (2016). Long-term care providers and services users in the United States: Data from the National Study of Long-Term Care Providers, 2013–2014. National Center for Health Statistics. *Vital Health Stat 3*(38).

Hudson, R. B. (2016). Social service and health planning agencies. In D. B. Kaplan, B. Berkman (Eds.). *The Oxford handbook of social work in health and aging* (2nd ed., pp. 171–179). New York, NY: Oxford University Press.

Kemper, P., Komisar, H. L., & Alecxih, L. (2005–2006). Long-term care over an uncertain future: What can current retirees expect? *Inquiry, 42*, 335–350.

Lawlor, D., & Thomas, M. A. (2008). *Residential design for aging in place.* Hoboken, NJ: Wiley.

Lawton, M. P. (1998). Environment and aging: Theory revisited. In R. J. Scheidt & P. G. Windley (Eds.), *Environment and aging theory: A focus on housing.* Westport, CT: Greenwood Press.

Lewin, K. (1935). *A dynamic theory of personality: Selected papers of Kurt Lewin.* New York, NY: McGraw-Hill.

Miller, S. C., Mor, V., & Burgess, J. J. (2016). Studying nursing home innovation: The Green House model of nursing home care. *Health Services Research, 51*(Suppl. 1), 335–343. doi:10.1111/14756773.12437

Oswald, F., & Wahl, H.-W. (2013). Creating and sustaining homelike places in residential environments. In G. D. Rowles & M. Bernard (Eds.), *Environmental gerontology: Making meaningful places in old age* (pp. 53–77). New York, NY: Springer.

Peace, S. (2013). Social interactions in public spaces and places: A conceptual overview. In G. D. Rowles & M. Bernard (Eds.), *Environmental gerontology: Making meaningful places in old age* (pp. 25–49). New York, NY: Springer.

Rabig, J., Thomas, W., Kane, R. A., Cutler, L. J., & McAlilly, S. (2006). Radical redesign of nursing homes: Applying the Green House concept in Tupelo, Mississippi. *The Gerontologist, 46*(4), 533–539. doi:10.1093/geront/46.4.533

Rantakokko, M., Portegijs, E., Viljanen, A., Iwarsson, S., Kauppinen, M., & Rantanen, T. (2016). Changes in life-space mobility and quality of life among community-dwelling older people: A 2-year follow- up study. *Quality of Life Research, 25*, 1189–1197. doi:10.1007/ s11136-015-1137

Rowles, G. D., & Bernard, M. (2013). The meaning of place in residential and public spaces. In G. D. Rowles & M. Bernard (Eds.), *Environmental gerontology: Making meaningful places in old age* (pp. 1–24). New York, NY: Springer.

Shin, J. (2014). Living independently as an ethnic minority elder: A relational perspective on the issues of aging and ethnic minorities. *American Journal of Community Psychology, 53*, 433–446. doi:10.1007/s1046401496506

Spillman, B. C., & Lubitz, J. (2002). New estimates of lifetime nursing home use: Have patterns of use changed? *Medical Care, 40*, 965–75.

16

Family and Friend Relationships, and Caregiving

Social relationships influence physical and mental health at all points in the lifespan, including later life. Social support and engagement of social networks are associated with positive mental health, and can offer significant support for independent living even in frail older adults. However, relationships can also have negative effects on well-being, introducing emotional drama, disruption, or burden. In this chapter, we describe how relationships are linked with mental health in later life. The following vignettes illustrate a few of the many complicated ways in which relationships and health, including mental health, are intertwined in later life.

> Janet is exhausted by evening from her job and volunteer work, but when her friend swings by to pick her up to go the mall to walk, she will go because she doesn't want to miss time with her friend or to let her down.

> John was advised to reduce salt and fat in his diet, and to lose weight in order to reduce risk of heart attack or stroke. Every time he gets this message from a health provider, he clams up with nothing to say because he knows that the daughter with whom he lives produces a lavish dinner each night as a sign of her love, and he must show his love by appreciating the meal enough to have seconds.

> Vivian has no appetite, especially when she is home for long days by herself. Her doctor is worried about the amount of weight she has lost in the last year, and encourages her to use nutritional supplements and to eat larger meals. None of it is appetizing if she eats alone.

Aging and Mental Health, Third Edition. Daniel L. Segal, Sara Honn Qualls, and Michael A. Smyer.
© 2018 John Wiley & Sons, Inc. Published 2018 by John Wiley & Sons, Inc.

Social Networks in Later Life

Over the course of our lives, we build social relationships from multiple domains of our lives—family, school friendships, intimate partners, work relationships, mentors, neighbors, even pen pals. By our fifth or sixth decade, we tend to have built a large network of relationships. Kahn and Antonucci (1980) referred to this as our *social convoy*, an accumulation of people who journey through life with us. Although we do not hold onto all relationships forever, we do accumulate people who stick with our convoy over years or even decades.

The size of one's network is correlated with well-being. Older adults with larger and more diverse networks have better health than those with smaller, more constrained networks (Windsor, Rioseco, Fiori, Curtis, & Booth, 2016). Larger networks afford you more choices from which to meet social needs. People who perceive their relationship networks to be supportive also have better health than those who lack support in their social network. Of course, perception is in the eye of the beholder, so we have to be open to perceiving social support *and* the supportive people have to be there.

Aging and the structure of social networks

Researchers have studied relationship networks all around the world by asking participants of all ages to list their relationships and then individually place each one into one of three concentric circles that represent the level of closeness (see Figure 16.1; Antonucci, 1986). Classic studies documented that older adults almost universally report fewer acquaintances than younger adults but older adults sustain stable networks of family and close friends in the inner circles (e.g., Lang & Carstensen, 1994). Multiple studies also showed that satisfaction with the network is higher among older

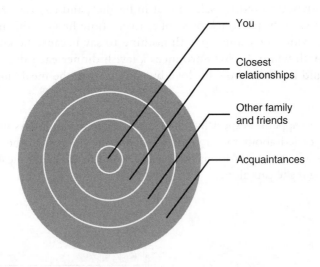

Figure 16.1 Social network circles.

than younger adults, with older adults less interested in seeking additions to their networks (Lansford, Sherman, & Antonucci, 1998).

Why do networks shrink with age, and how do people sustain the same value from smaller networks? Networks may shrink for both intentional and uncontrolled reasons.

Older adults tend to prune their networks over the lifespan, creating a smaller but equally important network structure by later life, according to Socio-Emotional Selectivity Theory (SST; Carstensen, Isaacowitz, & Charles, 1999). SST postulates that the motivations for investing in relationships change across the lifespan. Young adults are motivated to use relationships to learn how the world works, a social motive focused on information-seeking that is less salient with advanced age. Other social motives such as emotion regulation and support for identity are retained or grow in importance in later life. As vitality and other resources diminish, older adults reduce their investment in acquaintances in order to invest more heavily in closer relationships that support emotional well-being.

Later life is also a time of involuntary social loss as friends and family members die or move away. Coping with social losses is a major challenge in later life that can undermine well-being if not addressed effectively (Rook, 2009). Some losses are permanent and irreplaceable, such as the death of a marital partner of 60 years, or of a long-term business partner or professional colleague. As noted in Chapter 15, geographic relocation to new housing, often in a new neighborhood to be near family members leads to social losses as well as potential new relationships. Older adults describe multiple positive and negative reactions and social consequences of relocating (Löfqvist et al., 2013). New relationships may serve some of the lost social functions, but cannot replace the long-term shared history that provides emotionally salient memories and identity that constitute a personal narrative.

Effects of relationships on well-being in later life

Engagement with the social network has distinct benefits to mental health even though frequency of contact declines in late life. Longitudinal research shows that declining frequency of social interaction in advanced old age is associated with changes in functional health and subjective health, and that these changes are associated with lower levels of positive affect and life satisfaction (Huxhold, Fiori, & Windsor, 2013). Interestingly, emotional support tends to remain stable with advancing age. In other words, mental health benefits from sustained engagement in social relationships, but declining health is associated with decreased social engagement.

Loneliness and absence of perceived support are major risk factors to physical as well as mental health. Loneliness has a strong association with depression and anxiety in later life (Hawkley & Cacioppo, 2010; Losada et al., 2015). Perhaps more surprising is the growing evidence that loneliness is among the stronger risk factors for physical illness and death (Hawkley & Cacioppo, 2010). Although the biological mechanisms by which loneliness influences health are still under investigation, evidence suggests that blood pressure and changes in brain structure and functioning may mediate the risks of loneliness to health (Cacioppo, Capitanio, & Cacioppo, 2014;

Hawkley, Thisted, Masi, & Cacioppo, 2010). Loneliness adds risk to negative effects of depression, with severely depressed lonely men at particular risk (Holvast et al., 2015; Holwerda et al., 2016). Clearly, a sense of satisfaction with one's social network is of profound importance to health and well-being.

Of course, relationships can also negatively affect our lives. Relationships that induce negative emotions also add stress and undermine well-being (Rook, 2015). Relationships can elicit positive and negative reactions simultaneously, as well. Ambivalence, or simultaneous, conflicting feelings and beliefs, characterizes many family relationships. Adult children and aging parents commonly experience periods of tension as well as warm connection. Some relationships are experienced as chronically difficult, often due to mental health problems in a member. These relationships create particular challenges in caring for aging adults, a topic that has been the focus of books for distressed families (e.g., Lebow & Kane, 1999). In the vignettes below, Doris illustrates the common experience of families who desire enhanced social connection for a loved one yet cannot force the person to take advantage of opportunities. Sandra and Joel have had a positive relationship in the past, but find their closeness hard to sustain during the very busy phase of mid-life.

> Doris's children encouraged her to move from her suburban house into a senior apartment complex so she could have more social connections. Unfortunately, Doris experiences a similarly isolated and lonely lifestyle as she did in her home, being reluctant to participate in the many social opportunities at the complex.

> Sandra and Joel never felt that they had time to focus on their own mental or physical health while they reared their four children, worked in their small business, and provided leadership in their church. Having gained 10 pounds each decade, both now lament their excess weight, low energy, and high stress. Their frustrations produce constant bickering between them. Looking ahead to their old age, they wonder if they will live to enjoy the "golden years," and wonder if they would be happier apart.

Generally, however, older adults report more satisfaction from relationships as compared with younger adults (Luong, Charles, & Fingerman, 2011). The reasons seem to be that older adults use strategies in relationships that emphasize positive aspects of relationships, avoiding conflict. Simultaneously, others respond to older adults with more positive social behaviors than they do younger adults. The social advantages of aging can be compromised by environmental and personal factors that limit access to social relationships, limit willingness to engage in them, or limit the satisfaction derived from them.

Aging also can be a period when care needs escalate to a level that requires others to step in to provide support and services, commonly called *caregiving*. Most caregiving work is done by families or close friends who have a long-term historical relationship, which makes this a unique type of relationship that is discussed in more detail below.

Family Caregiving Relationships and Mental Health

Families are the primary care system for humans, including older adults (Qualls, 2016), providing 75–90% of their long-term care (Kaye, Harrington, & LaPlante, 2010; Thomas & Applebaum, 2015). Some families have responsibilities for other adults who need long-term assistance as well, creating extraordinary demand on those families. Responsibility for supporting persons with mental illness, traumatic brain injury, and physical or intellectual disability is almost certain to be carried by families, and typically lasts for decades. Thus, meeting the long-term-care needs of older adults occurs in a context in which families are often already engaged in caregiving for other adult members.

> Lori and John support their son Joseph in 1,000 ways that no one else knows about so Joseph can live semi-independently in the community despite the instability in daily living skills that his schizophrenia produces. Their parents' aging is now demanding more support as well, and they are increasingly aware that their own personal aging is also affecting their energy and resources to support Joseph. They try to face realistically the important questions about how they will care for their parents and their son simultaneously, and what will happen to Joseph after they [Lori and John] can no longer support him.

Caring and caregiving

Caring for each other is a primary function of families. Families demonstrate remarkable resilience in handling the cycles of heavier and lighter demands for care across the lifespan (Henry, Morris, & Harrist, 2015; Walsh, 2016). Although stress is associated with many periods of the life course (e.g., parenting toddlers and teenagers), families generally manage quite well. The same is true in later life, when families generally show remarkable resilience to the shifting care needs of multiple generations simultaneously (Coon, 2012).

Caregiving is a more involved set of roles and responsibilities than adults typically expect to perform for each other, even in families. The National Alliance for Caregiving (NAC) defines caregiving for adults as "unpaid care to a relative or friend 18 years of age or older to help them take care of themselves," including "helping with personal needs or household chores. It might be managing a person's finances, arranging for outside services, or visiting regularly to see how they are doing" (NAC & AARP, 2015, p. 3).

The areas of assistance needed by aging care recipients are referred to as activities of daily living (ADLs) which—as discussed in earlier chapters—are often divided into two groups: basic and instrumental. Basic ADLs include bathing, dressing, feeding, toileting, transferring, and ambulating. Instrumental ADLs (IADLs) include the functions that allow one to live independently, such as management of finances, appointments, transportation, and cleaning of living space. Also included in the instrumental ADLs are shopping, food preparation, and laundry. Age-related declines in vision, hearing, and mobility can reduce an older adult's ability to manage any or all of these skills independently, but the person may retain decision-making roles in arranging for assistance. As noted in Chapter 8, age-related cognitive impairments due to neuro-cognitive disorders or dementias often impact the IADLs fairly early in the progression of the disease, sometimes without the person's awareness of the scope of deficits, whereas basic self-care skills are retained longer.

Although families do not typically expect periods of intensive caregiving in their futures, families indeed provide caregiving work when the need arises. Thus, care-giving has become a normative aspect of family life. The NAC estimates that 34.2 million adults in the United States provide care to an adult aged 50+ in the course of a year (NAC & AARP, 2015). In a given year, that is about 14.3% of the entire population. Over the course of time, almost all families will experience caregiving in some form.

The NAC survey describes the caregiver and care recipient dyads in considerable detail (NAC & AARP, 2015). The prototypical caregiver is a mid-life woman caring for an aging parent, although spouses are the preferred first-line caregivers. The mean age of family caregivers is 49.2 years, and 60% are female. The vast majority are car-ing for relatives (85%), with 82% of those caring for a single adult and the remainder caring for two or more adults. Care recipients' average age is 69.4 years, with 47% of them over age 74. Almost half of the care recipients live in their own homes (47%) but 35% live with their caregivers and 18% are in a long-term-care residence or others' homes. The residential arrangement influences the amount of time caregivers spend. Caregivers living with the care recipients spend the most amount of time, with 62% of co-residing caregivers spending 21+ hours/week. Families experience many positive and many negative aspects of the caregiving lifestyle. The vignette below reminds us that dwindling social relationships are among the many effects of caregiving.

> Kendra provides all of her wife's care needs lovingly in their home. As her wife's dementia has progressed, Kendra finds it harder to get out into the community. She has completely lost touch with almost all of her friends. She doesn't have time to dwell on it, but she really does notice her feelings of loneliness.

Effects of caregiving on families

Caregivers to older adults show positive as well as adverse effects on their physical and mental health in particular conditions. For years, evidence accumulated about the negative effects of caregiving. The burdens of chronic care increased the risk of depres-sion as well as physical health problems and mortality (Pinquart & Sörensen, 2005). More recent research on population samples suggests that the research methods of earlier studies might have overstated the negative effects of caregiving because in large population samples, caregivers to older adults show reduced mortality and morbidity along with greater positive sense of purpose and meaning when compared with noncare-giving controls (Brown & Brown, 2014; Roth, Fredman, & Haley, 2015). Populations providing significant numbers of tasks for long periods of time to persons with dementia are the group for whom caregiving appears to pose the clearest health risks.

When family members become caregivers, they add this role to historical relation-ships that have lasted decades. Those relationships had preexisting structures and dynamics that shape the process by which they adopt caregiving roles, the meaning of those roles, and the challenges faced when adding extraordinary care roles to existing care patterns. The vignette below illustrates how life long personality difficulties influence the caregiving experience.

Karen's mother has always been difficult. While growing up, Karen worked hard to keep the peace with only intermittent success. Somehow, her mother always ended up upset, drawing attention to her needs over those of her children. Now that her mother needs hours of personal, intimate daily care assistance, Karen is keenly aware that no caregiver, family or professional, will be able to satisfy her mother.

By later life, families have created alliances and bonds, roles and rules for operating as a family, and have accumulated hurts and pride that provide a backdrop on which families begin to navigate caregiving challenges related to age-associated diseases and disabilities. Caregiving requires families to rearrange roles to accommodate the extraordinary care needs of members whose health has compromised daily functioning and self-care capabilities. As you can imagine, this can be exceptionally difficult.

Trajectories of caregiving

The onset of family caregiving can be sudden or subtle. Sudden onset health crises such as stroke, traumatic brain injury, back injury, myocardial infarction, or advanced stage cancer can change relationship structures in an instant. Other diseases such as dementias, chronic obstructive lung disease, diabetes, and congestive heart failure actually begin long before their symptoms become noticeable. In many cases, the symptoms arise slowly and without clear signals that a problem has begun. In the latter case, the family typically eases into caregiving, simply stepping in to provide assistance on some tasks and gradually taking on more responsibilities over time.

Linda's children have helped her with household repairs for years, and began helping her pay bills two years ago. Now they realize that they need to track her medical appointments because she has missed several appointments, and someone needs to check on how she takes her medications. Her children are not sure how they will manage it all, and the oldest daughter fears that everyone will expect her to organize everything, which seems overwhelming. When the doctor diagnosed Linda with Alzheimer's disease, the burden felt even heavier.

Caregiving episodes go through stages that are defined by the care recipient's deteriorations in functioning (see Figure 16.2). Declining functional health requires changes in the frequency and scope of caregiving support needed to sustain safety and health. Figure 16.2 illustrates that the family is in an existing structure at the time the illness or condition begins. At some point, the evidence of the changes in the care recipient prompts the family to shift into caregiving roles. The family may or may not recognize the scope of those changes, so they may not identify yet as caregiver(s), but in fact are functioning as such. During the progression through early, middle, and late stages, caregiving responsibilities increase, often requiring the family

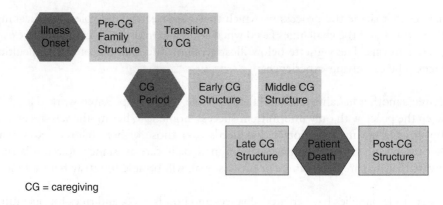

CG = caregiving

Figure 16.2   Stages of family caregiving.
Source: Adapted from Qualls & Williams (2013).

to include formal (paid) caregivers to assist. This could come in the form of a residential placement, home health providers, or personal care assistants who supplement the work the family is able to do. Paid care is often triggered when the person needs physical assistance in transferring from bed to chair and toilet, becomes incontinent, or has sleep interruptions. The death of the care recipient again provokes a change in the family as it shifts roles from being organized around caregiving to other patterns.

Some of the more challenging aspects of care are handling difficult behaviors resulting from dementia, such as repeated questions, confusion about time, lack of awareness of deficits, and changes in personality style. Families report being challenged by having to make decisions about driving: When is it safe to let a care recipient continue to drive? Even more challenging is the decision to take away driving privilege (Liddle et al., 2016), which may be contested by the older person who is not aware of his or her own deficits.

> Linda's son, Paul, was the one designated to tell his mother that she could no longer drive. He brought her favorite food to share over dinner, and broached the topic gently. But, as he feared, Linda became angry, left the table, and stomped off to her bedroom. On the way, she muttered, "So this is what it feels like when your kids take over, even after all you have done for them." Paul felt terribly guilty, and told his sisters that he refused to have anything more to do with the plan to take away her car.

Caregiving families have many other critical roles. With advanced frailty or cognitive impairment, the oversight and coordination of care responsibilities fall to family. When vulnerable, older persons must rely on others, most often family members, to advocate for them. However, among the most important roles of family members is emotional support and support for continuity of identity. Formal care providers who engage with elders for the first time know nothing of their history or preferences so families must create a social and personal context for the aging person. Also notable is the technical health care that families now provide, including many tasks that historically were only provided by health professionals, such as cleaning a tracheotomy or administering insulin shots.

Although the demands of caregiving add roles to lives that are often already role-loaded, caregiving also adds dimension to relationships that family members describe as gratifying and meaningful (Brown & Brown, 2014; Lloyd, Patterson, & Muers, 2016). Families often point out positive aspects of caregiving. Intimacy and closeness may increase during episodes of care. New roles emerge that allow people to relate in new ways. A previously fiercely independent person who could not accept assistance from a family member may open possibilities for new dimensions of a relationship.

Support for social relationships

Since the mid-20th century, communities have created gathering places to foster relationships and activities for older adults. Senior centers offer recreational and learning opportunities. Congregate meal sites provide options for healthy eating in a social environment. Programs like Silver Sneakers® and yoga classes draw older adults into physical activity in group settings. Colleges and universities often offer older adults options for joining classes on a reduced fee basis. The local Area Agency on Aging in each region can be one point of entry for identifying programs and activities with a social component (see www.eldercare.gov to find the local Area Agency on Aging).

Support groups are available to assist older adults and their family members in coping with health and behavior challenges. Disease-focused support groups (e.g., Alzheimer's disease, Parkinson's disease, depression, and bipolar disorder) are often key sources of social support for coping with challenges. Alcoholics Anonymous, Narcotics Anonymous, and Al-Anon (for families) assist people with challenges related to substance abuse within a social context that is a critical component of their intervention strategy.

Older adults with long-term challenges with emotion regulation may find it difficult to form and/or maintain relationships. Mental health professionals can offer counseling services to help the older adult build skills or work through difficulties that get in the way of healthy relationships. Interventions like Dialectical Behavior Therapy are equally effective in helping younger and older adults manage their emotions, a key challenge in relationship formation (Lynch et al., 2007).

Caregiving groups are now available in many settings. The disease-focused support groups noted above are offered for caregivers and persons living with the disease. Area Agencies on Aging now offer caregiver counseling, often using group formats, to educate and support caregivers while reducing the sense of loneliness that is often a painful component of facing the decline of a loved one. Hospitals and long-term-care facilities often offer family groups for similar reasons.

Families sometimes face substantial challenges restructuring their relationships to accommodate caregiving (Qualls & Williams, 2013). For example, families who have long-term conflicted relationships are likely to address caregiving challenges using the existing relationship structures and patterns, including dysfunctional ones (Lebow & Kane, 1999). Even families with structures that maintain the family's desired level of connectedness and support through acute situational crises during the first half of the life course may need to adapt to longer-term caregiving demands. Role restructuring may be particularly important in families caring for a person with cognitive impairment whose relationships can no longer function in the same way.

Interventions to Assist Families

Family therapy for later-life families has not received the theoretical or empirical attention that has been devoted to child-rearing families (Qualls, 2014). Most models of family therapy emerged in work with child-rearing families with goals that involved parenting, such as focusing on aligning parents in parenting approaches or assisting parents in handling their marital conflicts directly rather than through the children. In later-life families, clarity often must be reached about the decision-making axes because no longer is it as simple as the parents-are-in-charge.

Many later-life family challenges require some preliminary clarification of the family structure in order to determine how the problem fits into the overall family structure. Is there a problem with defining decision-making authority over some domain of a person's or a family's life? After one parent's death, the marital decision-making structure is lost, and a new structure must emerge. A widow or widower may be the sole decision-maker about finances, health, etc. or may draw upon one or more others. Disagreement among the children or siblings may emerge about who is now in the decision-making system or about how the shift occurred. Marital couples may bring adult children into decisions in new ways as the aging parents become frailer, or they may resist involvement even when decisions are past their capacity to make alone or to implement on their own. Family structures evolve significantly in later life due to illnesses, disabilities, and death, and those shifts are not always equally valued, respected, or appreciated by all family members. In short, keeping people on the same page is not a simple task when they no longer share the same residence or even live in the same part of the country.

Activation of family processes that have served family members well in previous periods of the lifespan can enhance family resilience in later life (Qualls, in press). With decades of experience of a variety of life challenges, later-life families can draw upon past experiences to identify strengths and limitations of their normative processes, and can also note examples of successful adaptation to expand the options the family might typically consider in the current moment. The family resilience framework offers research and clinical possibilities that are just now being explored in later-life families (Coon, 2012; Henry et al., 2015).

Restructuring the family system to incorporate caregiving and care recipient role shifts are among the larger structural changes faced by later life families (Qualls, 2014). Fundamental shifts in reciprocity in communication and service provision require role changes that are often profound. The role of daughter or son may change substantially after a parent becomes cognitively impaired due to stroke or dementia. The role of spouse changes in fundamental ways when one person's health is so fragile that their shared life revolves around the ill person's health. The history of the relationship is not lost or fully subverted. The family must figure out how to maintain former and current relationship values and meaning, writing a new narrative about how to be a functioning family in the face of altered roles.

Caregiving has been identified as a new normative life phase in families. Transitions into, and through, caregiving/care-receiving family structures are remarkably varied in timing, sequence, and interaction of individual and family well-being. Just as parenting children is a heterogeneous experience, so caregiving of older family members is influenced by the nature of the care recipients' needs, the personalities of all involved, the structures and processes of the families, and a myriad of contextual variables. No single pathway into or through caregiving can be identified.

Interventions to assist caregivers are available, but do not cover the needs of heterogeneous illness and disability populations who face diverse challenges. Some caregivers primarily need information whereas others need intensive intervention (Burgio & Gaugler, 2016). Notably, a large volume of research exists about caregivers to persons with dementia. Several empirically supported interventions have been studied in a sufficient number of rigorous studies to meet the standards of evidence needed to be listed in the Registry managed by the Substance Abuse and Mental Health Services Administration (Substance Abuse and Mental Health Services Administration, n.d.). Two such approaches are the REACH II and the New York University counseling approach (e.g., Belle et al., 2006; Mittelman, Ferris, Shulman, Steinberg, & Levin, 1996). Successful approaches to intervention are now understood to require flexibility and tailoring to meet the needs of the particular family and to activate support for caregiving from other family members as well as the primary caregiver. However, a similar research base does not exist for interventions for most other illnesses, leaving clinicians to adapt from existing evidence-based interventions and opening opportunities for researchers.

Caregiver family therapy (CFT) offers an organizing structure for interventions with caregivers of any illness or disability at any stage of the difficulty (Qualls & Williams, 2013). Although in early stages of empirical testing, the approach offers a systematic strategy for assessment and intervention planning that allows therapists to select evidence-based intervention approaches at an appropriate time for a particular caregiving situation. As depicted in Figure 16.2, caregiving is an adaptation of a family to some new illness or disability that shapes an existing family structure. Transitions in care needs are often gradual, eliciting changes in the emotional and practical support of family members and their caregiving roles. The transitions often involve role changes in more than just one dyad of caregiver and care recipient, and thus therapists benefit from understanding and considering the broader family system in the course of the intervention.

The CFT intervention process is organized around six tasks as depicted in Figure 16.3. At intake, a therapist can identify whether the family has a clear name for the problem. The name includes a diagnosis and accurate understanding of the illness or condition, along with the parameters of the immediate problem.

> Pamela finds her husband's behavior highly frustrating even though she can also empathize. George's increasing vision loss from macular degeneration is a source of intense frustration and helplessness for him multiple times each day. Pamela is insightful about the psychological as well as the functional ramification of George's vision loss, yet is overwhelmed emotionally by his needs. She defines her problem as "needing space" from the constant demands. The therapist notices that Pamela's satisfaction with the marriage has dropped significantly as well, so inquires if that would be another problem they need to name.

With a clear problem to address, therapy can proceed to examine the care structures. What types of care might be helpful to this family? What resources are available

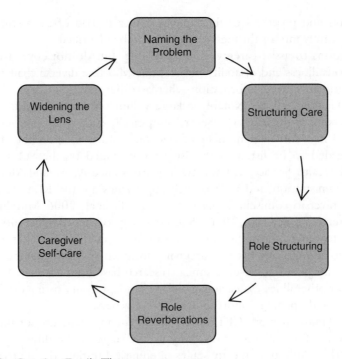

Figure 16.3 Caregiver Family Therapy components.
Source: Adapted from Qualls & Williams (2013).

in the family and in the community? What would a good care structure contain, from perspective of caregiver, care recipient, and others?

Implementation of care structures inevitably involves structuring of care roles. Who will do what for whom, when, how, and where? What is the meaning of those care roles? Do they represent large or small changes? Will they seem subtle or overt? Will change occur rapidly or gradually? The meaning of caregiving and care-receiving roles often needs to be explored, and sometimes needs to be formally negotiated. Once established, the family can consider the reverberating impact of those roles. Do the role structures related to caregiving impact other roles? For example, is Pamela's role in caring for her husband impacting her relationship with her children and grandchildren or her work life? A key question here is whether the role structures can be sustained.

Caregiver self-care during a period when extraordinary care is being managed is often tough to prioritize and sustain. Caregivers sometimes resist even taking on the task of self-care, pointing to the level of demand as too high to allow space for their "selfish" self-care actions. Others readily appreciate the importance of caring for self in order to be capable of caring for the care recipient. The initial care structures and roles may be identified as not sustainable, and require a revision of the overall strategy to meet the care recipient's needs in order to allow space for basic self-care of a primary caregiver.

CFT ends with an exercise in widening the lens to anticipate future changes and to look at the broader family network. Anticipation of future changes builds in an expectation for change in the care system and strategies. Changes in care recipients' functional abilities drives the family back through the questions addressed so far. What will be the new emerging problems? What care structures will be needed to address them? What role changes will that require, and what will be the reverberations of those changes in the caregiver's life? How will self-care be adapted in the new context? Widening the lens to look at the broader family network is intended to ensure that unintended consequences of the care structure for the lives of other family members are identified. If a mid-life woman has taken on large parent-care responsibilities, are there negative effects on her marriage or children and grandchildren? Can anything be done to ameliorate those, or at a minimum, to assess any associated risks?

> Pamela accepted that more care providers were needed to be incorporated into the care structure. She and George identified three people who could provide regular support services each week, affording Pamela time away from the house on a regular basis, and providing ongoing support with the tasks George found most frustrating. She appreciated being free from some of his moments of frustration, and free to reengage in aspects of her life that she had put on hold. The couple was referred for couples therapy to address the meanings of these important changes.
>
> Pamela and George both became engaged in identifying self-care opportunities, and they found new intimacy in bonding together to build each other's well-being. When they widened the lens, they could speak of the future with more directness and less fear. They identified the changes that would require new care structures, and were invited to return as needed for therapeutic help during those times. Pamela recognized that their children and grandchildren were no longer being nurtured by them regularly, a loss that the entire family acknowledged. The CFT therapist coached Pamela to engage in direct conversation about the impact of George's vision loss on all of them. She also explored opportunities to reengage the broader family in ways that would support her while meeting their needs for "grandma time." By widening the lens, the family saw opportunities to again change the care structure (and thus care roles) in ways that reduced the burden on Pamela while increasing opportunity for positive exchanges among children, grandchildren, Pamela, and George.

CFT is designed to be used flexibly, selecting among the six domains of work only those for which a caregiving family requires assistance. As in the case of Pamela above, the CFT therapist often works only with one member of the family, but consistently views the entire family system as being involved and affected. The family system lens opens the focus beyond the immediate caregiving situation, to consider how the broader family system is impacted by changes in the care recipient and caregiver. Sustainability of successful care strategies will be undermined if the strategies do not fit well within the overall family system. Empirical evaluation of the CFT model is in the early stages, with preliminary evidence of a positive impact of the approach and of treatment fidelity (O'Malley, 2017).

Summary and Conclusions

Relationships are critically important to mental well-being in later life, just as they are across the entire lifespan. The interaction of social relationships with physical and mental health is now well established, even though the mechanisms through which their influence is activated is not fully understood. Families serve particularly important roles when physical, cognitive, or psychological functioning is compromised. Caregiving episodes require substantial adjustment for the persons giving and receiving care, as roles change many times over the course of a chronic illness. Multiple opportunities exist for building new relationships in later life and for renegotiating existing relationships to adapt to age-related changes.

Critical Thinking / Discussion Questions

1   Do you believe that people who select isolated lives will be found to suffer with poor health as the national data suggest? Why or why not?
2   Under what conditions would you expect caregivers to show mental health problems?
3   How do you look at your own social future differently based on reading this chapter?

Website Resources

Eldercare Locator: Area Agency on Aging
www.eldercare.gov
National Alliance for Caregiving
www.caregiving.org
American Society on Aging
www.asaging.org
American Psychological Association: Caregiver Briefcase
http://www.apa.org/pi/about/publications/caregivers/index.aspx

References

Antonucci, T. C. (1986). Hierarchical mapping technique. *Generations: Journal of the American Society on Aging, 10*, 10–12.

Belle, S. H., Burgio, L., Burns, R., Coon, D., Czaja, S.J., Gallagher-Thompson, D., … Martindale-Adams, J. (2006). Enhancing the quality of life of dementia caregivers from different ethnic or racial groups. *Annals of Internal Medicine, 145*, 727–738.

Brown, R. M., & Brown, S. L. (2014). Informal caregiving: A reappraisal of effects on caregivers. *Social Issues and Policy Review, 8*, 74–102. doi:10.1111/sipr.12002

Burgio, L. D., & Gaugler, J. E. (2016). Caregiving for the chronically ill: State of the science and future directions. In L. D. Burgio, J. E., Gaugler, & M. M. Hilgeman (Eds.), *The spectrum of family caregiving for adults and elders with chronic illness* (pp. 258–278). New York, NY: Oxford University Press.

Cacioppo, S., Capitanio, J. P., & Cacioppo, J. T. (2014). Toward a neurology of loneliness. *Psychological Bulletin, 140(6)*, 1464–1504. doi:10.1037/a0037618

Carstensen, L. L., Isaacowitz, D. M., & Charles, S. T. (1999). Taking time seriously: A theory of socioemotional selectivity. *American Psychologist, 54*, 165–181.

Coon, D. W. (2012). Resilience and family caregiving. In B. J. Hayslip & G. C. Smith (Eds.), *Annual review of gerontology and geriatrics. Vol 32: Emerging perspectives on resilience in adulthood and later life* (pp. 231–249). New York, NY: Springer.

Hawkley, L. C., & Cacioppo, J. T. (2010). Loneliness matters: A theoretical and empirical review of consequences and mechanisms. *Annals of Behavioral Medicine, 40(2)*, 218–227.

Hawkley, L. C., Thisted, R. A., Masi, C. M., & Cacioppo, J. T. (2010). Loneliness predicts increased blood pressure: 5-year cross-lagged analyses in middle-aged and older adults. *Psychology and Aging, 25(1)*, 132–141. doi:10.1037/a0017805

Henry, C. S., Morris, A. S., & Harrist, A. W. (2015). Family resilience: Moving into the third wave. *Family Relations, 64*, 22–43.

Holvast, F., Burger, H., de Waal, M. W., van Marwijk, H. J., Comijs, H. C., & Verhaak, P. M. (2015). Loneliness is associated with poor prognosis in late-life depression: Longitudinal analysis of the Netherlands study of depression in older persons. *Journal of Affective Disorders, 185*, 1–7. doi:10.1016/j.jad.2015.06.036

Holwerda, T. J., van Tilburg, T. G., Deeg, D. H., Schutter, N., Van, R., Dekker, J., ... Schoevers, R. A. (2016). Impact of loneliness and depression on mortality: Results from the Longitudinal Ageing Study Amsterdam. *The British Journal of Psychiatry, 209*, 127–134. doi:10.1192/bjp.bp.115.168005

Huxhold, O., Fiori, K. L., & Windsor, T. D. (2013). The dynamic interplay of social network characteristics, subjective well-being, and health: The costs and benefits of socio-emotional selectivity. *Psychology and Aging, 28*, 3–16. doi: 10.1037/a0030170

Kahn, R. L., & Antonucci, T. C. (1980). Convoys over the life course: Attachment, roles, and social support. In P. B. Baltes & O. G. Brim (Eds.). *Life-span development and behavior* (Vol. 3, pp. 253–286). New York, NY: Academic Press.

Kaye, S., Harrington, C., & LaPlante, M. (2010). Long-term care: Who gets it, who provides it, who pays, and how much? *Health Affairs, 29*, 11–21. doi: 10.1377/hlthaff.2009.0535

Lang, F. R., & Carstensen, L. L. (1994). Close emotional relationships in late life: Further support for proactive aging in the social domain. *Psychology and Aging, 9*, 315–324.

Lansford, J. E., Sherman, A. M., & Antonucci, T. C (1998). Satisfaction with social networks: An examination of socioemotional selectivity theory across cohorts. *Psychology and Aging, 13*, 544–552. doi:10.1037/0882-7974.13.4.544

Lebow, G., & Kane, B. (1999). *Coping with your older parent: A guide for stressed out children.* New York, NY: Avon Books.

Liddle, J., Tan, A., Liang, P., Bennett, S., Allen, S., Lie, D. C., & Pachana, N. A. (2016). "The biggest problem we've ever had to face": How families manage driving cessation with people with dementia. *International Psychogeriatrics, 28*, 109–122. doi:10.1017/S1041610215001441

Lloyd, J., Patterson, T., & Muers, J. (2016). The positive aspects of caregiving in dementia: A critical review of the qualitative literature. *Dementia: The International Journal of Social Research and Practice, 15(6)*, 1534–1561. doi:10.1177/1471301214564792

Losada, A., Márquez-González, M., Pachana, N. A., Wetherell, J. L., Fernández-Fernández, V., Nogales-González, C., & Ruiz-Díaz, M. (2015). Behavioral correlates of anxiety in well-functioning older adults. *International Psychogeriatrics, 27*, 1135–1146. doi:10.1017/S1041610214001148

Löfqvist, C., Granbom, M., Himmelsbach, I., Iwarsson, S., Oswald, F., & Haak, M. (2013). Voices on relocation and aging in place in very old age – A complex and ambivalent matter. *The Gerontologist, 53*(6), 919–927. doi:10.1093/geront/gnt034

Luong, G., Charles, S. T., & Fingerman, K. L. (2011). Better with age: Social relationships across adulthood. *Journal of Social and Personal Relationships, 28*(1), 9–23. doi:10.1177/0265407510391362

Lynch, T. R., Cheavens, J. S., Cukrowicz, K. C., Thorp, S. R., Bronner, L., & Beyer, J. (2007). Treatment of older adults with co-morbid personality disorder and depression: a dialectical behavior therapy approach. *International Journal of Geriatric Psychiatry, 22*, 131–143.

Mittelman, M. S., Ferris, S. H., Shulman, E., Steinberg, G., & Levin, B. (1996). A family intervention to delay nursing home placement of patients with Alzheimer's disease. *Journal of the American Medical Association, 276*, 1725–1731.

NAC & AARP. (2015). *Caregiving in the US* (Research report). Retrieved from http://www.aarp.org/content/dam/aarp/ppi/2015/caregiving-in-the-united-states-2015-report-revised.pdf

O'Malley, K. A. (2017). *Caregiver family therapy: a pilot study of treatment fidelity, acceptability, and efficacy (Dissertation)*. University of Colorado at Colorado Springs.

Pinquart, M., & Sörensen, S. (2005). Differences between caregivers and noncaregivers in psychological health and physical health: a meta-analysis. *Psychology and Aging, 18*, 250–267. doi: 10.1037/0882-7974.18.2.250

Qualls, S. H. (2014). Family therapy with ageing families. In N. A. Pachana & K. Laidlaw (Eds.), *The Oxford handbook of clinical geropsychology* (pp. 710–732). Oxford, England: Oxford University Press.

Qualls, S. H. (2016). Caregiving families within the long-term services and support system for older adults. *American Psychologist, 71*, 283–293. doi: 10.1037/a0040252

Qualls, S. H. (2017). Therapeutic interventions for caregiving families. In W. A. Bailey & A. Harrist (Eds.), *Family caregiving: Fostering resilience across the lifespan* (pp. 29–42). New York, NY: Springer.

Qualls, S. H., & Williams, A. A. (2013). *Caregiver family therapy*. Washington, DC: APA Press.

Rook, K. S. (2009). Gaps in social support resources in later life: An adaptational challenge in need of further research. *Journal of Social and Personal Relationships, 26*, 103–113. doi:10.1177/0265407509105525

Rook, K. S. (2015). Social networks in later life: Weighing positive and negative effects on health and well-being. *Current Directions in Psychological Science, 24*(1), 45–51. doi:10.1177/0963721414551364

Roth, D. L., Fredman, L., & Haley, W. E. (2015). Informal caregiving and its impact on health: A reappraisal from population-based studies. *The Gerontologist, 55*, 309–319. doi:10.1093/geront/gnu177

Substance Abuse and Mental Health Services Administration. (n.d). *National Registry of Evidence-based Programs and Practices (NREPP)*. Retrieved from http://www.samhsa.gov/nrepp

Thomas, K. S., & Applebaum, R. (2014). Long-term services and supports (LTSS): A growing challenging for an aging America. *Public Policy and Aging Report, 25*(2), 56–62. doi: 10.1093/ppar/prv003

Walsh, F. (2016). *Strengthening family resilience* (3rd ed.). New York, NY: Guilford.

Windsor, T. D., Rioseco, P., Fiori, K. L., Curtis, R. G., & Booth, H. (2016). Structural and functional social network attributes moderate the association of self-rated health with mental health in midlife and older adults. *International Psychogeriatrics, 28*, 49–61. doi:10.1017/S1041610215001143

17

Ethical Issues in Work
with Older Adults
Advanced Care, Financial Decision-Making,
and the Impacts of Climate Change

Consider the following case examples:

Louise was 93 when she had "the talk" with her primary care physician. Her daughter, Ellen, accompanied her. Dr. Fisher said, "Louise, you know we should talk about an advanced directive for you. You've already had the EMTs [Emergency Medical Technicians] at your house once. If you have another fall, it might take a while to find you and revive you. If we were able to bring you back, you might not like the results." "No, I guess not," Louise answered. Ellen joined in: "Mom, are you saying you would not want to be revived? You wouldn't want people to help you?" "I've lived a long and good life. If my time is up, I'm ready," Louise answered.

Sandy Erikson insists that a new orthotic shoe will eliminate the pain she experiences when walking, despite repeated explanations of the structural damage to her foot from diabetic neuropathy. At each case consultation, she listens patiently to the explanations, and demands that her doctor provide her with a prescription for a new shoe. Sandy faces amputation, sooner or later, as a required strategy for limiting infection. Amputation is an immediate solution to the pain, but hard for her to accept. She seems unable to grasp the information or recall it from meeting to meeting. The physician has begun to question whether Sandy has the capacity to make the amputation decision alone (Lichtenberg, Qualls, & Smyer, 2015, p. 555).

When Jennifer, his only daughter, discovered that Daniel Horn's bank account was near empty, she was shocked and terrified. Her brother, who has Daniel's financial durable power of attorney, just built a new house that seemed extravagant but Jennifer cannot imagine he would actually steal from their father. The social worker at the skilled nursing facility where Daniel lived dreaded telling Jennifer

---

Aging and Mental Health, Third Edition. Daniel L. Segal, Sara Honn Qualls, and Michael A. Smyer.
© 2018 John Wiley & Sons, Inc. Published 2018 by John Wiley & Sons, Inc.

that the facility bill had not been paid for three months. Jennifer and her father's attorney contact you for help in documenting that Daniel did not have capacity to gift $300,000 to her brother as he claimed (Lichtenberg, Qualls, & Smyer, 2015, p. 565).

These examples reflect the importance of our starting assumptions about older adults, their capacities, and their rights.

The contexts of care matter. They affect the client and the clinician, shaping the framing of both problems and potential solutions. In this chapter, we will consider two types of frameworks to illustrate the impact of contexts: ethical and societal. Our goal is to illustrate the power of contexts, enabling you to reflect on the impact of current contexts for care and caring. We will use two domains—advanced care and financial decision-making—to illustrate these themes.

The three case examples presented above embody contrasting and, at times, conflicting ethical principles at work in later life: autonomy, beneficence, nonmaleficence, and justice (Harnett & Greaney, 2008; Hughes & Baldwin, 2006; Zarit & Heid, 2015). Autonomy here refers to the individual's ability to decide what happens to him or her. For example, Louise clearly wants to make the decision regarding an advanced directive. Beneficence refers to the goal of doing good for those you are entrusted to care for, including your clients and their family members. In Sandy Erikson's case, her physician wants to protect Sandy and make sure she understands the consequences of her decisions. Nonmaleficence reflects the ancient Hippocratic warning: First do no harm; the aspiration here is to avoid harming clients and their loved ones. In Daniel Horn's case, his daughter is concerned that her brother may be harming their father financially. Finally, the principle of justice calls for treating people fairly and equally.

Oftentimes these principles come into conflict around crises or difficulties for older adult and their families. In this section, we will use two examples—advanced care directives and financial fraud and abuse—to illustrate the challenges clients and clinicians face.

Advanced Illness and Advanced Care Directives

As we outlined in Chapter 2, most older adults have one or more chronic conditions. The diagnosis and treatment of these conditions is often complex and often involves ethical issues. For example, the average Medicare beneficiary with one or more chronic conditions sees eight different physicians per year (Hudson & Lindberg, 2014). Each treatment team may be concerned about balancing two ethical principles: avoiding harm for their patient (nonmaleficence), and doing good for their patient (beneficence). Greenlee (2014) argues that different practice communities balance these concerns in different ways. For example, those who focus on treating older adults tend to try to avoid overtreatment, whereas those who specialize in working with patients with disabilities are more likely to be concerned about not denying life-sustaining treatment to their clients.

During the last decade or more, public policy and clinical practice have emphasized "patient-centered" or "patient-driven" care as one element in managing the complexity of late-life care. Patient-centered care is "respectful of and responsive to individual patient preferences, needs and values" so that the patient's values "guide all clinical decisions" (Institute of Medicine, 2001). The federal Patient Self-Determination Act (PSDA), for example, requires that clinicians honor the choices of the client regarding end-of-life care (Greenlee, 2014), whether to choose or refuse treatment. As Stuart (2014) noted, this shifts the conversation from "what's the matter with you" to "what matters to you."

Discussions of patient preferences initially began by focusing on advanced directives—the patient's wishes for end-of-life care. More recently, however, the emphasis has shifted to another aspect of disease and disability transitions: advanced illness. Advanced illness is a "period of illness when functioning and quality of life decline and where the efficacy of continued treatment is open to medical and ethical question" (Hudson & Lindberg, 2014, p. 79).

As Greenlee (2014) notes, advanced care planning requires that the clinician and client work together to clarify important choices: which types of care they want to pursue, who will provide it, and who will speak for the client if the client is unable. In answering these questions, the client's own balancing of autonomy, beneficence, nonmaleficence, and justice shape specific discussions of the client's changing abilities, needs, required or desired services and supports, and the hoped-for outcomes of care. These discussions are hard work for the older person, her family, and the care team working with her. In many cases, there are no simple answers or solutions to which everyone agrees.

Stuart (2014) warned that there are challenges of time, space, and treatment models that make it difficult to assure that we are carrying out the client's wishes. For example, advanced directives are usually recorded at a single point of time. Consider the case of Louise at the opening of this chapter. Her doctor urged her to specify her advanced directives—which type of care she preferred and who would speak for her in case she could not express her preferences. Louise did so and eventually died three years later, without revisiting those choices. Stuart (2014) warns, however, that advanced directives that "record a snapshot of preferences... break down later when clinical urgency dictates actions that the ill person could not have foreseen, or did not want to think about, earlier in the course of illness" (Stuart, 2014, p. 102).

Stuart (2014) refers to a "silo of space," by which he means the separate treatment domains of hospital, office, home, and long-term care. Increasingly, clinicians working with those with advanced illness must coordinate between and among settings of care to provide an integrated approach to carrying out the client's wishes.

Breaking down the treatment silo requires a flexible plan of both treatments and palliative care that are responsive to the client's preferences and changing abilities as disease progresses. Stuart summarized the optimal outcome for the client:

> It is a comprehensive plan formed through shared decision-making, supervised by the personal physician, and carried out by a trusted team at the ill person's own pace in the safety and comfort of home. This method produces fully informed patients who express their wishes clearly and receive exactly the care they want—no more and no less. (p. 103)

Note that this outcome optimally provides neither too much nor too little treatment, following the client's desires and preferences. But the question remains: How can we achieve these goals with our clients?

What does success look like with advanced directives and advanced care?

It is important to define success for the process of advanced directives and advanced care at both the individual and societal level. For individuals, success includes clarifying the client's personal goals and then determining her preferences for care (Stuart, 2014). For society, success includes a "triple bottom line" of improved quality of care, improved population health, and constraining per capita growth in health care costs (MacPherson, 2014). We will return to the societal stakes in and approaches to advanced care later in this chapter. First, though, we will focus on the individual and how to assure that we know his or her preferences and that we faithfully carry them out.

Older adults and their families are increasingly interested in advanced directives. For example, between 2000 and 2010, the percentage of those 60 and older who died with an advanced directive increased from 47% to 72% (Silveria, Wiitala, & Piette, 2014). However, the rates of completion vary by setting, ranging from 28% of home health agency clients, to 65% of nursing home residents, and 88% of hospice users (US Government Accountability Office, 2015). Oftentimes, mental health professionals in these settings may be involved in discussing options with older adults and their families.

Sabatino (2014) pointed out that initially conversations about advanced care started with advanced directives and end-of-life planning. The two most prevalent documents used to record an individual's wishes were either a living will or a Physician's Order for Life Sustaining Treatment (POLST). Greenlee (2014) summarized the usefulness and limitations of living wills and of POLSTs:

> A living will spells out treatment decisions and directions for use of life-sustaining measures such as mechanical breathing (respiration and ventilation), tube feeding, or resuscitation. Living wills cannot cover every possible situation, so people can name someone to make care decisions for them through a durable power of attorney for health care that names a health care proxy. When there is no named health care proxy, states generally have rules about how families make care decisions. Health care providers and insurance companies need the individual's permission to share personal information with the health care proxy…
>
> A POLST makes sure that decisions about care at the end of life are written as medical orders that health care providers must follow. The POLST should list the medical care people do or do not want, given their current health condition. The POLST should include decisions for cardiopulmonary resuscitation if a person's heart stops or if they stop breathing. Without a POLST, emergency care providers generally must provide such medical treatment to keep people alive. Not every state has POLST, and some states have similar forms *that go by different names.* (p. 84)

Since there are variations by state, it is important to understand the current legal and regulatory environment of each state you are living and working in (Greenlee, 2014).

Living wills and POLSTs used to be "state of the art" mechanisms for capturing the client's preferences and wishes. Sabatino (2014) recently outlined many other options available to older adults, their relatives and friends, and the professionals working with them. He emphasized the importance of communication between and among the older adult, the family members, and the health care team carrying out the older adult's preferences.

Carpenter (2015) recently reviewed the challenges and opportunities for geropsychologists who work with individuals and families at the end of life. He noted that clinical geropsychologists bring a range of expertise to these issues: an understanding of life-span development; the interactions of biological, psychological, and behavioral functioning; and expertise in clinical assessment, psychological treatment, and research.

At the same time, Carpenter (2015) highlighted several gaps in our current knowledge and approaches to treatment. Prime among these are measurement issues: We still have a lot to learn about the reliability and validity of measures of psychological functioning (e.g., personality, memory, depression, etc.) under the stresses of end-of-life concerns. He summarized the concern well: "Coherence, acceptance, forgiveness, dignity, and peacefulness are important ideas that circulate in end-of-life care, but efforts to measure them are rudimentary" (Carpenter, 2015, p. 585).

Similarly, Carpenter (2015) outlines a number of psychological interventions that may be useful to individuals and families facing end-of-life issues, ranging from facilitating consideration of advanced planning before a diagnosis through assisting in behavioral coping and grief work. He acknowledges, though, that there are few well-documented intervention approaches. One exception to this generalization is meaning-centered group therapy (MCGT, based on the theoretical work of Victor Frankl). Recent research has documented the positive impact of MCGT on the individual's sense of meaning, faith, spiritual well-being, symptom-related distress, and desire for death (Breitbart, Poppito, et al., 2012; Breitbart, Rosenfeld, et al., 2010). Carpenter and Mulligan (2009) also outlined a process of working with family members to assess their views of parental care needs and wishes. The compiled views of family members allowed the therapist to highlight areas of agreement and areas of disagreement on potential care decisions.

Carpenter (2015) stressed the interdisciplinary nature of end-of-life work, with clinical teams often including nurses, social workers, and psychologists, as well as family members and clients themselves. Fortunately, there are resources available for clinicians working with client and families facing end-of-life issues (e.g., Qualls & Kasl-Godley, 2011; National Consensus Project for Quality Palliative Care, 2013).

When turning to advanced care issues, Sabatino (2014) offered a helpful distinction between getting started and advanced discussions regarding advanced illness and advanced directives (see Table 17.1 and Table 17.2).

Advanced care: Getting started

Sabatino (2014) highlighted several approaches to getting started. For example, Ellen Goodman, a former newspaper columnist, and her colleagues started the Conversation

Table 17.1 Resources for starting the conversation about advanced care

Resource	Description	Sample content	Source
The Conversation Starter Kit	Designed to help talk about end-of-life care	"What do you need to do or feel to be ready to have the conversation?"	www.theconversationproject.org
Consumer Tool Kit for Advanced Planning, from the American Bar Association	Discover, clarify, and communicate what is important when facing serious illness	How do you select a health care proxy? Are some things worse than death? The proxy quiz for family & physician	www.ambar.org/healthdecisions
The Go Wish Game	A card game for sorting out your values and priorities in end-of-life decisions	Using a deck of 36 cards (available in several languages), with phrases and wishes on each card. You rank your top 10 priorities.	Available for purchase from www.codaalliance.org
Prepare website	Prepare for medical decision-making	Choose a medical decision maker. Decide what matters most in life.	www.prepareforyourcare.org
Death Cafe or Death Over Dinner	Gatherings of friends or strangers to discuss death and end-of-life preferences over coffee, cake, or dinner	An agenda-free discussion in which attendees decide on the topics covered.	www.deathcafe.com www.deathoverdinner.org

Source: Adapted from Sabatino (2014).

Table 17.2 Comprehensive advanced care planning tools

Resource	Description	Sample content	Source
Five Wishes	"The most widely used advanced directive or living will in America"	Five key questions. For example: What kind of medical treatment do you want or don't want?	www.agingwithdignity.org
Caring Conversations	Free online workbook to help you reflect, talk, appoint & act	Resources to clarify your personal values, start conversations, and appoint a health care agent	www.practicalbioethics.org
Thinking Ahead: My Way, My Choice, My Life at the End	Free workbook and videos to help clarify personal preferences and end-of-life choices	Where I want to be… How I want to be cared for… Where I want my things to go… How I want to be remembered…	www.dds.ca.gov/ConsumerCorner/ThinkingAhead.cfm
Giving Someone a Power of Attorney for Your Health Care	A "bare bones" health care power of attorney, valid in all but five states	Provides solely for the appointment of a health care agent, without specifying an individual's preferences for care	www.ambar.org/healthdecisions
My Directives	A universal advanced digital directive	Specify your decisions, your preferences, your health care providers, and your circle of family & friends in a digital archive	www.MyDirectives.com

Source: Adapted from Sabatino (2014).

Project (www.theconversationproject.org), designed to help people prepare to have a conversation about their end-of-life preferences with their family members, their physicians, and other important people in their lives. They point out that, although 90% of people say that talking with their loved ones about end-of-life care is important, 27% have actually done so. Similarly, 80% of people say that if seriously ill, they would want to talk to their doctor about wishes for medical treatment toward the end of their life. However, only 7% report having had this conversation with their doctor. Their project helps prepare for "the conversation."

The American Bar Association Commission on Law and Aging has developed a helpful tool kit for advanced planning. Its web resources include information about state variations in advanced directive requirements. In addition, it provides a proxy quiz for family members and health care providers to assess the congruence between the individual's preferences and what those who may have to make decisions for them think those preferences are (see Box 17.1).

The Coda Alliance is dedicated to facilitating advanced care and advanced directive planning. It has developed the Go Wish card game (available at www.codaalliance. org). The card game allows individuals to establish their priorities and share them in a "gamelike" setting. The basic game comes in a two-pack set. Since it is in a card game format, it may be a way to ease into a conversation for some people.

Box 17.1   A Proxy Quiz: Sample Items

Developed by the American Bar Association Commission on Law and Aging.

1   Imagine that you had Alzheimer's disease and it had progressed to the point where you could not recognize or converse with your loved ones. When spoon-feeding was no longer possible, would you want to be fed by a tube into your stomach?
   a.   Yes
   b.   No
   c.   I am uncertain
2   Which of the following do you fear most near the end of life?
   a.   Being in pain
   b.   Losing the ability to think
   c.   Being a financial burden on loved ones
3   Imagine that…
   You are now seriously ill, and doctors are recommending chemotherapy, and this chemotherapy usually has very severe side effects, such as pain, nausea, vomiting, and weakness that could last for 2-3 months.
   Would you be willing to endure the side effects if the chance of regaining your current health was less than 1 percent?
     a.   Yes
     b.   No
     c.   I am uncertain

Dr. Rebecca Sudore and her colleagues at the University of California San Francisco developed the Prepare interactive website (www.prepareforyourcare.org) to help older adults and their families make medical decisions and end-of-life decisions. The website is available in both English and Spanish and features audio and video prompts that can be experienced individually or with family members. The website is premised on the fact that three out of four people will be unable to make some or all of their medical decisions at the end of life. Therefore, it is important to identify a medical decision-maker who understands your preferences.

Perhaps the least formal resource is the Death Cafe website (www.deathcafe.com). With a stated purpose "to increase awareness of death with a view to helping people make the most of their (finite) lives," the website provides tools for those who want to organize a community discussion or a gathering of friends.

Comprehensive advanced care planning tools

Sabatino (2014) outlined several comprehensive advanced care planning tools. As with the "conversation starters," these are tools that older adults can use with their family members or with health care staff to clarify their preferences for advanced care and end-of-life care.

Aging with Dignity is a private, nonprofit organization dedicated to safeguarding "the human dignity of people as they age or face serious illness." The organization advocates for quality care for individuals near the end of life. One of their main tools is the Five Wishes document, which assists individuals in specifying their preferences in nontechnical language to more effectively capture their preferences. The Five Wishes document is available in 28 languages in either hard copy or an online version. Aging with Dignity has also worked to ensure that in 42 states individuals can express their end-of-life wishes in their own words, instead of in state-written documents. In addition, Aging with Dignity staff and volunteers provide assistance to individuals and families through their website and through workshops.

The Center for Practical Bioethics is a freestanding nonprofit organization dedicated to raising and responding to ethical issues in health and health care. The Center has set as one of its priorities the improvement of advanced care planning and shared decision-making. It offers a free workbook, *Caring Conversations*, that guides individuals and families through several steps: reflecting on the individual's values and preferences; talking with family members and health care team members; appointing those who will speak for the individual when she cannot, including forms for appointing a durable power of attorney for health care decisions; and acting to communicate these decisions to family members and other involved in the ongoing care decisions.

The California Department of Developmental Services developed a free workbook and videos, *Thinking Ahead: My Way, My Choice, My Life at the End,* to assist individuals and families in establishing and communicating personal preferences about end-of-life choices. The materials are available in English, Spanish, and Chinese and focus on the individual's personal preferences and end-of-life choices. Although the California Department developed the *Thinking Ahead* materials for those individuals with developmental disabilities, the videos and workbook are useful for others, including older adults and their families.

The American Bar Association's Commission on Law and Aging has published *Giving Someone a Power of Attorney for Your Health Care: A Guide with an Easy-to-Use Legal Form for All Adults*. The Commission designed this guide to be used with a tool such as its *Consumer Tool Kit for Health Care Advanced Planning*, described earlier. The guide provides a multistate health care power of attorney that is valid in all states in the US, with the exception of five states: Indiana, New Hampshire, Ohio, Texas, and Wisconsin. (This is a good reminder to check on the rules and regulations in your own locale and state!)

A private, US corporation, ADVault, Inc., has developed the first all-in-one online advanced care planning tool and digital archive, *My Directives*. This free service helps you specify your values and preferences, identify treatment options, and share this information with your health care providers. It also gives the family members and friends you choose access to this information. Using an encrypted, secure database, *My Directives* makes your documents available around the clock to health care providers and others you specify. For older adults and their families who are comfortable with the digital environment, this option may promote broader discussion of preferences and next steps.

As Sabatino (2014) noted, developing a set of advanced directives is an important first step. Equally important, however, is making those directives available to those who need them in a time of decision-making. *My Directives* is an example of one site that offers a registry of your preferences. Others are available, without the integrated advanced directive preparation, such as the America Living Will Registry (www.alwr.com), DocBank (www.docubank.com), the MedicAlert Foundation (http://www.medicalert.org), and the U.S. Living Will Registry (www.uslwr.com). Many states have also developed registries.

The American Bar Association's Commission on Law and Aging, under Sabatino's leadership, has created a smartphone application, *My Health Care Wishes* (www.americanbar.org/groups/law_aging/MyHealthCareWishesApp.html) to help individuals and family members share important information. The app allows you to store your own and others' health care advanced directives, key health information, and health care contact information on your smartphone. It also allows you to send advanced directive documents to health care providers or other family members using email or Bluetooth connections.

In a time of increasingly complex advanced care and end-of-life decisions, health care providers working with older adults play an important role in assuring that the older adult's preferences for balancing autonomy, beneficence, and other values are honored. This requires understanding the ethical, legal, and technological tools to assure that all who are involved (older adults, their family members and friends, and their health care team) have a shared set of assumptions and a shared action plan in advance.

The societal stake in advanced care and advanced planning

As pointed out earlier, the societal definition of success in advanced planning includes a "triple bottom line" of improved quality of care, improved population health, and constraining per capita growth in health care costs (MacPherson, 2014). With 10,000 older adults joining the Medicare ranks each day, concerns about both program costs and quality will continue to rise in the coming decades (Stuart, 2014). In 2014, for example, the net cost of Medicare ($505 billion) was 14% of the US Federal budget outlays (Kaiser Family Foundation, 2015). Notably, the Medicare budget is projected to nearly double between 2015 and 2025, rising from $527 billion to $981 billion, driven primarily by the aging of the population (Kaiser Family Foundation, 2015).

The costs of care, however, are not evenly shared. Within Medicare, 10% of the program's beneficiaries account for nearly 60% of the total costs (Kaiser Family Foundation, 2015). Moreover, patients with chronic illness in their last two years of life account for 32% of Medicare spending (Dartmouth Institute, 2011). However, as Greenlee (2014) pointed out, 43% of older Medicare beneficiaries who died in 2009 used hospice services before death; many more could have benefited from this type of support. In addition, there are large regional variations in patterns of care, including hospitalization (Goodman, Esty, Fisher, & Chang, 2011).

As Stuart (2014) points out, however, cost containment is not the only metric of success in advanced care. He described the Advanced Care Project, co-sponsored by the Coalition to Transform Advanced Care and by the AHIP (America's Health Insurance Plan) Foundation's Institute for Health Solutions. Their analysis drew on evidence from existing plans with common elements: team based-care management, connecting across settings (home, outpatient, long-term care, hospitals); a mix of disease-specific and palliative care that is responsive to changing illness and individual preferences; and planning on an ongoing basis, responding to changing circumstances. Success has been demonstrated in both clinical and financial outcomes: high levels of hospice acceptance, patient and referring physician satisfaction; significant reduction in hospitalization and intensive care days; and significant cost savings (Stuart, 2014). In contrast, care integration approaches do not achieve these outcomes without focusing on the seriously ill cohort involved in advanced care (Brown, Peikes, Peterson, Schore, & Findrakoto, 2012).

The lesson for those working with seriously ill older adults is clear: Care integration, focusing on options that are responsive to the client's preferences, will achieve optimal outcomes for the individual and for society as a whole. Despite the difficult and uncomfortable nature of having discussions about end-of-life issues, it is often the psychologist's role to address these issues and propel discussions forward.

Financial Fraud and Abuse

Consider the following situation:

> An 84-year-old man with mild to moderate Alzheimer's disease can no longer manage his money or even shop at the local grocery store, but when taken to a bank, he signs a notarized reverse mortgage and loses $240,000 to his handyman who has secretly befriended the man over a six-month period. What is needed for the financial services industry to help prevent financial exploitation of this type while simultaneously not infringing upon the rights of its customers? (Lichtenberg, 2016, p. 165)

This case, like the case of Daniel Horn presented at the beginning of the chapter, highlights older adults' vulnerability to potential financial fraud and abuse. Both individually and collectively, the stakes are high. In the United States, older adults comprise 13% of the population and 21% of the households, but they hold 34% of the nation's wealth, holdings estimated to be more than $18 trillion (Marson & Sabatino, 2012). Sadly, the population that has amassed the greatest wealth is at the greatest risk for exploitation (Marson, 2016).

Hudson and Goodwin (2016) highlight the ethical issues that accompany the risks of financial fraud and abuse:

> There are ethical issues that compound detection and intervention efforts. Values of privacy, autonomy, and choice come up against those of paternalism, supervision, and control. Who can and should "take away the financial keys" has clear moral, legal, and affective dimensions, which clearly complicate whatever empirical understandings of a given situation may suggest. (p. 2)

Stiegel (2012) warned that financial capacity and financial exploitation are linked. Older adults may lose their financial skills or judgment or their ability to detect financial fraud or exploitation.

Despite these potential risks, most older adults have not adequately planned for the financial aspects of retirement. For example, Lusardi and de Bassa Scheresberg (2016) paint a troubling picture of Americans close to retirement. Drawing on data from the 2012 National Financial Capability Study, they found that only 47% of their pre-retiree survey respondents (ages 51–61) had tried to determine how much money they will need in retirement. At the same time, more than half did not pay their full monthly amounts on their credit cards; 43% admitted having too much debt. Lusardi and de Bassa Scheresberg (2016) point out that these habits are linked to the individual's overall financial literacy (skills like numeracy and the capacity to do calculations related to interest rates, understanding inflation, understanding risk diversification and of stocks and mutual funds, understanding interest payments on a mortgage, and understanding the relationship between interest rates and bond prices). Financially literate pre-retirees were 10% more likely to have planned for retirement (Lusardi & de Bassa Scheresberg, 2016). In addition, those with educational advantages were much more likely to have planned:

> Respondents with undergraduate degrees are 24 percentage points more likely to have a retirement account than those without degrees (83% vs. 59%). This gap is dramatic even when employment status and income are considered…Simply stated, nearly 30% of respondents appear to lack any form of retirement account. (p. 24)

Lichtenberg (2016) cautions that decision-making capacity assessment is a key element in identifying financial exploitation. Lichtenberg and his colleagues (Lichtenberg, Ficker, & Rahman-Filipiak, 2015; Lichtenberg, Stoltman, Ficker, Iris, & Mast, 2015) used a "person-centered" approach to develop both a screening scale and a comprehensive decision-making scale. Four key assumptions constitute their patient-centered approach. They believe that:

(1) People are more than the sum of their cognitive abilities, (2) their values matter, (3) the context of their life matters, and (4) they make decisions based on what is important to them and not according to how good they are at remembering things or solving new problems (Lichtenberg, 2016, p. 16).

These assumptions highlight the importance of emphasizing the older adult's strengths as well as deficits (Lichtenberg, Qualls, & Smyer, 2015). In addition, their approach focuses on the subjective experience of the person with dementia and the importance of hearing her priorities.

Their assessment approaches evolved from a conceptual model of financial decisional abilities (FDA) (Lichtenberg, 2016). The FDA model includes attention to financial situational awareness (income streams; concerns about spending); psychological vulnerability (e.g., loneliness; depression); susceptibility to undue influence (e.g., allowing others to access your accounts); and factors that affect the current financial decisions.

A number of behaviors could trigger concerns about an older adult's susceptibility to financial fraud or abuse (Lichtenberg, 2016). For example, an older adult's inability to recall earlier discussions regarding financial issues, having difficulty handling paperwork, or getting lost or appearing disoriented in the bank building—all are cause for concern. In addition, family members' accompanying the older person when they had not done so before or a previously uninvolved relative's claims to the older person's resources is another warning sign.

Drawing on earlier work of Appelbaum and Grisso (1988), Lichtenberg and his colleagues highlighted the older adult's functional abilities needed to make a financial decision, including:

An older adult's ability to (1) express a "Choice (C)," (2) communicate the "Rationale (R)" for the choice, (3) demonstrate an "Understanding (U)" of the choice, (4) demonstrate "Appreciation (A)" of the relevant factors involved in the choice, and (5) ensure that the choice is consistent with past cherished "Values (V)." Intellectual factors, unless they are overwhelmed by the impact of contextual factors, are the most proximal and central to the integrity of financial decisional abilities. (Lichtenberg, p. 16)

Lichtenberg's screening and assessment instruments reflect his emphasis on intellectual factors.

Marson (2016) also emphasizes intellectual factors, highlighting the impact of brain aging and cognitive disorders such as Alzheimer's disease and other dementias (Marson & Sabatino, 2012). Because of these changes, older adults develop new and progressive problems as they try to manage their household finances or make other financial decisions.

In contrast to Lichtenberg, however, Marson (2016) has focused on applying neuroscience techniques to understanding the causes of problems in financial decision-making. As discussed in Chapter 8, neuroscience assesses the relationship among the brain's and the nervous system's structure and function and behavior. In the case of financial decision-making, neuroscientists focus on the brain structures, networks, and connectivity that mediate the cognitive skills underlying financial decision-making (Knight & Marson, 2012). As Marson (2016) put it:

> Critical questions about financial capacity that a neuroscientist might seek to answer include: (1) What are critical neural and cognitive components for financial autonomy and independence in cognitively normal adults? (2) How do financial abilities break down in the presence of injury or diseases like Alzheimer's, thereby diminishing financial capacity and financial independence? (3) Can we identify structural and network changes in the brain that can predict diminished financial capacity in the elderly, and lead to early detection by clinicians of older adults at risk for diminished financial capacity? (Marson, 2016, p. 13)

Neuroscientists interested in financial decision-making capacity have focused on the brain's "default-mode-network" (DMN) because of its role in episodic memory, arithmetic operations, financial judgments, and engagement in internal thought (Greicius, Krasnow, Reiss, & Menon, 2003; Marson, 2016). The DMN is also vulnerable to Alzheimer-type neuropathology (Buckner, Andrews-Hanna, & Schacter, 2008; Buckner et al., 2009; Marson, Kerr, & McLaren, 2015). Marson and his colleagues have begun to use magnetic resonance imaging to identify neural substrates linked to financial decision-making capacity among older adults with neurodegenerative disorders (Marson et al., 2015). This growing area of inquiry holds promise for identifying brain structures and networks responsible for older adults' financial decision-making, but for now the assessment is a clinical one, often done by psychologists and other mental health professionals.

In summary, there are at least 5 million cases of financial abuse against older adults in the United States each year, but law enforcement or government officials learn about only 1 in 25 of them. If mental health professionals have significant concerns about elder abuse (financial or otherwise) for one of their clients, they are mandated to report those concerns. With the aging of society, issues of financial decision-making capacity will be increasingly important. As problems develop, older adults, their family members, lawyers, or those in financial services (e.g., bank employees) may ask clinicians to assess the older adult's capacity for engaging in financial decision-making (Widera, Steenpass, Marson, & Sudore, 2011). Psychologists have much to offer—from patient-centered assessments to neuroscience-based approaches.

Aging and Climate Change: Another Context for Concern

Thus far, we have focused on two contexts and their impacts on older adults: the legal and ethical frameworks of advanced care planning; and the legal and ethical issues of financial decision-making and potential fraud and abuse of older adults. In this section, we highlight another context with a significant impact on the health and mental health of older adults: global climate change (Reser & Swim, 2011).

Among climate scientists, there is little doubt that climate change is real and is human caused: 97% of climate scientists concur on this assessment (Cook et al., 2013;

Cook et al., 2016).[1] The Third National Climate Assessment in the United States (Melillo, Richmond, & Yohe, 2014) outlined the projected changes in temperature, precipitation, and extreme weather events for the rest of this century. The average US temperature has increased about 1.5 degrees Fahrenheit since 1895; temperatures are projected to rise between 2 and 11.5 degrees Fahrenheit or more by 2100. In terms of precipitation, we can anticipate that "wet areas will get wetter, dry areas will get dryer." Equally important for our purposes, extreme weather events—heat waves, floods, and droughts—have become more frequent and more intense and are projected to continue this trend.

A recent review (US Global Change Research Program, 2016) highlighted the impact of climate change on the health and mental health of vulnerable populations (young children, older adults, and those with disabilities) and communities (see Figure 17.1).

This assessment is consistent with earlier reviews (Centers for Disease Control, 2014; *The Lancet*, 2015) highlighting those who are vulnerable by virtue of age (children and older adults) or chronic conditions, or those who are living in certain geographic areas at particular risk for extreme weather events associated with climate change such as floods, droughts, or heat waves.

In its 2014 climate change adaptation road map, the US Department of Defense (DoD) labeled climate change a "threat multiplier" (US DoD, 2014). While the DoD

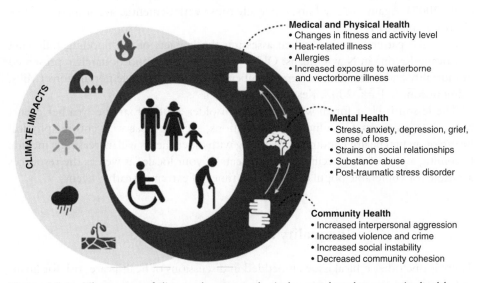

Figure 17.1   The impact of climate change on physical, mental, and community health. *Source*: Adapted from the US Global Change Research Program (2016). Retrieved from https://health2016.globalchange.gov/downloads

---

1   Van der Linden and his colleagues (2015) have called this scientific consensus a "gateway belief" since increasing public perception of this consensus is "significantly and causally linked with an increase in the belief that climate change is happening, human-caused, and a worrisome threat."

was focused on security threats, the concept of threat multiplier can also apply to the threats to older adults' physical health and mental health. What are older adults' threats that can be multiplied by climate change? Geographically, approximately 20% of older Americans live in a county in which a hurricane or tropical storm has made landfall in the last decade; most don't have the resources to relocate out of harm's way. Financially, 80% of older adults in the United States rely on Social Security as their primary source of income (Ekerdt, 2016); they may not be able to afford additional expenses associated with extreme heat, drought, or flooding. In terms of functional limitations, more than 40% of older adults have one or more functional limitations; these may be exacerbated by adaptations required by climate change. As pointed out in Chapter 2, more than 60% of older adults have at least one chronic condition; these conditions likewise may be exacerbated by extreme weather events or may impair older adults' ability to adapt to those events.

Consider, for example, the impact of heat waves. Christenson and her colleagues (2013) analyzed the mortality records associated with a heat wave in 2012, at that time the fourth warmest July in Wisconsin. They found that vulnerable populations were overrepresented among the fatalities: 70% were 65 years old or older; 75% had a cardiovascular disease; more than half of the fatalities (52%) had a mental health condition; and half of those were taking psychotropic medications. This is consistent with earlier reports on the greater risk of those taking psychotropic medications for mortality and morbidity in heat waves, presumably because of impaired thermoregulation (Bouchama et al., 2007; Bulbena, Sperry, & Cunillera, 2006; Martin-Latry et al., 2007). Again, older adults, especially those with dementia, are at increased risk (Luber et al., 2014).

A similar pattern emerged when assessing the impacts of the flooding following Hurricane Katrina in New Orleans: Older adults were disproportionately represented in mortality and morbidity, as were members of other vulnerable populations (Mills, Edmondson, & Park, 2007; Kessler et al., 2008).

The lesson is clear for those working with older adults: Extreme weather events pose a particular risk for vulnerable populations, such as those with chronic physical health or mental health conditions. Working with older clients will increasingly include becoming aware of the specific climate threats of your locale, as well as the resources available for vulnerable populations during times of extreme weather events.

Inequality and Issues of Justice

There is one other ethical issue embedded in discussions of health care, risk for financial abuse, and the impacts of climate change: justice or fairness. Access to resources for coping with these issues is not evenly distributed among older adults. Indeed, as Hudson (2016) points out, when it comes to inequalities in later life—either economic or health-related—we need to take a longitudinal view, looking across the life course, at "the cumulative accretion of opportunities and constraints over time and throughout the life course" (p. 39).

Through a process of cumulative advantage or disadvantage (Crystal, 2016), older adults arrive at later life with different economic and social capital. Indeed, Abramson (2016) points out that "a massive body of research shows that the first important fact in understanding the relationship between inequality and aging is that who gets the chance to grow old is unequal" (p. 69).

Currently, the United States is experiencing what Crystal (2016) has called a "Second Gilded Age," with levels of income inequality comparable to those of the original Gilded Age of the late- 19th century. For example, as mentioned in Chapter 6, Crystal (2016) recently summarized earlier analyses on late-life inequality:

> Between 1983–84 and 2010, the share of total income received by 65-to-74 year-olds in the lower 40% of the income distribution went down from 17% to 14%, while the share of the best-off 20% increased from 46% to 48%. For people 75 and older, the share received by the lower 40% decreased from 15% to 14%, while the share of the top 20% increased from 47% to 50%, with the lower 80% receiving only 50%. (p. 43)[2]

Hardy (2016) summarized the relationship between economic well-being and health status: "Health and wealth increase in tandem, with those having more resources also enjoying better health" (p. 53). She notes that differences in socio-economic status (SES) stand as a proxy for unequal distribution of resources. These differences are linked to different patterns of risk reduction, diagnoses, treatment, and outcomes (Phelan & Link, 2010). For Hardy, a broader view of SES includes health habits, social networks, and the ecology of neighborhood resources that either ameliorate or exacerbate the challenges of aging.

Neighborhoods and social networks matter when it comes to health challenges and advanced care (Abramson, 2015). They shape not only the services available, but even our ability to formulate choices for care. It is worth reiterating Abramson's (2016) assessment which we gave in Chapter 6: "The reality is later life is not the end of inequality, it is inequality's end game." He recently summarized the situation well:

> "Just as unequal wealth and disparate neighborhood resources shape how we age, so do the network inequalities that carry over into our final years…the inequalities that shape our opportunities from birth also structure our final years. Advantages and disadvantages accumulate."(pp. 70–71)

---

2 Stiglitz (quoted in Crystal, 2016, p. 46) reminds us that inequality is the result of a series of choices: "Inequality is a choice….Of the advanced economies, America has some of the worst disparities in incomes and opportunities, with devastating macroeconomic consequences…American inequality… has worsened as we have underinvested in our infrastructure, education and health care systems, and social safety nets. Rising inequality reinforces itself by corroding our political system and our democratic governance….For these reasons, I see us entering a world divided not just between the haves and have-nots, but also between those countries that do nothing about it, and those that do. Some countries will be successful in creating shared prosperity…others will let inequality run amok."

Similar concerns arise when focusing on the impacts of climate change (Moore & Nelson, 2010). Poorer neighborhoods, populations of color, and those most vulnerable are more likely to be affected by both extreme weather events and the longer-term impacts of climate change (O'Neill, Zanobetti, & Schwartz, 2005; White-Newsome et al., 2009).

When working with older adults on their advanced care plans or issues of vulnerability to financial or environmental threats, it is essential to understand their current ecology of care and its history. Larger issues of justice and fairness may affect not only which services are available, but also how each older adult frames and exercises her choices and preferences.

Summary and Conclusions

In this chapter, we have highlighted ethical issues that face many older adults, their family members, and those who work with them. Using the examples of advanced care, financial decision-making, and the health and mental health impacts of climate change, we have illustrated the trade-offs among autonomy, beneficence, nonmaleficence, and justice. Each individual and each family makes decisions about end-of-life care and financial issues. Increasingly, older adults and families will also be affected by extreme weather events and climate change health impacts. In each domain, ethical issues form the foundation of individuals' explicit or implicit decisions. Mental health clinicians are often called upon to help clarify the ethical issues at work in each of these important areas.

Critical Thinking / Discussion Questions

1 In your clinical practice, you are seeing a very old woman and you gently bring up the topic of advance directives and end-of-life planning. She tells you, "I'm only 100. I'll deal with this later." How would you respond to her to help engage in the process of end-of-life planning?
2 What steps can (and should) be taken to help older adults deal with issues of climate change in your community, your state, and your country?

Website Resources

Eldercare Locator: Advance Care Planning Fact Sheets
Fact sheet written for consumers, covering planning, as well as advanced illness for those with cancer and dementia. Hospice and palliative services are differentiated and the fact sheets cover the needs of caregivers.
http://www.eldercare.gov/eldercare.NET/Public/Resources/Advanced_Care/Index.aspx
The National Institute on Aging at the National Institutes of Health
Provides basic information on advanced planning topic and helpful links
http://www.nia.nih.gov/health/publication/advance-care-planning

Centers for Disease Control and Prevention—Give Peace of Mind: Advance Care Planning provides basic information on this topic and helpful links
http://www.cdc.gov/aging/advancecareplanning
National Academy of Social Insurance, 2014—Respecting Choices: A Case Study for Incorporating Advance Care Planning Into Person and Family-Centered Health Care Delivery
http://www.nasi.org/sites/default/files/research/Health_Policy_Brief_09.pdf
American Bar Association Commission on Law and Aging
http://www.americanbar.org/groups/law_aging/resources/health_care_decision_making.html#1
Centers for Disease Control and Prevention, Public Health Grand Rounds, 2014—Climate change and health: From science to practice.
http://www.cdc.gov/cdcgrandrounds/archives/2014/december2014.htm

References

Abramson, C. M. (2015). *The end game: How inequality shapes our final years.* Cambridge, MA: Harvard University Press.

Abramson, C. M. (2016). Unequal aging: Lessons from inequality's end game. *Public Policy & Aging Report, 26*(2), 68–72. doi:10.1093/ppar/prw006

Appelbaum, P. S., & Grisso, T. (1988). Assessing patients' capacities to consent to treatment. *New England Journal of Medicine, 319,* 1635–1638. doi:10.1056/NEJM198812223192504

Bouchama, A., Dehbi, M., Mohamed, G., Matthies, F., Shoukri, M., & Menne, B. (2007). Prognostic factors in heat-wave related deaths: A meta-analysis. *Archives of Internal Medicine, 167,* 2170–2176. doi:10.1001/archinte.167.20.ira70009

Breitbart, W., Poppito, S., Rosenfeld, B., Vickers, A. J., Li, Y., Abbey, J., ...Cassileth, B.R. (2012). Pilot randomized controlled trial of individual meaning-centered psychotherapy for patients with advanced cancer. *Journal of Clinical Oncology, 30,* 1304–1309. doi:10.1200/JCO.2011.36.2517

Breitbart, W., Rosenfeld, B., Gibson, C., Pessin, H., Poppito, S., Nelson, C., ...Olden, M. (2010). Meaning-centered group psychotherapy for patients with advanced cancer: A pilot randomized controlled trial. *Psycho-Oncology, 19,* 21–28. doi:10.1002/pon.1556

Brown, R. S., Peikes, D., Peterson, G., Schore, J., & Findrakoto, C. M. (2012). Six features of Medicare coordinated care demonstration programs that cut hospital admissions of high-risk patients. *Health Affairs, 31,* 1156–1166.

Buckner, R. L., Andrews-Hanna, J. R., & Schacter, D. L. (2008). The brain's default network: Anatomy, function, and relevance to disease. In A. Kingstone & M. B. Miller (Eds.), *The year in cognitive neuroscience* (pp. 1–38). Malden, MA: Blackwell.

Buckner, R. L., Sepulcre, J., Talukdar, T., Krienen, F. M., Liu, H., Hedden, T., ...Johnson, K. A. (2009). Cortical hubs revealed by intrinsic functional connectivity: Mapping, assessment of stability, and relation to Alzheimer's disease. *The Journal of Neuroscience, 29,* 1860–1873.

Bulbena, A., Sperry, L., & Cunillera, J. (2006). Psychiatric effects of heat waves. *Psychiatric Services, 57,* 1519–1519.

Carpenter, B. D. (2015). Geropsychological practice with people near the end of life. In P. A. Lichtenberg & B. T. Mast (Eds.), *APA handbook of clinical geropsychology. Vol. 2: Assessment, treatment, and issues of later life* (pp. 579–599). Washington, DC: American Psychological Association.

Carpenter, B. D., & Mulligan, E. A. (2009). Family, know thyself: A workbook-based intergenerational intervention to improve parent care coordination. *Clinical Gerontologist, 32*(2), 147–163. doi: 10.1080/07317110802676825

Centers for Disease Control. (2014). *Climate change and health: From science to practice. Public Health Grand Rounds.* Retrieved from http://www.cdc.gov/cdcgrandrounds/archives/2014/december2014.htm

Christenson, M., Geiger, S. D., & Anderson, H. A. (2013). Heat-related fatalities in Wisconsin during the summer of 2012. *Wisconsin Medical Journal, 112* (5), 219–223.

Cook, J., Nuccitelli, D., Green, S. A., Richardson, M., Winkler, B., Painting, R., Way, R., … Skuce, A. (2013). Quantifying the consensus on anthropogenic global warming in the scientific literature. *Environmental Research Letters, 8*, 024024.

Cook, J., Oreskes, N., Doran, P. T., Andereegg, W. R. I., Verheggen, B., Malbach, E. W., … Rice, K. (2016). Consensus on consensus: A synthesis of consensus estimates on human-caused global warming. *Environmental Research Letters, 11*, 048002. doi:10.1088/1748-9326/11/4/048002

Crystal, S. (2016). Late-life inequality in the second gilded age: Policy choices in a new context. *Public Policy & Aging Report, 26*, 42–47.

Dartmouth Institute for Health Policy & Clinical Practice. (2011). *The Dartmouth Atlas of Health Care.* Retrieved from http://www.dartmouthatlas.org/keyissues/issue.aspx?con=2944

Ekerdt, D. (2016). Gerontology in five images. *The Gerontologist, 56*(2), 184–192. doi:10.1093/geront/gnu077

Goodman, D. C., Esty, A. R., Fisher, E. S., & Chang, C.-H. (2011). *Trends and variations in end-of-life care for Medicare beneficiaries with severe chronic illness.* Retrieved from http://www.dartmouthatlas.org/downloads/reports/EOL_Trend_Report_0411.pdf

Greenlee, K. (2014). Making our own decisions about serious illness. *Public Policy & Aging Report, 24*, 81–85. doi: 10.1093/ppar/pru026

Greicius, M. D., Krasnow, B., Reiss, A. L., & Menon, V. (2003). Functional connectivity in the resting brain: A network analysis of the default mode hypothesis. *Proceedings of the National Academy of Sciences USA, 100*, 253–258.

Hardy, M. (2016). Societal legacies of risk and protection in the reproduction of health disparities. *Public Policy & Aging Report, 26*(2), 53–57. doi:10.1093/ppar/prw004

Harnett, P. J., & Greaney, A. M. (2008). Operationalizing autonomy solutions for mental health nursing practice. *Journal of Psychiatric and Mental Health Nursing, 15*, 2–9. doi: 10.1111/j.1365-2850.2007.01183.x

Hudson, R. B. (2016). Cumulative advantage disadvantage: Across the life course, across generations. *Public Policy & Aging Report, 26*, 39–41. doi:10.1093/ppar/prw007

Hudson, R. B., & Goodwin, J. (2016). Elder wealth, cognition, and abuse. *Public Policy & Aging Report, 26*, 2–4. doi: 10.1093/ppar/prv036

Hudson, R. B., & Lindberg, B. W. (2014). Advanced illness care: Issues and options. *Public Policy & Aging Report, 24*, 79–80. doi: 10.1093/ppar/pru034

Hughes, J. C., & Baldwin, C. (2006). *Ethical issues in dementia care: Making difficult decisions.* London, England: Jessica Kingsley.

Institute of Medicine. (2001). *Crossing the quality chasm: A new health system for the 21st century.* Washington, DC: National Academy Press.

Kaiser Family Foundation. (2015). *A primer on Medicare: Key facts about the Medicare program and the people it covers.* Retrieved from http://kff.org/medicare/report/a-primer-on-medicare-key-facts-about-the-medicare-program-and-the-people-it-covers

Kessler, R. C., Galea, S., Gruber, M. J., Sampson, N. A., Ursano, R. J., & Wessely, S. (2008). Trends in mental illness and suicidality after Hurricane Katrina. *Molecular Psychiatry, 13*, 374–384. doi:10.1038/ sj.mp.4002119

Knight, A., & Marson, D. (2012). The emerging neuroscience of financial capacity. *Generations, 36*(2), 46–52.

The Lancet Commission. (2015). Health and climate change: Policy responses to protect public health. *The Lancet, 386*(10006), 1861–1914. doi: 10.1016/S0140-6736(15)60854-6

Lichtenberg, P. A. (2016). New approaches to preventing financial exploitation: A focus on the banks. *Public Policy & Aging Report, 26*, 15–17. doi:10.1093/ppar/prv032

Lichtenberg, P. A., Ficker, L. J., & Rahman-Filipiak, A. (2015). Financial decision-making abilities and financial exploitation in older African Americans: Preliminary validity evidence for the Lichtenberg Financial Decision Rating Scale (LFDRS). *Journal of Elder Abuse & Neglect, 28*, 14–33. doi: 10.1080/08946566.2015.1078760

Lichtenberg, P. A., Qualls, S. H., & Smyer, M. A. (2015). Competency and decision-making capacity: Negotiating health and financial decision making. In P. A. Lichtenberg & B. T. Mast (Eds.), *APA handbook of clinical geropsychology. Vol. 2: Assessment, treatment, and issues of later life* (pp. 553–578). Washington, DC: American Psychological Association.

Lichtenberg, P. A., Stoltman, J., Ficker, L. J., Iris, M., & Mast, B. T. (2015). A person-centered approach to financial capacity: Preliminary development of a new rating scale. *Clinical Gerontologist, 38*, 49–67. doi: 10.1080/07317115.2014.970318

Luber, G., Knowlton, K., Balbus, J., Frumkin, H., Hayden, M., Hess, J., …Ziska, L. (2014). Human health. Climate change impacts in the United States: The Third National Climate Assessment. In J. M. Melillo, Terese (T. C.) Richmond, & G. W. Yohe (Eds.), *US Global Change Research Program*, 220–256. doi:10.7930/J0PN93H5

Lusardi, A., & de Bassa Scheresberg, C. (2016). Americans' troubling financial capabilities: A profile of pre-retirees. *Public Policy & Aging Report, 26*(1), 23–29. doi:10.1093/ppar/prv029

MacPherson, A. L. (2014). Person-centered advanced illness care at the intersection of politics and policy. *Public Policy & Aging Report, 24*, 86–91. doi: 10.1093/ppar/pru030

Marson, D. (2016). Commentary: A role for neuroscience in preventing financial elder abuse. *Public Policy & Aging Report, 26*(1), 12–14. doi:10.1093/ppar/prv033

Marson, D., Kerr, D., & McLaren, D. (2015). Financial decision-making and capacity in older adults. In K. W. Schaie & S. Willis (Eds.), *Handbook of the psychology of aging* (8th ed., pp. 361–388). London: Academic Press.

Marson, D., & Sabatino, C. (2012). Financial capacity in an aging society. *Generations, 36*(2), 6–11.

Martin-Latry, K., Goumy, M. P., Latry, P., Gabinski, C., Bégaud, B., Faure, I., & Verdoux, H. (2007). Psychotropic drugs use and risk of heat-related hospitalisation. *European Psychiatry, 22*, 335–338. doi:10.1016/j.eurpsy.2007.03.007

Melillo, J. M., Richmond, T. C., & Yohe, G. W. (Eds.), (2014). *Climate change impacts in the United States: The Third National Climate Assessment.* US Global Change Research Program.

Mills, M. A., Edmondson, D., & Park, C. L. (2007). Trauma and stress response among Hurricane Katrina evacuees. *American Journal of Public Health, 97*, S116–S123. doi:10.2105/AJPH.2006.086678

Moore, K. D., & Nelson, M. P. (Eds.). (2010). *Moral ground: Ethical action for a planet in peril.* San Antonio, TX: Trinity University Press.

National Consensus Project for Quality Palliative Care. (2013). *Clinical practice guidelines for quality palliative care* (3rd ed.). Pittsburgh, PA: Author.

O'Neill, M. S., Zanobetti, A., & Schwartz, J. (2005). Disparities by race in heat-related mortality in four US cities: The role of air conditioning prevalence. *Journal of Urban Health, Bulletin of the New York Academy of Medicine, 82*, 191–197. doi:10.1093/jurban/jti043

444 *Ethical Issues in Work with Older Adults*

Phelan, J. C., & Link, B. G. (2010). Social conditions as fundamental causes of health inequalities: Theory, evidence, and policy implication. *Journal of Health and Social Behavior, 51*(1 Suppl.), S28–S40. doi: 10.1177/0022146510383498

Qualls, S., & Kasl-Godley, J. (Eds.). (2011), *End-of-life issues, grief, and bereavement: What clinicians need to know.* New York, NY: Wiley.

Reser, J. P., & Swim, J. K. (2011). Adapting to and coping with the threat and impacts of climate change. *American Psychologist, 66,* 277–289. doi:10.1037/a0023412

Sabatino, C. P. (2014). Advance care planning tools that educate, engage, and empower. *Public Policy & Aging Report, 24,* 107–111. doi:10.1093/ppar/pru018

Silveria, M. J., Wiitala, W., & Piette, J. (2014). Advance directive completion by elderly Americans: A decade of change. *Journal of the American Geriatrics Society, 62,* 706–710. doi: 10.1111/jgs.12736

Stiegel, L. A. (2012). An overview of elder financial exploitation. *Generations, 36*(2), 73–80.

Stiglitz, J. E. (2013, October 13). Inequality is a choice. *The New York Times.* Retrieved from https://opinionator.blogs.nytimes.com/2013/10/13/inequality-is-a-choice

Stuart, B. (2014). Advanced care: Provider issues, health system buy-in, and best practices. *Public Policy & Aging Report, 24,* 102–106. doi: 10.1093/ppar/pru019

US Department of Defense. (2014). *2014 Climate Change Adaptation Roadmap.* Washington, DC: US Government Printing Office. Retrieved from https://rfflibrary.wordpress.com/2014/10/15/department-of-defense-2014-climate-change-adaptation-roadmap/

US Government Accountability Office. (2015). *Advance directives: Information on Federal oversight, provider implementation, and prevalence. GAO-15-416.* Washington, DC: US Government Printing Office. Retrieved from http://www.gao.gov/products/GAO-15-416

US Global Change Research Program. (2016). *The impacts of climate change on human health in the United States: A scientific assessment.* Crimmins, A. J., Balbus, J. L., Gamble, C. B., Beard, J. E., Bell, D., Dodgen, R. J., …L. Ziska (Eds.). Washington, DC. doi: 10.7930/J0R49NQX

Van der Linden, S. L., Leiserowitz, A. A., Feinberg, G. D., & Maibach, E. W. (2015). The scientific consensus on climate change as a gateway belief: Experimental evidence. *PLoS ONE, 10*(2), e0118489. doi:10.1371/journal.pone.0118489

White-Newsome, J., O'Neill, M. S., Gronlund, C., Sunbury, T. M., Brines, S. J., Parker, E., … Rivera, Z. (2009). Climate change, heat waves, and environmental justice: Advancing knowledge and action. *Environmental Justice, 2,* 197–205. doi:10.1089/env.2009.0032

Widera, E., Steenpass, V., Marson, D., & Sudore, R. (2011). Finances in the older patient with cognitive impairment. *Journal of the American Medical Association, 305,* 698–706.

Zarit, S. H., & Heid, A. R. (2015). Assessment and treatment of family caregivers. In P. A. Lichtenberg & B. T. Mast (Eds.), *APA handbook of clinical geropsychology. Vol. 2: Assessment, treatment, and issues of later life* (pp. 521–551). Washington, DC: American Psychological Association.

Epilogue

In this book, we have tried to provide a framework for assessing effective mental health treatments for older adults. In doing so, we have provided a snapshot of the most current theoretical and practice concepts. Effective geropsychological interventions will continue to evolve as a function of three elements: the changing characteristics of cohorts of older adults in the future, developments in the basic understanding of the processes that affect geriatric mental health, and alterations in the public policy contexts that affect the provision of mental health services for older adults.

Today's older adults represent a unique intersection of individual and historical time. There are some indications that tomorrow's older adults may arrive in later life with different patterns of mental health and mental disorder. For example, today's younger and middle-aged adults appear to have higher rates of depression than the current older adults did at a comparable point in their lives and thus are bringing higher rates of mental disorder with them into later life. In addition, the older adults of the future may arrive in later life with increased experience with, and increased expectations regarding, mental health treatment: They may rely more upon mental health services, thereby demanding greater access and efficacy from the mental health system. Finally, tomorrow's older adults will arrive in later life with a different set of experiences of historical and personal life stresses. Together, these patterns may alter the rates and presentation of mental disorders in the future.

Just as the older adults of the future will change, so will our understanding of three areas that shape the development and implementation of mental health services for older adults: gerontology, mental disorder, and effective mental health treatment. Study of the basic processes of aging continues to uncover a more differentiated view of the processes and prospects of normal aging. At the same time, inquiry regarding the precursors of mental disorder in later life remains an important part of the scientific agenda. These investigations of the processes of aging and mental disorder will be accompanied by continued scrutiny of the most effective treatment approaches for older adults and their families. Increasingly, these will involve interdisciplinary collaboration. In short, the knowledge base for effective practice will continue to evolve. And to us, that is exciting!

Changes in the older adults themselves and in our understanding of the processes of aging will certainly force changes in the public policies that affect geriatric mental health practice. For example, current debates regarding the fiscal health of Medicare, Medicaid, and Social Security will certainly shape the scope and costs of mental health services for older adults in the future, as well as access to those services. For example, we may see increases in funding for interdisciplinary collaboration to serve older adults more effectively.

Whatever the emerging policy consensus, the provision of geriatric mental health services will be a function of that policy context, along with the characteristics of the older adults of the future and the evolving understanding of aging and mental health. This book provides a foundation for treatment today and the unfolding of treatment options in the future.

Index

Aging and Mental Health, Third Edition. Daniel L. Segal, Sara Honn Qualls, and Michael A. Smyer.
© 2018 John Wiley & Sons, Inc. Published 2018 by John Wiley & Sons, Inc.

Assessment   98–105
  Cognitive aspects   90–93
  Development of   89–90
  For older adults   224
  Mood monitoring   102–103
  Self-administered   224
  Treatment   105–112
  Third-wave   112
  Trauma-focused   303–304
Cognitive-Behavioral Social Skills
      Training   258
Cognitive bibliotherapy   224
Cognitive distortions   91–92, 93
Cognitive impairment   23
  (See also Mild cognitive impairment and
      Neurocognitive Disorders)
  and Chronic pain   332
  and Depression   190
  and Housing   397–398, 400
  and Sexual intimacy   315
  and Schizophrenia   253
  Vascular   189
Cognitive maturation   32
Cognitive processes   90–91
Cognitive Processing Therapy   303–304
Cognitive Rehabilitation and Exposure/
      Sorting Therapy   297
Cognitive theory   91–93
Cognitive training   180, 198
Cohort differences   34–35, 46
  and Schizophrenia   251–254
Collaboration   33, 36, 38
Community-based services   383
  and Schizophrenia   254–256
  Home and community based services
      (HCBS)   395
Comorbidity   10–11
  and Anxiety   287–289
  and Schizophrenia   253
  and Sexual dysfunction   318
  and Sleep disorders   324
  Definition of   10
Competency   195
Complete State of Sexual Health   315
Confusional states   11
Context
  Climate change   436–438
  Complexity   32–33
  Ethical   424
  Health care industry   377

Historical   46–47
Individual differences   26–30
Mental Health   14–15
Physical environment   29
Physical health   35–38
Race/Ethnicity   33
Social   32–33
Societal   424
Continuing care retirement community   21
Coping Orientations to Problems
      Experienced scale   129
Coping
  and Depression   217
  and Environment   132–133
  and Illness   127
  and Social losses   409
  Basic coping strategies   124
  Decentering   54
  Dispositional coping   129
  Downward social comparisons   54
  Negative coping strategies   124
  Problem-focused vs. emotion-focused   124
  Teaching/Training   109, 136, 259
Countertransference   39, 84
Cultural factors   35
Cross-sectional approach   27
Cyclothymic disorder   231

Default-mode-network   436
Defense mechanisms   71, 76–77
Deinstitutionalization   384–385
Delirium   182–184
  Common causes   183
  Diagnostic features   183
  Prevalence   183
  Prognosis   184
Delusional disorder   245
Dementia (see Neurocognitive Disorders)
Dementia praecox   242, 250
Depression   9, 75, 120, 136
  and Chronic pain   326
  and Cognitive impairment   190, 192
  and Sleep disorders   326
  and Successful aging   50
  Assessment   218–221, 226
  Care management model   226
  Definition of   208
  Depression-Executive Dysfunction
      Syndrome   218
  Early-onset   211